Cultural Politics and Irish Education
Since the 1950s

In memory

of my Parents,

Thomas and Theresa O'Sullivan

Horgan's Buildings

The Lough Parish

Cork

Cultural Politics and Irish Education Since the 1950s

Policy Paradigms and Power

DENIS O'SULLIVAN

IPA
INSTITUTE OF PUBLIC
ADMINISTRATION

First published 2005
by the Institute of Public Administration
57–61 Lansdowne Road
Dublin 4

ISBN 1 904541 267

British Library cataloguing-in-publication data
A catalogue record for this book is available from the British Library

Cover design by Slick Fish Design, Dublin
Typeset in Times New Roman by Carole Lynch, Sligo
Printed in Ireland by Betaprint, Dublin

Contents

The author and publisher gratefully acknowledge the support received from the National University of Ireland Publications Scheme and the University College Cork Arts Faculty Research Publications Fund towards the production costs of this publication.

Acknowledgements

Interpretive research makes demands on time. The understanding of cultural politics in this book is part of an evolving process of inquiry and its writing has required the exclusive commitment of my research during the past five years. One of the ironies of the contemporary management of academic life is that such a research focus incurs penalties. The assistance I received from individuals and organisations is, therefore, all the more appreciated. The support from the National University of Ireland and the Faculty of Arts, University College Cork, through their schemes of assistance towards the production costs of scholarly publications, was particularly encouraging.

My most immediate debt is to the publishers, the Institute of Public Administration. Tony McNamara, whom I first approached at the IPA, concurred with the rationale of my proposal as a contribution to our understanding of ourselves, and was swift in his support. Eileen Kelly saw the project through from its early stages with efficiency and good counsel. I am grateful to both of them, to Eleanor Ashe for her copy-editing skills and to their colleagues in the publication process. I could not have expected more from a publisher.

I wish to thank the following who were kind enough to respond to queries or help with sources: Peter Archer, Colin Baker, Nano Brennan, Denis Burns, Gerard Casey, Centre of Adult and Community Education, NUI, Maynooth, Pat Clancy, Paul Conway, John Coolahan, CORI, Áine Cregan, Jim Deegan, Claire Dooley, Francis Douglas, Educate Together, Equality Studies Centre, UCD, Ted Fleming, *Gaelscoileanna*, Tom Garvin, Jim Gleeson, Attracta Halpin, Joan Hanafin, Damian Hannan, Mary Horgan, Des Hourihane, Eilís Humphreys, Áine Hyland, Irish Countrywomen's Association, Liz Kiely, Máirín Lankford, Library staff at University College Cork, University of Edinburgh and Institute of Education, University of London, Anne Lodge, Fiachra Long, Gemma Lynch, Tom Mullins, National Adult Literacy Agency, Pat Naughton, Niamh Ní Mhaoláin, Orla O'Donovan, Ombudsman's Office, Barney O'Reilly, Ted Owens, Secretariat of Secondary Schools, Ciaran Sugrue, Hilary Tovey, David Waddell, Mary Wall, Kevin Williams. My apologies to whoever may have been inadvertently omitted.

I would like, in particular, to acknowledge the support and collegiality of the academic and administrative staff of the Department of Education, University College, Cork, over many years.

The preparation of the manuscript for the publishers was substantially the work of Kay Doyle who brought a speedy efficiency and unfailing good humour to what was a lengthy and often tedious task.

I am grateful to the following journals for giving me the opportunity to explore ideas and interpretations that have contributed to the development of the conceptualisation and applications of cultural politics in this book: *European Journal of Education, Journal of Education Policy, International Journal of Lifelong Education, Journal of Educational Thought, Economic and Social Review, Compare, Studies*. An abridged version of Chapter Eleven appeared as 'Gender Equity as Policy Paradigm in the Irish Educational Policy Process', *Economic and Social Review*, vol. 30 (1999), pp. 309-336.

As always, my most enduring indebtedness is to my wife, Marie, who continues to sustain me, and to our family who contributed in their diverse ways, with a special hug for grandson Eoin for keeping me on my toes!

Introduction

This is a study of the cultural politics of Irish education. Its content is the relationship between understanding and action, and how educational policy is shaped by the meanings that come to be shared by those who influence policy. It is derived from an ongoing research project, commenced in the 1980s, on the cultural politics of Irish education from the 1950s to the present. In this, intersubjectivity is conceived as a realm of political action, and cultural phenomena such as language, classifications and theories are treated as resources in the advancement of particular kinds of educational change. Existing references to this realm of the policy process in Irish educational studies 'gloss' it as conceptually and procedurally uncomplicated. An essential prerequisite, therefore, was that the cultural dimension in educational policy be theorised to allow for its components to be mapped and disentangled. It was for this purpose that the construct of policy paradigm was developed.

The need to identify and schematise the construct of policy paradigms initially arose from attempting to analyse the cultural dimension in educational policy making in such substantive areas as the link between education and the economy, religion and equality. In the Irish experience, to speak of cultural issues in educational policy is to be interpreted as referring to the target areas or the content of decision making, be they normative (Irish language and heritage) or aesthetic (the 'arts'). Culture considered as intersubjectivity or shared meanings as a factor in educational policy across the full range of educational issues would be acknowledged, and it is not uncommon for commentators on educational change to speak of the need for, or existence of, 'paradigm shifts' or 'conceptual leaps', or of how values and ideologies predispose policy makers to favouring particular lines of educational action. If pressed, there would be an acceptance that cultural products such as symbols, narratives or spectacles can be used as resources in negotiating the policy process. But that is as far as the exploration goes, or indeed can go, due to the conflation of meaning, people and social structure, not to mention their individual components, in existing policy analysis.

While there are numerous instances of criticism and analysis of policy issues, what little study exists of the policy process in the timeframe covered by this book, largely from the 1950s to the turn of the millennium, is predominantly historical in conceptualisation and methodology (Coolahan, 2000; Farren, 1995; Hyland and Milne, 1992), occasionally supplemented with constructs from the

American behavioural political science tradition (Ó Buachalla, 1988), or to be found in descriptive/analytical (Randles, 1975; Walshe, 1999; White, 2001) and memoir-type (O'Connor, 1986; Hussey, 1990) publications. These approaches have their own important and distinctive contribution to make to an understanding of the Irish educational policy process, and the paucity of such studies has to be regretted. But it is not in the nature of these disciplines or approaches to place meaning and 'how it's produced, how it circulates, and its negotiation, excesses, and articulations to power' (Ellsworth, 1997, p. 10) at the centre of their enquiries. This is also true of the growing body of evaluation studies of educational policies and programmes which serve the developmental needs of programmes themselves or fulfil the evaluation requirements of their funding source.

The social sciences might have been expected to be an obvious home for the study of meaning-making. Yet, in Kane's (1996) criticism of the dominance of positivistic approaches in the broad family of the social sciences in Ireland she bemoans the loss of 'fact to science and meaning to literature'. She might well have including the loss of interpretation to history. This is not to engage in boundary disputes between disciplines or to seek to claim territorial rights on particular forms of social inquiry. Rather, the point is to draw attention to the weakness of the theorisation of Irish life as distinct from the collection of data in the social sciences in general in Ireland, a criticism that has been shared by historians (Lee, 1989) and sociologists (Bonner, 1996; Tovey and Share, 2000). The experience of the Celtic Tiger and the onset of the millennium have stimulated a number of interpretive studies that begin to correct this imbalance (Crowley and Mac Laughlin, 1997; Kirby, 1997; Allen, 2000; Corcoran and Peillon, 2002; Kirby, 2002; Kirby *et al.*, 2002; Coulter and Coleman, 2003).

Irish political studies largely mirror the social sciences' emphasis on fact gathering in its research on voting patterns, party support and general political mobilisation deploying a conceptualisation from behavioural political science (Chubb, 1970, 1992; Coakley and Gallagher, 1999) and latterly from social movement research (Connolly, 2003). There are also research strands on the historical study of political ideologies (Garvin, 1981) and on the operation of the structures of government and public administration (Chubb, 1970, 1992; Coakley and Gallagher, 1999; Collins, 1999). Culture as a political variable is to be found in the study of the role of norms and values (Girvin, 1989) and thought (Lee, 1989) as they operate at ideological, institutional and individual/collective levels of political life (Fitzgerald and Girvin, 2000). From political studies, Garvin (2004), in his attention to ideas in political change, and O'Carroll's (1991, 2002) vein of research on the politics of culture and representation come nearest to the domain of cultural politics that this study seeks to conceptually map, name and apply to the Irish educational policy process.

It should not surprise that in the study of the Irish educational policy process, or indeed of Irish education in general, a vast domain of scholarship has escaped mention, let alone use. This would involve cultural studies, semiotics, post-colonial studies, structural and post-structural approaches to the study of language, discourse studies and interpretive or critical policy studies. In the Irish experience it is in studies of literary works, cinema and the arts in general (Kiberd, 1995; Gibbons, 1996; Lloyd, 1999), and most notably in the Field Day *Critical Conditions* series, that these bodies of concepts and approaches are most likely to be in evidence, a reality that is in line with the observations of those who remark on the role of literature rather than the social sciences as a source for the study of meaning-making in Irish life (Bell, 1991; Kane, 1996). The loss to educational policy studies can be exemplified by the questions that await addressing.

How is education understood and what meaning does it have in Irish society? What variations exist in this regard among key social configurations or over time? How are these changes and variations to be characterised and explained? Are those who speak about education always communicating in terms of common meanings? If not, how do they maintain the communication without experiencing disruption? How is change to be understood in terms of its nature and dynamics?

How is language used in the policy process such as, for instance, in policy documents? How are they organised as structures of representation of current practice, problems and policy proposals? What rhetorical methods are used to present a point of view or proposal? What appeals are used to claim validity for them? How is educational reality structured through language? Which interpretations of education and society are foregrounded and which are sidelined, even to the extent that they lack a terminology to give a structural space in language to them? Who reads policy documents and what interpretations do they take from them? How do these relate to what the authors might have intended?

What regulatory mechanisms are at work when policy matters are being debated? What cannot be said? What must be spoken of? What identities and justifications are likely to convince? Who gets to speak? What position is accorded to them in the construction of meaning? What happens to those who break the rules of such encounters?

What are the taken-for-granted realms of educational thought and practice and how did they achieve that position? What meanings did they dislodge as they emerged? What developments in education have come to be accepted as representing progress and not others? What principles, appeals, authorities etc. are at work in establishing their progressive orthodoxy? How can the absence of such debates as 'back-to-basics' anti-progressivism in pedagogy, falling standards or cultural content be explained? Why are there no liberal economic, free market or right-wing discourses on education? Why are radical explanations of educational phenomena almost exclusively confined to the academy?

How does participation in the act of meaning-making about education get implicated in individual psychology? Are some individuals constituted as authorities as education comes to be understood in different ways and are others devalued in the process? Does self-image, ego or identity become implicated in how educational thinking develops? How much self-awareness is there of this on the part of the participants?

It is not unlikely that raising these questions in the public discussion of Irish education would experience resistance. One source would be the belief that educational policy can be adequately analysed without going beyond the data and approaches of current affairs – agenda setting, interest group activity, consultation, etc. – and that a more elaborate conceptualisation of its content and processes would represent an unnecessary theoretical obfuscation with little to contribute to understanding. There is also a broadly-based sentiment that education is too important to be allowed to become a political issue and that any kind of action or inquiry that might seek to disrupt the assumption of a consensus on education is not to be welcomed. This *cordon sanitaire* around education as a public good is clearly threatened by the questions listed above because of the manner in which they have the effect of excavating hidden power circuits in Irish education that routinely escape identification and naming.

Both sources of resistance came into play when in the mid-1990s I suggested to RTÉ that they might address such issues in the format of a Thomas Davis lecture series. This highly successful example of public service broadcasting had in the past brought scholarship on a diversity of social issues to a more general audience. Yet education had never been chosen as worthy of a series in its own right. When I proposed that such a series could usefully coincide with the publication of the White Paper on Education and serve to provide the conceptual and theoretical context for its public discussion, the negative response betrayed an inability to see educational policy making as an area of scholarly inquiry: the respondent felt that the topic could be best dealt with in news and current affairs where political balance could be more easily assured. Likewise, commentaries on contemporary Ireland, in terms of its society, economy and culture, only marginally engage with the institution of education, if at all, and it is the exception that devotes a chapter to it (Crowley and Mac Laughlin, 1997; Kirby, 1997; O'Hearn, 1998; Allen, 2000; MacSharry and White, 2000; Nolan *et al.*, 2000; Clinch *et al.*, 2002; Corcoran and Peillon, 2002; Kirby, 2002; Kirby *et al.*, 2002; Coulter and Coleman, 2003). It remains difficult for education to gain attention for reasons other than as a provider of skilled workers for the economy, a mediator of unequal life chances, or a manifestation of inadequate public service funding.

The academy cannot offload its responsibility for this omission on to the media or public perceptions about educational inquiry in general. The fact that the cultural domain as a site of contestation in the educational policy process receives scant attention owes much to the absence of a mapping of its terrain of a kind that is suitable for educational inquiry. Unless the shared meanings that feature in directing educational policy along particular lines are capable of being subjected to a conceptual apparatus that facilitates their delineation and makes possible a description of their dominion, character and impact then the 'glossing' of this dimension of the educational policy process will continue, and the contribution that the issues, concepts and approaches which the study of interpretation, signification, representation and regulation can make will be lost.

Since the most striking feature to emerge from an analysis of official Irish educational thinking from the 1950s is its insulation from competing/contesting viewpoints, and the associated mechanisms such as those of editing, filtering or excluding discordant meanings through which the orthodoxy of its understandings was maintained, Kuhn's (1962) concept of paradigm suggested itself as a suitable starting point. The concept of paradigm was the core construct in his widely debated study of the development of scientific thinking and was conceived of as a regulating and normalising framework of thought incorporating a particular vision of the world, definitions of appropriate research issues, the existence of a community of believers, the regulation of intellectual inquiry, and mechanisms of legitimisation and exclusion. In the event, it contributed less than expected to the development of the construct of policy paradigm: no more than a number of suggestions for exploration, particularly arising from Kuhn's emphasis on the boundary maintenance function of a paradigm, together with a convenient label for the construct. An application of policy paradigm that is more faithful to Kuhn is to be found in Hall's (1993) analysis of macro-economic policy making in Britain between 1970 and 1989.

I had been interested in theoretical boundaries – how they operate, the manner in which they effect closure on thought, and their shaping of behaviour – ever since while still a young teacher I had found myself perplexed by Sertillanges's (1962[1948]) recommendation in *The Intellectual Life* that enquiry should submit itself to working within a Thomist framework, or any one framework. That was in the mid-1960s and the book had been bought in a sale for one shilling and sixpence, further reduced from two shillings from its original price of six shillings! I maintained this interest in interpretive frameworks over the years and this was reflected in articles which argued for a greater use of the European phenomenological tradition in Irish educational research (O'Sullivan, 1976) and which studied the models of childhood and child-care intervention embodied in teacher consciousness and child-care thought and practice with a view to revealing their internal logic and interests (O'Sullivan, 1979, 1980c, 1984a). I first used the concept of paradigm in this context in an article in the *Sociological Association of Ireland Bulletin* entitled 'Pedagogues under Threat, Paradigms Rule OK' (O'Sullivan, 1984b), and I developed it in terms of policy paradigms in a critique of the insulated understanding of equality of educational opportunity in Irish educational policy (O'Sullivan, 1989a). A further elaboration of the construct of policy paradigm which distinguished between its components and sought to conceptualise its regulatory power and experience of charge followed (O'Sullivan, 1993a). Alongside this conceptual development, policy paradigm was used to explore aspects of Irish educational policy (O'Sullivan, 1992a, 1992b, 1996a, 1999b) as well as the process of educational reconstruction in central Europe (O'Sullivan, 1996b, 1998).

The concept of paradigm has much in common with the constructs formulated by a number of writers within educational, social and philosophical studies – Mezirow's perspectives, Foucault's epistemes, Bourdieu's habitus/field, Lakatos's research programmes, Hesse's networks and Quine's webs of belief (Fay, 1987; O'Sullivan, 1993a). Paradigm had the merit of already being well known in educational studies and was routinely used by way of description. What was required was an elaboration of the concept along lines that would be suitable for educational analysis.

I was mindful that paradigm was being used in much the same way as the concept of ideology is sometimes used in social analysis. In drawing on the concept of ideology it has been very difficult to avoid its association with 'false consciousness'. This is true even of those theorists who actively set themselves against such a positivistic stance whereby it is considered possible to specify which world views are misrepresentations, distortions or false (Apple, 1979; Giroux, 1983). Furthermore, there is the ensuing implication of enslavement and manipulation. One is a victim of ideology which acts in the interests of those who have power in society and whose creation, however unconsciously, ideology is. Policy paradigms make no such assumption or suggestion about distortion or victimisation. Certain policy paradigms can indeed serve such negative functions. They have the capacity to make opaque, to narrow one's viewpoint or range of explanations, or to delude. But these are not necessary features of a policy paradigm which as an analytical construct makes no special claims on what is true, real or valid. A policy paradigm may well act ideologically; it may equally illuminate, invigorate, raise consciousness or liberate. Those interests that a particular policy paradigm actually serves remain a matter for analysis and contestation.

The early efforts to give substance to the understanding of a policy paradigm as an interpretive schema that operated in a regulative manner in relation to the process of educational policy making are captured in the following working definition. *Policy paradigms are cultural frameworks that govern the policy process. They embody linguistic, epistemic, normative, affiliative and procedural dimensions. They regulate what is to be defined as a meaningful problem, how it is to be thematised and described, what is to be considered worthy as data, who is to be recognised as a legitimate participant, and with what status, and how the policy process is to be enacted, realised and evaluated.*

Initially, I drew on theories of language, conceptualisation and ideas as well as sociological treatments of social control and collective behaviour. Later, as the politics of interpretation gained in prominence in educational policy studies throughout the 1990s, I was introduced to a broader and deeper range of theories, languages and traditions of analysis that were to prove productive in schematising the construct. Early on, I also came to recognise the danger of slipping into an unduly idealist interpretation of the policy process in which culture would be seen as some abstract system of ideas moving forward according to its own principles and in which mind was accorded precedence over matter. The material dimension had to be acknowledged, and the manner in which meanings, thoughts and ideas are implicated in power relations, personal biographies, social interaction and individual benefit and advantage had to be accommodated within the schematisation of the construct of policy paradigm and its subsequent application in policy analysis.

Unlike the primacy accorded to culture by some post-modern commentators (Crook *et al.*, 1993), it is not the purpose of this cultural politics approach to the study of the policy process to posit culture as the master plan from which educational planning and change is directed. As well as internalising culture, people act to maintain or change it and they do so within social structures that are themselves both the product and consequence of agential/cultural dynamics. What prioritising of culture occurs in this study is by way of seeking to identify a cultural dimension to the social and individual facets of educational policy making and to construct a conceptual apparatus for its more precise description and analysis. Culture, in other words, is accorded prominence as a research issue rather than as a privileged social force, albeit one that is implicated at all levels of social structure and action.

For readers unfamiliar with the theoretical areas drawn on in this process of schematising the construct of policy paradigm it might be useful by way of an introductory orientation to have some of its dimensions spelt out at this stage. A paradigm is understood as a framework of meaning, how something is looked at, interpreted and represented as people seek to make sense of and give order and coherence to the world around them. A policy paradigm is an interpretive framework employed in relation to the processing of aspects of policy making. As an analytical construct it can be seen to have the following features:

- Conceptualisation: how something is thought of in a distinguishing manner
- Signification: how it is symbolically communicated
- Representation: distinguishable strands of knowledge
- Materiality: its implication with action, interests and power
- Legitimation: how it is justified and made to appear valid

- Social formation: the social actors who share its meanings
- Psychological: its impact on their sense of self
- Political: its positioning in social and political power circuits
- Change: its experience of qualitative change in its individual dimensions and overall structure.

Part One provides an outline of the recurring concepts of culture, paradigm and power and identifies and explores some of the issues and sources that come into play in dealing with the cultural politics of education. This is followed by a detailed elaboration of the construct of policy paradigm in terms of the features identified above and the issues they raise. Part Two traces a major shift in how Irish education has been understood since the 1950s and describes it in terms of a move from a theocentric to a mercantile paradigm. The implications of this cultural reconstruction of education for aspects of the operation of schools and the relationship between the people within them are described, the forces and processes involved in the change are isolated, and the manner in which this changed understanding of the institution of education successfully competes in its interplay with modernist sources of meaning-making in relation to equality, difference, virtue and control is explained. Relevant developments in other educational systems such as those of the US, England and Australia are introduced as a foil to the Irish experience. This section is drawn more generally than later ones and some readers may find it helpful to move to it after reading the summary of the construct of policy paradigm at the beginning of Chapter 2 before returning to its fuller schematisation later in the chapter.

The substance of Part Three relates to how educational processes are considered to be morally implicated in the life chances of people and refers to all the meanings that are being processed when people speak about equality of educational opportunity, justice and fairness in education and its impact on people's experience of life. I refer to this realm of meaning-making as the LEM (life chances, education and morality) domain of culture, and I track its activity initially over the 1960s, paying particular attention to the recognisable policy paradigms that developed from the 1970s in relation to employability, socio-economic disadvantage, (Christian) communitarianism, gender, and ethnicity and egalitarianism.

Part Four delves in even greater detail into the dynamics of the analytical components of a paradigm. It begins with variations in how childhood is conceptualised and it demonstrates how different understandings of childhood have been implicated in change and contestation relating to classroom pedagogies and the needs of children in care. With a view to exploring the role played by social actors as forces in cultural politics there follows an examination of the experience of named participants in educational policy debate in such areas as funding and social justice, the education of adults, and religious control of education. Finally, what is understood as adult education, how it has been constructed through actions and ideas as a field of knowledge and practice, is analysed from the 1960s.

It goes without saying that in operating on such a wide canvas of educational meanings it was necessary to be selective. This is true throughout the substantive chapters but it is particularly true of Part Three on life chances, education and morality. A guiding principle in the selectivity was the contribution that educational features or episodes might make to a more general understanding of the processes of cultural politics, how they might present exemplars of processes with relevance and application beyond their specific substance, and, inevitably, my own interests and competence. This necessary selectivity and the aspiration to model the cultural politics perspective are reflected in the title *Cultural Politics and Irish Education*. The book does not aspire to being a comprehensive study of the cultural politics of Irish education since the 1950s.

It has become routine to outline the authorial position in interpretive studies such as this. The sources drawn on – developments in education, existing practices, official documents, academic writing, collective advocacy, etc. – are deployed more in illumination than with evidential intent in a positivistic sense. It represents the lived ethnography of education as experienced by a liminally positioned social actor. It is the perspective of someone of working-class origins, a religious sceptic, whose part-time university study of sociology was combined with a teaching career, and who is now located in and totally funded by a university in an Irish provincial city. Its standpoint is from the verges of class and religious identities, disciplinary and professional ideologies, and state power. I would not be so presumptuous as to claim to 'speak truth to power' (Said, 1994) because of this vantage point, but the absence of clear-cut allegiances and the associated fractured habitus are likely to promote less predictable modes and targets of inquiry. Ideologically, the author subscribes to the politics of hope, to the view that people can through individual/collective action change their world. By revealing the interests served by the play of meanings in the field of educational policy, this book demonstrates how scholarly effort can contribute to this empowerment. Though ideological in its approach to social action and intellectual role, it is not teleological and assumes neither the inevitability of progress or social improvement nor the right or capacity to specify, in the form of a substantive and incorrigible social vision, what the end product of such a process should be. For the study of cultural politics, the existence of such closure in the form of authoritative knowledge must invite investigation of how it achieved and maintains that status.

As Feyerabend (1978) discovered, this kind of inquiry into the current verities can attract dismissal, even derision. Every era and social configuration within it assumes that certain 'truths' are beyond question or require defence. Tovey and Share's (2000) very fine *A Sociology of Ireland* provides a pertinent illumination:

in recounting the development of sociology in Ireland, it appeared to be self-justifying for them to deplore the attempt by some Catholic clergy to appropriate it in its early days in their opposition to socialism and Leninism while applauding the advocacy of emancipation as a guiding principle for the discipline among some contemporary Irish sociologists. Studying how, under what conditions, and with what mechanisms closure in truth-seeking is successfully achieved is always easier in relation to an historicised past rather than an institutionalised present. But there are degrees of closure in social analysis and unless one is to be endlessly and recursively reflexive it is impossible to move forward outside of a system of assumptions. This is the 'conundrum of culture' (Smith, 2000, p. 9), the fact that what one is hoping to study is itself part of our fabric of the taken-for-granted. Conceptualised as ideology, as I have argued elsewhere (O'Sullivan, 1993b), it is a conundrum that is near-impossible to resolve when acting with commitment in relation to educational programmes. Analysts are social actors and cannot be beyond culture/ideology. What I have chosen to do is to declare what I can of my operating principles, by no means a straightforward task, and to strive for as open an analysis as is feasible by drawing on a diversity of disciplines, theories and ideologies that effect a form of mutual interrogation.

I expect that certain categories of thinkers together with educational practitioners may find aspects of this book disconcerting. Sociological and cultural theorists will find that the use of concepts is not always faithful or even reverential to their original meanings, and that theoretical debates have been left unpursued. Contributing to this is my experience of having independently developed constructs such as *emergent, nodal point, redemptive* and *generative* before discovering them in the terminology of other theoretical systems. Educators who pride themselves as practical people in their negotiation of the flow of life in schools and classrooms and come seeking immediate answers are likely to be perplexed by an approach which treats their self-description, not as an uncontestable virtue, but as another validity-enhancing mechanism deployed in the politics of cultural production. Those ideologically demanding will remain dissatisfied with my efforts to describe my authorial position, querying, as a recent journal reviewer did in the manner of a 1950s' confessional, how far I was willing to go!

The aim of the study is both grandiose and humble. It is to contribute through the schematisation and illumination of the construct of policy paradigm to the 'conceptual literacy of critique' (Hogan, 1982), in relation to the production, circulation and modification of meaning in the shaping of educational policy. To paraphrase Foucault (1985), its task in this regard is to find new ways of thinking about such processes rather than colluding in their legitimation. I hope others will be attracted to this area of study and will find some aspects of this schematisation of policy paradigm helpful, and that further studies will follow on the cultural politics of Irish education.

Part One

Conceptual Orientation

The central task of the Conceptual Orientation is the schematisation of the construct of policy paradigm. This involved deciding on how it was to be internally differentiated, and selecting and identifying what are to be its analytical components. A number of guiding orientations operated in approaching this task:

- that it would provide a sufficient level of complexity, but no more, to facilitate the differentiation and description of the Irish educational policy process in terms of the production and consumption of meaning and its implication with power, benefit and change
- that it would be a dialectical construction, produced through the interplay of concept and application, moving back and forth between constructs and their use; and in consequence be open to on-going modification in the light of material and symbolic change and its understanding
- that while privileging the cultural sphere in the focus of the research, it should be an integrated theoretical construct capable of accommodating the diverse points of entry to the explanation of the forces that influence the direction policy takes.

This latter aspiration was essential in the light of the centrality accorded to cultural politics in the study and the need to avoid assuming an exclusively idealist approach to the study of policy change. Privileging intersubjectivity and cultural production as research issues demanded that they be contextualised within a more diversifying characterisation of society and social change. This is captured in the early working definition of a policy paradigm outlined in the Introduction which incorporates linguistic, epistemic, discursive, social, psychological and political dimensions. Two requirements follow from this which are also addressed in the Conceptual Orientation. Firstly, it will be necessary to outline the intellectual resources drawn on from the broad family of the social sciences and to describe the manner of their deployment. Secondly, issues relating to the place of the individual, the social and the cultural in social explanation are identified in the light of the cultural starting point of the study. This will draw the analysis into tensions that recur in sociological inquiry in relation to objectivity and subjectivity, idealism and structuralism, structure and agency, and culture and ideology. Not alone are the varied intellectual resources drawn on functionally ambivalent in this regard, some of these introduce additional challenges in their tendencies towards relativism and nihilism. Since there is no best or self-correcting point of reference in engaging with these tensions, I will describe the model of society and social action that I have found useful in seeking to negotiate between them.

The core concepts of culture, paradigm and power, the theoretical resources used and the sociological issues that arise are explained, assuming no specialised knowledge on the part of the reader, in Chapter 1. In Chapter 2, an analysis of the principles involved in its construction are followed by the schematisation of the construct of policy paradigm.

Chapter 1

Policy Paradigms and Cultural Politics

The twin concepts embodied in cultural politics are those of culture and power. In this study, the concept of paradigm intervenes to describe a cultural form, the particular aspect of culture that is the focus of this study and the object of schematisation. This leads to a description of the intellectual resources recruited to advance the study of cultural politics and the models of society and social action employed to accommodate the sociological issues that arise in the light of its focus and methods.

Culture

Since culture is the recurring point of reference in this study, a convenient beginning is to attempt to convey some understanding of its meaning as a sociological concept. This is neither a straightforward nor an uncontested task. Culture has been acknowledged by those who have sought to study it to be one of the most difficult concepts to define. Williams (1983) included it in his 'keywords' in human knowledge but contended that it was one of the two or three most complicated words in the English language. Smith (2000, p. 4), who also acknowledged its importance, cautioned that it can be 'a slippery, even a chaotic concept', and Surber (1998, p. 4) introduced his discussion of culture by warning that 'history has left us with no generally consensual definition of culture, nor could any completely satisfactory definition be given'. Yet, to judge by the scale of scholarly writing on the topic and the identification of 'cultural turns' in a number of specific areas within the social sciences, interest in culture as the focus of academic inquiry seems to be greater than ever. Something of the paradox of its appeal is captured by Jenks (1993, p. 2) in his monograph on *Culture* in the Routledge Key Ideas series when he confides that '… only a confident and wise person would begin to pontificate about it and perhaps only a fool would attempt to write a book about it – thus I begin.'

All writers on the subject point to its multiple points of reference, of which Finlayson's (1999a) listing is representative: in agriculture to refer to cultivation, in biology meaning bacteria, cultivation in the sense of a refinement of a particular quality, the artefacts of a society such as its paintings, music and writing, or the way of life of a people to include their language, customs, values, religion, economic, social and political systems, and their history and traditions. The fact that it is a feature of the conceptual apparatus of sociology, anthropology, cultural studies, post-colonial studies and geography contributes to the diversity of its meanings.

Seminal writers on the subject such as Williams as well as the authors of recent texts, monographs or chapters dealing specifically with culture cope with the variety of its usage by distinguishing between a number of domains of understanding and application in which culture is the central organising concept. Jenks's (1993) typology captures four broad areas of usage of the concept of culture and allows us to proceed through a process of exclusion and refinement to a specification of how it is to be used in this study.

Culture as a Cerebral Category. In this interpretation culture is seen as a general state of mind which carries with it the idea of perfection as an aspiration of individual human achievement or emancipation. At one level it might be a reflection of an individualist quest for personal development. But it also has links with the theme of redemption in Marx's writings on false consciousness and in the deliberations of the Frankfurt School. Its origin can be traced to the work of Romantic literary and cultural criticism, particularly that of Matthew Arnold. For Arnold, culture was the study of perfection, which would cultivate beauty and wisdom through contact with the best that has been thought and known, as well as the cultivation of a right reason.

Culture as a Collective Category. In this understanding culture relates to a state of intellectual and/or moral development in society. This understanding of culture links it with the idea of civilisation and with the evolutionary theories of Darwin as well as with the assumptions of those who pioneered anthropology, in so far as they felt it possible to assess a culture in terms of its primitivism, degeneration or progress. It also supplied imperialism with its ideology of the 'white man's burden', the obligation of those who were civilised to culturally improve those who were not.

Culture as an Aesthetic Category. Culture is viewed as the corpus of art, literature, music and intellectual work within any society. This is the most common and everyday usage of the term 'culture'. It carries with it the idea of standards, achievement, appreciation and cultivation that can also spill over into exclusivity, elitism and private languages.

Culture as a Social Category. Here culture is equated with the total way of life of a people. It is this all-encompassing domain that has come to be the focus of enquiry within sociology, anthropology and more recently, cultural studies.

Since it is this final understanding of culture, the social science perspective, which informs this study of cultural forces in Irish educational policy it is important to elaborate as to how it differs from the other more humanities-based normative-evaluative interpretations. Griswold (1994) highlights the following points of contrast.

Firstly, the normative-evaluative approach designates some cultures and some cultural works as better than others, believing as it does that culture has to do with perfection. In contrast, the social science approach avoids evaluation in favour of relativism. Evaluations may be made in terms of the impact that a culture has on the social order but not of the cultural phenomenon itself. Secondly, the normative-evaluative approach assumes that while a harmony between culture and society is possible it is rarely achieved and, in fact, culture often finds itself opposing the prevailing norms of a particular era. The social science approach assumes a close association between culture and society and involves extensive debate on the relative influence of culture, social structure and individuals in shaping the social order.

Thirdly, since the normative-evaluative perspective fears that culture is fragile and can therefore be lost or diminished, it holds that cultures must be carefully preserved through educational institutes, cultural centres such as libraries and museums, and social movements. Social science emphasises the persistence and the durability of culture rather than its fragility. Culture is seen more as an ongoing activity than as something that needs to be preserved in a museum or a cultural centre. Culture is not what is reposited in such an archive but rather the way in which people live their lives. Fourthly, the normative-evaluative understanding invests culture with the aura of the sacred, in a sense removing it from everyday existence. Social science assumes that culture can be studied empirically like any other social phenomena since it is not fundamentally different from other human products and processes.

While the problem of meaning is clarified by these comparisons it is not resolved by them. Half a century ago the anthropologists Kroeber and Kluckhohn (1952) could even then identify 160 different meanings among the multitude of definitions of culture available within the social sciences, and there is no evidence that social scientists have become less prolific in formulating or championing their own definitions in the intervening years. Furthermore, it is a specific component of culture that is the focus of the cultural analysis of Irish education being advanced in this book. The most accessible way to begin to clarify what aspect of a culture is to be isolated for consideration in this study is to make the distinction between cultural objects and cultural forms.

Cultural objects are tangible, visible or audible (Griswold, 1994). They are often instantly recognisable phenomena. Not directly referential or reflective of meaning, they are objects, behaviours or sounds that are vested with meaning for a particular social group. They would have been labelled and named in the process of becoming part of the cultural inheritance. For individuals, they will form the content of their socialisation into a culture and can be mobilised to influence their behaviour, instigating them even to feats of bravery and sacrifice. In his *Notes Towards the Definition of Culture*, T.S. Eliot (1962[1948], p. 31) provides us with a readily recognisable enumeration of English cultural objects: 'Derby Day, Henley Regatta, Cowes, the twelfth of August, a cup final, the dog races, the pin table, the dart board, Wensleydale cheese, boiled cabbage cut into sections, beetroot in vinegar, nineteenth century Gothic churches and the music of Elgar'. In the same vein there is Daniel Corkery's (1931, pp. 12-13) assertion, in recalling attending a hurling match in Thurles among a crowd of '30,000 onlookers ... all sorts of individuals present, from bishops to tramps off the road ... an assembly of a number of the nation's individual souls', that to 'belong' there, to be 'one' with this gathering it was necessary to be '100 percent' Irish, as distinct from Anglo-Irish. Clearly as cultural objects, Henley Regatta and the Munster Hurling Championship have more significance for their respective peoples than a competition between flimsy sailing craft and the hitting of a ball with implements fashioned from ash. Cultural objects are to the forefront in the ethnographic approach to culture whereby it is seen as the totality of what has been produced by human activity, to include knowledge, skills, beliefs, art, morals, custom, law, etc. This interpretation fulfils the spirit of inclusiveness and democracy and avoids hierarchies and evaluation in a manner that is characteristic of the social science perspective on culture. But it needs to be seen as a concrete backdrop, a realm of illustrative referents, for the less tangible cultural forms which constitute the focus of this study of Irish educational policy making.

While the phenomena through which cultural forms become recognisable as such will themselves be cultural objects, cultural forms are abstract constructs and not easily acknowledged as forms until they have been codified and named. For Eliot and Corkery, their use of cultural objects such as Henley Regatta and the Munster Hurling Championship rely on the established forms of Englishness and Irishness for them to have the significance they have in their respective analyses. But cultural forms do not declare themselves or come ready-named. And even if it appears that some distinguishing principle is at work in delineating and setting cultural objects apart from one another, the identification and naming of that principle is an interpretive act. Cultural forms, therefore, refer to the structuring conventions that operate within a culture in relation to the meanings, associations, images, connotations and definitions which invest cultural objects with their significance and by which, for instance, what is conservative, religious, patriotic, fashionable etc. is designated as such. In Geertz's (1975, p. 5) metaphor, they are the 'webs of significance' which people spin and are suspended by. What is foregrounded in this study are the conventions by which cultural forms within the Irish educational policy process are established and maintained and their impact on social structure and action.

This approach to cultural analysis does not identify neatly with any particular position among the many that have formed within the broad social science perspective on culture. Given the centrality it accords to cultural forms it might appear to be in the German idealist tradition. But it does not accept the *a priori* status of such forms or of their principle of change in terms of an internal dialectic. While the approach assumes the existence of regulative and patterning forces within the culture it does not claim, as Lévi-Strauss's structural anthropology would, that these can be traced to universal and deeply-embedded patterns of the human mind. The study contains much data-gathering in the form of policy documents and actions in relation to Irish education reminiscent of the 'Boas Revolution' of detailed fact-gathering in anthropology. But it differs from it in its aspiration to theorise the regulative principles involved. In line with Weberian *verstehen*, the role of interpretive action on the part of social actors is acknowledged in the shaping of culture; but so also is the social situation, including conflict over resources, of those actors, though without succumbing to materialist reductionism.

Cultural forms do not exist in a social or political vacuum. They have implications for social interests, personal identity and political programmes and are in turn open to modification by them. To have influence over the structuring principles of a culture is to have the capacity to advance one's social project and world view, to shape the self-definition of others and to legitimate or destabilise the nature of power relationships that exist. It can be said, to reverse the sociological adage, that those who succeed in making their view of reality stick enhance their power. And all the more so since the shaping of a people's understandings and feelings about themselves and their world impacts at the deeper and more resistant cultural level within their own consciousness, identities and intersubjective engagements, in contrast with their more accessible behaviours and actions. Culture is a site of power struggles, and the contestation in relation to cultural forms is a pivotal if less tangible level of such struggles since cultural forms embody the rules by which a culture arranges its meanings. This study is concerned with the cultural forms that pertain to the educational policy processes in Irish society and it is in this sense that it has been labelled a study in the cultural politics of education. To advance our analysis further we now need to look at the concepts of paradigm and power.

Paradigm

The term educational policy paradigm is used to refer to cultural forms which govern the substance and process of educational policy making. As described in the Introduction, they regulate what is to be defined as a meaningful problem, how it is to be thematised and described, what is to be considered worthy as data, who is to be recognised as a legitimate participant, and with what status, and how the policy process is to be enacted, realised and evaluated.

Barrow and Milburn (1986) trace the word paradigm to the Greek verb *paradeiknumi*, meaning 'to exhibit beside' or 'show side by side'. It is suggestive of comparison, but it is comparison for the purpose of identification and has come in practice to mean an example or pattern. Plato called his account of the ideal state in his *Republic* a paradigm, an exemplar, and the term has been used in a wide range of disciplines to mean a formal model or type. Its use in this study follows a similar orientation within the cultural realm. However, since in the social sciences paradigm is a term that is inextricably associated with the work of Thomas Kuhn on the processes of scientific discovery and change it is essential to begin with Kuhn's formulation and use of the concept.

In *The Structure of Scientific Revolutions* (1962) Kuhn takes as a starting point his dissatisfaction with the convention that scientific knowledge expands and develops by a process of accretion. In questioning the existence of cumulative and developmental lines of change in the history of scientific enquiry and discovery, he stresses the necessity to locate older scientific theories within their own contexts of assumptions, concepts and methods. Kuhn related these intellectual climates to one or more scientific achievements which supply a particular scientific community with a foundation of law, theory, application and instrumentation which it considers adequate for further scientific exploration. Research that proceeds on these foundations is referred to as 'normal science', a term that is closely related to paradigm, as a model from which emerge coherent traditions of scientific research. Examples of such traditions would be what are referred to as Ptolemaic or Copernican astronomy, Aristotelian or Newtonian dynamics, corpuscular or wave optics, and so on. Research within each of these traditions would be regarded as paradigmatic in the sense that it shares the conceptual and methodological assumptions of a particular scientific achievement and proceeds to explore the agenda of research that is prescribed by the tradition. Kuhn identified three classes of problems which constitute this agenda of research: the determination of facts regarded by the paradigm as significant, the matching of facts with theory, and the articulation of theory. Its most striking feature is how little it aspires to produce innovation. The emergence of novel theories require a paradigmatic crisis as a necessary precondition. Confronted with anomalies, scientists view existing paradigms in a new light. Competing interpretations and a willingness to move outside of the agenda of inquiry and debate over fundamentals constitute the symptoms of a transition to a new paradigm. The scientists involved in such a paradigmatic shift are described by Kuhn as often speaking of the scales falling from their eyes, or of 'lightning flashes' that clarify a previously-obscure puzzle. For Kuhn, this is what is meant by a scientific revolution.

Kuhn's account of how scientific communities advance their understanding of the world and, in particular, the assumptions under which they conduct their enquiries proved to be particularly attractive to the social sciences. From the 1960s onwards, the social sciences were diversifying in their approach to the study of society and this was happening at a very explicit level involving disputation and confrontation among advocates of competing perspectives. Kuhn's version of truth-searching and intellectual activity allowed participants in this debate to regard themselves as adherents of a particular paradigm which within its own field of inquiry conferred legitimacy on their scholarly activities. In this way irreconcilable differences about how society was to be conceptualised, how human behaviour could best be explained, how societies change and what was to constitute the data of analysis could be 'bracketed', the opposing schools acknowledging their differences and contenting themselves with the pursuit of their own agenda and methodology of research within their own paradigm.

For one such subset of sociologists, loosely described as antipositivists, Kuhn's formulations had a particular appeal in that they contributed to the validity of their criticism of the application of research models from the physical sciences to social inquiry. Greatly influenced by ideas such as those of Popper on the testing of truth claims, falsification and the scrutiny of all hypotheses and beliefs in the spirit of an open society, the positivist tradition promised much to the social sciences. Positivists believed that if society could be studied in the same manner as the physical world the science of sociology could develop and lay claim to authority in much the same way as did the physical sciences. Progress in understanding social life was seem to be contingent upon the emulation of the methods of physical sciences. If Kuhn were to be believed, however, the 'hard' sciences proceeded on the basis of assumptions and conventions as did the 'soft' sciences. Gaining knowledge of the external world could in no sense be seen as a value-free exercise that operated independently of those who conducted the research. Physical science could make no special claim in this regard.

Within educational studies the appeal of Kuhn's theories proved to be no less attractive. As Barrow and Milburn (1986) point out, some educational theorists explicitly outlined the rationale of their research by reference to Kuhn's specification as to how scientific knowledge progressed. These argued that particular traditions of research on teaching, curriculum etc. should proceed as 'normal science' according to which researchers would adopt distinct research agendas which sought to clarify the detail of a particular approach by means of quantification, refining associations and specifying antecedents and consequences. For the most part, however, paradigm was used more indiscriminately within educational studies. Some have used it to label specific theories such as those of Pavlov and Skinner on conditioning, different approaches to teaching (frontal, dialogical, collaborative etc.) and different methodologies of research (qualitative v. quantitative). It has been used extensively to denote the value base for different types of programmes and to distinguish between different philosophies of education such as those derived from functionalism, critical theory and feminism. In consequence, they point out, the term paradigm came to be bloated to the point where it 'means almost anything and virtually nothing' and caution that 'if not entirely removed from our educational vocabulary it should be used only with extraordinary care' (pp. 239-240).

Given the varied use of the concept of paradigm in *The Structure of Scientific Revolutions*, educationalists could scarcely be blamed for finding a variety of applications for it by way of a descriptive, discriminative or prescriptive device. One commentator (Masterman, 1970), described by Kuhn as sympathetic, claimed to have found 22 different uses of paradigm in the text. In a postscript to the 1970 edition Kuhn himself acknowledges two broad uses:

> on the one hand, it stands for the entire constellation of beliefs, values, techniques, and so on shared by the members of the community. On the other, it denotes one sort of element in that constellation, the concrete puzzle-solutions which, employed as models or examples, can replace explicit rules as a basis for the solution of the remaining puzzles of normal science (p. 175).

The first of these meanings is described by Kuhn as sociological, the second as scientific exemplar. It is essential therefore to outline how Kuhn's use of paradigm differs from the proposed application of the concept in this study of the Irish educational policy process.

An essential point of departure concerns the target phenomena of the analysis. Kuhn is interested in the process of scientific inquiry, in the manner in which knowledge of the physical word is produced. His content is the components and processes of physical phenomena and their inter-relationships, the planets and their constellations and orbits, the study of heat and light, movement and time. The end product is the growth of knowledge, its refinement, predictive capacity and explanatory power. The processes by which this end is attained involve quantification, the mapping out of the physical world, experimentation, formal enquiry, the matching of facts to theory and the communication of results at conferences and in academic journals. The agents engaged in these processes and pursuing these ends are recognisable through their allegiance to a particular paradigm. This allegiance is easily established. Kuhn points out that to an extent unparalleled in most other fields of inquiry scientists will have undergone a similar education and professional initiation and in the process will have absorbed the same texts and literature and drawn similar lessons from them. As well as the major groupings such as those of chemists, physicists, zoologists and the like, there are sub-groups within these – organic chemists and protein chemists, solid-state physicists and high-energy physicists and so on. At an even more specific level it is necessary to delineate membership of scientific communities by reference to attendance at special conferences, the distribution of draft manuscripts and galley proofs prior to publication, and to formal and informal communication networks through correspondence and citations.

In contrast, the target phenomena of educational policy paradigms are structuring forces within a culture which shape how the process of education is understood, communicated and prioritised. As such they are less tangible, strain conceptualisation and are not amenable to quantification. The end product is the shaping of the social institution of education, change in relation to education processes and ultimately social change. The processes involved include conceptualisation, discourse, the exercising of choice, social configuration, decision-making and the formulation and enactment of educational policy. Allegiance to a particular policy paradigm is not easily recognised and may be even most invisible of all to its own adherents. Adherents and agents of a paradigm are less easily categorised in terms other than their allegiance to it since they potentially include the totality of the people and not a particular profession or sub-group such as scientists.

As well as charting the points of departure from Kuhn's use of paradigm it is equally important to isolate those dimensions from Kuhn's specifications that have a relevance for the extrapolation of the distinguishing characteristics of a cultural paradigm. Two sequences of telling quotations relating to the influence of a paradigm and the implications that follow in the wake of paradigmatic change suggest a number of significant features which a cultural paradigm could be expected to exhibit.

> Successive paradigms tell us different things about the population of the universe and about the population's behaviour ... But paradigms differ in more than substance, for they are directed not only to nature but also back upon the science that produced them. They are the source of the methods, problem-field, and standards of solution accepted by any mature scientific community at any given time. As a result, the reception of a new paradigm often necessitates a redefinition of the corresponding science. Some old problems may be relegated to another science or declared entirely 'unscientific'. Others that were previously non-existent or trivial may, with a new paradigm, become the very archetypes of significant scientific achievement. And as the problems change, so, often, does the standard that distinguishes a real scientific solution from a mere metaphysical speculation, word-game or mathematical play. The normal-scientific tradition that emerges from a scientific revolution is not

only incompatible but often actually incommensurable with that which has gone before (p. 103).

> ... one of the things a scientific community acquires with a paradigm is a criterion for choosing problems that, while the paradigm is taken for granted, can be assumed to have solutions. To a great extent these are the only problems that the community will admit as scientific or encourage its members to undertake. Other problems, including many that had previously been standard, are rejected as metaphysical, as the concern of another discipline, or sometimes as just too problematic to be worth the time. A paradigm can, for that matter, even insulate the community from those socially important problems that are not reducible to the puzzle form, because they cannot be stated in terms of the conceptual and instrumental tools that the paradigm supplies. Such problems can be a distraction ... One of the reasons why normal science seems to progress so rapidly is that its practitioners concentrate on problems that only their own lack of ingenuity should keep them from solving (p. 37).

From these quotations it is possible to anticipate the following properties of a cultural paradigm:

- a description of the world or of whatever aspect of it the cultural paradigm addresses. In describing reality a cultural paradigm will structure the components of that reality and confer labels which allow it to be publicly known and promulgated
- a theory of the nature of that reality which supplies explanations relating to its origins, influences, causes and effects
- a specification of the problems and priorities, of what should command attention or excite emotions
- performative prescriptions outlining approaches for resolving these problems, acting in the light of these attitudes and responding to these feelings
- a truth regime which asserts the validity of the cultural paradigm's descriptions, theories, specifications and performative prescriptions
- exclusionary claims about these validity assertions which set them apart from the claims of other cultural paradigms
- the legitimation of authorities who are entitled to represent and interpret the perspective of the cultural paradigm.

These are not neutral processes. They are implicated in advancing the interests of particular ideologies, collectivities and individuals as well as in their suppression. How is this political dimension of these cultural processes to be articulated? How do cultural paradigms feature as cultural politics? Specifically, how are cultural paradigms to be seen to operate in the policy process in education? This requires a conceptualisation of power, what it is and how it operates, that implicates the cultural sphere. In the Irish context this demands a conceptualisation of power that proclaims what is distinctive about cultural politics and how it represents a point of departure from the behavioural approach to politics and policy-making.

Power

Power infuses society. It is manifested in the most diverse realms of social interaction and at all levels of the social structure, from grand political manoeuvres to intimate dyadic relationships. Like most sociological concepts in general use its meaning can appear to be deceptively simple. Yet as Lukes (1978) points out, to use the term 'power' is to invite a litany of questions. Is it a property or a relationship? Is it a capacity or the exercise of that capacity? Who possesses it and how is it distributed throughout society? Must the exercise of power be intentional? Must it involve coercion or the threat of force? Does the concept require that there be conflict or resistance? If so, must the conflict be manifest or may it be latent? Must it relate to subjective interests about which the actors are aware or can it involve objective interests unknown to the participants? Social theorists cannot avoid power if they aspire to anything approaching a comprehensive theory of society and there now exists a voluminous literature, a variety of conceptual formulations and terminologies and, inevitably, a series of controversies on the topic.

The *locus classicus* of the sociological phenomena involved is Weber's discussion of power, authority and legitimacy. Weber's (1964[1930], p. 152) most relevant definitions are framed in terms of the interaction of individuals. Thus, power (*Macht*) is 'the probability that one actor within a social relationships will be in a position to carry out his own will despite resistance'. Imperative control (*Herrschaft*), usually identified with authority, is 'the probability that a command with a given specific content will be obeyed by a given group of persons'. Weber points to the sources of motivation of actors to display obedience to commands: personal advantage, affective motives, custom, solidarity. But, he argues, no system of authority limits itself to such appeals as a basis for guaranteeing its continuance. In addition, 'every such system attempts to establish and to cultivate the belief in its legitimacy' (p. 325).

Weber (1964, p. 328) distinguishes between three 'pure' types of legitimacy. These are 'ideal types' in the sense of being abstractions and are unlikely to be found in their pure form in real life. The validity of legitimacy claims can be based on rational, traditional or charismatic grounds.

- Rational: based on 'a belief in the "legality" of patterns of normative rules and the right of those elevated to authority under such rules to issue commands'
- Traditional: 'resting on an established belief in the sanctity of immemorial traditions and the legitimacy of the status of those exercising authority under them'

- Charismatic: derived from 'devotion to the specific and exceptional sanctity, heroism or exemplary character of an individual person, and of the normative patterns or order revealed or ordained by him'.

Etzioni (1964), in his application of Weber's concepts, drew attention to how crucial it was to realise 'the nature of the power increment which legitimacy bestows' (p. 51), an observation that has become a truism in studies of the functioning of educational institutions as agents of social control, cultural transmission/imposition and status and economic role allocation (Bourdieu and Passeron, 1977).

A weakness of these formulations is that they address power in the context of the relationships between individuals. The collective dimension of power, the pursuit of class, ethnic or gender interests, is not to the fore in these definitions. This is especially so where collective interests are conceived as being irreducible to the desires and wants of individual agents and participants in political and social life. Neither do Weber's conceptualisations adequately engage the cultural dynamics of power of the kind that are being employed in this analysis of the policy process in Irish education. These omissions are responded to in what has come to be known as the community power debate.

The starting point for this debate is the work of the American sociologist C. Wright Mills (1956). Mills argued that behind the facade of its democratic structures American society in fact was dominated by a power elite. This integrated minority comprised those who occupied the pivotal positions within the major institutions of society. These included large corporations, the military and the federal government. While these may appear to be three distinct elites, their unity and cohesiveness is strengthened by virtue of social background, common educational experience, geographical location and informal association. Not alone are they likely to share similar values and beliefs and assumptions about the world but there is also likely to be considerable interchange of personnel between the three groupings. It is these who make the key decisions about society in a manner that excludes ordinary people from the real decision-making process and renders them passive in the political process. Hunter's (1963) study of the distribution of power in Atlanta, Georgia is usually taken as a manifestation at local level of Mills's notion of the power elite. In this study, Hunter claimed to have identified a small decision-making group largely comprised of businessmen and politicians. Through its regulation of the mass media and the flow of finance this group was said to influence local political decisions relating to such topics as urban development and taxation.

A weakness of Hunter's methodology was that in seeking to establish who had power in a community he used what is known as the reputational method, which involves asking prominent members to identify those whom they considered to have power. This weakness has been commented on by a number of social theorists, the most influential of whom has been Dahl (1961). Dahl studied the power structure of New Haven, Connecticut and claimed to have found a pluralistic structure in which power was diffused throughout the various groups and individuals with no one group holding the ultimate power on all issues. Dahl (1957) had earlier defined power along the following lines: 'A has power over B to the extent that he can get B to do something that B would not otherwise do.' In studying power, Dahl argued that it was essential to first identify central issues on which there might be disagreement, isolate the key decisions within these areas and then discover who had influenced actual decisions. For Dahl, power can only be analysed after there has been an examination of actual concrete decisions on recognisable issues. To test the hypothesis of the ruling elite Dahl maintained that it would be necessary to show that on these key issues there was in fact the existence of conflict and that it could be demonstrated that the preferences of the so-called ruling elite ran counter to those from any other group who might be interested in the issue.

In contending that power can only be understood through the analysis of actual decisions, Dahl attracted the criticism of Bachrach and Baratz (1963). They argued that Dahl had simply concentrated on one face of power when in fact there were two:

> Of course power is exercised when A participates in the making of decisions that affect B. But power is also exercised when A devotes his energies to creating or reinforcing social and political values and institutional practices that limit the scope of the political process to public consideration of only those issues which are comparatively innocuous to A. To the extent that A succeeds in doing this, B is prevented, for all practical purposes, from bringing to the fore any issues that might in their resolution be seriously detrimental to A's set of preferences.

Bachrach and Baratz are here drawing on Schattschneider's (1960) well-known concept of the 'mobilisation of bias'. This refers to the process by which some issues are organised into politics while others are organised out. This is considered to occur in all forms of political organisation in the sense that they have a bias in favour of the exploitation of some kinds of conflict and the suppression of others. Influenced by this notion, Bachrach and Baratz would argue that Dahl's approach is too behavioural in that he unduly emphasised the importance of observable decisions with the result that no account was taken of the fact that power can often be exercised by confining the scope of decision-making to relatively safe issues. It is important, they would argue, to examine both decision-making and nondecision-making and therefore necessary to study potential issues which nondecision-making prevents from becoming actual.

In *Power: A Radical View*, Lukes (1974) proposes a third face of power and in the process reconceptualises the earlier faces of power along the following lines. The pluralist perspective on power, advanced by Dahl and his supporters, is characterised by Lukes as involving a '... focus on *behaviour* in the making of *decisions* on *issues* over which there is an observable *conflict* of (subjective) *interests*, seen as express policy preferences, revealed by political participation' (p. 15). Lukes concludes that the two-dimensional power associated with Bachrach and Baratz involves '.... a *qualified critique* of the *behavioural focus* of the first view (I say qualified because it is still assumed that nondecision-making is a form of decision making) and it allows for consideration of the ways in which *decisions* are prevented from being taken on *potential issues* over which there is an observable *conflict* of (subjective) *interests*, seen as embodied in express policy preferences and sub-political grievances' (p. 20).

While Lukes regards the two-dimensional view of power as representing a major advance over the one-dimensional view he considers it nonetheless inadequate on three accounts.

Firstly, Lukes believes that two-dimensional power remains too committed to behaviourism, that is to the study of overt actual behaviour. In the process it gives, he argues, a misleading picture of the ways in which individuals and, above all, groups and institutions managed to exclude potential issues from the political process. Lukes maintains that bias in the system is not maintained simply by a series of individual acts. It is also imposed by the socially structured and culturally patterned behaviours of groups and the practices of institutions. In this regard he criticises Bachrach and Baratz for following the individualism of the pluralists too closely and consequently for failing to see that the power to control political agendas and exclude potential issues cannot be fully analysed unless it is seen as a function of collective forces and social arrangements. Secondly, Lukes criticises the two-dimensional view because of its association with actual and observable conflict. As Lukes puts it, A may exercise power over B by getting B to do what A wants to do but A also exercises power over B by influencing, shaping or determining what B wants. According to Lukes, the problem with Bachrach and Baratz and the pluralists is that they suppose that because power, as they conceptualise it, fully shows up in cases of actual conflict it follows that actual conflict is necessary for power. But, as Lukes argues, this is to ignore the crucial point that the most effective and insidious use of power is to prevent such conflict from arising in the first place.

Lukes's third criticism of the two-dimensional view of power relates to its insistence that nondecision-making power only exists where there are grievances which are denied entry into the political process in the form of issues. According to Lukes, it seems to be assumed that if people felt no grievances then they have no interests that are harmed by the use of power. This he regards as highly unsatisfactory. He argues:

.... is it not the supreme and most insidious exercise of power to prevent people, to whatever degree, from having grievances by shaping their perceptions, cognitions and preferences in such a way that they accept their role in the existing order of things, either because they can see or imagine no alternative to it, or because they see it as natural and unchangeable, or because they value it as divinely ordained and beneficial? To assume that the absence of grievance equals genuine consensus is to simply rule out the possibility of false or manipulated consensus by definitional fiat (p. 24).

Lukes summarises his three-dimensional view of power as involving '... a *thorough-going* critique of the *behavioural focus* of the first two views as too individualistic and allows for consideration of the many ways in which *potential issues* are kept out of politics whether through the operation of social forces and institutional practices or through individuals' decisions' (p. 24). In the three-dimensional view of power this can occur in the absence of actual, observable conflict which may have been successfully averted, though there remains an implicit reference to potential conflict. While this potential may never in fact be actualised, Lukes advances the view that what may be involved here is latent conflict, which consists of a contradiction between the interests of those exercising power and the real interests of those they exclude. These latter may not express or even be conscious of their real interests.

Lukes's theory of power has itself been reworked (Clegg, 1989) and continues to generate debate and claim a place in any overview of the understanding of the concept (Hindess, 1996). But power is a field of research that has also developed substantially and theoretically in ways that do not explicitly connect with Lukes, such as the feminist study of patriarchal power and the centrality of discourse in post-structuralist approaches (MacKenzie, 1999). Its function at this point is to explain the nature of the departure involved in making the transition to a cultural interpretation of political action in the context of the privileging of observable behaviour over meaningful action as the object of attention in Irish political and policy studies.

In rejecting behaviourism, stressing the centrality of culturally patterned behaviour, and in recognising that power can operate, perhaps even best operates, where real grievances go unrecognised because of the nature of one's under-standing of the world and one's place in it, Lukes edges the discussion of power towards the realm of culture. Since paradigms, as cultural forms, operate as structuring principles within a culture it might well be argued that the control of cultural paradigms constitutes a fourth face of power. Thus, it could be said that to understand the operation of power in society one needs to study the formation of paradigms and, of course, since they are never static, their qualitative change over time. At the very least, what the concept of paradigm contributes to the study of power in society in the first instance is a greater focusing and delineation of the features of Lukes's third dimension. In sharpening the conceptualisation of what Lukes refers to as perceptions, cognitions and preferences, it advances a more refined analysis of the phenomena and processes involved in regulating political decisions through cultural action.

As is explained in the second-next section, using Lukes as the point of entry to the field of cultural politics is not unproblematic. It does, however, serve to lead us to the characteristic content of the field as the meanings that pervade the policy process and to the policy paradigms as the structuring principles that operate, in the manner of the distinction between cultural objects and cultural forms, in their production, circulation and modification. But this no more than fixes what is and what is not to be the object of attention in cultural politics. It will now be necessary, mindful of its application within Irish educational policy, to outline the theoretical traditions, areas of study and specific modes of inquiry from within the broad field of the social sciences that provide cultural politics with a repertoire of theories, concepts, techniques and exemplars of cultural inquiry.

Cultural Politics: Sources

Intersubjectivity, a key dynamic in the politics of meaning, has a long lineage in sociology. Giving primacy to the manner in which people, individually and collectively, understand their world, how this process of knowing is best understood, the mechanisms of its production, and its consequences for human action is a feature of a number of prominent sociological traditions. Weber's (1978[1922]) concept *Verstehen* alerted sociologists to take account of the subjectively-intended meaning of an act. In arguing that if we define something as real it can become real in its consequences, Thomas (1923) was to highlight the impact of the definition of the situation, whatever its 'reality' might be, on the actor's behaviour. Schütz (1972[1932]) focused *inter alia* on the structure and functioning of the mental constructs – the typification and relevance systems – embodied in the social world. Human interaction as the site of meaning-making involving processes of self-presentation, interpretation, negotiation and self-definition is the target of symbolic interactionism.

While these perspectives stretch back over one hundred years, their influence within the sociology of education was retarded by the dominance of a structuralist interpretation of the interaction of individual, school and society, initially under the influence of Durkheim and later through the introduction of Marxist theories, in which social actors were treated as recipients, through a process of socialisation, of their understanding of the world. In this view, 'socialisation is usually thought of as something that happens to or is done to the individual – the focus is not on the active shaping of his life by the individual but on the plasticity and passivity of the individual in the face of social influences' (Danziger, 1971,

p. 14). Wrong's article 'The Oversocialized Conception of Man' (1961) appears as a seminal source of resistance to the image of the person as someone who is completely moulded by society. Having reacted against such abstractions as economic, political, sexual or libidinal, and religious man, it would be ironic, he argued, if sociology were to contribute to the reification of yet another abstraction, that of 'socialised man'. Wrong was to be repeatedly quoted over the years, particularly as theoretical innovations within sociology conceived of the person as an active and creative participant in social life.

Of the theoretical perspectives which emerged in a turning away from structural functionalism within educational studies, phenomenological and symbolic interactionist perspectives are most relevant to the study of understanding and meaning. Central to the phenomenological approach is the thesis that such everyday realities as concepts, roles, and institutions are socially constructed, i.e. they are human products created by people. Phenomenological sociology is a sociology of subjective meaning, and in its application to socialisation theory and research the effect has been to establish the socialisee as subject as well as object (Dreitzel, 1973). Symbolic interactionism is concerned with the manner in which meanings for gestures, social positions, behaviour etc. are transmitted and negotiated in social interaction. It contends that it is by means of such processes that individuals are 'linked to, shaped by and in turn create, social structure' (Denzin, 1971). In contrast to structuralism, phenomenology and symbolic interactionism stress the active participation in socialisation of the individual.

In *The Social Construction of Reality*, Berger and Luckmann (1967) attempted a reformulation of social theory in terms of these traditions. In this they set out to avoid the mechanically-determined view of the individual as in Durkheim while avoiding the implication of Weber's thinking that society is a creation of the individual. In its attempt to 'build a bridge between the objective and subjective features of social life' it has been described as a 'radical departure' (Layder, 1994, p. 86). Its main affect on education was to popularise the proposition that society is a social product, something that has been produced by social processes. Young's (1971) *Knowledge and Control* sought to reformulate the study of educational processes along constructionist lines, and to encourage educators to see teachers' categories and classifications, academic curricula and forms of assessment as 'sociological inventions to be explained likes men's other inventions, mechanical and sociological' (p. 41). This came to be known as the 'New Sociology of Education' following the subtitle of the book, *New Directions for the Sociology of Education*, and was widely influential in the English-speaking world. In relativising existing practices and taken-for-granted assumptions in education, nothing was held to be given and fixed as of fact or right. Its justice agenda led it to being described as 'radical possibilitarianism' (Whitty, 1985, p. 77).

The deterministic branch of Marxism made its contribution in the form of Bowles and Gintis's (1976) *Schooling in Capitalist America* which followed in the tradition of the structural Marxism of Althusser (1971). Later, 'softer' versions of Marxism, which accorded more autonomy to culture and individual action than in the classical Marxist 'domination from below' in its base/superstructure characterisation, found their way into education through the 'discovery' of Gramsci's (1971) writings, in particular his concept of hegemony. Hegemony describes a situation in which the understandings which prevail in social, cultural and political life, to the point that they represent common sense and normality, are those of the dominant class who, in consequence, exercise economic power invisibly and without coercion. Since this process of control is never complete, there will always be groupings who resist integration into the hegemonic culture. These counterhegemonic movements make culture 'a site of struggle among competing interests and their expressions' (Surber, 1998, p. 87).

More segregated in Britain, these strands of thinking came together, with other related influences such as Freire's cultural action and conscientisation and the Frankfurt School's critical theory, in the US to produce its tradition of cultural politics. This is described as follows by Apple (1996, p. 21) one of its earliest contributors:

> The terms that are used to describe social and educational life are also active forces in shaping it. One of the most crucial aspects of politics is the struggle to define social reality and to interpret people's inchoate aspirations and needs. Cultural politics in education is not only about whose visions of the family, the government, identity, and the economy are to be realised in our institutions and in our daily life. All of these *are* of great importance, of course. However, cultural politics is also, and profoundly, about the resources we employ to challenge existing relations, to defend those counterhegemonic forms that now exist, or to bring new forms into existence … this is part of a conscious collective attempt to *name the world differently*, to positively refuse to accept dominant meanings, and to positively assert the possibility that it could be different.

The influence of Berger and Luckmann's constructionism and Gramsci's cultural turn in Marxist theory did not end there. We shall see below how they later impacted on the areas of policy studies and cultural studies.

Not unrelated to these developments in the sociology of education but constituted in such terms as policy sociology (Ozga, 1987), policy science (Deleon, 1994) and policy scholarship (Grace, 1989) is the specific sub-discipline of policy studies. As Peters and Marshall (1996, p. 137) point out, policy studies has been receptive to the methodological developments within the social sciences since the 1970s, and like them '… has passed through a positivistic phase where policy problems were seen in predominantly technical and administrative terms to admit the relevance of hermeneutical and critical modes of analysis'. This is also subject to regional variations in approach and emphasis. In the US, policy science is in the older tradition of political science with its roots in administrative responses to social problems and the management of conflict and social disorganisation, and with a strong emphasis on policy implementation and evaluation. Ozga's (1987) policy sociology, which she describes as 'rooted in the social science tradition, historically informed and drawing on qualitative and illuminative techniques', is a characteristic British formulation. What has been described as the 'discursive turn' in policy studies, under the influence of Foucault's writing, is strong in Australia and New Zealand and represented in the Australian-based journal *Discourse: Studies in the Cultural Politics of Education*. Inevitably, there are points of fusion and overlap. For example, Stephen Ball, King's College, London could claim to be among the pioneers in the application of Foucault's constructs and techniques of inquiry to educational policy studies. There is also a distinct political dimension to much of the British and Antipodean research, with a commitment to change along the lines of anti-market emphases in education, anti-racism, social reform and feminism which seek to expose, and work towards the overthrow of, systems of domination (Ball, 1994; Troyna, 1994; Prunty, 1985; Taylor, 1997).

Foucault and post-structuralism in general continue to represent a fruitful resource for the study of cultural politics. The rejection of the closed meaning of a text derived from its deep structure, the assertion that texts can be read (interpreted) in different ways, that they change in meaning through the interplay with other texts, and that this can happen in a non-linear shifting fashion all suggest fruitful lines of inquiry in exploring the politics of meaning-making in educational policy. Foucault is particularly productive as a source for the study of meaning and power because of the prominence he accords to the power/knowledge relationship. This is not a simplistic matter of contending that 'knowledge is power' or 'power is knowledge'. As Foucault (1983) points out, if they were identical he would have been saved 'a lot of fatigue'. It is the relationship between them that has been the object of his extensive studies, the stroke or dash dividing them being interpreted as holding the words 'together and apart, showing both their presupposition of each other and their difference from each other' (Gore, 1993, p. 51). This is captured in *Discipline and Punish* in which Foucault (1979, p. 27) asserts that 'power and knowledge directly imply one another; there is no power relation without the correlative constitution of a field of knowledge, nor any knowledge that does not presuppose and constitute at the same time power relations.' This sense in which power and knowledge are 'two sides of a single process' is applied to educational policy studies by Ball (1990, pp 17-18) in the following suggestive manner:

Discourses are, therefore, about what can be said, and thought, but also about who can speak, when, where and with what authority. Discourses embody meaning and social relationships; they constitute both subjectivity and power relations … Words and propositions will change their meaning according to their use and the positions held by those who use them. Knowledge is that of which one can speak in a discursive practice. Meanings thus arise not from language but from institutional practices, from power relations, from social position. Words and concepts change their meaning and their effects as they are deployed within different discourses.

In his incorporation into educational studies, some of the weaknesses of Foucault's approaches are evident. Not all applications are as grounded in educational practice as those of Ball. Best and Kellner's (1991, p. 70) criticism of Foucault's account of power 'as an impersonal and anonymous force which is exercised apart from the actions and intentions of human subjects' is apposite in relation to studies of educational discourse which treat it apart from subjects and the social. This involves the neglect of the distinctive contribution of symbolic interactionist and phenomenological traditions. For Layder (1994, p. 112) this is due to Foucault's rejection of the 'interactive-dimension' of meaning; 'that element of meaning that is produced through inter-subjective processes of negotiation, definition and general forms of creativity that are brought into play whenever and wherever human beings mix socially'. Again we find Ball (1994, p. 2) attempting a reconciliation in his appropriation of Foucault's theories in policy studies by seeking to establish an affinity between his methods of exploring discursive formations and ethnography, with its attention to '"situated" discourses and "specific tactics" and "precise and tenuous" power relations operating in local settings'.

Within the policy science tradition, there is also evidence of a shift in the direction of the social constructionist perspective in the work of Rein and Schön (1977) and Dery (1984) who recognise the significance in policy making of the different frames of reference which participants in the policy process bring to it as they determine what is to be defined as a policy problem. Bacchi (1999, p. 30), however, detects a 'lingering positivism' and a solution-focused perspective. She finds that while the structuring role of language, metaphors and concepts in the formation of policy is recognised, the assumption seems to be that the participants can reflect on these constraints, acknowledge their impact as a source of tension and conflict, and reach a 'reasonable' solution before progressing further. Nonetheless, this reaching out to the cultural in what has been a predominantly behavioural area of inquiry corresponds to the kinds of linkages and extensions that this study is attempting to achieve in giving the cultural a more effectively-theorised position in Irish educational policy studies.

Another area of study that straddles social and political studies is social movement research. Its consideration of the link between culture and collective action is particularly relevant to the study of cultural politics. Following della Porta and Diani (1999), social movements can be characterised as informal interaction networks involving a plurality of individuals, groups and/or organisations with a shared set of beliefs and a sense of belonging, engaged in political and/or cultural conflicts for the purpose of promoting or opposing social change. Research on social movements has expanded since the mid-1970s, though it has displayed little interest in educational issues (McAdam *et al.*, 1996; della Porta and Diani, 1999). An exception is Davies's (1999) study of an educational lobby group in Canada which drew on the technique of frame analysis as used in the study of culture and collective action and mobilisation. In fact, Davies decries the absence of detailed cultural analysis in the educational policy process in North America generally. The concept of frame is used to refer to '… an interpretive schema that simplifies and condenses the "world out there" by selectively punctuating and encoding objects, situations, events, experiences and sequences of actions within our present and past environment' (Snow and Benford, 1992). Their effect is to 'locate, perceive, identify and label' (Goffman, 1974) in the manner in which one knows the world. Indeed, the application of Goffman's concept of framing to social movement research was itself instigated by the 'glossing' of the role of ideas and sentiments in research on the mobilising practices of social movements (Snow *et al.*, 1986). Yet, recent surveys of this field have concluded that 'frame analytical methods remain undeveloped' (Benford, 1997) and remark on 'a lack of conceptual precision in defining what we mean by "framing processes"', pointing out that it has come to mean 'any and all cultural dimensions of social movements' (McAdam *et al.*, 1996, p. 6). This is despite the wide use of the term 'framing' in social movement research and the existence in its initial formulation of differentiation between framing processes – bridging, amplification, extension and transformation (Snow *et al.*, 1986). Benford (1997) recognises the potential of constructionism.

In arguing for the development of the concept of framing he suggests that 'the question is not what's going on here, but under what conditions do people believe in a particular version of reality. In multiple versions of reality?' Benford's diagnosis of the weaknesses of frame theory and his prescriptions for its elaboration are pertinent to the schematisation of the construct of policy paradigm. Among the weaknesses of social movement framing studies, he lists the neglect of systematic empirical studies, a descriptive bias, static tendencies, reified constructs, a neglect of human agency and emotions, reductionism and an elite bias. To overcome these shortcomings he recommends '… systematic studies across time, movements, and cultures … conceptual clarification … (moving) beyond naming frames to studying framing processes analytically … take into account the multi-organisational fields of social movements … greater attention devoted to the negotiated, contested dimensions of movement framing processes; the restoration of actors, emotions, and talk ... focus on non-elites as well as elites ... integrating structural and cultural perspectives.' These are relevant to the theoretical development of cultural politics but limited because of the focus of the application in social movement research. Whatever analytical construct is developed to interpret the cultural dimension of the educational policy process, it will need to accommodate meanings and understandings that are less knowingly tactical in their use and specifically named and codified in their communication than the ideational mobilisation strategies of social movements.

Cultural studies is an obvious resource for the study of cultural politics. The Centre for Contemporary Cultural Studies at Birmingham University has made a significant impact on this interdisciplinary area of study. There, again, we find the influence of Gramsci's conceptualisation of hegemony with its highlighting of cultural struggle on its research programme and personified in the writings of its first two directors, Richard Hoggart and Stuart Hall. While within its educational inquiries it is Willis's *Learning to Labour* (1977) that has impacted most on the US approach to cultural politics, and in particular on the writing on critical pedagogy, it is its studies of the development of educational thinking, policy and change in post-war Britain that resonates most with this study. In fact it was the first of these studies, *Unpopular Education* (Education Group, CCCS, 1981), that made the author realise the loss to Irish self-understanding in the absence of such an inquiry into the development of contemporary Irish education.

Finally, two areas of scholarship, feminism and post-colonial studies, are exemplars in distinct ways for how the schematisation of a policy paradigm might be advanced. This is apart from the contribution of studies in the cultural politics tradition that adopt a feminist perspective. Feminist scholars have consistently approached major schools of thought and canonical writers in terms of how they might advance or retard the feminist project. Whatever reverence or admiration there might be for them, scholarly traditions and innovations are dissected not only for what within them is sympathetic, compatible or threatening but, more strikingly, for what can be modified or adapted for feminist purposes. This disrespect for theoretical and canonical purism or orthodoxy serves as a positive role model in the conceptual refinement of a policy paradigm as an analytical construct in studying cultural politics. So also does post-colonial studies, in the variety of its definitions (Ashcroft *et al.*, 1999). What distinguishes this area of study as a resource for cultural politics is its innovativeness in the constitution of concepts to facilitate the identification, delineation and naming of subject positions and the processes of their formulation in the interplay of dominant/dominated and settler/indigenous cultures.

Cultural Politics: The Individual, The Social and The Cultural

The relationship between the social and the cultural, between the behavioural and subjective dimensions of power, the connection between social change and cultural change and the role of the individual agent will recur throughout the study. These issues will emerge both in the explication of the concept of policy paradigm that follows and in the analyses of substantive policy processes in Irish education that are conducted in the light of this conception. In studying a particular aspect of the social order it is very easy to focus unduly on it in a manner that appears to set it in isolation, to see other social features in terms of it and perhaps to assume that all other aspects can be explained by reference to it. In this study of the cultural politics of Irish education it is necessary to avoid privileging culture through the corralling of power issues within particular institutions or levels of society.

This cannot be resolved by assuming that there is any one best or self-correcting point of reference to begin one's analysis. While situating cultural politics within the community power debate and using Lukes as the point of departure is productive, in the light of the behavioural orientation of Irish political and policy analysis, it does bring with it weaknesses and limitations. These are not distinctive to it and they are best confronted by drawing them out from his analysis and indicating what remedial or corrective forces can be built into the conceptualisation that follows.

Lukes's treatment of the perceptions and interpretations of individuals as a basis on which other people exercise power over them calls into question the entire constellation of social processes which shape the individual. Most obviously, they include child rearing, family processes, schooling and religion. Less adverted to are the formative influences of mass media, occupational experience and social movements. If the impact of these processes on people are such that they act in a manner that serves the interests of others rather than themselves, these processes need to be viewed in terms of social control rather than personal development. At a moral level this suggests the existence of a bias in the cultural definitions, values, and meanings which these processes of formation transmit. Such an interpretation is in the Marxist tradition that the ruling ideas in any era are always those of the ruling class and views power as operating at the level of social classes rather than individuals (Poulantzas, 1979). It is the substance of that approach to ideology which defines it as a way of knowing the world which acts, unknown to oneself, against one's best interests. This has to be rejected as too exploitative an understanding of culture on which to ground the study of cultural politics and, given some of the post-structuralist sources drawn on above, too dualist and truth-claiming in designating objectivity and delusion, oppressor and oppressed.

Theoretically, as an explanation of social behaviour, the cultural approach to power can be criticised for being unduly idealist. It can be accused of privileging the orientations, thoughts and definitions from within the cultural realm to the neglect of individual psychology, coercive power and structured action. It can easily give the impression that social behaviour is conditioned from above and that what fundamentally moves society are the ideas of the time. This has traces of the Hegelian proposition that if you control the ideas of people you regulate the world. In this view human motivation, personal values and social roles have no independent standing in their own right but rather exist as epiphenomena of the structuring processes that emanate from the realm of culture. In Lukes's analysis, his deprecation of the behavioural approaches to power fails to recognise that the explicit, observable processes such as those of agenda setting, nondecision-making and 'mobilisation of bias' which constitute the explanatory variables of the behavioural approaches have themselves the capacity to bring about change at the subjective level which Lukes privileges. It can be argued that the direction of the influence is in no sense a one-way process.

The third difficulty has to do with the status of the individual actor in the cultural approach to power. What space does it allow for the creativity and choice of individuals? Does it see them as the products of their formation, incapable of reflecting on these influences or transcending them in any way? The weight of Lukes's third face of power requires that the behaviour and orientations of individuals be accepted as human propensities that can be at least heavily formed or circumscribed by forces outside their control. This lies uneasily with some of the fundamental tenets of theories which stress human agency such as those of Weber, phenomenology and symbolic interactionism mentioned in the previous section. To emphasise human agency is to regard people as being in control of their lives, of having the capacity to intervene and shape the conditions of their existence and in that sense contributing to the direction that the world takes. Not only do human agency theories focus on the meanings which actors give to their action but they assume that meaningful behaviour can be understood in the light of the actors' own accounts and descriptions. And while the process of constructing meaning is not an individualist exercise but is conducted at an intersubjective level in interaction with others through processes of negotiation and redefinition, the emphasis is nonetheless at the level of individuals rather than in terms of imposing and constraining structures that operate on the individual from above.

If human agency is about conferring meanings on events, acting in a motivated manner and setting objectives which guide behaviour, then the characteristic proposition of the third face of power, that these very meanings, motivations and objectives are themselves shaped by forces external to the individual, seems to leave little space for a distinctive personal contribution. Lukes's conception of power seems to allow little or no possibility for the reflective, creative or quizzical. In the absence of an allowance for human agency the individual in the third face of power emerges as a victim of experience, as a 'cultural dupe'.

A final limiting feature of the entire community power debate, and not unique to Lukes's proposition, is its association of issues of power with 'grand' decision making, state policy formulation and the establishment of major civic and economic goals. This should not surprise since this tradition of inquiry has developed within the political sciences, with the focus of analysis on the public sphere following from this political orientation. The impression can easily be given that power is not an issue at the more micro-level of interpersonal relationships. This can have a distorting effect on the study of power in society, blocking off from scrutiny an entire realm of power disparities and dynamics that, as feminists have pointed out, though operating as the interpersonal level, are not in any sense 'private' in their consequences for individuals, groups, communities and society in general. As we have seen in the previous section, writers such as Foucault, for instance, who have written on the manner in which the state exercises power over individuals by means of discipline, training and surveillance, nonetheless emphasise that power infuses all relationships and is expressed in discourse through which individuals and groups reflect and extend the power relationships between them. Furthermore, for Foucault the exercise of power at the macro level of society is rooted in the manner in which discourse at the interpersonal level operates to construct identities, legitimate knowledge and establish authorities.

The tensions of the kind revealed in Lukes's conceptualisation of power, between objectivity and subjectivity, idealism and structuralism, agency and structure and culture and ideology recur in the social sciences and will not be resolved here. The diverse sources outlined in the previous section on resources for the study of cultural politics are not alone functionally ambivalent in this regard but some of these in turn introduce additional challenges in their tendencies towards relativism and nihilism.

Because of these theoretical tensions and the diversity of contributory conceptual schemes and research agendas, the author has found it useful, as a stabilising foil, to draw on an older theorisation of society which draws selectively from Parsons. Sociological commentaries since the 1960s have not been sympathetic to Parsons, where his work is routinely castigated as deterministic, consensual and politically uncritical, though there have been efforts to rework some of his ideas, most notably by Alexander (1985). In the present context two aspects of Parsons' theory have been found to be useful – the principle of emergence and his layered, macro-micro, conceptualisation of society – when reworked in a manner that exploits their potential for the task in hand.

Parsons wished to construct a general theory of action which placed human intention and orientation at its centre. Ironically in the light of his subsequent status, he sought to set his distance from deterministic theories of the social world which represented the individual actor as an element constrained within a wider system of laws. Voluntarism is fundamental to this theory of society and, as Gouldner (1971) has pointed out, Parsons was intent on establishing a counterpoint to any image of a repressive or deterministic society of the kind to be found within, for instance, Marxist analysis where capitalist classes and economic imperatives are seen to dominate the lives of people. For Parsons it was essential that there would be some dimension of voluntarism in social action since, without this critical element of freedom, action would become mere behaviour, leaving no room for such notions as consciousness, norms or ends except in so far as they are considered to be epiphenomena having no causal or explanatory significance in themselves and representing no more than structured reflections of other forces. According to Parsons, any adequate general sociological theory must be an action theory. By this he meant that its focus must always be the idea of actors consciously directing themselves towards situations by reference to various kinds of goals and values and standards, and behaving in the light of this orientation. This view acknowledges that not all behaviour is action. But Parsonian theory is based on the assumption that there are significant realms of human conduct which do in fact qualify as action and that it is these kinds of behaviours which must be the stuff of sociological analysis. In Parsonian theory action is to be differentiated from behaviour when in the relationship between action and situation there is a recognition of the interplay of 'subjective processes or orientation, conceived as causally relevant intervening mechanisms and not as epiphenomena and … explicitly formulated notions of ends or goals and of normative standards, conceived as ideal elements which function to structure the actor's orientation to situations' (Devereux, 1961).

In *Towards a General Theory of Action*, Parsons and Shils (1976) differentiate between the psychological, social and cultural aspect of concrete systems of action. Firstly, there is the personality which they define as the organised system of the orientation and motivation of action in any one individual actor. Secondly, there is the action of a number of actors in the same situation conceived as the process of interaction which, through a process of differentiation and integration, forms a social system. While this social system is made up of the relationships between individuals, it is a system which is organised around the problems arising from social interaction rather than around the problems which arise in connection with the actions of an individual actor. Personality and social system are acknowledged as being intimately interrelated but they are considered to be neither identical with one another nor explicable by one another. As they put it, 'the social system is not a plurality of personalities' (p. 7). Thirdly, the cultural system has its own forms and problems which are not reducible to those of either personality or social systems or even of both together. The cultural system is considered to be distinctive because it is not in itself organised as a system of action apart from its embodiment in the orientations of concrete actors, though it does exist as a body of artifacts and as a system of symbols. Because the cultural system operates both as an object of orientation and as an element in the orientation of action it must be articulated both with personalities and social systems.

In asserting the distinctiveness of the three components of concrete systems of action – personality, social system, culture – and in arguing that they are not reducible to each other, Parsons and Shils are here anticipating the principle of emergence. By emergence Parsons means that systems have properties which cannot be explainable in terms of the parts which go to make them up, and that at various levels of organisational complexity new forces and processes tend to emerge. Emergence is central to Parsonian theory since, just as it follows if you are to have any theory of action as distinct from behaviour then you must accept the principle of voluntarism, so it also follows that if you are to have a causally relevant theory of sociology you must accept the principle of emergence. Layder's (1994) explication of the personality, social and cultural systems of Parsonian theory serves to explain the principle of emergence in more concrete terms.

The personality system is made up of motivational elements such as a person's beliefs, feelings, emotional attachments, desires and objectives. These have been incorporated into individuals' subjective responses to the social world as a result of their own distinctive personal biographies. Such biographies include family influences, those of subsequent social contexts like peer groups and work groups and leave a formative impact on personality. They also include various internalised beliefs and moral standards that are current at any one time in society. Motivational needs may push people to seek gratification generally in terms of the solutions laid down in socially acceptable forms of behaviour. In that sense the personality system overlaps with other systems. Nonetheless, it is in itself a unique amalgamation that results from this complex of influences and as such has to be understood as a system in its own right with its own emergent properties.

In order to communicate and cooperate effectively with each other, people establish certain understandings and agreements about the nature of their relationship. In this way they develop a set of common expectations about their future behaviour and this over time tends to shape their orientation to each other. In a fully developed social system such as modern society these expectations become institutionalised. By this is meant that they become part of the accepted fabric of society which people have to take into account when formulating their behaviour. The emergent properties of a social system derive from the fact of this institutionalisation in that it confers a reality and a controlling force that transcends the sum total of the personalities that participate in the social system.

Processes of emergence need to be seen in a longer term perspective given the nature of the cultural system. Human interaction over long periods of time creates cultural products not only in terms of artifacts like furniture or buildings or different styles but also in terms of different forms of knowledge, literature, art and traditions. In this sense the cultural system is the storehouse of the cultural forms of human products that represent the history and traditions of a particular society. Thus the emergent features of a cultural system are reflected in the sedimentation of values and traditions that constitute the cultural heritage of a society.

This division of society obviously represents a simplification of reality. Society neither exists nor is experienced in segments. In asserting the principle of emergent properties in relation to personal, social, and cultural systems, Parsons was not in any way suggesting that these systems were totally free-floating. He recognised that each of these aspects of the social order was constrained by every other and by the fact of heredity. For Parsons the challenge was to formulate a theoretical system which would allow for the interplay of all of these types of factors to be conceptualised and analysed. Irrespective of how his theory of society developed and the criticism it attracted, the utility of these analytical orientations for this attempt to establish the context for the study of cultural politics is that they provide a macro-micro template of the components of society without unduly privileging any one component as a force for explaining social stability and change.

Parsons' framework recognises the 'reality' of the segments of society that are neither reducible to nor independent of one another. It acknowledges the autonomy and interdependence of parts, agency and formation, individual and social, structure and culture. Its macro-micro spread, its 'ontological depth' in Layder's (1994, p. 33) usage, establishes the different layers of society as objects of inquiry in their own right, but with a realisation that this can never provide more than a partial contribution to sociological explanation, and that it is foolhardy to assume that the understanding of either the individual, the social or the cultural can ever be expected to yield up some holy grail for the interpretation of each other. This refers to what Archer (1988, 1998) has described as the 'fallacy of conflation'. She argues that while the problem of structure and agency can be considered to be at the core of the many ontological tensions in social theory internationally of the kind addressed in this and the previous sections – such as subjectivism and objectivism, voluntarism and determinism, and macro and micro – the parallel problem of culture and agency which raises identical difficulties has been overshadowed. She sets her position against three varieties of conflationism – upward, downward and central – in relation to theorising the link between culture and agency. Upward and downward conflation are examples of epiphenomenalism which render either ideas or people as an epiphenomenon (reflection) of the other. In the former, cultural features are formed and transformed by such unconstrained forces as economic interest and elite groups and agents that operate independently and influence all before them. In the latter, a culture's values and ideologies are seen to shape social life and individual behaviour to the extent that human agents are reduced to bearers of its message – *träger* – through processes of internalisation or mystification. In each of these, an aspect of social life – culture or agency – is rendered passive.

In central conflation – represented by Giddens's structuration theory – both are deprived of their autonomy. This is because they are presented as being so tightly constitutive of one another that any examination of their interaction is precluded. As Archer (1988) points out, 'the net effect of conflation is that the possibility of gaining explanatory leverage on cultural dynamics from the interplay between "parts" and "people" is relinquished from the outset' (p. xiv). This is in contrast to what Archer is seeking: 'a theoretical stance which is capable of linking "structure and agency" or "culture and agency", rather than sinking the difference between the "parts" (organisational or ideational) and the "people", who hold positions or ideas within them' (p.xii). Here, Archer is advocating analytical dualism. This she distinguishes from philosophical dualism which suggests that one is dealing with separate entities. For Archer they are only analytically separable in the sense that it is useful to treat them separately with a view to theorising about their interplay. This approach of analytical separatism is central to the study of culture and the ontological status attached to it in both the conceptual and empirical analyses that follow.

The influence of these orientations – emergence, ontological depth of society, analytical separateness – should be evident throughout the study: in auditing the selection of social variables considered necessary for the analysis; wherever there are moves to contextualise and stabilise in the face of privileging and fragmentation; and, while making cultural politics its research priority, in acknowledging other sources of influence on educational policy making from within the macro-micro web of society and in establishing points of intersection with them. This should be immediately evident in the incorporation of the psychological and social as well as the cultural in the schematisation of the construct of policy paradigm that follows in the next chapter.

Chapter 2

The Schematisation of the Construct
of Policy Paradigm

This Chapter outlines the schematisation of the construct of policy paradigm which supplies the language and concepts to be deployed in the study of the cultural politics of Irish education that follows. Some sense of the diverse theoretical positions, disciplines and areas of study that are available as resources in attempting such a conceptual mapping has been provided in the previous chapter on studying cultural politics. Needless to say, it was not possible to include all the rich insights by way of concepts, language and approaches that these suggested. Nor were the theoretical resources that were used always deployed in precisely the manner in which they were originally formulated. A brief note on the rationale of the schematisation in terms of its principles of selection and modification of existing thought is, therefore, appropriate.

Throughout, the schematisation of the construct of policy paradigm was experientially grounded. The test of the construct's elaboration, in terms of its delineation and description of its components, was the extent to which it served to clarify and refine the description and interpretation of the cultural component in the process of shaping educational policy in real life, political contexts. Far from being a matter of imposing a theoretically-derived set of concepts on data, the schematisation of the construct arose from issues in the cultural politics of Irish education from the 1950s. The process was one of ongoing abrasion between concept and data in which concepts were used to enter and chart newly-identified features of educational reality and were in turn accepted, extended or rejected depending on how adequately they classified, named and explained these dynamics. The spirit of the principle of 'Occam's razor' prevailed, that entities should not be further subdivided unless this added to understanding. Or as Occam put it, 'It is vain to do with more what can be done with fewer' (quoted in Russell, 1967, p. 462).

A consequence of this process of honing the conceptual apparatus in the light of the Irish educational policy process was that concepts and perspectives from the broad family of the social sciences, some with conventional, others with variable meanings, were used with a contextually-specific meaning and function. The result is theoretically eclectic and utilitarian while seeking to avoid the sociological depthlessness to which theoretical pluralism is vulnerable. In this it aspires to a 'disciplined eclectism' (Layder, 1994, p. 222) and operates in the spirit of Best and Kellner's (1991) 'multiperspectival' social theory which seeks to accommodate the interconnection between the social, cultural, economic and political dimensions in the context of a complex social system. The ongoing nature of the schematisation also means that it continues to evolve, as is indicated by earlier published versions (O'Sullivan, 1989a; 1993a), according as further substantive applications suggest the need for additional units or features, refinements or deletions.

The orientation is primarily educational, and privileges Irish education in its conceptualisation. As such, to draw on an old distinction, it is an exercise in educational sociology rather than in the sociology of education. It would be surprising if it did not contribute to the theory of cultural politics or if the schematisation of the construct of policy paradigm did not have a wider application beyond Irish education (O'Sullivan, 1996b; 1998). But it was produced in the first instance to get a purchase on the operation of Irish educational policy making.

This disposition towards conceptual selection and elaboration can be likened to that of a *bricoleur* as used by Lévi-Strauss and defined by Derrida as 'someone who uses the "means at hand", … those which are already there, which had not been especially conceived with an eye to the operation for which they are to be used and to which one tries by trial and error to adapt them, not hesitating to change them whenever it appears necessary, or to try several of them at once, even if their form and their origin are heterogeneous' (quoted in St Pierre, 2000). As mentioned earlier, feminists have a long tradition of adapting and combining theories in this fashion in their political work and similar practices are to be found in the conceptualisation within literacy, cultural and post-colonial studies.

These orientations share a number of points of common sympathy with Ball's approach to the study of policy sociology in terms of contemporary educational policy analysis. He argues that in the study of complex social issues such as policy, which involve forces from all the layers of the social system, including political structures, culture, social interaction and individual interpretation, 'two theories are probably better than one', and that what is needed is 'a toolbox of diverse concepts and theories – an applied sociology rather than a pure one'. He is seeking 'to replace the modernist theoretical project of abstract parsimony with a somewhat more post-modernist one of localised complexity' (Ball, 1994, p. 14). Indeed, the 'toolbox' imagery has been endorsed by writers as diverse as

Vygotsky, Foucault, Bourdieu and Giddens in relation to the use of their theories and constructs.

Within the eclectic approach to theory adopted, post-structuralist approaches and insights are regularly drawn on. This is particularly evident in the centrality of the analysis of discursive and non-discursive practices, and their constitution as message-sending systems, that invite inquiry into their construction, reconfiguration and reception in the production of educational meanings. Yet, the applied focus of the approach adopted to the study of Irish cultural politics is at odds with the radical scepticism about the human subject, knowledge, truth and rationality which is at the heart of post-structuralism (Henriques *et al.*, 1984; Sarup, 1988; Nicholson and Seidman, 1995). To be faithful to post-structuralism is to find oneself 'lost in the play of discourse – not by any means an unrewarding experience, but one that can be frustrating for those who want to know exactly what is going on' (St Pierre, 2000). In fact, for post-structuralists, wanting to know what is exactly going on is an inadmissible question (Bové, 1990). While not presuming to seek to know 'exactly' what is happening in the Irish educational policy process, this study does aspire to advancing the understanding of some of its central and recurring processes. This forces the analysis to seek points of stability, fixity and structure in the flow of Irish educational meanings.

This in turn raises issues relating to human agency. As indicated earlier, it is assumed that human actors have the capacity to question and bring about change; they are not merely carriers or points of intersection of discourses. Yet, they do act in politically constrained contexts. Both sides of Marx's famous dictum have to be accommodated, that 'Men make their own history, but they do not make it just as they please; they do not make it under circumstances chosen by themselves, but under circumstances directly encountered, given and transmitted from the past' (quoted in McLellan, 1978, p. 137). It will be necessary to explore the circumstances – political, cultural, social and discursive – in which social actors find their capacity to act as agents in shaping the direction of education enhanced or diminished.

In accepting the reality of constraints in social action but refusing to admit to despair or the impossibility of critique, empowerment and commitment, the approach adopted here lines up with Rosenau's (1992) affirmative rather than sceptical post-modernists. Having said that, the underpinning ideology is not redemptive. In this regard, it distinguishes as Layder (1994, p. 223) does between general theories of society which are 'closed and intolerant of evidence and ideas which they cannot easily absorb or explain and those which are open to the possibility of new modes of thinking and to revision in the light of new empirical evidence'. Sheridan (1980, p. 221) in his description of Foucault's genealogy as 'the unmashing of power for the use of those who suffer it' warns that the genealogical method is also 'directed against those who would seize power in their name'. The author takes the spirit of that warning too much to heart to aspire to anything more than contributing to understanding, itself by no means an apolitical act.

Before proceeding to outline in detail the dimensions of the schematisation of the construct of policy paradigm a brief summary and tabular overview might help.

Table 2.1 outlines the schematisation of the construct of policy paradigm. From this it can be seen that it allows for the description of a policy paradigm along the following dimensions: its epistemic, discursive, social and psychological components; the extent and depth of its dominion; and the nature and character of its experience of change.

The analytical components of a paradigm are constructs to facilitate the description of a paradigm's features and to allow for their classification and delineation. They are not the substance of a paradigm but rather the tools of discrimination. The conceptualisation/language nexus provides a paradigm with the scaffolding for the delineation, classification and labelling of reality and its analysis benefits from a range of theories including those of structuralism and post-structuralism on the relationship between language, thought and reality. Themes are what can be meaningfully spoken of in a communicative encounter and texts their expansion and elaboration through narrative, analysis, imagery and performance. Performatives are proposals for action. The analysis of a paradigm's discourse can usefully draw on a number of traditions from the Greek notion of rhetoric or persuasive communication with its repertoire of figurative speech to Foucault's discourses, understood as expressions of power in the context of specific varieties of knowledge.

Table 2.1 Policy Paradigm: An Analytical Schema

Analytical Components			
Concepts/ Language	Themes/Texts/ Performatives/ Discourse	Associative Forms/ Authorities	Identities/ Subjectivities
Dominion			
Framing	Cultural Penetration/ Intertextuality		Political Positioning
Change			
Expansion/ Contraction	Intensification/ Simplification	Systematisation/ Diffusion Mutation	Merging/ Factioning Rupture

Associative forms address the social configurations of the agents who constitute a paradigm's intersubjective community, the extent and nature of their affiliation (e.g., atomised, diffuse, social movement, primary etc.) and allows for a consideration of how they become membershipped to the paradigm. A paradigm's authorities are those within these social configurations who legitimate the meanings of its texts as real and proper and are available to be called upon in their defence or arbitration. Identity recognises the psychological dimension in an individual's engagement of a paradigm and acknowledges that subjectivities can be constituted through paradigmatic membership and indeed experience fracture and fluidity through multiple and shifting membership as well as through paradigmatic change.

The dominion of a paradigm is a function of how weakly or strongly framed are its boundaries, the nature and range of the cultural phenomena it penetrates and where within the policy-making process it is dominant. A doxic paradigm is the ultimate in dominion in that not alone does it penetrate all aspects of life and all agents but there is no awareness of another reality outside of it.

Policy paradigms are always changing even at times when they appear to be static and beyond question. Here the work of Archer (1988, 1996) on cultural change was found to resonate theoretically with what emerged practically from the analysis. As a paradigm expands it incorporates a wider range of reality within its remit. A wider realm of ideas, discourse, people are incorporated within its influence. This can take the form of additional themes taking their flavour from the paradigm, previously unconvinced groups sharing its meanings, and gaining a foothold throughout the policy community. Conversely, a contracting paradigm will be seen to concede aspects of ideational, discursive and collective life. Unlike expansion, intensification results in more dense policy paradigms. It refers to a process of 'filling in' rather than 'filling out'. The result is a complex socio-cultural phenomenon, a developed network with interconnections and inter-linkages. This elaboration of a policy paradigm occurs within its components as well as in the character of the relationship between them. Intensification is produced by a more specialised set of agents than those who fuel the expansion and contraction of a paradigm. Its currency is research findings and theoretical developments. In a reversal of intensification, simplification results in a sparse paradigm. Theories are reduced to assertions, the language becomes sloganised and there is a paucity of legitimation.

Where a paradigm experiences continuous expansion and intensification it begins to take on the features of a system. In expanding it will have infused a greater swathe of reality that is meaningful to educational decision making; in intensifying, the interconnections between various features of a paradigm will be articulated and refined. Through these joint processes of 'filling out' and 'filling in', a paradigm systematises. This can be observed when it begins to exhibit such features as strong framing, protective strategies and reproductive mechanisms. Mutation also involves expansion/contraction of the components of a paradigm. But in this case the change does not take the form of incremental additions or subtractions. The defining characteristic of mutation is the reworking of an element of a paradigm to the extent that it facilitates the emergence of a new paradigm. The emerging paradigm is experienced as a outgrowth from the base paradigm. In merging, paradigms gain through the act of partnership. In a reversal of this process, paradigms may subdivide and form two or more autonomous structures. The rupture of a paradigm signals its demise as a coherent force in the shaping of the policy process. In reality, even in the more explicit and codified domain of science, as Archer points out, any theory can be saved from apparent falsification. Even more so with meaning, diversity and pluralism are more likely than elimination.

Analytical Components

Concepts/Language

Concepts

Concepts are boundaried categories of thought which we use to structure and make sense of the world. It was Kant who, in opposition to Hume and the empiricists and the rationalism of Descartes, drew the distinction between the data of experience and the categories in terms of which we know this experience. He puts it as follows: 'that all our knowledge begins with experience there can be no doubt ... but though all our knowledge begins with experience, it does not follow that it all arises out of experience' (quoted in Copleston, 1964, p. 13). What is being argued here is that to know reality is to engage in an interpretative exercise. This means that the mind imposes on the base material of experience its own forms of cognition and that we cannot know reality except through the medium of these forms. Kant believed that the categories through which we gained our knowledge of the external world were the same for all sentient beings. He considered them to be permanent and unalterable, believing that this is what made the world one and communication possible. Those who questioned the *a priori* status of our categorical system and saw change and difference in how we understood the world, would nonetheless have recognised the significance of what Berlin (1980) describes as the 'category spectacles' through which we interpret reality. Berlin draws attention to the profound differences which 'wearing different sets of spectacles, using different categories, thinking in terms of different models, must make to men of different times and places and cultures and outlooks' (pp 8-9). These relate to notions of cause and purpose, *good and evil, things and persons,* rights, duties, justice, truth etc. They include different interpretations of society ranging from Plato's geometrical pattern, through the mechanical model of Hobbes's and Spencer's organic imagery, right down to the contrasting visions of the communitarian agenda and Margaret Thatcher's assertion that there was no such thing as society.

Even more fundamental than the expectation of dispute between those who hold different conceptions of reality is the debate within philosophy on the extent to which they can be said to even understand one another. Davidson (1984) describes conceptual relativism as a 'heady and exotic doctrine'. Its implications are stark for human understanding and communication since there can be no translating from one conceptual scheme to another once it is claimed that the components of one scheme have no true counterpart in the thinking of those who subscribe to another scheme. This problem will again arise in relation to language as a mechanism for translating conceptual schemes. At this point what conceptual relativism draws our attention to is the sense in which people can appear to live in different worlds.

The shaping of one's conceptualisation of the world is a feature of personal socialisation both at the primary level of becoming a competent member of society and at the secondary stage of induction into educational, social and occupational sub-worlds. Even at the childhood stage, this involves individual variations and responses, be they conceived in terms of the 'lone scientist' constructing knowledge through action on objects (Piaget) or in social interaction with peers and adults making sense of the culture within a shared context (Vygotsky) (Wood and Attfield, 1996, p. 35). A key point in this development is the progression from an awareness of particular persons, objects and emotions familiar through daily contact to the incorporation of categories which reach beyond the child's known and existing experience. This significant development introduces such basic concepts to children as father, mother, drink, food, anger, joy in the sense that, for instance, their own father is now known as a member of a general category of fathers, categorised by the concept of fatherhood or the familiar smiles of their mothers are recognised as a pattern of facial expressions which have an established cultural meaning.

Later in life more complex concepts like motivation, cause, effect, proof are introduced and regularly used in schooling in coming to terms with the humanities and sciences, and elsewhere in the flux of social, occupational and bureaucratical activity. These represent the filters through which the world is progressively known and internalised. They help to make sense of the buzzing mass of stimuli by establishing a structure through their differentiation and integration: not alone does the concept of father associate those who qualify but its sets them apart through the concept of mother, for instance, from all those who are mothers in society. It, therefore, influences our perception of reality, what we really select from experience and how we organise it and interrelate its parts. In this manner one becomes a participant in a view of reality that is particular to a social group, culture or era. As Davidson (1984, p. 183) puts it, conceptual schemes are 'ways of organising experience; they are systems, categories that give form to the data of sensation; they are points of view, from which individuals, cultures or periods survey the passing scene'.

As well as varying in the light of, for instance, personal upbringing, education and professional membership, one's repertoire of concepts will be influenced at a more global level by one's place in time and space. Concepts are cultural and historical phenomena and can be seen to vary between cultures and over time. Colour concepts, for instance, may be more elaborate in one culture than another where the darkness/brightness of objects might suffice. Concepts can vary in significance; the relational concept of cousin remains in modern times but the obligations and prescriptions associated with it are greatly diluted, and what remains differs between urban and rural areas. Concepts can be rendered meaningless as charity and theft might be in total communism.

Concepts operate at various levels of complexity. A great number of people, perhaps the majority, never find it necessary to go beyond the unconscious use of concepts in their daily life. Others build their careers and professional knowledge around the study of concepts like thinking, feeling, heat, light, intelligence and planets. What is used at one level in an operational way may be comprehended and labelled more diversely in a scientific study of the relevant phenomena. In place of the operationally defined concept of group, for instance, sociologists in their analysis of society may demand any of three concepts – social category, collectivity and group – which make finer distinctions and points of demarcation possible. Similarly, a botanist will describe even the most commonplace of flowers by a Latin term which establishes its taxonomic status.

Ausubel *et al.* (1978) who have studied the conceptual maps incorporated in what they refer to as 'prior knowledge' have attempted to describe how cognitive structures develop and expand. They identify three major principles: hierarchical structuring (new concepts subsumed under more general or inclusive concepts); progressive differentiation (the acquiring and setting apart of concepts from existing ones); and progressive reconciliation (the establishing of linkages between related sets of concepts). Barrow (1981) describes this expansion in the refinement of one's conceptual repertoire as 'conceptual finesse' and proposes it as a key objective of the educational system. Others regard an awareness of the conceptual maps which people bring to a situation as an important starting point for self-knowledge and as the basis for personal transformation (Deshler, 1990). In his studies of the conceptual development of children, Vygotsky distinguished between two types of concepts – scientific concepts which are formed through a process of systematic and hierarchical thinking and everyday concepts which are context-specific and lack systematisation. According to Vygotsky, the process of their interaction is not one of domination or replacement: in Kozulin's words, Vygotsky made it a point to argue that 'spontaneous concepts in working their way upwards towards greater abstraction, clear a path for scientific concepts in their downward development towards greater concreteness' (quoted in Daniels, 1996). These are no more than examples of processes relevant to the functioning of conceptualisation within policy paradigms from what is an extensively studied area in philosophy and cognitive psychology with a strong empirical tradition (Estes, 1996).

It has been argued that, theoretically at least, it should be possible to interpret experience in the light of a totally novel set of concepts. Strawson (1966) argues that it is possible to imagine varieties of worlds very different from the world of our understanding. Kuhn (1962) speaks of incommensurable systems of concepts. Yet, given its incorporation in life-long socialisation, even those who subscribe to such relativist positions, and argue that there is nothing absolute about our conceptual inheritance, would nonetheless find it difficult to argue that conceptualisation can be purely a matter of personal choice. Experientially, there is a distinct collective dimension in how one views the world in the sense that it can signal membership of, for instance, social, religious and ethnic groups, incorporate symbols of solidarity and consequently be used both to exclude and coerce. Culturally-prescribed concepts are invested with considerable power. They define boundaries of normality and demand allegiance for the purpose of meaningful human contact. To deviate from what is accepted may well result in a disruption of social life, lack of comprehension, and even the labelling of the innovator as a genius or schizophrenic. One wonders, for instance, how 'sexism' or 'racism' would have been received by previous generations as categories for culturally integrating certain features of social relations. To analyse why certain concepts dominate at any given time and the process by which they change requires the consideration of the social interests involved, particularly in the case of the concepts central to the key institutions of society. At its most fundamental there is an ontology implicit in a repertoire of concepts in that 'concepts reflect and embody in their meaning beliefs about how the world operates' (Fay, 1987, p. 44).

The concepts used by individuals, groups, movements, cultures or eras will, therefore, influence how and with what level of innovativeness, stability, complexity, reflexivity and regulation, reality is comprehended and understood. Even the very act of inviting an arbitration on the concepts deployed in interpreting experience is restrained by the fact that in advancing such an invitation one has to make use of existing conceptual frameworks. It follows, therefore, that for a policy paradigm to regulate the conceptual framework through which the educational process is known and interpreted is to exercise control over the policy process at a deep and hidden level of structure. The conceptual apparatus sanctioned by a policy paradigm is a crucial element, and any analysis of the policy process, if it is to be other than culturally superficial, must engage the conceptual component of its paradigm. It equally follows that this is not a straightforward task, and for the same reasons – the normative power, the cultural embeddedness, the connotations of reality, and the social interests vested in the conceptual frameworks deployed within an intersubjective community.

Language

Concepts are abstractions and maintain a very precarious claim on reality in the absence of being labelled. The relationship between language, concepts, and reality is much disputed. Positivism, structural linguistics, semiology, linguistic analysis and post-structuralism all suggest their own interpretation and differ in the location of their emphasis. To what extent is the world available to be known as something 'out there' independent of the modes of knowing (e.g. concepts, language) of the knower? Is our understanding of what is true or real a function of the structure of the language we use to describe the world? Can we really justify the depsychologising of the sending and receiving of signs? Is the system of social signification all that really matters in determining meaning? Is it necessary to admit to a less closed or fixed set of relationships between the messages we communicate and the means of their communication? Or is the issue a conceptual one which can be settled by an analysis of the concepts used by people in living and making sense of the world (Winch, 1958; Kearney, 1986; Fay, 1987; Surber, 1998)?

Exploring the role of language in the shaping and maintenance of policy paradigms benefits in the first instance from the insights of the structuralist tradition in linguistic analysis. This perspective adopts Durkheim's interpretation of social facts as 'things'. The implication of this is to establish the social rather than the psychological in the study of human behaviour and, in particular, to draw attention to the constraining influence which social facts, though produced by human interaction, exercise over individual behaviour. For Durkheim, the sign systems used in communication like the social institutions of family, education, religion and economy, and the practices and regularities in social and moral behaviour '... all function independently of the use I make of them' (Durkheim, 1982[1895], p. 51).

Saussure's structural linguistics is credited with having been influenced by Durkheim's ideas. He incorporates the distinction between social facts and their manifestation in human behaviour in his distinction between *langue* and *parole*, between language as a system and actual speech. It was *langue*, the aspect of language which corresponds to social facts, which Saussure considered to be the primary object of linguistic analysis. This serves to heighten the interpretation of language as coercive and it is this sense of language operating as a regulative mechanism that Saussure pursues when he explores the consequences that follow from the arbitrary nature of the signs which make up a language system. By this it is meant that there is no intrinsic link between the signifier and what it signifies. In drawing out the implication of this, Saussure sought to discredit the notion of language as a system that named a preexisting world of objects, concepts and ideas. He contended that 'not alone does each language produce a different set of signifiers, articulating and dividing the continuum of sound in a distinctive way; each language produces a different set of signifieds; it has a distinctive and thus "arbitrary" way of organising the world into concepts or categories' (Culler, 1990, p. 23).

In the anthropological explorations of Boas, Sapir and Whorf, these themes of language as a regulative and arbitrary system are contextualised in relation to cultural variations in the linguistic systems for naming and interpreting the world. According to what has come to be known as the Sapir-Whorf hypothesis, a group's understanding of the world is shaped by its linguistic habits to the extent that those who do not share the same linguistic background cannot be said to live in the same world. While Sapir (1933) would acknowledge that the latent content of all languages is similar, he argued that how it is experienced and understood is shaped and differentiated according to the language of the speaker: '… no matter how sophisticated our modes of interpretation become, we never really get beyond the projection and continuous transfer of relations suggested by the forms of our speech … Language is at one and the same time helping and retarding us in our exploration of experience, and the details of these processes of help and hindrance are deposited in the subtler meanings of different cultures.' Sapir described the move from one language to another as being psychologically parallel to passing from one geometrical system of reference to another. The geometrical image also appealed to Whorf. Dineen (1967) recounts his example of the difficulty a European would experience in discussing geometry with the Hopi Indians. For Europeans the analysis of Newtonian geometry would be unproblematic since its requirements of space and time were to be found in most European languages. The Hopi language, on the other hand, does not contain such a distinction of time. It was in such a sense that Whorf spoke of being unable to discuss the 'same' world with the Hopi.

There are similarities between the Sapir-Whorf hypothesis and Wittgenstein's (1967[1953]) later writings on language-games. This refers to his belief that there are multiple patterns of language use following their own specific rules that implicate the participants in forms of life that are incommensurable with one another. Apart from the obvious extension of the Sapir-Whorf hypothesis to shifting intra-cultural variations in language use, Wittgenstein's language-games differ radically from Sapir-Whorf in their highly sceptical implication that all language is 'impossible, indeed unintelligible' (Kripke, 1982, p. 62).

Grace (1987) has distinguished between two viewpoints within the structuralist approach to language. These he labelled as the 'mapping view' and 'reality construction view' of language. The basic assumption of the mapping view is that 'there is a common world out there and our languages are analogous to maps of this world' and that differences in the details of that mapping from one language to another '... may be thought of as differences in the way they "divide the common world up" – in the way they "classify" its phenomena' (p. 6). In the reality construction view emphasis is placed on the imperfect view of the world provided by our senses. All we can do is theorise about reality and construct models of the world which are reflected in the languages we speak.

It can be argued that the dichotomy is not as sharp as Grace suggests. Mapping out the world of experience through language can be quite a creative exercise and involve acts of shaping and formation that range beyond the function of language as a nomenclature. Equally, language does not create reality but can be said to construct it in the sense that it helps to regulate what is real to people and what constitutes their understanding of their world. Grace accepts that the difference is one of emphasis but that it pertains to an emphasis that has major implications for how we think of language. Here it serves to heighten a number of issues that are pertinent to how language might function in the construction, maintenance and destabilising of policy paradigms.

Firstly, there is the question of the dynamic link between conceptual change and linguistic change. Consider Culler's (1990, p. 22) example of the signifier 'silly'.

> ... a 'silly' person was once happy, blessed, and pious. Gradually this particular concept altered; the old concept of 'silliness' transformed itself, and by the beginning of the sixteenth century a 'silly' person was innocent, helpless, even deserving of pity. The alteration of the concept continued until eventually a 'silly' person was simple, foolish, perhaps even stupid.

Culler argues that if language were a nomenclature we would have to say that there exists a number of distinct concepts and that the signifier *silly* was attached first to one and then to another. His interpretation is otherwise: that '... the concept attached to the signifier "silly" was continually shifting its boundaries, gradually changing its semantic shape, articulating the world in different ways from one period to the next'.

To arbitrate on this, one would need to know if at the time when 'silly' meant 'blessed' and 'pious' there were also concepts such as stupid, innocent and pitiful, and if so what signifiers were used to differentiate between such concepts and 'silly'. This is to advert to a core tenet of Saussure's linguistics, that it is the system of relationships through differentiation that is important. It is not particularly helpful to be told that 'silly' shifted its articulation of an individual's psychology unless there is an exposition of how 'silly' fits into its relevant system of signification. Furthermore, one would need to explore the fluctuating impact of superstition, religion and psychology on the understanding of human personality to the extent that it changes the way we mentally delineate and give meaning to traits in the manner in which we think about human behaviour.

Pursuing this kind of analysis points to the difficulty in drawing a distinction between bringing a thought into being and putting it into words, between thinking and its codification. It also raises the possibility that the potentialities have not been yet exhausted for the creation of new languages and cultural systems which will allow us to differentiate the universe in novel ways and speak of it in a fashion that we cannot even dream about now.

A related issue is the existence and status of concepts which have not been encoded in language. Derrida (1981, p. 19) concludes that maintaining the essential distinction between signifier and signified '... inherently leaves open the possibility of thinking a concept signified in and of itself, a concept simply present for thought, independent of a relationship to language, that is of a relationship to a system of signifiers'. On the other hand, in a famous passage in the preface to the *Tractatus*, Wittgenstein (1961[1921]) seems to relegate unnamed thinking to a realm of, at best, contingent existence.

> What can be said at all can be said clearly; and whereof one cannot speak thereof one must be silent. Thus the aim of the book is to draw a boundary of thinking, or rather – not of thinking, but of the expression of thoughts: for in order to draw a boundary of thinking, we should have to be able to think both sides of the boundary (we should have to be able to think what cannot be thought). It will therefore only be in language that the boundary can be drawn, and what lies on the other side of the boundary will be plain nonsense.

Wittgenstein's later writing has been described as shifting perspective (Finlayson, 1999b) on this issue, and indeed forgetting, no longer understanding, or refuting this assertion (Malcolm, 1988). Relevant here is a series of passages from notebooks and letters reproduced by Malcolm (1988, p. 65) in which Wittgenstein writes on how he believes that the constituents of thought 'correspond to the words of language' and that 'thinking is a kind of language'. Malcolm, in fact, points to the affinity with Chomsky's idea of the individual's innate and endowed capacity for language. He quotes from Fodor (1976) who speaks of 'the language of thought' as an 'inner code' or 'internal representational system', and he proposes that 'learning including first language learning, essentially involves the use of an unlearned internal representational system'.

This allows us to revert back to Wittgenstein's assertion that 'whereof one cannot speak, thereof one must be silent' and to question, at least, its more popularised interpretations. The study of semiotics has pointed to alternative mechanisms of communication to speech and writing, such as graphic representation, styles of dress, patterns of consumption and routines of behaviour. The realm of unencoded thought is suggested by a personal awareness of hunches and intuition. Similarly, satirical and ironic genres of communication and non-rational and para-normal representations testify to a set of mental formulations that have yet to be named in a manner that signifies their location within the relational system of a particular language but which nonetheless exists in a meaningful way for the individuals who engage in them. The source and formation of these realms of thought may also be studied as a structural process in that they reflect cultural myths, the operation of the unconscious, repression and guilt.

Finally, how capable are all languages of expressing all possible thoughts? Searle (1969, p. 19) has advanced the 'principle of expressibility' which he defines as 'the principle that whatever can be meant can be said'. In its extreme form, the mapping view of language fully supports this principle. Since according to this view all languages are descriptions of a common world, and since whatever is said in any language must refer to that world, they share a similar base of reference. An extreme version of this is what is known as adamic language. This is explained by Steiner (quoted in Grace, 1987, p. 14) as follows:

> The vulgate of Eden contained, though perhaps in a muted key, a divine syntax – powers of statement and designation analogous to God's own diction, in which the mere naming of a thing was the necessary and sufficient cause of its leap into reality. Each time man spoke he re-enacted, he mimed, the nominalist mechanism of creation.

A more muted version would hold with the principle of expressibility but would recognise that the structure of a language will hinder/facilitate the expression of some rather than other ideas. This has given rise to the 'intertranslatability postulate' (Grace, 1987, p. 7), that what can be expressed in one language can also be expressed in any other language.

The reality construction view of language rejects these propositions and argues that what is said cannot in any satisfactory way be separated from the way in which it is said. It argues that just as culture and language cannot be separated to such an extent that one cannot say where one begins and the other ends, similarly one cannot draw a clear line between thinking and the encoding of thought.

If it is true that the contrasting propositions relating to these issues are incorrigible, in that, because of problems of hypothesis formulation and testing, they cannot be refuted or confirmed then their utility must lie in the insights and understanding they offer and the degree to which they shed light on different situations in which policy paradigms might apply. The following are some pointers:

- The manner in which the language of a paradigm is implicated in how it conceptualises the aspect of the world to which the paradigm pertains and the possibility of the endless deconstruction and reconstruction for that reality.

- The existence and processes of a realm of conceptualisation that awaits codification within the system of relationships which characterise a linguistic system and which, though 'ideal' in nature are nonetheless very real, negotiable and changeable to the participants.
- The experience of communicating across paradigms and of participants in one paradigm importing meanings from another. What is lost, misinterpreted, reformulated or gained in the process?

One of the limitations in adopting the structuralist view of language is that it can underplay change and the role of individuals as active sources of change. However factual, language is constantly changing. Saussure accepted the historicity of language but prioritised the synchronic study of language (the study of a language system at a particular point in time) over the diachronic study of language (its study over time). Saussure argued that however language might have evolved what was important for the individual was its contemporary state. But Saussure acknowledges the role of individual action in arguing that change originates in *parole*, in linguistic performance, and through modification in aspects of the realisation of language, the system, *langue*, is affected. According to Saussure (1983[1916], pp 84-85) what is happening is that 'certain elements change but without regard to the connexions (*sic*) which integrate them as part of the whole' causing a disturbance of its 'equilibrium' and bringing 'a new system into being'.

If not teleological, the role of motivated (to use the term differently from Saussure) *parole* must be considered. As Culler (1990, p. 37) acknowledges, language does not exist as a series of totally homogeneous synchronic states. 'In a sense', he argues, 'the notion of a synchronic state is a methodological fiction', since to speak about the linguistic system of any language is an abstraction from variations that exist at any one time.

As well as what the participants in a linguistic community inherit by way of the variability of its linguistic resources, Bakhtin, Voloshinov and Medvedev, in collaboration it is argued (Wertsch, 1991), have drawn attention to the dialogical nature of language use, to the fact that to speak is to respond to a previous utterance while seeking to address a specific audience. The implication is that 'all language responds to previous utterances and to pre-existing patterns of meaning and evaluation, but also promotes and seeks to promote further responses. One cannot understand an utterance or even a written work as if it were singular in meaning, unconnected to previous and future utterances or works. No utterance or work, (they) argue, is independent or what they term "monumental"' (Allen, 2000, p. 19). In this view, Saussure's privileging of the synchronic study of language 'loses sight of the social specificity of language and confines it to something as abstract as a lexicon or dictionary' (Allen, 2000, p. 19). Both Saussure and Sapir-Whorf have been faulted for tending to assume that language systems are homogenous and uniform and for downplaying the variety of language use in social and political contexts, Sapir-Whorf appearing 'to make language seem as if it were the mystical product of the community', and Saussure making 'the community sound like the mystical product of language' (Finlayson, 1999b).

Not only does situating language in the context of its worldly use draw attention to the fact of changing meanings, it also highlights the realisation that cultural values are at work when we describe and classify phenomena: 'when we give things a label, we also give them a standing, a position in a pecking order and an estimate of their moral worth. We place values on the things we talk about through the very words we use. In turn, these words only make sense within the systems of values we share within social communities' (Smith, 2000, p. 50). Barthes (1973) sought to extend the structuralism of Saussure to take account of these cultural systems in which communication takes place. To this end he introduced the terms denotation and connotation as a means of acknowledging the polysemic nature of signs – their ability to assume different meanings – depending on the cultural reference system in which they function. Denotation operates at the level of language (the first order semiological system) and involves a description of the thing in question, whereas connotation draws on a higher order of signification (the second order semiological system) that implicates the prevailing historical and cultural meanings available to the participants in the communication. Surber (1998, p. 175) takes as an example the photograph of a bald eagle: 'the photograph itself is a sign that denotes a bald eagle. However, in addition to the first order object, most of us would think almost immediately of other, related signs, such as the American flag, patriotism, or perhaps endangered species, all of which constitute part of the eagle's connotation for most contemporary Americans.'

Once the possibility of change in the regulative system of language through the speech practices of individuals and groups is situated in the context of variable usage, values and individual action, it is easy to see how the politicisation of speaking makes sense. To speak is potentially to make assertions about how our understanding of the world is to be confirmed or restructured. Leaving aside the content of its propositions, ideas and ideologies, to use language in a particular way has the capacity to be fundamentally subversive. Predictably, this is the approach to language adopted by the exponents of critical approaches to society who see the possibility of disrupting and changing the linguistic dimension of unequal power relationships and structures. McLaren (1995, p. 100), one of the leading interpreters of critical pedagogy, for instance, asserts the capacity of people to shift meaning '... by critical self-reflexivity ... in order to effect acts of political transgression'. Within the feminist critique of language, Cixous has been described as choosing 'not to take the route that denies sexual difference(s) but to accede to a play of differences that would not turn into oppositions. Mocking

Freud's statement that describes women as the black continent, Cixous intimates that black is a neutral term until it is charged with a negative value in a system of oppositional hierarchies. Rejecting a dialectical use of binary terms, she writes the way males see women but revalorises the terms' (Conley, 1992, pp 37-38).

But it is important to recognise that the political use of language in meaning-making that disrupts power structures and systems of concealment will itself be constrained by the weight of established orthodoxies and the interests they serve. While recognisng the social embeddedness of language use, structural constraints in language have to be acknowledged unless the task of reconfiguring meaning is to be reduced to one of individual agency and voluntarism. The historical era in which people operate and the social and cultural context of their linguistic engagements are never static and will yield different possibilities for modifying the relationships between signifiers themselves and between them and the different orders of signifieds which they realise. This is captured by Voloshinov (2000[1929], pp 23-24):

> ... (the) *inner dialectic quality* of the sign comes out fully in the open only in times of social crises or revolutionary changes. In the ordinary conditions of life, the contradiction embedded in every ideological sign cannot emerge fully because the ideological sign in an established, dominant ideology is always somewhat reactionary and tries, as it were, to stabilise the preceding factor in the dialectical flux of the social generative process, so accentuating yesterday's truth as to make it appear today's.

Bourdieu (1991), who also recognises the need to understand language as social practice as well as a system, attempts to find a space between the extremes of structure and agency with his theory of habitus. In the process, his research agenda and empirical investigations represent a transition to the study of discourse, to how language use is implicated in social institutions, stratification, authority and power.

These issues arising from the structuralist approach to language will recur at various points of this chapter and throughout the subsequent substantive analyses both in their own right and as points of departure and reference in the light of the post-structuralist approach to language, culture, social action and power. They specifically emerge in the next section when we deal with the linked concepts of discourse, texts, themes and performatives. Later, dealing with the framing of a paradigm, the role of language in establishing the strength of a paradigm's boundaries is considered, as well as efforts to cope with this boundary maintenance function within the confines of language itself.

Discourse/Texts/Themes/Performatives

Discourse

It is best to begin with Benveniste's (1971, p. 209) definition of discourse which adopts a very broad understanding of the concept and the practice to include '... every utterance assuming a speaker and a hearer, and in the speaker, the intention of influencing the other in some way'. As Benveniste points out, this includes any kind and level of oral expression ranging from trivial conversation to the most formal of orations, as well as the diverse forms of written work such as memoirs, diaries and scholarly and academic texts. As such, there is a danger of seeing discourse as so universal and diffuse that it evades systematic analysis. In describing discourse as '... what is said and written and passes for more or less orderly thought and exchange of ideas', Cherryholmes (1988, p. 2) identifies a central feature of all discursive practices: that they follow the conventions and routines of rule-governed action and that at the most basic level of being accepted as discourse in the first instance they are required to satisfy a number of basic conditions relating to intelligibility, meaningfulness and predictability.

Three approaches to the study of discourse can contribute to an understanding of the role of discourse in the construction, maintenance and communication of policy paradigms. The oldest approach dates from the ancient Greeks and derives from the study and art of rhetoric, the power of persuasive communication. Unlike grammar, which specifies the rules of correct language use, rhetoric concerns the planning and enactment of public speaking in political and legal contexts. This meaning is indicated by its Greek root, *rheo*, meaning 'to flow' or 'to gush forth'. Condit (1990) in her study of campaign discourse in the US, has drawn on features of classical rhetoric to illuminate how those who seek to advance the case of particular political positions or groupings organise their discourse to maximise the likelihood of it appearing truthful and compelling. This includes the use of figurative speech such as metaphor, synecdoche (substituting a part of an item for the whole of another), and metonymy (replacing a precise name for something with a quality or a characteristic). A study of tropes, the collective category for forms of figurative speech, is more typical in literary studies but its utility in the study of other forms of discourse has come to be increasingly recognised: 'attention is now being increasingly given to how rhetorical devices shape our experience and our judgements, how language serves to promote the possibilities of certain kinds of action and exclude the practicability of others' (Sarup, 1988, p. 52).

The *Handbook of Discourse Analysis*, in four volumes (Van Dijk, 1985), was an attempt to document the state of development of a second approach, the interdisciplinary area of discourse analysis (*textwissenschaft*). This began to develop a coherence as a distinct area of study in the 1970s, drawing together and seeking to find a common focus for those from a diversity of backgrounds in anthropology, sociology, mass communications research, linguistics, semiotics, etc. with a shared interest in language use, texts, conversational interaction and communicative events. As an example of the variety of theoretical and descriptive approaches in this new interdisciplinary field, Van Dijk (1985, p. xi) points to the study of narrative, the attention paid to natural forms of language use, the computer-simulated study of text processing, the ethnography of teaching and the analysis of style and argumentation. All of this suggests many applications in the study of the discursive practices of policy paradigms.

A third approach derives from Foucault's study of the power/knowledge relationship in discursive practices. According to Foucault, discourses are expressions of power in the context of specific varieties of knowledge. They are manifestations of a society's 'regime of truth', that is 'the types of discourse which it accepts and makes function as true; the mechanisms and instances which enable one to distinguish true and false statements; the means by which each is sanctioned; the techniques and procedures accorded value in the acquisition of truth; the status of those who are charged with saying what counts as true' (Foucault, 1980, p. 131). To enunciate a discourse is therefore to speak with authority about a particular area (such as medicine or law) having followed the rules governing the operation of truth regimes which can vary according to historical, social and economic contexts. But in any professional relationship the distribution of power is not symmetrical. Thus, the ability to successfully use a discourse and to be accepted as a communicator of authoritative knowledge 'also implies that this facility is employed in relation to people who lack such command and have no legitimate claim to such knowledge' (Layder, 1994, p. 97). Yet, it is an essential feature of Foucault's study of discourse that he does not see power as something that is possessed. Rather, it is considered to circulate and not in any sense to follow the binary pattern of master/slave, oppressor/oppressed, superior/subordinate, etc. Foucault suggests that '… an analysis of power should concentrate not on the level of conscious intention but on the point of application of power' (Sarup, 1988, p.82). This shifts the focus from questions relating to the identity and intentions of those who have power to enquiries concerning its function, production, regulation and social affects (Bové, 1990). The relevance of this mode of thinking about power, knowledge and language for the study of educational policy was recognized by Ball (1990, p. 22).

> Discourse provides a particular and pertinent way of understanding policy formation, for policies are pre-eminently, statements about practice – the way things could be or should be – which rest upon, derive from, statements about the world – about the way things are. They are intended to bring about idealised solutions to diagnosed problems. Policies embody claims to speak with authority, they legitimate and

initiate practices in the world, and they privilege certain visions and interests. They are power/knowledge configurations *par excellence.*

Bacchi (2000) groups Ball with a growing body of scholars who adopt the broad approach of 'policy as discourse'. Among the many issues revealed in her detailed analysis of the meaning of discourse and its political context among these scholars, of particular relevance here is the difficulty of imagining social or political change given the totalising manner in which the policing function of discourse is represented. Foucault has been widely interpreted to mean '… that every attempt to reform society, to give people more freedom ineluctably become its opposite – a technique of domination. No matter where or when, it is the same as it ever was – social control' (Lacombe, 1996). Bacchi advises that 'policy-as-discourse analysts need to spend more time theorising the "space for challenge".' This is apt since discourse can often appear in social and political studies to be anonymous, without an author, or in which the individual is represented as no more than the intersection of discourses. In applying the insights of Foucault and the general post-structuralist approach to discourse in the study of policy paradigms it will be important to identify contradictions, multiplicities and modifications in the life of discourses. This acknowledges the regulative power of discourse without assuming the existence of a sealed epistemic system. It believes that a society's 'regime of truth' is neither monolithic nor immutable.

Texts

Rather than use discourse to refer to a field of power-bearing knowledge on a particular topic, such as in speaking of medical or legal discourse in the tradition of Foucault, it seems more discriminating to deploy the concept of 'text' to isolate within cultural production a strand of established meaning-making with the potential to yield an identifiable body of knowledge. This distinction allows discourse to be used more generally to refer to what is said and written while retaining for texts the regulative function identified by Foucault. Distinguishing between discourse and text in this way also isolates the role of non-discursive forces, such as practices and images, in text production. Because a text can be realised through discursive and non-discursive signification, where there is the possibility of confusion in using text in its conventional sense 'work' will be used instead.

As used here, a text is constituted by the development of a theme over time through the dynamics of multiple sources of signification. As such, a text can be extensive and ambitious in what it seeks to assert, and in such instances is likely to have a complex structure involving master, subsidiary and counter-texts. Equally, a text can be less substantial and be realised by a series of articles or books or recurring pattern of social action (single-sex schooling, the expansion of multi-denominational schooling, evaluative practices). What they have in common is the working through of a concept, theory or idea by means of its expansion, defence and application. The most accessible use of texts in this study is where they are selected as instantiations of policy paradigms and, as such, provide us with pathways of excavation back to a paradigm's underpinning and defining understandings. This is never a matter of simply reading off a policy paradigm from a text.

At any time, it is possible to identify an infinite number of texts that could be considered to offer interpretations that are in some sense relevant to educational issues. Even with globalisation, particularly in relation to the flow of educational ideas and practices, only a limited number will come into play as serious contenders in influencing the cultural interpretation of educational phenomena in any one country or system. Yet, despite this narrowing of the field of knowledge, when all the varieties are considered from substantial master texts (e.g. Christianity) to more specialised subsidiary texts (e.g. parental involvement), selectivity becomes necessary. Two principles of selection will be applied: the explanatory force of a text in relation to a substantive policy paradigm, and the exemplary character of the text as a model of a particular dimension of a policy paradigm's dynamics.

As well as being a selective exercise, using texts as a means of revealing a policy paradigm's distinctive understandings is also interpretive. Texts do not always announce themselves in the terms by which they become named in analysis. Re-interpretation of religious education as indoctrination is an obvious example. Nor is it necessary that they would be knowingly produced as a sequence of educational ideas and proposals, or that the social actors who contribute to their construction would recognise themselves as being involved in a common exercise. What is important is the configuration of discourses and practices that can be judged to have an independent impact as a body of knowledge on how educational phenomena are to be understood, represented and politically engaged with. The implication of identifying and naming the contributory sources in the politics of meaning in this selective and interpretive fashion is that a similar episode in the production of knowledge could find itself configured and re-configured in the construction of different texts depending on which aspect of educational reality is the target of the analysis. This resonates with Derrida's imagery of texts as tapestries, making the task of deconstruction '... a process of unravelling various strands of the tapestry, tracing them back to other tapestries in which they are already interwoven and following them where they might lead beyond the texts at hand' (Surber, 1998, p. 207). It also anticipates the concept of intertextuality, which will be used later to analyse a paradigm's dominion in terms of the interplay of texts within a culture. This reflects the early application of intertextuality by Kristeva and Barthes as designating 'the way in which a culture is structured as a complex network of codes with heterogeneous and dispersed forms of textual realisation. It formulated the codedness or textuality of what had previously been thought in non-semiotic terms (consciousness, experience, wisdom, story, gender, culture, and so on)' (Frow, 1991).

Points of stability are provided by the manner in which policy paradigms are made to become real in texts in the sense that they constitute the recognisable and lived content of communication and interaction between human actors, operating individually or collectively, in actual political situations. As well as existing as recognisable contributions to the stock of human knowledge, texts can also attain orthodoxy. To varying degrees and in appropriate settings they will command use and allegiance. Texts can also be subsumed in ongoing routine practices in the case of non-discursive texts. All of this enhances their facticity, 'fixes' their representation amid their endless articulation and re-articulation of meaning, and disguises the politics of their construction and change (as distinct from the more explicit and behavioural politics of their prescriptions). One of the tasks in the study of cultural politics must be to uncover the principles of inclusion and exclusion at the level of meaning in the production of texts that reveal the hidden operation of policy paradigms.

There is a long tradition of structuralist approaches to the analysis of texts, in the form of myths (Lévi-Strauss, 1969[1949]), folk tales (Propp, 1958[1928]) and literary works (Barthes, 1970). These seminal studies have been followed by the application of their techniques of analysis to the study of western movies, detective novels and television programmes (Smith, 2000). They relate, however, to clearly delineated texts or clusters of texts often as a feature of specific works. Also, in some of these early structuralist accounts of texts consideration of their historical, social and political contexts is deliberately excluded. Nonetheless, because of their concern to reveal the deep structure of a text, which can be disguised beneath the surface appearance, by identifying its rules, codes and binaries, they suggest fruitful lines of enquiry. They can also be usefully adapted, as Eco attempted with the accommodation of hermeneutics within structuralism, and Kristeva with its extension through Lacan's psychoanalysis (Surber, 1998). These facilitate the analysis of texts ranging from single identifiable works such as policy documents to the 'imagined', though real in their material impact, complex configurations of discourse and practice. Overall, the repertoire of approaches is immense once one is willing to draw on different theoretical traditions and disciplines. As we have seen in the approaches to the study of discourse, these can include the rhetorical tactics by which a text seeks to establish itself as true, the function of grammar in the communication of meaning, the creation of subjectivities, and the principles of inclusion and exclusion. Since in any policy context the operation of power is central, Janks's (1997) specification of the relevance of critical discourse analysis (after Fairclough, 1995) is of universal significance:

(discursive practices) are tied to specific historical contexts and are the means by which existing social relations are reproduced or contested and different interests are served. It is the questions pertaining to interest that relate discourse to relations of power. How is the text positioned or positioning? Whose interests are served by this positioning? Whose interests are negated? What are the consequences of this positioning?

This focus on the operation of power and interests will narrow the analysis of texts within more manageable limits. This is reflected in according a primary place within the analysis to the study of themes and performatives.

Themes/Performatives

In seeking to lay bare a policy paradigm through the analysis of texts, the place of themes and performatives is of particular significance in this present study of Irish cultural politics. Themes represent the point of entry of a meaning to a culture, and performatives the transition from meaning to prescription for educational change.

Themes are what can be meaningfully communicated within an intersubjective community. Ball's (1990, p. 32) analysis of the impact of James Callaghan's widely quoted speech at Ruskin College, Oxford, in 1976 serves as an example of this process both at the level of acceptance and expurgation. He interprets the Prime Minister's intervention as making it more difficult to defend comprehensivisation and progressivism from their critics. To do so would be to invite being labelled as 'both subversive, damaging to the interests of children and the nation, and reactionary, irrationally persisting with old, disreputable ways' and 'to court exclusion from the arenas of policy'. As a corollary, the themes of the New Right – standards, authority, industrial linkages – gained entry to policy debate. As one of its advocates argued '… we have pushed back the boundaries of what is sayable, and now there are a number of things, which are sayable which weren't sayable ten years ago'. Ball's examples illuminate a number of mechanisms in the regulation of themes. These include the contextual constraints on what can be said in one setting and not in another, changes in the logic of these norms through the discursive reconfiguring of, for instance, professional or 'responsible' subjectivities, as well as the self-censorship exercised by the social actors acting either tactically or in the gaze of these favoured subjectivities.

Those who consciously experience dismissal or derision in attempting to add a viewpoint or perspective to policy debate can develop coping strategies which seek to neutralise these constraints. A common tactic is what is referred to in social movement research as the accumulation of 'idiosyncrasy credit'. This involves seeking to enhance the likelihood of getting an audience for unorthodox views by building up a conventional image through what one does and says. Themes may also at times appear or be made to appear as elements of 'idle talk' (*gerede*) – snap judgements, hasty evaluation, jocose opinions – that functions to fill aural space and ease social interaction rather than advance authentic communication (Heidegger, 1962[1927]). Yet, even in idle talk, there is a testing of the cognitive and communicative tolerance of a theme. And it constitutes a testing ground that involves no statement of intent or commitment. Attributing a view to a third party or communicating it in the passive voice also provides the speaker with a similar defence. Such tactics allow for themes to be filtered into the policy process without political threat.

There is a danger in interpreting thematisation within the confines of agenda setting. Thematisation is culturally prior to agenda setting in that its objects of analysis are the meanings and interpretations that shape the form of the issues that come to be in competition for even a place in policy debate. This distinction between a policy option competing for political action and the history of its cultural production is central to the characteristic domain of cultural politics. For Bacchi (2000), the starting point in treating policy as discursively produced '... is a close analysis of items that do make the political agenda to see how the construction or representation of those issues limits what was talked about as possible or desirable or as impossible or undesirable'. A necessary condition for the existence of a topic in policy debate is the tolerance of its meaning and language within the culture. They must be expected to make sense to the participants in the communicative encounter. To have the status of a theme is to be recognised and understood, to constitute valid elements of discourse. Where those in communication are failing to make meaningful contact there will be incomprehension. Theorists who postulate the untranslatability thesis in relation to conceptual schemes and languages would treat this as the inevitable failure of sealed cultural systems to interpenetrate. More dynamically, thematisation points to the processes of production and reception in the construction of meaning.

Situated between cultural possibility and political possibility, between what can be thought or spoken of, and possible orientations for educational change, respectively, themes represent a grey though important realm of the policy process. A delicate tension is represented in having the status of a theme. While a conceptualisation, interpretation or viewpoint can, as a theme, be seen to have a meaningful place in educational discourse there is no necessary implication for the direction of educational policy. Themes may be essential elements in the establishment of a proposition as a policy option, but in having the status of a theme, there is no guarantee that they will ever be included in the policy agenda as possibilities to be considered and assessed relative to others with a view to directing educational practice.

Performatives are prescriptions for educational change. Accordingly, they are more recognisable elements of the policy process than such constructs as concepts, language or themes. They also represent the point at which conventional policy studies begin their consideration of the policy process. Influencing the agenda in policy-making – keeping items off as well as putting items on – is conventionally seen as an indication of the relative power of the participants in the policy-making process. To have one's favoured line of educational change taken sufficiently seriously within the policy community to be considered for possible implementation is a necessary achievement for an individual or social configuration intent on influencing the direction of the educational system. But this is to advert to what is most visible. Socio-political processes – advocacy, lobbying, influence, power, forming coalitions, accepting compromises, making deals – are clearly involved in gaining prominence as a performative. These socio-political processes are public if only in the sense of being explicit to the participants, as in the case of otherwise private or covert arrangements 'behind closed doors'. What needs to be kept in mind is that dimensions of the policy paradigm from the pre-debate level influence what can be made salient, spoken about and communicated in a manner that is meaningful to participants.

The establishment of a line of action as a performative, therefore, is influenced by the filtering and delineating function of these paradigmatic components. The political players do not select from some infinite set of performatives and succeed or not succeed in having their favoured option considered for implementation depending on their strength within the socio-political process. What are considered to be available as performatives would have been influenced by the conceptualisation of the educational system, its labelling and thematisation. Little of this may be recognised with the result that the power of a paradigm is at its greatest when it operates at this covert level of pre-debate. This is not to devalue the significance within the policy process of the designation of performatives. Rather, it situates this component of a text within the history of its production, in particular serving to identify the anticipatory and structuring influences that shape the pool of performatives from which the policy agenda is set. The circulation of performatives is nonetheless a distinct stage within the policy process involving all the socio-political processes of advocacy, negotiation, etc., and should not be seen as a mere epiphenomenon or representation of less visible structuring forces within a policy paradigm.

There are countless opportunities for intervention in the cultural and historical space between the entry of a theme into a culture and its manifestation as a performative in policy discourse. A theme may come to dominate the discourse on education; equally, it may experience marginalisation and be deemed to be appropriate and tolerable only in certain contexts – the academy, idealised, speculative or utopian discourse, or in relation to other educational systems, for instance. It may attract extensive theorisation, defence and application or it may remain an inspirational thought or idea with long-term rather than immediate relevance. A theme can expect to mutate intertextually as it comes into play with other ways of speaking and thinking about education. This is to advert to the emergent influence of social and political factors.

As a theme is constituted as a text – the process of textualisation – it is open to deployment within different textual patterns with implications for material interests. It will be beneficial for some individuals and social configurations to have a particular theme accorded a prominent and influential place in educational discourse and practice. Those who sense a threat in such a topic becoming a feature of the collective understanding of education, and the manner in which education is routinely spoken of and acted through, will wish to retard its dominion. What happens to a theme when viewed in this manner as a political resource will depend on the existence of individuals who become infused with it, collective interests that develop and communicate it, and the receptiveness of the political system to its distinctive impact. And this is only to consider the construction of a policy issue as a proposal for educational change and not to advert to its success or otherwise in influencing the enactment of policy. Passion, mobilisation and political opportunity are important for cultural production as for political change. Cultural politics is never bodiless or socially free-floating.

The next two sections engage with such components of paradigm formation – its social dimension in the shape of the varieties of associative forms which an intersubjective network might take, the specific roles in relation to legitimation, authority and leadership which members play in its formation, advancement and change, and the manner in which individual psychology becomes implicated with paradigm engagement and membershipping.

Associative Forms/Authorities

Associative Form

The associative form of a paradigm refers to the character of the relationships between the actors involved. Some conceptual refinement is required if the particular forms that association between participants in a paradigm can take are to be adequately delineated and named. Sources for this conceptualisation are to be found in writings on the individual and society, solidarity, social integration and collective action that reach back to the beginnings of sociology. The conceptualisation that follows draws explicitly on a tradition that spans more than a century and includes Tönnies, Weber, Cooley, Davis and Giddens. I identify six varieties of association – categorical, atomistic, collective, primary, exclusionary and bureaucratic – which can be usefully deployed in the description and analysis of the social, 'peopled' dimension of the existence, development and expansion of paradigms.

Categorical Association

Social categories are no more than statistical groupings. They involve the linking of people through an act of classification and delineation. They exist conceptually rather than experientially. Characteristics such as income level, age, height and shoe size provide a basis for categorical association. Typically, the characteristic shared is not perceived by those represented to have any significance for how they might relate to one another. Accordingly, they see no sense of mutual interest, common values or a shared life-situation. All that can be said of categorical association, that has a significance for the analysis of policy paradigms, is that it has potential for mobilisation and transformation to higher forms of association as individuals are membershipped into particular policy paradigms. Parental status and sex have experienced such a transition in educational policy in recent decades.

Atomistic Association

Social aggregates have a common focus that may involve no more than the coming together of people. There is no necessary sense of sharing. The relationship between the participants is atomistic. Those watching a television programme at any one time, a queue waiting for a bus, a cinema audience, those being transported in a lift and motorists in a traffic jam are examples. While there is likely to be an awareness of the existence of others, the goal of the moment does not require that any cognisance be taken of one another apart from whatever is demanded by the rules that apply to such encounters – waiting one's turn, not jumping the queue or quietness in the cinema. Though atomistic, if the people involved share a common focus and physical space, transformation to more socially-significant associative forms is a possibility. A large student group in a lecture theatre exemplifies this. From the students' point of view the focus is on the lecture. The encounter does not require communication, empathy, or solidarity between students. The goals of the learning programme can be effectively achieved by maintaining an atomistic stance. Yet, if the encounter persists over time it is likely that, through attraction and repulsion, a sense of common interest, and social contact outside of lectures, a higher-order associative form will develop.

But while social atoms, individuals have no ties of obligation, friendship or common interest which might constrain their behaviour. Their invisibility, as in a television audience, reduces the possibility of surveillance. For this very reason, because atomistic association allows participants to 'remain themselves' it is inappropriate, even to the point of being dysfunctional, in policy paradigms because of the individualised interpretations and uncoordinated action it facilitates. Membershipping culturally-atomistic agents to a particular educational paradigm is often a feature of staff-development days, school transformation and curriculum and pedagogical change apart from, though usually related to, the skills, contents and practices which such encounters seek to influence.

Collective Association

Collectivities, on the other hand, experience the existence of a bond – a common grievance, allegiance, set of values or heritage. There is an awareness of a common membership, though those who share this collective identity do not require physical contact. In the case of such collectivities as nationalities or religions, frequency of interaction involving the total collectivity would be impracticable. Collective association can make inroads on the private and personal. One may be required, or indeed feel obliged, to submerge personal interest or inclination in favour of the goals of the collectivity. Equally, the identities highlighted and made salient and socially relevant through collective association may well conflict with established allegiances, values and inclinations. Collective association is a basic requirement for a policy paradigm if it is to have a coherence and impact.

A pivotal associative transition for a policy paradigm is the cultivation of a sense of collectivity where a lower-order associative form previously existed. Social movements represent the most extensively-researched example of such mobilisation and membershipping to policy paradigms generally. The membershipping process itself – its structure, processes and rituals – also invites analysis (O'Sullivan, 1993b).

Primary Association

Groups, like collectivities, have a sense of membership, an obligation to fellow members and collective loyalties, and a common sense of values. But they exhibit the additional characteristic of frequency of interaction. The most heightened manifestation of these characteristics is to be found in what have been called primary groups. Cooley's classic definition is as follows:

> By primary groups I mean those characterised by intimate face-to-face association and cooperation. They are primary in several senses, but chiefly in that they are fundamental in forming the social nature and ideals of the individual. The result of intimate association ... is a certain fusion of individualities in a common whole, so that one's very self, for many purposes at least, is the common life and purpose of the group. Perhaps the simplest way of describing this wholeness is by saying that it is a 'we'; it involves the sort of sympathy and mutual identification for which 'we' is the natural expression (quoted in Davis, 1969).

Rather than talk in terms of primary groups as opposed to secondary groups, Davis is of the view that it is more appropriate to refer to the primary character of association defined by closeness, smallness, durability, intimacy, intensity and solidarity. As a consequence primary association facilitates the surveillance, control and socialisation of participants.

Since it is difficult to maintain the primary character of an association once membership increases, it is most likely to be a feature of a paradigm's emergence or of specific cells or sites or interaction within it. However, where a paradigm's ideas are in sympathy with the qualities of primary association, as in the case of the women's movement, special efforts will be made to preserve intimacy, intensity and non-hierarchical structures as the membership expands.

Exclusionary Association

Goffman (1968) described the phenomenon of the 'total institution' as an organisational form in which the fulfilment of the members' full range of needs and the enactment of their daily routine are confined to its social parameters and purview. An associative version of the 'total institution' is to be found where a paradigm, as he puts it, 'captures something of the time and interest of its members and provides something of a world for them; in brief ... has encompassing tendencies' (p. 15). Exclusionary association can be quite explicit in the distancing, and even segregation of members, from adversarial, dysfunctional or potentially contaminating forces.

By cultivating an ingroup/outgroup distinction, exclusionary association enhances solidarity among members. Threats from outside forces heighten the need for mutual support, the recognition of common interests and the transcending of differences. Such threats may be real, imagined or contrived. Erikson's (1966) study, *Wayward Puritans*, describes how in a New England puritan community phases of witch hunting and public fear of attack from forces hostile to the community coincided with the dissolution of religious orthodoxy, loyalty and the internalisation of the community's beliefs among its members. The sense of siege, apparently contrived, had an integrating effect in making salient and affirming the social, moral and religious rationale for the community's existence.

The more a paradigm encompasses the lifeworld of individuals the greater will be their conformity. Heretics, doomsday scenarios, moral outrage and the demonising of adversarial forces are particularly functional in paradigms with a widely-dispersed membership. Heightening the emotional and cultivating a sense of urgency serve to compensate for the absence of primary association, with its intense, regular face-to-face contact and mutual support, and help to sustain identification with and loyalty to a paradigm. Exclusionary association through ingroup/outgroup delineation also sharpens a paradigm's profile when, in its early stage, it seeks to publicly establish its identity. What Donoghue (1992, p. 157) said of the practice of cultural nationalism in his Irish schooling – 'we defined ourselves by not doing certain things' (English games, music, religion) – is equally recognisable in the mobilising strategies of paradigms.

Bureaucratic Association

The more a paradigm expands, intensifies and systemalises the more its associative form takes on the features of a formal organisation including those described by sociologists as bureaucratic. The seminal writings of Weber on bureaucracy have been distilled by contemporary sociologists (Giddens, 1993) to yield a number of distinctive bureaucratic characteristics.

A bureaucracy operates within fixed areas of jurisdiction with clear boundaries between what is and what is not within its domain. This principle of boundaried expertise pervades its organisation so that each official knows where the responsibilities and obligation of the office, section, department etc., begin and end. Hierarchical organisation is a key feature of bureaucracies. This can take the form of a system of national and regional headquarters and local offices, as well as a pyramid structure of authority with stratified powers of decision-making and supervision. Written rules govern the operation of bureaucracies which specify, in detail and allowing for all conceivable eventualities, how particular cases are to be dealt with and what are the powers and responsibilities of the bureaucracy's officers. Authority within a bureaucracy is associated with the office rather than the individual occupying it. Accordingly, the conduct of the office is to be guided by the written rules of procedure within its hierarchy of supervision rather than by the personal tastes or feelings of its human incumbent. Policy paradigms that display characteristics of the formal organisational/ bureaucratic associative form are not only better structured for the successful penetration of the policy process but also for recruitment, adaptability and reproduction. Practices of corporate and religious representation and advocacy in the educational policy process provide illuminations of such features. Because of their social visibility and differentiation, and the practice of documenting their defining rationale, they are more amenable to analysis, though it can be expected that a feature of their protective armoury would be their obfuscation of efforts at such inquiry.

All social systems are liable to differentiation. Within the social system of a paradigm, members will vary in the contribution they make and the roles they occupy. Depending on the level of systematisation of a paradigm and the degree of bureaucratisation of its associative forms, these roles and functions can be expected to be multiple and diverse. Here the analysis is confined to one such cluster of functions – those who can be said to occupy authoritative roles within the paradigm.

Authorities

To isolate for attention the authoritative roles that people play in the shaping and penetration of policy paradigms is to recognise that individuals have the capacity to advance, extend, defend, justify, classify, modify, recruit, proselytise etc. in a manner that acknowledges them as more than 'carriers' of paradigms or publicists for their texts. The following are no more than examples.

Modernisers target for intervention within a paradigm attachments to traditional practices and beliefs considered to be discordant with defining features of modern society. These would include such characteristics of modernity as social and economic differentiation, technology, improved material standards of living, urbanisation, secularisation, or at least the relegation of religion to the private sphere, tolerance of difference, equality of opportunity and democracy. Aspects of a paradigm that are sympathetic to society changing in this direction are approved; any impediments or what might be dismissed by outsiders as primitive, reactionary or unenlightened are identified as weaknesses, rendering the paradigm vulnerable to marginalisation. All the assumptions, categories and values of modernity are a feature of the moderniser's psychological makeup: justice, separation of church and state and social and economic progress. Modernisers see themselves as part of a teleological process: theirs is a contribution to historical evolution which is rule-governed and incorporates a destiny. They are recognisable in the manner in which they seek to modify a paradigm with the intention of making it more relevant and meaningful in the society of its time.

Conservers are orientated to the maintenance of tradition and to resisting the modification of paradigms to the point that they can be regarded as post-traditional (Giddens, 1996b). Tradition in this usage is bound up with collective memory, rituals, guardians and combines moral and emotional dimensions. While tradition is associated with endurance and stability, traditions, both in their actuality and remembrance are always changing. If the construction of tradition is variable, so also are those who present themselves as its guardians and act to preserve its authenticity and integrity. Conservers project themselves into a paradigm's discourse at a point in which they feel tradition to be under threat or in danger of dissolution. Their engagement may take the form of resisting specific practices, proposals, or adaptations, or they may be in the mould of Ball's (1990) cultural restorationists whose concern is with broader issues of heritage, values, standards and ways of life.

Vanguardists see themselves as having a leadership role in bringing about change in society. Their diagnosis is that vested interests, inertia, a lack of organisation among those who would benefit from change requires that action be taken to advance new social arrangements. People cannot be relied upon to take the initiative on their own behalf. Vanguardists regard themselves as being privileged in relation to their diagnosis of the situation and their capacity to show leadership. The basis of this is rarely specified, or it tends to be linked with flashpoint experiences, educational formation or personal qualities (O'Sullivan,

1993b). Political vanguadism is associated with the role of the party in Lenin's theory of radical change which saw the proletariat as being incapable of releasing itself from its trade union ideology without the direct action of the Communist Party (McLellan, 1995). In education, vanguardism has been identified among the exponents of critical pedagogy such as Giroux and McLaren (Jóhannesson, 1992).

According to critical pedagogy, teachers are crucially placed to assist in the development of an emancipated society. This is because they have the opportunity to create in their pedagogy the conditions for the formation of oppositional discourse which not only criticises establishment thinking and practices but also provides for a disposition of hope and possibility. Teachers who have penetrated the disabling and restrictive ideologies of conventional schooling and commit themselves to a form of pedagogy that advances a more just society are described as transformative intellectuals. Jóhannesson (1992) has integrated a number of Giroux's writings on transformative intellectuals to indicate that their role involves creating solidaristic relationships in the classroom which are based on trust. Vanguardists reach out beyond a paradigm's boundaries in a targeted fashion to members of naturally sympathetic paradigms or, more generally, accentuating examples of intertextuality with a view to membershipping others and coopting paradigms through a process of sharing, initiation, and reformation.

A paradigm, like social movements or ideologies, will have among its membership intellectuals who interpret its features and activities and theorise about its role in society. A number of types of intellectual activity have been identified (O'Dowd, 1996). Mannheim looked to the freefloating intellectual to overcome the tendentialist world views of particular social classes and to facilitate some kind of balance and synthesis in interpreting social and political life. This is made possible, he argued, because intellectuals represent '… such a relatively unattached middle stratum which is open to the constant influx of individuals from the most diverse social classes and groups with all possible points of view' (Mannheim, 1949, pp 143-4). Mannheim warns that this should not be interpreted as claiming that an individual's class links disappear. Rather, what he is asserting is that the intellectual stratum is situated between classes and, while it is affected by class interests, '… these interests represent a variety of classes and in their interaction they subject the individual to all sorts of intellectual tendencies which are thus tied one with another' (Larrain, 1979, p. 116). Gramsci (1971, p. 60) disputed this conceptualisation of the relatively disengaged and synthesising intellectual. Far from operating in a mutually balancing manner, according to Gramsci, the intellectuals of the ruling class '… exercise such a power of attraction that, in the last analysis, they end up by subjugating the intellectuals of the other social groups; they thereby create a system of solidarity between all the intellectuals, with bonds of a psychological nature (vanity, etc.) and often of a caste character (technico-juridical, corporate, etc.).' Gramsci distinguished between this category of intellectual and the organic intellectuals of each social group 'who give it homogeneity and an awareness of its own function not only in the economic but also in the social and political fields' (p. 5).

Following Mannheim, it is possible to imagine some manifestation of free-floating intellectuals operating as border intellectuals at the intersections of paradigms. Thus positioned, they have the capacity to become agents of renewal, resuscitation, differentiation, political positioning and change through their 'raiding' of the resources of other paradigms at the point at which they share language, subjectivities, etc. However, they remain vulnerable, if not quite to the subjugation that Gramsci speaks of, at least to a strategic hybridity and shifting allegiances. Like the freefloating intellectual, the organic intellectual characteristically contributes to the intensification, legitimation and framing of a paradigm, but unlike them they remain embedded within it even to the point at which it defines their identity.

It needs to be kept in mind that all members of a paradigm have the potential to contribute to its development, as distinct from its maintenance, through their active participation in the intersubjectivity that sustains it. Theirs may not be the more identifiable contribution of modernisers, conservers, vanguardists or intellectuals, etc. Yet, in this regard it is well to remember another assertion of Gramsci (1971), that while everyone is engaged in intellectual activity in society, only some are accorded the standing of intellectuals.

Attention to associative forms and social differentiation in the study of policy paradigms is essential in the light of the need to incorporate the social and connect with political action in the broadest sense. It is an acknowledgement that people embody policy paradigms in their consciousness of the world, that they flow between them at the intersubjective level in social configurations that vary in their visibility, self-awareness, intimacy, surveillance and control, organisation and resources, and that within these social systems members are differentiated in their roles and functions. Without this social context, paradigms are in danger of being understood in an unduly idealist sense, as forms of bodiless shared thought or as language systems or discourses that merely implicate people at the point of their intersection and, consequently, are theorised in an unhelpfully reductionist/conflationist manner.

Identities/Subjectivities

As well as the social context of paradigms, individual psychology is also a factor in understanding the engagement of people with paradigms, their degree of personal investment in them, and the impact this has on how they regard and define themselves.

Identities

A person's identity represents the intersection of culture, society and individual psychology. What constitutes personal identity, its viability as a construct and the forces that contribute to its construction have been the subject of ongoing debate within the social sciences for many years. Within critical psychology a number of developments have sought to move the study of the individual away from reductionist explanations which focus almost exclusively on intra-individual processes while ignoring the historical, political and ideological contexts in which people come to understand the world and their place within it. From within these developments social identity theory provides a productive starting point for the analysis of the role of the self in the operation of policy paradigms.

Tajfel (1978) defines social identity as 'that part of the individual's self concept which derives from his knowledge of his membership of a social group (or groups) together with the value and emotional significance attached to that membership'. Andrews (1991), who has used social identity theory in a study of political commitment, points out that while this understanding acknowledges that people belong to more than one social group, it does not consider the complex dynamics that such multiple group membership will entail. These psychological dynamics include 'the process by which individuals identify the salience of particular social groups which comprise their world view … the organisation of an individual's social world, and consequently the way in which an individual perceives herself and others' (p. 26). Furthermore, and this introduces the cultural dimension, Andrews later points out that 'the concepts which one uses to identify oneself are not only a reflection of aspects of self-perception (both real and idealised), but are also themselves socially constructed' (p. 27). As such, personal identity will be internally labelled and redefined in terms of the language of political, religious and social inheritance.

As with group membership, participation in a paradigm can also be a source of one's sense of social identity and in this way embody similar features and processes. Paradigms will contribute to the internal language by which identities are established, and the construction of reality embodied in a paradigm can act as a backdrop against which a person's self understanding in relation to social action and change is defined. Given the variability in their associative forms, paradigms will impinge with different degrees of intensity, comprehensiveness and centrality on a person's self-definition and create problems of ordering and prioritising. To paraphrase Gurin and Marks (1989), some paradigm members are likely to possess antennae that are tuned to receive group-relevant information that others miss. For these people, paradigm membership has become so central to the self that the identification with it can be activated by minimal cues.

Subjectivities

As with social identity theory, the difficulties created by the multiple membership of paradigms need to be entertained and confronted. The difficulties go beyond those recognised by social identity theorists. For even among those who recognise the fluidity and the problems created by multiple group membership there is the acceptance of a stable point of reference, a sense of self or a personal vantage point which is capable of overseeing such difficulties as self-definition, group allegiance or divided loyalties. This is the point of departure for the post-structuralist critique of the unitary subject. The target of this critique is what is referred to as the Cartesian subject, as captured in the dictum of its originator, Descartes, 'I think, therefore, I am'. As Sarup (1988, p. 1) points out, the term subject is quite different from the term individual and presumes a thinking, free agent capable of independent uncoerced thought: '... fully conscious, and hence self-knowable ... not only autonomous but coherent ... a narrator who imagines that he speaks without simultaneously been spoken'.

In critique of this, we find a range of prominent thinkers in the post-structuralist tradition questioning the unity of the subject, its capacity to reflect on itself and to initiate social change. In Laclau and Mouffe's (1985, p. 115) summary, what is being questioned is 'the view of the subject as an agent both rational and transparent to itself, the supposed unity and homogeneity of the ensemble of its positions, and the conception of the subject as origin and basis of social relations'. Lyotard's (1984) seminal criticism of metanarratives (foundational, moral and epistemological theories and master accounts of human progress and emancipation) incorporates a denial of universally-valid knowledge and of a single knowing subject. Instead, there is a diversity of subjects, knowledges and minds reflecting different histories and social settings. Lacan's target is the humanist concept of the autonomous individual with an integrated personality. He argues that the unconscious is structured like language and that there cannot be a subject without language. As with language, representation of the unconscious, as in dreams and slips of the tongue, are indicating something quite different from what superficially appears to be the case. This view of the person centres the unconscious structural action of multiple meanings rather than the representation of the ego at the conscious level. For Lacan, the person is '... a split subject, whose conscious images of self-identity are perpetually decentred by unconscious desires. There are no individuals ... only dividua or divided ones' (Kearney, 1986, p. 273).

The problems that such a denial of subjectivity as anything other than fractured, multiple and porous, creates for a breathing, thinking and acting individual are described by Haraway (1994) from a feminist perspective:

> It has become difficult to name one's feminism by a single adjective ... identities
> seem contradictory, partial and strategic. With the hard-won recognition of their

social and historic constitution, gender, race, and class cannot provide the basis for belief in 'essential' unity. There is nothing about being 'female' that naturally binds women. There is not even such a state as 'being' female, itself a highly complex category constructed in contested sexual scientific discourses and other social practices. Gender, race, or class consciousness is an achievement forced on us by the terrible historical experience of the contradictory social realities of patriarchy, colonialism, racism and capitalism.

When she goes on to pose the questions, 'Who counts as "us" in my own rhetoric? Which identities are available to ground such a potent political myth called "us", and what could motivate enlistment in this collectively?', she might well be speaking of the personal recognition of paradigmatic membership, its significance for one's identity and the fluid processes of inclusion and exclusion.

To the extent that the post-structural critique of the human subject denies the existence of an autonomous ego, a god's eye capable of having a perspective on oneself in all its diversity, it can be fundamentally disabling and nihilistic. Foucault (1973, pp 342-343) appropriately reserves a 'philosophical laugh' for those '... who refuse to think without immediately thinking that it is man who is thinking'. The implication of the absence of a faculty of self-awareness that itself rises above all the other self-definitions and identities that we embody means that there is no basis for any integrated self knowledge much less the meaningful and coherent communication of such self-understanding to others. This clearly is far removed from the aspiration of the enlightenment dream for humanity of a self that is there to be known, a reflective subject capable of realising and knowing itself and a political agent participating in the shaping of history according to its true and self-defined interests. In the post-structural critique, contingent, partial, fragmentary, even superficial, are the adjectives that necessarily qualify our access to our own identity. Yet, a receptiveness to contradiction, incoherence and limitation in self-definition is likely to more faithfully capture the complexities of the relationship between the self and a paradigm. As with social identity, paradigmatic identities will be influenced by cultural diversification and change in a manner that move them away from singular, personal identity-statuses (Waters, 1994, p. 351).

For the purpose of applying these insights in studying the functioning of personal psychology in the operation of policy paradigms, it will be necessary to distinguish between subjectivities and identities. In the process, this study seeks some fixed points of reference within the fluidity claimed by post-structuralist analysis in studying the self. This is partly for heuristic purposes but mostly because it is felt that the continuing utility of classical socialisation theory, in particular the process of internalisation, has been unfairly distanced and sidelined by these newer conceptualisations. Identity and subjectivity are terms that are often used interchangeably, indicating the degree of overlap between them. Here, subjectivity will be used to refer to the way one *is*, not necessarily with awareness. In this definition, subjectivity is consistent with the idea of defining the self in multiple ways in the light of social and cultural membership. As such it is possible to speak of a social actor assuming different subjectivities or subject positions. But because of the centrality of meaning-making within a paradigm it will be necessary to move beyond social affiliation to consider the role of texts in making available subjectivities to social actors.

For Althusser (1971), subjectivities are formed by individuals being recruited to texts (ideologies) through an act of 'interpellation or hailing' in which they recognise themselves in the meanings of the text. This does not address the possibility of refusals: why, given the multitude of texts available to social actors, they do not explore a range of them before acknowledging a 'best fit' for themselves. While the phenomenon of human choice lies uneasily with post-structuralist thought, it is clear that prominent writers in this tradition seek to reinstate human agency in such forms as transgression and resistance. As Butler (1995) argues, it is possible to be active in relation to the subjectivities made available and engaged with in discourse: 'My (subject) position is mine to the extent that "I" – and I do not shirk from the pronoun – replay and resignify the theoretical positions that have constituted me, working the possibilities of their convergence, and trying to take account of the possibilities they systematically exclude.' But she cautions:

> It is clearly not the case that 'I' preside over the positions that have constituted me, shuffling through them instrumentally, casting some aside, incorporating others, although some of my activity may take this form. The 'I' who would select between them is always already constituted by them. The 'I' is the transfer point of that replay, but it is simply not a strong enough claim to say that the 'I' is situated; the 'I', this 'I', is constituted by these positions, and these 'positions' are not merely theoretical products, but fully embedded organising principles of material practices and institutional arrangements, that matrix of power and discourse that produces me as a viable 'subject'.

In Woodward's (1997) reading of Althusser, also, it is considered possible for a social actor to fulfil the demands of a role while refusing to be interpellated by it. As used in this study of policy paradigms, subjectivities are ways of being that attract degrees of psychological investment. They can be engaged with tactically or refused even in the face of coercion. Nonetheless, the structuralist problematic of how we are often translated from active to docile bodies quite willingly (Smith, 2000, p. 95) will need to be accommodated. Paradigms offer incentives to social actors to invest in the subjectivities they constitute within their texts. Althusser (1971) draws on Lacan in explaining the attraction of capitalist subjectivities, to those who are regulated and exploited through them, as a means of resolving unconscious tensions. Less psycho-analytical explorations would consider personal biography and habitus (Bourdieu, 1977), social benefits, affiliative needs, political advantage and the need for the reassurance of a 'narrative of the self' (Hall, 1992).

While the post-structuralist position on the self is that there is no stable 'I' observing the interplay of an individual's subjectivities, for the purpose of analysis I reinstate a sense of predictability and typification in distinguishing between identity and subjectivity. In using the term identity I acknowledge that some subjectivities will play a more dominant role than others in how people define themselves or are so defined by others across time and context. Identity is less text- or context-specific than subjectivity. The reconstitution of subjectivity as identity can emerge from within the person and be socio-psychological in nature or it can be a function of power, a consequence of definition by some external process with the capacity to fix that position for the purposes of social and political life. Religion can be all-consuming as a source of identity because of strong belief in its tenets or by virtue of being set apart for persecution by others. Defining the 'Orient' (Said, 1978), slaves under slavery and Jews during the Holocaust are other examples of enforced identities. Social actors can also be successfully defined in social life in terms of a paradigm. For the most part, however, a paradigm will be said to inform an identity when its meanings become sedimented within a person, in a manner reminiscent of the process of internalisation of classical socialisation theory, but which acknowledges the diversity and fluidity of the self. In such situations, a paradigm's texts can be expected to be dominant in how people will respond and act. In this process, a policy paradigm adds to its resources those of human psychology.

Dominion

Having identified some of the analytical components of a policy paradigm we now turn to the question of its influence in society. This section examines a paradigm's coherence, the nature of its constitution and the extent to which it can be said to exist and operate in a distinctive manner. Then it turns to the cultural pervasiveness of a paradigm, the extent to which its meanings colonise those of other cultural texts, while recognising their interpenetration and interdependence. Finally, a paradigm's dominion is considered in terms of its political positioning, the extent to which it informs the thinking of the state and the policy-making institutions.

Cultural paradigms vary in the depth and range of their engagement of society. Religion supplies a template of how a comprehensive and encompassing paradigm might operate in a society, supplying for its believers cosmic explanations of the universe, theories of the person, criteria for identifying truth and error, together with authorities, identities, collective allegiance and psychic and affective reassurance. On the other hand, cultural paradigms can relate to a wide range of aspects of the social structure, such as landscape (Schama, 1995), the calibration of time and colour (Whorf, 1954[1927-41]) and the classification of food (Douglas, 1984) that are more specific and more loosely political in their reverberations. So it is with educational policy paradigms. The manner in which society, the economy, social institutions such as the family or education itself, social change, and life stages such as childhood, adolescence and adulthood are defined, interpreted and positioned, to say nothing of private/public, state, justice, knowledge and intelligence, will differ in their potential for impacting on educational policy. Restraints and possibilities such as these for the dominion of a policy paradigm, derived from its positioning within the social structure, are not built into this schematisation of a paradigm's dominion. It is felt that these variations are best addressed substantively as specific paradigms are selected for study. In the chapters that follow these variations in the social positioning of a policy paradigm are acknowledged in the priority accorded to the transition from theocentric to mercantile paradigms, which refer to such a central pillar of society as a social institution, and the distinction drawn between this and the concepts, agents and texts of Part Four which are treated as social phenomena and processes with a more specific penetration of the social structure. These are not theorised here in terms of a paradigm's dominion. Rather, in describing and tracking the nature and techniques of its influence on the policy process, three axes of the dynamics of a paradigm's dominion – its structuration, interplay of meaning, and power – considered in terms of Framing, Cultural Penetration/Intertextuality, and Political Positioning, are selected as most productive in explaining its dominion.

Framing

The framing of a paradigm refers to its boundaries and how weak or strong are their definition. Framing relates to the degree to which the components of the paradigm are set apart from those that are considered to be external to a paradigm. This is most obviously a matter of consciousness and culture, of how reality is individually and collectively conceptualised and understood. But it is socially grounded, embedded in biographies and social space, and implicates power. In a world of multiple meanings, the sense of fixity constructed by a closure on interpretation (Eco, 1976) induces security and a feeling of belonging. With the awareness of other members of one's sub-world comes solidarity and integration. For those who succeed in establishing themselves as authoritative – witchdoctors, philosophers, religious, academics, activists or experienced participants – closure restricts the field of would-be pretenders, enhances their self-justification and confers symbolic and material power.

The concept of framing is to be found in the writings of a number of sociologists including Goffman (1974), referred to earlier in terms of the cultural framing of social movements, and Bernstein (1971). In educational studies, Bernstein's related concepts of classification and frame, as applied to the organisation, transmission and evaluation of educational knowledge, are well known. For Bernstein, classification, '... refers to the degree of boundary maintenance between contents', while framing refers to the degree of control which the participants (teachers and pupils) in the educational encounter possess over aspects of the transmission of knowledge. Both aspects of insulation and regulation adverted to in these definitions are included in the concept of framing as used here in relation to the nature of a paradigm's delineation.

The more a paradigm achieves a coherence across its various dimensions the more it takes on a character which will allow it to be set apart from what it is not. The clearer the delineation the sharper will be the differentiation that is possible between paradigms. Conversely, anything that distorts this distinctiveness will weaken a paradigm's frame. Polyvalent concepts, translatable language, non-specific themes, authorities who have yet to establish their legitimacy or are beginning to have it questioned create permeable boundaries. Another source of fuzziness would be a contradiction between any number of possible combinations of dimensions that designate a paradigm: language inadequately capturing thought, authorities employing a discordant discourse, and identities disrupting otherwise appropriate forms of association. While the overall strength of framing is a function of its holistic integration as a distinctive entity, it is quite likely that some components of the paradigm are more important than others in determining the tightness of its framing. Conceptualisation, language, discourse and identity appear to have such a status.

Concepts contribute to framing in a manner that is not fully encompassed in the analysis of language. There is an independent conceptual force in framing that has some distinctive properties. This realm of unencoded or partly coded thinking by its nature is difficult to penetrate through the routine practices of influence such as representation, dialogue or contestation since these rely largely on language. Because of this it introduces a particularly robust or evasive element to the definition of boundaries. On the other hand, to successfully alter this realm of thought is a much less public act than any conversion that has been linguistically mediated and represented. As such, it evades or elides the public realm. It is silent and all the more effective as change because of the fact that it side-steps discursive practice.

The tradition of utopian discourse illuminates some of these features. In his comprehensive survey of utopian propositions and schemes throughout history, Kumar (1991, p. 3) concludes that utopia's value 'lies not in its relation to present practice but in its relation to a possible future. Its "practical" use is to overstep the immediate reality to depict a condition whose clear desirability draws us on, like a magnet.' In stepping out of one reality into another there is the challenge of constructing in the minds of others what this hypothetical world might look like. This is apart altogether from the practical problem of creating such a world. As Kumar's account makes clear, conventional concepts have been drawn on to communicate such a conceptualisation. He identifies the four characteristics of the utopian vision as harmony, desire, hope and design. These are derived respectively from archetypal varieties of the ideal society: the golden age, a time of simplicity and sufficiency involving harmonious relationship between people and nature; the age of paradise, a land of exuberance and plenty; millenarianism, with its belief that a new era characterised by peace is at hand; and the ideal city or perfect commonwealth. Nonetheless, while one relies on language a deficit remains which retards the mental transportation of people from the conventional and lived to the ideal and aspirational. Kumar's (1991, p. 3) quotation from H.G. Wells's *A Modern Utopia*, first published in 1905, characterises this: 'Our business here is to be utopian, to make vivid and credible if we can, first this facet and then that, of an imaginary whole and happy world. Our deliberate intention is to be not, indeed, impossible, but most distinctly impracticable, by every scale that reaches only between today and tomorrow.' In seeking to stir the imagination, broaden horizons, disrupt complacency about what is possible and raise hopes of a better life, utopian discourse reaches out to a realm of thought that is only faintly captured, if at all, in language. Where, however, such appeals to the unthinkable are successful their effect is potentially radical in the manner in which they redefine the boundaries of possibility. Not surprisingly, one finds many radical educators proclaiming the need for a revival of utopianism in the manner in which we conceptualise the range of futures that are possible through educational change (Apple, 1979; Giroux, 1997).

Language opens up possibilities of regulating people's organisation of the world and of their experience of it. It provides a method of naming experience and thus delineating and drawing boundaries around components of reality in such a way as to objectify and confirm what might otherwise remain in a limbo world of intuitions, feelings and hunches. The capacity of language to be at once stabilising and disruptive of thought and society is recognised by Sartre: 'Words wreak havoc when they find a name for what had up to then been lived namelessly' (quoted in Bourdieu, 1977, p. 170).

If we accept that a crucial mechanism in the structuring of a person's conceptual organisation of the world is linguistic usage then language must be recognised as an important factor in the framing of a paradigm. The imaging of reality through language, and the curtailment exercised by this process of imaging through the selective use of language, has the capacity to advance a distinctive reconceptualisation of the world. In this way, according to Ball (1990, p. 25) who draws on Baudrillard's process of 'imposition of the real', 'discourse is self-generating, self-reinforcing ... where the opposition between things as presented and what's really going on begins to dissolve. Signs take on a life of their own, their own circulation.'

The less the language of a paradigm is translatable the greater will be its capacity to contribute to strong framing. This is because of the linguistic boundaries that can be constructed around a set of ideas that give them an identifiable character in discourse. An extreme position in the intertranslatability debate would argue that a language circumscribes reality to the extent that there is no representing a perspective on reality outside the resources of that language. In its feminist application, Lorde (1984, p. 112) famously observed that 'the master's tools will never dismantle the master's house.' In a similar theoretical vein, Daly (1979) contends that the distorting capacity of male language is so great that a new terminology has to be constructed, what she refers to as a gynomorphic vocabulary. Davidson (1984) dismisses this general view with obvious irritation:

> Whorf, wanting to demonstrate that Hopi incorporates a metaphysics so alien to ours that Hopi and English cannot, as he puts it 'be calibrated', uses English to convey the contents of sample Hopi sentences. Kuhn is brilliant at saying what things were like before the revolution using – what else? – our post-revolutionary idiom. Quine gives us a feel for the 'pre-individuative phase in the evolution of our conceptual scheme', while Bergson tells us where we can go to get a view of a mountain undistorted by one or another provincial perspective.

While it is not possible to record the responses of these writers to Davidson's criticism, others have recorded their efforts to grapple with this problem. In his critique of the family as a conditioning device, Cooper (1976, p. 29), the alternative psychiatrist and follower of R.D. Laing, laments: 'I have of course used the language that I find archaic, essentially reactionary and certainly discrepant with my thinking. "Family words" like mother, father, child ... the connotation of "mother" takes in a number of biological functions, primary protective functions, a socially over-defined role, and a certain legal "reality".' Because of this, Cooper feels constrained in his efforts to question 'the fatuity and danger of the fetish of consanguinity' while confined to a language that underlines roles defined by blood relationship. But, unlike Daly, he does not suggest a new language. More like Derrida (1978), he is using discourse which tactically borrows from a heritage the resources that facilitate the destabilisation of the heritage itself. Derrida's practice of *sous rature*, usually translated as 'under erasure', is designed to advance this deconstruction from within a tradition. The idea is that since the word is inadequate it is crossed out, but since it is necessary for communication it remains legible. The dynamics of renegotiating the meanings of words will arise in the next section on Intertextuality.

Be it in the efforts of those who seek to construct a new language with a view to advancing paradigmatic change or those who grapple with the existing language of a paradigm to advance a critique of its fundamental tenets, there is the shared recognition that language is critical in establishing the boundaries of perspectives on reality.

Bernstein (1971) has usefully drawn attention to the 'identity' dimension of classification/framing, proposing that where these are strong they will lead to an enhanced sense of membership and a specific self-definition. While Bernstein's observations relate to curriculum organisation and transmission they are also pertinent to the operation of paradigms. He speaks of forms of curriculum organisation which create an 'identity which is clear cut and bounded' and where identity is 'pure'. There is an abhorrence of 'mixed categories and blurred identities, for they represent a potential openness, an ambiguity, which makes the consequences of previous socialisation problematic'. Bernstein gives as an example a student with a first degree in psychology who might wish to read for the higher degree in sociology. He describes the transfer requirements as 'a process of resocialisation into a new subject loyalty'. This is required because any attempt to weaken or change the classification/framing of the subject area 'may be felt as a threat to one's identity and may be experienced as a pollution endangering the sacred. Here we have one source of the resistance to change of educational code.' Applied to the framing of paradigms these propositions suggest a number of lines of enquiry which link frame strength, identity, membershiping and socialisation.

As a general rule, particularly where identity is implicated, the impetus will be towards strong framing. In terms of individual psychology this will arise from people's need for meaning as well as to believe that their ideas and behaviour operate in a coherent manner. Where cases of cognitive dissonance arise through loose framing, one can imagine individuals finding ways of reducing this dissonance by avoidance, redefinition etc. or, to invoke a post-structuralist interpretation of the self, through the assumption of multiple subjectivities. These strategies, in turn, will impact on the paradigm and act as a source of change. This introduces another general rule of paradigms: their inclination to modify rather than dissolve.

The anthropological work of Douglas (1984) on social classification and ordering and on the response of people whose cosmologies are under threat is seminal. As well as influencing Bernstein, James and Jenks (1996) have drawn on it in their analysis of the defence of the categorising of childhood as 'innocent' in the light of the James Bulger murder case in 1993. Using mass media response, they demonstrate how in an attempt to maintain the traditional 'interpretative frame' by which children's behaviour is understood, acts of violence by children are individualised as atypical, abhorrent cases. They explain this resistance to any blurring of the framing of childhood as a hedge against 'existential anxiety' arguing that the child has come to symbolise 'the solidity and adhesion of the past' in an era of late-modern uncertainty. The definition of childhood as 'innocent', they argue, reflects the aspirations, altruism and longings of the adult condition and conclude that 'in an historical era during which issues of identity and integration ... are, perhaps, both more unstable and more fragile than at any previous time, such a loss would impact on the everyday experiences of society members with disorientating consequences'.

Bourdieu's (1977) distinction between doxa and orthodoxy allows us to calibrate the definitional capacity of a paradigm's boundaries. And it achieves this in a manner that qualitatively distinguishes between different kinds of framing and the tensions involved in maintaining them, and the distinctions between them, in existence. Doxa refers to the universe of what is undiscussed and, therefore, undisputed, 'the sum total of theses tacitly posited on the hither side of all enquiry, which appear as such only retrospectively when they come to be suspended practically' (p. 168). It incorporates the absolute form of legitimacy 'since it is unaware of the very question of legitimacy, which arises from competition for legitimacy, and hence from conflict between groups claiming to possess it'.

Orthodoxy, on the other hand, refers to the universe of discourse, the realm of available opinions and arguments, but in a manner that explicitly defines some ways of thinking as erroneous or untrue. When the limits of doxa are pushed back, and its arbitrary character revealed, it becomes necessary for those who subscribe to the established view to systematise and rationalise it. Orthodoxy involves the answering of questions which under doxa remain unposed. Orthodoxy requires legitimation of positions in a way that doxa does not. As Bourdieu points out, the control exercised by orthodox positions, in sanctioning some world views and opposing others, conceals a more fundamental censorship that operates through maintaining a distinction 'between the universe of things that can be stated, and hence thought and the universe of that which is taken for granted' (pp 169-170).

Framing is at its strongest when a paradigm attains a doxic status. This is the ultimate in framing in that there is no awareness of another reality outside of the paradigm from which it must distinguish itself. The conceptualisation and explanation of the world represent the boundaries of coherent thought, common sense and normality. It experiences no challenge because there is no world view, interpretation or vision to be set against it. In fact, so deeply structured is a doxic paradigm that its existence as a paradigm is unknown to those whose consciousness it regulates.

Framing refers to a paradigm's sphere of 'inside' and 'outside', its distinctiveness from other interpretations, the extent of its ambiguity, linkages with other texts and insulation from sources of change. Psychologically, it relates to a participant's sense of belonging, exteriority or 'otherness'.

To paraphrase Bernstein, by way of application to paradigm formation and maintenance, the following questions will require explication:

- What are the antecedents of variations in the strength of a paradigm's framing?
- How does a given frame structure perpetuate itself and what are the conditions of and resistance to change?
- What formative experiences are realised through variations in the strength of framing?

When viewed in terms of the instantiation of paradigms as texts, the impulse towards strong framing, be it due to the orientation towards coherence in thought and identity or through tactical differentiation, generates its own instability in the manner in which it will incorporate other (discordant) texts in the delineation of its boundaries. The only exceptions to this will be in the cases of truly doxic paradigms where the boundary is deemed to be between sense and nonsense. By establishing its distinctive message in opposition to those of other texts, it can indeed set itself apart as different but it does so in a manner that establishes the meaningfulness of the 'other' in determining its parameters. The more this is repeated in the positioning of texts in their relationships with each other, the more a text's distinctiveness will be understood in terms of its relationships to a complex network of other texts. Thus, while strong framing is oriented towards the closure of a text's meaning, the multiple acts of differentiation involved in establishing its boundaries open up avenues of interpenetration. In terms of a text's dominion, this introduces both opportunities and threats. This is considered in the next section on Cultural Penetration/Intertextuality.

Cultural Penetration/Intertextuality

The cultural penetration of a paradigm's meanings, and their institutionalisation within a society as the rationality for its operations, is an important axis of a paradigm's dominion. In seeking to establish closure, a paradigm's textualisation will have acknowledged and implicated other texts. But if it is to ensure the influence of its meanings it must do more than use these multiple textual nodal points of engagement as opportunities for self-definition. It has to engage in 'culture wars'. The concept of intertextuality can help us to understand something of the complex nature of such cultural competition within the educational policy process.

The concept of intertextuality, and the questions and approaches it has generated in relation to how meanings, in their circulation, negate, oppose, interrogate, parody, support, modify or otherwise interrelate, are instructive for studying the competition between policy paradigms, and specifically their instantiation in texts, in shaping educational policy. The effect is to reconfigure the constructs of domination and suppression in how education is to be understood in a manner that acknowledges that, even when a particular view of education appears to be dominant, what it is considered to have displaced is rarely absent or unimplicated in the rationale of its dominance, and that in culture wars, as in state diplomacy and physical conflict, tactics are borrowed, positions exchanged, ground conceded, compromises made, affinities acknowledged and slogans shared as texts circulate the meanings of the policy paradigms they instantiate.

Intertextuality is a term developed by Julia Kristeva in the 1960s under the proximate influence of the writings of Saussure and Bakhtin but which has existed as a phenomenon in some form for as long as there has been discourse about texts (Worton and Still, 1991; Allen, 2000). At the core of the theory of intertextuality is the assumption that a text 'cannot exist as a hermetic or self-sufficient whole, and so does not function as a closed system' (Worton and Still, 1991, p. 1). Literary texts have been routinely analysed from this perspective but the theory has also been employed in the study of the non-literary arts such as cinema, painting, music, architecture and photography (Allen, 2000). There are two obvious reasons why such works cannot be said to exist as sealed, self-contained or terminal creators of meaning: all the influences which their producer will bring to the act of creation, and the dialogue and interpretation involved in the act of reading, viewing or listening. Works of social science are explicitly intertextual in this sense in that they exist as points of departure from an existing body of knowledge by means of quotations, references, dissent, development, application or refinement, and in turn invite a similar treatment from those who read them and engage with them in subsequent works.

The understanding of text used in this study as a strand of meaning-making realised through a sequence of discursive and non-discursive signification lacks the material presence of a literary, artistic or discursive work and, as such, does not always lend itself to citation, reference or quotation. Yet, as we have already seen, in the early works of Kristeva, Barthes and others, intertextuality was also used 'to designate the way in which a culture is structured as a complex network of codes with heterogeneous and dispersed forms of textual realisation' (Frow, 1991). In other words, they believed that social structure as a whole, and not only a specific representational work, could be thought of as a network of interlinked texts. This suggests that the insights derived from the study of the latter should at least be tested for their suitability for the illumination of the former. The implication for the study of cultural politics is their capacity to extend and render more complex its use of the constructs of domination, subordination, contestation and resistance. These are the dualisms through which cultural politics in general, and critical pedagogy in particular, have been analysed in the US and beyond. This can be illustrated from the work of the leading writers in this field.

McLaren (1995, p. 30) explains how the influence of the combined perspectives from within critical theory broadly conceived 'provoked a conceptual recasting of schools as more than simply instructional sites':

> They may instead be considered as cultural arenas where heterogeneous ideological, discursive, and social forms collide in an unremitting struggle for dominance ... This new perspective has ushered in a view of the school as a terrain of contestation. Groups from dominant and subordinate cultures negotiate on symbolic terms; students and teachers engage, accept, and sometimes resist the ways school experiences and practices are named and legitimated. The traditional view of classroom instruction – of learning as a neutral or transparent process antiseptically removed from the concepts of power, politics, history, and context – can no longer be credibly endorsed.

Similarly, for Giroux (1997, p. 133) what is at issue is 'the recognition that schools are historical and structural embodiments of ideological forms of culture; they signify reality in ways that are often experienced differently and actively contested by various individuals and groups':

> Schools, in this sense, are ideological and political terrains out of which the dominant culture in part produces its hegemonic 'certainties'; but they are also places where dominant and subordinate voices define and constrain each other, in battle and exchange, in response to the socio-historical conditions 'carried' in the institutional, textual, and lived practices that define school culture and teacher/student experience. In other words, schools are not ideologically innocent; nor are they simply reproductive of dominant social relations and interests.

The texts that participate in this cultural contestation at the level of schools and classrooms are ripe for a close analysis along the lines of studies of intertextuality in a manner that suggests how the study of a policy paradigm's dominion might be progressed.

An extension of Frow's (1991) theses on intertextuality, adapted in terms of the relationships between policy paradigms, would propose the following:

- Texts are not self-contained but are differential and historical.
- Texts contain 'traces and tracings of otherness'; they are shaped by the existence, repetition and transformation of other texts.
- Texts can be represented within one another, and act as preconditions, restraints or justifications.
- Any aspect of a policy paradigm – conceptualisation, language, themes, performatives, authorities, members – can operate as a nodal point of interplay between texts.
- The meanings generated in the interplay of texts are not dependent on the 'authorship' of the participating texts.
- Designating authorship and points of origin is an interpretive exercise.
- In textual interpretation a detailed knowledge of its substantive field is less important than the ability to identify the paradigm that it instantiates.

- Unilinear causality is rejected in favour of accounts of the circulation of meanings and their textual integration and loss.

At many points, the discourse of cultural politics/critical pedagogy in the US tradition seems to invite such a reconfiguration of the relationships between texts. Apple (2001), for instance, demonstrates the role of a shared vocabulary in the competition between economic and citizenship texts.

> Diametrically opposite policies often are wrapped in exactly the same vocabulary, something neo-liberal and neo-conservative educational 'reformers' have recognised all too well. A fine example today is the struggle over the meaning of democracy. We are witnessing a major transformation of our understandings of democracy. Rather than democracy as a fundamentally political and educative concept its meaning is being transformed into primarily an economic concept. Thus, democracy is increasingly being defined as consumer choice. The citizen is seen as a possessive individual, someone who is defined by her or his position in market relations.

In his analysis of the ideological transformations of Reagan and Thatcher, Apple (1989) also identifies other nodel points of intertextual contact in the success of market forces, free competition, private ownership and profitability over individual need, common good and public welfare in educational policies:

> This occurs *not* through imposition, but through creatively working on existing themes, desires and fears, and reworking them. Since the beliefs of people *are* contradictory and have tensions because they are what some have called polyvocal, it is then possible to move people in directions where one would least expect given their position in society. Thus, popular consciousness can be articulated to the right precisely because the feelings of hope and despair and the logic and language used to express these can be attached to a variety of discourses.

Marshall (1997, p. 7) clearly illuminates the multi-site communication between texts that renders problematic the seamless and uncompromised penetration of any single text in its influence on policy and practice.

> As policies are implemented through a conglomeration of sites and agencies, educators' abilities to alter, resist, translate, opportunistically adopt and remake policy are well-documented … Communications get distorted in loosely coupled systems. Policies are managed and translated to fit the values and meaning systems of powerful decision-makers with ongoing district and site needs and constraints. Analyses of policy implementation must look for policy slippage and symbolic policy compliance, and recognise that policies will create arenas of struggle – sometimes just over resources and turf, but more often over ideology, over what is and is not valuable and useful.

But while there are many points of reaching out to approaches that employ less dualistic roles, unidirectional influence, and authorial self-confidence, and assume multiple and interacting interpretations, the US variety of cultural politics/critical pedagogy and its derivatives have difficulty in achieving an independence of thought from the conventions and imperatives of enlightenment redemption. The following quotation from McLaren and Giroux (1997, p. 23) exemplifies this:

> There is no single discourse or discursive community that holds the franchise on truth. The very possibility of discourse presupposes a multiplicity of interpretations … If this is the case, then every reading is also a misreading. If truth is subordinate to its effects and if all of textual reality can be placed *sous rature* – including our visions of liberation and emancipation – then it seems to us that we need to abandon our truth claims and a language of interpretation purged of distortion and direct our efforts at challenging those narratives that justify one percent of the population controlling the lives of the rest by exploiting their labor and by colonising their capacity to resist – to dream or to think otherwise.

While beginning with an apparent engagement with the implications of the post-modern denial of the grand narratives of liberation and emancipation, McLaren and Giroux conclude by retreating to the security of modernity's confident identification of oppressor and oppressed and a self-designated vanguard.

The analysis of the dominion of a policy paradigm cannot afford to ignore the challenges posed by intertextuality which must rather be seen as presenting opportunities to elaborate on the constructs and modes of analysis of cultural politics/critical pedagogy and greatly expand its illuminative power. In adopting an intertextual approach to the cultural penetration of a policy paradigm it continues to be appropriate to speak of domination, suppression, exclusion and marginalisation but in a fashion that recognises that the texts involved are never hermetically sealed from one another despite their positioning, or totally self-contained, self-sufficient, independent, or secure.

Political Positioning

For a thought to be widely influential it is not necessary that it be widely held. Not all social interpretations have an equal chance of informing educational policy and practice. Some social actors have the capacity to make their understanding of a situation become 'real' even for those who would disagree with them. The final element of a paradigm's dominion encompasses these realities in the manner in which paradigms engage with and penetrate the policy-making process. It is important that this should not be seen in terms of diffusion and adoption studies which track the penetration of a stable set of ideas or practices throughout an otherwise unaltered social system. No policy process exhibits a *tabula rasa* awaiting a paradigm's inscription. There will always be an existing set of paradigmatic components, conceptualisations, language, discourse, authorities etc., of whatever provenance, that must be engaged with. In this, there are likely to be few Pauline conversions; the modification of both resident and challenging paradigms is more likely to be the norm. This experience of cultural change will in turn modify aspects of the policy process itself. As well as influencing intersubjectivity, with possible changes in educational practice, paradigmatic change can result in changes in the membership of the policy community, their inter-relationships and mode of working with one another, and facilitate newer associative networks and techniques of knowledge production. In seeking to chart the different sites of influence within the overall policy-making process with a view to identifying where a paradigm might be most likely to have an impact on decision making, the immediate problem is one of theorising the policy community itself. This is because opinions differ on where within the policy community it would be most beneficial for a paradigm to gain a foothold. When we look at the membership of the policy community – the state apparatus, varieties of collective activism within its area of jurisdiction as well as an increasingly-diverse range of international bodies and agencies – we find considerable variation in the interpretation of how these operate and influence the pursuit of policy goals.

The over-arching social institution in relation to policy making is the state and any changes in its dominant paradigms will have implications both for the substance and the process of policy making. The recent interest in the state as a concept in Irish sociological writing has not produced agreement as to how the state might be best defined. This diffuseness characterises international debate on the topic. Weber's definition of the state as a relatively stable organisation that enjoys a monopoly of the legitimate use of force, a territory over which it exercises sovereignty and an administrative apparatus for putting its directives into practice routinely represents the extent of consensus. The institutional stretch of the state as distinct from its influence raises questions as to whether local government, state-sponsored bodies, the educational system or even political culture itself should be included as part of the state.

Even if we draw back the state to its central core we find an institution that is in no sense monolithic and includes a legislature, cabinet members together with advisers and programme managers, the civil service, the judiciary, the police and army, and an array of advisory and consultative bodies. Because of its multi-faceted character any attempt to conceptualise how the state operates in relation to society can, at best, take the form of 'ideal type' depictions. Briefly sketched, these representations yield manipulated, pluralist, populist, interventionist and corporatist models of the state (Dunleavy and O'Leary, 1987).

The manipulated state acts in a manner that serves the interests of a limited segment of society. The dominant interests have been variously identified as the church, the bourgeoisie, major industry and corporations, or the military, considered individually or collectively as members of the power elite. Marxist inspired, in some versions the state is granted a relative autonomy if only to keep the different factions within the power elite in step for their common good. The pluralist state is seen to be beset with a wide range of interest groups which are well organised, assertive and present the state with conflicting demands. The state acts as an impartial referee adjudicating on the relative merits of the claims being made for resource allocation and legislative change. The populist state is said to perform in the image of the collective psyche of society. In its pure version it appears almost metaphysical: in its preferences, values and instincts the state behaves in union with the collective will of society. The interventionist state pursues an explicit agenda of change. It aspires to rising above sectional interests and *ad hoc* decision making, and perceives itself generally to be working towards a better society as guardian of the common good, in particular defending the interests of those who are badly organised or otherwise marginalised. In the corporatist model the state expands to incorporate within its policy-making mechanism significant groups, usually representing the economic interests of labour and capital from civil society, with a view to regulating conflict between them and creating a more orderly and predictable environment for the pursuit of state goals.

Even as 'ideal type' classifications these serve as useful points of reference in analysing changing institutional patterns of policy making particularly in so far as it involves the structured exercise and operation of power. The manipulated state exists where power is held by a few whereas the pluralist state assumes a dispersed distribution of power. The populist state incorporates the vision of power held by the 'people'. The interventionist state is often associated with central planning of the kind found in statist and socialist regimes. Integration and partnership underpin the corporatist state. A few illustrations from Irish experience should help to contextualise these patterns and suggest how they might be deployed in analysing the political positioning of policy paradigms.

Even interventionist states are best viewed as sites of paradigmatic interplay rather than application. Insider accounts of the workings of coalition governments testify to this, if indeed such testimony was needed (Finlay, 1998; Duignan, 1996). They demonstrate how foolhardy it would be to assume that policy decisions, let alone the associated discourse that precede them at cabinet meetings and advisory documents, could be attributed to a singular paradigm inviting easy interpretation and recognition. The contribution of civil servants to policy discourse is much documented both generally (Lee, 1989) and in relation to education (Ó Buachalla, 1988). Programme managers and special ministerial advisors are sources of new ideas on education (Harris, 1989) and have been acknowledged as such by former ministers (Hussey, 1990). Walshe (1999) provides a revealing glimpse, in his comparison of the different drafts of what came to be the 1992 Education Green Paper, of the different interpretations of the function of schooling, management and control which individual ministers and their respective advisors brought to this work. Legislation not directly relating to education, a judiciary given to expansionist interpretations of the constitution, and state-appointed commissions and inquiries are all potential contributors of changed understandings, of which those relating to childhood and children and young persons' rights (Lynch, 1998) is just one example, that have a bearing on educational policy making.

Increasingly, the state operates against a broader background of more global influences. Membership of the European Community since 1973 has exposed Irish policy makers to directives from the European Commission, judgments of the European Court, and a host of policy statements together with grant-aid inducements which influence how issues are conceptualised, spoken of and socially constituted as problems which the state is willing to confront. For some, this is to be regretted as a lack of sovereignty. For others, it exposes Irish policy to modernising influences and provides a point of reference and appeal for liberalising interests within the state and society. Recognising the power of global economic forces, it has been argued that Irish industrial development since the 1950s could be better understood as an example of dependency capitalism rather than modernisation. This has assumed a number of versions. Crotty (1986) describes the Irish situation as neo-colonial. O'Hearn (1995) recommends dependency reversal based on local democratic structures and green sentiments, and Coulter and Coleman (2003, p. 29), in the wake of the Celtic Tiger, yearn to 'speed the day' to 'a form of society that is genuinely human and sustainable'. More muted examples are provided by the Telesis (NESC, 1982) and Culliton (Industrial Policy Review Group, 1992) Reports which urged a greater targeting of indigenous industry for support and expansion. Jacobsen (1994, p. 201), however, points out that international economic forces do not determine the precise policy responses of a country. In fact, they can become a resource in the hands of state actors who interpret and promulage international forces in a manner that supports their policy choices. As he puts it, 'external forces and agents are (far from tame) pieces on the domestic political game board in the pursuit of domestic advantages.' Similar processes of selection, filtering and legitimation also operate in relation to the use of international discourse and practice in education.

Where the cultural influences on policy form part of a taken-for-granted realm of knowing, in its extreme form as doxa, their power is likely to be concealed. Whyte's (1980) conclusion that there were few instances where the Roman Catholic Church had sought to directly intervene in the enactment of legislation can also be interpreted as a measure of the power of an institution which could rely on its successful shaping of the cognitions and understandings which state officials, elected and permanent, would bring to the task of policy making. Those who possess such cultural power have less need to engage in public advocacy and protest. Yet for the Roman Catholic Church, that same cultural power over individual participants in the policy process has waned at a time when more explicit intervention has been undermined as modernist critique of church-state relationships dislodge religious ideologies to the private sphere. And as further evidence of how paradigmatic change is implicated in the shifting nature of the policy-making site, we find in turn an acceptance of the integration of the texts of the new social movements, such as feminism, environmentalism and peace, into the state's discourse.

Because of this diversity and change in its personnel, structures and practices, knowing where the state begins and ends as a force in policy making is challenging. This is further exemplified in efforts to estimate the extent to which the integration of significant interests in society within its policy-making mechanisms can be said to constitute corporatism. There has been no shortage of viewpoints (Hardiman and Lalor, 1984). In *Pay, Politics and Economic Performance in Ireland, 1970-1987*, Hardiman (1988) concludes that, despite numerous consultative bodies and tripartite structures, these have not developed as significant subsystems of the state, but rather have come and gone as the needs of the organised interests dictate. 'Neocorporatist sentiments rather than institutions' have been diagnosed by Breen *et al.* (1990, p. 176) and 'corporatist practices rather than a corporatist system' by Peillon (1995). And yet, as Peillon, citing the Programme for Economic and Social Progress (1991-1993) and the Programme for Competitiveness and Work which immediately followed it, goes on to point out that 'as soon as the end of corporatism in Ireland is announced, another corporatist framework is set up'. Furthermore, these frameworks, now more numerous than ever, stretch beyond the pay and industrial relations arena and the resolution of conflict between competing interests (O'Donnell and Thomas, 1998). Studies of Bord na Gaeilge (Tovey *et al.*, 1989) and the corporatist tendencies in relation to educational interests as reflected in the National Council for Curriculum and Assessment and in numerous commissions/committees of inquiry (O'Sullivan, 1992b) seem to confirm, at the very least, the emergence of a strong corporatist political culture throughout the 1990s.

Within these corporatist arrangements, as well as the more tangible bargaining over salary and welfare increases and anti-poverty initiatives etc., there is also the potential for negotiation, not necessarily explicit, over the cultural assumptions of the communication between the participants. This can relate to the reconceptualisation of issues and problems, to the addition of new themes, and to changes in those designated as authorities, all of which can occur in relation to the most material of performatives. Contrasting models of the state may be employed in such general terms as 'making choices between Boston and Berlin', or 'rolling back the nanny state'. One would not routinely expect participants to speak in terms of paradigm wars or shifts even in cases when such was the nature of their engagement. CORI, a prominent member of the Third Social Partnership Pillar, drawn from the community and voluntary sector, which was incorporated into the negotiations leading to the ratification of Partnership 2000, is exceptional in this regard.

CORI (Healy and Reynolds, 1993, 1998) have argued that the source of many of the social and economic problems faced by Irish society lies in the dominant paradigm underpinning public policy-making. This they describe as mechanistic, involving progress being seen mainly in terms of economic growth, economists becoming the ultimate authorities on most areas of public policy, and GDP accepted as an end of policy in itself. Their proposed alternative paradigm, one of 'right relationships', would be 'underpinned by a global ethic', a 'broader understanding of the concept of citizenship', and involve 'genuine progress indicators in the (overlapping) economic, political, cultural and social areas' (Healy and Reynolds, 1998). It scarcely needs to be stressed that it is not necessary for there to be this theorised level of discourse for policy discourse to operate at a paradigmatic level.

Along with other members of the Third Pillar, CORI has also been credited with recognising the power implications of being a participant at the terminal point at which social and economic policy is determined. They are said to have regarded their involvement in consultative bodies such as the National Economic and Social Forum and *ad hoc* task forces as 'participation without power': 'that their relative inability to exert any discernible influence on the direction of public policy was institutionalised and perpetuated by the lack of full social partner status and their continued exclusion from the formal negotiation process for the national agreements' (O'Donnell and Thomas, 1998). While these concerns are valid in terms of the capacity of participants in the policy process to imprint their own meanings on the framing of policy, it is in danger of overstating the distinction between policy discourse and decision making. Policy makers do not select from an open-ended set of options. The range and substance of the performatives from which policy is determined will have a longer genesis involving cultural shaping and filtering. Their formation will occur in many sites, involving consultative bodies, where processes of conceptualisation, thematisation, naming, legitimation and exclusion etc. will act as resources in moving what it is considered appropriate for policy makers to negotiate about in one direction rather than another. It is nonetheless an important reminder that the actors, social configurations and sites involved in this process do not have equal power and that the social and economic understandings of some will be better positioned to become official state policy.

Pluralist explanations of the state assume the existence of a set of well-organised interests capable of representing and asserting their position and concerns in national policy debate. The conceptualisation of collective activism of this nature in Ireland is largely in terms of interest groups. One large-scale study of Irish political culture in the early 1970s (Raven and Whelan, 1976) suggested that the Irish were slow to form interest groups and appeared to confirm the conclusion of some earlier small-scale studies that they preferred to bring their personal grievances to the attention of their elected representatives. In this interpretation the familiar pattern of brokerage and clientelism in the Irish political system is seen to suppress latent collective action among those who share common dissatisfactions. Whatever validity this reluctance to organise in pursuit of a common goal had some thirty years ago it seems to have dissipated quite quickly. In the third edition of *The Government and Politics of Ireland*, Chubb (1992, p. 125) described as 'a comparatively recent phenomenon', 'the enormous scale of pressure-group activity, which is a feature of government and administration today'. The greater urge to mobilise appears to be particularly striking in relation to issues that affect the quality of life such as environmental concerns about industrial sites and waste disposal, and the provision of services such as hospitals, educational facilities, post offices and roads (Curtin and Varley, 1995). Overall in Irish society, Peillon (1995) sees the process of social differentiation of people according to various types of economic activity, outlook and values as a feature of an advanced industrial society which in turn leads to a proliferation of organised interests. He measures this in term of the expanding list of associations contained in the *IPA Yearbook and Diary,* finding that 'the list has grown quite considerably over the last twenty years ... One gets a picture of a society made up of a great variety of pressure groups, representing particular interests or values and jostling one another in their attempt to influence the State'.

Interest groups vary considerably among themselves and it is possible to differentiate between them in relation to a number of dimensions such as lifespan, focus, resources and capacity for mobilisation which affect their impact on policy. As a conceptualisation of collective activism, interest group analysis of this kind can be productive where the objectives are explicit and instrumental or, if they aspire to more abstract cultural change, it is codified as a principle or idea. Such is the nature of policy paradigms, even in the form of their instantiation in texts, that a wider range of associative forms, along the lines that have been outlined earlier, is required to describe the collective dimension of those who act psychologically or socially as their carriers and enunciators. Otherwise, it is difficult to know how such features as unnamed meanings, non-discursive contributions to texts, and a membership that is not always determinable can be socially positioned in the first instance. Overall, the social study of shifting meanings of a kind that pays attention to such details as shared conceptualisations, language, themes, performatives etc. needs to acknowledge that intersubjectivity as a process is a more universal activity than interest group mobilisation and action. Implicitly, this is a feature of research which has analysed the impact of social movements on policy in relation to organic farming (Tovey, 1999), women (Connolly, L., 1997) and the environment (Yearley, 1995).

The brief explication of some of the variations and dimensions involved in a paradigm's political positioning, and their implications for its dominion in the determination of educational policy, is restricted not merely by virtue of space but also by the cultural orientation of this study. The limited treatment of more explicit political structures and processes is a function of the analytical extraction of culture, for the purpose of its conceptual elaboration and scrutiny, from the policy process. As acknowledged in the previous chapter, this is an artificial, though functional, exercise: the reality of policy making is the integration of its cultural, social and psychological dimensions in a fashion that proclaims the interrelationship and interdependency between meaning, social structure and people. As well as incorporating aspects of this integrated nature of the policy process, the inclusion and treatment of political positioning in the schematisation of a paradigm's dominion suggests some of the linkages that are possible with the broad field of political and, more specifically, policy studies. Some specialisms, approaches and developments within these areas, such as those influenced by social constructionist theories and what has come to be known as the 'new institutionalism' (Healy, 1998), are more susceptible than others to according significance to the cultural dimension of policy studies. Inevitably, there will be policy researchers who quite legitimately will prioritise more observable political processes, as I have the cultural realm. Whatever the analytical emphasis, however, all theorists acknowledge, however implicitly, the use of language, ideas, justifications, interpretations, arguments etc. by participants, programmes and policies within the political process for which this schematisation of the cultural sphere of the policy process provides a conceptual literacy.

In conclusion, a policy paradigm's dominion will be greater the more it exists as a coherent interpretive force, the more it gains supremacy over other cultural interpretations, and the more it informs the understandings of policy makers. It may seem incredulous that any paradigm could achieve total dominion in the present globalised era. With such apparent freedom of ideas and the rapid dissemination of information, whatever is proclaimed is open to challenge almost immediately irrespective of location. The tribe, community or country insulated from outside influences, or even knowledge of an alien world, no longer exists as in the past. Herodotus describes the mutual incomprehension experienced when a people who cannibalised their dead and those who cremated theirs became aware of each other's practices (Ryan, 1970). The latter were reported to have been outraged at the lack of ancestral respect, the former incredulous at the wanton wastage of food. The sealed cultural worlds that made these sentiments possible have in the popular view been consigned to history. Yet westernisation, 'McDonaldisation', 'end of history' theses, and the advocacy of liberal democracy suggest taken-for-granted assumptions about quite fundamental principles of human development, economic organisation and political structures that enjoy exceptionally wide currency. Ultimately, by definitional fiat, to be able to recognise a policy paradigm with total dominion would be to deny it such a commanding status. One has, therefore, to hold open the likelihood that there are dominant paradigms holding sway in the world that await recognition and naming.

Change

So far, no attempt has been made to make qualitative distinctions in relation to the varieties of paradigmatic shifts that are relevant to this analysis of cultural politics. In reality, paradigms are in constant flux. To speak of change, therefore, is to refer to the modalities in the manner of their development and restructuring. Six kinds of modality have been identified for the purpose of the study – expansion/contraction, intensification/simplification, systematisation/diffusion, mutation, merging/factioning and rupture. All of these features of paradigmatic change were observed, inferred or extrapolated from the substantive analysis of the operation of policy paradigms in the Irish educational policy process. Reference has already been made to the manner in which what emerged empirically in this regard from the research resonated with Archer's (1988, 1996) analysis of cultural change. In particular, the author is indebted to Archer's imagery and classification of change in such areas as systems of belief and scientific theory, though these have been modified and adapted for the task in hand. Perhaps, in retrospect, it should not have appeared so uncanny as it did at the time that the dynamics of meaning-making in as specific a site as the educational system of a nation state should be found to mirror those of codified thought across a range of publicly-formulated bodies of knowledge. Such was the degree of congruence and confluence that it is difficult to estimate where the agency of Archer, author and research process began and ended.

As we have seen in the previous chapter, Archer's analysis of cultural change is theoretically suited to the exploration of paradigmatic change, particularly because of the manner in which she seeks to avoid the 'fallacy of conflation' and attempts to sketch the dynamics of the interaction between culture and the social system. In order to unravel the dialectical interplay of culture and human agency over time, Archer proposes the operation of endless three-part cycles of Cultural Conditioning – Socio-Cultural Interaction – Cultural Elaboration. The first element, the anterior cultural conditioning, refers to how the prior development of ideas, which itself arises from earlier interaction, conditions the current context of action, confronting agents with unproblematic and problem-ridden sets of beliefs, theories and ideas. While Archer acknowledges the constraints on the actors in such a situation she equally asserts their capacity to be reflective, creative and strategic in responding to the situations in which they find themselves. In advancing their interests, justifying their position or countering resistance, individuals will take advantage of inconsistencies in what they have culturally inherited and generate new forms of pluralism, combinations and specialisation in the field of ideas. In this way, the elaborate and recurring sequences through which culture is transformed are the joint products of the culturally-induced context in which individuals find themselves and their socio-cultural responses to it. As Archer (1988, p. xxiv) succinctly puts it, 'cultural elaboration is the future which is forged in the present, hammered out of past inheritance by current innovation.'

Unravelling this process is no straightforward task since by the time a feature of the culture is analysed it may appear to be complete and self-contained. The dynamics through which it proceeded to attain such an integrated character are difficult to replay and the contestation, competition, losses and gains that went into its having its current shape can be easily obscured to analysis.

Expansion/Contraction

As a paradigm expands it incorporates a wider range of reality within its remit. As with colonisation, it extends the territory it controls. A wider realm of ideas, discourse, people are incorporated within its influence. This can take the form of additional themes taking their flavour from a paradigm, previously unconvinced groups showing allegiance, and gaining a foothold in the policy community. Obversely, a contracting paradigm will be seen to concede from its control aspects of ideational, discursive and collective life.

An expanding/contracting paradigm takes the form of an incremental process. The addition and subtraction involved is reasonably amenable to social analysis. As well as the incremental nature of the change, another factor rendering it more transparent than most is the political activity which orchestrates this kind of paradigmatic change. Much of this is likely to be in the public domain, the stuff of newspaper correspondence, interest group representation and publicised negotiations. In fact, it is quite easy to see this process of political activity as no more than the pursuit of material advantage and strategic manoeuvring, and to ignore the cultural resources that are being deployed and altered in advancing a social project. In drawing attention to this intersection of the social and the cultural, to the fact that actors are positioned in both domains simultaneously, Archer argues that to explain sociologically the outcome of conflict situations it is necessary to introduce cultural factors such as the legitimatory armoury that forms part of most of the struggles and transactions. Whether or not an interest group knows it in advance, she contends, once it proceeds to act as such it enmeshes itself in a particular form of cultural discourse, and its associated problems of correcting, protecting and justifying its ideas, if it is to be successful in the pursuit of its more behavioural objectives. As Archer (1988, p. 284) argues, 'empirically and theoretically the cultural penetration of the structural field has to be recognised, for the same sociological reason as before – that social groups not only have interests, resources and power but they also have ideas (and if certain groups would like not to have some of these around, then their opponents certainly would)'. With each phase of expansion, new threats and competitors arise and new sets of mechanisms emerge as paradigms seek to defend their interests in the face of the expansion of what is now recognised as their potential coloniser. As a paradigm contracts, and becomes progressively a less serious competitor, not alone will it cease to be treated with suspicion and hostility but it may even attract the benign tolerance of paradigms that are still in the ascendant.

While the expectation would be that an expanding paradigm is also one that is growing in power, and obversely that a contracting paradigm results in a loss of power, this need not necessarily be the case. The addition of themes to an existing set of concerns may dilute the coherence of a paradigm and loosen its framing. New policy options can result in a lack of focus for political action where the project is an emerging or assertive one, or for state planning where it has already attained an official standing. Likewise, converts are not always of the kind that one would wish to recruit.

Intensification/Simplification

Unlike expansion, intensification makes for more dense policy paradigms. It refers to a process of 'filling in' rather than 'filling out'. The result is a complex socio-cultural phenomenon, a developed network with interconnections and interlinkages. This elaboration of a policy paradigm occurs within its components as well as in the character of the relationships between them. Intensification is more visibly produced by a more specialised set of agents than those who fuel the expansion and contraction of the paradigm. Its currency is conceptualisation, research findings and theoretical developments.

One of the more obvious factors instigating intensification is an external challenge of a kind that attempts to refute a paradigm's precepts. Archer (1988, p. 209) provides a revealing illustration of the consequences of such confrontation from the mid-nineteenth century controversy between Pasteur and Poucher on whether the micro organisms responsible for putrefaction were introduced from the air or were spontaneously generated in certain circumstances. When a commission pronounced in Pasteur's favour it suppressed opinions for some years. Later, when the controversy was revived, Pasteur and others were forced to undertake further research as a result of which new problems emerged and old problems were revived. However, as Archer points out the historical development of density can often emerge independently of real or imagined external threats. Where there is confidence in the validity of its basic precepts among those involved in the paradigm there can be what Archer describes as a 'self-absorption' to the point at which refutations are disregarded and verifications become the contact points of reality. In such situations, 'the autonomous and preoccupying activity' of intensification has 'its own dynamics which engage in the absence of external threats or regardless of them' (p. 182). 'Cultural embroidery' (p. 158) this may appear to be but its impact can be totalising and encompassing for the identity of the participants.

Intensification requires the existence of a cadre of intellectuals and a culture of intellectual life. It is necessary that there be a tradition of inquiry and the establishment of roles in society committed to such an inquiry in relation to the substantive content of the paradigm. Within education, those who assume this role of intellectual, in the sense of interpreting, systematically analysing and representing the processes of education, can be drawn from the state apparatus, the professional teaching bodies, interest groups, as well as from the more obvious academic settings. The drawing together of these in the form of working parties, councils, commissions, committees of inquiry and conferences can be the occasion, through policy refinements and strategic statements, for the intensification of the paradigm at the level of ideas, individual and collective life.

The reversal of intensification – simplification – results in a sparse paradigm. Theories disassemble and language becomes less precise and distinctive. Because of the relative lack of elaboration of its meanings, it can appear blunt. Accordingly, it can be variously experienced as oppositional, threatening or inviting, depending on how its cryptic messages are interpreted.

Systematisation/Diffusion

Where a paradigm experiences continuous expansion and intensification it begins to take on the features of a system. In expanding it will have infused a greater swathe of reality that is meaningful to educational decision-making. In intensifying, the interconnections between the various features of a paradigm will be articulated and refined. Through these joint processes of 'filling out' and filling-in', a paradigm systematises. This can be observed when it begins to exhibit such features as strong framing, protective strategies and reproductive mechanisms.

There is now a much clearer sense of what the paradigm is not as well as what it is. As it becomes internally more dense its self-image and identity sharpen in focus. In being confident about itself, a paradigm is much more specific in its identification of the 'other'. This finer delineation sets it apart and projects it as a distinct entity. As such, it is much better placed to demand and command loyalty, if only in the sense that with a more easily-defined membership there are fewer ideational ambiguities in which waverers can take refuge. But organisationally, through the development of roles and practices, it will develop strategies both to shore up loyalty to its orthodoxies and to protect its members from the contaminating impact of competing paradigms. Censorship or other forms of restricted exposure, derision, dismissal as unscientific or extreme are the crudest mechanisms for guarding members from the influence of competitors. Building up conviction and loyalty through socialisation rituals or events are likely to be more effective. Spokespersons, standardised responses and answers to doubts, queries and contradictions are also features of the defence armoury of the systematised paradigm.

With systematisation comes the impetus to perpetuate itself through the cultivation of promising new supporters, building one's beliefs into more permanent forms and having the paradigm propagated more widely. To paraphrase Archer (1988, p. 179), an island of ideational order with an integrated community aptly describes a systematised paradigm.

In a reversal of systematisation, a paradigm experiences diffusion. Framing weakens, authorities speak with a less coherent voice and a range of expertise that is less comprehensive. Association becomes less structured, formal or differentiated and membership uncertain.

Mutation

Mutation also involves expansion/contraction of the components or a paradigm. But in this case the movement does not take the form of incremental additions or subtractions. The defining characteristic of mutation is the reworking of an element of a paradigm to the extent that it facilitates the emergence of a new paradigm. The emerging paradigm is experienced as an out-growth from the replaced paradigm. An example of mutation at the cosmic level is provided by the re-interpretation of the universe that was made possible as bigger portions of it became amenable to a naturalistic explanation. For religious adherents who wished to reconstruct their faith along rationalistic lines the resulting mutation took the form of 'its miracles becoming metaphors, its sacraments becoming symbols, spirituality becoming depth-psychology, its priests becoming social workers and its ethics becoming a code of social fraternity. In sum, this represented a shift towards naturalistic explanation, mundane application and this-worldly justification' (Archer, 1988, p. 170).

Since with mutated paradigms the growth is organic, the sense of dissonance, confrontation and contestation is greatly reduced. As a strategy of change, therefore, mutation has distinct advantages. Without dissonance there is a reduced psychological, personal and social disruption for the adherents. Loss of support is minimised. The basis for systematic opposition is diminished since the change appears to be no more than a restatement, a new way of speaking, a case of old ideas redressed in a new form.

Merging/Factioning

In merging, paradigms adopt a particular kind of expansion. They gain in substance through the act of partnership. Obviously, this will be pre-signalled by virtue of their compatibility in their ideas, collective life or individual members. But the context of the fusion is a crucial element. This is the difference between the continuing in existence of autonomous compatible paradigms and their merging to form a more comprehensive structure of influence on the policy process. The dimensions of merging paradigms which form the bridgehead between them will influence the degree to which the merger is ideas-, policy- or people-led.

The process of merging can be a slow one in which paradigms fuse over an extensive period of time. This need not be a continuous process with one dimension after another losing its individual identity. It allows for regression, faulty alliances and ideological tensions; in other words, taking a step backwards before progressing towards an accommodation.

The nature of the accommodation eventually arrived at may not be one of equal partnership. Rather than a coalition of equals, it might resemble a form of co-optation in which one of the paradigms gains the support of the other's propositions and theories and the allegiances of its members, while maintaining a dominance in the shaping of its merged character and control over its future development.

No matter how even and balanced the merging of paradigms might be, but particularly where co-optation is evident, there will always be tensions, conflict and dissent accompanying the process. This may result in the loss of members who may in turn form the base of a new paradigm or align themselves with an existing more compatible one. While such a scenario has the potential to destabilise and demoralise, it can also be an impetus for the further intensification of the new paradigm as it seeks to develop a consistency, avoid the loss of future members and generally fill in the gaps, streamline itself and edit out inconsistencies.

In a reversal of the process of merging, paradigms may factionise and form two or more autonomous structures. This will involve the undoing of many of the above interactions relating to the bridgeheads, pacing, divided loyalties, a sense of membership and range of influence. While factioning is synonymous with contraction, paradoxically it may result in an enhanced impact on the policy process. This would be the case where, in factioning, a paradigm partitions off less coherent aspects of its thinking, releases less committed or affiliated members and abandons policy options which have ceased to have appeal. The result may be a policy paradigm that is more coherent in its ideas, more vigorous in its membership and more focused in its direction for policy.

Where the parting of the ways leading to a factioning of a paradigm follows internal disputes and disagreements or personality clashes, the subsequent paradigms resulting from the divorce will begin their life, initially at least, in an oppositional relationship. While paradigms routinely find themselves in such a relationship of disagreement with one another, the tension, confrontation and competition that follows sub-division is rendered particularly potent by virtue of how well-informed on each other's position the protagonists will be. Individual deserters may cause embarrassment and, if they leave in sufficient numbers or regularity, engender instability and self-doubt among the remaining members. They are also available for recruitment to alternative paradigms. But where a paradigm factionises as a result of disagreements and dissent, there is a ready-made and well-informed source of confrontation. It is akin to the differences between heretics and schismatics. Individual unbelievers are always less of a threat than a new school of thought or belief.

On the other hand, the factioning of a paradigm can be an uncontentious occurrence, the result of a long process of benign disengagement or of a more sudden parting as a response to a precipitating circumstance which highlights diverging strands. Either way, the relationship between the resulting paradigms can range from compatibility to growing mutual irrelevance. In either case of parallel development there will be degrees of aloofness and introspection as each paradigm enters a new phase of development.

Rupture

The rupture of a paradigm signals its demise as a force in the shaping of the policy process. There are potent psychological restraints on the rupture of a paradigm. People are sustained and affirmed by the continuity of their beliefs, and even where the intensity of their commitment might wane, conversion to competing systems of thought is less likely. Few welcome the dissipation of personal identity that can result from the dramatic recantation of their beliefs. Likewise, who desires the social isolation of disengagement from the affiliative experience of paradigmatic membership?

An even more fundamental impediment to rupture than individual psychology is the difficulty in achieving the complete eradication of an idea. Ideas do not die. Advocates may lose listeners, supporters and sympathisers. They rarely change their own allegiance. A set of policy prescriptions often lives on in the structure and content of the educational system. As Archer (1988, p. 169) points out, even in science any theory can be saved from apparent falsification. There is nothing, she argues, in science that forces a theory to go under and compel its supporters to admit defeat. As she puts it, 'Survival is always possible, the question is, on what terms?' Some strategies of survival, indeed, may well be conducive to the intensification of the paradigm as propositions are refined and less defensible ones are shed in the face of contradictory evidence. Where accommodation is through *ad hoc* hypotheses or linguistic reinterpretations of theory it can signal degeneration. In the case of scientific theories, 'survival through *ad hoc* devices means that a theory loses its empirical character. Adherence to it is no longer because of the theoretical purchase gained or the empirical world: instead it is a matter of commitment where the empirical domain is drawn upon to prop up the theoretical structure. This spells degeneration but not extinction.'

This degeneration can lead to a loss of dominion for the paradigm. Ultimately, it can be rendered incapable of defending itself against charges of irrelevance, fundamentalism, extremism, divisiveness or whatever other label is employed by its opponents to effect its marginalisation. Nonetheless, Archer is correct in maintaining that the result of competitive contradiction is elaboration, diversity and pluralism rather than elimination.

In the analysis that follows, these variations of paradigmatic change will be further calibrated in terms of a paradigm's components – those conceptual/linguistic, discursive, social and psychological dimensions which all paradigms exhibit and which allow them to be productively differentiated from one another. Adopting a framing and, particularly, an intertextual approach to the study of the cultural pervasiveness of paradigms represents a further complexity in the study of paradigmatic change in so far as it renders less positivistic and self-contained its various statuses and stages. The implication of such change for a paradigm's dominion touches at the core of this study. It refers to the knowledge, and the framing and intertextual dynamics of its production, which informs the policy-making process. But, more deeply, at the intersubjective level, it directs us to the changing structuring principles that guide these dynamics in a manner that implicates the ontological depth of society.

Epilogue to Part One

The object of this book is to explore the cultural politics of Irish education, how meanings are produced, circulated and negotiated within the context of the Irish educational policy process. It would be tautological to describe this as a study of politicised meaning since meaning, the processes of meaning-making and contestation always implicate power. This evokes Foucault's power/knowledge construct: knowledge, what it is and how it is structured and named both confers and assumes power, while power creates and benefits from the configuration of knowledge. Reworking Andersen's (2003) example of the dead seal found on a beach, which he uses to illustrate discursive battles as a conflict over which signifiers are to be tied to which signifieds, provides illumination as a distanced non-educational example. In this instance, competing signifiers might include the will of God, the unrelenting, amoral whim of nature, global warming, pollution, and over-fishing affecting the seal's food supply, which variously seek to establish its meaning in terms of how it is to be understood, defined, explained, moralised and politicised. These are the cultural forms which compete to give significance to, and in the process recruit, the presence of a dead seal on a beach.

In the chapters that follow, these processes of meaning-making will be explored in relation to the personnel, practices, values and assumptions that constitute the social institution of education, in terms of how the experience of education might be said to be implicated in what people become, individually and collectively, and to more specific objects of contestation such as particular age and developmental stages, the provision of financial support to educational organisations, and the control of their character and processes. Be it a teacher at the head of a classroom, a child seated in a desk, differences in educational achievement and participation, a crucifix on the wall, the syllabus, or legislation, there exists the potential for contestation in relation to what it is, how it came to be and what action it requires that constitute the cultural politics of education. The multi-layered and dynamic nature of this process can easily be obscured as participants in the policy process seek to bring about or resist specific varieties of policy change – the dilution of church control, the greater involvement of parents, the re-introduction of undergraduate fees and the privatisation of universities. As the example of the dead seal on a beach illustrates, more than a once-off ideational and discursive moment in the understanding of governance, participation, rights, and efficiency is involved. Even where a signifier is successfully applied, there is the question of its ongoing existence in terms of its coherence, stability in engagement with other meanings, and dominion, modulated between doxa and rupture. Also at issue is the nature and degree of association between those who share such meanings, its psychological significance for them and their social and political power. This is to recognise the issues surrounding the place of the individual, the social and the cultural in the theorisation of cultural politics that have been illuminated against the background of the diverse intellectual resources deployed in approaching the schematisation of the construct of policy paradigm.

The task of Part One has been to address these issues and to describe these scholarly sources as a preamble to the schematisation of the construct of policy paradigm. Considered as an interpretive framework, with linguistic, epistemic, discursive, social, psychological and political dimensions, this supplies a conceptual literacy for thinking and speaking about meaning. Recognising the dense nature of the cultural dimension of the educational policy process, it facilitates a more discriminating communication about its processes and components. It achieves this by differentiating between the structuration of meaning through concepts and language, its discursive and non-discursive development and elaboration, and its 'peopled' features of association, authority and identity. Its dominion distinguishes between conceptual, intertextual and political dimensions. Varieties of qualitative change are used to allow for the fine-tuning of cultural shifts. This schematisation of the construct of policy paradigm was developed through the abrasion of concept and application. With the added variable of the contextual and substantive nature of educational change over the past half-century, it will be found that not all of these dimensions will be equally employed in the analysis that follows in the subsequent chapters. This variable usage will provide a further dynamic for the modification of the construct, and methodological and conceptual issues of this nature will be explored again in the Conclusion.

Part Two

The Cultural Reconstruction
of Education:
From Theocentric to
Mercantile Paradigm

One of the most recurring and characteristic themes of Irish educational analysis has been the influence of the Roman Catholic Church (henceforth, depending on context, also referred to as the church or the Catholic church) on Irish educational policy and practice. However its power is conceptualised, traced and measured, commentators agree that from the 1960s onwards it diminished in capacity and range (Fahey, 1992a; Hornsby-Smith, 1992; Nic Ghiolla Phádraig, 1995; Kenny, 1997; Inglis, 1998a; Fuller, 2004).

What is less clear from these commentaries is what is considered to have replaced the Roman Catholic view of education as an overarching principle of the educational system. Cultural nationalism, with which it had been explicitly linked in the process of nation building since the formation of the state, also loosened its grip on education over the same period and did not benefit from what might otherwise have been a monopoly in defining the institution of education. Remarkably, there have been few attempts to theorise the changes experienced by education as a social institution since the 1950s. Though focusing on a specific aspect and sector respectively, Wickham's (1980) study of state educational policy in terms of interacting national and international contexts and O'Reilly's (1989) analysis of the development of the VEC system according to Archer's conceptualisation of the evolution of educational systems are exceptional in this regard. Otherwise, for those who have sought to chart the changes experienced by the Irish educational system during this period the implicit model adopted appears to be modernisation theory. Historical texts that include the period (Murphy, 1975; Lyons, 1979; Brown, 1985; Lee, 1989; Keogh, 1994), which vary greatly in the attention they devote to education, together with dedicated overviews of educational change (Sheehan, 1979; Coolahan, 2000; Breen *et al.*, 1990) all select, as significant, changes that are synonymous with modernisation: equality of opportunity, greater access and mass education, fading influence of religion and tradition, rational and quantifiable procedures in decision-making and reorientation of the curriculum in the light of the needs of the economy.

A telling attraction of modernisation theory to Irish audiences is that it appeals to the 'anti-ideology' orientation that prevails in Irish political culture, well captured in Gallagher's (1981) ascerbic assertion that 'the "end of ideology" dawned in Ireland before ideology had even arrived.' Modernisation theory can accommodate the assumption that once the church and state are kept at a distance, decisions about education handed back to elected representatives and state officials, representative structures put in place to involve the relevant interests, and the content of education made responsive to the demands of economic roles and the challenges of modern life, the ideological battles have been, if not won, at least resolved. Indeed, the thesis pervades the EU White Paper on Education and Training, *Teaching and Learning. Towards the Learning Society* which proclaims 'the end of debate on educational principles' (European Commission, 1996, p. 42).

Wickham (1980), alone, adverts to criticism of modernisation theory by those who argue that dependency – on larger capitalist formations – might represent a more accurate characterisation of the nature of the change involved. Dependency theory is to be found in a number of interpretations of Irish economic development since the 1950s (O'Hearn, 1995; Kirby, 1997). Predictably, since modernisation theory has never been systematically or assertively promoted – exemplified in Clancy's (1995b) guarded application – in relation to Irish educational development during this period, these critics have not turned their attention to education.

What is surprising, given the fading influence of cultural nationalism and the emergence of Europeanisation within Irish educational policy and practice, is that post-nationalism (Kearney, 1997) has not been deployed to delineate and trace shifting senses of Irishness, identity and narratives of the past in curricular and policy discourse (but see Waldron, 2004). Similarly, post-colonialism, apart from passing references (Lynch, 1989) and rhetorical flourishes – 'just how "Gaelic" is the self-image of a country which, within the past decade, has had a Minister for Education who could not speak the Irish language' (Kiberd, 1995, p. 648) – has not featured as an orienting or explanatory perspective. The increasing uses of multiculturalism and interculturalism in education tend to be more by way of description, aspiration, advocacy and legitimation than as reflexive and analytical constructs. The phenomenon of Irish educational change since the 1950s awaits theorisation.

In approaching the task of theorising Irish educational change from the perspective of the cultural reconstruction of the institution of education, it seemed productive to view the span of development since the 1950s in the first instance in terms of a transition from an institution that had God at its centre to one in which 'trade/exchange' is at its core. In labelling these as theocentric and mercantile respectively, and analysing them in terms of my schematisation of the construct of policy paradigm, they were found to have the potential to not alone illuminate what is suggested by the nature of the dualism but, more importantly, for accommodating themes raised in previous treatments of Irish education by way of their paradigmatic and textual relationships.

Chapter 3 begins by providing an ideal-typical overview of the contrasting meanings and practices involved in the transition from a theocentric to a mercantile paradigm in the reconstruction of Irish education, and situates it against the doxic-like prescriptions of the church at the beginning of the period under review, specifically in relation to the primacy of its role in education in contrast to the subsidiarity of the state. Chapter 4 seeks to explain the circumstances in the 1960s which allowed the state to become more activist in relation to educational policy and change against the background of the social and economic crisis of the 1950s and the economic reconstruction that followed. The role played by the human capital paradigm, and specifically by *Investment in Education*, published in 1965, is at the core of this explanation. But the longer term significance of *Investment in Education* is also traced in the light of the manner in which distinct interests – state officials, politicians, teachers and parents – drew out, in a process of mutation, from the discourse it facilitated, new themes relating to the legitimacy of state activity, commercial and economic models, schools encompassing quantifiable and manageable resources both physical and human, and an educational public. This chapter concludes as the boundaries of the human capital paradigm became less coherent and it experienced factioning as these emergent themes yielded texts in their own right. This textualisation that followed the mutation and factioning of the human capital paradigm is characterised asa process of detraditionalisation in Chapter 5. Five texts are selected as strands of meaning-making about education, rather than in terms of their immediate instrumental effects on the system – commercial, managerial, vocational, consumer and market. In a process of complementary intertextuality, that involves mutual support, validation and extension, these realise meanings beyond the range of what they textually produce individually to generate the mercantile paradigm. Educational transformations in other educational systems along New Right and Neo-Liberal lines are used to particularise this Irish experience in educational reconstruction. Finally, Chapter 6 describes the culture wars relating to how education was to be understood in an Ireland in which religion had progressively ceased to be a dominant contributor to public knowledge and understanding since the 1960s. Within the dynamics of predatory intertextuality, the mercantile paradigm is pitted against the modernising discourse of a society that would have understood itself as outward and forward-looking, industrialising, more affluent, and freeing itself from the traditional restraints of nation, religion, economic self-sufficiency and circumscribed opportunity. But it will also be seen that the theocentric paradigm, from which both were setting their distance, was not unimplicated. Four areas of cultural production – equality, difference, virtue and control – which would have been identified with a modernising educational system, both in terms of its understanding and materiality, have been selected as the terrain for the engagement. What emerges is how difficult it is to avoid the predatory engagement of the mercantile paradigm – becoming implicated with it, allied to it, neutralised or destabilised by it. A number of interpretations of the status of these culture wars relating to the understanding of Irish education as a social institution are identified in terms of manifestations of detraditionalisation and post-modernism in Irish society at large, and these are pursued in the Epilogue.

Chapter 3

From Theocentric to Mercantile Paradigm: The Erosion of Doxa?

While there is a vibrant and expanding literature on the topic of markets and marketisation in education, well-captured in Marshall and Peters's (1999) handbook *Education Policy*, much of public discourse refers to a more specific set of issues (e.g. choice, competition) in the *provision* of educational facilities than what is encompassed by a mercantile paradigm. Marketisation has also been used to refer to more wide-ranging changes in the *experience* of education in all its dimensions – curriculum, school ethos, teaching, pupils, parents, public etc. – which capture aspects of what is involved in the transition to a mercantile paradigm of education (e.g. Chitty, 1989; Ball, 1990; Flude and Hammer, 1990; Kenway *et al.*, 1993; Gewirtz *et al.*, 1995; Beck, 1998; Gewirtz, 2002; Willmott, 2002). Some studies, while concentrating on the narrower understanding nonetheless recognise that to speak of markets and education is to allow for a comprehensive debate on educational change that does not confine itself to the trading of educational services in market or quasi-market conditions. Marginson's (1997) *Markets in Education* intimates this wider application in its specification of the characteristics of market production in education and is particularly suggestive for their theorisation. As well as the production of scarce commodities, a defined field of production (schooling, training, higher education), monetary exchange between producer and consumer, and competition between producers, markets are also described in terms of market subjectivities, 'the attitudes and behaviours appropriate to market production, consumption and exchange' (p. 30). These subjectivities are seen as both the conditions and effects of markets in that markets are considered as social contexts that form and foster certain kinds of personal change and retard and penalise others. Marginson acknowledges that 'Subjectivity is more complex than *homo economicus* would suggest, but markets nevertheless leave their mark, calling up hard-headed consumers, and efficient and entrepreneurial producers' (p. 30).

But the transition to a mercantile paradigm is more than a response to market-like conditions in schools. It represents a broader cultural transformation which valorises trade/exchange dispositions together with the social settings and organisational forms which exemplify them to the extent that they become normative. The construct of trade/exchange is used to describe this transition because of the manner in which it mirrors the set of socio-cultural phenomena identified in a cluster of socio-economic theories, in particular the exchange theory of Homans (1961) and Blau (1964), in which rationality is central. Indeed, as Waters (1994, p. 56) points out, 'the trading relationship is the paradigm for formal sociological theories emphasising rationality as the primary defining characteristic of human society.' Surprisingly, given its obvious potential for the conceptualisation of marketised relationships, this body of sociological writing has been substantially ignored in the theorisation of markets and education. Along with exchange theory, such theories include the writings of Marshall and Pareto on the construct of utility, the standard used to estimate the value of an item involved in an exchange; public-choice theory, which explains collective behaviour including political structures in terms of individual economic behaviour; and rational-choice theory (also referred to as game-theoretic or analytical Marxism) which seeks to deal with the problem presented by uncertainty about outcomes for a reliance on calculating individuals committing themselves to collective interests (Waters, 1994).

However, these theories differ in scope and aspiration from what is being contended here, in that they seek to build a theory of society on the back of calculating individual action which, in describing the transition to a mercantile paradigm of Irish education, characterises a cultural shift over a particular time in a specific context. In this process of cultural change, it is argued that people become constituted as exchange theorists. Homans's (1961) *Social Behaviour*, a primary influence on exchange theory, was itself acknowledged by him to be based on behavioural psychology and elementary economics. This is reflected in his envisioning of social behaviour 'as an exchange of activity, tangible or intangible, and more or less rewarding or costly, between at least two people' (p. 13). As Blau (1964), in *Exchange and Power in Social Life*, argues, social exchange can be universally observed once one is sensitised to this conception of it. He details and develops this and theorises the constructs and processes involved. In this, he is seeking to explain the complex structures of society by beginning with the simpler processes that pervade the daily associations between individuals. Blau excludes conformity with internalised norms from his definition of social exchange which he uses to refer to 'voluntary actions of individuals that are motivated by the returns they are expected to bring and typically do in fact bring from others' (p. 91). Tellingly, for its deployment here, Blau quotes La Rochefoucauld (1940) in the introduction to *Exchange and Power in Social Life*:

> Gratitude is like mercantile credit. The latter is the mainstay of business; and we pay our debts, not because it is right that we should discharge them, but in order more easily to borrow again.

The actors in Homans's and Blau's social exchange theories were operating in societies that differ from the context in which the mercantile paradigm is being diagnosed. Globally, major shifts have occurred in trust, risk, expert knowledge and authority that are relevant to the analysis. This necessitates the appropriation rather than the direct application of their theories in specifying the trade/exchange subjectivities and practices that characterise the mercantile paradigm. These include:

- the individualisation of felt needs and wants
- utility, the capacity to satisfy felt needs and wants, established as the orientating value of social exchange
- differentiation of interests and the separation of one's own interests from those of others
- a calculus of benefit and loss in the act of exchange
- a drive to maximise individual benefit and to minimise loss
- an orientation and capacity to compete
- privacy/anonymity: the act of exchange demands only that the necessary requirements for the transfer be made explicit
- mobility and flexibility in pursuit of utility
- regulated affectivity in the calculation of benefit and loss
- feelings of responsibility for others suspected as interference or intolerance of difference
- risk management through the formalisation of the social requirements of exchange in preference to a reliance on trust, loyalty and obligation
- the assumption by the participants in social exchange that these subjectivities and practices are reciprocated
- mercantile performances themselves become sources of personal satisfaction and fulfilment (skilled and discriminating in trade/exchange) and of identity formation (patterned consumption and need satisfaction).

The impact on education is felt in the totality of its manifestations – institutional, organisational, relational and substantive. This transition is not about the existence of competing conceptualisations of education such as public service versus tradeable good. Rather, it seeks to explore how trade/exchange – being prepared for it in relationships, institutions and organisations that are shaped by it – has fundamentally reconstructed what education is thought to be about, including those constructs that would have been understood as non-market or anti-market such as public sphere, civil society, common good, altruism and vocation.

Comparatively, this resonates with debates elsewhere on the marketisation of education and on the impact of 'New Right' and economic liberalism on educational policy. What such educational systems have in common – England, the US, Australia and New Zealand are examples – is a background of welfare state, anti-racist, and equality interventions. In this they differ from the Irish experience in which the vision of education that preceded the mercantile paradigm was one inspired by a Roman Catholic world view. Inevitably, local conditions and traditions shape the form that such transitions will take, and necessitate differentiation in the manner of their labelling if they are to avoid being subsumed within globalised conceptualisations. Rather, the comparative perspective will allow us to establish foils to reveal the particularism of Irish educational change since the 1950s.

By way of an overview, the theocentric and mercantile paradigms of education can be sketched from official sources such as the reports of the Council of Education which was largely active in the 1950s and such contemporary reports as those of the National Economic and Social Council, the Industrial Policy Review Group, the 1992 Green Paper, as well as ministerial statements from the 1990s when the mercantile features of education began to assume a recognisable pattern.

According to the Council for Education *Report on the Function and Curriculum of the Primary School* (Council of Education, 1954), 'the school exists to assist and supplement the work of parents in the rearing of children. Their first duty is to train their children in the fear and love of God. That duty becomes the first purpose of the primary school. It is fulfilled by the school through the religious and moral training of the child, through the teaching of good habits, through his instruction in duties of citizenship and in his obligations to his parents and the community – in short, through all that tends to the formation of a person of character, strong in his desire to fulfil the end of his creation' (p. 94). It argued that for the Irish people, who 'through many centuries ... had striven to secure the freedom to have their children taught in schools conducted in accordance with the parents' religious concept of life ... religion was not merely one of many subjects to be taught in the school: it was the soul, the foundation and the crown of the whole educational process, giving value and meaning to every subject in the curriculum' (p. 130). It quoted with approval a note in the programme of religious instruction:

> of all the parts of a school curriculum, religious instruction is by far the most important, as its subject matter, God's honour and service, includes the proper use of all man's faculties, and affords the most powerful inducements to their proper use. Religious instruction is, therefore, a fundamental part of the school course. Though the time allotted to it as a specific subject is necessarily short, a religious spirit should inform and vivify the whole work of the school. The teacher – while careful, in the

presence of children with different religious beliefs, not to touch on matters of controversy – should constantly inculcate, in connection with secular subjects, the practice of charity, justice, truth, purity, patience, temperance, obedience to lawful authority, and all the other moral virtues. In this way he will fulfil the primary duty of an educator, the moulding to perfect form of his pupils' character, habituating them to observe in their relations with God and with their neighbours, the laws which God, both directly through the dictates of natural reason and through revelation, and indirectly through the ordnance of lawful authority, imposes on mankind (pp 131-132).

The Council of Education *Report on the Curriculum of the Secondary School* (Council of Education, 1962) continues this emphasis: 'the purpose of school education, then, is the organised development and equipment of all the powers of the individual person – religious, moral, intellectual, physical – so that, by making the fullest use of his talents, he may responsibly discharge his duties to God and to his fellow men in society.' According to this report the aim of the school was to prepare pupils 'to be God fearing and responsible citizens' (p. 88).

In stark contrast, by 1990 the major national advisory council on social and economic matters (National Economic and Social Council, 1990, pp 313-314) was arguing that in the educational system 'the principles of consumer representation, participation, and accountability should be reflected in management and decision making structures.' It criticised the absence of a formal appeal mechanism for parents at primary level, and at second level the fact that there was no formal system whereby parents can 'obtain factual and evaluative data about schools, in order to make appropriate educational choices'. The Council concluded, 'the absence of accessible data on schools, of the type indicated above, touches on the issue of accountability. How can the effectiveness of the educational system be ascertained, and accountability then enforced, if systematic data on the performance of the system is not available? ... There is a need to consider the role of information systems and performance indicators within the educational system. The use of such analytical techniques would allow educationalists to account for resources used and to assess the effectiveness of the educational system.'

In its main recommendations, the Culliton Report (Industrial Policy Review Group, 1992, p. 52) gave pride of place to the following criticisms of the educational system:

> The contribution of productive enterprise to our social and economic objectives should be an issue of primary importance at all educational levels to de-emphasise the bias towards the liberal arts and traditional professions.

> A higher priority must be attached in the education system to the acquisition of usable and marketable skills. This is evident both from the perspective of the requirements of industrial development and for the employment prospects and self-fulfilment of young people.

The Green Paper (Department of Education, 1992, p. 11) mirrored these sentiments, claiming that 'in the business world there is a wide recognition that many Irish young people tend to lack:

- the range of technical skills needed in today's industry
- the communication and other interpersonal skills sought by employers
- the critical thinking, problem-solving ability and individual initiative that an enterprise culture requires
- the language skills to work and win markets across the EC, and to take part in tourism-related activities.'

In a newspaper interview the Minister for Education who released the Green Paper, Séamus Brennan, was even more explicit: 'we have to put an enterprise ethos into our system. We have probably relied too much in the past on the academic side … it may be a coincidence, but we have the highest unemployment rate in the European Community. We also have the highest emphasis on academia. That may be a coincidence, but I don't think so. I suspect there is a link' (quoted in Bonel-Elliott, 1997).

Theocentric and Mercantile Policy Paradigms

Using the theocentric paradigm as the foil inevitably foregrounds some features of the mercantile paradigm while neglecting others. As we shall see later, the mercantile paradigm proved to be an expanding cultural production that assumed a character that is inadequately conceptualised as the 'other' of an understanding of education in which God is at the centre of its rationale. Nevertheless, the extent of the cultural shift involved can be better identified and explained if we begin by itemising from the perspective of the theocentric paradigm some aspects of the changed thinking about education. In the event, it would appear that this exercise captured the evolving future of Irish education even more prophetically than it factually represented its reality at the time of its initial formulation in the 1990s.

This is to advert to the dual function of the juxtapositioning that follows. It operates both as an ideal-typical manifestation of educational meanings under contrasting policy paradigms and as a specification of material reality in the sense of being embedded in practices that privilege, marginalise and exclude. It is necessary, for the moment, to leave open the task of fine-tuning their dominion – their status as systems of knowledge and the nature of their political and cultural penetration. What follows is an orientating analysis of how the change experienced by Irish education since the 1950s can be understood. Some of the more salient contrasts between the theocentric and mercantile paradigms in this regard are summarised in Table 3.1 and are now developed.

Table 3.1 Contrasting Manifestations of Theocentric and Mercantile Policy Paradigms in Education

	Theocentric	*Mercantile*
Aim	Determined by unchanging Christian principles	Determined by the consumers of the system
Ownership/Control	Christian authorities	Individual/collective initiatives
Policy-making	Expert-based	Broadly-based
Role of Users	Beneficiaries	Vigilant
Role of Educators	Trustworthy professionals	Requires visibility and accountability
Schools	Solidaristic communities	Commercial/service organisations
Pedagogical Relationship	Paternalistic	Contractual
Evaluation	Truncated, incomplete	Quantifiable
State	Subsidiary	Managerial

Aim

For the theocentric paradigm, the aim of education is a settled matter, to be determined by unchanging principles based on a Christian view of human nature and destiny. In contrast to this dogmatic prescriptiveness about the purpose of education, the mercantile paradigm assumes a populist approach holding that what education is for is a matter for consumers of the system, such as pupils, parents, civic leaders and business interests, to decide.

A fundamental shift in cosmology is involved in this change. The demands of eternal destiny, salvation and the after-life were as real and relevant to education in the theocentric paradigm as were the needs of living on earth. Once one works within these supernatural parameters the sentiments of the Council of Education are eminently rational in their specification of pupil virtues and educational aims. They only appear remarkable to those whose cosmic view is more restrictive and materially-based, and who regard the role of education as being derived from a specification of the demands of a full life on this earth – the needs of industry, the challenges of citizenship, and social and personal development, while also allowing for a spiritual dimension. Or to put it more bluntly, attempting to keep a clean moral slate in this life in the pursuit of everlasting happiness in union with God in a limitless after-life is open to being interpreted as a more rational strategy than pursuing material success through the CAO *numerus clausus* system.

The populism adopted in the mercantile specification of educational aims is to be understood as meaning 'coming from the people' in a fashion that is almost metaphysical in contrast with the majoritarian tendencies of democracy. It is what 'people' are 'known' to think, what is deemed to be 'obvious', in this instance, about what education is for, and that scarcely requires elaboration. The much-criticised failure of the 1992 Green Paper to outline its philosophy of education must be viewed in the light of this assumption of the obviousness of the aims of education. The similarity between the mission statements of quite diverse schools, be it in terms of religious ethos, clientele or academic focus, reflects this assumption and underscores the unstated logic of the Green Paper's omission. In such a situation, education is whatever it can be made to be and is quite a pliable cultural construct. This is reflected in the manner in which new aims and objectives accrete to the institution of education not only with each new educational report but with a wide realm of advocacy that may be only vaguely related to education. In so far as this translates into school subjects, modules, programmes or approaches, teachers have drawn attention to the increasing demands on them and on the school timetable, sometimes describing the phenomenon in term of 'curriculum overload'.

But this transition runs deeper than the practicalities of pedagogy and curriculum. It represents a fundamentally-changed logic in establishing what the educational process is to be in society – from a unitary vision to a hollowed-out mechanism of power/knowledge without an essential content or substance. This is not merely a question of education being used to serve the interests of a particular substantive doctrine or ideology, and thus 'denying to education – to the actual conduct of teaching and learning – any effective integrity of purpose as a practice in its own might, i.e. as a practice entitled to certain rights which are inviolable, but also accountable' (Hogan, 1995, p. 11). In the mercantile understanding of education it is its *plasticity* as a social institution that is celebrated along with the texts, authorities and their social configurations that in their time are established as reliably capturing the public's mood and needs.

Ownership/Control

If the purpose of education is to lead people to God and to facilitate them in reaching their eternal salvation, it follows that the designated religious authorities – church, religious personnel – can claim privilege in relation to the ownership, management and general control of schools. On the other hand, if consumers are entitled to decide what education is for they must also be facilitated in establishing schools, through individual or collective initiative, according to their philosophy of life, if the existing school system is unresponsive to their demands.

This transition adverts to the distinction between constitutional entitlements and cultural possibilities in relation to the ownership of schools. Writing for a foreign readership in the London-published *Educational Year Book* of 1951 on 'The Constitutional Position of Education in the Republic of Ireland' (subsequently reprinted by Cork University Press in 1952) O'Rahilly could legitimately claim in relation to Article 42: Education,

> Perhaps, at least to outsiders, the most significant and surprising aspect of this article is that it does not contain so much as a casual mention of the Church, which, as such, is not conceded any constitutional right in education. The only institution (except itself) in which the state acknowledges the right of education is the family. The only exception recognised is the case of the moral or physical disability of the parents. Then, and only then, may the state endeavour to supply the place of the parents, i.e. by carrying out the duties which they are unable to perform. Constitutionally, vis-à-vis our mixed state, the Catholic Church is recognised only in so far as it represents the families.

In pointing out that Irish schools are *de facto* but not *de jure* denominational, O'Rahilly concluded that 'if a sufficient number of parents in any locality wished to establish an interdenominational or a nondenominational school, there is nothing to prevent them, and they have a valid claim to the financial help of the state' (p. 6). But O'Rahilly reflected more accurately the cultural politics of school ownership and control at that time, apart from the more obvious limitations imposed by financial impediments, in the following passage in which he refers, albeit obliquely, to the presumption of the Roman Catholic Church to speak authoritatively, and not merely representatively, in this regard for Roman Catholic parents:

> insofar as the Catholic Church, as an organisation for implementing parental rights, has a constitutional status in education, every other religious denomination has an equal status. Looked at from the inside, as regards ourselves who admit its supernatural authority, the Catholic Church is much more than a natural association of parents. But as regards the Constitution of this State, we have, though numerically preponderant, the same status as the Church of Ireland or the Jews. Each of these bodies is recognised educationally only as it represents the parents who agree to send their children to the respective schools.

This helps explain the difference between what was likely to happen at that time in relation to school ownership as distinct from what was constitutionally admissible. The change represented by the mercantile paradigm involves a recasting of the power/knowledge assumptions between Roman Catholic Church authorities and people such that the disjunction between culture and constitution became progressively diminished.

Policy-making

Policy-making in the theocentric paradigm is a matter for experts since the knowledge, skills and understandings that this process of formation requires are not universally distributed. Decision-making needs to be in the hands of a knowledgeable few. For the mercantile paradigm, the process of decision making must be more widely based and facilitated by public information about the system.

The identity of those who are constituted as authorities shifts in the process. So also does the nature and basis of their authority, together with the character of the policy discourse their interaction generates. Most obviously, religious authorities were replaced by those whose knowledge and experience was in the secular domain. Papal Encyclicals and episcopal pronouncements were displaced from the 1960s onwards by World Bank policy, OECD Reports, EU funding protocols and whatever was deemed from time to time to constitute 'best practice' elsewhere. But the sacred/secular dualism does not fully capture the depth or spread of the change involved. Reference points in policy making may have become less insular but there was nonetheless selectivity in what was chosen from the vast corpus of global thinking and practice in education. Some sources were accorded an entitlement to a voice in policy making because of technical or specialised knowledge in pedagogy, assessment, evaluation, management or curricular content, others because of their distinctive experience, and more who could claim to represent specific interest groups.

Public consultation in the form of regional and national meetings on educational policy signalled the more broadly-based character of policy making. Increasingly, these consultative events assumed the role of culturally-signifying spectacles in which the changed process of policy making was represented as transparent, accessible and democratic. But more is involved than the assertion or enactment of democratic procedures. What constitutes expertise in the policy-making context changes, in terms of its legitimisation – technical knowledge, experience, representative voice – as do whatever texts are appropriated or displaced in policy discourse, and what social actors are involved. A recurring feature of this discourse is its lack of theoretical complexity or reflexivity.

Role of Users and Educators

In the theocentric paradigm, the complementary roles of user and educator are those of beneficiary and trustworthy professional, respectively. Clients of the system need do no more than use it in an unreflexive and trusting manner to derive its benefits. In this view, professionals are dedicated and committed to the ideals of the educational system and they can be relied on to act in the pursuit of the best interests of those who are in their charge. In the mercantile paradigm, however, the delivery of an educational service is seen as something approaching an amoral activity. The self-interest of educators must be reckoned with and users of the system are required to be vigilant. Because trust in educators is not sufficient to protect the users' interests, the processes and standards of education need to be visible and answerable to the public.

Self-regulating moral accountability which relies on professional formation and collective identities is replaced by contractual accountability. This feature of the transition to a mercantile paradigm is reflective of the analysis of risk in a post-traditional society (Giddens, 1996b, p. 42). For Giddens, to live in a world of multiple authorities is to have to cope with the absence of a 'super-expert' to whom to turn, and in consequence to have to factor into risk calculation the risk involved in selecting one expert over another. This social condition has been described as 'risk society' (Beck, 1992) in which 'experts are undercut or deposed by opposing experts. Politicians encounter the resistance of citizens groups, and industrial management encounters morally and politically motivated organised consumer boycotts' (Beck *et al.,* 1994, p. 11).

Within the mercantile paradigm, risk management involves elements of a transition to both economic and methodological individualism. Economic individualism refers to a social order which is understood to be enhanced through individuals' pursuit of their own interests. Methodological individualism approaches the understanding of institutions such as schools as the 'result of a particular configuration of individuals, their dispositions, situations, beliefs and physical resources, and environment' (Lukes, 1990, pp 114-115). In this view, the functioning of all social institutions should always be understood in terms of decisions and actions of individuals. In Popper's conclusion (in Lukes, 1990, p. 114) 'we should never be satisfied by an explanation in terms of so-called "collectivities".' For instance, in the calculation and management of risk in relation to the instrumental quality of teaching, we find parents suspicious of the collectivism of whole school evaluation while favouring systems of regulation and monitoring at the level of the individual teacher. For Giddens (1998) 'risk society' has been linked to "reflexive modernisation", a 'coming-to-terms with the limits and contradictions of the modern order.' In contrast, what the mercantile paradigm exhibits in the Irish context is traces of naïve modernity, an assumption and expectation that all aspects of the educational system (and society itself) can be definitively known and predictably controlled and regulated. Within the mercantile paradigm, risk invites not calculation and democratisation but countering and surmounting.

Schools

Where schools are founded on the pursuit of God's plan for humanity, those who participate in its activities are bound together by a sense of membership of a common community of believers. It is this solidarity through a sameness of philosophical outlook that Durkheim referred to as mechanical solidarity. In the mercantile paradigm, schools are to be understood and assessed according to the same commercial principles as any other organisation offering a service, such as efficiency, cost effectiveness, quality control and surplus and deficit in relation to market requirements. Solidarity is organic, derived from a mutual interdependence of calculative roles.

Traditionally, in Roman Catholic social teaching and formal pronouncements, and very immediately in face-to-face discourse, the intimacy and communality of mechanical solidarity was communicated through the use of family type tropes – Mother Church, Children of God, God the Father, God's Family etc. Not alone did this affiliative imagery represent the primary nature of church-regulated institutions but it also carried with it, in the hierarchical relationships of family life, the normality of disparities of power and the legitimacy of authoritative sources and agents. Church discourse is replete with these figurative practices in the representation of its collective relationships. Some examples are quite florid. In justifying the primary entitlement of the church to involvement in the educational process, Kavanagh (1966, pp 89-90) quotes a Papal Encyclical which appeals to 'that supernatural office of motherhood whereby the Church, Christ's spotless bride, bestows upon men the life of divine grace and nurtures and fosters it by her sacraments and teachings. "None can have God for his Father," says St Augustine, "if he refuses to have the church as his Mother."' Kavanagh concludes that 'here is stated succinctly the reason for the church's stand on education. The church acts on the authority of Christ, the Son of God' (p. 90).

The 'collective conscience' of mechanical solidarity allows little scope for difference, choice or individuality. The norms governing behaviour are as much a part of society as of its individual members. Dissent, deviation and rejection evoke shock and outrage, and are accordingly punished with exemplary intent, not only to bring the sinner to heel but to affirm the collective spirit that has been violated.

Mechanical solidarity is neither distinctive to religious collectivities nor without its appeals. The transition to the organic solidarity of the mercantile paradigm in the form of the interdependence of a commercial organisation involves the same disruption that Giddens associates with what he refers to as the 'disinterring and prolematisation' of traditional modes of living and understanding. This involves the loss of the security and affective underpinnings that come from 'the mechanisms of anxiety control that traditional modes of action and belief provide' (Giddens, 1996b, p. 18). The anthropological construct of *préstation totale*, used to describe a form of exchange that involves the totality of the social personality of the giver, and in which symbolism, meaning and ritual are embedded in the interaction, helps to characterise the transition involved. In the theocentric paradigm the experience of schooling was understood as that of a neophyte member of a community of believers being inducted into the totality of its understanding of life by those knowledgeable and positioned to conduct this process of initiation. Increasingly, in the mercantile paradigm church schools are represented as service organisations funded by their taxpayer users in a manner that repositions the traditional intermediaries of Church and State and establishes a direct conceptual linkage between a service provider and its clients.

This contrast appears to mirror the conclusion of those anthropologists who argue that exchanges in primitive and traditional societies were richly and thickly layered in meaning by comparison with the more limited involvement of the self in individualised market economies (Mauss, 1990[1952]). While such a contention seems to characterise the changed nature of schools in the transition from a theocentric to a mercantile paradigm, there is a danger of seeing contemporary exchanges as purely functional and lacking in meaning. While relationships within schools are less total and more considered under the mercantile paradigm they nonetheless embody the meanings of trade/exchange in their assumptions of rational engagement, calculation of risk, pursuit of personal benefit and market equality. These values are further reflected in the manner of the state's monitoring of the taxpayer's investment in schooling. Whereas in the past the school represented to parents what church/state understandings of education were, under the mercantile paradigm it finds itself caught in a pincer action with the users/funders of its services increasingly defining its nature while the state as the people's agent oversees its operation in terms of commercial principles and instrumental efficiency.

Pedagogical Relationship

At the focused level of the pedagogical relationship, the core of the educational process, the theocentric paradigm conceives of teachers not just in *loco parentis*, but also as church/state agents concerned with the ultimate salvation of the pupil and empowered to act as they will know best to further assist in that salvation. In the mercantile paradigm, the relationship is contractual, based on increasingly circumscribed and specified responsibilities and entitlements.

Clancy's (1983) research on primary school principals in the 1970s helps to explain the paternalistic/formative nature of the pedagogical relationship in the theocentric paradigm. He points out that when the theocentric paradigm was prominent not alone was there a dominance of religious personnel in Irish schools but lay teachers were accorded something of a quasi-religious standing such that they were considered to be 'part of a "sacred order" ... linked to the core values of society ... (which) the advent of secularisation does not seem to have emptied ... of its special moral qualities'. The significance of being positioned in this way for the manner in which it allowed teachers to presume to know what was best for children is analysed by Clancy in terms of the boundary exchanges between school personnel and parents. Traditionally, the service ideal, embodying the norm of selflessness and exclusive commitment to the pupils' welfare, in the ideology of professionalism was 'considered to provide an adequate safeguard for the apparent paradoxical exclusion of the client from occupational decision-making'. Enjoying the status of sacred rather than profane, with its associated status socialisation and control, further enhanced the professional power of teachers to make judgements on what was best for students. Being religious or quasi-religious added a further boundary dimension to that of professionalism in the era.

The mercantile paradigm more successfully than secularisation undermined these boundary maintenance techniques such that in the mercantile paradigm parents demand to be consulted about what is done in school, the programmes and experiences to which their children might be exposed, risks to their health and safety, educational decisions affecting their career prospects, and are increasingly willing to challenge (legally, if necessary) school decisions that in the past would have been mutually regarded as internal operational matters. In such a situation, the actions of teachers become circumscribed by protocols, directives and legislation. More significantly, it becomes unremarkable that teachers and teaching should be regulated and monitored by external and formal mechanisms.

Evaluation

Since in the theocentric paradigm, education aspires to influence one's status in the next life, evaluation of its effectiveness through worldly measures is necessarily incomplete and truncated. The mercantile paradigm, however, asserts that the success of the educational system can be quantified by the use of pivotal indicators, and that students themselves can have, and indeed are entitled to have, their educational achievements measured, labelled, classified and graduated in terms of national and, increasingly, international protocols and credit transfer systems (National Qualifications Authority of Ireland, 2003). How different are the sentiments of the Report of the Council of Education (1954, p. 90) in which it seeks to correct 'certain misconceptions' relating to the function of the primary school:

> Exaggerated stress on the utilitarian aspects of education has led to the demand for immediate tangible results, produced, after the fashion of modern manufacture, in accordance with specifications. Education is certainly a process, but the school is not a machine nor are its pupils raw material to be mechanically moulded into finished

products. The success of the primary school can be only partially assessed at its termination, for it is not at 13+ but at 33 that the average man has taken his place in life. Much of the success of the primary school, as, we may grant, much of its failure, will always remain hidden from the human mind.

State

Finally, the state in the theocentric paradigm is obliged to assume a subsidiary role, playing second fiddle to the church, which along with pupils, whose interests they represent, are considered to have prior rights in relation to education. While the state is also a secondary force in the mercantile paradigm, its role is a more active one in managing both the demands of the various interests in the market place of education and the educational process itself, and of facilitating the efficient use of public resources and the provision of a quality service to its clients. In terms of policy-making, the establishment of the Council of Education, in the words of the Minister for Education, Richard Mulcahy, at its launch in 1950, as 'a permanent part of the organism which is the Ministry of Education' (reproduced in Hyland and Milne, 1992, p. 26) reflected a vocational social order. This was in line with Catholic social teaching which advocated that those actively participating within a particular occupational sphere should be incorporated into the process of formulating state policy pertaining to it. While the state became more activist in educational policy-making from the 1960s, the role accorded to it within the mercantile paradigm would also be one of restraint and refraction in which, in contrast to the formulation and advancement of autonomous political objectives, it would find itself managing situations, resources and people in pursuit of what popular sentiment demanded and competing interest group activity would allow. In fact, it is possible to trace a pathway, with no more than a few transitions, from subsidiary to managerial state.

While the reports of the Council of Education are routinely positioned as the cautious and conservative foil to the adventurous and progressive educational initiatives of the 1960s, the corporatism they represented, far from losing face, was to be resurrected in some form in every decade since. The Fine Gael (1966) Just Society programme of the mid-1960s, appealing to Pádraig Pearse's 'The Murder Machine', proposed that 'primary responsibility' for all aspects of policy including teaching methods should be transferred to a Schools Committee, comprised of those 'directly engaged in the work of education, so that educational decisions will in future be taken for educational reasons rather than being based on extraneous political considerations' (p. 6). Supporting this, with responsibility for future physical and human resources, they proposed an Educational Planning Committee as one of the vertical committees within a vocationally reorganised National Industrial Economic Council.

A draft Bill to establish an independent Examinations Board was ready in 1976 but was not proceeded with (Hyland, 1990). The Interim Curriculum and Examinations Board operated from 1984 to 1987 when it was followed by the National Council for Curriculum and Assessment which attained statutory status in the Education Act (1998) as an advisory body to the Minister. The 1992 Green Paper and the voluminous submissions that ensued were separated from the 1995 White Paper by the National Education Convention of 1993. It was during these latter two decades, and particularly during the 1990s with its discourse of consultation, transparency and partnership, that corporatism's potential for the state's management of its relationship with the organised interests of civil society and the general public became more evident. The current round of *Your Education System* meetings (Department of Education and Science, 2004), during the spring of 2004, continue the managerial model.

In the theocentric paradigm it was the church and its teaching that held the state in its subsidiary position; within the mercantile paradigm it is on behalf of the users and funders of education – parents, tax-payers, industry, employers – that it exercises its managerial function.

The Theocentric Paradigm as Doxa

As with all transformations, cultural or otherwise, the question of how the transition from a theocentric to a mercantile paradigm of education occurred, and more pointedly, how those interests who had most to lose allowed it to happen must be confronted. As Archer (1984, p. 2) put it '… to understand the nature of education at any time we need to know not only who won the struggle for control, but also how: not merely who lost, but also how badly they lost out.' The fact of the transformation is all the more noteworthy because of what is generally considered to have been the doxic status of the theocentric paradigm until the 1960s. The Roman Catholic world-view appeared all-encompassing in its dominion, not merely in relation to education, a status reflected in the constraints on what could be publicly said and who could speak, and in the nature of its discourse and its legitimatory appeals and sources. It was well nigh uncontestable because of what it must have regarded as the extent of its internalisation in individual consciousness. We will wish to question this as we seek to explain its contraction in Chapter 5. We will also be dealing more extensively in Chapter 15 with the role of social actors, of human agency, in challenging aspects of church teaching and practices relating to the governance of education. But for the present it is necessary to pursue this commonplace perception of the theocentric paradigm as doxa in order to fully explore the dynamics of its transformation.

In Ireland, the church had always claimed a primary role for itself in education and a superior right in relation to the state. This claim would have been based upon the official teaching of the church as represented in papal encyclicals and other formal statements from Rome. These prescriptions on education from the church would have been disseminated by means of such publications as *Primer of the Principles of Social Science* (Cronin, 1957) and *Manual of Social Ethics* (Kavanagh, 1966) to secondary school pupils, university-level students of sociology, adult education students of social studies and members of study groups within the associations of the Catholic social movement (O'Sullivan, 1989b). Kavanagh, citing the encyclical *Divinii Illius Magistri* (1929) of Pope Pius XI, outlined church teaching in the following terms:

> Education is first and supereminently the function of the church. That puts the whole subject immediately into its proper perspective. The church is responsible for bringing the souls of men for whom Christ died to eternal happiness and so, logically, she must exercise her authority in education, which plays so vital a role in man's formation ... This authority of the church extends not merely to specifically religious education but to all branches of teaching ... Even physical training is not to be regarded as outside the scope of her maternal function, for this, too, is a thing which may be either beneficial or harmful to Christian education (pp 89-90).

This was the basis of the church's campaign for Catholic education. It recognised that the state had certain rights in education. It had the duty of supplementing the parents' efforts to educate their children or to provide for children where the parents neglected their duties. In recognition of financial support the state had the right 'to fix standards and to prescribe tests' (Cronin, 1957, p. 28). But these state rights were 'subordinate to the prior claims of the church and the family' (Kavanagh, 1966, p. 91). Parents were recognised as having the primary right and duty of educating their children. But the rights and duties of parents and church in this regard were considered to be complementary.

> The rights of the church derive from the supernatural order; the rights of the family from the natural order, but there is perfect harmony between them ... These family rights are tenaciously defended by the Church. The rights of the family are prior to those of the state, and it is the duty of the state to respect and uphold them (Kavanagh, 1966, p. 92).

These anti-statist sentiments reflected the principles of subsidiarity in church social teaching. According to this principle no larger body should do what a lesser body or individual can best do for themselves, and was meant to protect individual citizens against a statist moulding of needs, a sapping of personal initiative, an insensitive state bureaucracy and the designs of totalitarian regimes. The immediate source of this resistance to statism was the Papal Encyclical *Quadragesimo Anno,* which appeared in 1931, and its influence on the direction on the Catholic Social Movement of the 1940s (Whyte, 1980). The similarity between the principle of subsidiarity and the liberal precept that the state should not do what is best done by individuals, what it is best for individuals to do themselves and what might unnecessarily add to state power (Mill, 1978[1859]) is deceptive and obscures significant differences. For classical liberals the individual is the primary source of goodness and worth. In Catholic social teaching individual autonomy would have been circumscribed by church teaching and 'informed' conscience. Though generally concerned with the freedom and dignity of the individual, church social teaching such as the principle of subsidarity was open to being exploited by interest groups in society to retard government action and preserve the status quo as occurred during the Mother and Child controversy.

These prescriptions on the place of church, family and state in the provision of education and the formulation of educational policy were reflected in the articles on education in the 1937 Irish Constitution and were almost universally unquestioned. In 1957, in what continues to be a widely-quoted speech, the Minister for Education, Richard Mulcahy, appeared to acknowledge the primacy of the church in educational planning.

> Deputy Moylan has asked me to philosophise, to give my views on educational technique or educational practice. I do not regard that as my function in the Department of Education in the circumstances of the educational set up of this country. You have your teachers, your managers and your churches, and I regard the position as Minister in the Department of Education as that of a kind of dungaree man, the plumber who will make the satisfactory communications and streamline the forces and potentialities of the educational workers and educational management of this country. He will take the knock out of the pipes and will link up everything. I would be blind to my responsibility if I insisted on pontification or lapsed into an easy acceptance of an imagined duty to philosophise here on educational matters (Quoted in O'Connor, 1986, p. 1).

It might be assumed that a certain amount of posturing has to be allowed for in the Minister's statement, and that it is no more than indicative of the nature of power relations at the time that he felt it politic to acknowledge his subsiduary role. In that era, it has been said that the Minister for Education was sometimes jocosely referred to as 'Minister Without Portfolio' (Tussing, 1978, p. 67). It seems most likely that for Mulcahy, a member of the Knights of St Columbanus, these perceptions of the rightful place of church and state in the policy process were a reflection of the central place of Catholicism in shaping his identity. In this regard he was not alone among senior politicians. Some years earlier in the decade John A. Costello, as Taoiseach, had proclaimed in the Dáil, 'If the hierarchy give me any direction with regard to Catholic social teaching or Catholic moral teaching, I accept without qualification in all respects the teaching of the hierarchy and the church to which I belong,' and on another occasion, 'I am an Irishman second, I am a Catholic first' (both quoted in Keogh, 1994, p. 209).

Small wonder, then, that the church would have been so self-confident in its prescriptions. The discourse of writers such as Kavanagh and Cronin was meant to be explanatory and educative rather than analytical or polemical. It had something of the character of Heidegger's (1962[1927]) *speech as assertion* (*Aussage*) serving the purpose of designating and spelling out for others the uncomplicated, valid nature of things, in this case as they pertain to the provision, control and direction of education. Justification or speculation about the church's role in education would have been unnecessary and redundant since what was being asserted was based on dogma and faith rather than on rational analysis. When called upon, popular thinking would have celebrated the involvement of the church in education by reference to the traditional contribution of priests and religious teaching orders, their provision of opportunity and the sacrifices made in the interests of the education of the Irish people over a long period of foreign domination.

The Church could therefore be said to have entered the period under review in a strong position to continue to shape the cultural understanding of education. It would seem to have achieved such a dominance in influencing the understanding of education among those involved in the policy process that it could be said to have come as near to establishing a doxic paradigm as can be possible in modern society. There are many indicators of this. Its conceptualisation and language permeated policy discourse. Its performatives expanded to all aspects and levels of education. The distinctiveness of its discourse – figurative speech, non-symmetrical – is only recognised as such retrospectively. Its penetration engaged the constitution, the identities of policy makers and the pulpit. It appeared natural, obvious and without credible contestation. With its elaborated system of knowledge production and mechanisms and agencies for its dissemination and reproduction it constituted a systematised paradigm.

As with all diagnoses of doxa, this lies uneasily with the subsequent reality of social and cultural change, and suggests the need to seek out the subjugated identities, tactical subjectivities, and discordant texts that became obvious only after the veil of doxa had been lifted. The status of doxa carries its own limitations. It includes a sense of omnipotence and self-belief that hinders its receptiveness to even the mildest of questioning. The more successful it is, the more it will confuse acquiescence and behavioural conformity with internalisation. Once it ceases to be doxa it opens itself immediately to the charge of totalisation. In this event, the codification of its authoritative knowledge that signifies systematisation provides a comprehensive resource for its critics, and where these are dissident members, apart from being well-informed, they carry the emotional trauma of identity shifts, bridge-burning events, and the sense of deception and lost innocence that feature so predominantly in Irish writing.

From the point of view of seeking to explain the emergence of the mercantile paradigm, the most significant subordinated though un-subjugated text within the theocentric paradigm was what I refer to as 'careerism'. This strand of meaning-making about education would have been realised and sustained at various levels of society, achievement, expectation, opportunity and knowledge. These include the practical skills and subject areas of vocational schools, the preparation for no more than qualifying performances in matriculation and other entry tests of those confidently aspiring to follow parents into middle-class and professional occupations, and most salient and best recorded, the intense competition for the limited opportunities for social mobility through educational achievement for those from lower middle-class, working-class and more modest farming backgrounds.

Whatever of the assertion in the Council of Education Report on the Primary School (1954), referred to earlier, on the impossibility, indeed the impropriety, of presuming to assess the outcomes of primary schooling within the time-frame of a pupil's primary schooling, the practices and priorities of religious schools valorised the preparation for examinations as a route to middle-class and professional careers. Schools communicated this careerist text by means of discursive and non-discursive mechanisms that can be gleaned from the manner in which schools represented themselves in advertisements and prospectuses and in their lived culture as recollected in autobiographical and semi-autobiographical accounts of school life in the decades prior to the 1960s. I have previously drawn attention to some of these sources – McGahern's (1965) account in *The Dark* of the tension in his class in the 1950s as the Leaving Certificate approached, and the tactics used to divert and distract their emotions, and McElligott's (1986) excoriation of what he regarded as the examination-obsessed schools during his teaching career covering the same period (O'Sullivan, 1992a). A more comprehensive coverage is provided by O'Donoghue (1999) to support his contention that 'from the early 1920s to the 1960s, Irish secondary schools were largely concerned with preparing students for the Intermediate and Leaving Certificate examinations' (p. 87).

These include advertisements for elite private schools that promised not only preparation for scholarships and entry to university and courses of study for the professions, but also 'special grinding' to meet the additional requirements of these examinations. A similar school is described as concentrating on public examinations in pragmatic response to the demands of parents. A reference to McGahern's *The Dark* is used to emphasise what was at stake: 'You had to get high in the honours to stand a chance in the cut-throat competition for the scholarships or ESB (Electricity Supply Board) or training college or anything … They knew too it was get honours or go to England.' Other sources evoke the frequent tests, 'the diligent rabbiting away at the work' (John Banville), the extra tuition provided by the Christian Brothers outside of school hours, and the close scrutiny of pupil progress and application, by fellow pupils as well as teachers and parents. While O'Donoghue confines his study to secondary schools, similar patterns of extra-tuition, special classes and targeted notes were a feature of preparation for post-primary school scholarships and competition for entry to the teacher training preparatory colleges in senior grades of primary schools.

Because of the gendered understanding of career, all-girls' schools accorded a special place to the role of housewife and mother. But they were not free from the dominance of public examinations. Girls from small-farm backgrounds found themselves competing for entry to nursing and teacher training, with some schools identified by their proficiency in preparing for the latter. In the case of more elite all-girls' schools, expectations were higher. Maeve Binchy (Bennett and Forgan, 1991) remembers that the nuns in her school in the 1950s hoped they would 'go on to get degrees'. In the same era, Nuala O'Faolain (1996, p. 42) recalls that while they were expected to be 'more than exam-passers', they were nonetheless 'expected to be the best in Ireland at school subjects.'

For the theocentric paradigm there was nothing obviously discordant, much less threatening, about this textualisation of education for career. Preparation for motherhood was consistent with the primacy accorded to the mother by the church for religious transmission (Inglis, 1998a). Nuala O'Faolain was 'ostracised' by the nuns because she 'didn't go straight to the chapel to thank God for coming first in French' (p. 42). Justification of examinations as character-building were available from educational authorities (O'Donoghue, 1999) and the secondary school programme of study – a grammar-type curriculum with a strong literary-classical emphasis – could be rationalised in terms of personal and moral development (Council of Education, 1962). Above all, there was the confidence in the totalising character of the theocentric paradigm that could accommodate cultural nationalism as well as careerism. O'Donoghue (1999, p. 89) writes of 'an unwritten consensus … that the central core (of subjects) offered effectively satisfied the demands of religious education, the needs of the Gaelicisation process and the scope of "general education" suitable for clerical occupations, entry to professional training and dealing with the general problems of life'. For the theocentric paradigm there was no doubt about where the ultimate values resided and this confidence continued as these three texts assumed more distinct identities from the 1960s. As the early manifestations of the mercantile paradigm first presented themselves as themes to be recognised, acknowledged and engaged with in the 1960s, it was the worldly meaning of education embodied in the careerism of day-to-day life in schools that provided it with a base for its future popular dominion. A meaning of education that had been constructed and maintained by religious, in an era when it was presumed to be subject to supernatural values, was to prove to be a church-made Trojan horse that ultimately facilitated the replacement of the theocentric with the mercantile paradigm as the dominant understanding of education. Intertextually, the subordinated careerist text of the theocentric paradigm would provide the popular and parental subjectivities that contributed to its contraction.

More generally, for the Irish church as an institution the 1960s unleashed a period of change that was characterised by a questioning of its role in society. This was evident outside of the church in the modernising features of the era: the rationality and individualism of industrialisation and economic growth, the questioning of authority and appeal to democratic principles, and privatisation and urbanisation. The Vatican Council (1962-1965) sought answers to questions about the church itself that had scarcely been posed in Ireland. Part Four traces the fortunes of the church from this period of change onwards, paying particular attention to the role of human actors as agents of change. Such is the popular and well-recorded understanding of the 1960s as a period of questioning, both general (Tobin, 1984) and religious (Fuller, 2004), that it is not necessary to further elaborate on it here before proceeding to trace the emergence of state activism in educational policy and its greater assertiveness in initiating change.

Chapter 4

State Activism, *Investment in Education*, and the Human Capital Paradigm

It is generally acknowledged that in the 1960s the state became more activist in relation to education policy and more directive in pursuing specific educational change. Dr Hillery's press conference as Minister for Education on 20 May 1963, when he announced a series of initiatives in relation to post-primary education including comprehensive schools, a technical Leaving Certificate and a common Intermediate Certificate, is routinely regarded as epitomising this new confidence and independence. It will equally be admitted that the state's initiatives were often diluted and that its own commitment varied over time and across the range of policies that it had proclaimed. But, irrespective of the effectiveness of this new assertiveness on the part of the state, the immediate task is to seek to explain its emergence in the light of the subsidiary role that it appeared to have previously accepted for itself in educational policy making. The context is the economic planning embarked upon by the state in the 1950s and specifically the human capital theme in educational discourse, which it begot, itself a pivotal development in the construction of the mercantile paradigm. We begin the analysis of this transformation by examining the role of *Investment in Education*, published in 1965, and regarded as the benchmark for the beginning of modern Irish education.

Investment in Education

Investment in Education (IIE) was the work of a survey team appointed by Dr Patrick Hillery as Minister for Education in 1962. Its membership was comprised of two economics lecturers, Patrick Lynch of UCD and Martin O'Donoghue of TCD, William J. Hyland, a UN statistician, formerly of the Central Statistics Office, Dublin, and a mathematician, Pádraig Ó Nualláin, who was an Inspector of Secondary Schools. In an introductory note the survey is described as having been 'organised in co-operation with the Organization for Economic Co-operation and Development (OECD) as a project under the educational investment and planning programme of the organization'. The OECD contributed financially and 'provided technical support and information on related developments in member countries'.

IIE has come to be regarded as a major modernising force in Irish society. It is credited with rescuing Irish education from its concern with character development and religious formation pursued through the medium of a general education largely comprised of literary and classical studies. *IIE* is said to have reconceptualised education as a social institution, directing attention to the needs of the economy and the imperative that schools respond to the technological requirements of industry. It is also claimed that it gave prominence to the principle of equal educational opportunity and introduced a quantitative dimension to Irish educational policy making. It has been variously described as a 'water-shed' (Breen *et al.*, 1990, p. 141), 'epoch-making' (Lyons, 1979, p. 652), 'a radical ideological departure in Irish educational thinking' (Brown, 1985, p. 250) and 'the most important study ever made of the Irish educational scene' (O'Connor, 1986, p. 111). At a commemorative conference to mark the thirtieth anniversary of its publication it was acknowledged as '*the* foundation document' of modern Irish education (Clancy, 1996).

In cultural terms, *IIE* is generally regarded as having produced an abrupt shift in relation to the conceptualisation of Irish education. The established dominion of general education is considered to have been successfully confronted by the modernising imperatives of international educational policy represented in *IIE* and dislodged by a new set of problems, such as manpower needs, principles like that of equality of education opportunity, and a more positivistic approach to educational understanding and planning. But, above all, *IIE* is perceived to have normalised the link between schooling and the economy, fundamentally redefining the role of the educational system in society and giving vocational relevance the status of a taken-for-granted educational aim. In Gibbons's (1996, p. 83) colourful characterisation, it 'set out to remove the school from the sacristy and place it in line with the need for greater technological change in Irish society'.

The role played by *IIE* in Irish educational change is indeed pivotal, but this general view of its significance inevitably requires refinement and extension if its contribution to the transition from a theocentric to a mercantile paradigm is to be explicated. There is a danger in seeing *IIE* as an autonomous, sealed and textually explicit work, that 'carried' a particular policy paradigm and succeeded in steering Irish education on a new cultural trajectory that continues to be followed. Such a mainstream understanding of its contribution understates the complex character of its cultural significance while glossing the mechanisms of its influence. Here, *IIE* is treated as a material point around which concepts, language, performatives and authorities were strategically structured and mobilised, having previously existed in inchoate, unnamed, unstructured or unestablished forms. In this approach, *IIE* is considered, in the final analysis, not in terms of whatever message the authors were seeking to communicate, but rather as a work that was made to function as a resource for normalising the introduction of new themes, not necessarily or obviously inherent to it, to Irish educational discourse. This, in turn, is viewed as an achievement of agents and social configurations who had a material and symbolic interest in the formalisation of these constructs and their acceptance as themes within the discourse.

But to pave the way for this distinctive cultural approach to the impact of *IIE*, it will be necessary to address it more conventionally in terms of the flow of codified ideas, in particular human capital theory, and locate it within the process of economic reconstruction that began in the 1950s, itself a response to the social and economic crisis of the mid-1950s. A brief summary of some of its projections and conclusions in relation to labour force needs and educational supply should give something of the distinctive and innovative character of the report.

IIE was a study of trends in the use of the human and material resources in the Irish educational system that sought to estimate the demands that were likely to be made on these resources in the light of the needs of the economy in the years ahead. The report began with a description of the existing educational system and of the number of qualified people it was likely to produce if no changes, other than those officially announced at the time, were to be made. This was followed by an examination of employment patterns and a forecast of the number of people with various levels of qualifications expected to be required to meet the projected needs of the economy. Contrasting these indicators of supply and demand the report considered the possible alterations that were required if the adaptation of the system to changing economic needs was to be facilitated.

The projected manpower demand for the period 1961 to 1971 was for 40,000 professional and technical workers, 20,000 employers, managers and salaried employees, 80,000 skilled manual workers, 113,000 intermediate non-manual workers and 197,000 farmers, agricultural and other workers. This demand was then translated into educational requirements by establishing an educational target for each occupational level. These targets were set by reference to defined or accepted standards where these existed, trends in competitor countries, projections of current trends, and employers' requirements as expressed in job advertisements.

The number of students who would leave full-time education with various educational qualifications during 1961-1971 was estimated and due allowance was made for such factors as not entering the labour force. With the projected supply of people with various educational qualifications estimated it was possible to compare them with projected requirements for the same period. Table 4.1 expresses the resulting comparison between the projected educational qualifications of those expected to enter the labour force during 1961-1971 and the target qualifications which such persons might be expected to possess. It can be seen from Table 4.1 that the projected outflow from the educational system would not meet the targets set for Junior Certificate Level, while those with no post-primary qualification would be in much greater supply than was likely to be required by employers.

Table 4.1 Supply & Demand by Educational Qualifications 1961-1971 ('000)*

	Third Level Qualifications	*Senior Cert*	*Second Level Junior Cert*	*No Post-Primary Qualifications*
Supply to Labour Force	32	78	110	230
Labour Force Demand	31	73	186	160
Labour Force Supply or Deficit	+1	+5	-76	+70

*Adapted from Table 8.4 *Investment in Education*, p. 201.

The educational targets established, of course, were based on contemporary standards and had been applied only to the projected output of the educational system during 1961-1971. If such targets had been applied to the total 1971 labour force there would have been significant deficits at all levels from Junior Certificate upwards, a testimony to rising educational standards. The survey team concluded in this regard that 'if the proposition that education has a beneficial effect on productivity is accepted, measures which tend to bring the educational levels of the labour force as a whole closer to present day standards should be promoted' (p. 204). Accordingly, it recommended that deficiencies in basic education, particularly among the younger members of the labour force, be corrected and that retraining arising from redundancy and change of occupation together with refurbishing, broadening and updating be provided. No further breakdown of the occupational categories referred to above was attempted. However, the survey team felt it necessary to consider the question of the future demand for and supply of technicians. It estimated that approximately 750 technicians per annum would be needed whereas it was considered unlikely that the output would be more than 400 annually. If the ratio of three technicians per technologist was to be accepted it was the view of the survey team that by the end of the decade under consideration the deficiency would have assumed 'formidable proportions' (p. 219).

The Human Capital Paradigm

The details of these findings of *IIE* were much less significant than its overall approach to education, the terminology used, the questions asked, what it defined as a problem, what it considered as data and the conceptual framework within which it operated. All of these elements were broadly consistent with manpower planning, human resource development and, specifically within education, with human capital theory which were influential internationally in education at this time. This took the form of the determination of 'appropriate' educational levels in the light of market forces, such as employers' expectations and practices in competitor countries, the introduction of notions of 'deficit' and 'surplus' in relation to education credentials and, more strikingly, in relation to people with particular levels of educational achievement, attention to the needs of the economy in devising the curriculum, and the quantification of educational phenomena by means of costings, inputs, outputs and participation rates. Overall, education was seen as investment in people as components of the energising, well-being and maximising of an economy in much the same way as one might view investment in physical plant and new technology.

In its own words:

> ... the educational system in all its branches may be regarded as one of the biggest industries and certainly the most important, in the country ... Because of the scale of human and material resources involved, if for no other reason, these resources should be allocated in the most rational way (p. 351).

> ... a country must seek in designing its educational system to satisfy, among other things, the manpower needs of the future. If the range and levels of skills required to convert economic potential into economic achievements are not available a country is unlikely to have the resources needed to provide education of the quality and variety that is being increasingly demanded. As education is at once a cause and a consequence of economic growth, economic planning is incomplete without educational planning. Education, as well as having its own intrinsic values, is a necessary element in economic activity (p. 350).

IIE was in no sense doctrinaire in this theorisation of education. It acknowledged the acceptance at that time of the likelihood of a relationship between education and economic growth but warned that there was 'no general agreement on the precise nature of the relationship and the temptation to add to the dogmatic generalisations already made about it should be avoided' (p. 369). It was with reservations, relating to the relationship between output and employees' educational occupational content, assumptions relating to future pricing and output, and the reliability of long-term forecasting of the economic requirements of education, that it endorsed the manpower approach as the 'most tangible basis'

(p. 382) for an assessment of such requirements. Far from being euphoric about the potential contribution of economics and economists to education, it was cautious and restrained in advocating an interdisciplinary approach: 'Short or medium run educational needs might be estimated on the basis of an overall "manpower" forecast for the economy. Longer term needs, which are ultimately the more important, could be assessed (if at all) only after much educational/ sociological/economic research' (p. 386). Indeed, some years later one of the economist members of the survey team was to write that education was 'too serious an area to be left in the hands of economists' (O'Donoghue, 1971, p. 219).

These themes of *IIE* would not have been found in the *Report of the Council of Education on the Curriculum of the Secondary School* published in 1962, the same year in which the *IIE* survey team was constituted. Described as 'highly defensive and conservative' (Mulcahy, 1981a, p. 13) in tone, this report of the Council of Education operated, as we have seen, within a theocentric paradigm. In its statement of general educational aims it conceived of the school in terms of cultural and religious transmission, it stressed its subsidiary and complementary relationship with family and church, and proclaimed the ultimate purpose of education to be the overall development – religious, moral, intellectual, physical – of the person. *IIE* did not immediately challenge this view of education and, as we shall see, excluded engagement with the overall aims of education in appealing to its terms of reference and the competence of the survey team. Its immediate point of departure was in relation to the Council of Education's conceptualisation of the curriculum of the secondary school.

This identified the secondary school with general education, articulated in terms of the aim of a general education: the all-round development of the person and preparation for life; as well as in relation to the curriculum of a general education: the humanities, classical and modern languages, mathematics and the sciences. Specialised preparation for a particular skill or profession was distanced from this provision of general education. In fact, in justifying more practical subjects such as woodwork and domestic science, the report commends the contribution which these subjects could make to general education through their cultivation of general capacities and attributes (Mulcahy, 1981a).

It would, however, be incorrect to regard *IIE* as the first attempt to advocate an educational response to the needs of the Irish economy. Within the first decade of the new state, the Commission on Technical Education in 1927 had recognised that the existing secondary schools did not prepare pupils specifically for entry to employment at the age of 16. The Vocational Education Act, 1930, the only major piece of legislation governing education enacted by the new state until the late 1990s, was meant as a response to this weakness of the system. It was designed, through a system of vocational schools, to respond to the needs of industrial and agricultural production, with particular reference to the patterns of production and employment in the neighbourhood of the schools. In the view of O'Reilly (1989), 'Vocational Education can be seen as the main element of the manpower policy of the new state: as part of the infrastructure to promote agricultural and industrial production.'

However, these initiatives in manpower planning were confined to lower status occupations and to what were to be less prestigious state schools, and did not infringe on the more dominant tradition of general education provided by high-status and religious-controlled secondary schools (Mulcahy, 1981b). In fact, it is likely that the success of the state in its vocational initiatives can be attributed to the fact that it did not infringe on the secondary school sector. What *IIE* participated in achieving was the extension of this economic planning approach initially to the entire post-primary sector, including most notably secondary schools, and ultimately to third level as well. It helped to normalise the practice, reflected in state educational policy, demands of employers, and the concerns of parents of using industrial and commercial models and needs as key points of reference in determining the structure and content of education as a whole. But to fully appreciate the role played by *IIE* in this regard it is necessary to locate it in the context of the attempt, commencing in the late 1950s, to reconstruct the Irish economy.

Economic Reconstruction

Throughout the 1950s it became increasingly obvious that Ireland was in the grip of an economic crisis. As Breen *et al.* (1990, p.35) put it, 'the real question people asked in the 1950s was not whether the state should expand but whether the nation would survive.' A litany of economic and social ills characterised the period, including high inflation, balance of payments crises, industrial and agricultural decline and massive emigration. The human statistics are particularly evocative: 'some 400,000 persons left to seek employment elsewhere, mainly in Great Britain during the decade. Approximately one person out of every five born since Independence and resident in 1951 had emigrated by the end of the decade; for those in the younger age groups the rate of departure was nearly twice as great ... In many years, emigrants almost equalled the number of births' (Breen *et al.*, 1990, p. 35).

The policy response of economic planning was orchestrated by civil servants together with academic advisors rather than politicians (Fanning, 1983; Lee, 1989; Breen *et al.*, 1990). In this regard, T.K. Whitaker, appointed Secretary of the Department of Finance in 1956, is the key figure. His *Economic Development* published in 1958 provided the inspiration for the *Programme for Economic Expansion* usually referred to as the *First Programme* which was published later that year. In the view of one contemporary commentator, no less an observer than the subsequent Taoiseach, Garret FitzGerald, *Economic Development* represented 'the snatching by the Department of Finance of the initiative in planning' (quoted in Lee, 1989, p. 343). Within the state apparatus, economists were in the ascendant. It is from this point that it becomes productive to trace the emergence of the human capital paradigm in terms of both its short-term and long-term impact on Irish educational policy.

A key redirection in economic development, along with a move from protection to free trade, was the encouragement of foreign-owned manufacturers with a strong export commitment to locate in Ireland. In support of this the *First Programme* committed itself to giving special consideration 'to the need for ensuring an adequate supply of personnel, with the requisite knowledge and skill, to all levels of industry' (*Programme for Economic Expansion*, 1958, p. 39). Apart from recommendations on education for agricultural and rural development, however, neither *Economic Development* nor the *First Programme* elaborated on how education in general might contribute to economic recovery. This was to follow in the *Second Programme for Economic Expansion* in 1963, which promised that 'special attention will be given to education, training and other forms of "human investment"' (*Second Programme for Economic Expansion*, 1963, p.17):

> Since our wealth lies ultimately in our people, the aim of educational policy must be to enable all individuals to realise their full potential as human persons … Better education and training will support and stimulate continued economic expansion. Even the economic returns from investment in education and training are likely to be as high in the long-run as those from investment in physical capital (p. 13).

Treating education as the development of human resources generated a particular set of issues in educational discourse and planning. These included the choice between levels of education for investment and development, the tension between quality and numbers, the balance to be struck between formal classroom-based learning and on-the-job learning, maintaining incentives and reconciling individual and social needs (Harbison, 1967). These were to form the agenda for the analysis of Irish education emanating from the broader state apparatus in the subsequent decades. Official policy statements, the deliberations of government-appointed inquiry and advisory bodies, and the educational problems confronted by state-sponsored research agencies all bore the influence of these human capital concerns of the educational planners and later of industrialists, the business sector and employers (Coolahan, 1984b; Gleeson, 2000).

As well as the specification of what constituted a meaningful and pressing educational problem changing in line with the issues generated by the human capital paradigm, the identity of those who were accepted as legitimate commentators on educational issues also changed. Economists came to be accepted as the natural sources of informed and analytical observation on social issues in education in a manner that equated society with the economy. Indicative of the shift was the fact that in major lecture series and publications reviewing contemporary educational developments and policy it was economists who were routinely invited to contribute (Sheehan, 1979, 1982; Barlow, 1981; Tussing, 1981; Walsh, 1981). Economists had dislodged the pedagogue – an educational practitioner, typically from the humanities, possibly a headmaster, and frequently a priest or a member of a religious congregation – as the native educational authority. Eleven of the twenty-nine members of the Council of Education appointed in April 1950, for instance, had been religious, and of the twenty-three listed as having university qualifications only four were from outside the humanities. In contrast, as we have seen, the *IIE* survey team contained two economists, a statistician and a mathematician, all lay. Its National Steering Committee was drawn from technical, scientific and vocational areas of expertise in the public and private sectors and the trade union movement. All were lay, with the exception of Dr J. Newman, Professor of Sociology, St Patrick's College, Maynooth. And as the identity of educational authorities changed so also did the style of discourse: the pedagogue offered comment and wisdom on the basis of experience and reflection, usually communicated by means of anecdote, axiom and ideals, while the economists purported to describe the system as it was, based on empirical verifiable data. This positivistic assertiveness was to prove an important factor in heading off possible challenge and contestation.

Though in no sense a cipher, *IIE* operated within the same human capital paradigm as did the Irish economic planners of the late 1950s. In fact, it has all the indications that the acceptance of the OECD suggestion, at its 1961 Washington Conference, that such a survey be carried out was a feature of this reconstruction project. We have seen how *IIE* proclaimed the necessity of educational planning for economic development. Senior civil servants would have been familiar with the broad intent of the OECD in this regard. Seán O'Connor (1986, p. 62), later to be Secretary of the Department of Education, recalled the cultural context of the Washington Conference as follows:

> The OECD had set up a study group on the economics of education and from its work grew a conviction of the importance of education in economic growth to the extent that education was canvassed as the most important factor in economic recovery ... The Washington Conference was held in an atmosphere of certainty about the importance of education and the urgent need for increased resources for education. The theme of the conference was economic growth and investment in education and experts in different countries spelt out the need for more resources for education to an audience of professional economists and educational experts as well as government representatives with responsibility for educational policy and general fiscal policy.

O'Connor's characterisation of the event is corroborated in Marginson's (1997) account of the dominion of human capital theory among state planners of education at that time. He describes the Washington Conference as one of the 'showpiece policy gatherings' (p. 93) at which the speakers were led by the same advocates of human capital theory who wrote on the topic for the leading academic journals and acted as consultants to national governments. The conference was chaired by Philip Coombs, the US Assistant Secretary of State for Educational and Cultural Affairs, who argued for the absolute necessity of closer links being forged between economic and educational policy than in the past. The message of this 'new faith' (p.106) was simple: 'the duty of authorities was to expand education as fast as schools and universities could be built and teachers trained. The same programmes that provided equality of educational opportunity, the career open to all the talents, would generate the national wealth which would pay for all' (p. 93). For the OECD, education was the key to modernisation.

O'Connor goes on to point out that Ireland sent two representatives, both high-ranking civil servants, one from each of the Departments of Finance and Education, an indication of the importance attached to the issue under consideration at the conference. In fact, following an open invitation from the OECD, Ireland was the first of the member states to volunteer, in the words of Dr Patrick Hillery (1963), the Minister for Education of the time, 'to carry out pilot studies of their educational system in the light of their probable long-term economic and scientific needs'.

IIE was not an accessible publication. Spread over two volumes of detailed statistical tables and appendices it was written in guarded academic prose. We shall see later how this reticence as to the policy implications of *IIE* was interpreted at the time as a recognition of how sensitive educational policy still was in the 1960s. The technical nature of the report, however, meant that in the absence of human issues or obvious controversy *IIE* was not of itself likely to fire the public imagination. In fact, *IIE* contained only one specific recommendation, though Tussing (1978, p. 65) argues that 'this is probably because the force of its factual findings in many instances made specific recommendations superfluous.' This interpretation has too much of the theoretical mop about it (Salter and Tapper, 1981) – its effect is to soak up a complicated flux of conceptual and propositional issues involving considerations of interest, contradiction and contestation and represent them as a rational and linear current. Had *IIE* been, as seems to be generally assumed, a discordant and isolated challenge to the dominant understanding of education as typified by the *Report of the Council of Education on the Curriculum of the Secondary School*, it could without great difficulty have been ignored and condemned to the fate of similar reports of external authorities before it. Referring to such an authority, a Swedish economist who sat on the 1934-1938 Banking Commission, Lee (1989, p. 625) observes that senior civil servants 'deluged Jacobson with praise, and ignored any of his recommendations they found distasteful'.

In the first instance, *IIE* acted, not as a source of paradigmatic penetration, but as a means of extending and legitimating a paradigmatic shift that had already occurred within an influential sector of state policy-making. The educational policy paradigm forming within a sector of the state apparatus, namely the Department of Finance and its economic advisors, now had to expand and engage educational thinking beyond this core site of influence if its role in the economic reconstruction that began with the publication of *Economic Development* was to become a reality. But the agents and social configurations that were the most likely targets of such colonisation were to assert their own cultural agency when exposed to the human capital paradigm. They may have been receptive to it but they were far from pliable. They were to draw out from the human capital discourse, that *IIE* had given a material presence to in education, new themes in the light of their material and symbolic interests. Their membershipping to the human capital paradigm may have been publicly uncritical but their engagement with it was a dynamic one that expanded its boundaries and eventually precipitated its factioning. To analyse how this occurred it will be necessary to sharpen the focus of the analysis to consider the micro-political processes relating to individual and collective interests among those involved. But first, the insignificance of contestation needs to be explained and the factors that headed off or contained potential or residual contestation explored.

Contestation and Containment

The lack of contestation in relation to the economic reconstruction of the late 1950s has been commented upon (Breen *et al.*, 1990), though retrospectively as we have seen in Chapter 3 the nature of the redirection has been questioned because of its undue reliance on foreign investment, a failure to utilise native resources, the absence of democratic participation in the decision-making processes, and the ultimate ceding of substantial industrial and financial power to forces outside of the state. There were some expressions of unease in relation to the paradigmatic shift represented by *IIE*. Ó Catháin, a Jesuit educationalist and university lecturer, wondered about the danger of over-emphasising the economic aims of education to the neglect of the formation of the intellect and will of the individual person, while the President of the Association of Secondary Teachers of Ireland (ASTI) asserted that 'what we must seek to ensure is that the economist occupies the place he should in education and that is, of course, a minor place' (both quoted in O'Connor, 1986, p.121). These sentiments were echoed at the widely-publicised (*The Irish Times*, 4 December) and evocative 'Student Teach-In' at University College, Cork in 1967 by Fr Liam Ryan, a Lecturer in Sociology at the College, who warned of the dangers of economists directing the future of the educational system to the neglect of considerations of ideals: 'Ideals tended to be associated with impracticality; in fact, ideals were gold dimly seen in the distance and worth attaining for their own sake. Without ideals, life merely made cynics' (Ryan, 1967a).

A general theme of the 'Teach-In' – too great a readiness in Ireland to import package solutions to its problems from countries which differed from it – was supportive of these concerns about the impact of the human capital paradigm on educational planning. If, however, *IIE* did indeed cause 'a considerable stir in Irish education circles' (Coolahan, 2000, p. 168), expressions of reservation or opposition were isolated and uncoordinated. The response to *IIE* in the newspapers of the time (OECD, 1969), the National Industrial Economic Council's (1966) commentary, reviews in such influential journals as *Studies* (FitzGerald, 1965), and at the symposium organised by the Statistical and Social Inquiry Society of Ireland (SSISI) (Cannon *et al.*, 1965/66) were positive, welcoming and congratulatory. There was little evidence of sustained confrontation from religious or other interests and none at all of mobilised contestation in relation to the paradigmatic shift that was occurring or to state activism in the formulation of educational policy.

Conceptually, the human capital paradigm as presented in *IIE* was not immediately discordant with character and religious development as an educational aim. The survey team had been careful to disclaim any inclination to comment on the aims of education or any authority to do so: 'It is not our function to say what the objectives of the education system should be or to say what priority or weight should be given to particular objectives' (p. xxxiii). They were equally careful to acknowledge the significance of these wider philosophical questions: 'We have tried to keep before our minds at all times the character and purpose of education and that the term "educational system" has little meaning if it is considered apart from the human needs which it is there to serve' (p. xxxiii). *IIE* presented itself as a value-free empirical exercise 'essentially fact finding and analytical in character' (p. xxxiii). All of this was consistent with the atheoretical conceptualisation of the social sciences at that time in Ireland as the empirical fact-finding wing of social ethics from which it was nonetheless epistemologically distinct. In this view, the mission of the social sciences would have been to produce facts rather than to debate values which in the Roman Catholic sociology of the time would have been derived from dogma, their validity an inappropriate topic for social inquiry.

Economists, so distinct from traditional disciplines of educational studies (Coolahan, 1984a), were ideally suited to introduce this empirical dimension to Irish education. Its implication for paradigmatic change was that the human capital paradigm could be seen as accreting to the theocentric paradigm by way of expansion through merging rather than confrontation. Indeed, the self-positioning of *IIE* discourse was such that it could be read as holding out the expectation and acceptability that such a merger would take the form of its co-optation within the theocentric paradigm. Those who wrote favourably about linking education with the needs of a growing economy did not consider themselves to be jettisoning education of its human, cultural and religious objectives. Few felt it necessary to affirm this. At the SSISI Symposium (Cannon *et al.*, 1965/66), Cannon (Headmaster of Sandymount High School and an official of the Federation of Irish Secondary Schools), citing Newman's educational vision, argued that 'important as the economic benefits of education may be, it should be stressed that they are incidentals rather than fundamentals, and that any system of education that loses sight of this essential distinction, is unlikely to prove fruitful in the long run, even in the strictly economic sense'. Yet, even in this instance, the caution is located in the appendices and appears almost as a superfluous afterthought, scarcely requiring proclamation.

Apart from these disclaimers of authority and expertise in relation to the objectives of education and their prioritisation, the general body of the report was cautious and hesitant. The one recommendation made was that a Development Unit be established within the Department of Education. This was interpreted at the time as an awareness by the survey team of the sensitivity of educational policy issues. It was seen as an alertness to the probability that, even in relation to topics on which they might reasonably be expected to have considered opinions in the light of their terms of reference, any hint of policy activism on their part was liable to be interpreted as an infringement on the jurisdiction of established interests. Milne's (Secretary, Board of Education of the Church of Ireland) description at the SSISI symposium was graphic:

> One feels as if the survey team felt itself to be, if not actually walking in a potential minefield, at any rate walking on eggs. One senses that the authors of the report – well aware of the dangers of outstepping their terms of reference, yet convinced of the urgent need that some of their findings be taken to heart, took refuge in the oblique phrase and double negative!

In reading the report, according to Milne, it was essential that it be understood in the light of such important features of the Irish educational system as its 'denominational and managerial basis'. For O'Meara (Professor of Classical Languages at UCD and a prominent commentator on education), speaking at the same conference, *IIE* 'did well, in my view, to be very sparing in its interpretation of the statistics it made available: if it had not done so, it would inevitably have aroused suspicion. The interests of religion and language movement have tended to overshadow cold analysis in Irish education'.

The role of the OECD as a sponsoring body was widely publicised and was crucial both in heading off possible contestation and in the report having the effect that it had. *IIE* is routinely referred to as an OECD report or more specifically as 'the product of OECD experts' (Tovey and Share, 2000, p. 165). It is spoken of as if it were a report of a foreign survey team. While the membership of the survey team was prominently listed at the beginning of the report it was the economist Patrick Lynch who tended to be identified with it, and then as chairman of the survey team. Even among Irish educationalists it is common to hear the findings of the report referred to as what 'they' uncovered about 'our' system. O'Connor describes the predicament of Patrick Hillery who, as Minister for Education at the time, had to decide whether or not to approve the setting up of the survey team: 'He had been long enough in office to know some of the shortcomings and inequities of the Irish educational system; he knew also that many more would be exposed by the survey. The OECD would publish details of these inadequacies for the world to see. If blame was to be assigned – and he never doubted that the picture painted by the report, when it appeared, would be grossly unfavourable – then his government would be the target. He could easily refuse, as many other countries did, and nobody might ever know' (O'Connor, 1986, p. 63).

Being associated with the OECD gave the report a neutral identity. The OECD could not be regarded as having an 'interest' in the issue being studied, in the sense that an indigenous analyst might be expected to have. As a large bureaucratic-like organisation it would be expected to cultivate the characteristic features of bureaucratic activity – among them neutrality and an absence of an affective orientation towards the object of its analysis. The response of the National Industrial Economic Council to the findings of *IIE* clearly represents this local perception of the affective neutrality of the report: 'the sober and detailed factual analysis in *Investment in Education*, by challenging complacency and conventional wisdom and leaving no excuse for ignorance of relevant facts, has given an impetus towards that critical examination of our educational system in all aspects that alone can lay the basis for permanent improvements' (NIEC, 1966, p. 31).

Expert knowledge and specialisation are other features of bureaucracy and the OECD association meant that *IIE* would be regarded as the product of expert authorities in their specialised fields of inquiry. Its deliberations would be given legitimacy by reference to the expertise of the survey team. As such it could not be easily dismissed. O'Connor (1986, p. 120) describes how, along with other senior civil servants within the Department of Education, he recognised the implications of the OECD involvement for the direction of educational policy: 'The importance of the report to the Department of Education cannot be over-emphasised ... We, officials of the Department, were well aware of the many faults of the system. Indeed, the Department support for the investigation was prompted to a very large degree by an anxiety to have a full and thorough investigation by an independent body of the ills of the system. In 1962, when the review was initiated, the Minister's (and the Department's) position in the educational scene was obscure and, at second level in particular, the Department's officials, perhaps without good reason, felt that any direction from them would be regarded as an intrusion. An independent report would demand Departmental action.' Similarly, Dr Hillery later recalled how Seán MacGearailt, Assistant Secretary at the Department of Education and his representative at the Washington Conference, had recommended that the OECD invitation be accepted:

> One day Seán MacGearailt came (they knew what I wanted – I had told them and I
> had written it down) and he said that there was this OECD study (we could get
> done). I said 'but Seán I know what I want', but he said 'this is the way to get it'
> and he was right. Now you had the force of an international body (quoted in Bonel-
> Elliott, 1994).

Seán MacGearailt was subsequently appointed chairman of the National Steering Committee for the *IIE* survey.

Not surprisingly, *IIE* was to be frequently cited by politicians (see Coolahan, 2000), senior civil servants (O'Connor, 1968) and academic educationalists (Craft, 1970). Indeed, *IIE* has been used to explain, support and legitimate a range of policy decisions which may have preceded it or were only obliquely derived from it (Bonel-Elliott, 1994, 1996). As one secondary teacher wrote with some exasperation, 'have we not had the OECD Report ... quoted and re-quoted as if it was Holy Writ' (Buckley, 1968). Ubiquitous in educational debate and analysis, the terminology, themes and problems of *IIE* dominated discourse on education and normalised the human capital paradigm in the manner in which Irish people at all levels communicated with each other about education. This influence on educational discourse reaches to the present where its semantic legacy is to be discerned in the mercantile paradigm. But to achieve this influence the human capital paradigm qualitatively changed in a distinctive manner that can be best illuminated by adopting a comparative perspective on aspects of the influence of human capital thinking since the 1960s.

Comparative Perspective: Human Capital Theory and Educational Policy

A comparative perspective on the fate of human capital theory will help to situate the distinctiveness and localised emergence of the cultural change in Irish education that *IIE* had made possible. Human capital theory did not stand still as a theorisation of human resource development through education. When viewed comparatively, this provides a foil that allows its experience of cultural mediation in the Irish experience to be distinguished as an emergent production in the context of the material interests and cognitive readiness of the social actors involved.

Human Capital Theory emerged 'phoenix-like' in the early 1960s through the writings and promotional activities of Gary Becker, Edward Denison and Theodore W. Schultz (Blaug, 1988), its birth attributed to Schultz's presidential address at the annual meeting of the American Economics Association in December 1960 (Blaug, 1968). Its proposition that investment in people produced a greater rate of return than investment in physical plant was as simple as the imperatives that followed for educational policy – the necessity to expand educational provision and equalise participation so as to mobilise all the talent of society for the promotion of growth. From small beginnings – a few papers in the 1950s to almost 2,000 in 1976 (Blaug, 1976) – Human Capital Theory intensified as a field of knowledge that was not without its dissent and confrontation. It was also to experience modifications in the policy documents of international bodies and individual educational systems. Marginson (1997) has identified four phases: First Wave Human Capital Theory of the 1960s, Screening Theory spanning the 1970s and 1980s, Second Wave Human Capital Theory of the 1980s and Market Liberal Human Capital Theory of the 1980s and 1990s. This conceptualisation and phasing has been developed from an Australian perspective. Table 4.2 presents an adaptation of this in the light of Irish experience.

It is possible to find evidence, albeit patchy and fluctuating, of these changing understandings of the functional link between schooling and the workplace and of how investment in education might contribute to a nation's growth in Irish policy discourse. Screening Theory is to be found in the 'Transition from School to Work' field of research which will be described in Chapter 8 on employability. In that chapter also, Second Wave Human Capital Theory will be reflected in state discourse and educational interventions in the 1990s relating to skill deficits within the ICT sector. The Market Liberal version of Human Capital Theory is more easily linked with particular social actors (some economists), controversies (state validation of Hibernia College's teacher education course), and policy episodes of which Tussing's treatment of educational funding priorities to be dealt with in Chapter 14 is an example, than with specific historical phases. Yet, it is also true that a contemporary exposition of how the development of human resources contributes to economic growth, by an economic consultant who has participated in educational policy discourse (Tansey, 1998), could be accommodated in the first wave stage of Human Capital Theory. He summarises his exposition of the effects of investment in human resources on Irish economic performance as follows: 'investments in education and training raise national productivity, both directly and indirectly, encourage a widening and deepening of the physical capital stock, remove structural barriers to economic growth and employment expansion and act to alleviate unemployment. Together, they all combine to sharpen the competitiveness of Irish output and enhance the prospects for further additions to employment' (pp. 108-109).

Table 4.2 Human Capital Theory and the Policy Process
(adapted from Marginson, 1997, Table 4.2, p. 116)

Theory	*Main Theoretical Assumptions*	*Popular Understandings*	*Governmental Practices*
First Wave Human Capital Theory (1960s)	Education leads to productivity, and investment in education leads to economic growth	Education delivers career jobs, status and higher incomes: increased demand for greater access to education	Expansion of education provision, supported by funding; equal opportunity to maximise human capital
Screening Theory (1970s-1980s)	Education credentials are a surrogate for individual productivity; education is a screening device that distributes jobs	The need to struggle for relative advantage: better credentials provide competitive advantage in the labour market	Cessation of increases in expenditure; programmes linking education to work; standardisation of qualifications
Second Wave Human Capital Theory (1990s)	Education augments the capacity to handle new technologies and other innovations	Strategic personal investment in education in 'cutting edge' areas (management, computing etc.)	Selective investment in education in high technology and management areas
Market Liberal Human Capital Theory (personalised and episodic)	Individuals invest in education until costs exceed the expected benefits, mostly, future earnings.	Educational investment and its financing are an individual responsibility: individualised investment (private schools, home computing, postgraduate courses) maximises relative advantage.	Programmes and policies to secure self-managing individual investment: the selective use of student assistance, 'talking up' participation, income contingent fees and loans schemes, etc.

The modification of Human Capital Theory as an academic body of knowledge and as an influence on educational policy does have a relevance for the emergence of the mercantile paradigm. But this resides less in its academic refinements or measurements of returns, though these remained as a resource for legitimation, than in the manner in which it supplies new themes to maintain an authoritative discourse on the link between schooling and the economy and the world of work. In the Irish experience these modifications of Human Capital Theory are not what shaped the meaning of the institution of education. What expanded the human capital paradigm and subsequently constructed the mercantile paradigm, were the themes that were drawn out, from the cultural opportunities provided by *IIE,* by local agents in the light of the cultural and psychological resources and material interests they individually and collectively brought to their engagement with the human capital paradigm.

This will be illuminated as we consider the positions and interests of those sectors of Irish society on which the paradigmatic change impinged – Department of Education officials, Ministers for Education and politicians in general, teachers and parents. As well as its generative contribution to the changing cultural definition of Irish education, this should further explain the containment of contestation to the human capital themes which *IIE* brokered into Irish educational understanding.

Agents and Collective Interests

Department of Education officials must have been more than a little bemused at the Department of Finance interest in education and their according it a significant role in economic recovery and development. With the Department of Finance now interpreting education as the development of human resources and as an asset in economic efficiency, Department of Education officials were unlikely to look a gift horse in the mouth. During the immediate past they would have smarted under a parsimonious and censorious Finance Department. Reviewing this period, Ó Buachalla (1988, p. 307) describes the Department of Finance attitude to education as follows: 'On expenditure, it was usually reactionary, controlling and cautious, on expanding educational opportunity it was less than enthusiastic.'

Ministers for Education during the period from the late 1950s to the end of the 1960s – Lynch, Hillery, Colley, O'Malley – were for various reasons anxious to be associated with development and change. Their approach to policy making appears to have been more assertive and activist than that of their predecessors. In this regard the statement of Lynch's immediate predecessor as Minister, Richard Mulcahy, quoted in full earlier, in which he likened his position to that of a plumber who would 'take the knock out of the pipes and … link up everything' and refused to 'lapse into an easy acceptance of an imagined duty to philosophise … on educational matters' (quoted in O'Connor, 1986, p. 1) is routinely cited by way of a foil. Lynch and Hillery emerge as politicians who, leaving aside any consideration of their interest in education, were eager to develop their career prospects. In fact, both moved on to the most senior ministries and ultimately to the positions of Taoiseach and President, respectively. O'Malley, a folk figure of immense proportions, is remembered as impetuous, with a keen sense of justice and a concern for the underdog (McElligott, 1986; O'Connor, 1986; Ó Buachalla, 1988). Of Colley it was said that 'from the time of his first election to Dáil Éireann (he) had made no secret of his interest in education, and his ambition to be Minister for Education' (O'Connor, 1986, p. 135). These politicians were likely to be responsive to whatever would justify expansion in education and prove to be sensitive to the wishes of the electorate. According to Ó Buachalla (1988, pp 201-202),

> Though lacking the support of a party policy document, these young ministers were unerring in identifying the potential public support for specific policies and in adopting these policies without delay. Because of this supreme pragmatism, few would question the validity of the claim in its 1977 manifesto, that Fianna Fáil was 'the party of Investment in Education and of free education'.

Lee's interpretation (1989, p. 587) that the 'market for educational ideas abruptly opened up, thanks to the recent activity of some politicians and new secretaries of education, Terry Raftery and Seán O'Connor' is too generous in its assessment of the openness of policy makers and too idealist in its attribution of the motor of policy change. What happened was not as neat as Weber's elective affinity of ideas. Nonetheless, in their intellectual and material dimensions, the subjectivities of influential decision makers, spanning finance and education and involving politicians and civil servants, did appear to coincide. The significance for educational policy was the extent to which the human capital paradigm, with its expansionist rationality as crystallised in the discourse of *IIE*, was to find acceptability within key sectors of the central state apparatus.

Among teachers, expressions of opposition to the prominence being given to the economic function of schooling were over-ridden by pragmatic self-interest. Teachers were alert to the manner in which their individual and collective interests would benefit from the view of educational funding as investment rather than consumption incorporated in the human capital paradigm. In the decade 1963/64 to 1973/74 public educational expenditure almost doubled as a percentage of GNP to 6.29 per cent (NESC, 1976). The numbers of secondary school teachers similarly doubled between 1967 and 1974 (Tussing, 1978, p. 67). But the benefits went beyond the individual level of expanded employment opportunities. Mobilisation and solidarity were enhanced. As well as increases in absolute numbers, membership of the Association of Secondary Teachers of

Ireland (ASTI) rose from 55 per cent of all full-time lay registered secondary teachers in 1968 to 96 per cent in 1974. This gave secondary teachers considerably more control over the achievement of state educational goals becoming, in consequence, a force to be reckoned with and meriting consultation in the policy-making process (Barry, 1989).

The 1960s was a period of considerable public interest in education. Peillon (1982, p. 150), echoing Ó Buachalla's observations above on the populism of the Ministers for Education of the time, speaks of education becoming 'a burning issue in Ireland, when the demand for reform became so insistent that the state was finally forced to take the initiative'. According to Kellaghan (1989), in retrospect much of the actual expansion of the 1960s and 1970s, despite 'a bow to manpower planning needs' in the policy statements of the era, seems to have been the result of 'an increasing popular demand for education to which policy makers, planners and schools responded'. It was not so much the intensity of the interest that was significant. What most represented a departure was a diffusion of the interest across a wider spectrum within Irish society. A significant change in consciousness occurred. Parents who previously would have dismissed secondary schooling as an experience suitable only for those 'with brains and money' (Ryan, 1967b), were now less confident about excluding their children from the possibility of further education after primary schooling. Participation rates at second level grew throughout the 1960s. This growth occurred independently of the policy changes that were enacted during the decade in relation to free post-primary schooling and free school transport which would have sustained and enhanced it (Tussing, 1976).

Explaining increases in educational participation is not a simple task. There are 'push' and 'pull' factors at work in determining how long pupils will persist in schooling. These include the extent and distribution of educational facilities, the perceived relevance of schooling, its satisfaction of needs, the demand for labour of varying levels of skill, and the degree to which educational certification is used in occupational selection. Of these, the most tangible is the pattern of employment opportunities available to school leavers. An analysis of employment opportunities for the period 1951 to 1971 (Breen *et al.*, 1990, p. 60) reveals a striking decline in demand for those categories of work which require little by way of formal education. Small farmers, agricultural labourers and unskilled manual workers suffered a combined decline of 244,700 positions over the 20-year period. During the same period there was an increase of 91,400 positions in the skilled manual and upper and lower non-manual categories, all of which would have required post-compulsory educational experience and, increasingly, specific certification levels. In 1961 over 40 per cent of the male work force was in self-employment, mainly in agriculture (Hannan, 1986). Whereas up to that time a third of young people could expect to inherit a family-owned business, occupational entry now became more formal, competitive and based on educational credentials (Hannan and Breen, 1987).

It is clear from the utterances and responses of politicians, most notably Dr Hillery's 1963 policy statement, that from the early 1960s there was a growing demand for greater educational provision. In particular it would appear that parents in rural areas wanted greater access to post-primary schooling for their children. The clientelist relationship between Irish public representatives and their constitutents, cultivated through the operation of constituency clinics which hold out the promise of advice, advocacy and the brokerage of influence (Hazelkorn, 1986), would have impressed upon politicians the desirability of expanding educational provision. That it was a human capital discourse that made it possible for civil servants and politicians to justify such expansion and investment was unlikely to impinge on parents. Parents, for their part, were always aware that whatever of the discourse of religious, cultural and character formation, and despite the general nature of the curriculum, secondary education was recognisably careerist. It would have been clear to all that secondary schools channelled the minority of pupils who attended them into different kinds and levels of work and prepared them to meet the entry requirements where these existed.

As we have seen, the fact that this selective function could be performed with measured and relentless expertise is widely recorded in biographical writings of the period. The National Industrial Economic Council (1966, p. 4) in its *Comments on 'Investment in Education'*, expressed the view that the main reason why the majority of those who stay on in school beyond the legal minimum leaving age actually do so is with a view to requiring 'the facts, arts, skills and attitudes' required for the work place. Significantly, when the expansion, justified on the basis of the human capital paradigm, did occur it was to the traditional secondary schools, most identified with the theocentric paradigm, that the pupils flocked. Non-vocational in the narrow instrumental sense they may have been. This is probably the basis for Tussing's (1978, p. 65) assertion about *IIE* that 'perhaps its most important conclusion was its demonstration of the utter lack of correlation between the curriculum and the subsequent careers of pupils.' Yet, parents appear to have correctly interpreted the continuing and widening careerist potential of general secondary education. This was facilitated by expansion in the public service and in the service sector, which itself accounted for 80 per cent of the increase in employment during the 1970s. In fact, the situation was such that educational supply and labour market demand remained roughly in equilibrium until the recession of the 1980s (Hannan and Breen, 1987). This allowed Breen *et al.* (1990, p. 135) to conclude that 'no radical changes in educational goals or curriculum were required to meet the nature of the jobs becoming available to most school leavers.'

Two texts on educational expansion appeared to co-exist. One, to be found among civil servants and politicians within the policy-making sector, justified expansion, to one another and to international bodies in human capital terms as a necessary contribution to economic development and manpower needs. The other, dominant among parents, demanded an expansion in educational provision with a view to benefiting from its careerist potential though with no more than a minimal insistence on a change to a more explicitly vocational curriculum. There would be little cognitive dissonance as they were membershipped to the human capital paradigm. The careerist function of existing secondary schools provided a link to which the development of human capital could be mentally coupled in the evolution of Irish educational thought. For parents, in the horticulture of ideas, the human capital paradigm was less an implant than at first appears and more an outgrowth from their careerist interpretation of general education to which it was grafted and from which it drew sustenance.

It is improbable that politicians, state planners, teachers and parents all collectively and seamlessly adopted a human capital theorisation of education. Nor was it necessary that such a penetration of consciousness be achieved at that time for the long-term cultural impact of *IIE* to be realised. In 'hailing' the consciousness of these interested agents within the educational process, human capital theory offered distinctive and personalised benefits and attractions. For Department of Education officials, the reconfiguration of education as investment rather than consumption provided a justification, indeed imperative, for increased funding. It presented politicians with economic reasons for acceding to populist demands for an expansion of educational provision. The working conditions of lay teachers stood to benefit and the influx of extra teachers could be expected to enhance their leverage in their collective power relationships with church and state. For parents there was the promise of greater educational access and opportunity for their children. Of these, it was parents who proved to be most immediately receptive to cognitive change in their understanding of education. For them the vocational conceptualisation of education that came to be circulated subsequent to *IIE* captured in language what had previously been known in a loosely signified manner as career, at that time framed in the gaze of the theocentric paradigm. Within a few decades the relationship would be reversed. Whatever its differential appeal and degree of penetration of individual and collective consciousness, the immediate significance of the engagement of state officials, politicians, teachers and parents with the traces of human capital theory in *IIE* was the manner in which it brokered the insertion of its themes, in such forms as conceptualisation, language and performatives, into Irish educational discourse.

Cultural Agency: New themes and Factions

But in this process of cultural change, the participants were not passive. As they had interests, so also had they cultural agency. As *IIE* had been a loosely framed manifestation of human capital theory, the human capital paradigm experienced further modification as it became a feature of educational discourse. In engaging with the themes of expansion, investment, human capital, economic development and skill needs in the light of their distinctive material interests, state officials, politicians, teachers and parents drew out related themes from those presented to them in the human capital paradigm. These included the legitimacy of state activism, the 'people' as an undifferentiated construct possessing entitlements, the valorisation of quantification and economic rationality, the identification of aspects of the educational process as resources (possessing potential utility but requiring exploitation and management in pursuit of state goals), and an expanded conceptualisation of parents as discerning participants as well as suppliers of pupils to the school system. As the vocationalism of the human capital paradigm had spoken in a recognisable manner to the careerism of parents, in this mutated form it provided the state with a distinctive sphere of educational knowledge independent of the church that it could call its own.

The implication of its mutation for the already loosely framed human capital paradigm, as a paradigm, was the steady erosion of its distinctiveness as an interpretation of education. Once it spread beyond the economic planning cadre its associative basis became progressively atomised. For many, including politicians, teachers and parents, their engagement had been partial and self-interested. The state itself had potentially wider interests and perspectives than the provision of human resources for the economy. Mercantile themes – the state as manager, populist generation of state goals, commercial models of schools, secular expertise, and rationality and quantification – were now in evidence within the culture. With these changes, the boundaries of the human capital paradigm became less coherent and the way was open for its factioning along the fault lines of these components – themes, members and authorities.

Chapter 5

The Mercantile Paradigm:
Complementary Intertextuality

Mediated through the work of *IIE* and the emergent responses of significant agents and social configurations, the human capital paradigm provided the state with both a distinctive educational discourse and the basis for an authoritative status (as moderniser, producer of educational knowledge, etc.) that did not immediately appear to threaten religious interests in education. It appeared to have recognised and deployed a sphere of meaning about education that it could call its own and a range of performatives that it could legitimately consider and pursue in the national interest. Whereas previously state discourse on education invoking national aims would have been predominantly cultural, and particularly linguistic, it was now speaking in terms of the economy.

Social change in general was on the side of the state and statist discourse from the 1960s. As it textualised the themes made possible by the mutation of the human capital paradigm, the theocentric paradigm was experiencing contraction. The material dimension of this was most immediately obvious. Numerically, the involvement of religious in teaching declined. Prior to 1960, religious teachers outnumbered lay teachers in secondary schools (Barry, 1989). By 1969/1970 the representation of religious among full-time recognised secondary teachers had decreased to about a third, and to about a fifth in 1978/1979. This numerical reduction was followed by the appointment of lay teachers as principals in schools controlled by the religious orders. The declining representation of religious among the teaching body can be explained by reference to two interacting factors. Firstly, there was the increased influx of lay teachers from the 1960s onwards to cope with the expansion in pupil numbers caused by free education, higher expectations, a rising school-going population and a growing credentialism in occupational entry. The number of secondary school teachers doubled between 1967 and 1974 (Tussing, 1978). Secondly, making itself felt during the 1970s, there was a decline in religious vocations and an increase in the number leaving the religious life. In 1978, for instance, for every ten who entered the priesthood or religious life, seven others died and eight left (Inglis, 1979).

Whatever the origins of this dramatic decline in religious representation, it was clearly not self-induced by the religious orders themselves. The reaction of the religious authorities, though not passive, was a good deal more acquiescent than anyone might have expected. Vigorous recruitment campaigns, exhortations to parents, school-based programmes, or vocation-conscious enrolment policies in designated schools never materialised. Yet, a few short decades previously, during a phase of increasing membership of the priesthood and religious orders, such recruitment practices had been the norm (Titley, 1983a). And while the appointment of lay teachers as principals in religious schools seems retrospectively to have been inevitable, given the decline in the number of religious teachers available for such administrative and leadership roles, few would have predicted, when demands for promotional opportunities for lay teachers were first advanced, that change in this regard would have been so rapid and painless. In 1968 the view from within the Department of Education was that there would be 'an explosion, maybe sooner than later' in relation to the absence of promotional opportunities for lay teachers in religious secondary schools (O'Connor, 1968). And even a decade later, it was clear from Tussing's (1978) analysis of the changing lay/religious balance among secondary school teachers that he expected the issue to be contentious, referring to it in the context of 'teacher militancy'.

It would fail to do justice to the dynamics and nature of the change in the theocentric paradigm to treat it as a mere coping response on the part of religions to their declining representation among the teaching body. Within the church the deliberations of the Second Vatican Council helped to create a more open and questioning approach to the role of the church in society. In the view of a Jesuit educationalist (Barber, 1989, p. 99), the council's document on education was 'unexceptional' but it was the documents on the church and the modern world, on the laity and on the religious life that greatly influenced education and religion providing 'a climate for change within the Catholic Church and indirectly within Irish education'. A more positive and welcoming approach to lay participation in church affairs and a greater inclination among religious to see their vocation in terms other than teaching were important sources of change. Most fundamental of all was the breaching of the doxic qualities of the discourse on the church's involvement in the control of education, particularly in relation to the role of the state. We have seen in Chapter 3 how in Ireland the church had always claimed a primary role for itself in education and a superior right in relation to the state, arguing that 'education is first and supereminently the function of the church' (quoted in Kavanagh, 1966, p. 89). Yet, by the early 1970s what had been the verities of a doxic-like, tightly-framed and highly systematised paradigm were becoming the subject of intense speculation and debate within the church.

We find evidence of this in the FIRE report *Future Involvement of Religious in Education* in 1973. This was a report of a working party involving lay and religious personnel appointed jointly by the Catholic Hierarchy and the Conference of Major Religious Superiors (CMRS). The fact that in its deliberations it was felt necessary and appropriate to engage in rational and analytical discourse involving a range of non-religious domains of life suggests something of a legitimation crisis, even among religious themselves, with regard to their role in education. Their recognition of tension and contradiction in the system they presided over and managed – particularly in relation to its manifestations of materialism, privilege and power – sets the report apart from previous thinking. The fact that the report was meant for private circulation excludes any possibility that the exercise was one of posturing or public relations. Paradigmatically, the following discourse, themes, authorities and legitimation are foreign to those propagated by Kavanagh and Cronin on the primacy of the church's role in education:

> Religious schools are less and less needed to provide a service in education: the state will increasingly care for that aspect. Many religious schools now do little more than duplicate, more efficiently perhaps, what could be done by lay men. They do not show the strengths which could characterise religious-run schools, either in serving those in greatest need or in sensitivity to the real needs of the children now for the first time seeking post-primary education ... The recommendations ... are suggested as the only means of at once collaborating in the service of national needs, recognising the legitimate aspirations of lay secondary teachers and their role in moral and religious education, and finally ensuring the survival of Catholic schools in the pluralist system (FIRE Report, 1973, p. 3).

There is strong evidence here that the defining characteristics that give a paradigm a doxic status – connotations of rationality and common sense, deeply structured in discourse and consciousness, publicly uncontested, an absence of conceivable alternatives and a non-recognition or misrecognition of contradictions or change – are at the very least in the process of being eroded. While there have been diverse views on the significance of the FIRE Report for subsequent educational practice (Barber, 1989; O'Sullivan, 1996a; Andrews, 1997; Walsh, 1997), paradigmatically it represents a breaching of the limits of what was thinkable, sayable and possible, most significantly within the church itself, in relation to the control and nature of education.

Of particular significance was the growing discrimination being exercised by the laity in engaging with church teaching. Keogh correctly identifies the publication of the encyclical *Humanae Vitae* in 1968 as a pivotal indicator in this regard. Its affirmation of traditional papal condemnation of artificial methods of birth control, he argues 'challenge(d) the laity to think for themselves and become, as a consequence, more independent of hierarchical structures' (1994, p. 267). Personal intimacy and pedagogical orientation may seem far removed from one another, but they shared a worldly space, that had come to be differentiated from the sacred and appropriated and defined in terms of lay authority and competence, in which lay people increasingly made decisions on the basis of personal experience and material needs. Rather than a rejection of church teaching, this is best understood as a reclassification of sacred and profane domains of power/knowledge.

In tracing the erosion of the church's regulation of the worldly understandings of people, it is appropriate in the light of the receptivity of parents, in particular, to the human capital paradigm, to revisit an issue left hanging in Chapter 3. This is the extent to which the consciousness of parents about education was ever fully penetrated by the theocentric paradigm. While proclaimed, in line with the principle of subsidiarity, as the first educators and as having a prior right in relation to the education of their children, parents would have been obliged to act as mute followers in the social formations that maintained and reproduced the theocentric paradigm. Such was the paternalism of the relationship, derived from the knowledge/power disparity involved, that church authorities experienced no difficulty in speaking for parents, and indeed, as the unquestioned experts, would have felt an obligation to them to do so. Ensuring the followership of parents would not have been a source of anxiety for the church. The smugness of certainty induced by a doxic-like paradigm, its Achilles' heel, allowed behavioural compliance to be interpreted as internalisation.

For parents, general education, seen in terms of its career potential, had been the predominant conceptualisation of education. While they would have dissented little, if at all, from the full range of church positions on education and, most particularly, not from the authority of the church's leadership and control in education, the framing of the theocentric paradigm was never as rigorous in the popular understanding as in official church and state discourse. Parents (and teachers) would have experienced no conflict between careerism and church teaching on education. They would have easily made their sense of the worldliness of schooling compatible with personal salvation. This was facilitated by the popular discourse of the pulpit in which, unlike linguistic revival where the school was the prime agent of the project, it was the home rather than the school that was allocated responsibility for the transmission of the faith. When the human capital paradigm, with its linking of the school and the workplace in a rationale for expanded educational opportunities, presented itself it had no difficulty in membershipping parents. In fact it represented a more natural cultural homeland for them. Not alone did they recognise in it an understanding of education that they shared but it also named and legitimated in official discourse what they had previously lived namelessly, subordinated and co-opted under the dominion of the theocentric paradigm.

The obvious worldliness of the economy allowed the state to enter the educational policy process with confidence and to become increasingly active. As the human capital paradigm expanded thematically, socially and politically, so also did the sphere of authority of the state. This more wide-ranging authoritative status was attained without obvious design or demand for new powers in a manner that was procedurally, culturally and politically compatible with Irish society as it was developing from the 1970s. The fact that it was by mutation that the human capital paradigm had expanded facilitated this, both in its nature and substance. As we have seen in the previous chapter, new themes were introduced to the cultural understanding of education by the mutation of the human capital paradigm. These included the legitimacy of state activism, populism and parental agency, the appropriateness of economic and commercial models and exemplars, and the educational institution as a system of identifiable, measurable and manageable resources. There was no public discourse, much less advocacy, of these additions to the core human capital themes of education as investment in economic development and the claims of the workplace on the content of schooling. As a series of unreflexive mutations, the entire process appeared as a seamless expansion – cognitively compatible, culturally unremarkable and politically unthreatening.

Yet, it was an emergent and interested production of agents and social configurations engaging with the traces of the human capital paradigm promulgated with the publication of *IIE* and eventually extending its boundaries – relating to themes, members and authorities – to the point of their disruption. While these would have felt that they were participating in the modernisation of Irish education, this study argues that the process is best understood in terms of detraditionalisation in Irish society at large. In an unreflexive haste to escape from aspects of its past, to make up as it were for lost time, change was sought in terms of its 'other' rather than of an independently-framed, desired future social order. This will be elaborated on in the Epilogue. Suffice is to say here that it was not a linear process. As well as the 'mixed temporalities and uneven development' that Munck (2003) diagnoses in contemporary Irish development, there were contradictory and ambivalent subjectivities that are not even captured in a traditional/modern hybridity of the self.

With the textualisation of the themes of the mutating human capital paradigm, – to which the new members and authorities generated by it contributed, along with the state – the human capital paradigm factions. The human capital paradigm contracted to its basis in economic theory and, as we have seen, continues to exist in modified forms within the field of economic research, and in a more specific sense within educational policy discourse. There, it provided another resource, along with the new strands of meaning-making and recognisible fields of knowledge production that it had originally facilitated, for the construction of the mercantile paradigm. From these five texts can be excavated – commercial, managerial, vocational, consumer, and market – to illuminate this process of paradigm formation. This selection does not exhaust the extent of cultural change in relation to education occurring at this time. Their labelling carries no value connotations. Nor is one seeking to address the benefits, appropriateness or limitations of the educational practices involved. The focus is on these texts as strands of meaning-making and not on their instrumental effects within the system.

The concern here is not to address the merits of particular educational practices *per se*, but to trace the cultural transformation that those texts signify and sustain, and reveal to analysis. It should be possible to treat these strands of meaning-making and knowledge production as instantiations of specific paradigms relating to school organisation, function, relationships and provision. Taking the broader view of the institutional perspective, as is done here, these texts are presented as manifestations of the cultural resources that, in their symbiotic, mutually-legitimating and generative linkages, construct the mercantile paradigm. This is an evolving and unfinished project in that it is scarcely possible to speak of a mercantile text as such. Rather, it is in intertextuality that the mercantile paradigm is produced and made available for analysis. A brief sketching of these five texts should allow us to progress the illumination of this process.

The Commercial Text

The commercialisation of schooling was reflected in the educational 'problems' of the 1960s – the viability of school units of varying sizes, economies of scale, efficient use of resources (be they specialist teachers, laboratories or woodwork/metalwork rooms) and society's need for the development of all its talents. Wastage, deficit, surplus and overlap recurred as the 'terminology of concern' about the system. This is evident in *IIE* itself and in the 'comments' on it by the National Industrial Economic Council (1966), particularly in what it recommended as the agenda for the enquiries of the proposed educational development unit. Schools were viewed under the influence of a commercial model, with all the measures, meanings, anxieties and objectives of the world of commerce, where unbalanced books, under-utilised resources and high unit costs were the salient vices and the imperatives for intervention. The context was increased demands for expenditure in the light of expanding participation that would last until the 1990s. The immediate impact on practice of this paradigmatic shift is debatable. The appeal of Minister of Education, George Colley, in what came to be known as his 'co-operation letter' to the authorities of secondary and vocational schools in 1966, requesting their co-operation in the pooling of post-primary facilities at local level is generally considered to have had a very limited affect. A year later, a ministerial proposal to rationalise the provision of university education in the Dublin area with a view to avoiding the duplication of faculties by Trinity College and University College, Dublin came to naught (Coolahan, 2000). At that time, a more material influence of this change of consciousness is to be found in the policy of amalgamating small primary schools which had been found to be the most expensive to build, maintain and staff. The Government policy of amalgamating and rationalising one- and two-teacher schools resulted in their reduction from 3,194 in 1962 to 900 in 1984, and created its share of national and local controversy (Coolahan, 1989).

A potent indicator of the penetration of the commercial text is the manner in which the Future Involvement of Religion in Education (FIRE) Report of 1973, referred to earlier, enunciated it in justifying the continuity role for religious in Irish education. It pointed to the flexibility with which religious could be deployed within and between schools because of their lack of permanent contract or security of tenure, or restriction to 'school hours', and the resultant benefits for extra-curricular activities, alternative programmes and special needs. As they put it, 'the obedience of religious is a material factor in the character of their schools' (p. 9). This illuminates the process of the replacement of the theocentric with the mercantile paradigm. It represents a point at which the advocates of religious involvement in education, who a decade earlier would have confidently asserted church teaching on its supreme power in education, found themselves participating, perhaps even feeling obliged to do so to make their arguments meaningful in the changing cultural understanding of education, in the commercial discourse of the emerging mercantile paradigm. Here we find the church enhancing the credibility of alternative educational meanings in using their logic, and signalling the disruption of the doxic status of church teaching on education as it seeks to reposition itself in the changing cultural scene.

Subsequently, viewing educational institutions along commercial lines became routine. Staff might complain about form filling and the inappropriateness of the techniques, and speak with derision about such practices as unit cost studies in the universities (Kane, 1996), but it has been commonplace for some time for universities to employ quantified budgetary protocols, process new course proposals along the lines of product development (costings, demand, resources), diversify their programmes in the light of market needs, be compared in terms of student completion rates, follow up on the labour market experience of their graduates and even conduct market research on what they should use as a trading name. At third level, also, there has been an encouragement to institutions to be less dependent on state funding and to seek out more financial support from industrial and commercial bodies through contract research, service provision, and endowed positions. Relatedly, there has been the development of alumni associations and economic fee-paying students (HEA, 2003). This is now deemed unremarkable and attaining doxic qualities. A fuller account, together with its theorisation, is provided in Skilbeck's *The University Challenged* (2001).

The Managerial Text

Educational institutions came to be regarded as human organisations pursuing a specific set of goals. As such, they were considered to have similar managerial needs – goal setting, policy making, job-specification, motivation, co-ordination of roles and sectors, decision making, implementation, evaluation, managing change, and internal and external communications – to organisational settings that in the past would not have been regarded as having much in common with the task of education. The recognition was associated with the emergence of certificate and post-graduate diploma courses in educational administration from the late 1970s. In his review of these courses during the 1980s, Diggins (1990) explains that their development 'coincides with the development of a greater awareness among educators of the importance of educational administration in the effective and efficient running of schools'. The context was one of financial cutbacks, school closures, rationalisations and amalgamations. Teacher mobility was low and few new teachers were being employed. Reflecting an international pattern, the proper management of one's existing resources as distinct from demands for more was accentuated. As Diggins puts it, 'there is an increasing awareness of the necessity for school based/focused staff development programmes … (which) in turn require even greater understanding of the leadership role, of theories of motivation and practices and calls for more administrative skills.'

But these courses provided more than skills; they also contributed to the provision of new subjectivities and discourses. School principals, who in the past would have been practising teachers and viewed as *primus inter pares* (not necessarily benign) now occupied distinct roles. The extent of this shift is exemplified by the formation of separate associations for principals at primary and post-primary levels, the former amid some controversy with the INTO. For the Green Paper on Education (1992, p. 148) the principal was conceptualised as 'the chief executive of the school' and allocated standard management duties in a chapter entitled 'making the best use of resources'. There was dissent from this in the Report of the National Education Convention which expressed an anxiety that principals might be recruited from the ranks of professional administrators, arguing that 'the role of the principal as instructional leader clearly distinguished this position from that of the manager or chief executive in a business environment' (Coolahan, 1994, p. 43). This was reflected in the less threatening and discordant, though nonetheless managerial, treatment of the role of the principal in the White Paper that followed.

Greater specialisation within the teaching profession and posts of responsibility associated with designated duties further differentiated roles within schools that in the past were organisationally simple. The evolution of these posts of responsibility and their unrelatedness to the management needs of schools was considered by the National Education Convention in terms of middle management and a proposal for its reorganisation. Practical, operational issues received a great deal of attention in this regard – job specifications, training, induction, and the management of change, etc. However, different models of management were also discussed:

> One view was that the hierarchical nature of the present management structure in school was built on an out-dated industrial model and was unsuited to the needs of the institution. In its place an organic model, based on a collaborative concept of management, was proposed. This would seek to involve all of the staff in the management of the school and would promote group planning and management through a consensus approach (p. 49).

Apart from this, there is little evidence of an alertness among the participants at the Convention to issues of power, control and the possibility of new forms of regulation emerging. This is not to suggest that there was an unawareness of such issues but that there was an apparent confidence that *educators, educational* issues and *educational* values would prevail. The managerial themes from the discussions on policy formulation, the role of the Department of Education, quality assurance and intermediate educational tiers do not get to be discussed as such or even considered in the context of school management. Quality assurance in Higher Education seems to have been approached with an awareness of more threatening international trends. Yet, here also there is a sense of self-belief that the threat could be contained by self-initiation of procedures of peer review and audit within higher education institutions rather than waiting for the state to impose them from above.

The simplified managerial text being realised around this time reveals the extent to which managerialism has become well-positioned, particularly in higher education, in recent years. This is disguised by setting it alongside the English New Managerialism, the dominance of which in education and throughout the public sector has been extensively studied (Gewirtz *et al., 1995*; Clarke and Newman, 1997; Exworthy and Halford, 1999; Clarke *et al.* 2000; Gewirtz, 2002; Willmott, 2002).

The managerial text did not confine itself to organisational settings in education. It was also generated and deployed in proposals for the establishment of local education committees. This is just one strand of recurring knowledge production around constructs such as regionalisation, sub-national structures, intermediate or middle tiers on the governance of Irish education which also generate texts on local democracy/representation, efficiency and accountability (O'Reilly, 1992; Brown and Fairley, 1993; Coolahan, 1994; Walshe, 1999). The managerial text came to the fore in the 1990s with the controversy between the CMRS Education Commission and the Council of Managers of Catholic Secondary Schools (CMCSS) on the former's support for local education committees (Walshe, 1999). For the Education Commission, the strength of such committees was the manner in which they would act as a regulatory body, curbing the practices of individual schools, such as those relating to pupil admission, that have negative consequences for schools in disadvantaged areas. For the CMCSS there was the fear of an erosion of the autonomy of their schools. The Green Paper had proposed a greater devolution of budgeting and decision-making powers to individual schools. For those who believed that the failure of the educational system to adequately address the problem of underachieving pupils from deprived backgrounds would be further exacerbated by this proposal, local education committees were expected to replace competition with collective responsibility for inequality and disadvantage: 'our current system ensures that not only is there no institution responsible for the public or collective good, conceived of at a local community level in ensuring equality of access and treatment of each child (particularly the weaker child), but the high degree of competition between local schools almost ensures inequality of access and treatment' (Hannan, 1993).

A statist interpretation, which equates state policy with the pursuit of the public good, would favourably conceive of local education committees as mechanisms for the more effective penetration of state policy to the operational levels of schools and classrooms. As Breen *et al.* (1990) put it in reference to the proposals, for curricular and structural reform of post-primary schooling in the 1960s: 'had the state, directly or otherwise, owned the schools themselves then the prospects for the rationalisation of facilities and a comprehensive curriculum would have been much brighter' (p. 138). In the circumstances, 'it became impossible for the Department of Education either to direct enrolments into specific kinds of schools or to effect curricular changes that would ensure a substantial move to a more vocationally orientated form of education' (p. 137).

For the NESC, in two reports, *A Strategy for the Nineties* in 1990 and *Education and Training Policies for Economic and Social Development* in 1993, its support for local education structures was expressed 'not in terms of any particular reallocation of power, but rather on the basis of more effective service provision and more efficient use of available resources' (1993, p. 220). This was in the context of a rapid rise in public expenditure on education since the 1960s and its recommendation in its 1990 report on the need to review educational policy in the light of demographic change, constrained public funding, and a changing environment for education.

The discourse on local education committees generated, among others, a managerial text that held out the possibility of influencing the practices of individual schools in the absence of the power to direct change or demand compliance. Local education committees would achieve this effect by reconfiguring the way those who had material power over individual schools in the area related to one another and to other interests in the pursuit of their goals, using the standard managerial procedures of participation, negotiation, consultation, conviction, social pressure and inducements. But more than interpersonal relations are involved. As private institutions with a public service function, voluntary secondary schools would find themselves 'positioned in a new field of forces' (Clarke and Newman, 1997, p. 30) at the intersection of state and civil society that involved those to be represented on local education committees and organised interests as well as the state. This has been described as 'managerialised dispersal' (p. 29), a process of transferring tasks, roles and responsibilities outwards from the state in a manner that disperses power among other agents in its field of relationships. This needs to be seen as a political strategy that reconstructs the state and coordinates its education function: 'dispersal has meant the simultaneous shrinking of the state and the enlargement of its reach into civil society (through its engagement of non-state agents). As a strategy of state reconstruction, dispersal has realigned power in a complex way. Above all it has sought to discipline and transform the old institutional sites of power …' (p. 29). The context in which these concepts are being developed is the transformation of the British welfare state. While it has been applied here in relation to voluntary secondary schools, its implications run far wider. Nor can it be assumed that the effects of such a reconstructed state would necessarily be oriented to the common good and social democratic values, as some advocates of local education committees had hoped, or for that matter be even benign in nature.

This exploration of the managerial text in Irish education is not seeking to address issues of 'good' or 'bad' management practice or to be pejorative about what might be regarded as the introduction of inappropriate business models of decision-making in schools and colleges (Skilbeck, 2001). Nor is it necessary to implicate at this stage those structural changes associated with the New Managerialism, such as the distancing of the political centre from educational institutions by means of intermediate, semi-autonomous and increasingly lay, government-appointed committees and boards (Beck, 1998). Here, the interactionist and governmental understanding of managerialism is deployed to refer to a social technology of control and self-regulation through which the behaviour of others is shaped, coordinated and directed with a view to bringing about predetermined ends, getting them to do what is 'best' even in spite of themselves, or ideally because they have been brought to desire to do so. The latter produces self-regulating teachers which reduces the need for systematised surveillance and controls behaviour that cannot be readily reached and governed by legislation. This requires that teachers 'learn to be managed' (Ball, 1990, p. 122). Trust must be won by teachers through performances that exhibit and confirm such learning. In the process, they become more resources than agents, and professionalism is resignified in terms of managed, self-regulating subjectivities, or at least as adaptation to accommodating roles.

The managerial text can be discordant with the traditional understanding of teaching in terms of semi-autonomous, professional judgement and what remains of the quasi-religious status of teaching as vocation. In England, the New Managerialism is said to attempt to manage such tensions by fusing Neo-Taylorist with Post-Taylorist management practices (Gewirtz, 2002). The Neo-Taylorist orientation is to rationalise, regulate, set targets and performance indicators, and to reward those who demonstrate merit within these terms (Exworthy and Halford, 1999). But since this fits uneasily with professionalism and related public service tendencies such as collegiality and trust, Post-Taylorist collectivising practices are employed. These involve the formulation of mission statements and visions, and invitations to creatively contribute to organisational cultures of performance review and self-improvement. Professionals are then invited to be hailed in their occupational identities by this mix, and to see in these regulative practices and self-regulating subjectivities more contemporary forms of professionalism. This intertextual combination of Neo-Taylorist and Post-Taylorist management practices is recognisable as an emergent pattern in Irish education, in particular at university level. There it is presented as progressive and sensitive to academic values and is enhanced in its legitimacy by the absence of a counter-text, or one that disentangles its component texts, that cannot be diminished as nostalgia for a simpler era.

The more powerful primary and post-primary teaching bodies can be expected to oppose whatever they perceive to be undue regulation and monitoring of the work of teachers, and culturally resist the resignification of the construct of professionalism. In consequence, the managerial text needs conducive circumstances – the heightening of themes such as the pursuit of national, 'common good' aims, commercially-inefficient schools, 'under-performing' teachers, schools unresponsive to parental needs, etc. – to gain entry to discourse. Because of this, as we shall see later in the analysis of intertextuality, managerialism is more easily invoked in the wake of commercial and consumer texts. Thus positioned, managerial constructs and practices that otherwise might be experienced as conceptually dissonant and disruptive of communication achieve thematisation in discourse seeking to promote effective, efficient and quality schools. In such circumstances, the objections of teaching organisations can be counter-productive: they are liable to be signified as resistance to the modernisation of schools in general, luddite in defense of teacher self-interest, and used to further legitimate the rationale of the managerialism that is being challenged.

The Vocational Text

Assumptions about the necessity of vocationalising the curriculum experienced a penetration of discourse and practice in education to different degrees. Since the 1960s the need for the post-primary curriculum to embody a greater relevance to the demands of the work place had been a recurring theme in educational discourse. In this regard, the widely-quoted views expressed by Dr Patrick Hillery as Minister for Education in 1964 are more blunt than most:

> Secondary education ... is only one stream. What we really need in this country is the other stream, technical and scientific. We need to develop these ... if you were to give secondary grammar academic type of education to everybody, you would be wasting your money ... you would be getting too many people taking a course which is no use to most of them – we haven't jobs for them, we haven't need for them (quoted in Mulcahy 1981a, p. 21).

Public attention to schooling accorded a high priority to vocational relevance. Programmes and schemes which sought to prepare young people for the world of work attained a high profile in the mass media and in the manner in which the government and Department of Education represented the Irish educational system to outside bodies (Department of Education, 1984b).

State representation of post-primary schooling tended to accentuate the provision and uptake of languages and scientific, commercial and technological subjects. In particular, the pattern was to emphasise how government policy had responded to criticisms of the second-level curriculum as being 'excessively academic in content and method – a criticism implied ... in the OECD study *Investment in Education*' (*White Paper on Educational Development*, 1980, p. 44). Agencies such as ANCO (The Industrial Training Authority) and the YEA (Youth Employment Agency), later amalgamated under FÁS (Foras Áiseanna Saothair), assumed increasing responsibility for the more instrumentally-vocational preparation of young people for the labour market. Such programmes achieved a normative status as a socially-concerned response to the growing problem of youth unemployment during the 1980s. The activism of these vocational preparation and training programmes caused them to be valorised when contrasted with the traditional curriculum of the post-primary school which was castigated as irrelevant to the demands of the labour market and unresponsive to the needs of young people (Conniffe and Kennedy, 1984). The relationships between the state departments, education and training institutions and educational sectors involved have been characterised in terms of 'internal politics' (O'Connor, 1998) and 'tension and rivalry' (Gleeson, 2000). To argue that the high incidence of youth unemployment was a labour market rather than a curricular problem would have been to disrupt the paradigmatic assumptions of the discourse and risk exclusion from the policy community of concerned educators.

Accusations of an over-academic bias in the educational system continued into the 1990s, most publicly in the Culliton Report and Green Paper of 1992. Over time, the foregrounding of the school/work nexus produced the anachronism of the same educational system that had been accused of unresponsiveness to youth unemployment finding itself, within the decade, lauded for its contribution to the Celtic Tiger. As the 1990s progressed, while the labour market disadvantage of early school leavers remained in focus, there was now the new concern of skill shortages in the expanding economy, and the state response in the form of targeted training programmes such as the £250 million Educational Technology Investment Fund announced in 1997 (Gleeson, 2000).

The impact on the post-primary curriculum has been described as general rather than specific. A detailed analysis of the increase in vocationalism in Irish education from the late 1960s published in 1987 concluded as follows in the light of the nature of the vocational offerings and the numbers of students involved.

> The types of vocational education being offered in schools would seem for the most part to be the most general, designed to make students adaptable in the working environment rather than providing them with any occupationally specific skills or even skills of a group of occupations which utilise a range of similar skills (Lewis and Kellaghan, 1987).

This still remains a fair assessment of the current character of the formal post-primary curriculum, particularly in the light of the failure of the White Paper to endorse the Culliton Report's (1992) advocacy of a dual system of academic and vocational education at senior cycle. The introduction of the Leaving Certificate Vocational Programme modifies the situation somewhat as does the greater technicisation experienced by the post-primary curriculum as it broadened in recent decades (Drudy and Lynch, 1993). As well as interpreting this as an indication of the success of business and scientific sectors in defining what is appropriate school knowledge, it has also been traced more deeply to the emergence of economic self-interest as a 'cultural value' (Lynch, 1982; Clancy, 1995b).

Whatever about moving the curriculum in a more vocationally specific direction, aspects of it that would have been justified as general or liberal education have been reconceptualised in terms of their vocational relevance. Business and related studies and continental languages are examples (Sheehan, 1992). The Irish Business and Employers' Confederation lists among the merits of a broadly-based education the provision of trainable and adaptable workers (Gleeson, 2000). The skills and subjectivities cultivated by the newer pedagogies

– group work and projects, experiential and active learning and drama-in-education techniques – have been linked with the needs of new working practices, often referred to as post-Fordism (Piore and Sabel, 1984; Ashley, 1997), such as team work, 'flexible specialisation', multiple roles, short-run production, contract work, and increased autonomy and responsibility in outcentres and work units. In this manner, traditional texts on curriculum such as personal development, general and liberal education become diminished in their cultural meaningfulness and in their interpellation of subjectivities as their referents in terms of student formation are reinterpreted in a vocational text that doubly gains in dominion through the disablement of its competitors and the appropriation of their resources.

Indicative of this cultural shift is the existence of school-business linkages such as corporate support and sponsorship for school resources and events, but particularly the expansion of enterprise, junior achievement and mini-company schemes since the late 1970s. These encourage pupils, including those in primary school, to role-play business practices – company formation, raising capital, division of labour, market research, product development, production, distribution and sales – in a quasi-commercial setting. *The Irish Times* (9 December, 1999) carried a report of an event, which it sponsored, at which individuals including primary school teachers, who had made a contribution to bringing the business world into the classroom were applauded. A patron of the scheme, in presenting the awards, explained that 'the next generation had to learn about business at an early age if an enterprise culture was to be fostered'. A mini-company has been described 'as a business enterprise undertaken by young people using real money under circumstances where they can make decisions, take risks and sometimes make major mistakes without serious consequences. It is a simulation of the real business world where a school can provide a structured series of experiences aimed at helping the young participants to come to terms with aspects of the adult working world' (Ó Donnabháin, 1990). While there was considerable unease about the place of enterprise in the 1992 Green Paper, in terms of emphasis and curriculum change (Coolahan, 1994), this has not transferred to these school-business linkages which have been accepted as normatively unremarkable and even innovative.

The targeting of schools, parents and pupils in corporate promotions has attracted criticism and is the subject of departmental guidelines. Consumer education for young people has also been developed (Ní Aonghusa, 1997). What these safeguards and consumer-awareness programmes do not make problematic is the manner in which the taken-for-granted presence of school-business programmes in schools, and the energy, activity and publicity activated by them, represent a non-discursive contribution to the construction of the vocational text as well as constituting pupil subjectivities relating to trade/exchange that valorise economic self-interest. The unremarkable reality that members of the local business community are likely to be more visible than parish clergy in Catholic secondary schools acts as a trope of the transition from a theocentric to a mercantile paradigm.

The vocationalisation of the curriculum has been most apparent at third level. This occurred through the establishment of new educational institutions such as the Regional Technical Colleges (later Institutes of Technology) and the National Institutes of Higher Education (later Limerick and Dublin City Universities), as well as through the expansion of science and technology programmes in the traditional universities. In the most recent national survey, of first-time entrants to third-level institutions in 1998, it was found that the university sector thus expanded still accounted for fewer of the new entrants than the Institutes of Technology, while technology was the field of study of the largest percentage (26%), followed by commerce (21%), humanities (17%) and science and agriculture (14%) (Clancy, 2001). In fact, comparatively, a feature of the expansion of higher education in Ireland continues to be the high proportion of students taking short-cycle sub-degree level vocational courses.

The Consumer Text

Conceptualising parents and pupils as users rather than recipients and beneficiaries of education constructed a consumer text, effectively reworking an older parent participation text. In her address to the National Parents Council at Easter 1991, Minister for Education, Mary O'Rourke argued that 'we need to openly address the issue of "Parent Power" alongside "Teacher Power" and "Church Power"' (O'Rourke, 1991). To this end she recommended active Parent Associations, a clear strategy for parental involvement to be built into the policy of individual schools, and full participation of parent representatives in Board of Management decision making. These recommendations were subsequently communicated to schools in circular 24/91 'Parents as Partners in Education' (Department of Education, 1991).

Like earlier advocacy of the role of parents in education this must be understood in its context. Religious encouragement of greater parental involvement, pioneered by the Christian Brothers in the 1970s, has been described as a 'means of marshalling the support of parents in maintaining the status and preserving the character of religious-owned schools faced with changes which were perceived to be a threat to their future' (Walsh, 1997, p. 277). The subsequent establishment of the National Parents' Council in 1985 had the effect of diluting the power of the Congress of Catholic Secondary School Parents' Associations, that had grown from the activism of the National Federation of Christian Brothers Schools Parents' Councils, and the constitution of a less confessional parental voice in education. The Minister for Education, Gemma

Hussey, who established the National Parents' Council, recorded how at its first meeting the delegates of the Catholic Secondary School Parents' Association were 'peering frostily' at her (Hussey, 1990, p. 163).

In the 1990s, parents were being recast as consumers and were routinely described in this manner in state and policy discourse. We have already seen how the NESC's Report *A Strategy for the Nineties* (1990, pp 313-314) had championed the principle of consumer representation and criticised the absence of accessible factual and evaluative data about the quality of schools to allow parents to make appropriate educational choices. At third level it spoke of parents and students exercising 'a degree of choice in relation to institutions and courses', and argued that 'as "consumers" they are organised and formally represented (through Students Unions) in the educational system'.

The traces of the Total Quality Management movement were discernible in discourse. In this, organisations were encouraged to orientate their activities, relations with their public and self-assessment and self-regulation in terms of the needs and demands of their users. 'Quality' and 'consumer' became inextricably linked in this discourse that expanded to areas as diverse as business, engineering, food industry, human services, information services and the public sector. Murgatroyd and Morgan's (1992) *Total Quality Management and the School* was to be its most influential representation in education.

The 1992 Green Paper devoted a full chapter to quality assurance and it also figured prominently in the chapters on Higher Education, The Teaching Profession and Ireland as an International Education Centre. Working parties, pilot schemes, structures and personnel devoted to the assessment and assurance of quality became routine in higher education institutions. At second level 'quality' was to be found in mission statements, prospectuses and course and programme guidelines and objectives. Richard Bruton, as Fine Gael spokesman on education, became a consistent advocate of the quality management principles. Sensing that 'quality management concepts are viewed by many within the education system as something threatening rather than fulfilling', he sought to allay the fears of teachers in an opinion piece in *The Irish Times Education and Living Supplement*, 17 March 1998. 'Quality improvement', he explained, 'goes to the heart of modern management. It involves systematic analysis of what an organisation does, benchmarking against other players and reorganising their work so that they operate as a more cohesive team to improve results.' He advocated comparisons between schools using less crude measures of quality than examination results, opportunities for parents to fill out confidential questionnaires each year about their experiences and, invoking the managerial text, 'strong personal development policies' to enlist the support of teachers.

The Market Text

Overall, there has been little discursive production of a market text in which schools, third-level institutions and training institutes are represented as competitors, offering choices of service to educational consumers. What has been said or written, positively or negatively, to realise such an understanding of education is oblique and unsustained. An era in which third-level institutions were encouraged to be less dependent on state funding and to seek out more financial support from industrial and commercial bodies through contract research, service provision and endowed positions also experienced the abolition of undergraduate fees. The 1992 Green Paper proposed that 'the maximum possible operational and management autonomy will be accorded to schools and colleges' (p. 156). Similarly, in her reported response to the OECD examiners at their Paris meeting following its 1991 report on Irish education, the Minister for Education Mary O'Rourke indicated a preference, over regionalised administrative structures, for greater budgetary control to be devolved to individual schools. Yet, the two Ministers involved, Séamus Brennan in the case of the Green Paper, shifted position on the virtues of making individual schools more autonomous (Walshe, 1999). Nonetheless, the signing of the Bologna Declaration which seeks a united European approach to higher education initiated an explicit phase of market discourse that continues. It was described by the chairman of the Higher Education Authority as a 'wake-up call' to those involved in higher education to learn to compete in a global market place, 'in what will increasingly be a more demanding international environment' (Oliver, 2001).

Yet, it is through the non-discursive mechanism of actual provision of education and the practices and subjectivities within schools and among parents and pupils that the market meaning of education is substantially produced, communicated and maintained as a way of understanding education. In Ireland, parents have always been free to seek a place in the school of their choice for their children (OECD/CERI, 1997). While this freedom was constrained by practicalities of space and transport, as well as local or school conventions on entry policies, the existence of a market of educational services and providers has long been a feature of parental consciousness about education, even among those who had difficulty in benefiting from it. In urban areas it has been both a public and unremarkable practice for parents to send their children to schools other than their local one on the basis of such factors as size, medium of instruction, religious/lay staffing, sexual composition, academic reputation, games, disciplinary climate and provision for special needs. Even in rural areas, Hallak and McCabe (1973) found that in the 1960s parents in Sligo were clearly selecting between the available post-primary schools in the region on the basis of more than unreflexive convenience. In some instances, this market behaviour became quite explicit in cases, not uncommon in rural Ireland, where parents, dissatisfied with local school provision hired private transport to avail of a preferred school outside of the area. This is apart from those parents who sent their children to boarding schools (Mac Cárthaigh, 1980). Overall, it has been estimated that a half of all second-level students do not attend their nearest school (Hannan *et al.*, 1996).

From the perspective of the schools themselves, seeking to attract a greater share of the available pupils is not a new phenomenon. There are records of tension, rivalry and occasional disputes in relation to the movement of pupils between primary schools (O'Connell, 1969). It has been routine for decades for post-primary school principals to make recruiting visits to the senior classes of local primary schools. The examination results of individual pupils, involving levels of achievement, 'calls to training', university scholarships and offers of state employment were published in local newspapers. Now it is not uncommon for schools to produce promotional brochures and videos, organise open days to promote the school and represent it in a particular manner, and to be conscious of the need to be seen to participate in educational, sporting, cultural and artistic events and competitions and to publicise successes. School policy on the timing of the school day, allocation of holidays, uniform, additional subjects and activities both during and after school hours became increasingly responsive to market trends and the practices of competitors. A falling school-going population has fuelled this competition for pupils. Competition is more explicit at third level where the share of first preferences under the CAO system, and their academic quality, and the percentage of national research funding won in competition are viewed and publicised as indicates of an institution's success.

The most explicit signification of an education market is the operation of profit-driven provision of educational services. Grinds, in the form of the provision of private tuition, have developed in some instances into tutorial centres that are availed of to supplement regular schooling. But there are now in existence, at both second and third level, full-time educational institutions that constitute a response to the existence of a market for educational services. In 1992, the Green Paper adverted to the 'major growth' (p. 178) in this area. At second level such institutions have received a hostile reception from the teaching associations. At third level they have been treated with suspicion by the state, with the Green Paper proposing an approval and registration process on a cost-recovery basis 'in the interests of consumer protection' (p. 178). The state's acceptance in 2003 of an on-line teacher education programme of a private provider, Hibernia College, may suggest a changed orientation.

There is little evidence of any advocacy of the creation of such educational markets as a matter of educational policy in the pursuit of quality and efficiency. But, nonetheless, in the past decade or so the earlier awareness of choice has elaborated to a conceptualisation of education as a service to be bought and sold that continues to be textualised by means of a largely non-discursive market signification through the production and provision practices of schools, the consumption practices of parents and pupils, and the expansion of commercial ventures in education. The effect has been the reworking of the meaning of public service that erodes the public/private dualism and that conflates the emerging sense of 'voice' with 'exit' and 'choice' (Levin, 1991) as the mechanism by which parents can exercise control over the schooling their children receive. What were agents of a theocentric/state project are increasingly providers of educational services in a trading environment.

Complementary Intertextuality

There is no sense in which the centrality of trade/exchange in the institutional understanding of education can be revealed by a sealed reading of these texts, considered individually or even collectively. In any event, commercial, managerial, vocational, consumer and market texts are themselves extracted by processes of interpretation and selection from the mosaic of cultural signification relating to Irish education. Within these parameters, it is the cultural transformation produced and revealed by these texts rather than their sum that represents the limited instantiation of the mercantile paradigm. This takes the form of a complementary intertextuality in which mutually supporting, validating and symbiotic texts realise meanings that range beyond what they textually produce individually.

It is easier to understand this dynamic by beginning with the interdependency of the consumer and market texts. To act as a consumer requires the existence of some version of an education market. To be able to make choices in how one educates one's children, it is necessary that there be diversity in the nature of the education provided by schools and colleges together with an absence of prohibition in accessing them. Conversely, the existence of an education market presents parents (and pupils) with choices, and positions them as consumers, obliging them to judge and choose.

But consumer and market texts do not merely sustain one another in a fixed loop. They also mutually intensify and systematise each other. If seen in paradigmatic terms in relation to people and systems in education, they exhibit a tendency to merge around nodal points of conceptualisation, performatives and subjectivities. In the process, other themes are implicated (recruited) from within the cultural tapestry of which both texts are a part and from which they have been analytically extracted. Rights and consumer discourse from other social sites besides education, themes of risk and its regulation, together with associated legislation and structures of monitoring, protocols and agencies, relating to the use of services are obvious examples. A range of practices and issues – from the weight of schoolbags to the publication of school league tables are infused – and provide a material presence for the consumer/market conceptualisation that is sustained, normalised and expanded in the process. Specifically, the 'exceptionalism' claimed for education, in opposition to treating it in trade/exchange terms along with other varieties of transfers in social life, is undermined.

The commercial and managerial texts operate in a similar dynamic in relation to the social setting in which educational transfers take place. A common sequence in discourse is where contesting one invokes the other. Teachers who might express the view, for instance, that specific proposals for change, derived from the commercial world, are inappropriate where educational relationships and contexts are involved, are often materially repositioned and culturally re-signified as problems themselves – fearing change, unadaptable, resisting modernisation, etc. – requiring managerial intervention in the form of re-skilling courses, programmes on 'coping with the challenges of change' and general staff-development days. Skilbeck (2001, p. 114) has attributed nostalgia and false memory to those academics who unfavourably contrast the use of management and business procedures in universities with collegial-style forms of decision-making traditionally associated with universities. We have already seen how personal development opportunities have been recommended for teachers who express concern about the introduction of monitoring mechanisms to the work of schools. One of the effects of the managerial text is to conceptualise teachers as resources in a manner that increases its compatibility with the commercial text and renders unremarkable themes relating to the recording, monitoring and auditing of teachers' work. This is further confirmed and extended by the vocational text in which the service provided by schools – as end product of tradeable qualifications or as process of engagement between teacher and pupil – becomes instrumental and technical, amenable to quantification. Health and Safety, Equality and Education and Welfare legislation is invoked in a process that normalises the manner in which teachers-and-pupils and teachers-and-teachers relate to one another through the construction of protocols, prohibitions and designation of 'best practice'. The role of 'trust' in the pedagogical relationship is dissipated, professional judgement, even teacher agency itself, becomes circumscribed and vocation is recast as dedication to one's attributed role. Education's claims to be unique among service providers are stripped away. This signals a defining point of transition in the cultural transformation of education as it comes to be successfully thematised in terms of trade/exchange. Within intersubjectivity about education this conceptualisation can now circulate without special pleading or disruption of communication, and has the potential to interpellate individual subjectivities and experience textualisation throughout culture and society. This process is facilitated as exchanges such as we have seen above between the meanings of those five texts and their total cultural field recur extensively and recursively in culture and time.

This new representation of education in the culture was neither actively nor independently advanced by people acting politically in seeking to bring about either a new understanding of education or a specific alteration or redirection of how the system operated. While the intertextuality of these five texts introduced individual themes that characterise the mercantile paradigm, its pivotal achievement was to erode the legitimacy of schools as sites of interaction that were entitled to abrogation from their individual 'modernising' demands. The theocentric paradigm had achieved this corralling of the forces of transformation by appeals to the supernatural nature of its project. With change, metaphysical, high-culture and humanistic characterisations of schooling were effective in turn. But with the erosion of the legitimacy of education's 'exceptionalism' came the opening up of its cultural production to penetration from wherever markets, consumers and providers engaged in trade/exchange.

The funding and resourcing of schools cannot be expected to operate without attention to the question of its proper use. Schools will never be self-regulating. As part of the society in which pupils live, business, commerce and industry need to be represented on the school curriculum. Parents will rightly want to influence the nature of their children's education. In the five texts selected for attention, we find a variety of understandings about these matters, often produced by different agents but nonetheless engaging with one another in a mutually-reinforcing, validating and intensifying fashion such that the ultimate cultural transformation was of a kind that their detraditionalising progenitors were unlikely to have expected and perhaps even at odds with what they would have aspired to in its implications for the educational system.

This did not involve a mystical, idealist set of processes. The transformation was substantially effected by ordinary people in lived situations with routine material interests who reshaped, in establishing new linkages, relationships and relevances, their intersubjective engagement with the institution of education. It was not, however, a steady, unchallenged progression.

The teacher unions have the power to resist, and at least delay, the material implications of the mercantile paradigm. Because of the nature of its intertextual production it lacked a distinctive discourse and designated authoritative agents. Its associative status experienced difficulty in making the transition from the atomistic to the collective because of the absence of a discourse of mobilisation that would confirm common sentiment and perception. It needed a dedicated language, a collective existence and a monumental work or social project to coherently frame it. To date, the ASTI dispute with the government in 2000/2001 provided it with its best single episode of favourable circumstances for its instantiation and development as a paradigm. Apart from the salary claim involved and the related issues of teachers' working conditions, the policy conflict that characterised the dispute was the ASTI opposition to the application of benchmarking procedures to the work of schools, on the basis that it industrialised education and was unsuited to the nature of the educational process and the professional character of the teacher's role. Yet, the public response from a diversity of sources was to repeatedly challenge the 'exceptionalism' of schools and teaching. Common arguments were: that stress was now a feature of all kinds of work where, unlike teaching, it included the fear of redundancy; the multiple nature of the teacher's role was paralleled in the expectation of multi-skilling in the post-Fordist contemporary workplace; teaching was substantially a repetitive exercise in which similar lessons were given year after year; the equivalent of 'underperforming' teachers in industry and commerce would not be tolerated; teachers should be open to evaluation as were other workers. As one prominent journalist (Browne, 2000) argued, if society is satisfied to measure the achievement of pupils in the Leaving Certificate with career-determining implications, why should it be considered improper or impossible to similarly assess, measure and compare their schools and teachers?

This was not an uncontested interpretation of the work of schools and teachers. Apart from challenges from teachers themselves, as well as from the general public, there were differences within the policy-making process itself, between parent bodies, for instance, on the construction and publication of 'league tables' of schools. Yet, it seemed clear that in the heightened conflict and discourse of this long-running dispute a wide range of individuals from government, media and employers' organisations, as well as those who were parents and private-sector employees, came to recognise themselves as belonging to a like-minded social configuration in their conceptualisation of schooling, teaching and learning with other forms of trade/exchange experienced by them in their social and occupational lives. Ironically, what was widely seen, even with the distance of hindsight (Oliver, 2003), as the inflexible, defensive and embittered hard-done-by stance of teachers during the dispute would have confirmed the appropriateness of the mercantile conceptualisation in the manner in which themes of differentiation of interest, maximising individual benefit and flexible commitment were realised, and, in the light of this, the need for protocols to regulate and ensure predictability and equilibrium in exchanges between teachers and parents and pupils. Whatever the merits of the teachers' objections to benchmarking, the nature of their campaign would have confirmed for many the need for some such regulation of the exchanges involved in their work. This had the potential of a cultural flash-point, allowing the more vigorous and enthusiastic 'believers' to make explicit and name the basis of this shared conceptualisation. This potential has yet to be fully realised: it is the rare intellectual who seeks to frame it within theorised parameters and, apart from the print media's now routine practice of publishing rankings of schools and colleges in terms of overall quality, 'feeding' universities etc., there is no significant social project that explicitly proclaims itself, with whatever use of language, as seeking to advance a mercantile reconstruction of education. The mercantile paradigm exists more collectively than it did. But it is lived rather than named in its infusion of what have become unremarkable practices and expectations in the relationship between education and its public.

Because of its intertextual production, the mercantile paradigm lacks a distinctive discourse and established authoritative agents. Its associative status experiences difficulty in making the transition from the atomistic to the collective because of the absence of a discourse of mobilisation that would confirm common sentiment and perception. On the other hand, because it is ineffectually framed in all but conceptualisation and performance, its apparent untheorised and 'unpeopled' character makes it difficult to target for challenge and contestation. Yet, this is also a source of its vulnerability: because of its reliance on conceptualisation and performance to maintain its meaning, the mercantile paradigm's boundaries, being both unnamed and unmonitored, are more open to penetration and possible co-optation. This double-edged sword in the armoury of the mercantile paradigm will come into play in the culture wars between the mercantile and the modern to be examined in the next chapter. Whatever of this audit of its strengths and weaknesses in achieving dominion, as will be argued in the Epilogue, what every revisitation of its status since the 1990s reveals is a growing clarity in its expansion and intensification.

Comparative Perspective

The fact that it is possible to regard these five texts on school organisation, personnel, aims, users and provision as independent strands of interpretation, naming and prescription, indeed as instantiations of distinct paradigms relating to these dimensions of education, disguises the totality of their contribution to the mercantile paradigm. This is cultivated by the manner and agency of their production. The state may have become more activist from the 1960s but it was never interventionist. Throughout, the approach to change was staggered and cautious, the antithesis of holistic planning as attempted in some educational systems (Corson, 1986). This was most obvious in its relationship with the church where it was obliged to recognise its material power as manifested in church ownership of schools and its legal and constitutional entitlements in relation to their management and control. A recurring reflection of this has been the shifting nature of policy and practice on the structure and nature of post-primary schooling revealed by, for instance, Dr Hillery's 1963 announcement of comprehensive schools, rationalisation initiatives, the 1970 Community School document, the 1980 Education White Paper, the 1984-1987 Programme for Action in Education and the 1992 Education Green Paper. Despite the existence of economic planning which begot the human capital paradigm and the OECD involvement, there was no explicit plan for educational change. The approach has been described as 'pragmatic gradualism': 'moving things forward on a gradual path, testing responses, slowing down or speeding up developments as circumstances permit' (Coolahan, 1989).

Parents who had initially become involved in the process as individual constituents of politicians proceeded to collective representation by means of formal parent organisations and corporatist-like structures such as the National Parents' Council. More explicit corporatist structures such as the Interim Curriculum and Examinations Board and the more representational National Council for Curriculum and Assessment formalised the contributions of teacher and managerial bodies, a process that expanded in interest group representation and intensified in consultative practices during the 1990s. Economists, employers, business groupings and employment-creating bodies also individually participated. Effectively, these texts were to appear as populist productions, supported by a growing statist discourse from across these interests. From the 1970s, the church itself by means of episcopal statements and the advocacy of church bodies, in contrast to its earlier discourse of subsidiarity, was calling for state action on a range of social issues such as poverty and housing as well as education (O'Sullivan, 1996a). As the years progressed, religious-inspired justice ideals were joined by capitalist, social democratic, social rescue, health and civic rationales in advocating state action in pursuit of the common good, social transformation, a vocational curriculum, modulated bodies, shaped identities, and the amelioration of an increasing litany of social ills from teenage pregnancy to political apathy. This can be rightly interpreted as pluralist advocacy in which diverse interests make competing demands on the state. In Ireland, given the legacy of restraints on the state's autonomy and capacity in the making and enactment of educational policy, its effect was to normalise state activism and confirm its authoritative status in relation to educational knowledge and change. But this status was as much a product of popular sentiment as state initiative in a process in which each invoked the other and in which the state moved forward, in discourse as in practice, within the bounds of measured and cautious possibilities.

Comparatively, what distinguishes the Irish experience of replacing a theocentric with a mercantile paradigm is that, unlike cultural transformations of a similar scale in other educational systems, it happened largely without advocacy. While there have been calls for the separation of church and state and criticism of the power, even monopoly, of the church in Irish education, it would be difficult to find an example of support for the specific cultural and material shift that is identified here as the emergence of the mercantile paradigm. To use our nearest neighbour as a foil, there has been no equivalent of the Black Papers on Education, Callaghan's Ruskin speech, Thatcher, Hayek or the Education Reform Act. Specific facets of the transition would have had their supporters. But overall it appears as a transformation without agents, but one in which the work of social actors from different ideological positions nonetheless achieved a coordinated effect that was to have material and symbolic consequences.

The policy debate following Chubb and Moe's (1988, 1990) research on private and public schools in the US, and specifically their arguments on the implications for school effectiveness of their environmental context in terms of the logic of politics and markets, is an appropriate point of entry to this debate in selected countries on schooling in the light of market concepts and orientations. Supplementing existing national data, Chubb and Moe (1988) argued that private schools outperformed public schools on academic grounds and that this can be explained by virtue of their ability 'to make their own decisions about policy, organisation and personnel subject to market forces that signal how they can best pursue their own interests'. They concluded: 'Given their substantial autonomy – and given the incentives for autonomy that are built into the system – it is not surprising to find that principals are stronger leaders; that principals have greater control over hiring and firing; that principals and the teachers they choose have greater respect for, and interaction with, one another; and that teachers – with conflict or formal requirement – are more integrally involved in policy making'. They prescribed as the key to school improvement, not school reform but a pulling back from direct democratic control and the creation of private schools or market-based and autonomous public schools.

Criticisms of Chubb and Moe targeted methodological, policy and ideological aspects of their arguments. Yet, it became a widely quoted source in policy debate internationally. In Australia, Marginson (1997) has traced its influence on a number of proposals relating to the funding of education and parent and student choice. It fuelled the advocacy of the Education Reform Act in England and Wales and, specifically, the local management of schools, the stripping of local education authority power, consumer choice and management discourses (Halpin and Troyna, 1995). In the US, Conway *et al.* (2001) concluded that 'with the publication of Chubb and Moe's *Politics, Markets and America's Schools* (1990), the neo-liberal thrust in education reform gained social scientific respectability'.

This should not surprise. Chubb and Moe's recommendations on the rolling back of the state and on the regulative effect of the marketplace in which the participants operate as self-interested individuals, found a sympathetic ideological climate in the New Right thinking that had come to prevail in these political systems. The New Right is used to describe a reaction against Keynesian social democracy that had held sway since the 1930s and the post-war years and favoured a managed capitalism and government intervention in the interests of curbing instability and unemployment rather than an economic order based on a self-regulating market (Heywood, 1997). For the New Right, Keynesianism came to be identified with 'a politicised economy, an economy where decisions are made by public agencies, and with economic strategies which rely heavily on government expenditure and thus on high taxes and high levels of public sector borrowing ... (resulting) it is argued, in inflation and government overload' (Ball, 1990, p. 36). The writings of free-market economists Hayek, of the Austrian School, and Friedman, of the Chicago School, both long-time critics of Keynes, formed the economic thinking of the New Right. They were highly critical of government intervention which, they argued, even when it was well-intentioned, inevitably had damaging effects in cultivating dependency and a dilution of initiative. They believed in the self-regulating nature of the market and its ability to deliver growth, efficiency and prosperity. These finally found a receptive environment in the era of inflation and unemployment in the 1970s, and are identified with Thatcherism and Reaganism in the 1980s with their themes of the 'nanny state', rugged individualism and entrepeneurialism.

New Right education policy never transferred to Ireland as a model for macro-educational policy. As we have seen, many of the themes of New Right educational discourse – consumer rights, performance indicators, devolved budgets, private investment in education, enterprise, corporate linkages, new forms of school management, quality and efficiency – were successfully inserted into Irish educational discourse and experienced varying levels of textualisation. But in their representation they were never explicitly linked in pursuit of a neo-liberal restructuring of education. Whatever receptivity there might have been for New Right thinking to become a participant in the cultural politics of Irish education it was systematically undermined by representing it, synecdochecally, as the construct of 'Thatcherism'. As a trope, the power of synecdoche lies in the manner in which it invites the substitution of part of something for the whole of something else. Unlike the most basic of tropes, the metaphor, which in this case would have operated by equating 'Thatcherism' with New Right thinking, manifested in her party's and government's policies, it was a construct described as 'Thatcherism', selectively and locally shaped, that performed the act of substitution. In the local construction of 'Thatcherism', it was successfully positioned to mean cutbacks, anti-education and anti-teacher policies, low standards of pupil achievement, indiscipline, teacher shortages and low morale, but also arrogance, anti-Irishness and Empire. Any theme that could be semantically linked to 'Thatcherism' was suspect. The effect was to create the perception that 'the Right was bereft of intellectually respectable arguments' (Beck, 1998, p. 120) and to establish the English educational system as a negative role model in a manner that rarely required explicit justification. The teachers' associations were to the fore as agents in this process of representation and substitution but academic educators and the media also contributed.

Such is the exclusionary power of 'Thatcherism' in Irish policy discourse that throughout the 1990s discourse on performatives relating to enterprise as a school subject, the publication of the examination results of individual schools, school and teacher evaluation, performance indicators and benchmarking reveals how their advocates were obliged to resort to disclaimers and special pleading, idiosyncrasy credit-building techniques, dilution and alteration of terminology in an effort to establish them as themes in policy discourse. It would be wrong to infer from the manner in which 'Thatcherism' was used as a term of derision to undermine the creditability of such themes that the cultural politics of Irish education was hostile to the underlying principles of New Right educational thinking. As used in Irish discourse on education, 'Thatcherism' related to performatives rather than the neo-liberal conceptualisation of people, society, motivation and prosperity and their associated legitimatory armoury. Thus when we look at the detail of the deployment of 'Thatcherism' as a synecdoche for New Right thinking we find that what were being protected and culturally ring-fenced were teachers' interests and working conditions rather than some overall principle of education. This suggests that the vein of research, relating to what is broadly referred to as 'policy borrowing' (Finegold *et al.*, 1992; Halpin and Troyna, 1995; Vickers, 1995) could benefit from incorporating in the politics of policy insulation, the manner in which the formation of 'cautionary texts' from experiences elsewhere are deployed as filtering mechanisms in regulating the entry of new ideas.

Substantially, the consequence was that unlike England where the underlying and more durable transformation effected by Thatcherism related to 'rationalities and technologies of government' (Rose, 1993), in Ireland the transformation took a cultural form independently of social and political movements in education broadly referred to as the New Right. The dominance of the mercantile paradigm is not without its material implications in terms of the governmentality of education, a problem for the state in Ireland as in England. This has taken the form of representative and populist demands for action relating to ineffective teachers, grievance mechanisms for parents and pupils, and evaluative information about school standards and efficiency, and their quality of service such as the length and organisation of the school year and the timing of parent-teacher meetings.

New structures of control and regulation relating to the higher education sector and the processes of accreditation and certification are already in place. Local education committees were proposed and rejected. A policy of allocating some of the functions of the state department of education to separate agencies featured in both Green and White Papers on education and is being pursued.

Whole School Evaluation is being advanced as the means of regulating, at a remove, practices in individual classrooms, the most challenging of tasks in the governmentality of education. But the power of teachers in Irish education is such – their representation on the NCCA, review bodies and the Teaching Council is but a manifestation of this (Granville, 2004; Sugrue, 2004) – that these structures and mechanisms of control are less developed and less threatening to teachers than in England. If the mercantile paradigm continues to expand, populist demands for the regulatory and disciplinary practices routine in other relationships of trade/exchange to be applied to schools will not alone strengthen whatever inclinations the state may have in this regard, but will oblige it to act as the auditor and guarantor of standards and efficiency in what remains a quasi-market in education.

The comparison with Thatcherism's experience with trade unions is instrumental here. The ASTI industrial action of 2000/2001 may have been nothing on the scale of the miners' strike but it could well constitute a turning point in the power of teachers in the manner in which it demonstrated, in the responses of the public and the media, the dominance of a mercantile interpretation of teachers and teaching in terms of their functions, obligations, reward and motivation, and governmentality. While it would be too glib to predict that Irish education is set to experience Thatcherism in the absence of Thatcher, it does seem likely that the cultural shift represented by the mercantile paradigm will produce real material consequences in new modes of governmentality in education. But if it is valid to describe Thatcherism as 'authoritarian populism' (Hall, 1980), in Ireland the new forces of regulation and control will be ushered in by means of a managerial populism in which the state, positioned (or self-positioned), as the agent of popular sentiment, will approach its task in a technical rather than an explicitly ideological or interventionist role. This and other possibilities for the relationship between the state, society and people in the formulation and implementation of educational policy will be explored in the Epilogue.

Chapter 6

The Mercantile Paradigm and Modernist Discourse: Predatory Intertextuality

The boundaries of the theocentric paradigm began to contract in the 1960s with the effect of increasingly releasing from its control the designation of appropriate themes, performatives, authorities and modes of discourse. These would have concerned the vocation of teaching, the control of schooling, the role of parents and the laity and the contribution to be expected from the state in the resolution of educational and social problems. As this process of contraction progressed, the position taken in Irish consciousness about these issues became less fixed, more open to analysis and speculation, involving a wider range of personnel entitled to contribute, and much less subject to dogma and received wisdom. Substantively, the lay teacher came to be accepted as the norm in the general staffing of schools and, increasingly, in positions of educational leadership, the prior right of the church in the control of schooling and anxiety about state involvement were less likely to be asserted, and a concern for weaker sections of Irish society, together with a critique of its inequalities, pervaded church discourse and action.

This reflected changes that were broader than education and relate to the function of religion in Irish society. The extent to which the concept of secularisation adequately captures the nature of these changes has been disputed (Fahey, 1992a; Nic Ghiolla Phádraig, 1995; Tovey and Share, 2000). If secularisation is taken to mean that religiosity withers away with increasing industrialisation and modernisation it proves to be an inappropriate description of Irish social change from the 1960s. The expression of religiosity persists but now assumes a loosely institutionalised form reminiscent, it might be argued, of the nature of religious practice and experience in Irish society prior to the modernisation of the church in the nineteenth century. More appropriate to the current Irish situation is the understanding of secularisation as a growing differentiation of society in terms of institutions, forms of knowledge and expertise which result in a diminished significance, power and visibility for religion in political, civic and social life, retreating perhaps ultimately to the private sphere.

But the implications of this contraction and associated secularisation for the cultural interpretation of education were more wide-ranging and fundamental than their material consequences in the staffing and control of schooling. As the theocentric paradigm contracted it facilitated the emergence of a more varied discourse and practice of education, incorporating a new language, themes, authorities and identities reflected in new school types, bodies of educational knowledge, educational roles, social configurations, and the advocacy of diverse subjectivities as the object of curriculum change. The successful penetration of the human capital paradigm, and its subsequent mutation and fracturing in Irish educational consciousness, was already paving the way in this regard. But this influence was being forged in a manner that allowed it to be cognitively segregated from, or co-opted under, the theocentric paradigm. As the latter contracted, it might appear that the emerging mercantile paradigm was being presented with a hollowed out educational institution awaiting its inscription. The opportunity was certainly there. But, it was not in any sense an uncontested cultural space. The 'culture wars' relating to how education was to be understood in an Ireland in which religion had ceased to be a dominant and extensive contributor of public knowledge and cultural interpretation are evident from the 1960s and continue.

But while the theocentric paradigm was ceasing to be the pre-eminent combatant in these culture wars, it was not unimplicated in the intertextuality that constituted their engagements. Since it represented the understanding of education that was being replaced, in some instances materially, it established, at least initially, the cultural terrain of themes and authorities on which aspiring definitions of education had to establish themselves, obliging them to legitimate themselves in relation to what had gone before while ensuring that they were not being out-manoeuvred by fellow usurpers. In selecting mercantile and modernist paradigms as the combatants in this regard, and arguing that it was the former that most successfully went on to define the institution of education, it needs to be continuously kept in mind that they were not alone in the cultural production of education or isolated from the other texts with which this connected them. What was involved was a different, more predatory, kind of intertextuality from the complementary intertextuality that features so prominently in the construction of the mercantile paradigm itself.

As the theocentric paradigm contracted, the themes that were made explicit and valorised were ones that were believed to epitomise a modernised new Ireland, outward and forward-looking, industrialised and affluent, freeing itself from the regulating pieties of religion, nation, and economic self-sufficiency. In education, the human capital themes of cultivating society's talents as resources in the generation of economic growth, and the articulation of the content and objectives of schooling in terms of the requirements of the workplace, were positioned in historical and general textualisation of Irish social change in terms of such modernist discourse. It is quite valid to decipher modern tendencies in the cultural change experienced since the 1960s. What is questionable is what has become of them and what their current status is in terms of an ongoing cultural politics. Specifically, they need to be considered in interaction with the mercantile paradigm, which is the task of this chapter. Theoretically, as we have seen in the previous chapter, it will also be necessary to later explore if constructs other than modernisation might more productively explain Irish educational change and its social context over the period. One can isolate four areas of cultural production – equality, difference, virtue and control – relating to education which would have been considered to epitomise a modernised educational system, both in terms of its understanding and materiality. These are generated from educational discourse derived from academic and policy-related research, state-led proposals for educational change, and curriculum innovation, legislative activity, advocacy and representation by interested individuals and social configurations, as well as a wide range of behaviours and practices.

A core modernist theme is that of equality as a principle for the allocation of educational resources and opportunities which seeks to break the dominance of inherited status and facilitate its replacement with a status that is achieved through individual talent and effort, effectively freeing people from nature and tradition. A willingness to recognise differences in society is treated as an indication of the transition from mechanical solidarity as the basis of social life in traditional societies in which a sense of sameness is heightened to generate cohesiveness and allegiance to the social order. In modernising, previously devalued, hidden or suppressed differences are acknowledged as legitimate dimensions of society among citizens who commit themselves to public engagement on the basis of rational debate. In such a social order, tolerance, mutual respect and the obligations of inter-dependence become the ideals which the school system seeks to reflect and cultivate. Deciding on what is virtuous behaviour becomes a more contested process in a society in which life is legitimately lived according to different value systems. Dogma and prescription no longer suffice and individual freedom is asserted in the choice of political, social, economic and religious beliefs within the parameters of shared civic virtues. Schooling in such a situation requires among its aims the cultivation of the capacity and disposition to participate in the public sphere, and to make responsible choices in terms of one's own needs and one's obligations to others and to society in general. The sovereign state with control over its institutions is a hallmark of modernity in which those who exercise power must be accountable and submit to the public will in the form of an electorate or bodies or agencies sanctioned in terms of popular franchise.

As the chapter develops and the engagement between the mercantile and the modern is considered in each of these four areas of cultural production, it will be necessary to refine and extend what modernist understandings of the person, rationality, equality, society, social obligations, responsibility, entitlements, etc. might entail. In the absence of such an elaboration in Irish educational discourse this is a heuristic exercise to facilitate the clearer illumination of the intertextuality, which is the focus of the analysis. But calibrating the modernity of education in such a manner is complicated by the different forms which modernity has taken, and by the existence of disputes as to how they should be named and explained (Kenway *et al.*, 1993; Hall *et al.*, 1992; Bauman, 1995). For this reason, it is useful to draw on a foundational contributor to modernity in the form of Enlightenment Thought, itself in no sense unitary (Outram, 1995), which is consistent with the intellectual/cultural rather than a social, economic, technological or bureaucratic emphasis of the analysis. Two key elements of Enlightenment Thought have fuelled modernity: rationality, particularly according to the principles of scientific inquiry; and teleology, the sense of participating in the historically-driven advancement and perfection of society. This held out not merely great hopes but exceptional promise: scientific knowledge would deliver people from oppression to freedom; society was not a victim of its past and could rationally fashion its own destiny; social institutions were human rather than natural or divine products and could be designed for the benefit of all rather than for the few (Seidman, 1998). As for terminology, while recognising that 'modernity' and 'modernist' are sometimes given different meanings, the former designating all the intellectual, social and political changes that ushered in the modern world, the latter referring to a cultural movement in the late nineteenth century that involved a critical engagement with modernity, we use the terms here interchangeably (Kumar, 1995).

Even on the basis of this cursory account, which leaves aside the variations associated with political ideologies such as those of socialism, social democracy, and liberal and neo-liberal democracy (Habermas, 1996), it is possible to see how modernist themes connect with some of the key features of the mercantile paradigm. Both accord a high priority to the individual, rationality, mobility, privacy, autonomy, self-determination, circumscribed commitment and affiliation, open negotiable social orders, dispersed power, equal treatment, achieved status, and the erosion of privilege. The relevance of intertextuality as an approach to studying the dynamic nature of their interrelatedness is further suggested by the manner in which the mercantile and the modern often appear to use a common language – choice, individual freedom, achievement, reason – and yet realise different meanings. Further trajectories are added by their need not only to distance themselves from the theocentric paradigm, but to do so in their own distinctive way. With appropriate data, this analysis is capable of fine-tuning, across all the dimensions of a paradigm – its components, dominion, and nature of change – the ebb, flow, mutation, exclusion and suppression of meanings in determining what becomes the dominant understanding of Irish education. What is being attempted here is more limited, due to space and the purpose at hand which is to demonstrate how at the turn of the century it was the mercantile understanding of the person, society, and its appropriate functioning, that most succeeded in culturally shaping Irish education, while recognising the ongoing nature of the contestation and positioning. This is broadly sketched and necessarily selective but nonetheless representative of Irish educational change up until around the turn of the millennium and beyond in some instances.

Equality

Ireland, in common with other educational systems, has problems with uneven rates of participation and achievement across a range of significant categories within society. It is in relation to these disparities that the question of equality is routinely discussed. Accordingly, equality is constructed as a state policy issue in its softer manifestation of equality of educational opportunity rather than in its more demanding version as egalitarianism and social reconstruction. Class differences in educational opportunity have been the focus of attention since the 1960s, gender differences came to be recognised during the 1970s and particularly in the 1980s, while since the 1990s Travellers have successfully claimed entitlements in education because of their distinct ethnicity. These will be discussed in their own right in terms of the intersection of life chances, education and morality in Part Three. Since the 1990s, also, people with disabilities are becoming more assertive in claiming that they experience unequal educational opportunities in seeking to develop their potential, and at the time of writing are demanding rights-based legislation to ensure that their needs are met.

Because of the scale of disparities in achievement and participation involved, the numbers affected, and its recurrence in Irish policy discourse, it is the cultural production of class inequalities in education that is isolated for analysis. Clancy's (2001) representation of these disparities, reproduced in Table 6.1, is particularly illuminative and captures vividly the key issues better than any other set of statistics.

Table 6.1 Educational Transitions: Differential Participation and Achievement Rates by Fathers' Socio-Economic Group
(Source: Clancy, 2001, p. 79, Table 31)

Fathers' Socio-economic Group	Percentage reaching Leaving Cert (LC) Level	Of those reaching LC Level		Of those with at least 5 passes in LC % enrolled in Higher Education	Of those with at least 2 Cs at Hons Level % enrolled in Higher Education
		% with at least 5 passes	% with at least 2 Cs at Hons Level		
Farmers	88.8	95.9	67.8	63.5	78.5
Other Agricultural	71.7	90.4	52.2	54.8	79.6
Higher Professional	92.0	99.0	86.9	77.2	83.3
Lower Professional	93.8	95.7	82.3	73.7	78.9
Employers & Managers	90.7	95.6	67.5	63.0	78.1
Salaried Employees	89.7	97.9	69.0	66.9	82.7
Intermediate Non-Manual	83.8	96.5	69.2	62.3	78.5
Other Non-Manual	76.7	91.1	47.0	48.6	77.6
Skilled Manual	79.8	94.8	55.4	49.7	72.6
Semi-Skilled Manual	75.1	89.9	47.1	38.1	60.7
Unskilled Manual	65.4	87.9	43.0	38.1	68.5
Total	80.6	94.2	60.2	56.2	76.4

At the basic level of participation considered, it demonstrates that one-fifth overall fail to make it to Leaving Certificate level. The retention rate varies significantly by social class. The figure for the children of unskilled manual parents is about two-thirds, while the figure of 92 per cent for children of higher professional families comes within the range of universal participation in the terminal examination of post-primary education. The next disparity that Clancy draws our attention to is the level of achievement of those who stay on to sit the Leaving Certificate. The lower level of achievement considered – at least five passes – yields further but not dramatic class differences. About 12 per cent from an unskilled manual background, as opposed to 6 per cent overall, effectively fail the Leaving Certificate. At the higher level of performance, achieving at least two Cs at honours level, we find quite dramatic differences between the higher professional group (86.9 per cent) and the unskilled manual group (43 per cent). This has major implications for one's capacity to compete for places in higher education. However, class continues to be a force in making this transition to higher education even for those with similar levels of achievement. For those with a minimum pass level, about three-quarters of the higher professional group as opposed to just less than two-fifths of the unskilled manual group transfer to higher education. For those with 2 Cs at honours level, the respective figures are 83.3 per cent as opposed to 68.5 per cent.

Initiatives aimed at furthering equality of educational opportunity from the 1960s include free post-primary schooling and transport, third-level grants and the Rutland Street pre-school intervention programme for disadvantaged children, one of the earliest of its kind in Europe. However, since the 1980s, efforts to combat socio-economic disadvantage have become a more specific feature of state educational policy. These interventions embody a number of features. The idea of pre-school compensatory education has been revived to be followed by targeted allocation of resources to ensure low teacher pupil ratios and better capitation grants in designated disadvantaged schools. Specific targets in terms of participation rates for low-participating groups have been set throughout the educational system. For those who fall through the net, second-chance programmes are available for unqualified school leavers and for adult recipients of social welfare. Initiatives seeking to widen access from socio-economically disadvantaged backgrounds to third-level education continue (Osborne and Leith, 2000). The range of interventions is extensive and varied (Murphy, 2000). In general, in terms of formal policy statements, these are characterised by a change of focus from inequalities in access and participation to the underdevelopment of talent and potential.

Yet, when one examines the policy issues that the principle of educational equality generates one finds a basic focus on an individual's opportunity to access and participate in specific educational levels. Repeatedly, equality is seen in terms of equity in the progression of pupils through the educational system and is represented as a theme of official discourse in a manner that is informed by the mercantile paradigm or at least neutral towards it. Achievement gained in attention since the 1980s but this came to refer to how far one progressed rather than how one performed in relation to one's peers. Insofar as there has been attention to issues of achievement in equality discourse, it has followed in the tradition of what will be referred to in Chapter 7 as the 'distant other', those pupils at the extremes of low achievement who since the 1980s have been constituted as the educationally disadvantaged. It continues to be remarkable that so little public discourse about equality in education addresses the full extent of social class differences in achievement at all its levels revealed by Clancy in Table 6.1. A key factor in this omission is the suppression of social class inequality in achievement as a theme by the construction of disadvantage in terms of low achievers requiring improvement and inclusion within a more acceptable achievement range. Despite the efforts of egalitarians and communitarians, to be discussed later, it continues to be difficult for equality to attain a cultural form, such as a principle that encompasses collective issues of social justice, that cannot be accommodated by the mercantile paradigm or co-opted by it.

Early debate from the 1960s on equality of educational opportunity was in the context of the human capital paradigm. The tapping of unrealised talent was seen as socially beneficial, indeed even essential if the economy and production were to be fully energised. As the Education Minister, Dr Patrick Hillery, put it in justifying the extension of the provision of scholarships in 1961: 'It is directed towards bringing forward, for the benefit of the country as a whole, the best talent that the country is producing, and that from whatever economic level in which such talent is to be found' (quoted in O'Sullivan, 1989a). In the 1990s with the growth in the economy a more contemporary variant of human capital theory is again in evidence in influential national and international reports (Gleeson, 2000). According to this, the demands on education are now even more comprehensive, no longer merely requiring that those with talent would be recognised and developed, but that all pupils should be adequately trained for the increasingly higher technological demands of modern industry.

Consistent with this, concern for low-achieving school leavers is repeatedly represented in terms of their experience in the labour market. One's chance of getting employment, the length of time one remains unemployed, the level of the labour force one enters, of course, all have implications for individual status and reward. However, variations in employment rates across those with different levels of educational credentials are repeatedly treated in a manner that elides the distinction between employability and employment chances. The data on which such interpretations are based are derived from the annual school leavers' surveys, now carried out by the ESRI on behalf of the Department of Education and Science, and based on a stratified random sample, interviewed 12-18 months after leaving the official second-level educational system. The 2002 survey (Gorby *et al.*, 2003), of those leaving between September 2000 and August 2001, demonstrates how the prospects of school leavers securing employment one year after leaving school improve consistently with each level of educational attainment. While 55 per cent of school leavers without qualifications were found to be unemployed, the corresponding figure for those with a Junior Certificate fell to 26 per cent and to 10 per cent for those with a Leaving Certificate. Overall, the association between increasing educational attainment and greater labour market success became more pronounced over the twenty-one surveys since 1980, and particularly so over the past decade. In terms of odds ratios, while unqualified school leavers were two to three times more likely to be unemployed than those with a Leaving Certificate in the early 1990s, by 2002 this differential had grown to over seven times.

In the employability discourse that appropriates these data, low achieving/ early school leavers are represented in mercantile terms and specifically so in relation to their violation of its conventions of social engagement and subjectivity. Rather than consider these figures as examples of the hiring practices of Irish employers, they have been treated as indicators of the capacity of young people to fulfil the requirements of available positions. The issue is constructed as a problem of labour market preparation and readiness. Low achieving/early school leavers are positioned as deviant participants in a mercantile world. Not alone are they considered to be deficient in the skills and knowledge that would render them employable but their subjectivities are suspect in their potential to disrupt the processes of trade/exchange. Their disposition towards the labour market – unmotivated by its opportunities, unwilling to compete on its terms, unable to segregate their self-interest from the alienating tendencies of the school/labour market nexus – serves as an exemplar of an alternative and disturbing understanding of social and economic exchange. Policies aimed at extending participation in education and improving credentials are represented as having the potential to reduce unemployment and social welfare spending, and supply competent workers to the labour force. Bringing those who leave school early with minimal or no qualifications to higher levels of achievement is therefore seen as benefiting all through the raising of the skill levels of the labour force, and through the reduction of unemployment and the costs of social welfare. Less publicly, 'social inclusion' objectives in relation to low achieving/early school leavers at once confirm the virtues of the social system from which they are assumed to be 'excluded' and seek to co-opt their culturally-destabilising potential. This does not involve the direct suppression of citizenship themes, which have been even more formalised in such curricular areas as CSPE and SPHE, through the dominance of labour market preparation understood in mercantile terms. What happens is more subtle, penetrating and silently non-discursive as citizenship itself comes to be reconceptualised around the entitlements and expectations of individuals to mercantile competencies and subjectivities.

The report *Educational Disadvantage in Ireland* (Kellaghan *et al.*, 1995) illuminates these sentiments. This report was prepared at the Educational Research Centre, Drumcondra for the Combat Poverty Agency and was publicly acknowledged in a foreword by the Minister for Education, Niamh Bhreathnach, as a scholarly work that would inform her policy on combating educational disadvantage. In the preface to their report the authors link educational disadvantage with 'severe difficulties at school' resulting in young people, beginning '... their adult lives without the knowledge and skills required for a productive life in contemporary society'. They see this situation as having three important implications.

> First, it means that our educational system is not providing all children with the opportunity to realise their potential and to access further training in the labour market. Second, failure to develop the talents of many individuals has the effect of diminishing the level of 'human capital' of the nation, so reducing its capacity to compete economically. There is a need to raise national educational standards which will require paying particular attention to the lowest achievers in the system. Third, failure to create a situation in which all individuals can contribute to economic activity results not only in foregoing benefits but gives rise to actual costs, for example, in supporting the unemployed and in dealing with disaffection and other personal and social problems (p. xiv).

In its introduction to the report, the Combat Poverty Agency describes as its philosophy 'that education is a fundamental social right and that the education system and schools within that system should provide a vision of society which is committed to the values of social equity and justice'. This alludes to the more collective and modernist vision of the role of schooling in creating a more just society that tends to be submerged under the influence of the mercantile paradigm. Ironically, the discourse also excludes evidence that would question its construction of low achieving/early school leavers' subjectivities as discordant with mercantile rationalities. Comparative figures from the OECD (cited in Clancy, 1995a) indicate that competitor countries have not found early school leaving and minimal qualifications to be insuperable impediments to integrating young people into the labour force. This was to be mirrored subsequently in the 1990s as those targeted for retention in greater numbers to leaving certificate level were otherwise attracted to the buoyant labour market.

An analysis of the scholarly and policy discourse which informs the rationale of programmes targeting the disadvantaged 'distant other' reveals how difficult it has been for it to move beyond an understanding of the person that is predominantly psychologistic and atomistic. This individualism, aetiological, ontological and methodological in nature and consistent with the mercantile paradigm, persists alongside the acknowledgement of complex social, economic and cultural influences on disadvantage. Yet, people are projected in a psychologistic/atomistic fashion devoid substantially of a social and, particularly, of a cultural dimension. They could be social isolates were it not for an acknowledgement of families and communities which nonetheless remain 'black-box' and aggregated rather than relational constructs. Culture is understood in the thin rather than the 'thick' sense (Geertz, 1975), as a veneer of values, attitudes and characteristic practices. At most, the recognition of an intersubjective life, cultural patterns and their pervasiveness in identity and habitus, local social structures, even norms, reference or peer groups, but particularly the structural positioning of people, is limited.

The psychologistic/atomistic conceptualisation of disadvantage is evident in the manner in which the distribution of disadvantage has been addressed in relation to the designation of areas and schools as disadvantaged. Great emphasis has been placed on the fact that disadvantaged pupils, be they defined in terms of early school leaving or in terms of the receipt of free medical care and reading standards, are distributed throughout the country and not predominantly in the large public authority areas most identified with deprivation, unemployment and social problems. The following quotation is typical of a number of these arguments (see also Hannan, 1987; Nolan and Callan, 1994).

> While the concentration of disadvantage is found to be greatest in Dublin, in absolute numbers the greatest percentage of disadvantaged (60.7%) are found in rural areas, followed by Dublin (25.5%). The percentages in other urban areas (4.3%) and in towns (9.5%) are relatively small. When the figures for distribution of disadvantage are compared with figures for designation of schools under the Scheme of Assistance for Schools in Designated Areas of Disadvantage, we find that provision at primary level in Dublin is considerably better than in other areas (Kellaghan *et al.*, 1995, p. xi).

There is no recognition here of the collective experience of disadvantage or its structural dimension, be it at local community or school level. It can be argued that the existence, impact and strength of the cultural dimension, the sense of identity and closure including self-limitation, and the capacity of others to set boundaries that exclude and experience internalisation are all likely to be more intense in areas where there is a concentration of disadvantaged pupils than in a context in which disadvantaged pupils are more widely dispersed in terms of homes and schools. Similarly, the significance of material deprivation – income, housing, etc. – for educational progress and aspirations may be greater in urban than in rural areas, where land ownership, however minimal, and family and local traditions and culture cultivate identities and expectations that contrast with the identities and forces of exclusion and self-exclusion to be found in the large deprived urban areas (O'Hara, 1997). In a submission to the Minister for Education and Science in 2003, the Educational Disadvantage Committee (2004) recommended that issues of this nature be addressed in relation to the identification and targeting of the educationally disadvantaged. What is at issue here is not merely a question of accuracy or efficiency in designating schools as disadvantaged but more fundamentally a question of how the on-going understanding of disadvantage is constructed.

A consequence of the psychologistic/atomistic view of disadvantage is that disadvantaged areas are seen as geographical entities that contain a concentration of disadvantaged individuals. The significance of having areas designated as disadvantaged in this view is that they allow efficient and convenient access to disadvantaged pupils. The importance of area is administrative rather than structural, collective or cultural. Areas are perceived to be aggregates of individuals. It can reasonably be inferred from a number of intervention programmes that schools with a high representation of disadvantaged pupils are acknowledged to be facing accentuated difficulties because of this, and it is in this regard that norms and peer groups are likely to be invoked. But the accommodation of the social dimension resides in the attribution of impediments to a school's efforts rather than as a force within a pupil's habitus which is more routinely relegated to the 'distal' sphere of influence.

This stratification of sources of influence on educational achievement suggests a line of explanation for the persistence of the psychologistic/atomistic focus of scholarly and policy discourse on disadvantage. It points, in the epistemology of its explanation, intervention and evaluation, to the mediation of the mercantile paradigm's privileging of exchange between individuals in understanding and reshaping social life. This is revealed in a number of very laudable aspirations and practices in action on disadvantage. These include seeking to construct the most effective and efficient intervention strategies, not only to have the most positive impact on the greatest number of those designated as disadvantaged but to be able to estimate the effectiveness of aspects of the interventions, with a view to matching impediments to school success with strategies that in turn can be further refined and used. This finds affinities with a positivistic/empiricist orientation to the understanding of educational disadvantage, giving priority in intervention and evaluation to what appears most immediately visible, tangible and 'real'. As a corollary, there is, for the purpose of intervention, a distancing of those structural and cultural factors which cannot be as readily differentiated, isolated and measured as can indicators of the specific cognitive and behavioural skills and abilities of individuals. In some cases, there can even seem to be an incredulity as to their ontological status (Kellaghan, 2001). The socio-cultural approach to learning recently advanced by Conway (2002) for disadvantaged contexts has the advantage of challenging the individualist epistemology of cognition and learning from within the discipline of psychology itself, seeking to reconstitute the field of pedagogical practices in a manner that is more accommodating of social and cultural forces. It is too early as yet to say what its impact on policy will be. Sociologists, for their part, have not been successful in articulating social structure at a level other than macro-change, which tends to further confirm its 'distal' conceptualisation. Indeed, the methodology of much of the more prominent policy-related sociological research in Ireland itself embodies assumptions about the relationship between the individual and the social that do little to challenge or offer alternatives to the psychologistic/atomistic orientation (Nolan *et al.*, 2000).

Increasingly, as the 1990s progressed, a community discourse was deployed to refer to instances of social mobilisation and action, social pathologies and service provision. And even within these limited parameters of the social, as Ryan's (1994, pp 202-203) early evaluation of the Home-School-Community Liaison (HSCL) scheme operating in disadvantaged areas points out, the community-based aspect of the scheme received less emphasis than the cognitive-behavioural objectives in the operation of the programmes. There is a reference to community in only one of the aims of the HSCL scheme and it is limited to enhancing 'active cooperation between home, school, and relevant community agencies in promoting the educational interests of the children'. The evaluation distinguished between two types of community-based programmes. One recognises that to create the optimum conditions for a child's development it is necessary that many agencies which support child development should work in partnership with the family. The other type of programme recognises that 'the problems of disadvantage very often have their origins in the conditions of the communities in which families live, communities that may lack services, organisation, and leadership', and therefore regards 'development of the community itself as a pre-requisite to sustaining the effects of any intervention that may be implemented to support children's development'. The report, however, concludes that 'both the aim of the scheme and the way in which the programmes have developed suggest that the former type of programme is what was envisaged in the HSCL scheme'. Yet, it needs to be acknowledged that it is in local initiatives, be they in relation to university access (Osborne and Leith, 2000) or support for disadvantaged schools (Morgan, 1993; Deane, 2003), that one is likely to find practices, such as institutional linkages, with the potential to intervene in how educational possibilities are structured within the culture of disadvantaged areas.

As well as recognising the distinctiveness of individual identities, a modernist understanding of the social dimension of people's lives also incorporates an alertness to the systemic and structural relationships in which they find themselves positioned, particularly insofar as these can limit and impose restrictions on the ability of people to act autonomously in pursuit of their own self-fulfilment and collectively in advancing social progress.

These twin modernist themes of constituting individuals as subjects rather than objects who are acted upon and the collective orientation to social improvement are introduced by Cullen (1997) in his observations on the absence of a discourse on social change in relation to area-based partnership approaches and other community initiatives designed to combat educational disadvantage. He distinguishes between theoretical approaches which focus on the role of individual achievement and those which emphasise institutional and structural features in creating social change: 'the first approach might lead to interventions that are focused on individual capacity-building, personal development and education, training and job placements, the second is perhaps more likely to influence the formation of strong, independent community – and other – institutions that can effectively interact with and possibly change social, economic and political structures.' His purpose is to draw attention to his conclusion that while there appears to be an assumption that area-based partnerships are addressing the structural issue, 'in reality there is, in fact, no real debate going on about whether or not this is the case or, indeed, whether it may be the case in some locations and not others' (p. 28).

These observations of Ryan and Cullen relating to the limited consideration of the social structures within which the disadvantaged are obliged to live their lives in interventions that aspire to improve their opportunities betray the regulative effect of the mercantile paradigm in suppressing, editing out, reconceptualising or otherwise excluding from the textualisation of disadvantage the kinds of modernist themes raised by these writers.

Along with the persistence of psychologistic and atomistic understandings of disadvantage in research and policy discourse, this draws attention to the operation of different understandings of rationality and the subject and their role in society and social behaviour. The enlightenment rationality of modernity is driven to seek out all impediments to individual self-direction however inaccessible, be they through internalisation, mystification or structuration, and does so in a spirit of participating in a teleological process of advancing the ultimate perfection of society. Mercantile rationality is impatient with such vague and nebulous themes, with what it would regard as unreal social objectives and the attribution of restraints and restrictions on individual behaviour. The criticism of the then Chairperson of the Higher Education Authority (Lindsay, 1994), that the author's efforts (O'Sullivan, 1989a) to raise issues of social justice in relation to unequal achievement within the Irish educational system were attempts to use schools as agents of social engineering, is characteristic of such an understanding of the relationship between the individual and the social. In an antithesis of teleology, its focus is on the point-of-contact between individuals – accessing and exiting different stages of education, the learning exchanges of the classroom, and the career choices of the labour market – in the specification of educational objectives. In modernism, to be a subject is to be embedded in society destined to reflexively engage with others in its understanding and perfection; for the mercantile, subject-status is attributed through the pursuit of one's interests, including the choice of whatever subject positions one considers it most beneficial to adopt. As we shall see in Chapter 9, this performative (here-and-now, immediate, activist) orientation of the mercantile paradigm is consistent with the deferral and dispersal of the meaning of disadvantage that occurred since the 1990s, and the avoidance of dissonance and contestation that it facilitated, as intervention was established as the core of its textualisation.

Another feature in the debate on equality that is relevant to the individualisation of disadvantage is the re-emergence of poverty as a social problem. The extent, distribution and characteristics of people designated as living in poverty has been studied extensively since the 1980s. In 1988 the results of a major national study of poverty and income distribution conducted by the Economic and Social Research Institute (ESRI) for the Combat Poverty Agency were published (Callan *et al.,* 1988). Its core findings were to reconceptualise the problem of inequality in terms of income. The effect was evocative and focused, and more direct than any consideration of social class in its impact. Its key conclusions and those of subsequent similar studies were to become the standard fare of media coverage on inequality.

The ESRI had identified three poverty lines – 40 per cent, 50 per cent and 60 per cent of average disposable income. While the researchers did not favour the use of any single poverty threshold, the Combat Poverty Agency was 'of the opinion that anyone living on incomes below any of these three lines is in poverty' (p. ii). The import of this was that one in three of the population was defined as living in poverty. It was difficult for a concept like social class to compete with the explicitness and concreteness of such a finding. When the report sought to identify who the poor actually were and which sectors of society were most vulnerable to poverty, of particular relevance to education was the following equally compelling and quotable conclusion:

> The increase in the number of children being brought up in poverty is significant – all the more so in view of the decline in the birth rates since 1980 which might have been expected to lessen child poverty. Over six out of every ten households below the lowest poverty line contain children (p. iv).

In time, the initial shock impact of poverty discourse dissipated. This had benefited from older associations between hunger, third-world famine images and poverty. According as living in poverty came to be culturally redefined in contemporary western terms, public guilt and responsibility declined. This was accentuated in the buoyant employment market of the 1990s in which people were increasingly held to be accountable for their own material situation. A more persistent consequence of poverty discourse for the understanding of educational inequality has been the manner in which it has distracted from structural definitions of disadvantage, most obviously in terms of social class.

In fact, as researchers such as Whelan (1994) pointed out, the extensive research on class, social mobility and educational credentials could be clearly linked with the experience of living in poverty. In calculating the risk of poverty by class of head of household, Whelan estimated that while only one in a hundred of higher professional and managerial families experience poverty the figure was about a half for the families of unskilled manual workers. He summarises the conclusions of a multivariate analysis of the net effects of class origins, social class, education and labour market experience on the risk of poverty as follows:

> A household headed by a person currently in the professional managerial class and in employment, with no previous experience of unemployment and with some educational qualification, has a zero probability of being in poverty. On the other hand, where the head of household is an unemployed, lower working-class person with no qualifications, from a working-class background and having been unemployed for 15 per cent of his or her potential time in the labour market, the probability of the household being poor approaches one (pp 140-141).

Furthermore, some indication of the independent impact of class background and the absence of educational qualifications is provided by the finding that 'a household headed by a person currently in the lower working class who is in employment and possesses some educational qualification and comes from a non-working-class background has one chance in twenty-five of falling below the poverty line; where the qualification is lacking and working-class origins are involved, the risk rises to one in eight' (p. 141).

Nonetheless, the exclusion of class as a theme in state discourse found its apotheosis in the 1992 Green Paper. In it, social class does not figure as a means of conceptualising differences in the experiences, inequalities, or culture of pupils that were deemed relevant to benefiting from education.

It constituted no challenge to the mercantile paradigm to speak of poverty so long as wealth and its cultural valorisation were not regarded as part of the problem. There is no threat in advocating or organising programmes to assist those who are disadvantaged in accessing the market place. Nor is there in the promotion, identification and development of talent and ability according to existing principles by which merit is defined, identified, named and stratified. It would be much more disruptive, even at the communicative level in the first instance, to speak of social class hierarchies and relationships and the nature of the boundaries of closure, exclusion and legitimation that structure the class system, to question the yardsticks by which merit is assessed, or to take issue with the reward structure, communal obligations and enterprise and profit-seeking values that dominate in the processes by which wealth is acquired. In short, where there is no questioning of the organisation, values, principles or personal virtues of the mercantile, the treatment of disadvantage will be substantially neutral towards it. It may even be supportive because of the manner in which it co-ops elements of social conscience and moral concern both in terms of ideas and agents from modernist discourse.

In the absence of these themes, discourse on poverty elicits a further coping response from the mercantile paradigm, alongside the construction of the low achieving/early school leaver as a deviant competitor in the labour market. Rather than being viewed in terms of their restricted access to social, cultural and political life, the poor are defined in the context of a consumer society. In Bauman's (1998, p. 38) words, they are interpreted as 'flawed consumers':

> As in all other kinds of society, the poor of a consumer society are people with no access to a normal life, let alone to a happy one. In a consumer society, however, having no access to a happy or merely a normal life means to be consumers *manquées*, or flawed consumers. And so the poor of a consumer society are socially defined, and self-defined, first and foremost as blemished, defective, faulty and deficient – in other words, inadequate – consumers.

As with the reworking of the civic rights of low achieving/early school leavers as an entitlement of deviant producers to the capacity and motivation to compete in the labour market, the orientation of the mercantile paradigm is to redefine the quality of life of the poor as their inadequacy, as consumers, to choose from the vast array of goods and services available and to successfully compete for those that are most sought after. Once discourse on poverty is amenable to such reconceptualisation, at the very least it does not challenge the meanings of the mecantile paradigm.

Since the 1960s there has never been a difficulty in introducing modernist themes of equality to intersubjectivity about Irish education. What is more questionable is what happened as they circulated within the cultural production of Irish education. A number of examples, all of which will be outlined in greater detail in later chapters, should be instructive in illuminating the fate of efforts to conceptualise equality in a manner that perceived people, society and education other than according to the mercantile paradigm.

The writing and research of those who have been described (by Lynch and O'Neill, 1994 following Karabel and Halsey, 1977) as 'equality empiricists' sought to represent the problem of educational inequality in terms of social class. Clancy's research on participation in third-level education has been particularly noteworthy in this regard, succeeding as it has in reaching a wide audience through frequent media citations. The persistence of the findings – to date, there have been four surveys in the research programme, 1980, 1986, 1992 and 1998 –, the clarity of the reporting and the force of the figures have meant that class relationships are kept in focus as a means of identifying the problem of inequality in education. A specific manifestation of this impact is provided by the role played by the secretariat of the National Education Convention (Coolahan, 1994) of which Clancy, along with other sociologists, was a member, in reaffirming the significance of socio-economic factors in educational disadvantage and in isolating this variety of disadvantage from the more general concern for special needs and related support and intervention of the 1992 Green Paper. It can be argued that its influence is to be found in the greater emphasis on socio-economic status in the White Paper's consideration of equality.

A. Dale Tussing, a visiting American economist, was more successful than most in expanding the themes of educational discourse on equality. As well as raising the question of equity in the distribution of scarce resources, Tussing (1981) introduced themes of stratification, elitism and the structuring of inequality, claiming that state aid to fee-charging second-level schools contributed to '... the perpetuation of elitism and class stratification through the school system'. Minor changes followed in the funding of fee-paying schools. But more significant in the overall context of Irish thinking was the fact that the financing of education came to be recognised as a topic about which there could be disputes of principle and values relating to equality. The content of a number of official and advisory body reports suggests that Tussing played a role in having equity and social justice accepted as themes within the policy community, particularly in relation to the funding of third-level education (O'Sullivan, 1992b). Yet, in contrast, a socially regressive intervention, the abolition of undergraduate fees was introduced in 1995. Nonetheless, what Tussing had sought to thematise was that disadvantage was socially constructed and that privilege was a factor in its production.

Sustained public dissent from the mercantile paradigm of education is to be found in the activities of the Conference of Religious of Ireland (CORI), formerly the Conference of Major Religious Superiors (CMRS). Its Education Commission describes its goals as including 'identifying root causes of injustice' and 'challenging unjust structures'. It sees society '... as made up of interdependent rather than independent units ... and recognises that the circumstances of poor people will not change unless the circumstances of people who are not poor also change'. While the Commission conceptualises the problem as the link between education and poverty and seeks to identify ways of breaking this link, 'it suggests that the most effective strategies are ones which seek to empower those who are poor in ways which will enable them to challenge the unjust structures which give rise to inequality and disadvantage in our society' (CMRS, 1992c, pp v-ix). With the benefit of a permanent secretariat and full-time committed personnel, and carrying the (albeit diminishing) moral authority of the church, CORI inserted modernist (*inter alia*) themes into discourse through a sustained series of publications, conferences and specific responses to state discussion documents, policy statements and interventions.

More a feature of academic and activist discourse and drawing its rationale for change from a radical enlightenment orientation to the perfection of society rather than from a Christian theology of social transformation is the egalitarianism of Kathleen Lynch of the Equality Studies Centre at University College, Dublin. Highly critical of what it perceives as the limitations of liberal understandings of equality of educational opportunity, it proposes equality of condition as an objective for the educational system. This argues for more than offering an equal chance of success and failure, which leaves the hierarchies of wealth, power, prestige and recognition unaffected. The objective of equality of condition is to seek to eliminate the hierarchies themselves (Lynch, 1996). From its university base, this radical aspiration for social change has access to students, the state and its corporatist structures, public policy discourse, and activist and community organisations.

Yet, despite these invitations to understand equality otherwise, the mercantile paradigm persists and strengthens in its regulation of the meaning of equality in policy discourse and action. Two questions are initially suggested. Firstly, how successful were these modernist insertions into discourse in maintaining their credentials as modernist themes as they circulated and were culturally processed beyond the immediate agents and social configurations of their production? Secondly, did they experience textualisation to the point, culturally and politically, at which they participated as forces to be reckoned with in understanding how education is implicated in the variability of life chances through the full range of their dimensions?

The answer to the first is a qualified 'no', the answer to the second more consistently negative. This invites a further question as to the intertextual strategies by which these restrictions on the cultural penetration of modernist equality themes were achieved or facilitated. While such culture wars have been an on-going feature of the cultural production of education since the 1960s, two varieties of cultural engagement relating to what is later referred to as the life chances, education and morality (LEM) domain – linguistic skirmishes around the language of LEM from the 1960s and the textual manoeuvring around educational disadvantage in the 1990s – are central.

Linguistically, the deployment of equality of educational opportunity from international policy discourse during the 1960s can act as a base from which to illuminate the subsequent shifting semantic status of the language of LEM. As shall be argued in Chapter 7, by the end of that decade equality of educational opportunity had established itself as the obligatory linguistic usage (overdetermined signifier) when referring to LEM principles. Yet, its contribution to the structuration of Irish understanding of the LEM domain was minimal (underdetermined signification) in its accommodation of native meanings. Even then, themes such as the school as an agent of social reconstruction, as within the comprehensive school ideal, or the structural attribution of inequality, were short-lived in communication. Since then, equality of educational opportunity has been joined by other signifiers within its semantic field – equity, inclusion, cohesion, disadvantage, class, stratification, elitism, egalitarianism, social reconstruction – but these continue to operate in a form of knowledge production that relies on action, programmes, protocols and selection criteria for its realisation and advancement rather than on theorised intentional language. The effect is to expand the vocabulary of LEM, to include modernist themes, without fixing their meaning through linguistic differentiation, resulting in a series of shifting signifiers both in meaning and in their relationships with each other. In such a context, it becomes difficult to successfully maintain a theme in intersubjectivity through a reliance on any single signifier. Even, as in the case of egalitarianism, where there has been a sustained effort to 'fix' its meaning as a theme, through a specification of how it differs from other understandings of equality and a specification of its performatives, it can still find itself ignored, co-opted, resisted or de-legitimated.

More effective in coping with discordant texts is the non-confrontational strategy adopted in the cultural production of educational disadvantage during the 1990s. Due to developments within sociology of education from the 1980s, a range of often-incommensurable texts and counter-texts on educability, variously privileging constitutional limitations, material conditions, cultural forces, and political and economic structures, were available as potential contributors to this process. In the event, many of these texts are evoked in the construction of disadvantage but they are brought together in what is described in Chapter 9 as *pastiche*, a cultural form of non-generative consensually-driven mixing of traces of texts, as distinct from an intertextuality that draws paradigms into an engagement that creates an intersubjective dynamic. *Pastiche* promotes little dissonance that cannot be eased by non-reflexive negotiation, compromise and pragmatism and allows intervention to be quickly foregrounded in discourse. This strategy of appearing to accommodate a text while disengaging from its submerged complexities and contradictions is to be discerned in the depthless processing of many modernist equality analyses and prescriptions. Examples include the reconstitution of unequal achievement as low-achieving 'distant others', the realisation of social structure as community, and the valorisation of action over understanding.

Nonetheless, however unstable and truncated in textualisation, these modernist themes and textual traces do circulate in official discourse on equality. For those so politically motivated, a project awaits in the re-signification of equality and in the excavation of its texts to reveal their modernist origins. Exemplars exist in feminist and anti-racist demands for ethical language, in the fixing of the semantic relationship between multiculturalism and interculturalism by the advocates of the latter, and in how the signification of intelligence was destabilised by the discourse of multiple intelligences. This at least would be a first step in making explicit what is being excluded from, or restrained within our understanding of equality to the benefit of the mercantile paradigm.

Difference

The tendency to regard Ireland as a homogeneous, integrated society was a feature of nationalist ideology, nation-building strategy and Catholic social teaching all of which conceived of society in terms of consensus rather than conflict. To suggest otherwise, that the 'nation', the 'people', the 'Irish' or 'Catholic Ireland' might be in need of differentiation to take account of complexities of distinct identity, values and lifestyle would have been disruptive, in its assertion of new groupings and categories, of the self understanding of Irish culture. As this pertained to education it constituted a case study of boundary politics.

An early assertion of difference in contemporary Irish education has been the multi-denominational school movement now operating under the umbrella of Educate Together. Áine Hyland, Professor of Education at University College Cork, and one of the founders of the movement, has traced its origins, struggles and achievements (Hyland, 1989, 1996). She describes how she and her husband, Bill, a member of the *Investment in Education* survey team, having returned to Ireland from abroad, sought something other than the denominational school system for their children in the early 1970s. Along with other like-minded parents, they set up the Dalkey School Project in Dublin in 1975 for those committed to what was referred to as a multi-denominational option within the national school system. The movement experienced resistance but political support eventually grew and at the turn of the century there were some 20 schools throughout the country affiliated to Educate Together which is also recognised by the Department of Education and Science as a consultative body, and as such took its place at the National Education Convention in 1993. As well as the logistical problems of funding, premises and bureaucratic regulations that assume denominational schooling, Hyland (1996) also notes the opposition of a conservative Catholic group. As she puts it, 'it was as if we were in some sense dangerous radical subversives about to undermine the structure of society,' and quotes from a pamphlet distributed in the Dalkey area by this group calling on local people to contact their elected representatives or to write to the Minister for Education objecting to the proposed school on the basis that it was 'atheistic ... divisive ... hostile to religion ... a precedent for major trouble in other areas'. For reasons that were unlikely to have been considered by this oppositional source, such a movement had indeed the capacity to be disruptive given that conflict relating to cultural categories is fundamental to how society and its institutions are to be understood. In the event, the multi-denominational movement, though educationally transgressive, was not culturally disruptive. For though it challenged the dominion of denominational schooling while remaining within the national school system, it did so in terms of the conventional, cultural coordinate of religious belief.

One has to be struck by the unrelenting commitment of the leaders and early participants of the multi-denominational school movement. A less visible factor in the success of the movement was the manner in which it benefited from the emerging engagement between theocentric, mercantile and modernist themes. Most obviously, the mercantile emphasis on choice and diversity in the provision of services in line with the expressed wishes of consumers is totally consistent with the assertion of difference in the realm of religious sentiments, together with the demand to have that difference acknowledged and catered for in the nature and organisation of educational provision. What was even more significant, and ironically so, was the manner in which the multi-denominational school movement drew on the privileging of religious belief over other realms of commitment (such as social, economic or political principles) to be found in the theocentric view of education. The theocentric paradigm, in the significance it attached to the religious domain in the definition of one's values and world view found itself, with the assertion of rational self-determination of belief, holding the door open for its opposite pole, religious non-belief as well as all intermediate and lateral points to include varieties of socio-religious positions. The effect was that of a palimpsest (Ashcroft *et al.*, 1998) in which the theocentric text, overwritten but not erased by modernity's rationality text, yielded a dense classification of conscience and belief that valorises not just a specific denomination but religious belief and non-belief in the widest sense. Merging the categories of the overwritten, 'rationalised' theocentric text with the principles of the mercantile, the multi-denominational school movement effectively legitimated a new classification of the users and types of educational services. But it achieved this innovation through a process of diversification and superimposition rather than disruption of the existing cultural categories of religion, identity, conscience and world view.

The re-emergence of Irish-medium schools since the 1980s under *Gaelscoileanna* (The National Organisation for Irish-Medium Schools) can also be considered in terms of the construction of difference – in this case the classification of linguistic communities within Irish society. Whatever the motivation for this growth of Irish-medium schooling, having experienced a consistent decline within the mainstream educational system since the 1960s, as they evolved they became implicated with a minority rights discourse. Those whose preference was for the Irish language argued for their entitlement to educational as well as to state services and recreational and cultural facilities through the medium of Irish. This rationalisation represented a departure from the language policy of the state which designated the Irish language as the native language of the Irish people rather than the chosen language of those Irish people who might voluntarily opt for it over English as their preferred medium of regular communication. There were obvious benefits to be derived from adopting a minority rights text in the context of a European Union committed to respecting cultural diversity. But, once the unity of the Irish 'people' in the designation of linguistic communities was disrupted, and language acknowledged as a matter of choice rather than ethnic ascription, it opened the way for those who felt no affinity with Irish to seek abrogation from the requirements of the state's Irish language policy. If those who wished to use Irish as a medium of communication could claim special treatment in pursuit of their cultural values, then equally those who did not include the learning and speaking of Irish in their cultural preferences could feel entitled to exemption in this regard. This argument gained sustenance from the politico-ideological environment of *rapprochement* in Northern Ireland during the 1990s and specifically from the discourse of confidence building and mutual respect among the different traditions on the island. An early manifestation of this argument is to be found in the proposal recorded by Watson (1996) that there should be schools with Irish as the medium of instruction, schools with Irish as a compulsory subject, and also a new type of school in which Irish could be an optional subject. This assertion of cultural difference and choice continues and seems likely to be voiced even more vigorously in the future.

Along with the multi-denominational initiatives, the *Gaelscoileanna* movement represented a modernist intervention in relation to doxic objectives of Irish education – religious formation and linguistic revival – but it did so in the manner in which it embraced the Irish language as a chosen heritage rather than as an ascribed and inescapably essentialised indicator of Irishness. The multi-denominational schools were facilitating parents with an understanding of education other than the theocentric and in giving lived expression to it in the manner in which they educated their children. The *Gaelscoileanna* movement allowed parents to engage anew with the distinctive position of Irish within society and education but according to an interpretation of cultural identity that stressed the active and selective engagement of people with their past as distinct from an objectification of identity in terms of historical and external forces.

Yet, the manner in which these assertions of religious/secular and linguistic differences take the form of the structural differentiation of pupils in different school types has been interpreted as threatening modernity's ideal of a common citizenry. In support of this, schools in which all sectors of society, religious/secular, ethnic, social, etc., learn and interact in mutual recognition and respect according to shared civic values are seen as microcosms of democratic society and as a lived preparation for it. One suspects that this might have been what the Report of the National Education Convention (Coolahan, 1994, p. 25) had in mind when it observed that 'the state may have to strike a balance in responding to pressure groups so as to prevent an undue fractionalising of the school system'. Sugrue (2000) is more explicit. Referring to multi-denominational and Irish-medium schools, he argues:

> ... reliable, if anecdotal, evidence from school principals in both school types, suggests that parents select such schools, in preference to more local national schools, for reasons of social class and elitism, and avoidance of direct contact with church control, rather than commitment to a deeply held conviction about the country's official first language or to pluralism. While such schools tend to have a particular ethos, and may, in some respects be more inclusive, they facilitate also a degree of social segregation that was avoided when everyone, regardless of class, colour or creed, attended the local national school, despite its denominational nature ... There is need therefore for strategic planning in education that considers the consequences for civil society of funding a more diverse school provision.

Multi-denominational and Irish-medium schools are themselves responses to historically-created situations. Advocates of both school types might well respond by arguing that their separateness from the mainstream was forced on them by its failure to accommodate their different aspirations for their children's education in a satisfactory manner. Whatever about responsibility for the lack of accommodation, the material consequence has been the structural differentiation of primary school provision with implications for the cultural status of the modernist theme of citizenship.

When situated in their changing cultural context, modernist dimensions of both school types can themselves be seen to be vulnerable. A significant mercantile threat to the modernism of multi-denominational and Irish-medium schools, and indeed to their distinct defining rationale, is its capacity to culturally re-signify them as manifestations of Post-Fordist production, as initiatives in educational provision that respond to the requirements of specialist configurations of differentiated and discriminating consumers in the form of niche markets. In such a re-interpretation, they come to be represented as boutique schools, brands with discerning appeal, distinguishable from high-street Fordist products, attractive to mercantile subjectivities that take self-confirmation from being active and discerning consumers and doing so in a public and visible manner, at once experiencing and declaring one's mercantile credentials.

Schools may seek to resist these threats to their modernist principles through induction and on-going educational programmes for parents and achieve some success in this regard. But no organisation can insulate itself from social and cultural change. As Catholic schools have experientially accommodated in their ethos and practices to the erosion of the theocentric regulation of lifestyle since the 1960s, in a similar process of cultural penetration multi-denominational and Irish-medium schools will experience being chosen by parents because of the fact, apart from the substance, of their difference and its alignment with mercantile subjectivities of market alertness, judgement, and activism.

In contrast, asserting difference while integrating within mainstream schools has been the policy trend in the education of Travellers. Their claim to cultural distinctiveness and demand that it be recognised in educational practice and provision has been a feature of policy discourse since the 1980s. This has been argued on the basis of their endogamous nature, distinct language, values and lore, shared sense of a common history, and patterns of mutual identification with the settled community (Rigal, 1989; Kenny, 1991). It represents a major shift in the official definition of this group since the 1960s when the policy was one of sedenterisation and settlement of Traveller families and the treatment of Traveller children as culturally deprived in attempting to benefit from education. The acceptance of the distinct ethnic identity of Travellers is reflected in the Green and White Papers which proposed modules on Traveller culture in teacher preparation courses and in the school curriculum. Underachievement and low participation rates, particularly at post-primary level, were treated as problems of cultural difference and ethnicity rather than deprivation, and specific targets have been set. While the 1995 White Paper speaks of Traveller children being 'encouraged to enjoy a full and integrated education within the school system' (Department of Education, 1995, p. 26), the thrust of policy discourse is that they should not become assimilated or absorbed, and that the distinct identity of Travellers would be reflected in schools, as in policy, in a spirit of interculturalism (Coolahan, 1994, p. 126). This will be discussed in greater detail in Chapter 12.

If these successful assertions of difference in education are to be applauded as manifestations of modernity, an on-going test of such an interpretation will be the nature of the relationship between established and newly-differentiated social configurations and their associated identities. As with the entitlement to linguistic choice, there appears to be a public willingness to financially support special provision for Traveller education. What is more suspect is how open people are to accepting that they have obligations to others of different belief, lifestyle, etc. that go beyond financial support, such as recognition, political power and cultural penetration, with the potential to impinge on one's liberty of choice, cultural standing and regulation of identity/orientation be it religious, linguistic or nomadic/sedentary, among others. This refers to the distinction between the minimal obligations of trade/exchange, in which self-interest and its collective pursuit are valorised as collectively beneficial, in promoting greater efficiency, choice, quality and optimum happiness, and those of socially-encumbered understandings of the individual which stress the socially-constituted limitations on choice, social responsibilities, mutual obligations and restrictions on behaviour in the interest of a public or common good, however ideologically shaped. This is as relevant to newly-asserted, as it is to more established, identities. It is particularly pertinent to the final example of accommodating difference in education considered – the case of the Leaving Certified Applied.

The official view on the restructuring of the senior cycle curriculum in terms of three programmes – the Leaving Certificate, the Leaving Certificate Vocational and the Leaving Certificate Applied – was that it recognised and rewards the diversity of abilities and interests which pupils exhibit at this level now that the great majority of young people remain in education until the end of post-primary schooling. Recognition of difference carries with it values such as acceptance, validity and parity of esteem. Views differ on the extent to which the new Leaving Certificate Applied (LCA) programme embodies these values or is likely to reflect them in its operation. Gleeson and Granville (1996) see the LCA as one among a 'comprehensive range of quality educational programmes reflecting and recognising a variety of forms of intelligences and experiences' as 'part of the response to the unequal distribution of the cultural capital of educational achievement' in the context of the 'orientation of educational policy towards the provision of a diversity of programmes to match the changing needs of Irish society'. Nonetheless, they argue, as a central point of their assessment that what will be required will be a 'formal and specific system of direct and reserved access to further education, training and employment for those successfully completing the programme'.

Tuohy and Doyle (1994) are less sanguine. They wonder if the new LCA will contribute to the 'structure of failure', be concentrated in deprived areas and reproduce a new stratum of perceived low-status, effects that are at odds with the aim of social cohesion and cultural unity embraced by the Maastricht Treaty of the European Union whose Social Fund helped to finance the new LCA. They specifically raise questions about the selection of pupils for the LCA:

> Will the teachers avoid a type of thinking which suggests that discipline problems are solved by consigning students to the new course outside the mainstream classroom?

> What criteria do they use to recommend students to the different programmes and how do they avoid impressionistic judgements which assign potentially 'difficult' students to programmes which take them out of the mainstream of school life?

relating to the validity of the LCA qualification in the market place:

> (Students) also need assurances on how their chosen programme will be valued by society and by employers, and on the options open to them when they leave school for employment or third level.

and concerning the implications for common citizenship:

> Can separate tracks coexist in a school which focuses on developing a comprehensive understanding of the world and on promoting a sense of community

in which there is justice and equity? What will be the effects of such differentiation on young impressionable boys and girls, searching to discover their own talents and to express and develop these in a complex and changing world?

Given the association between low achievement and social class at senior cycle as indicated in Table 6.1, the likelihood remains that selection (including self-selection) for the LCA will be a function of social class, mediated through the differential *realisation* of potential. As such it can be accommodated within the mercantile paradigm as an intervention that directly targets the deviant labour market participant and holds out hope in time for the 'flawed consumer'. What Gleeson *et al.*'s (2002) case study of the implementation of the LCA in four schools demonstrates is that such concerns must persist; but it equally attests to a diversity, in the aspirations for the LCA, in the efforts of teachers to engage with pupils and in school culture, that holds out possibilities for change.

Virtue

A distinguishing feature of the theocentric paradigm was the very explicit and directive manner in which it pronounced on what might be generally labelled as virtue. This covered a wide span of behaviours and dispositions including the social domain of charity and justice, personal qualities such as truthfulness, patience and temperance and the duties of citizenship including obedience to lawful authority, all mentioned in the Council of Education reports of the 1950s and early 1960s, as well as more specific areas such as sexual behaviour and the sanctity of the family. An uncompromising aspect of educational programmes relating to these virtues which operate within the frame of the theocentric paradigm was their confident prescription of right and wrong based on church teaching derived from revelation and natural law. As the theocentric paradigm lost its controlling power, the legitimacy of this prescriptiveness became less secure. What had been the certainties of the religion class and of the general practices and ethos of Catholic schooling became less compelling to students and invited open challenge and dissent. A new set of values was emerging which centred itself on the individual and proclaimed the priority of personal autonomy, self-direction and choice. Behaviour, most publicly relating to alcohol, drugs and sex, which in the past was differentiated in terms of 'right' and 'wrong', was increasingly treated in terms of personal choice. The function of educational programmes addressing such matters was seen to be the preparation of young people for the making of these choices rather than their instruction in what constituted proper, correct and moral behaviour. As Dorr (1989), one of the earliest advocates of a change in approach to dealing with values in the educational system, put it, 'young people in school are already exposed to a great diversity of conflicting views on what is worthwhile in life and are near the point of leaving whatever shelter the home and school provide and of taking charge of their own lives ... I believe that it is vital that they be prepared to meet the challenge and that this cannot be done either by ignoring controversial issues or by by-passing the controversy and teaching them "the correct answers", as if this were as simple as teaching them the facts of History, Geography or Science.'

The obvious tensions between the teaching of correct behaviour and the facilitation of lifestyle choices came to a head in relation to a range of new programmes variously described as social and health education, life skills, human relationships, pastoral care, and education for living which developed from the 1970s. These were offered in post-primary schools in association with Youth Associations, Health Boards and the Health Education Bureau, and sought to expand the traditional curriculum beyond its cognitive/intellectual focus and its emphasis on examinations (Crooks and McKernan, 1984). It was not until 1994 that the Department of Education became directly involved in this area when it was the initiator of the development of what was described as a relationship and sexuality education programme (Inglis, 1998b). These programmes were targeted by sections within the Catholic church as a source of threat to religion and religious values. Many apparently overlapping and fluid Catholic interest groups have participated (Mac an Ghaill *et al.*, 2004; Kiely, 2004). This study draws particularly on the contribution of the better known Family Solidarity (1987) and on the theorised contestation of the Public Policy Institute of Ireland (1993) which describes itself as committed to promoting 'the common good in the light of natural law and Christian principles in an ecumenical spirit'. Two of their pivotal criticisms are relevant here: the wide interpretation of health education and the moral relativism and subjectivism of the programmes.

Far from being confined to what the Public Policy Institute of Ireland described as the commendable and uncontroversial 'nits and hygiene' (p. 43) understanding of health education, that is promoting healthy living in terms of hygiene, diet, exercise and the dangers of alcohol, tobacco and drugs, the critics of the programmes pointed to components dealing with family living, morality, human growth and development, relationships and sex education, all of which should more properly feature in the Christian formation of young people. Quite simply, the domain of moral belief and principle was considered to be under invasion from a predominantly secularising set of influences in a manner that disguised both the intrusion and the paradigm shift involved. On this point, Archbishop Kevin McNamara (1987) of Dublin was the most explicit critic of these programmes from within the institutional church:

> While appreciating the need for health education in our schools, and commending the
> efforts to make it available, one may reasonably ask that programmes presented

under the heading of 'health education' should, to avoid misunderstanding and confusion, confine themselves to what is normally understood by health and not seek to gather into the net of health education practically the whole range of a pupil's personal and social life and how, in the wide range of a pupil's relationships with others, moral decision-making and moral behaviour should be guided.

The methodology of these programmes included group discussion, socio-drama, role play and value clarification techniques, and followed approaches from training manuals developed initially in North America. Of these, the values clarification technique developed by Raths *et al.* (1966) has been repeatedly criticised for the manner in which it teaches that 'there are no absolute rights and wrongs' (Family Solidarity, 1987). As Dorr (1989) argues, the values clarification technique seems to start from an awareness of the multiplicity of conflicting values in the modern world, and assuming that no single one of them is capable of being rationally justified over another, considers it unacceptable just to teach set values. Instead, the technique offers strategies for getting pupils to be clear and consistent in the values they opt for, to choose them freely and to think through the consequences of so choosing. As he puts it, 'what the strategies claim to do is to help people judge whether the values they profess verbally are *truly* values they are committed to and live by. This is very different to the question whether those values, or any other values, are *true* values, as opposed to false or illusory values.'

By far the most widely-quoted and rhetorical criticisms of the values clarification techniques is to be found in Manly's *The Facilitators* (n.d.). She accuses the formulators of the techniques of being 'total moral and philosophical relativists' and of being 'subjectivists and emotivists'. She sees the values clarification approach as an invitation to young people to abandon the values they were reared with and encourages them to say 'I now find this value unattractive, it doesn't suit my personality or self concept, so I'll throw it in the dustbin. It's just not my style' (pp 55-57).

This debate, with these criticisms recurring, was again activated by the inclusion of a section on the health promoting school in the 1992 Green Paper. But it was the Stay Safe Programme for primary schools that generated the most wide-ranging and public confrontation on these issues at that time.

Conceived as a response to child abuse and bullying, the programme was tested in the Eastern Health Board region in a joint venture with the Department of Education and introduced nationally to schools in the early 1990s. There were twelve lessons in the programme, each of about thirty minutes duration, dealing with such experiences as getting lost and coming into contact with strangers, bullying, and touches that make one feel 'unsafe'. The most contested feature of the programme was the approach to teaching children to use the distinction between 'yes' and 'no' feelings to discriminate between abusive and non-abusive acts. Gerard Casey (1993a), a philosophy lecturer in University College, Dublin and a member of the Public Policy Institute of Ireland, has been the foremost critic of this emotive/affective approach to teaching children to distinguish between right and wrong. As he puts it, 'the blindingly simple point I would make is this: even supposing that children are able to make the appropriate affective discrimination there is no necessary correlation between feelings of any kind and acts that are objectively right and wrong.' He goes on to argue, and elsewhere (Casey, 1993b) to give examples, that 'children can get "yes" feelings both when abused and when not abused, and "no" feelings both when abused and when not abused, so that the "yes" and "no" feelings method cannot discriminate between acts that are abusive and acts that are not.' His argument is that the purpose of moral education is to train young people's feelings in such a way that 'their emotional response to moral situations will be appropriate and will reinforce and make possible sensible moral choices'. He also draws on Archbishop McNamara's (1987) published lecture on curriculum and values cited earlier: 'true values ... rest on what a person ought to do, on what is in conformity with the real good of the human person and society, a good that cannot be discerned by feelings or spontaneous emotional reactions, but only by the God-given gift of reason'.

The introduction of the Department of Education initiated programme, Relationships and Sexuality Education (NCCA, 1996), continued the conflict. This programme originated from an Expert Advisory Group established by the Minister for Education, Niamh Bhreathnach in 1994 following the 'grotesque, bizarre, unprecedented and, most of all, unacceptable discovery of two dead babies within a month' in that year (Inglis, 1998b, p. 1). The response to the programme in *RSE in Catholic Schools. A Resource for Teachers and Boards of Management* (1997, p. 5) was explicit:

> The Catholic school in the formulation of its policy should reflect Catholic moral teaching on sexual matters. Even more fundamentally, it needs to be specific in excluding approaches which are inconsistent with the foundations of Catholic moral thought.

Alongside this can be found Alvey's (1998) fear that RSE wouldn't be 'free of religious undertones' because of the state's willingness 'to placate the doctrinal concerns of the catholic authorities'. A recurring feature of this ongoing conflict is well-illuminated by a study of the public controversy surrounding *Exploring Masculinities*, an optional social, personal and health education module that may be offered in single-sex boys schools during Transition Year or senior cycle of post-primary schooling (Mac an Ghaill *et al.*, 2004). It demonstrates how, whatever the substantive status of social, personal and health education themes in school initiatives, their presence in material works, programmes and practices are prone to being deployed to function as cultural flashpoints around which further cultural battles, of the broadest kind about issues of religion and correct living, can be publicly staged.

What needs to be kept in mind is that far from being a conflict between those who propose a value-laden education and those who don't, the tension is between different understandings of the person, relationships with others and society, and how these ought to be reflected in the classroom. On the one hand, there is the view of the Public Policy Institute of Ireland (1993), firmly grounded in the theocentric paradigm, that education should be premised on 'belief in the human person as possessed of an eternal destiny, as morally free but in need of formation in virtue' since this is considered to be 'an essential element in the self-understanding of the vast majority of our people' (p. 43). On the other hand, developers of these programmes (e.g. McKernan, 1988; McIntyre, 1993) project their targeted pupils as rational subjects with the capacity, given suitable training in coping with social pressures, enhancing self-esteem, and in clarifying values, together with appropriate knowledge, to make autonomous choices. This reflects the enlightenment subject capable of knowing itself and, being both knower and known, placing its knowledge, fears, inhibitions and restrictions under scrutiny and, rising above these restraints, making choices for itself, individually and self-aware. To this extent the enlightenment subject is shared by both modernist and mercantile paradigms. What separates them is the manner and the extent to which they depart from ethical individualism, according to which the sole moral objective of an individual's actions is personal benefit.

There is little divergence from this in the mercantile assumption in social and sexual exchanges that whoever one is engaging with has been similarly positioned as a rational subject, unless there are obvious contraindicators such as those of age or mental capacity. While embracing ethical individualism, the mercantile paradigm nonetheless incorporates an expectation that self-interest promotes the basis for social improvements and enhanced happiness, freedom and efficiency. Modernity's ideal of co-responsibility for social progress conflicts with ethical individualism, and the distinction between both paradigms in this regard is stark in relation to macro-social objectives such as equality. However, the divergence is less clear in relation to such an area as sexual relationships insofar as it pertains to that social realm which modernity, most extremely in liberalism, defines and distinguishes as a private sphere in which one may live one's own life in one's own way. A consequence is the instability of the intertextual relationship between the mercantile and the modern in relation to such a social realm. As reflected in RSE programme discourse, this generates a bivalent signification of the social and ethical dimension of interpersonal relationships, fluctuating between the secular and civic virtues of social responsibility, mutual respect and tolerance and their mercantile configuration as indifference, apathy, privatism and anonymity.

Ironically, modernity's secret ally in stabilising a social and ethical, as distinct from an individualistic, interpretation of responsibility is the theocentric text on sexuality from which relationship and sexuality type programme discourse distances itself in its proclaimed unwillingness to judge or to preach. This is apart from the political accommodation of religious interests in the state's acknowledgement that the parameter for the delivery of such programmes must be the policy of the school regarding the spiritual, moral and ethical development of pupils as drawn up through the collaborative involvement of parents, teachers and board of management. The characteristic theme of sexuality as part of God's plan for procreation and the human race and its formative and prescriptive textualisation may be absent from programme discourse. But neither is it treating sexuality as any other commodity that can be implicated in social exchange. Mercantile self-interest is signified in the centrality accorded to 'risk', particularly in terms of health (disease, unwanted pregnancy), in its foregrounding of sex and sexuality. Yet, throughout its discourse, a social ethic (not necessarily secular) is implied in appeals to 'responsible' behaviour as in the aspiration that 'the pupil becomes more responsible in making choices and decisions in all aspects of life, and particularly those relating to sexuality and relationships' (NCCA, 1996, p. 5). But this ethic is never quite asserted, much less described. Rather the discourse relies on the cultural legacy of the theocentric text's privileging of sex and sexuality, furtively 'raiding' a cultural resource that it has differentiated itself from as a paradigm.

We have seen the bivalent signification of virtue in terms of individualistic and social ethics in the interplay between the modern and the mercantile. The theocentric paradigm adds a further strand of meaning-making to be employed within the intertextuality. It can be seen to be implicated as the moralistic, judgemental and preaching 'other' used to differentiate relationship and sexuality programmes and define their modernity. But it is also the unstated (and perhaps unknown) cultural source for the legitimation of the exceptionalism of sex and sexuality over other dimensions of social relationships that feature in these same programmes to warrant a more social ethic than mercantile self-interest would otherwise allow. This exemplifies the multi-text nature of the intertextuality involved in signifying virtue in the context of relationships and sexuality programmes that their progressive advocates would proclaim as modern, at once 'a force of emancipation which challenges and replaces outdated, inappropriate attitudes to life' while 'enabling young people to counteract the colonising effects of the media, market forces and consumerism' (Inglis, 1998b, pp 173-174).

Control

Controversy regarding the control and management of schooling can be traced to the nature and representation of the governance of education in the Irish Republic.

Irish education is largely an aided rather than a state system with almost all primary schools and the majority of post-primary schools owned by religious authorities. While within the theocentric paradigm this would have been unremarkable, and its anti-statist character totally consistent with the Roman Catholic principle of subsidiarity, it came to be contested from the 1960s onwards. Here, we concentrate largely on developments in relation to school governance, religion and the Roman Catholic Church in the 1990s, and then only for the purpose of analysing the interplay of the cultural resources employed by the protagonists.

This contestation drew on a number of routine representations of the existing system of school governance in policy discourse. Firstly, problematising its doxic status, there was the empirical demonstration of the comparative distinctiveness of the Irish system of school governance: 'the structure of the education system in the Republic of Ireland is unique among the countries of the European Union ... unlike other EU countries where the norm is the publicly owned and publicly controlled school, in Ireland the norm is a privately run school' (Hyland, 1996). Secondly, the extent of public funding to the private institutions involved was highlighted: 'the state pays over 80 per cent of the capital costs of building and facilities, and over 90 per cent of current expenditure if one includes teachers' salaries' (Coolahan, 1994, p. 23). Finally, there was the casting of religious ownership of schools in terms of self-appointed authority, unmandated power and unresponsive control. 'Many have been concerned', claimed Michael D. Higgins (1991), a former government minister, 'that control of education has been ceded away from the public and given to an authority that does not seek its mandate from the public will, that involves transcendental authority, above and beyond a democratic will.' These themes reflect the construct of the modernist state as the prime agency of sovereignty within a particular territory, legimated by notions of popular will, implicit contractual agreement and universal franchise, and with authority over previously privileged groups, both spiritual and temporal. In Crook *et al.*'s (1993, p. 221) description, processes of modernisation produce 'the state as a container of rationalised power based on claims to sovereignty, and as the creator and protector of citizenship rights', becoming 'a corporate manager, securing a "grand armistice" between warring socio-economic interests' and supplying functions that include 'internal and external stabilisation, economic regulation, infrastructural development, the amelioration of social problems and social-political legitimation'. It was with such an understanding of the state that the authors of *Understanding Contemporary Ireland* (Breen *et al.*, 1990, p. 123) concluded that 'despite the shift of the financial burden of education on to the State, the degree of control possessed by the State over the system remains limited ... the capacity of the Irish State to carry through educational policy is restricted by the nature of the system.'

It would be wrong to assume that Roman Catholic schools did not acknowledge or respond to the concerns of a modern state. A variety of arrangements and special provisions were put in place for pupils whose parents objected to the religious or the specifically Roman Catholic aspects of schools, where such schools were pragmatically the only sources of education available to them. As Roman Catholic parents and school staff themselves became less orthodox in their religious practices and more individualistic in their interpretation of church teaching, especially in relation to their personal lives, schools adapted in their expectations, assumptions, exhortations and excoriations in a manner that sometimes brought them into conflict with Catholic parents who would have wished for a more 'authentic' assertion and modelling of church teaching. In contrast to the fears of the 1970s, state efforts to rationalise post-primary school facilities were treated with less suspicion by the religious authorities by the mid-1980s. Indeed, as Walsh's (1999) analysis of this process of adaptation to state planning points out, faced with decreasing religious personnel, it went beyond closure and amalgamation to include withdrawing religious from teaching, from principalships, from boards of management, and planning for when they might withdraw totally from the trusteeship of schools. Yet, the Roman Catholic Church never theorised its position, or indeed acknowledged some of these changes in church schools, be it in relation to the vindication of individual religious rights within its schools or the nature of its power relationship to the sovereign state. Specifically, it never sought to create a post-subsidiarity text that would accommodate the issues and contradictions for a modernist state in effectively having as its substantial provider of education throughout its territory a church body operating a network of private, state-funded schools. The fact that Article 42 of the Constitution 'acknowledges' and 'guarantees to respect' the status of parents as 'the primary and natural educator of the child' indicates the challenges involved in constructing such a text; but it should equally have suggested the urgency, for the church, of addressing the issues involved in a more proactive way in the light of the social and cultural transformations occurring in Irish society.

In contrast, what publicly signified the church's position on the issue of control were such performances as mobilising parents in defence of Catholic schools (Walsh, 1997), and defending their interests during the establishment of community schools in relation to their formation and location (Owens, 1989) and the issues of deed of trust and reserved places (O'Flaherty, 1992). It was atypical interventions such as the Eileen Flynn case of the early 1980s and the unrepresentative conspiratorial discourse of Vera Verba (1975) that served as tropes for, respectively, unbridled church power and an irrational fear of modernisation. In attempting to rebut such representations, since the time of the FIRE Report of 1973 apologists for the existing system found themselves drawn into the emerging mercantile discourse, seeking to compete on the basis of its logic, less inclined to invoke the theocentric paradigm without adequately engaging with the modern. Common arguments included the relative efficiency of religious schools in the use of public funding when compared with more publicly-controlled schools, the extent of state control in terms of curricular content, public examination requirements and the registration and inspection of teachers, the fact that the parents of the children who were availing of this publicly-funded education had themselves contributed to it as tax payers, and legalistic appeals to the Constitution. As we shall see in Chapter 10, the extensive discourse of CMRS/CORI on education focused on issues of justice in the light of the Gospels. School ethos and the quality of religious experience in schools also featured (Hogan and Williams, 1997; Feheney, 1998b).

What remained neglected was what Dunne (1997) referred to as the 'institutional-political' question. The church was arguably better-placed than any of the interests implicated in the processes of control and power in education, having within its membership (Dunne, 1991; Lane, 1991; Cassidy, 1992; Drumm, 1997) and institutions (Williams, 1997, 1999) intellectuals capable of producing the most conceptually-refined and theoretically-grounded cultural resources for such a task. The process of textualisation was in evidence in a revised and expanded version of a paper first delivered by Dunne (1991) at the CMRS (1991) Conference, *The Catholic School in Contemporary Society*, in which he explored the tensions between the Catholic school and civil society, together with some options for Roman Catholic schools. Perhaps this process was pursued and a sustained interpretation of the 'institutional-political' question exists within the church that acknowledges ongoing adaptation at school level and suggests constructs, protocols, or possibilities for confronting the issues involved. If so, it was not evident in public policy discourse during the 1990s at a time when the governance of education came to be thematised. For whatever reason, at a time when it would have been to its advantage to have done so, the church failed to insert an effective text into the cultural production of the church-state relationship in education that acknowledged the social and cultural transformations impinging on it and the experiential adaptations of its schools.

This was both the cultural backdrop and context for the initiatives by the state during the 1990s in the form of policy discourse and legislation in relation to the governance of education. The 1992 Green Paper proposed that all aided secondary schools and primary schools with five teachers or more would have an eleven-person board of management with a rotating chairperson, the composition of which could not guarantee a majority for the five nominees of the trustees or owners. Boards of management had been a feature of primary schools since 1975. There was to be 'minimal intervention' (p. 143) from the owners/trustees and from the Department of Education. It stipulated, as a condition for funding, the establishment of a 'representative board of management with the necessary authority to manage' (p. 154). In its response, the CMRS (1993b) declared itself favourable to the principle of boards of management, but felt that 'the proposed reduction in the number of trustee nominees and the proposal of a rotating chairperson would not be justified in view of the responsibilities which trustees bear and would continue to bear' (p. 64). The patrons and trustees of Catholic schools again adopted this position at the National Education Convention, arguing that they needed to appoint majorities on the boards and nominate the chairperson so as to protect the religious ethos and social mission of their schools. However, it was reported (Coolahan, 1994, p. 27) that 'both the Catholic bishops and the CMRS declared that they were open to discussions with the Department and other relevant bodies on alternative, effective mechanisms by which the continuing religious ethos and social mission of their schools could be protected'.

Subsequently, when the 1995 White Paper was published its policy intentions in this regard found favour with religious authorities: 'the government is committed to maintaining the diversity of school types, recognising the pluralism of Irish society and the rights of parents to provide for their children's education in schools of their choice, subject to curricular and financial constraints' (p. 63). So also did its recognition of the distinctive role of the patrons of religious schools: 'the functions of patrons/trustees/owners/governors relate to the original promoters and founders of schools, the most important of which is ensuring the continuity of the ethos of the school concerned, including a distinctive religious ethos' (p. 146).

Because of this, the provisions of the Education Bill (1997) came as a shock to religious authorities. As David Meredith (1997), secretary of the Church of Ireland (Anglican) Board of Education explained:

> so why is the Education Bill dominating the headlines and generating so much heat? I can only suggest that the heat generated is in direct proportion to the divergence between the 1995 White Paper and the 1997 Bill. Why there should be a divergence at all is a mystery. But divergence there is and in areas of quite considerable sensitivity.

The coalition of religious interests that emerged has been described as 'an unprecedented alliance', constituting an 'historic moment' in Irish education (Pollak, 1997a). Representatives of almost every religious faith involved in Irish education gathered, Roman Catholic, Anglican, Presbyterian, Methodist, Quaker, Muslim, and claiming the support of the Jewish community, to oppose what they regarded as a threat to the denominational character of their schools. The strength of feeling can be gauged from the fact that the kind of language used had not been heard for decades: 'statutory takeover of our schools', a 'great fear' that the church's running of schools would be undermined resulting in schools 'controlled by the state'. At the press conference, the senior education spokesman for the Anglican community, Archdeacon Gordon Linney, referred reporters to what he described as the 'brilliant analysis' of the Bill by the Roman Catholic Church's Conference of Religious. This analysis (CORI, 1997a) proposed a number of modifications to the Bill for the purpose of making the role of patron and the relationship between patrons and boards of management more explicit. The most fundamental of these modifications, and one from which all the others are derived, was as follows: 'the patron of a school has a right to require that the school protects and promotes particular principles and core values' (p. 22). It argued that this clarification was necessary to do no more than enshrine the commitment and principles of the White Paper in the Education Act.

Was this to be seen as the government of the day seeking to assert state sovereignty within the limits imposed on it by its Constitution? And is the advocacy and opposition of these religious interests to be interpreted as resistance to the efforts of a modernising state to disperse the control of schools more widely throughout the citizens of the state, to include parents, teachers and members of the business community, and in the process dilute the regulatory power of 'the non-elected holders of religious office' (O'Toole, 1997)? This seems to have been the understanding of the coordinator of the National Parents' Council – Primary, Fionnuala Kilfeather, at its Annual Conference. She was reported (Pollak, 1997b) to have declared that she was 'disturbed to hear reports that some patrons and some political parties have been seeking to weaken the responsibilities of the boards of management and to give more power and control to the patrons'. She urged the Minister for Education to 'push ahead' with her 'democratic reforms', and warned that no matter who owned the school property, 'the education that takes place in schools is not "owned" by any one group. It belongs to us, the citizens of Ireland.' O'Toole (1997) was less sanguine about the modernising credentials of either the Education Bill or the modifications demanded by CORI, criticising them as 'a "choice" between a great deal of church control on the one hand and almost total church control on the other'.

To this extent, modernist categories and principles were employed as protagonists sought to define the nature of the issues involved. However, the root metaphor of the market was also prominent in policy discourse on the governance of education, drawing heavily on the primacy of the tax payer-funder of education, on the image of paying the piper and calling the tune, on the principle of responsiveness to the wishes of the users of the service, and on the virtues of a market for educational services within which consumers could function.

School governance was not an issue that appeared to concern large sections of the population. As the Report of the National Education Convention (Coolahan, 1994, p. 31) observed, the great majority of parents appeared 'to retain a preference for denominational education for their children'. At the very least it can be said that there was a widespread acceptance of it. Anecdotally, it would appear that arrangements made by Roman Catholic schools for an increasingly-diverse range of religions represented within their student bodies, meet with general approval. As for the parental perspective on school governance, it seemed to engage little with the modernist nature of its mechanisms and more with its mercantile performativity in the form of delivering academic results and responsiveness in its day-to-day operations to the users of its services.

The treatment of the provision of denominational, multi-denominational and secular education in the Report of the National Education Convention contained a judicious selection from within modernist and theocentric texts in a manner that excluded mercantile appeals. It sought to assert the modernist theme of the state as vindicator of the rights of minorities and individuals, be they motivated by religious belief or the absence of it, while also acknowledging the entitlement of religious authorities to establish and operate schools according to a particular ethos and to receive state funding. It proclaimed the virtues of citizenship in the mutual accommodation of differences, through dialogue and agreed protocols, while being educated in shared publicly-funded school space, rather than an increasingly diversified market of educational services. It concluded: 'without affecting the rights of religious authorities to establish schools with a clearly defined ethos, and to be aided by the state, there needs to be much wider agreement on the rights of nonbelievers, or other minorities within (such) schools' (Coolahan, 1994, p. 33). It was in this regard that the absence of a church text on a new understanding of the interests of church and state in its schools, notwithstanding references by the CMRS at the Convention to 'issues of civil liberties' (p. 33), appears most obvious. Indeed, the Convention's background paper prepared by its secretariat in the light of responses to the Green Paper identifies some of the key themes that such a text might have developed as a contribution to the resolution of the issues that arise in the light of the public/private character of church schools: 'while protecting the rights of majorities, the rights of minorities must not just be tolerated, but treated with respect and an outgoing policy be adopted to facilitate the accommodation of their needs' (p. 153).

At this stage, the conflict surrounding the 1997 Education Bill may seem no more than another episode in church-state wrangling over the control of schooling, the issues legally determined to the advantage of religious authorities by the Education Act and the Employment Equality Act of 1998 and the Equal Status Act (2000). Yet, culturally the tensions surrounding the role of the church in the governance of education revealed by that episode remain unresolved and its inadequate cultural resources and truncated understandings persist. What seems to have happened both in the extensive policy debate as a preamble to the Education Bill (1997) and in the response to it (Walshe, 1999), is that a number of distinct themes were inadequately differentiated from one another. It is possible to identify at least five themes, operating in a sliding relationship to one another – mutating, fusing, appropriating, and forming an unstable base for attempts at communication:

- The entitlement of committed agents to establish and maintain schools in accordance with their principles, be they religious, secular, linguistic or otherwise
- Casting such agents or their successors in commitment as representative agents of those parents who opt to avail of their educational services
- Vindicating the interests of those pupils who do not share the foundational commitment of the schools they are attending
- Facilitating the participation of groups with legitimate interests in the management of the school
- Arranging for the financial answerability to the state of organisations in receipt of public funding.

These themes are applicable to denominational, multi-denominational schools and *Gaelscoileanna*, but it is in relation to Roman Catholic schools that the issues involved are most challenging and universally experienced. In the realisation and prioritising of these themes, in their interaction and in the manner in which efforts were made to build them into convincing discourse by the protagonists, all three paradigms – theocentric, modernist and mercantile – are evident in the shifting meanings that circulated in the policy discourse that ensued. Both modern and mercantile paradigms experience difficulty with religious belief and particularly with religious agency in society. Modernity is perplexed by the persistence of religion and its failure to rupture in the face of the teleology of modernisation. It is uneasy with the non-rational character of religious belief and uncomprehending of how shared civic norms can be agreed with people who do not submit to rational procedures in determining values, choosing personal philosophies and directing their lives. Relatedly, modernity fears that in its recognition of a superordinate authority, religion compromises, indeed challenges, the sovereignty of the state. The mercantile is intolerant of any kind of inflexible commitment, be it religious or secular, that might limit the capacity of participants to reposition themselves in the light of changing contexts of trade/exchange. Affective loyalties and attachments, unregulated by rationality in the pursuit of one's best interests, are regarded negatively, destined to inhibit individual initiative and adaptability and social efficiency and diversity. For its part, as we have seen, following the policy initiatives concerning school governance during the 1990s, the theocentric paradigm was invoked more defensively, drawing on legal and constitutional appeals but also on constructs such as subsidiarity that were more reminiscent of an earlier era.

The status of the five themes listed above depended on the extent to which they were realised and their subsequent processing in the texts embodied in these paradigms operating individually but usually in some form of engagement with one another. When processed in modernist and mercantile texts, the themes of committed and representative agency were merged in policy discourse on the governance of church schools. Even the modernism evident in the Report of the National Education Convention (Coolahan, 1994) which was tempered with an acceptance of denominational education, did not quite differentiate between them. Along with other committed agents such as the founders of multi-denominational schools and *Gaelscoileanna*, it recognised the mission of the religious patron in wishing to ensure 'that certain fundamental beliefs, values and culturally valuable practices are effectively taught and learned/internalised within the schools they set up'. But it then appeared to subsume such committed agency under representative agency: 'the patron/trustee in this sense stands for, or acts on behalf of, a body (usually organised) of people who wish their children to be educated within a particular religious, ethical or cultural tradition' (p. 24). Yet, these varieties of agency are conceptually distinct with implications for rights and obligations. It was such a distinction that Archdeacon Linney was attempting to make when he argued that 'our church schools and other religious educational foundations are really entrusted to us by those who went before us, and it is our duty to hand them on to those who succeed us in circumstances which are consistent with their foundation' (quoted in Pollak, 1997a). While the context and logic are different, Edmund Burke's famous distinction, in his communication with the electors of Bristol, between being elected as a member of Parliament to follow one's convictions rather than to act according to the wishes of the electors is a useful parallel (O'Brien, 1992, pp 74-75).

At the roundtable discussions on school governance in 1994, Bishop Flynn sought to contain the theme of financial answerability to the state within the limits of practices of accountability. He argued: 'the state has a right and an obligation to see that money paid to schools is well spent. But there is a big difference between making a school accountable for its use of state grants and interfering with the running of the school' (quoted in Walshe, 1999, p. 108). However, financial answerability was more usually deployed in discourse in mercantile terms as a theme to boost the entitlement of clients of the educational service to participation in school policy-making, rather than relying on modernist justifications in terms of democratic values of a kind which favour participation at the most immediate level of decision making. In fact, the requirement of financial answerability came to be prioritised in legitimating the exercise of power in the governance of education. As an editorial in *The Irish Times* (1997) put it, 'there is a need for some belated statutory recognition that the elected government which pays the piper of the national education system has the right to call the tune, or at least a significant part of that tune.' In the same editorial we find the representative agency of patrons highlighted to the exclusion of their committed agency in a manner that effectively denied the validity of the latter: 'the churches may own the sites of schools; they don't own the education that goes on inside them … on the eve of the twenty-first century increasingly well-educated and independent-minded Irish parents – whether Catholic, Protestant, Muslim or of no religion at all – are the best judges of their children's education'.

As indicated above, committed agency is alien to the mercantile paradigm with its valorisation of flexible, adaptable and entrepreneurial producers and service providers whose primary commitment is to commercial viability rather than to a specific product. Occasionally, beyond the confines of the policy discourse on the governance of schools, this contrast between entrepreneurial and committed agency is made explicit. In an address to a conference on the topic of economic values and the common good, organised by the Irish Centre for Faith and Culture, Mr John Dunne, Director General of IBEC, as reported by McGarry (2000), likened the Roman Catholic Church in Ireland to that of a monopoly 'undergoing the necessary process of change following deregulation and market liberalisation'. He pointed to the dangers of monopolies becoming detached from the needs of consumers:

> Put bluntly, it doesn't matter how good your product or service is if it does not meet the needs of the consumer. This approach is as relevant to the church as it is to business. As in business, it is pointless bemoaning economic and social change, denying the reality, demands and needs of the lives of ordinary people.

The inevitable outcome of an organisation that refused to or was incapable of adaptation was 'a loss of competitiveness and erosion in market share'.

It is not in the nature of the membership of the theocentric paradigm to be responsive, be it to modernist democratic appeals or mercantile consumer demand, if it is to require the renouncing of the founding commitment of church schools. Who then is to vindicate the rights, even represent the interests, of those pupils who do not share in the founding commitment of the school type they attend? And what would be the relative contribution of modernist and mercantile paradigms to such discourse and action? Whatever about the role of the state and school board of management in this regard, what is most relevant here is the inadequate thematising by church spokespersons of the nature of the obligations of the current agents of the founding commitment of church schools to such pupils. In its failure to contribute a text to policy discourse on its public education role, in terms other than its fulfilment of the secular requirements of the state in relation to curriculum, teacher qualifications and inspection, standardisation of the school year, etc., the church appeared to refuse the engagement with modernist texts on education such as were offered during the National Education Convention. But, far from being conducive to such intertextuality, the modern/mercantile failure to differentiate between committed and representative agency in the church's involvement in education, subsuming the former under the latter, contributed to subjectivities more disposed to tight framing and the maintenance of boundaries.

What the discourse of the time demonstrates is the difficulty experienced by a society addressing issues relating to religion and the politics of education with the cultural resources of a 1990s Ireland in which post-theocentric subjectivities were particularly alert to any suggestion of the persistence of church influence in society. Indeed, since then the manner in which protagonists and commentators in the 'Dunboyne Debacle' (Carr, 2002), which involved the dismissal of the principal of the local interdenominational *gaelscoil* but was made to function as a 'cultural flashpoint' in relation to church power, positioned themselves discursively indicates more regression than progress in relation to both cultural resources and subjectivities. Leaving aside the issue of employment rights, the discourse of the controversy reveals – in the letters to the editor and news coverage of *The Irish Times*, and among columnists (e.g. Holland, 2002) and subsequent commentators (Bacik, 2004) – an incomprehension, at its mildest, of the interdenominational principle and intent, among those for whom multi-denominational/secular education had become doxic, that mirrors the experience of the multi-denominational movement when it sought to gain acceptance thirty years earlier. Following Pareto, doxa as well as elites circulate, each by their nature oriented to applying the lash rather than seeking to understand or accommodate.

What the events of the 1990s recounted in this section on control represent for modernist/mercantile intertextuality is an ignored opportunity on the part of the church to sponsor and incorporate into its understanding of the governance of education some of the more positive constructs of modernity such as dialogue, acknowledging, respecting and accommodating difference, and mutual respect and shared civic virtues in the occupancy of a 'public-within-a-private' sphere; or better still to draw on its intellectuals to develop new hybrid constructs, in a manner that could have challenged the more mercantile-derived influences on the politics of education.

An Irish Post-Modernism?

Notwithstanding the legislation of the late 1990s, the demise of the theocentric paradigm is destined to be confirmed in the educational planning of the future. Religiosity seems set to persist as a force in people's lives and denominational schools are likely to continue to serve the wishes of parents who desire, with diverse levels of engagement and orthodoxy, to have their children educated within a specific religious ethos. But the collective cultural orientation on which Irish educational ideas will draw, be it in terms of the view of the human person, individual freedom, social obligation, personal virtue or social progress, will be derived less and less from a world-view that places God and his intentions for the world and its people at its centre. The most effective contender to replace the theocentric paradigm in the reconstruction of Irish education is the mercantile paradigm, and not modernity as might have been expected.

One can only speculate on the fate of the modernist cultural production around the themes addressed in this chapter – equality, difference, virtue and control. As currently constituted, they cannot avoid the predatory engagement of the mercantile paradigm, becoming implicated with it, allied to it, and neutralised or destabilised by it. To continue as the more vulnerable intertextual partners to the mercantile paradigm opens them to editing, modification and co-optation in line with its understandings of the values, principles and relationships of trade/exchange. This is not without its benefits. A real improvement can appear to follow through doing no more than sailing in the wake of a larger cultural force, as would have been the case with social virtues such as charity in a religious era, individual freedoms under liberalism and the expansion of public services in communist regimes. There are obvious attractions in reducing early school leaving and underachievement, recognising distinctive identities and traditions within the school, preparing pupils for lifestyle choices, and introducing participative structures in the governance of education. But from a modernist perspective these benefits may be short-term, ephemeral and, most likely, deceptively progressive. The real consequence may be a narrowing of the imperatives of equality, a fragmentation of the basis for civil society, behaviour bereft of a social morality, and a formalist understanding of citizenship and democracy. Above all, the mercantile paradigm attains a dispensation from critique. For the more areas of life and their representation that a paradigm can penetrate, the more its dominion is expanded, possibly to the point at which it achieves a taken-for-granted standing of unquestionable normality, a doxic status.

It is quite clear that there are those, most notably in relation to equality, who would wish to rebuff the advances of the mercantile paradigm, re-negotiate the meanings involved, and seek a reconstruction of Irish education that is more authentically modernist. This chapter contributes to this, in its description of some of the intertextual dynamics involved, by mapping out the cultural terrain that has to be contested. This encompasses the understanding of the subject in terms of its constitution and social action, the place of rationality, the responsibilities of citizens, the teleology of progress and the ethical basis of social interaction. What the chapter equally reveals, in the susceptibility of modernity to penetration by the mercantile paradigm, are the contradictions/limitations of modernity's enlightenment legacy – rationality's delegitimation of other truth-determining mechanisms, the possible self-deception of a subject that is both knower and known, the ambivalence of progress, and the instability of its social ethics. Rather than seek to reinstate modernity's enlightenment project in the reconstruction of Irish education, it might be argued that we need to acknowledge where we are, and in the manner of this chapter benefit in hindsight from making public the complex intertextuality that is shaping our contemporary understanding of education. Issues to be addressed in the Epilogue include the proposition that the mercantile paradigm is what emerges when a society in (understandable) haste to detraditionalise uses naïve (unreflexive) modernist appeals without quite engaging with their implications or contradictions, and whether in the Irish context with its background of the theocentric paradigm this produced a particularistic, context-specific variety of post-modernism.

Epilogue to Part Two

In attempting to track and characterise the cultural transformation experienced by the social institution of education over the past half-century, the designation of a theocentric education as the point of origin in this transition is unremarkable. It would equally be difficult to dispute that there has been dramatic change in this regard. But, what has become of education as a social institution has not, to date, been substantially addressed. The author first began to detect what seemed to be a patterned manifestation of trade/exchange in the discourse and practice of Irish education from the early 1990s (O'Sullivan, 2000). Then, its status appeared as emergent. Regular revisitation of this diagnosis confirmed a growing clarity and pattern of expansion and intensification. This persists and seems to be accelerating. At the time of writing, in the summer of 2004, developments have already occurred, such as the handing over of a teacher education programme to a private profit-making educational provider, deliberation from within the state on the privatisation of universities, and support from the Information Commissioner and High Court for the publication of inspectors' reports on schools, that a few years ago one would have expected to occur no sooner than in a decade. The cultural reconstruction of Irish education as a mercantile institution was outstripping my ability to keep revising the drafts of its analysis and description. Furthermore, with schools constrained by legal requirements, fear of litigation, conditions of partnership and benchmarking agreements, contractualism that will be even further necessitated for, *inter alia*, the effective regulation of pupil behaviour, and consumer-alert parents increasingly engaging with schools as organisations providing services, both monitored and measured, to their individual children, it is difficult to see how this spiral can be interrupted. Substantial non-exchange behaviours and subjectivities remain in the non-calculative contributions of teachers to extra-curricular activities and in general professionalism and collegiality in schools. But these are vulnerable to erosion in future negotiations on pay, promotional opportunities and conditions of service, and to atomisation as residual rather than emergent forces in the cultural construction of education.

Against the background of the doxic-like prescriptions of the church on education in the 1950s, Chapter 3 provided an ideal-typical overview of the transition from a theocentric to a mercantile paradigm in the reconstruction of education, and sketched some of the contrasting meanings and practices involved, in terms of educational aims, school ownership and control, pedagogical relationship, role of state, etc. In Chapter 4, the publication of *Investment in Education* in 1965, in the context of human capital theory, was treated as a key point of reference in explaining the emerging activism of the state in policy-making. Its longer-term significance in the transition to a mercantile paradigm was tracked from the cultural production its human capital traces occasioned, to which state officials, politicians, teachers and parents contributed, and in the manner in which themes relating to the legitimacy of state activity, commercial and economic models, schools conceived as quantifiable and manageable resources, and an educational public, began to circulate in Irish intersubjectivity on education.

The burden of the diagnosis of the transition to a mercantile paradigm rests on the analyses of the cultural production of education that follow in Chapters 5 and 6. These dealt with two varieties of intertextuality, complementary and predatory respectively, and are best interpreted as concurrent processes in the cultural production of the institution of education. Even as the mercantile paradigm was being structured as a complementary intertextual production that involved agents and texts deploying modernist subjectivities and themes, it was assuming the role of predator of its cultural progenitors. It would succeed in modifying, diluting and narrowing dimensions of Irish cultural production, such as those relating to equality, difference, virtue and control that merited testing against the yardstick of modernity. The effect was to compromise modernist understandings of equality, civil society, social morality, citizenship and democracy. But this was the effect of on-going culture wars in which modernist resources are never quite subjugated and those of the theocentric paradigm can be both silently invoked and more tactically and publicly transformed and appropriated. Furthermore, these culture wars reveal the contradictions, limitations and instabilities of modernity's enlightenment legacy, such as rationality's delegitimation of other truth-determining mechanisms, the possible self-deception of a subject that is both knower and known, the ambivalence of progress, and the instability of its social ethics.

The intertextual processes involved in these culture wars are complex and their understanding may benefit from the use of image and metaphor. They can be likened to the components (lines, dots, etc.) that, in different arrangements, form optical illusions and variable cartoon-like representations. The image of a tapestry with its different threads, colours, textures and designs creating diverse overall impressions, evocations and effects has been used earlier. A particularly effective metaphor for intertextuality is provided in the prologue to E. Annie Proulx's (1993) novel *The Shipping News* which takes the form of a quotation from Clifford Ashley's (1944) *The Ashley Book of Knots*:

> In a knot of eight crossings, which is about the average size knot, there are 256 different 'over and under' arrangements possible ... Make only one change in this

'over and under' sequence and either an entirely different knot is made or no knot at all may result.

This captures the processes of restructuring, appropriating, reforming and disassembling meaning that are at the heart of intertextuality. The current status of these culture wars relating to the understanding of the social institution of Irish education was described as a context-specific variety of post-modernism. In this the traces of modernity holding out the promise of release from a theocentric society would contribute to modernity's destabilisation, while the 'pre-modern' social order yielded not to modernity but to a post-modern disassembling of sociality and a fragmentation of identities.

We have interpreted the orientation to change in these transformations in terms of detraditionalisation in Irish society at large. In haste to escape from aspects of its past, change was sought in relation to its other rather than to an independently-framed, desired, future social order. In this regard, a comparison with the independence movement and the post-independence project of nation-building is instructive: emancipation from British rule and colonialism was replaced as an aspiration by release from what was experienced as a closed, isolated, socially-static and church-dominated social system. There was an investment of faith in a future whose virtue would be its difference from the past. Educational change was no more than a refraction of this. Instead of grappling with possible educational futures, there existed manifestations of a naïve (unreflexive) modernisation, features of which persist. Throughout the 1980s, Mulcahy (1981a, 1981b, 1989) drew attention to the failure to address the issue of aims and objectives of the post-primary school curriculum, be it in terms of their specification or implications. Yet, the lack of objective-setting in Irish education was itself no more than a by-product of a more pervasive defect – the absence of a habitus of reflexivity amidst social change. This will be described later in relation to the liberal functionalism of the curriculum development movement from the 1970s. But it also had been a feature of the invocation of human capital theory and populist educational expansion from the 1960s which bore implicit, taken-for-granted objectives. Over time, responding to the needs of a growing/more technological/knowledge-based economy, preparing pupils for school-to-work transitions, and facilitating social inclusion would appear unremarkable and unquestionable. This non-reflexivity in relation to Irish educational change, and the consequent inadequacy of self-knowledge within the system, is captured in the OECD (1991) *Reviews of National Policies for Education. Ireland* which goes on to describe it as having behaved 'reactively rather than pro-actively' (p. 36).

More widely in society there was a failure to detect the implications for social morality and solidarity in the individualisation of subjectivity, association, mobilisation and social action (Beck and Beck-Gernsheim, 2002). The same individualism that, from the 1960s, facilitated the assertion and acceptance of difference, the redesignation of the domains of sacred and profane, and the challenging of restrictions on life chances would welcome and embrace a diminished sociality and a low-tax regime, and regard the financial benefits that ensued as no more than its entitlement. Should it have really surprised that keeping the church apart from the state, the nation from the self, and society from human subjectivity and association would have been followed by the hand of the state being repulsed from individual pay packets? The race to escape from the past had distracted from the dangers of a future which neglected the structural imperatives that the traditional solidarities of nation, religion and community had supplied.

In the late-1990s some features of Irish social, cultural and political life relevant to this unreflexive detraditionalisation were sketched (O'Sullivan, 2000). Processes of secularisation and the erosion of the orthodoxies of Irishness from the nation-building phase had left a void, both in terms of self-definition and culture. Attempts to contain/resolve the Northern Ireland conflict had found the notion of Europeanisation an attractive strategy for submerging disputes about territory, allegiance and identity. The globalisation of the mass media presented culture as a matter of choice and personal taste, largely irrelevant to nation and identity. The world of the Celtic Tiger was increasingly a geography of markets rather than political territories, peoples or cultures. All of these influences forced a disruption of cultural inheritance and contributed to identities that sought to define themselves in the first instance in a manner that asserted their difference from their past. It was in this regard that multi-culturalism was deployed as a trope for progress. Sources for self-definition such as religion and nation had been excluded and the dominant politically-centrist ideology provided no collectivising appeals. The private world of personal and family consumption took precedence, with social action increasingly found to be most vibrant in mobilisation around short-term association addressing populist, single-issue objectives derived from individual risk, i.e. mercantile association and mobilisation. The moral debates of the 1980s and their successors ran far more deeply than the diagnosis of a 'second partitioning of Ireland' (Hesketh, 1990) would suggest. Rather, they revealed the fluidity of moral subjectivities and the frailty of the public sphere.

Criticisms such as these are not uncommon and are most concentrated in Kirby *et al.*'s (2002) *Reinventing Ireland*. But to advance them is to be accused of blind nostalgia for the pre-modern (Munck, 2003) and to invite the celebration of contemporary Ireland as a post-traditional society – opulent, secular, global, pluralist and multi-cultural. Where social and economic defects are acknowledged, two reactions tend to follow – their aetiology is tracked, not to the process of detraditionalisation, but to the effects of residues of the traditions themselves, and there is an impetus to revisit them for the purpose of further magnifying their pre-modern status. The latter pattern has been charted by Waters

(1997) with his usual perceptiveness and flair. It is as if with every manifestation of failure in contemporary Irish society there is a need to be assured that the past was even worse than had been imagined. This adverts to the dynamic nature of tradition. It is never static and as it was constructed in its living, so also can it be reworked to justify its internment.

Finally, to attend to the political context of this cultural reconstruction of education, two topics need addressing, the wider issue of the nature of politics that it manifests, and, more specific to educational policy-making, the managerial populism of the state. With regard to managerial populism, as the terms suggest, no evidence can be found of manipulation of public fears, prejudices, emotions, partiality or demonising that can be a feature of populist mobilisation strategies (Ionescu and Gellner, 1969). Nor could it be said that it necessarily invites the lowest common denominator in the substance of policy. Overall, educational policy seems to represent what people were considered to want or would tolerate, where the people were the broad mass of those who were active politically and likely to vote, modulated by what can be managed in engagement with the Department of Finance, and the main power interests of church and teacher organisations. This is cultivated by the broad social base of support for Fianna Fáil, the importance of transfers within the Irish electoral system and laterally by the predictability of coalition governments. No-one who is likely to vote at whatever level of preference can be neglected or ignored. In education, this is tempered by the de-politicisation of educational policy-making, the educational policies of particular parties being differentiated by degree rather than kind. Educational initiatives do not win elections or even seats as the abolition of undergraduate fees initiative of Niamh Bhreathnach demonstrates. Yet, sensitive issues are carefully policed within political parties themselves as evidenced in Noel Dempsey's efforts in 2003 to reintroduce undergraduate fees.

Nor are there parallels in Hall's (1983) analysis of Margaret Thatcher's populist tactic of (following Gramsci) transformism – 'the neutralisation of some elements in an ideological formation, their absorption and passive appropriation into a new political configuration'. According to Hall, this was achieved through a caring society being recast as an intrusive nanny state, the appeal of trade union collectivism replaced by a shareholder society, and the welfare state set against the image of a self-reliant British people. However, Hall does draw attention to the dangers of regarding populist politics as no more than 'a set of ideological con tricks'. Populist sentiments have a real and material base. But there are always multiple ways of interpreting one's educational needs in the context of social and economic conditions. While successive governments have sought at times to convince and, in recent decades, to consult, there is little evidence of a presentation to the public of a diversity of possibility, problematics or contradictions for educational change in which the state cultivates an intersubjective dynamic towards a generative role for society in policy deliberation. At the height of the debate leading to the publication of the 1995 Education White Paper, the author drew attention to the absence of a stimulus to reflexivity despite all the discussion that had taken place. The Green Paper had been published in 1992 and an 'open and democratic' process of consultation promised in the Fianna Fáil and Labour Parties' *Programme for a Partnership Government 1993-1997* (1993, p. 29). The round of meetings, public discussion and voluminous submissions, including a National Education Convention, was unprecedented. It was represented as an exercise in participatory democracy. The author disagreed with this interpretation, describing it as a 'truncated analysis of a limited range of options and possibilities for the organisation of the Irish educational system' (O'Sullivan, 1994a):

> For a genuine debate there should be options to discuss. If it aspires to be a fundamental examination of an issue, the horizons of these options should stretch beyond present practice. What is contestable should be admitted. The existence of contradictions, tensions, dissent and dilemmas should not be shirked. In particular, the culturally taken-for-granted should be made visible and available for analysis. All of this is especially necessary for those who are not professionally familiar with the topic. For parents and the public in general, knowledge about the educational possibilities and the issues involved is a prerequisite for participation. They need to be fully informed if they are to be engaged. The appearance of a full analysis of the Irish educational system has been cultivated. This illusion is politically conservative and fundamentally antidemocratic. While the debate proceeds within unsensed constraints, the grandiose self-deception that we are participating in an open analysis, with 'everything on the table', remains unthreatened.

Before that, and since, there has been little from the state to suggest to the people that they might think otherwise about education, particularly to recognise it as a contested institution, or that the state sees its role in relation to society in this generative sense. In this regard, the state tends to take the procedurally less-challenging option in democratic politics, a disposition that has been diagnosed more generally, and critically, in Irish politics in studies that stretch back further than the timeframe of this study (Girvin, 1989; Breen *et al.*, 1990).

Because the individual's interests, rights, guarantees and protection are at its core, the transformation involved in a mercantile reconstruction of Irish education may be read as a democratisation of the educational system. This is sustainable, but only if we deny the existence of other meanings of democracy besides the liberal model. How the politics of this transformation might be characterised raises quite critical issues about political forms, the state and its citizens, no more than two of which can be addressed here.

Mercantile education is consistent with the liberal model of democracy, with its pluralist view of the state as an administrative structure, regulated by a society of private autonomous individuals, interacting in competitive contexts and configurations. The task of politics becomes one of asserting one's interests and preferences with a view to gaining leverage in this regulation of the state through practices of representation and lobbying and the electoral process. Appropriately, the image of the market – of ideas and people presenting themselves and being chosen or rejected – is relevant. To these two components – administrative power and individual interests – the republican model of democracy adds solidarity and the orientation to the common good. With this, politics becomes more than a process of mediating private preferences to the government of the day. Rather, in Habermas's (1996) words, this involves a process in which a recognisable group of people 'become aware of their dependence on one another and, acting with full deliberation as citizens, further shape and develop existing relations of reciprocal recognition into an association of free and equal consociates under law'.

Solidarity, what it involves and how it might be established and maintained, is central to any critical engagement with the mercantile paradigm. This is because, in its constitution and construction, it instrumentalises solidarity and then works to erode it wherever it might persist – in Irish society at large the conversion of credit unions to localised banks is but one such contemporary threat. Reconstituting the solidarities of the past is no longer an option, even if it were desirable. As mobilising invocations, 'workers of the world', 'sisterhood', 'we the Irish' and 'Faith of our Fathers' have all experienced internal fragmentation. Difference, ontological and biographical, will need to be implicated in any solidarity that is constitutive of citizenship. In this it will be essential to distinguish between mercantile and constitutive interdependence. Perhaps, no more than mercantile solidarity, derived from contractual, partial and calculating association, will be available for some time to come, in the absence of a transformative flashpoint event – economic crisis, physical threat or political instability. It is all too easy to be deceived by false dawns.

The procedural and normative prerequisites for reconstituting political subjectivities relate to the second political issue that arises – the status and nature of the public sphere. The public sphere is used here to describe an intersubjective space for political intertextuality, in which meanings pertaining to the processes and direction of the polity circulate and interact, or more colloquially where political ideas collide. This is the dimension of democracy that was lacking and missed in the failure of detraditionalisation to recognise the implications of its naïve use of modernist themes and unreflexive construction of a mercantile institution of education. Such a politics has come to be described in terms of deliberative or communicative democracy, and ranges across many varieties for which Habermas's deliberative or discourse theory of democracy remains a fundamental point of reference. In place of the liberal individual actor and the republican collective actor, discourse theory works with 'the higher-level intersubjectivity of communication processes'. These 'subjectless forms of communication constitute arenas in which a more or less rational opinion- and will-formation can take place' (Habermas, 1996). Developing understandings of the public sphere that are less enlightenment-based – patriarchal, dispassionate and unitary – and encompass a diversity of contributors, perspectives and speaking styles, represents a recurring challenge to writers such as Young, Fraser, Phillips, Kymlicka, Cohen and Benhabib in addressing how democracy and difference might be accommodated (in Benhabib, 1996). This contributes to a broader debate on multi-culturalism, liberalism, and public and private spheres (Barry, 2001; Joppke, 2004). The cultivation of a public sphere that is accommodating, dense and diverse remains an urgent requirement for Irish politics at large. We will return to this in the Conclusion. In the meantime, we turn to a middle-range issue – that of life chances, education and morality – that cannot but feel the effects of how a society configures the relationship between its people and the quality of its political reflexivity in the widest sense.

Part Three

Life Chances, Education
and Morality

This section examines the paradigms that have formed around the intersection of life chances, education and morality (LEM). Unlike the more institutional definition of education that was the focus of Part Two, this relates to more middle-range issues and processes in the operation of educational systems. LEM refers to how education is implicated through its mediation of resources, restraints and possibilities in the character of a person's life course, in the sense of what one becomes in terms of identity, social and material status and power. Life *chances* is preferred over more contemporary possibilities such as life *politics* or life *style* though it encompasses their referents – 'autonomy of action', 'freedom from the arbitrary hold of tradition, from arbitrary power and from the constraints of material deprivation', and the capacity to participate in the 'disputes and struggles about how (as individuals and as collective humanity) we should live in a world where what used to be fixed either by nature or tradition is now subject to human decisions' (Giddens, 1996a, pp 14-15). This is because life chances, better than life politics, signals the existence of restrictions and limitations in what people become, and avoids whatever insubstantiality and transience is suggested by life style. Morality is included to stress that these are not merely technical issues and that questions of right and wrong are implicated in the mediation of resources, restraints and possibilities through the educational process.

One may ask why less cumbersome and more explicit concepts were not used. The reluctance to begin with obvious contenders such as equality and justice is because they are themselves particular configurations in the structuring of meaning in relation to what is at issue in the analysis. To orchestrate the scrutiny of meaning-making around such themes would be to limit one's gaze to that of their associated cultural constructs. As the bemusement of the sociology student at the variety of labels for the socio-economic group to which he belonged (perishing and dangerous classes, depraved, poor, deprived, disadvantaged, different, marginalised and excluded) testifies, words embody meanings that encompass explanations, moralities and categorical systems. Signification is important. To try to encapsulate in a few words, therefore, what is at issue without leaning towards one particular representation rather than another of what is meant to be an ongoing object of analysis is difficult. The more inclusive and accommodating is the analysis, the more the focus dissipates to encompass the totality of schooling and the diversity of its effects on individuals and society. The more the focus is on specific themes such as equality and justice the more their status as themes is obscured and they become unproblematic principles in their own right without a history and without contestation.

In contrast, the co-ordinates of life chances, education and morality provide a framework around which a variety of policy paradigms can be seen to form and structure themselves. As a conceptualisation it allows for a broader understanding of educational outcomes beyond the narrow occupational and economic effects of education to include personal, civic, relational and political development. It encompasses both individual and structural impediments to education within a variety of intervention sites (i.e. preschool, school, home, work, community, economic and political order). It recognises the diversity of differences considered relevant in relation to benefiting from education, e.g. class, finance, gender, ethnicity, disability, etc. It stresses that moral issues are involved in a manner that can accommodate statist obligations, individualistic rights and 'third-way' communitarianism. Nonetheless, as an act of signification LEM is an effort at cultural evasion that, while operationally functional, can never be more than partially successful. No analysis can be free from its historical or cultural context.

The existence of an LEM paradigm in any shape or form is not guaranteed in each and every society. It is possible to conceive of a cultural world in which questions of a moral nature generating themes of rights, duties and obligations might be underdeveloped in relation to how schools influence one's access to scarce resources and offices, or in which the linkages between life chances and education would be quite tenuous. The forms which LEM paradigms might take may be potentially diverse but they can also be absent or enjoy only the most rudimentary of existences in a society. To exist at all, the following are required within the conceptualisation, signification and discourse of society:

- An awareness of some aspect of life chances as they are affected by education, operating either directly on individual/collective resources such as capacities and dispositions which influence, provide options, reduce impediments, or indirectly in the shaping of society and the social order in which the dynamics of life chances are acted out. The former impacts on an individual's or group's capacities to compete, be self-determining or politicise, the latter influences the regulations and conventions governing such processes
- A system of categorisation that allows for differentiation and comparison in relation to benefits, control of scarce resources and offices, and identities
- A moral response, be it cognitively derived through a violation of principles or affectively based on a sense of concern, outrage or indignation.

A further mapping of the inter-relationships within the paradigm may be provided by the following:

- Explanations of how education has the effect it has on the specified life chances
- Proposals for action that reflect these explanations.

Theories of explanation and intervention allow an LEM paradigm to attain a sophistication as a cultural form through the range of phenomena which it encompasses and the inter-linkages that it establishes. As a codified and systematised interpretation of a sector of social reality it can lay claim to specialisation and objectification. But without some understanding of an association between life chances and schooling, a system of classification and a moral orientation, it is difficulty to imagine how an LEM paradigm can be said to have a cultural existence at all.

The experience of paradigm formation within the LEM domain begins in Chapter 7 with the wide deployment in state discourse during the 1960s of equality of educational opportunity, a central principle in international educational policy discourse at that time, as a concept used to communicate concern about fairness in accessing education. The extent to which this can be regarded as an organic cultural development or as imposition, the nature and character of the meaning-making involved, and the dynamics of paradigm formation/retardation are considered. It is represented as an era of 'paradigms postponed' in which opportunities for the intensification of equality of educational opportunity were offered and refused. Chapter 8 traces the emergence from the 1970s of employability as a policy paradigm that constructs the needs and identity of those whose chances of labour market entry are most precarious, in terms of their capacity to find work, as the crucial attribute capable of rescuing 'vulnerable' people from a reliance on social welfare and the experience of social exclusion.

The re-emergence in the 1980s as educational disadvantage of the socio-economic focus from the 'postponed' paradigm formation surrounding equality of educational opportunity in the 1960s is addressed in Chapter 9. Government policy and interventions, including early compensatory education, targeted resources, prevention, retention and re-entry programmes, third-level access schemes, inter-agency coordination, and social and economic development at local level, are characterised as a cultural *pastiche*, a configuration of knowledge and action that maintains a sufficient cultural consensus to allow for concerted action and on-going communication by an avoidance of the tensions and contradictions of its presuppositions and actions.

In Chapter 10, Christian Communitarianism is used to describe the approach to social policy proposed by the Conference of Religious of Ireland (CORI), formerly the Conference of Major Religious Superiors (CMRS), that emphasises the obligations of people to one another in their use of the world's resources, and grounds these obligations in their interpretation of texts within the Christian tradition. In terms of educational policy, this prioritises the life-world of the socially and economically disadvantaged, stresses unjust structures as distinct from individual experience in maintaining inequality as well as social transformation as a means of change, and incorporates an holistic understanding of the person. The structuring and membershipping capacity of this policy-directed action and discourse is studied in relation to otherwise disparate and secular communitarian themes generated by the Combat Poverty Agency, the community development movement, andragogical practices in literacy and adult education programmes, and in EU-sponsored interventions in local development, partnerships and anti-poverty initiatives.

Gender equity, which developed from the 1970s, and represents the most immediate deployment of the principle of equality of educational opportunity from the 1960s, is proposed in Chapter 11 as the most systematised paradigm within the LEM domain in Irish experience. This is explored in terms of its meaning, dominion, systematisation, engagement with counter texts, and the possibilities for the emergence of other understandings of gendered education. Finally, in Chapter 12, Travellers' ethnicity and egalitarianism are presented as paradigms with a generative potential to extend meanings of life chances beyond the distributive to the recognitive, disrupt embedded meanings through the deployment of utopian discourse, and achieve an integrative process between LEM paradigms given to isolation and absence of mutual engagement.

Throughout these chapters, three structuring features from the 1960s – 'distant other', sponsorship, and the pre-reflexive construct of fairness – are tracked in terms of their functioning and effects.

Chapter 7

The 1960s and Equality of Educational Opportunity: Paradigms Postponed

In his influential *Studies* article 'Post-Primary Education. Now and in the Future' published in 1968, Seán O'Connor, then assistant secretary of the Department of Education, presented equality of educational opportunity as a prominent objective of what he referred to as recent developments in Irish education. It was a fitting ideal to select. Dr Hillery's widely-quoted policy statement on proposals for changes in post-primary education in 1963 concluded that 'the whole plan is a move in the direction, not only of a better co-ordination in our entire educational system, but of equality of educational opportunity'. George Colley, who succeeded Dr Hillery as Minister for Education, was to use the same appeal in 1966 in his letter to the authorities of secondary and vocational schools, requesting their co-operation in the pooling of post-primary school facilities at local level (Colley, 1966a). At the end of the 1960s, in an introduction to a booklet for parents distributed nationally, *Ár nDaltaí Uile – All Our Children* (Department of Education, 1969), Brian Lenihan, the Minister for Education of the time described equality of educational opportunity as 'our most urgent social and educational objective'. In this formative period of modern Irish educational change equality of educational opportunity was the concept most utilised to orchestrate moral responses to differential educational participation and is an appropriate entry point to the process of the cultural production of LEM paradigms. This centrality accorded to equality of educational opportunity was novel to educational discourse in Ireland, coinciding with the international popularity of the concept in educational policy developments at that time.

Whereas equality of educational opportunity entered Irish educational discourse without ceremony or opposition, what is questionable is its contribution to Irish signification and thematisation in relation to LEM issues. Was it that Irish culture was taking on board the language, principles and imperatives of the principle of equality of educational opportunity, and that the referents of the principle were the same for the Irish as for the international educational community ranging from political parties, reforming educational systems or international agencies like the OECD (1961) or the World Bank (Jones, 1997)? How did this importation of language or thought interact with indigenous meanings? Could it be said that the emergence of equality of educational opportunity as a policy objective was an organic development representing some kind of fusion of cultural components to mutual benefit? Or was this an exercise in the colonisation of Irish culture, suppressing the inherited and giving dominance to the imported? It would be easier to explore these questions were it possible to identify distinctively-framed LEM paradigms influential within Irish society in the decades prior to the 1960s.

Antecedents

While there is a recognisable social radicalism to be discerned within the independence movement, which visualised a new social order, spoke of economic redistribution and worker democracy and conceptualised society along social class lines, once the Free State settled into a social conservatism the collective conscience was satisfied by a cautious improvement in the living conditions of the less well off, approached with hesitation. The cultivation of a collective sense of the 'people' in nation building and the post-colonial maximisation of native human resources suppressed conflict models of society. Concerns for the poor, those with exceptional needs, the underdog and the small farmer never threatened the conservative view of society which proclaimed the functional interpretation of the contributions, benefits and satisfactions of the mutually interdependent roles and sectors of Irish society, of which de Valera's 1943 St Patrick's Day speech is an unfairly much-parodied manifestation. The Catholic Church, which had the benefit of a long tradition of social teaching, refuted the class conflict interpretation of society as Marxist-inspired and advocated co-operative and community-wide initiatives in achieving social objectives, be they the improvement of living conditions in rural Ireland or coping with urban property. Its principle of subsidiary, which proclaimed that no larger or superior body should do what is best done by a lesser or smaller one, may have been motivated by a desire to protect people from bureaucracy and totalitarianism. But its deployment to suppress state action in relation to poverty, education and health in the Ireland of the 1940s and 1950s served the interests of more privileged sectors of Irish society.

When Pope John XXIII sought to correct this misuse of Catholic social teaching in *Pacem in Terris* in 1963 he could well have had the Irish experience of the preceding decades in mind in the manner in which, according to Dorr (1992, p.143), he criticised the '… ideological use of this teaching, i.e. its use as a cover and legitimation for resistance to the changes needed to promote social justice'. The significance of this appropriation of Catholic social teaching for our consideration of the formation of LEM paradigms is less its retardation of social welfare type policies and more its restriction of an LEM discourse from the very source that was best positioned, in terms of an intellectual class, history of paradigm construction and mechanisms of dissemination etc., to generate a moral commentary on life chances in education.

The other potential source of intellectual activity on educational issues, the teachers themselves, appears to have been similarly restrained in addressing such issues of principles, rights and entitlements in education. There is little evidence that teachers, through the voice of their representative organisations, communicated, much less generated, thematic resources for the formation of LEM paradigms. Nor would the intellectual and moral formation of teachers prior to the 1960s have been conducive to such an educational discourse, as Coolahan's (1984a) survey of the content of educational studies in teacher training programmes has demonstrated. In effect, the detailed histories of the two largest teacher organisations, the INTO (O'Connell, 1969) and the ASTI (Coolahan, 1984c), record the fine print of representations to governments, deputations, disputes and controversies without finding sustained reference to the role of education in reproducing unequal life situations and chances. Ó Buachalla's (1988) content analysis of the presidential addresses of both the INTO and ASTI at their annual congresses provides a useful overview. He found that for the INTO, equality of educational opportunity featured regularly as a topic during the first three decades of the twentieth century but not again until the 1970s. This Ó Buachalla attributes to the close links, through its general secretary, T.J. O'Connell, with the Irish Labour Party whose 1925 policy statement on education Ó Buachalla describes as a 'radical document' (p. 356). For the less well-established ASTI, it was not until the 1960s that national education policy featured as a central theme in its presidential addresses. Prior to the 1960s, the exceptionalism of the INTO's *A Plan for Education* (1947) is striking in its appeal to 'the philosophy and ideals of a genuinely democratic people' (p. 7) as a rationale for 'providing equality of educational opportunity for all its citizens' (p. 10):

> Equality of educational opportunity, it is quite clear, is still denied to the majority of our people, and both secondary and university education, which in practice are denied to the vast bulk of the population, are financed on a more generous scale than primary education (p. 10).

The omens for education may have been 'propitious' (Lee, 1989, p. 129), Pearse most notably having accorded a primacy to educational reform as the first task of a Free Ireland. Yet, the role attributed to education in the limited vision of social improvement to be found in the new state was itself restricted. Writing on education as an issue in the first and second Dáil, Ó Buachalla (1977) concluded that it 'does not seem to have received the political priority one might reasonably expect from the importance attached to its reform by many nationalist spokesmen in the first two decades of the century'. This characterisation can be said to have a more extended historical validity in relation to schooling as a social institution with the potential to impact on individual life chances and Irish social structure. That there should be 'little use for idealism and less scope for utopianism in the Irish Free State of 1923' (Lynch, quoted in Keogh, 1994, p. 37) can be explained by the pressing political and financial problems faced by the new state. What is less easily excused is the failure of even a social vision for education to surface for much of its first half-century.

The School Attendance Act of 1926 has been described as the 'main gesture' among the government's 'meagre measures … taken to implement the idea of equality of educational opportunity' (Lee, 1989, p. 131). Far from being a morally inspired attempt to equalise the life opportunities of the less well off through educational participation, this was directed to the general expansion of a minimal education throughout society. The Vocational Education Act of 1930, the only other major piece of educational legislation until the 1990s, despite its social positioning apart from the elite secondary schools, did not address equality issues, its function being the provision of technical skills for local industries and agriculture. In introducing the second stage of the Bill, the Minister for Education, John Marcus O'Sullivan, assured deputies that if they would 'bear in mind the disappearance from the countryside of carpenters, masons and harness-makers, they can grasp the importance that a practical system of continuation education might be, even from that point of view, to the country districts'. He specifically identified the group of boys and girls 'whose education comes to an end, so far as systematic control of it is concerned, at the age of fourteen unless they go into one of the existing technical schools'. But to the extent that this group caused concern, it was encapsulated in '… the boy who has left school at the age of fourteen and who stays about the farm, who is too young to get technical agricultural training and is in danger in the course of a couple of years of forgetting a great deal of what he learned in the national school' (reproduced in Hyland and Milne, 1992, pp 210-212).

One might expect issues of fairness, life chances and the needs of those with limited opportunities to arise in deliberations on the possibility of raising the school leaving age. The reports of the Commission on Technical Education, 1927 and of the Commission on Youth Unemployment, 1951, and the Council of Education's Report on the Function and the Curriculum of the Primary School, 1954 are among the major sources of evidence indicating the views of a wide range of interests as to what should be regarded as a minimum education. In coming to their conclusions, the improvement of the competitiveness in the labour market of those who are deemed to be disadvantaged in searching for work (as distinct from the employability of early school leavers), asserting children's entitlements to an extended education irrespective of family background, or any awareness of the impediments to availing of education derived from home background do not emerge as identifiable themes.

In the report presented to the Minister for Education by the Inter-Departmental Committee on the Raising of the School Leaving Age in 1935 we find that the thinking of those with more proximate influence on the policy-making process was no different. There is an unquestioning acceptance of the distribution of opportunity in society associated with a conception of segmented sectors of labour market competition: 'A large proportion of the employment obtained by juveniles in non-agricultural occupations is blind-alley employment as messengers etc., but it is difficult to see what better employment could be obtained for such juveniles by keeping them a year or two longer at school' (p 31). What principles exist in its deliberations are circumscribed by a concern to protect the state from additional financial demands: 'The parents of juveniles who enter blind-alley employment are generally in very poor circumstances and would be unable to keep them longer at school. If the school leaving age were raised, there would be a very strong demand for maintenance grants for the disemployed juveniles' (p. 31). One of the few cases for raising the school leaving age which the committee found convincing related to the dangers of idleness and the cultivation of a disciplined workforce: 'There are large numbers of young people between the ages of fourteen and sixteen who have not obtained employment and do not attend school. There is grave danger in their idleness which tends to make the young people unfit for employment' (p. 31).

The discourse on scholarships offers another opportunity to test for the existence of themes relating to differences in life chances and the role of education in diminishing or enhancing them. One might expect the primary function of scholarships to be unremarkably obvious: the provision of financial support to those who, though capable of benefiting from it, would otherwise have difficulty in continuing their education. When the Council of Education came to arbitrate on the desirability of intermediate scholarships in its 1962 report on the curriculum of the secondary school, it found it necessary to consider what it described as 'various arguments … used from time to time against the very principle of scholarships'. These included the arguments that '… the principle is radically evil, appealing to the motives of cupidity and desire for praise; that scholarships disturb the even tenor and leisurely progress which should be the hallmark of a true school; that preparation for scholarships leads to cramming rather than education of pupils, while school authorities tend to concentrate on prospective scholarship winners to the neglect of the average pupils' (p. 230). Though the council went on to justify scholarships on the basis of principle and 'well-established tradition' (p. 232), there was no mention, in its quite detailed consideration of the topic, of students of exceptional merit from financially less well-off families for whom scholarships might be the only mechanism for enabling them to enter senior-cycle secondary schooling.

The council's opposition to 'free secondary education for all', and its dismissal of it as 'untenable' and 'utopian' (p. 252) are frequently cited. Nonetheless, it did find it necessary to address what it described as this 'frequently reiterated demand' (p. 252), albeit in the final paragraphs of the report. It regarded the more qualified ideal of secondary education for 'all able and willing to profit by it' as worthy of consideration, arguing that its realisation 'could be accelerated considerably by the greater provision of scholarships' (p. 252). In this regard also, the council referred to its deliberations on scholarships in its first report on the function and curriculum of the primary school (Council of Education, 1954). There, having examined the various scholarship schemes for post-primary education, it 'conceded that the number provided out of public funds still falls very much short of what is needed. Furthermore, the annual value of these scholarships would on the whole appear to be too low' (p. 254). It went on to endorse the means testing of these scholarships and of reserving quotas on the basis of urban/rural areas, school size and sex. With regard to university scholarships, the 1962 Report concluded that provision 'from both the local authorities and from State funds is entirely and deplorably inadequate' (p. 246).

The inference in these references to free secondary education for students of ability and motivation, to the inadequacy of the number of scholarships available and to the desirability of means testing is that these schemes can serve a meritocratic-type purpose in the sense of providing financial support, or at least lessening the financial barriers, for students who have demonstrated a capacity and wish to benefit from secondary schooling. It seems clear that there are meanings pertaining to educational opportunity, impediments and educability being realised and communicated in this discourse. These themes may be confined to the realm of unexplicated assumptions and propositions and emerge without been named and without the benefit of a distinguishing language. Substantive limitations include a fixed understanding of personal abilities and an exclusively-financial interpretation of impediments to educational participation. But one can nonetheless detect, even at the level of finding it necessary to contest and oppose performatives relating to educational policy on access to secondary schooling, conceptualisations and themes that are a prerequisite for the emergence of an LEM paradigm.

Prior to the 1950s, it would appear that the prerequisites for LEM structuration are largely missing or exist only in the most rudimentary form in Irish cultural production. It does not associate variations in life chances with educational experience. Rather, a sense of a fixed social order prevailed in which the prospect of inheriting a family-owned business was substantial (Breen *et al.*, 1990). To the extent that education was implicated with the class structure, it was more formative than selective. Education provided the personal development and training, where such were required, for those ways of life and occupations that people were already destined for within that order. The allocation of scarce resources, offices and prestigious occupations was ascriptive rather than achieved. This helps to explain the salience of the limited opportunities to breach and violate those ascriptions on the basis of educational achievement through the competitive procedures for entry to the civil service, primary teacher training and the semi-state administration. For the great majority who did not participate in these procedures and felt remote from them, education was perceived, at its most benign, as a preparation for life (including the after-life) and work rather than for the educational competition for occupational and mobility opportunities. This contrasts with the situation that prevailed in Irish society in the later part of the century when the balance shifted in the opposite direction.

In such a fixed social order, differences in the life expectations of people were an unremarkable feature of social experience. In retarding the problematising of these differences, its doxic status concomitantly suppressed social differentiation and classification and an awareness that moral issues were involved. The culturally unremarkable neither invites nor requires theorisation.

Unlike the theocentric paradigm which was elaborate and systematised, realised through a distinctive discourse, interpreted by designated intellectuals, and enjoyed clear framing and an associative character that evoked primary intensity, in the beginning of the period under review moral issues arising from the nexus of schooling, society and individual life chances had only the most meagre of such resources on which to draw in articulating a set of representations, ideas and propositions. One is forced, therefore, to attempt to consider changes in collective understandings, priorities and prescriptions without the benefit of a distinguishing language, characteristic discourse or identifiable agents to differentiate between them. This greatly impedes attempts to chart the standing of LEM issues in Irish society in the beginning of the period under review and to establish the base from which the subsequent structuration of LEM paradigms emerged.

International Developments and Local Stirrings

In Europe the social reconstruction that followed the ending of World War II impinged directly on educational policies. The Butler Education Act of 1946, which introduced the tripartite post-primary school system to England and Wales together with the practice of selection at the age of eleven, and the beginnings of a comprehensive school system in Sweden were examples of quite contrasting policies that nonetheless were at one in attempting to correct for inequalities in the provision of opportunity and the realisation of talent, irrespective of its social origin. Studies in the political arithmetic and demographic traditions from the 1950s charted the extent of non-participation and early leaving in education. A succession of academic studies and European-wide policy developments in education succeeded in establishing the principle of equality of educational opportunity as a key imperative in relation to LEM issues (OECD, 1961). Initially, this research stressed inequalities associated with social class background, understood in terms of its material manifestation such as salary, nutrition, health care and living conditions. Later in the 1960s, with social class still the basis of societal differentiation, cultural attributes such as values, attitudes and ambitions gained greater prominence in attempts to explain variations in educational participation and achievement.

In this period, also, there was discussion as to what the principle of equality of educational opportunity might entail. This conceptual exploration is generally acknowledged to have been American in origin. There, race together with poverty were central themes in considering equality of educational opportunity in the context of what came to be known as the War on Poverty. In the deliberations that led to the Coleman Report, Equality of Educational Opportunity (Coleman *et al.*, 1966), the key report of this era, three dimensions of the principle – access, input and outcome – emerged. Equality of access demanded that no pupils should be denied access to educational institutions or courses of study on the basis of irrelevant considerations such as geographical location, financial position, religious belief or racial and social background. Equality of input drew attention to the possibility that schools in certain areas or schools attended by racial or social minorities might be less well-endowed in terms of societal investment. This included not just financial investment, physical plant and learning resources but also differences between schools in terms of teacher skills and morale and pupil cultures and aspirational levels. Outcomes related to the results of schooling, the actual effects on pupils as indicated by the length of their retention within the system, their attainment of learning objectives, possession of credentials and success in transferring to adult and working life. Clearly, equality of outcome is a demanding interpretation of the requirements of equality of educational opportunity. But, even if considered in terms of the modalities of particular groups, it placed education in a challenging compensatory role, a role that was emphasised in a host of compensatory programmes in the United States throughout the 1960s.

In Ireland, as we have seen from the Council of Education deliberations on scholarship schemes and free secondary education for all, themes consistent with this international discourse on equality of educational opportunity began to surface in Irish educational policy debate during the 1950s. An awareness of equality of input between types of post-primary schools can also be inferred from this time. In his book, *Reform in Education* (1958), the Professor of Classical Languages at UCD, J.J. O'Meara, called for an enhancement of status for vocational schools. This was to be repeated in 1963 in Dr Hillery's statement to the press in which he saw 'the bringing of the vocational stream throughout the country to a parity of standard and evaluation with the present secondary school stream' as constituting 'a very important educational and social reform'. Later that year, this was to be reaffirmed by the first part of the Second Programme for Economic Expansion. In fact Randles (1975) has argued that the improvement of the vocational system was a dominant feature of educational planning at this time. Whether this was due to its contribution as a system, as provider of technical skills etc., because it contained a concentration of less-advantaged pupils, or because state intervention in vocational education did not impinge on the church (O'Connor, 1986) can be debated. Nonetheless, it thematised fairness of treatment between school types.

The themes of access, availability, exposure and opportunity in relation to benefiting from education also surfaced in Dr Hillery's 1963 policy statement. In it he gave prominence, as one of the two weaknesses of the Irish post-primary educational system, to the fact that 'there are still areas of the country which have neither a secondary nor a vocational school within easy daily reach of potential pupils and where under the existing system such is not likely to be available in the foreseeable future'. The free education scheme was announced to the National Union of Journalists on 10 September 1966 by the Minister for Education, Donagh O'Malley. This innovation was directed he said at 'the basic fault of our educational structure … the fact that many families cannot afford to pay even part of the cost of education for their children'. The scheme he was drawing up, he asserted, would ensure that 'in future, no boy or girl in the state will be deprived of full educational opportunity – from primary to university level – by reason of the fact that the parents cannot afford to pay for it'. Such concerns about the geographical and financial impediments to gaining access to education were reasonably common at this time in Dáil debates and politicians' statements (Randles, 1975; Ó Buachalla, 1988).

A concern that the principle of equality should also prevail in relation to the performance of pupils and the benefits they derive from schooling was slower to emerge. As well as recognising the absence of this equality of outcome dimension of Coleman's formulation, it is also necessary to note that in extracting these concerns for access and input dimensions from the flux of cultural production at that time there is a danger that one gives a structure to the discourse that did not exist. Rather, these sentiments, far from originating in a discourse of individual entitlements or justice, must be seen as atomised expressions of concern motivated by a feeling that a pre-reflexive principle derived from the fairness/unfairness dualism of a 'spontaneous' folk realm of knowledge had been violated. For this reason, the centrality of equality of educational opportunity in official discourse of the era can be deceptive as an indicator of the status of LEM meanings at that time.

In attempting to tease underlying principles from the ministerial statements on rights and entitlements in education at this time, Greaney and Kellaghan (1984, p. 27) limit themselves to the observation that '… some government policy statements on equality of opportunity … seem to assume the operation of meritocratic principles'. They specifically cite two statements from Dr Hillery. In 1960, he stated that it would be an uplift to the morale of the country 'if it were generally understood that the child of even the poorer, if he is of sufficient ability, would have the opportunity of … climbing right to the top of the educational ladder'. In the following year, he identified as a 'serious defect in our social system … that the boy or girl who was poor but clever had often no adequate opportunity of receiving the entire course of education available'. If what is implied here is meritocracy, it appears to be confined to the principles governing access to educational resources alone. There is no suggestion in any ministerial statement of the era, a fact that Greaney and Kellaghan draw attention to, that such an expansion in educational opportunity was designed to lead to a meritocratic society in which old elites based on the privilege of birth would be replaced by those who had demonstrated merit (defined as ability plus effort) in their personal achievements. In fact, it is difficult to know if there is any real advance in such statements on the thinking that would have sustained the existing scholarship schemes for post-primary and third-level education. One might argue that scholarship schemes required exceptional ability on the part of their beneficiaries whereas Dr Hillery's understanding of the extension of educational opportunity in the first of the above statements merely demanded sufficient ability to benefit from the programme.

Making a judgement on the extent and depth of meritocracy intended by the policy-makers of the era is impeded by the absence of discussion on the concept of equality of educational opportunity at the time with the result that 'ministerial statements about equality escaped any detailed scrutiny and their possible implications have not been explored in any systematic way' (Greaney and Kellaghan, 1984, p. 26). Consequently, fine analysis of the statements of the time is unlikely to be productive as an indicator of the meanings being realised on LEM issues. An exception to this, albeit operating by exclusion rather than confirmation, is to be found in the explicit denial of 'political' or 'ideological' objectives for education in relation to the introduction of comprehensive schools, a form of restructured post-primary schooling that elsewhere in Europe had been associated with social change and not solely educational aspirations. This will be described in the second-next section, to reveal the persistence of one of the three indigenous features of the official LEM text throughout the 1960s – the folk moral construct of fairness. The realisation of the other two – 'distant others' as the target of moral concern, and sponsorship as the principle of intervention by society – rely on non-discursive communication, again confirming that within the variety of meaning-making mechanisms relating to the LEM domain in state policy at this time policy statements were only of minimal significance. These indigenous meanings would remain resistant to modification by the construct of equality of educational opportunity despite its wide deployment in the discourse.

Non-Discursive Textualisation: 'Distant Others' and Sponsorship

The absence of a language that would allow for a differentiation of meanings and the structuring of thought, and the overall non-discursive nature of the representation of meanings pertaining to equality of educational opportunity in state discourse, means that one needs to draw on other message-sending mechanisms to fully explore what in the first instance was the official text in cultural communication on LEM issues at that time. This also explains the one-way character of much of the communication. There appears to have been little by way of dialogue and much less contestation. Since there were few explicit statements of belief, justification or description there was little to explicitly question, contest or reject. From the mechanisms deployed to construct and disseminate the official text on LEM issues one can identify tropes, exemplars, cautionary tales, slogans, strokes and policy practice. Examples of tropes can be found in some of the official policy statements quoted earlier. These contain figurative speech such as 'poor but clever' and 'climbing right to the top of the educational ladder' that conveys a sense of opportunity and the possibility of surmounting circumstance. The imagery appealed to emotion and sentiment. It invited consensus rather than contextual analysis.

This anti-discursive character was shared by the practice of sloganising of which 'equality of educational opportunity' was itself a prime example. Slogan systems 'do not die from explicit rejection but through lack of attention ... when the general slogans in the system fail to capture the imagination, no longer command loyalty, and creative disciples fade away, the system dies' (Komisar and McClellan, 1961). This explains the limitation (and even the fallacy) of submitting the use of the concept of equality of educational opportunity to careful scrutiny and attempting a linguistic analysis of it as a construct. As a slogan 'equality of educational opportunity' was not used in a theorised fashion, as a feature of a social project or vision. Rather, it was grounded in appeals of a high moral loading which were considered to be self-evident, beyond dispute and not demanding justification from anyone educationally, economically or socially alert. In this way, it functioned to mobilise support and accommodate and integrate potentially divisive viewpoints. When operating effectively, the role of slogans is to suppress inquiry since to question what appears to be obvious is potentially disruptive or at least a distraction from the task in hand. For this reason, in Irish cultural production at this time equality of educational opportunity largely operated as a membershipping device recruiting a 'people' believing in fairness to a shared view on expanding opportunities in education. As a force in cultural production on Irish LEM issues it has much less significance.

For this reason also, when Donagh O'Malley announced his intention to introduce free post-primary education what he actually said, the written text he delivered on the occasion, was less potent than the nature of his actions as spectacle in establishing its cultural impact and as a source for retrospectively understanding the meanings of the time. It combines elements of impulsivity, side-stepping of bureaucracy, commitment to the underdog and an unwillingness to settle for half measures. Long regarded as one of the more flamboyant strokes in Irish politics, it communicated the need to act rather than think and appealed to the privileging of activism over reflection. In having to act with such immediacy and with what appeared as a lack of respect for administrative conventions, it proclaimed the moral imperative without a reliance on discourse. In fact, the most recognisable text on LEM issues at this time is to be found in policy enactment. A highly influential aspect of this was its identification of violations of equality of educational opportunity and its specification of those in need of state intervention. The thematising of primary school terminal leavers and its textualisation from the late 1960s is an example of this.

The extensive educational delay in Irish primary schools was quantified by *Investment in Education* in 1965. It found that in fourth, fifth and sixth standards, two-fifths of the pupils had been delayed for at least one year and about one in ten delayed for about two years or more. With the minimum school leaving age set at fourteen, pupils delayed for two years or more would be entitled to leave full-time education having completed their primary school course. Pupils who terminated their full-time education with their exit from the primary school came to be thematised as primary school terminal leavers. Hyland (1969) recorded a drop in the number of terminal leavers from eighteen thousand to ten thousand between the years 1964/65 and 1966/67. Despite the introduction of free education in September 1967, the percentage of primary school leavers becoming terminal leavers merely dropped from fifteen to thirteen in the school year 1967/68 (Rudd, 1972). This 13 per cent, according to Rudd, represented 'a hard core, those whom the administrative and economic changes were not affecting'.

This textualisation continued through an examination of the educational careers of a sample of terminal leavers during the school years 1966/67 and 1967/68. This revealed that their educational attainment was even lower than was immediately evident:

- Twenty per cent left from fifth standard or below.
- Twenty per cent left having registered less than half the required attendances in sixth class.
- Twenty-five per cent left having registered more than half but less than eighty-five per cent (average) of the attendances in sixth class.
- Fifteen per cent left having made eighty-five to one hundred per cent attendances in sixth class.
- Twenty per cent left having completed sixth and having made some progress in a subsequent year.

Furthermore, when the attendance records of the pupils in this sample for the primary school grades second to sixth were examined it was found that whereas 68 per cent had average attendances in second class, the percentages decreased gradually to 62 per cent in third class, 59 per cent in fourth class, 55 per cent in fifth class and 31 per cent in sixth class. Therefore, not alone did terminal leavers fail to receive any form of post-primary schooling, but a sizeable proportion could not be considered to have completed the primary school course; in fact, even though officially in attendance at primary school, their attendance records almost from the beginning of their school careers were drastically inferior to those of the average child.

This web of limited exposure to education is compelling as an example of educational inequality. It had the potential to act figuratively, as a metonym, substituting one sub group of those unequally benefiting from education for its totality. Perhaps it was meant to operate in this rhetorical fashion as a means of mobilising emotion, evoking outrage and mustering support. In effect, it communicated more at the denotative than connotative level achieving a more literal signification of the specific sub-group involved – terminal leavers as non-beneficiaries of free education. This reveals a structural feature of discourse on educational equality. Most publicly, it accorded a special position to those on the edge of society, 'hard cases', furthest removed from a normalised 'us'. Structurally, it operated as an orientation to establish educational inequality as the exclusive experience of 'distant others', those so different from 'us' as to be almost unknowable. In the instance of terminal learners, they were those who had been left behind, stuck in the impenetrable mud as the rising tide of educational opportunity lifted all other boats, however variably.

The 'distant other' proved to be a more enduring construct than the 'poor but clever child' of ministerial discourse in the targeting of concern and intervention in relation to LEM. In time it would assume many material forms as later chapters on employability and disadvantage will demonstrate. In the late-1960s, but particularly salient from 1970, the discovery of the deprived child, to be analysed in Chapter 13, worked to fix and sustain the place of the 'distant other' in educational discourse. Being problematised in this manner introduced an instability into the understanding of the 'distant other'. Were the pupils involved to be the more appropriate concern of social work, youth work, juvenile liaison, and welfare rather than educational personnel? Should intervention be refocused from schooling to social service provision and community programmes? And how was the 'distant other' to be theorised morally in terms of social risk, social rescue, philanthropy, human capital or children's rights? This instability was already in evidence in the differences in the prescriptions for intervening in educational disadvantage between social workers and educators in the Rutland Street Project during the 1970s (Holland, 1979) and, as we shall see in later chapters, persists to the present.

The official text continues in the policy responses to these limited educational experiences of terminal leavers. In terms of pupil progression, two interventions – circular 10/67 on pupil promotion and the raising of the school leaving age to fifteen – 'solved' the problem of terminal leaving (O'Sullivan, 1989a). Circular 10/67 of March 1967 directed that 'the normal procedure should be that a pupil is promoted to a higher standard at the end of each school year'. Semi-automatic promotion would ensure that few pupils should reach the minimum school leaving age while still in primary school, and the raising of the school leaving age from fourteen to fifteen further confirmed this. Terminal leaving, however, was a symptom of educational underachievement. It pertained to the effects of schooling, to pupil performance, in the first instance, rather than to pupil access to educational programmes. Circular 10/67 and the raising of the school leaving age confronted the access problem for terminal leavers in that it became the norm for pupils to receive some post-primary schooling. The failure to recognise the performance problem which underpinned terminal leaving was, however, to become a recurring absence in the understanding of unequal opportunity in education. Apart from constituting terminal leavers as 'distant others', their textualisation in this manner through policy enactment and practice further confirms, in its exclusions and intervention mode, the prioritising of activism over reflection, analysis and theorisation.

If the target group of the official text on LEM issues was the 'distant other', the principle of intervention was that of sponsorship, a principle that emanated from the manner in which the educational system allocated opportunity and managed mobility in general, and not just in relation to those who experience blockages or limitations in this regard. The dichotomy of contest/sponsored mobility, meant as 'ideal types', was developed by Turner (1961) to help illuminate what he described as the folk norms governing social mobility, in so far as they are mediated through the organisation of educational systems. As a pre-reflexive construct, the contest/sponsored dichotomy is particularly suited to the analysis of Irish educational knowledge at this time.

In contest mobility, elite status is likened to a 'prize in an open contest in which the contestants have wide latitude in the strategies they may employ' and where the processes and agents of assessment are widely dispersed. With sponsored mobility '... elite recruits are chosen by the established elite or their agents, the elite status is given on the basis of some criterion of supposed merit and cannot be taken by any amount of effort or strategy'. In the 1960s – a pivotal point of change in this regard – the following features of the Irish educational system indicate its leaning towards sponsorship in the manner in which it managed the development of talent:

- The emphasis on the needs of society and in particular those of the expanding economy is found consistently in the ministerial statements of the time, reflected in the development of the career guidance service and in efforts to enhance the vocational strand of post-primary schooling.
- The centralised character of Irish education made a unitary currency of mobility possible, provided the agents and the means by which suitable recruits for sponsorship could be recognised, while the traditional reference groups of a predominantly rural society, such as the church and the professions, exalted formal qualifications.
- The university system through its matriculation requirements regulated what was to be recognised as high status knowledge. The fixed and stratified social structure operated closure through its monopoly of elite credentials including educational linkages and affiliations.
- While formal selection was not a feature of schooling, early differentiation by scholarship class, post-primary school type and stream operated through recommendation, endorsement and internalisation.

Through its communication of sponsorship the operating text of the educational system supplied a rationale governing who was entitled to enhanced opportunities and indeed who was obliged to act in advancing equality of educational opportunity. Historical, though still recognisable, tropes in this textualisation included the attribution, development and subsequent career confirmation of 'character' and leadership qualities within private schools, and the selection, grooming and publicised successes of the Christian Brothers' scholarship boys. In the transitional 1960s, values of essentialism, philanthropy, paternalism, social efficiency and meritocracy variously circulated. It was not that individual entitlements or social justice were excluded: as a folk norm, sponsorship did not require explication and had succeeded in managing the limited mobility opportunities available in a fixed social structure in a manner that was consistent with its untheorised nature.

From the 1960s the agents and nature of sponsorship were changing. Education was actually becoming a more important force in regulating the labour force entry of each cohort of young people growing up in Ireland. More of them were staying on longer at school and college, the work available to them in a dramatically-changing occupational structure was employment- rather than inheritance-based, and recruitment to these predominantly white-collar positions was increasingly in terms of educational credentials. It was indeed valid in this context to describe the systemic role of education as one of 'discrimination and selection' (Breen *et al.*, 1990, p. 139). But the processes involved had become less personalised, individually-regulated or reliant on ritualised formation of subjectivities. Mobility regulation within this expanding and changing educational system became more contest-based, though it would be by no means equitable in its operation (Smyth and Hannan, 2000). Sponsorship, however, persisted as a principle in determining needs and priorities and allocating resources at the interface of life chances, education and morality. But rather than centring around the management of the recruitment of individuals as a feature of social mobility, sponsorship now took the form of endorsing social categories meriting special attention in education in a process that largely involved agents other than schools and teachers, such as the state and its corporatist structures, industrial and social interest groups, mass media, and international bodies including the EU and the OECD.

'Non-Political' Education: Comprehensive Schooling

A very accessible example of the absence of theorisation of the school/society interface, and the explicit exclusion of social justice and social change, from the LEM meanings of the era is to be found in the manner in which comprehensive schooling as a theory and a practice was introduced to Ireland. We have seen how official statements on equality of educational opportunity failed to allow for, much less intend, that the bringing into more advanced levels of the educational system of previously excluded pupils would have implications for society in its distribution of resources and offices. The introduction of comprehensive schools in 1963 provides an even more striking instance of the segregation of educational innovation and social change in the minds of policy makers. Unlike the discourse on the expansion of educational opportunity where one is obliged to identify silences, absences and omissions in this regard, the exclusion of social objectives in the discourse on comprehensive schooling was explicit and emphatic.

Though it can be argued that the American High School was the prototype comprehensive school, it was the European experience with comprehensive schooling that most impinged on Irish experience. There, comprehensive schooling was seen as an alternative to dual or tripartite systems of post-primary school systems, that normally involved selection and a differentiated curriculum. As developed initially in Sweden, and in later years in England and Wales, comprehensive schooling was a project geared towards social reconstruction and was not solely an educational initiative. Five aspirations for the effects of comprehensive schools were identified at the time of their introduction in England and Wales (Ford, 1969):

- Comprehensive schools would provide greater equality of opportunity for those with equal ability. According to this argument, early selection of pupils into different schools and educational programmes is likely to involve significant misplacement of pupils resulting in a mismatch of talent and opportunity. Because of their wide curriculum, comprehensive schools would be more likely to recognise and exploit the presenting talents of their pupils.
- Comprehensive schools would expand the pool of abilities in society. This was based on a more flexible understanding of the nature of ability, rejecting the idea of a fixed ability from birth and arguing that it can be developed by school experience.
- The occupational horizons of pupils in comprehensive schools would be broadened. It was felt that where there are different types of schools they tend to feed different occupations, not only because of differences in the actual programmes that they provide but also because of the manner in which pupils tend to form 'realistic' expectations of their occupational hopes.
- Comprehensive-school pupils would be less inclined to mix only with children of their own social background resulting in a greater inter-group knowledge, understanding and empathy, and ultimately in a society with a common core of social values.
- Comprehensive-school children would be less likely to regard the social class system as naturalistic, inevitable or a functional feature of society, and consequently be more open to policies which pursue a greater egalitarianism in society.

All but the first of these aspirations were contentious and instigated considerable public controversy in England and Wales. This was particularly true in the case of the more political objectives where advocates of comprehensive schools were accused of social engineering (O'Sullivan, 1972a). Nothing of this debate – its themes, discourses, texts, etc. – was experienced in Ireland as it considered the government's policy on comprehensive schooling.

Dr Hillery announced his intention to establish comprehensive schools in his 1963 statement to the press. These were to be state-financed, co-educational, non-selective, provide a wide curriculum incorporating both academic and practical subjects and involve a period of observation, particularly during the first year, when the pupils' aptitudes and talents would be identified. In that statement, Dr Hillery presented this innovation in post-primary schooling as an attempt to correct two main weaknesses of the Irish educational system. Firstly, he identified the problem of access in some rural areas where there was no post-primary school within easy daily reach and where none was likely to be provided under existing arrangements. Secondly, he drew attention to the 'haphazard way' in which many pupils find themselves in one type of post-primary school rather than in another, resulting in a mismatch of pupil ability and school programme. He pointed to '… children entering vocational school who might have benefited to a far greater degree from a more academic course … (and) large numbers in secondary schools who derived little benefit from the study of academic subjects but who might profit greatly from the more practical type of course provided in vocational schools'.

That was the extent to which comprehensive schools were meant to embody LEM issues. It is clear that the themes of access and pupil ability/school programme mismatch are both contained within the first aspiration of comprehensive schools – that they would facilitate a greater development of the existing talent of society. There is nothing in Dr Hillery's extensive statement that engages any of the more demanding aspirations of the advocates of comprehensive schooling, be they in relation to the nature of ability, occupational horizons, social knowledge or egalitarianism. In the Dáil, on 16 June 1963, when Dr Noel Browne pressed the Minister to explain the educational theory behind the proposal, Dr Hillery responded that '… to do what is possible is my job and not to have the whole matter upset because of some principle or ideal' (quoted in O'Sullivan, 1989a). Not that the Minister was subjected to much prodding in relation to the aspirations of comprehensive schooling. Political, professional, media and public attention centred on the possible location of the schools, the lack of information and consultation and the issue of administration and control. As if to copperfasten this restrictive, non-political understanding of comprehensive schooling, George Colley as Minister for Education in 1966 availed of a prominent article on the topic of comprehensive schools in a major Sunday newspaper to issue the following disclaimer:

> I feel I should begin by explaining what I mean by comprehensive education … It is necessary because of the misconception which many people have about it, to state as precisely as possible what comprehensive education is. Negatively, it is not anything ideological or political. Positively, it is a system of post-primary education combining academic and technical subjects in a wide curriculum, offering to each pupil an education structured to his needs and interests and providing specialist guidance and advice on the pupil's abilities and aptitudes (Colley, 1966b).

Describing this state intervention in school financing, structure and curriculum as comprehensive schooling may well have been no more than a badge of convenience to manage anticipated local resistance and to qualify for international funding (Barber, 1989; Bonel-Elliott, 1994). Like equality of educational opportunity, it highlights the danger of inferring shared meanings from the use of a common language. Unlike equality of educational opportunity, it was sufficiently explicit in excluding social, and particularly political, objectives to obviate the likelihood of misinterpreting the intentions of the policy makers of the era as other than concerned with a pre-reflexive understanding of fairness.

LEM Themes: Reception and Tolerance in Irish Culture

Contemporaneous with this largely non-discursive textualisation of LEM themes, loosely signified by the construct of equality of educational opportunity in state discourse, there existed a series of innovative and novel efforts at thematisation that had the potential to expand and elaborate the LEM domain of meaning. Throughout the 1960s Irish society was exposed to a great range of themes pertinent to LEM issues. As we survey the decade there is scarcely a year that did not make a noteworthy and distinctive contribution. These allow us to identify the content of themes to which Irish culture was exposed at this time and to chart their apparent failure to penetrate Irish educational thought. By this means we can assess the thematic tolerance of Irish culture by observing what it refused to accept as a resource towards LEM paradigm formation. It should also facilitate the analysis of the agents of exclusion and the identification of where within the policy-making process this boundary maintenance occurred.

In 1961 the London branch of Tuairim produced a pamphlet entitled *Irish Education*. Tuairim was founded in 1954 and described itself as a forum to facilitate the study and discussion of Irish affairs by young people. It sought to achieve its objectives by organising meetings and conferences, commissioning research projects and publishing the work of members or groups of its members. The London branch of Tuairim was inaugurated in 1960 and committed itself in the beginning to the serious study of political and social traditions in Ireland. Its pamphlet on Irish education was based on discussion papers read before the members of the London branch, documentation and submissions provided by organisations and individuals involved in Irish education, as well as on a questionnaire study of recent school-leavers.

The pamphlet was highly critical of the manner in which ideas about Irish education had been generated:

> Councils and committees with terms of reference which preclude the possibility of constructive recommendations and which are composed of people confidently expected to endorse existing policies and which are, in any case, too large, slow and verbose, have not illuminated even a corner of the blackout on educational thinking. The ideologies which have dominated our school courses for the last forty years have effectively screened us from educational developments in other countries throughout the world ... (p. 2).

It condemned the lack of research and the open discussion and publication of criticisms of the system which it claimed had resulted in complacency and a belief that no flaws existed in the system. It attributed this complacency to the interests of those groups in society who benefited from existing arrangements and who might stand to lose if the kinds of ideas typical of the LEM domain were to take root:

> Education has remained static for so long in Ireland because it suits powerful sections of society, the middle classes, the churches and the politicians, to keep it so. The middle classes can afford to send their children to the best private schools available… They can buy the ancillary services not offered directly by the schools: music and art education, specialised training and medical care. They have a vested interest in keeping the most remunerative and socially acceptable professions within their own circle. Their way of life is dependent on the availability of cheap, untrained labour. They complacently believe what's good for them is good for the country (p. 4).

It complained that 'boys for no obvious educational reason, are specifically excluded from the Domestic Science examinations' (p. 7).

In the following year, 1962, a remarkable document entitled *Investment in Education in the Republic of Ireland with some Comparative Statistics* was produced. It was compiled by the Federation of Irish Secondary Schools which drew its members from the Headmasters/Headmistresses/Proprietors of lay secondary schools. Arguing that 'modern trends – political, economic, social and cultural – are all directing attention towards the central role education could and should play in the community' (p. 1), it supported its argument for an expansion in education through the production of quantitative data. These were compiled according to the conventions contained in the UNESCO manual of educational statistics and drew on data pertaining to other educational systems from sources such as the OECD. It constructed participation rates in education for each of the Irish counties from Department of Education annual reports and census figures, identified trends in participation and examination performance in vocational and secondary schools, and estimated investment levels in Irish education, making comparisons where appropriate with other educational systems. The practice of supporting one's argument through the use of quantitative data on educational development incorporating international comparisons was quite unique.

As well as being a source of the themes which it contributed to Irish thinking on education, we also find, in the beliefs and practices that it considered necessary to debunk, some understanding of other themes prevalent in Irish thinking about education at that time, but which may not have otherwise been recorded or entered into the public domain. By way of assertion or contestation it introduced the themes of the nature of intelligence, educability and its development, as well as the social basis of restrictive ideas on the expansion of educational opportunity.

In addressing the question 'are there enough talented people in Ireland to be educated?', it concluded that 'in our view the answer is even if intellectual ability is a fixed quantity (and psychologists now hold that it is not, but that it may grow in suitable circumstances) there are many major sources of talent which are as yet largely untapped in Ireland' (p. 4). It supported this view by pointing to the relatively small percentage of children in Donegal between the ages of twelve and eighteen attending secondary schools concluding that 'we certainly have no reason to assume that the available supply of intellectual ability in Donegal is in any way smaller than in (counties with higher rates of participation)'. It went on to argue that '… the amount of ability available to enter higher or university education is at present limited mainly by the size of the field from which its students are selected' (p. 4) and, pointing again specifically to the situation of young people in Donegal, it estimated that at that time they had approximately only one-third of the chance of reaching university as that of a child from some other Irish counties.

It acknowledged the existence of opposition to its arguments for the expansion of educational opportunity:

> There are Irish men who, while willing to admit the force of economic and social arguments for educational expansion, nevertheless maintain that all or nearly all of those who might benefit from extended secondary education or from higher education are already being catered for, and that to extend the provision for education might lead to a lowering of the academic standards (p. 4).

Not alone does the report oppose this interpretation, expressing its conviction that '… the reservoir of intellectual ability as yet untapped by post-primary education in Ireland is larger than in most European countries' (p. 5), but it was particularly explicit in identifying the social base of this opposition and the interests which it served. It went on to express these views raising themes of privilege, power and social standing associated with the benefits of an extended education:

> It has not infrequently happened in other countries that the dominant class opposing the extension of higher education facilities has itself been traditionally educated … the favourite argument against development was the danger of dilution of values and the inflation of standards. It may be taken that in raising these arguments traditional education was less concerned with values than with holding on to the seats of power and influence. Such arguments are not totally unknown among some of our Irish people who have obtained the full benefit of secondary and even university education for themselves, but would wish to preserve these benefits as exclusive privileges for their own children rather than extend them to all the children of the nation (p. 5).

It went on to raise the themes of access and impediments in relation to educational opportunity:

> We are not without Irish critics who point with scorn to the eleven-plus examination in Great Britain and Northern Ireland as excluding certain children from the advantages of a Grammar School education, but who conveniently forget to estimate how many Irish children of high ability are excluded from secondary education either by the absence of secondary facilities in their area, or by the existence of a financial thirteen plus – factors only too evident in the secondary enrolment figures for Donegal, Cavan, Monaghan and Leitrim (p. 5).

Gender issues were also thematised. It drew comparisons between the academic attainment of pupils in the Irish Republic and pupils in England, Wales and Northern Ireland, and noted in particular '… that a significantly greater effort is being made to draw on the mathematical and scientific ability of girl pupils in Northern Ireland, England and Wales'. It concluded that these discrepancies '… reflect to a great extent the quality of the mathematical and scientific teaching in the girls' schools in the Republic of Ireland' (p. 10).

The Labour Party policy document on education *Challenge and Change in Education* followed in 1963. It recast the theme of privilege in terms of the class structure of Irish society and the discrimination associated with it and experienced by less well-positioned sectors of society:

> Education in Ireland today, despite the undoubted fact that increasing numbers of children are receiving post-primary education of one sort or another, remains essentially a part of a structure of social and financial class privileges which serve to prevent the full utilisation of the human resources of the community and which are in complete opposition to Labour's concept of a good society. Labour believes that post-primary education should be free to all children and that the opportunity to receive university and other forms of education should be made available to all those with ability to benefit from it (p. 1).

This policy document also perceived the function of education in correcting this situation to range beyond that of personal benefit, such as the social and economic improvement of individuals through educational participation, and argued for the use of education to reconstruct a different kind of society where there would be a greater emphasis on communal as opposed to individual values. It urged that education should '… strive to create good citizens, who recognise the needs and importance of the community as well as those of the individual, and who will play a full and constructive part in society' (p. 1). In committing itself to the policy of raising the compulsory school leaving age from fourteen to fifteen years of age as soon as possible and to sixteen years as soon as practicable, it argued, echoing almost word-for-word the INTO *A Plan for Education* (1947), that equality of educational opportunity was a core democratic value: 'An education which ends when the pupil is only on the threshold of mental and physical development is neither a liberal nor a so-called "vocational" education. The society which tolerates such a system is not truly democratic; for a democracy aims at providing equality of educational opportunity for all its citizens' (p.7). Furthermore, in its classification of social beneficiaries, it moves beyond social class categories to a conceptualisation based on mental handicap: 'the compulsory school leaving age of handicapped children should be sixteen years of age, and this educational provision should be free' (p. 7).

The Fine Gael *Just Society* programme yielded pamphlets and policy documents during the 1960s, including one dedicated to education, *Fine Gael Policy for a Just Society. Education* (Fine Gael Party, 1966). The *Just Society* programme was motivated by a need to rework society, in this case the creation of a social order derived from Catholic social teaching:

> The social and economic thought of the Fine Gael party has been informed and moulded by the social doctrines contained in the papal encyclicals. Most people in public life will state their acceptance of the teachings contained in the papal encyclicals ... It is our responsibility as lay men in politics to learn and appreciate these principles; to review the situation as it exists in Ireland; to form a judgement on that situation and in the light of these principles to decide how they should be implemented in this country at the present time (Fine Gael Party, n.d., p. 3).

It professed itself to being fundamentally concerned with making a reality of two concepts – freedom and equality: 'Irish society today denies the full realisation of these concepts for all citizens. It is therefore not a just society. We seek office to work towards a society in which freedom and equality are not concepts from an academic textbook but are expressed in real and tangible conditions which all our people can enjoy' (p.3). In the field of educational policy it declared the elimination of obstacles to equality of opportunity in education to be one of its two fundamental principles, and committed itself to raising the school leaving age, improving the financing of the school building programme, providing inducements to those schools that remained outside the free education system to join it, and providing maintenance grants to help overcome geographical disadvantage and for senior pupils from families with limited means.

As we have seen from Chapter 4 the most celebrated educational report of modern times, *Investment in Education,* was published at this time, in 1965. Reworking census figures, it identified significant variations in educational participation by occupational group and geographical area. It found that while just over half the thirteen to seventeen age group was in full-time education in counties such as Tipperary and Waterford, Donegal's rate was somewhat less than a third. Occupationally, there was a marked contrast between the participation rates of students from professional and white collar families and those from skilled, semiskilled and unskilled manual worker families, with the contrast becoming more marked the higher the age group and educational level. While the

Investment in Education survey team was careful to point out that it did not have the data on income differences between families, it later concluded that children of parents of certain social groups, including those with lowest income, were found to have a higher probability of failing to maintain their position in entry to post-primary school and university and other third-level institutions.

Through its use of the socio-economic classification scheme of the census *Investment in Education* offered a conceptualisation of Irish society along class lines, provided a terminology that allowed for a detailed social differentiation of the beneficiaries of education, and thematised a stratified society within educational discourse. This public breaching of the concept of a communal society in such an official publication cannot be understated in its potential for LEM paradigm formation. The classification system of the census did not conform to the conventions of social class categorisation. It treated farmers as a single undifferentiated category and did not follow an ordinal pattern (Clancy, 2001). Yet, at that time it normalised a way of speaking about the collective identity of those who participated to different levels in Irish education that resonated with social class imagery. It regularised the naming of categories such as professional, middle and working class in relation to educational participation. By reference to the indisputable statistical differences in educational participation that it yielded, the facticity of this class conceptualisation of Irish society was enhanced.

Investment in Education also gave specific consideration to the possibility of building economic redistribution into the educational funding policies of the state with the objective of improving the participation of children from the lower socio-economic groups. The impact of this redistribution would have been to fund the increased financial support for the children from less well-off families through holding the better off more accountable for the cost of their children's education. The report considered that the funding of post-primary and university education provided the greatest scope for such redistribution given that 'existing arrangements confer an automatic subsidy on all aided post-primary and university pupils' (p. 343).

Beginning at the post-primary level, it noted that the existing system of capitation grants was in effect a scholarship awarded indirectly to every pupil, and that this allocation of financial support took no account of ability or financial needs. It recommended for consideration, both in relation to this indirect subsidy and to the scholarship scheme proper, that such support might vary according to the financial circumstances of the families. The report further raised the possibility of abolishing the existing income-tax relief for children of 16 years and over who remain in full-time education with the view to using the financial savings to provide more scholarships. A third possible redistributive strategy which the report raised was the establishment of a system of variable capitation grants with the object of ensuring that at least some secondary schools in each area would be able to provide schooling at a low fee. In further noting that the existing system of capitation grants meant that schools charging higher fees were able to provide better facilities, it hoped that a variable capitation grant might '… reduce to some extent that disparity in educational opportunities' (p. 344).

The report followed a similar line of argument with regard to the financing of university education where the practice of block grants to individual colleges similarly meant a scholarship for each student. It suggested that there might be grounds for replacing such a system with a mixture of scholarships and grants conditional on scholastic attainment and/or family income, and recommended that 'students who did not satisfy those conditions might be asked to pay the full cost of their courses' (p. 345).

In supporting these recommendations, the National Industrial Economic Council (1966) drew attention to the underlying redistributive principle involved: '… it would mean that some part of the additional funds needed to encourage greater participation in secondary and university education by the children of the lower income groups would in effect be met in some part by parents in the higher income groups who would be paying fees in line with the full economic cost of post-primary and university education' (pp 24-25).

An early sociological contribution to public consciousness by an independent academic in the area of LEM was 'Social Dynamite' by Liam Ryan, priest and sociology lecturer at University College Cork, in 1967 (Ryan, 1967b). 'Social Dynamite' reported on a study of one hundred school 'drop-outs' from a corporation housing estate, referred to as Parkland, in an Irish provincial city. It proved to be a highly incisive account of the culture of the area, recording a high incidence of unskilled workers, low and precarious salaries, over-crowding and large families, a value system with little regard for planning or schooling, and an adolescent career pattern that led predominantly from primary school to work or unemployment. Written in a highly readable style with strong moral and social rescue dimensions, this evocation of the cycle of deprivation was frequently referred to in the media and reached a wide audience through serialisation in *The Irish Times*. The theoretical basis of the article was W.I. Thomas's (1923) 'definition of the situation' theorem which points to the centrality of our interpretation of the world around us, apart from its objective reality, in shaping our self-perceptions, hopes, expectations, personal decisions and social actions. In the consequences that follow from our definition of the situation we can create it as reality. As Ryan concluded, 'therefore, from an early age, and almost unconsciously, the child learns to define a situation in a way that favours the job rather than school, that favours today rather than tomorrow, that sees getting ahead as a combination of money and "pull", and stresses the inequalities of the "fine soft jobs" of the idle rich, and that kills any sense of their own dignity and importance and that kills any respect for their neighbourhood, their city or their country.'

The solutions offered were largely of a cultural and service nature – community centre, social worker, a better and co-ordinated social welfare and charity system, and a more varied primary school system. But Ryan also castigated the '… amused hostility … of the better educated classes who identify the area and its people with all kinds of deceit, shiftiness, and immorality…(and) are careful to segregate themselves and their offspring from these "undesirable and under-educated children"'. He also recognised that research such as his, however sympathetic, '… could underline the distinction between these people and the better educated classes, and so become a source of discrimination and segregation'. He raised the option of political action: 'all over the world today minorities are on the march demanding an end to discrimination and injustice. Minorities everywhere are finding a solution to their problems in political activity. There is no reason why the minority that is Parkland should not do likewise. Parkland is partly the creation of its residents, but it is also the creation of "officialdom" with its policy that urban populations need only roads and houses.'

In the Rutland Street Pre-School Project in Dublin, the state's first major intervention programme for areas such as Parkland, it was not the mechanism of political activism that was adopted but the American model of compensatory education. The Rutland Street Pre-School Project enrolled its first pupils in 1969. Research on the area during the 1960s had indicated systematically low levels of performance on standardised tests across a range of skills and competencies. A committee established by the Department of Education in 1968 proposed the project and part-funding was obtained from the Dutch Van Leer Foundation. Influenced by similar programmes in the United States it conceptualised the problem as one of educational disadvantage as defined by Passow (1970). This is evident from one of the earliest publications from the project (Ó hUallacháin and Kellaghan, 1969). In this '… a child is regarded as disadvantaged if he is unable to benefit fully from educational facilities because the skills and attitudes he brings from his cultural background to the school make adjustment in school difficult and unduly impede learning.' The theme of culture clash was also made explicit. It argued that 'the problems of the disadvantaged may be viewed as being fundamentally problems in adjustment to cultural demands' and posed the following questions:

> What does it mean for a child from a non-middle class background to go to a school that is staffed by middle-class people using middle-class language and modes of thinking and who have middle-class expectations for school children? What are the implications of going to a school that is committed to propagating middle-class values and standards, when one's own values and standards, and those of one's home are quite different?

The Rutland Street Pre-School Project was influenced by principles of cognitive development derived from Piaget's work. The programme was structured and teacher-directed with an emphasis on scholastic objectives. A feature of both project and 'Social Dynamite' was the concern for actual academic performance of disadvantaged pupils – the educational outcomes theme – as well as their retention in the educational system beyond the level of primary schooling.

This account of cultural work in relation to the LEM domain in the 1960s is unlikely to be exhaustive (Bonel-Elliott, 1996). Though no more than a selection drawn from accessible resources of the time, it nonetheless identifies the existence of efforts at cultural production that seemingly failed to penetrate state understandings in this field of meaning.

These themes offered to the cultural production of the LEM domain, and specifically to the elaboration of the construct of equality of educational opportunity, distribute themselves, albeit unevenly, over the dimensions of the LEM domain identified in the introduction to Part Three. These include the capacity to compete for resources and offices in society and the rules governing such competition, a social categorisation and delineation of beneficiaries, moral responses derived from principle or emotion, and explanations and interventions:

- Capacity to compete: unrecognised talent, undeveloped talent, mismatch of pupil talent and school programme
- Social categorisation: occupational levels, social class, gender, mental disability
- Moral responses: utilitarianism, society's needs for talent exploitation, fairness, democracy
- Explanations: availability of schools, financial impediments, cultural impediments to educability, personal internalisation of failure, culture clash between home and school
- Interventions: greater accessibility of suitable schools, abolition of fees, exposure to a wider curriculum, cross-subsidisation of the education of the less well-off by the more advantaged, politicisation and social action, pre-school compensatory programmes.

Given this range and diversity of themes, and even allowing for its uneven character, it provided Irish culture with sufficient discursive resources for the establishment of texts reflective of LEM paradigms. The question that has to be confronted is why this cultural production never occurred and why the textualisaton that ensued persisted largely as a non-discursive process. The agents of this cultural work were largely drawn from the intellectual or the broad state sector and were in no sense submerged or marginal voices, easily excluded from cultural production or the educational policy process. Nor could it be said that the themes were cognitively, culturally or even ideologically remote from the pre-theoretical constructs of fairness, 'distant others' or sponsored mobility within the state's text. They contained no more than an incipient realisation of collective or structural change and, not unexpectedly, little or nothing of the possibilities in schooling for suppressing or enhancing social or cultural identities. For the most part they could have been accommodated through a discursive theorisation of the concept of equality of educational opportunity, particularly in terms of a moral obligation and economic imperative to counter, by means of resources and facilities, economic and cultural impediments to accessing and benefiting from education experienced by individual or particular categories of pupils.

Truncated Cultural Production

In seeking to explore the restrictive character of cultural production on LEM issues at that time, Vygotsky's distinction between actual and potential development is illuminating. Though conceived in relation to the individual's conceptual maturation, Vygotsky's theory of ZPD (Zone of Proximal Development) transfers productively to the collective and cultural spheres of human experience. This should not surprise since a central feature of Vygotsky's theory of human development is the role of interaction within one's social and cultural context. The ZPD can be regarded as the interface between actual development and the most immediate potential development. Vygotsky (1978, p. 86) defined it as:

> *the distance between the actual developmental level as determined by independent problem solving and the level of potential development as determined through problem solving under adult guidance or in collaboration with more capable peers* ... The zone of proximal development defines those functions that have not yet matured but are in the process of maturation, functions that will mature tomorrow but are currently in an embryonic state. These functions could be termed the 'buds' or 'flowers' of development rather than the 'fruits' of development.

It is clear that the 'buds' of paradigm formation in the sphere of LEM existed in great abundance in Ireland during the 1960s, specifically in relation to equality of educational opportunity. But a more symmetrical equivalent in cultural formation of 'adult guidance' or 'collaboration with more capable peers' appears to have been lacking.

The strategies suggested by post-Vygotskians for the realisation of the potential within the ZPD (Vygotsky himself was rather silent on this matter) – instruction, modelling, demonstration, feedback, reinforcement, questioning, providing explanations and belief structures, recruitment of learners and engagement of their attention (Daniels, 1996) – have clear equivalents within the field of paradigmatic development. The stimulation, formation and systematisation of the LEM themes to which Irish culture was introduced during the 1960s required social and intellectual activities along the following lines:

- Linking the manifestations of access, input and outcome, and labelling them as such within a structure of differentiated meaning of inequality of educational opportunity
- Providing a sustained analysis of themes such as class, politicisation, culture clash, comprehensive schooling
- Substantiating and affirming by means of further manifestations or examples
- Contesting the appropriateness of descriptions of Irish society or education
- Providing counter interpretations or concepts
- Questioning the use of schooling as an agent of social engineering
- Seeking clarification of some aspect of a theme
- Estimating the cost of an intervention
- Organising conferences/study groups around particular themes
- Maintaining associations/networks to sustain meanings
- Publicising the results of deliberations on these matters.

To the extent that one can explore these matters retrospectively it would appear that interactions of this nature were striking in their rarity.

At that time, university education departments were understaffed, chairs were vacant and they lacked specialists or courses of study in areas such as sociology or the kind of philosophical inquiry that would be conducive to raising LEM issues. The social sciences were only beginning to emerge as independent sites of analysis from Roman Catholic apologetics. In none of these disciplines would there have been the time or the encouragement for research (Coolahan, 1984a; Drudy, 1991).

An exception was Craft's (1970) short but ambitious analysis of ideology and the economy in educational development in Ireland in which he drew parallels with the situation in Great Britain. He concluded that 'in Ireland, as in Britain, it is no longer thought acceptable that life chances should be allocated at birth, once and for all; it is increasingly felt that each child be encouraged to go as far as he or she can, to achieve at the highest level, regardless of social class, colour, religion, or any other ascribed characteristic'. This, he contended, '… is what is meant by the *democratisation* of education, the widening of opportunities for individual children regardless of social origin; the movement away from an ascriptive to an achievement-oriented society'. Furthermore, he detected in the educational policies of the era a '… fundamental belief in western social democracy. The maximising of individual freedom and self-fulfilment through a programme of community education devised and executed by elected government'. It is easy to criticise Craft for assuming the existence of an integrated paradigm of education and social policy of a kind that he was familiar with through 'the post-war consensus' (Education Group CCCS, 1981) in England and Wales on the basis of the existence of a few constitutive themes. Over-interpretation it may be but in modelling how equality of educational opportunity might be linked to broader social policies, sociologically named and illuminated in comparative perspective, it represents an example of the kind of support that LEM paradigm formation required in the 1960s. Not that the culture of the time was necessarily receptive to the introduction of new themes or to any of their stages of subsequent development within its LEM domain. It cannot be assumed that it was a 'willing learner'.

When American speaker Professor Eoin MacTiarnáin addressed the Conference of Convent Secondary Schools in 1960 he decried what he saw as 'a lack of native virile philosophy' and claimed to have detected a 'degree of class differences and an acceptance of the doctrine of class difference so shocking that I am compelled to refer to it in unjustifiably strong terms and call it a caste system'. Yet, the indications from both the response of the meeting and a subsequent commentary are that his criticisms elicited the themes of free education, state funding and an inactive Minister for Education rather than unequal social structures, critical awareness or theorisation (Randles, 1975). This is an example of alien cultural representations being reinterpreted or 'translated' in the light of indigenous conceptualisations, as intrusive constructs were denied the status of a theme. Class, caste and a critical theorisation of society failed to be accepted into the discourse of the engagement which nonetheless continued with more acceptable and less disruptive substitutes.

These examples from the extremes of the 1960s give some insights into the truncated dynamics of LEM cultural production at this time. In fact, it would seem that the most frequent fate of such innovative themes as have been outlined here from a selection of publications of the era was to be ignored. Thus, when they failed to survive in the discourse their exit was due to neglect rather than explicit rejection. The populist nature of both the state representation and parental reception of educational expansion from the late 1960s may go some way to explaining this. As has been indicated in Chapter 4 on the enthusiastic parental embracement of educational expansion at this time, to be further developed in Chapter 13 on the social context of the discovery of the deprived child, parents were beginning to dissent from ascribed educational expectations and becoming more aware of how educational participation could enhance their children's life chances. But the associative context was atomistic rather than collective. Two manifestations of this were to prove important. Firstly, it cultivated a commutative relationship between individuals – parent/pupil and educational provider – rather than a distributive relationship between the state and its collective citizens. Secondly, among parents, there was little sense of solidarity with or obligation to those who may have needed to benefit more than others from expanded educational provision. Indeed, populism would have suppressed differentiation between the educational beneficiaries in such terms. It should not surprise that it was more conducive to interpreting educational benefits in terms of the competitive positioning of one's offspring than to constructing a social morality around educational opportunity.

A more immediate restraining factor retarding the elaboration of the construct of equality of educational opportunity was the discursive context of its circulation as a subsidiary or subsumed component within the human capital paradigm. In the 1960s it was rare for equality of educational opportunity to stand alone as a necessary objective that required no further justification than the assertion that it constituted a basic requirement of a democratic society. There was little by way of public manifestation of outrage, indignation or shame. For the most part, the arguments supporting the provision of greater educational opportunities throughout society appealed as much to the social and economic benefits to a society with expanding manpower and leadership needs as to the benefits to those who would avail of this expanded education. Individualistic justifications that refer to questions of rights, entitlements, autonomy or self determination were not a feature of this discourse, much less a collective understanding of inequality between groups. While the sources of the innovative themes quoted from earlier were exceptional examples of cultural production in this regard, they nonetheless could not escape the constraints of the human capital paradigm.

The Federation of Irish Secondary Schools (1962) report *Investment in Education in the Republic of Ireland* argued that 'Selfishness is almost always short-sighted and the begetters of such arguments (against educational expansion) conveniently ignore the fact that the maintenance of such restrictions on educational facililties cannot fail to ultimately adversely affect our Irish economy, and thus indirectly injure both themselves and their families' (p. 5). Even the Labour Party policy document *Challenge and Change in Education* (1963), which contained by far the most explicit class indictment of Irish education, found it appropriate to justify a less discriminatory educational system not only '... on social or moral grounds, but (as) a basic economic investment':

> In the next few years this country is going to face enormous economic problems, problems which may indeed put our survival as an independent nation in question. It is, therefore, essential that planning in education should be an inherent part of our economic planning. Already shortages of certain types of skill are becoming felt in our economy, and at the same time there is a surplus of other skills resulting in under-employment and emigration (pp 1-2).

Investment in Education, as we have seen, provided the most unassailable factual basis for moral outrage. It, nonetheless, maintained a distanced amoral position on its findings on class disparities in educational participation, the political context of which has been explained in Chapter 4. It identified five main areas in which improvements might be sought:

- The number who leave school without having reached primary certificate level
- The lower rate of participation in post-primary education by children from unskilled and unemployed groups
- The high rates of early leaving from vocational schools
- The small proportion of vocational students to reach third-level courses
- The low rate of participation in university by many social groups.

It pointed out that there are many complex factors affecting the rate at which people in different circumstances participate in education, of which income is only one. It listed schools, their location, fee levels, entry requirements and curriculum, as well as the income, preferences for spending, environment and traditions of parents and potential pupils. Its concluding observation on this topic was cautious and restrained: 'The influence of such factors – social group, location etc – on participation in education has of course been observed in many countries. Experience in other countries has also shown that a significant improvement in participation by certain social groups can be a very slow and expensive process' (p. 176).

Even in relation to the various redistributive options in the financing of education which *Investment in Education* identified as a means of funding financial support for children of lower socio-economic groups to allow them to continue in education, the report was again reticent and restrained. It concluded:

> These are some of the possibilities. It is not suggested that any or all of them might be introduced. This would depend on the objectives which the State wishes to achieve by its expenditure. Nor is it suggested that the present system is without merit. For while the present method does have the effect of subsidising a relatively wealthier sector of the community, it also has some effect in stimulating participation on the part of this group. However, it would seem somewhat anomalous to continue such subsidies unless some comparable effort were made to increase participation on the part of poorer groups (pp 345-346).

The endorsement of *Investment in Education* by the National Industrial Economic Council in 1966 signals support from a comprehensive range of interests from within the broad industrial sector. The NIEC, the precursor of the NESC, was the main consultative body to the government on economic and employment issues. Its membership was nominated by the government itself, the Irish Congress of Trade Unions, the Federated Union of Employers and other employer organisations, state boards, and the Federation of Irish Industries. Quoting from and paraphrasing the sections of *Investment in Education* cited above, it replicated, almost word for word, its cautious and restrained approach to any possible intervention. It concluded that while 'the ideal is a society which strives after equal opportunity by ensuring access to the highest levels of education for all with the ability to benefit … equality of educational opportunity, however, cannot be achieved either easily or quickly' (p. 13). Its rationale was both communal and human capital in its logic:

> Of all kinds of inequality, inequality of opportunity is by far the most damaging to the ethos, efficiency and material welfare of a society. If those with the innate ability to benefit from it are denied access to further education, their reasonable ambitions are thwarted, their potential contributions towards achieving the society's objectives are reduced and social cohesion is endangered. The development of the economy and the growth of the society depend in a fundamental way on the quality of leadership. This quality is always in short supply, and if the field from which the leaders are chosen is smaller than the whole society, or if it is defined by any criterion other than ability, then it is being made even more scarce (p. 13).

Later, it expressed the view that low participation rates in post-primary schools and universities among lower socio-economic groups 'are probably a major cause of … manpower deficits' (p. 22), in particular the projected cumulative deficit of something in the order of seventy thousand for those with Intermediate Level or equivalent certification.

In suggesting a series of topics which the proposed development unit in the Department of Education might fruitfully examine, it included:

- the effects of raising the school leaving age on the demand for teachers, buildings and equipment and on participation rates
- the contribution of comprehensive schools to greater flexibility in the educational system
- how the administrative burden on school managers might be eased
- the possibility of further extending co-education in post-primary schools with the objective of more fully utilising educational facilities
- the feasibility of using school buildings and equipment on a 'double-shift' basis (p. 29).

Significantly, any of the issues which the report had earlier raised in relation to the pursuit of equality of educational opportunity, be they by way of impediments or interventions, failed to achieve a sufficient coherence in the scale of what was defined as an educational problem to be listed as a desirable research objective for the development unit.

Equality of Educational Opportunity: Signifier and Signification

Looking specifically at the conceptualisation of the LEM domain in terms of equality of educational opportunity, we now return to the question posed at the beginning of this chapter as to how it interacted with local meanings. In this we find little of Vygotsky's characterisation of everyday concepts working their way up to greater abstraction as they clear the path for scientific concepts in their downward quest for contextualisation. Irish debate at that time seems to have benefited little from the academic and political consideration of equality of educational opportunity elsewhere. Little or nothing of the language of this international discourse – access, input, effect; ascription/achievement; meritocracy/aristocracy; kinds, extent, distribution of ability – was employed in Irish debate. It is easy to obscure this silence because of the manner in which subsequent interpretation of the thinking of the time makes use of an academic terminology. This results in a merging of text and interpretation such that it becomes difficult to disengage their semiotics. For instance, policy makers of the time were committed to providing greater access to schooling and raised issues, such as those of selection and choice of programmes, associated with access. This attention, however, must not be confused with being aware of 'access' within a system of signification that establishes its difference from 'input' and 'outcome' in a fashion that serves to structure its field of meaning. Yet, to be retrospectively critical, as the present author has been (O'Sullivan, 1989a), of the emphasis on the access dimension in Irish educational policy at that time runs the risk of appearing to credit policy makers with such a differentiated conceptualisation of equality of educational opportunity. The most plausible conclusion must be that the use of equality of educational opportunity in Ireland at that time was no more than a slogan of convenience for an unchallenged indigenous system of meanings pertaining to LEM issues which was made possible by a broad compatibility between them.

In the state discourse of the time it can be said that equality of educational opportunity operated as an over-determined signifier with an underdetermined signification. It had become the socially sanctioned label by which concern about LEM issues could be made public, but in a manner that was culturally unspecific in the meanings that it realised. Equality of educational opportunity was what participants in educational discourse intoned when seeking to invoke an LEM construct, in particular when wishing to establish a principle or ideal, but it could tolerate a diversity of interpretations without a disruption of communication. In this manner it was possible for Irish policy discourse to appear to be modern and cosmopolitan without having to explicate, much less defend or compromise native LEM meanings. These persisted at the commutative level with fairness as the core moral construct. Far from colonising Irish LEM meanings, the contribution of equality of educational opportunity as a signifier to their structuration was minimal. Rather, it experienced a semantic hollowing-out as it was accommodated to the nature of Irish LEM knowledge at that time.

Giddens's 'double hermeneutic' rather than Vygotsky's mutual accommodation of the spontaneous and the scientific best captures the character of the dynamic involved. The 'double hermeneutic' refers to the two-way ties that link social science and the actions and institutions it studies. For while social scientists may take lay concepts and seek to fix and define their meaning to facilitate more accurate and precise descriptions of social processes, the agents who form the objects of their standardisation 'regularly appropriate themes and concepts of social science within their behaviour, thus potentially changing its character' (Giddens, 1984, p. 31). Not alone did Irish society appropriate the concept of equality of educational opportunity, but the manner of its deployment was protean, constituted as an empty signifier capable of assuming whatever meaning was required of it. What were to be the implications for LEM formation?

LEM Formation: 1960s and Beyond

In taking stock of the state of the cultural production of the LEM domain at the end of the 1960s it is essential to guard against potential sources of deception and delusion. Too much can be read into, and structures retrospectively imposed on, ministerial statements about educational opportunity, the state's expanding educational provision, and parents who were breaking with their inherited use and perception of schooling. The temptation to diagnose principles of meritocracy, democracy or equality of educational opportunity need to be restrained and circumscribed. Indeed, giving primacy to the concept of equality of educational opportunity in seeking to understand the status of LEM production at this time obfuscates more than it illuminates.

The 1960s can be described as a decade of paradigms postponed when an impressive array of themes with the capacity to intensify equality of educational opportunity as a cultural construct were offered to Irish discourse and refused, their potential allowed to remain unrealised. The social and cultural context of knowledge production of this nature – the absence of intellectual engagement, the dominance of the human capital paradigm, and the populism of educational expansion – was not supportive. The official LEM text was communicated largely by means of non-discursive mechanisms, such as policy practice, strokes and slogans, in which indigenous folk meanings prevailed and were allowed to circulate in their pre-reflexive form. The situation can be summarised in terms of the requirements for LEM formation outlined in the introduction to Part Three. In relation to life chances, it was expected that the sponsorship of pupils for educational progression and occupational entry would attain a wider relevance and application. The social differentiation required for the categorisation of the beneficiaries of expanding opportunities was restrained by the populism of the human capital paradigm and its relationship to educational expansion. It was those marginal to the new opportunities in education – the 'distant others' who constitute the most abiding categorical construct from this time. Morality was grounded on fairness in the commutative relationship between parents/pupils and educational providers, and collective constructs such as distributive justice and social change were excluded. There was a recognition of geographical and financial impediments to progressing in education, and interventions in this regard were visualised in terms of an expansion of educational facilities and the provision of financial support to students. The result was an untheorised, loosely-framed set of LEM resources that nonetheless remained resistant to modification because of their embeddedness in pre-reflexive folk understandings of society. The cultural basis for what would be later interpreted by Lynch (1987) as the dominant ideologies of Irish educational thought – consensualism, essentialism and meritocratic individualism – was already in place.

Looking beyond the 1960s and anticipating subsequent chapters, the most immediate deployment of the cosmopolitan principle of equality of educational opportunity is to be found in the construction of the gender equity paradigm which begins its work from the 1970s. This will be described in Chapter 11. There it will be seen that, in contrast to the 1960s, the discourse on gendered education drew explicitly and emergently, on both the concept of equality of educational opportunity and its specifications for educational policy, by reference to international policy discourse relating to human rights declarations and intergovernmental agreements. Furthermore, gender equity succeeded in becoming a systematised paradigm with an unambiguous interpretation of gendered education, explicit performatives, state integration, and a monitoring and reproductive mechanism, all in striking contrast to the experience of the largely socio-economic-focused use of equality of educational opportunity in the 1960s. Yet, while equality of educational opportunity was being recruited to gender equity, the loosely-framed, indigenous LEM meanings of fairness, sponsorship and 'distant other' find themselves employed in a new era of cultural production as curriculum development enters Irish educational studies, European grant-aided initiatives become a force, and Irish society was faced with an oil crisis, recession and youth unemployment. The effect was to maintain the human capital focus as the LEM construct of employability, the capacity to contribute to production, was established, both constituting and addressing the needs of a new category of 'distant other' – those deemed to be vulnerable to unemployment.

Chapter 8

Employability:
Polyvalent Conceptualisation,
Mutability and Co-optation

As a policy paradigm, employability addresses, and in the process constructs, the needs of those whose chances of labour market entry are most precarious, and posits the capacity to find paid work as the crucial attribute which can rescue them from reliance on social welfare and the experience of social exclusion. This represents, in the first instance, the 1970s' inscription on the construct of 'distant other'. Within the LEM domain of thought, the legitimation of employability emerges from the individual 'deficit' text on educability. When intervention programmes seeking to develop in disadvantaged children the skills and dispositions necessary to benefit from schooling are either non-existent or ineffective, the site of intervention changes from, typically, the earlier years of childhood to the teenage years when the consequences of their disadvantage become more public and explicit in the shape of school alienation, non-attendance, early school leaving, few qualifications or none, and unemployment. While the site of intervention changes, the explanation of their predicament and the recipe for intervention remains within the 'deficit' text in that the supposed inadequacies in the necessary skills and dispositions for educational success are replaced in the discourse by a failure to satisfy the requirements of the labour market.

In each case, the weaknesses are located in the person of the pupil, allocating responsibility, and varying degrees of culpability, to the most immediate agent of socialisation to which the pupil has been exposed – the home in the case of educability, the school in relation to employability. There is also a commonality in the rationale of their sponsorship, as a category of concern and intervention, which hinges on the aspiration to improve a person's capacity to benefit from the opportunities in their environment, the potential for learning in the school and the chances of employment in the labour market. At its most basic, employability is perceived as a means by which people can avoid material disadvantage, dependence on welfare, alienation and marginalisation and be thus assured of, at least, minimal life chances. As it developed, employability became linked to, and regarded as a necessary condition for, making a successful transition to adult life.

This attention to employability and the attainment of adult status may seem unremarkable. In the period under consideration in this book, few parents would have seen schooling as other than a preamble to work and a responsible adult life. Even in the research on popular response to compulsory schooling at the beginning of the state, which records substantial levels of non-attendance, the problem was seen as 'not so much a complete disregard among sections of the population for the benefits of schooling as a gap between what educational officialdom defined as an acceptable minimum and what popular voluntary practice yielded by way of school attendance' (Fahey, 1992b). As later commentators would remark, even those parents who supported their children through a liberal university education did not expect that they were being prepared for unemployment. But the practice of attending within the educational system to what was needed to satisfy the requirements of employment was general in nature and largely unfocused. Outside of the professions and the trades there was little that people with the most general of educational backgrounds would not be expected to turn their hand to. And for those with little and interrupted education there was a range of employment opportunities that relied on the physicality of the body rather than on educational formation. All of that was to change in the 1960s in the light of a more employment-based occupational structure, formal diversification of the labour market, and the credentialisation of the process of labour market entry.

Constructing the Employability Paradigm

The proximate origins of the employability paradigm can be traced to the curriculum development initiatives of the 1970s, though at that stage it assumed a muted and unexplicated form. The 1970s was the decade of curriculum development with a particular emphasis on making the curriculum relevant to life experience. With the introduction of the New Primary School Curriculum of 1971 there was also the feeling that the next target for innovation should be the second-level curriculum. Whatever its initial aspirations for systemic curricular change (Mulcahy, 1981a), as it progressed the curriculum development of the 1970s did not engage the entirety of the curriculum or the full range of the pupil population, and was unevenly experienced across school types. For secondary schools, the senior cycle of the post-primary sector, those transferring to third-level institutions and those likely to cope with the Leaving Certificate, curriculum development as distinct from syllabus change was for other people and institutions (Crooks and McKernan, 1984; Ó Donnabháin, 1998). Its targets were usually identified as those pupils who, in the wake of the increased participation following the expansion of post-primary schooling since the 1960s, were said to be unmotivated by the existing curriculum, had difficulty attaining at the required levels, became disengaged and disruptive in the classroom and had the potential to become early school leavers. It was thus lower-stream pupils, typically outside of the secondary school sector, who were first perceived to be in need of intervention in their transition from school to working life. Substantially, they appear to have been the 1970s' manifestation of the 1960s' primary school terminal leavers, repositioned within the educational system by policy changes, such as those on pupil progress and the raising of the school leaving age. It was around these 'distant others' that employability was initially constructed as a paradigm.

The problematising of these newly-identified 'distant others' in terms of their integration into the non-school world of labour market and adult relationships, as distinct from their potential for class and school disruptiveness, was a significant step in the construction of the employability paradigm. Prior to this, those who experienced school as uninviting, felt they had enough of it and left as soon as it was legally permissible or earlier were expected to 'find their level' within the labour market and adjust to adult role expectations and obligations. They were conceived of as no more than the initial group to be released from the educational system into the world of work and adult life.

The discourse of the European Social Fund (ESF) was the influential early source of the reconceptualisation of specific school leavers as a vulnerable group requiring intervention if they were to make satisfactory adjustments and transitions between schooling, work and adulthood. As outlined by O'Connor (1998), the ESF was established under Article 123 of the Treaty of Rome with a view to improving job opportunities in the community by means of grant aid for vocational training and to assist in the geographical and occupational mobility of workers. It refocused itself in the mid-1960s in the face of a growing unemployment problem and progressed through a number of stages to the mid-1970s when its conceptualisation of the school-to-work experience impacted on Irish consciousness and practice. In the process, the fund had been restructured, increased six fold with over 90 per cent of the total funding now going to vocational training. By 1977, following the enlargement of the community and increased unemployment throughout Europe, unemployed young people under 25, especially first-time job seekers, were included as one of three new 'at risk' categories to be targeted by the fund. Regionally, Ireland was also identified as an area with special problems in this regard. A further revision of the ESF followed in 1982 in the wake of the growth in youth unemployment. This was the origin of the 'training guarantee' to all young people deemed to be vulnerable to unemployment. This further targeting of young people resulted in them making up at least 75 per cent of those who benefited from the ESF. It has been noted that from that time young people, especially those who were long-term unemployed or who had inadequate training and education, became the focus of funding. This was further reinforced by the European Community Heads of Government in 1985 when they passed a resolution instructing member states to actively pursue measures proposed in the Adonino Committee Report which recommended that 'up to two years vocational training, in addition to compulsory education, should be made available as a matter of course to any young people who require it' (ESF Programme Evaluation Unit, 1996, p. 12).

The European Community involvement was never that of a neutral provider of financial support. It was rather a dynamic force in the shaping of Irish understandings on the link between young people, schooling and the world of work. This is evident in a series of Irish intervention programmes from the mid-1970s that have been variously instigated, shaped and influenced by this European discourse. These include the following:

- Pre-employment courses, initiated in 1977, and their successors. Initially, these courses were confined to vocational, community and comprehensive schools and targeted young people who failed to find employment having left school on reaching the school leaving age. These were redeveloped in 1984 as Vocational Preparation and Training (VPT) programmes and were extended to a number of secondary schools. Initially a one-year programme, in 1985 a second year was added. The target group continued to be early school leavers who were deemed to be inadequately prepared for the world of work. It has been estimated that the numbers enrolled constituted about a third of those leaving mainstream second-level schooling (Kellaghan and Lewis, 1991).
- Transition from school to adult/working life projects. The first cluster of these programmes ran from 1979 to 1982 and the second from 1983 to 1987. They originated in a decision of the Commission's Council and of the Ministers for Education meeting within the Council in December 1976 that measures 'be taken to improve the preparation of young people for work and to facilitate their transition from education to working life' (Department of Education, 1984b). The Curriculum Development Centres in Trinity College Dublin and Shannon were involved in these projects.
- Youthreach Programmes. These were aimed at young people between the ages of 15 and 18 years of age, who had left the formal educational system with minimal or no qualifications, who had been unemployed for at least six months and were likely to be socially and economically disadvantaged. Launched in October 1988 by the Ministers for Education and Labour, Youthreach was said to contain a 'guarantee of up to two years of co-ordinated education, training or work experience for unqualified school leavers' (ESF

Programme Evaluation Unit, 1996). Youthreach was delivered by means of two separate networks, Youthreach Centres funded by the Department of Education through Vocational Educational Committees and the Community Training Workshops associated with FÁS regional training centres. Youthreach was conceived as a two-year programme, the foundation year of which is devoted to basic life skills, general education and practical work training. A progression year for those who failed to find employment after the foundation year was also envisaged.

While some of these programmes of educational intervention were short lived, subject to change and adaptation and marginal to the mainstream educational system, their overall cultural impact was not in any sense transient. In their discourse and performance they established the distinctiveness of social configurations, age spans and statuses, communicated the basis on which they were deemed to be distinctive and set apart from others, and why and how society and schooling ought to respond to these definitions of life experiences, needs and interventions. What had previously remained undelineated as a distinct category of young people was now set apart from other leavers from the educational system. Early leavers were now regarded as a distinguishable group with peculiar attributes and needs. Their condition, in particular their change of role to that of worker and adult, which previously, unless issues of moral development were raised, would have been deemed to be unremarkable, was now seen as problematic and requiring intervention. This succeeded in isolating and normalising the sequence of experiences involved in the process of leaving full-time education, effectively establishing and calibrating what was deemed appropriate in relation to new groups and new experiences. Through a fusion of what was said and done in relation to these newly-constructed categories of people and experience, particularly in its conceptualisations, prescriptions for action and the themes that were raised, it was possible to speak of the transition to adulthood, young people and preparation for employment while communicating that all of these statuses, transitions and tasks had a more particularistic meaning in the discourse: they were not to be seen in a universalistic sense as relating to all young people who were leaving the educational system, seeking employment and entering the labour market. The reification of the attribution of membership involved in this also effectively obscured the differences within the group and allowed for employability to be shaped as a desirable aspiration for the group. The consequence of this in terms of paradigm construction was the manner in which it contributed to the establishment of new themes, texts, authorities and identities in the reconstitution of the 'distant other'.

A series of interacting forces with local, global, demographic, labour market and economic dimensions provided the context for this cultural production surrounding the school to work transition. In analysing their impact it is difficult to disengage their objective influence from the manner in which they operated as thematic resources in the discourse of the construction and penetration of the employability paradigm. It is not easy to disassociate the dynamics of the transition from school to labour market from the construction of it as a problem of employability. Be they considered as objective forces or discursive resources in cultural production, there is a commonality in the contextual features identified in studies of young people in the labour market (Hannan, 1986), youth unemployment (Youth Employment Agency, 1982), transition education (Kellaghan and Lewis, 1991) and early leavers (ESF Programme Evaluation Unit, 1996; National Economic and Social Forum, 1997) at this time:

- *Demography.* The fact that in the 1981 Census people under the age of 25 accounted for almost half of the total population was one of the defining signifiers of that era. Between 1971 and 1981 the overall population grew by almost half a million or just under 16 per cent. Each year during this period the population aged 15 to 24 grew by almost thirteen thousand (Youth Employment Agency, 1982; Kellaghan and Lewis, 1991)

- *Economic and labour market changes.* A decline in agriculture as a source of employment began in the early 1960s. In 1961 42 per cent of males were employed in agriculture whereas in the mid-1980s the figure was 18 per cent. A growth in the industry and services sectors to around 40 per cent each of total employment by 1981 compensated for this decline. The structure of employment opportunities also changed with a decline of 14 per cent in unskilled manual employment between 1971 and 1981. This was mainly felt in labouring work in agriculture, industry and in construction. By the mid-1980s it was estimated that over half of those working or previously employed as unskilled manual workers were unemployed. Employment opportunities expanded in highly-skilled technical and non-manual or white-collar employment, with higher professional, semi-professional, scientific and technical and managerial positions increasing by over 50 per cent between 1971 and 1981 (Hannan, 1986).

- *Certification.* Formal educational qualifications grew in significance for labour market entry. There was a dramatic shift from property based self-employment, particularly in agriculture, to employment by others, increasingly in large private and public corporate settings. Whereas over 40 per cent of the male workforce was self-employed in 1961 this had declined to around 25 per cent by 1981, and for young men entering employment for the first time, entry into family employment had declined to less than 10 per cent (Hannan, 1986).

- *Technological change.* The impact of technological change, particularly in the electronics field, was repeatedly stressed. This was expected to result in an opening up of new fields of employment in the services sector and in the manufacture of new products. While certain types of work were expected to become obsolete it was predicted that with a relatively young and well-educated workforce it should be possible to exploit these new technological opportunities (Youth Employment Agency, 1982).

- *World economy*. The state of the world economy, particularly in Western European countries, provided the macro context for the analysis of employability. Crises and recessions, involving high inflation, low growth and energy supply, were variously mirrored in Irish experience (Youth Employment Agency, 1982; Kellaghan and Lewis, 1991).

- *Youth employment*. Having fallen during the 1960s, largely due to increased educational participation, youth unemployment increased rapidly up to 1975 as those who had delayed their entry into the labour market were now seeking work at a time of a sudden downturn in economic activity. It was not until the final years of the decade that the situation improved (Youth Employment Agency, 1982). Subsequently, peaks of youth unemployment have been identified for 1983-1985 and 1992-1993 (McCoy and Whelan, 1996). Unemployment rates among the under-25s were up to one-and-a-half times that of the workforce generally and are reported to have increased fourfold between 1980 and 1985 (Kellaghan and Lewis, 1991). A similar vulnerability among young people to unemployment in Europe instigated interventions from the 1970s, such as the pilot projects on school to work transitions and the targeting of young people in the eligibility guidelines of the ESF mentioned earlier.

An important agent in the crystallisation of the employability paradigm into a coherent cultural construct was the Youth Employment Agency (YEA). It drew together all the thematic resources itemised above, and in its establishment, existence and operation, as much as in its discourse, contributed significantly to fusing them into a sustained text on employability. The YEA was incorporated as a limited company on 4 March, 1982 as provided for in the Youth Employment Agency Act, 1981. The fact that the Act also allowed for a 1 per cent youth employment levy to help defray the expenditure of the operation and interventions of the YEA ensured its impact on public consciousness. Yet, it is possible to underplay the contribution of the YEA in terms of programme initiation and social action in relation to young people experiencing difficulties in finding employment. In its policy statement, *A Policy Framework for the Eighties* (Youth Employment Agency, 1982), it conceded that there was 'virtually no area critical to the overall objectives of the agency where institutions with whom it can cooperate do not already exist and, in some cases, the programmes are already in place through which the objectives of the agency can be achieved'. As to its financial status, in its First Report and Accounts to 31 December, 1982 (Youth

Employment Agency, 1983), the Chairperson of its Board of Directors identified its lack of influence over the allocation of the youth employment levy as a major issue transcending the operation of the agency. Nonetheless, under its memorandum of association, the agency:

- was given an overall national responsibility under the Minister for Labour 'for the furtherance of the employment of young persons'
- was entitled to submit views on educational policy and its effectiveness in preparing young people for working life
- was obliged to provide for the extension as well as the integration and co-ordination of existing training and employment programmes
- was to show special concern for access by the disadvantaged to training and employment programmes
- was to encourage enterprise and self-help among young people
- was to assist voluntary and community organisations in the provision of employment.

The agency recognised that it was unique in having an integrated range of responsibilities across all of the services required to give effect to manpower policies for those between 15 and 25 years, that it had been given responsibility for coordinating the activities of the agencies already delivering services to this age group, and that its mandate was more comprehensive than that which had traditionally obtained within the scope of manpower policy in Ireland, extending as it did from the educational system through to job creation.

In advancing the textualisation of employability, the YEA succeeded in communicating about youth and employment while clearly signifying that it was not focusing on all young people or all school leavers, and that its concern was not employment but rather avoiding unemployment for those most vulnerable to it. The YEA was a contributory force in constructing a new category of concern and the more explicit and subsequently normalised specification about what constituted a successful transition to adult status. In focusing on the earliest of school leavers, those with few or no qualifications, those from the most economically deprived areas and backgrounds, and on the most basic levels of employment, the employability paradigm continued the focus on the 'distant other' as the target of concern in the Irish cultural construction of the LEM domain. But it was to prove to be a mutable product of cultural activity, most notably in relation to the instability of its conceptualisation of employability, and its liability to co-optation once deployed beyond the LEM domain, in transition from school to work studies and in curriculum development.

Instability: Polyvalent Conceptualisation of Employability

The employability paradigm went on to draw on other resources in establishing and developing itself and outlived the YEA which was eventually subsumed under FÁS. Among these, were the nodal points of contact with both what remained of the human capital paradigm and the emerging mercantile paradigm, particularly in its vocational text. This included the prescription that the skill needs of the economy should be matched by those of pupils as they are formed by educational programmes, definitions of self-fulfilment which established the centrality of employment in the individual's life path, and an expectation of 'trading qualifications for jobs' (Hannan *et al.*, 1998). This contact with related paradigms together with its adjustment and adaptation to the changing social and economic scene revealed its receptivity to mutation. It was most observable in the manner in which the salience and visibility of its repertoire of themes – world economy, youth unemployment, technological change etc. – varied from their first emergence in the 1970s up to the present. Less visible and more effective in facilitating adaptability to changed conditions and texts was the polyvalent nature of the underpinning conceptualisation of employability. This is indicative of loose framing, the benefits of which include flexibility in the specification of performatives and an inclusivity in its membership but with the vulnerabilities that follow from porous boundaries – in the case of employability, co-optation by avuncular interlopers in the shape of human capital and mercantile paradigms. Three conceptualisations of employability can be identified in its textualisation since the 1970s.

Strict employability encapsulates the sense of having met the requirements of an available position in the workplace and being capable of performing with competence its job specifications. It implies a range of personal capacities, attributes and dispositions which distinguish those who are employable from those who are unemployable, a specific set of requirements which must be met to achieve competance in the workplace and a process of matching the two – the objective job requirements and the individual's abilities. Relative employability refers to the likelihood of gaining employment. This allows for a less fixed matching procedure between the individual and the job requirements. It recognises competition between applicants for a position in a process in which the employer arbitrates on who is to be employed. In this process employability is determined by the options that employers have in terms of the market of human resources that presents itself to them and by the choices they make from within that range of options. Among the mediating variables intervening between the individual's attributes and becoming employed can be listed employers' interpretations and judgements about the inferences for behaviour to be drawn from the presenting attributes of the applicant and their option to redefine the job specifications in the light of the application process.

Strict employability addresses the question 'can an individual be employed?' This is never clear cut except perhaps in extreme cases and these are becoming increasingly rare with developments in 'Sheltered' and 'Special Provision' work arrangements in which account is taken of, and provision made for, physical or psychological factors which otherwise might render an individual incapable of performing the duties of a paid position. In that sense, strict employability is a near universal attribute to the extent that it becomes invalid to speak of a person being 'unemployable'. Yet, in keeping with the nature of the 'distant other' as a construct, during the 1970s it was unemployability that defined its relationship with the employability paradigm. Relative employability responds to the question 'is an individual likely to be employed?' This recognises and takes account of the structure of the labour market and the supply/demand relationship in terms of levels and kinds of skills. The most routine problematisation of relative employability in the discourse is where there is deemed to be an excess of low-skilled or unskilled individuals competing for a diminishing pool of manual and routine occupations.

As a construct, certified employability is a product of the credentialisation of skill and knowledge mastery, often in the context of distinct occupations and specific areas of designated expertise. To have been certified as competent in the designated area by an authorised body is to be deemed to be employable. As with all definitions of reality, the impact of certification depends on its ability to have its judgement accepted as true and valid. As well as an increasing use of existing qualifications (Intermediate and Leaving Certificate, etc.), recent decades have been characterised by the credentialisation of vast areas of labour market activities. This has resulted in work routines being subjected to standardisation, classification and naming as programmes of preparation are developed which aspire to transmitting a newly identified and calibrated skill and knowledge base of an area of economic activity. It further formalises the gatekeeping function performed by credentialisation in determining who is to be employed in the area. This can lead to situations in which existing workers who continue to perform their tasks with competence, and accordingly are strictly employable, find themselves failing to satisfy the requirements of certified employability. Nor is labour force activity left unchanged. In the process it becomes newly differentiated and distinguishable, reworked in terms of a variety of taxonomies of skill, common knowledge and activity type, and exhibits varieties of collectivising and professionalising tendencies.

This variability of conceptualisation yields a shifting textualisation of employability. In seeing the phenomenon of the pupil/labour market relationship in different ways, varying orthodoxies of knowledge, constructed in terms of different problems, subjectivities and educational achievement/population segments, follow. Being unemployable is presented as a problem of the pupils themselves, their skill and personality deficiencies, and targets the 'distant others' of society. Experiencing difficulty in finding employment translates into a critique of schools, their irrelevant and inappropriate culture and curriculum, and encompasses more of what are sometimes described as 'ordinary children' (McCulloch, 1998). Thinking in terms of validating employability through a certification process generates specifications relating to knowledge and skills, and concerns surrounding quality control, efficiency and international competition and standards that engage the majority of the country's future productive workers. Within the shifting texts, relative employability is particularly unstable. A common pattern is for the failure of pupils to find employment to be treated in a manner that obscures the question of why they were unsuccessful in gaining the albeit limited number of positions that they would have been deemed to be capable of performing competently. Their unemployability is invoked in a process that foregrounds their personal limitations rather than the structure and practices of the labour market. The textual transition is from relative employability to a denial of strict employability with the implications that follow for the reconfiguration of the knowledge involved – the demographic and educational profile of those encompassed, the bases on which they are considered to be a problem worthy of attention, and their subjective relationship with education, training agencies and the world of work.

'Transition from School to Work' Studies

At the discursive level, the textualisation of employability was advanced by means of extensive research studies on a common set of themes (Breen, 1984, 1991; Hannan, 1986; Sexton *et al.*, 1988). This has much in common with the 'transition from school to work' (TSW) field of study in Britain characterised by Raffe (1997) as 'policy related, descriptive and only weakly underpinned by theory'. This is despite the fact that the TSW field of study in Britain differed from its Irish counterpart in its origins and issues and in the nature of its enquiries. More noteworthy for the present analysis is that unlike the experience of the field of study in Britain, where it fragmented after 1980, in Ireland it remained a very recognisable and cohesive area of research in terms of themes and agents. This is due to the absence of the penetration of the area by developments such as cultural studies or youth studies and its location within the field of education, training and labour force studies. The implications for employability being realised through TSW studies was the penetration of human capital and mercantile themes and their marginalisation of life chances in favour of social efficiency and national productivity and competitiveness within the paradigm. When conceptualised within the LEM domain as the means by which 'vulnerable' young people might avoid dependency and limited life chances, employability has obvious nodal points of common meaning with those of TSW studies. It was its shifting textualisation, however, that positioned it as the less secure participant in the intertextual activity with the human capital and mercantile paradigms of TSW studies as they negotiated the meanings surrounding young people, schooling, training and work.

Because of the non-theoretical, policy-directed and largely descriptive nature of TSW studies, and their dominance in the textualisation of employability, its focus remained very concentrated while its development as a body of knowledge was substantially by means of empirical (as distinct from theoretical or thematic) intensification. The main source of this empirical intensification continues to be the body of data collected through the annual school leavers' surveys which commenced in 1980. As referred to in Chapter 6, these surveys are based on a stratified random sample of those leaving the official second-level school system. Interviews take place twelve to eighteen months after the respondents have left school. Data are collected about their current employment status, their level of educational achievement and their employment experiences. As well as providing a great deal of information about the employment/unemployment/further educational experiences of school leavers, the industrial sector and occupational category entered by those who gain employment and the salary levels achieved, variations are also recorded according to gender, educational achievement and social class background. Because the surveys have been running for some twenty years, it has been possible to record patterns of fluctuation and change over this period in relation to all of these measures and relationships (Gorby *et al.*, 2003), as well as to make comparisons with similar databases from other countries (Hannan *et al.*, 1995). This database has in turn been the point of departure for even more elaborate analyses of the transition from school to labour market.

The nature of the research questions posed by *Trading Qualifications for Jobs* (Hannan *et al.*, 1998), though untypically giving considerable attention to those with third-level education, exemplifies how detailed the filling-in rather than the mapping-out of the transition from the educational system to the world of work has become. The main research question explored in this study was the extent to which there is a high 'level congruence' in Irish education/labour market linkages, that is the extent to which entry to the Irish labour market is non-competitive between levels of education. The more specific features of this research question studied included the extent and nature of the congruence/correlation between school/college leavers' level of education and the occupational status of first job achieved; the extent to which first jobs provide a reasonable estimate of the medium-term occupational status achievement of the higher achieving school/college leavers; the role played by migration in 'successful' labour market integration for different levels of education; the extent to which third-level graduates who are deemed to be over-qualified for their occupations are rewarded for their better qualifications or greater human capital; and the extent to which third-level graduates who initially take up lower-status jobs are restricted in their subsequent career mobility chances.

This empirical charting of these linkages between educational qualifications, labour market competition and career chances, despite the increasing precision and detail of its hypotheses, remains within the conceptual limits of the employability paradigm. However, this allows for some flexibility in themes and performatives because of the polyvalent nature of the conceptualisation of employability within the paradigm which, as we have seen, can realise itself as strict employability, relative employability or certified employability. We find evidence of this in further analyses conducted on the data of the school leavers' surveys. This is the case with Breen *et al.*'s (1995) study of how employers interpret educational qualifications in making decisions about whether or not to employ school leavers, and about the wages they pay them. In foregrounding the decisions of employers in relation to who is to become employed, the conceptualisation is that of relative employability. The authors point out that given the availability of national public examinations, Irish employers can use these as predictors of a person's potential for productivity. In this analysis they stress the significance of the employers' interpretations and warn against distortions that can follow from failing to take account of how educational performance is perceived by potential employers in terms of its relevance to performance in the workplace. As they put it, 'the set of criteria potentially available for use by employers will depend upon the educational system, but which is used in any given context will depend upon which aspects of educational performance are perceived to be relevant by those who determine what these rewards will be.'

This entire body of description based on the original school leavers' surveys, their subsequent re-analysis and associated studies generates a very explicit performative discourse which is particularly evident in submissions and presentations to professional, advisory and policy-making bodies dealing with issues affecting young people, their education and life chances (e.g. Hannan, 1996). This produces a tightly-linked textualisation in which facts and performatives are inextricably linked and where there is an unproblematised transition from what is the case to what ought to be done. In *Pathways to Adulthood* (Hannan and Ó Riain, 1993) we find a departure from this in the manner in which it seeks to normalise the process of transition from school to adult status. This textualises the status transition process through a differentiation and sequencing of the stages that young people require to pass through before they are recognised by society at large as adults. The stages include being single/completed education/unemployed/at home; at home/employed/engaged in home duties/student; left home; married; parent; house purchased. They calculate that over 90 per cent of young people in 1987 had to pass through an earlier stage before they could proceed to a later one. But they regard the sequences as being normatively, as well as statistically, structured in the form of expectations, values and sanctions prevalent in one's family, social network and community. Further elaboration of this process is introduced by pointing to the existence of blockages in the transition process as well as to the possibility of regression.

The more themes are introduced in this manner, the more elaboration in the form of explanation or legitimation is required. There is an explicit statement of what is assumed but unstated in the employability paradigm – that success in the labour market is regarded as a 'crucial "threshold" achievement' (Hannan, 1996) in progressing normatively through the transition sequence from youth to adult status. This in turn is followed by justification of the centrality attributed to employment in the transition process – a source of economic independence, self-confidence, sense of control, autonomous action and general feelings of well-being – that is not routinely required in the employability discourse such is its doxic status.

By acknowledging equity issues and the needs of lower-achieving pupils, TSW studies were able to accommodate the LEM themes of employability but in a manner that left it vulnerable to co-optation, in the first stance, by the human capital paradigm. This will be developed later. But first it is necessary to record the existence of counter texts to the definitions and assumptions of TSW studies which offered discordant representations and understandings of young people, schooling and work that were to be specifically oppositional to the human capital orientation to employability and the deficit and unpoliticised cultural processing of the 'unemployable' 'distant other'.

Counter-Texts

Within the intellectual field of TSW studies, employability was exposed to a number of potentially disruptive themes in a consultancy report on socio-economic, particularly labour market, and institutional implications of the Irish pilot projects that formed part of the second EEC programme on Transition of Young People from Education to Working Life. In the published version of this report, *Schooling and the Labour Market*, Hannan (1986) drew attention to the functional nature of the assumptions of TSW studies, the limited range of school outcomes being considered, and the reproductive and legitimatory role of education in the context of unequal life chances. He pointed to the effective assumption of the kind of analysis that he had been invited to conduct, that the education system is subservient to the needs of the economy: 'that it has to adjust to economic transformation'. While he acknowledged that the educational system cannot influence the opportunities available to its leavers or how these positions are to be filled, he nonetheless argued that the education system had choices, in that 'what it currently produces or reproduces faciltitates, limits or conditions the way the economy and the polity works' (p. 57). It could choose to accept 'the current agenda set by economic and linked political interests – one which in these terms has to realistically accept high levels of unemployment for the forseeable future', in which case 'its function is to maximise the provision of highly skilled manpower for perhaps three quarters to four fifths of its graduates, while trying to ensure that these arrangements are held to be just or legitimate by the other quarter or one fifth' (p. 57). On the other hand, it can opt to acknowledge and attend to the 'equally important civic or political roles that school leavers have to play and which to a large extent condition or limit the nature of our economy and its "health"'. He worried about the future of a society 'if it is to be dominated by competitive, highly achievement-orientated individuals who, as a group, have developed a very weak collective civic culture' (p. 57), and how collectivistic agreements can be expected and effective leadership developed from a 'highly individualistic, competitive social and cultural base' (p. 58). His concluding remarks on the pilot projects asserted their relevance for all pupils and sought to alter the perception that they were exclusively intervention programmes for the 'distant other'. He regretted that they had 'such an uncaring reception from the academic secondary schools, both from the point of view of the better provision of education for those who achieve so little within their current provision, as well as the richer more integrated provision of education for the more able' (p. 58).

Had these themes achieved textualisation within the discourse on the experiences and destinations of young people as they leave the educational system, it seems unlikely that it could have been contained within the employability paradigm. This would not have instigated the rupture of the employability paradigm which in its various conceptualisations would have survived and continued to be sustained and communicated through the human capital paradigm. A textualisation of the themes raised by Hannan in *Schooling and the Labour Market* would have been far reaching, most likely resulting in at least a factioning of the employability paradigm. This is indicated by the new focus, direction and questioning that such a textualisation would have introduced. This would have included the following:

- The consideration of all pupils, and not just those underachieving or alienated from the education system, within the range of its performatives
- The impact of schooling on social and civic, and not exclusively on human capital and economic, outcomes
- Taking a holistic view of people, not focusing exclusively on their role in production
- Questioning the structure of, at least, rewards in the workplace
- Seeking to advance a civic culture informed by a sense of social obligation and communality

- Raising moral questions far beyond the narrow considerations of efficiency in integrating new members into the production process.

Textualisation along these lines had the potential to lead to the creation of a new policy paradigm or the substantial modification of others through acts of coalition or co-optation. Whatever the nature of the paradigmatic activity that would have ensued, one consequence seems clear, namely that it would have been more firmly rooted within, realised in terms of, and engaged with structural dimensions of the LEM domain of cultural production. In the event, this textualisation never occurred.

Hannan's thematisation of the functional assumptions, the reproductive and legitimatory roles of education and its relationship to production, the economy and the civic culture occurred within the TSW field that was shaping employability at that time. This was both advantageous and disadvantageous. Had textualisation occurred in relation to these themes it would have been difficult not to engage with them, be it by way of some form of accommodation or rejection. On the other hand, their failure to achieve a subsequent textualisation may well be seen as evidence of the restraining power of what had become a robust, tightly-framed intellectual field in its capacity to jettison what it interpreted as discordant, threatening or meaningless themes. Unlike Hannan's *Schooling and the Labour Market*, Kellaghan and Lewis's (1991) *Transition Education in Irish Schools* originated from outside TSW studies and explicitly sought to reveal, contextualise and challenge many of the key assumptions of employability. These include the following:

- Making the deficit assumptions explicit
- Distinguishing between strict employability and relative employability
- Questioning the changing needs of employment in the light of technological change
- Questioning what was meant by vocational education and education for employment
- Contextualising the concept of employability
- Recognising the constructionist dimension of the category of 'youth'.

Transition Education in Irish Schools distinguished between student deficit, school deficit and curriculum deficit assumptions of transition programmes. It argued that they fitted into an historical process which, especially during periods of economic recession, sought to establish a relationship between vocational training and schooling, and relatedly involved schools 'losing educational territory to training agencies' (p. 15). It drew attention to the inflation of qualifications required for entry into further training programmes and occupations and outlined what was involved in relative employability in a manner that clearly distinguished it from strict employability. Whenever there are high levels of youth unemployment, it pointed out, those with the lowest qualifications relative to other job applicants are going to be at a disadvantage irrespective of the absolute level of the qualifications they have. With the inflation of credentials, educational credentials are required for entry into an occupation 'not because they bear any direct relationship to what is technically necessary to perform the work in question but because they serve as a useful administrative device in selecting individuals' (p. 18). It is the distribution of educational qualifications and not the qualifications themselves that are important in such a scenario.

Thus, change in what is educationally required to gain access to further education, training and occupations occurs 'not because of any inherent change in the nature of the further education, training, or occupation, but simply because the distribution of educational qualifications in the labour force has changed over time' (p. 18). It questioned the view that technological changes were having a widespread impact on the skills required for most entry-level jobs. It gave publicity to the view that 'unemployment is not the result of deficiencies in individuals or in schools but rather the effect of defects in the economic system which fails to provide a sufficient demand for labour' (p. 17). Paraphrasing an OECD report, it interpreted the thematisation of transition to adulthood and working life as a response to the shrinking employment opportunities, arguing that 'if school leavers could have been absorbed into the economy, it is unlikely that preparation for working life would have loomed saliently as an educational issue at all' (p. 13). It drew attention to the manner in which a particular period of life had been identified as a stage called 'youth' and to the developmental and cultural characteristics that are said to characterise this stage as distinct from earlier and later points of development.

Some of these themes recur in the academic discourse on issues such as those of early leaving, unemployment and the appropriateness of preparation, relating to the transition of pupils from schooling to the workforce. In this, the dominance of labour market demands, employers' recruitment practices, credentialism and qualification inflation are recognisable. Occasionally there is a textual engagement with some of these themes. Hannan *et al.* (1995) endorsed the significance of credentialism, particularly during the 1980s, which they argued resulted in its institutionalisation in employers' recruitment practices as 'the entry level "qualification ratchet"' stayed locked at the higher level. However, they go on to argue that credentialism is not the whole story: 'structural changes are certainly involved as a longer term underpinning for employers' shifting preferences. One reason is a substantial decline in those unskilled manual and service jobs with minimal or no literacy and numeracy requirements, and with minimal requirements for discipline and responsibility (developed through, or signalled by, successful education and training).'

What little there has been of this textualisation is most likely to be found the more the discourse is academic rather than policy oriented. And this obtains even where the academic and policy oriented discourse involves the same authors. It serves to signal how discursive conventions derived from a multiple membership of different policy paradigms can regulate communication. This usually takes the form of a greater openness to disparate understandings, attributions and more complex relationships in the academic discourse. In the policy-focused discourse the understandings of the sponsoring or targeted associative network constrains what features of the academic discourse survive, and the need to generate performatives results in an emphasis on modalities of behaviour and on themes that are capable of yielding policies that are sympathetic to these understandings. Occasionally, in specifying performatives, there are attempts to remain faithful to a complex understanding of the experience of schooling and transition to the workforce of those most vulnerable to unemployment.

One such attempt is Fagan's (1995) advocacy of 'critical cultural pedagogy' in engaging with early school leavers, as an alternative to their traditional constitution through 'a psychologistic discourse with a pathological aversion to politics' (p. 154). This she criticises for the 'deficit approach' it takes to the 'social experience, knowledge, subjectivity and identity of early school leavers' (p. 154). She interprets their 'social relations of subordination' which leave them without a qualification, work or income as 'relations of oppression' (p. 157). To counter this, critical cultural pedagogy seeks to move 'subjectivities of early school leavers from a reactive political position to a more assertive and active political position' (p. 158). This suggests such performatives as teaching early school leavers their 'rights as democratic citizens', empowering them 'to negotiate politically' and to 'produce strategies for community representation' (p.159). This would require that they 'uncover the social forces of production' (p. 164) that influence them as school leavers and 'interrogate and deconstruct' (p. 165) their own explanations and understandings of their schooling, work situation and future prospects. It would seek to counter 'the strongest form of subordination ... when these young people feel that they cannot afford to imagine a long-term future' (p. 152). Throughout, Fagan distances her analysis from the reification and decontextualisation of early school leaving as a life experience: 'I am not attempting here to cite early school leaving as a founding moment or an original moment of suppression, to which all other forms of oppression can be related; rather, I am simply choosing early school leaving as a specific moment to enter the cultural processes that bring about specific relations of subordination, and from this awareness to suggest an appropriate cultural politics' (p. 151).

Employability never showed evidence of experiencing any of this as the contestation of its assumptions. The constitution of early school leavers as political agents was too discordant with their construction as 'distant others', particularly in terms of its sponsorship and social rescue dimensions. Their dependency status was sustained by the emerging text on the changing composition of post-primary school pupils which attained widespread legitimacy. Its discourse of discordant needs and motivations, and practices of curricular and assessment interventions asserted the existence of a new category of pupils, the product of expansion in education, who were unable to cope with the demands of post-primary schooling. These would have been regarded as educationally misplaced and in need of intervention, rather than subordinated and requiring politicisation. Indeed, leaving aside radical cultural politics, even the mild counter-arguments of general liberal education – exceptions include Williams and McNamara (1985), Geraghty (1988) and Kellaghan and Lewis (1991) – against the recurring demands for a greater emphasis on science, technology and vocational preparation in post-primary schooling routinely exempted the 'distant other' in their commentaries in the light of their educational 'unsuitability' and pressing employability 'needs'.

A number of sources suggest that those most in contact with young people in non-mainstream programmes – another form of signification for the 'distant other' – might be an important site of disengagement from aspects of the employability paradigm. The ESF Programme Evaluation Unit's report on *Early School Leavers Provision* (1996) identified dissent, among adults involved in these programmes, from both credentialism and attributions of deficit among the young people involved. It reported that 'many young people active in the youthwork sphere express anger at the perpetuation of credentialism because it has militated so severely against disadvantaged young people. Others claim that if education is to respond to market forces then youthwork with disadvantaged young people should, by definition, be centred as much on training for unemployment as for employment. Virtually all practitioners are agreed that the notion of attributing deficits to, or finding fault with, the young people concerned is seriously flawed in the current economic and employment context' (p. 43).

Those who play intellectual roles within these programmes and theorise their rationale, functioning and interaction with other forms of provision for young people, have been most explicit in this regard. Discordant concepts, language and themes recur in the writings of Dermot Stokes, National Co-ordinator of Youthreach. He argues that perhaps the most fundamental characteristic of the Youthreach approach is its emphasis on achievement, on an affirmative credit model. He goes on to argue that while 'the particpants may have learnt a great deal while they were at school ... their abiding impression of schooling is of ten or more years identifying what they cannot do'. Relatedly, the representation of the participants' future life course is not as production-focused: 'the young person is not seen as a unit of production that requires to be fixed. Rather, is it accepted that it is the system that has failed and needs to be revised. The objective is to help young people become independent, self-directing lifelong learners' (1999b). The instrumental needs of production also are less central. In speaking about the provision of an appropriate guidance and counselling service for Youthreach participants, he speaks of the need to introduce concepts like mentoring, brokerage and advocacy with a view 'to broaden the discussion, identify newer models and, perhaps, establish a broader frame for our understanding' (1999a). This would involve a championing of 'the young person rather than the system' (1999a). He also draws attention to the quality and the nature of the work which young people, particularly those with poor qualifications, will find themselves doing, and identifies as a key task 'the establishment of a new relationship with the world of work that will offer labour market entrants (and particularly those entering low skill employment) a continuing learning environment' (1999b).

Stokes adopts an oppositional discourse in seeking to establish the validity of his views in engaging others and in influencing policy. He argues that while there is a consensus, among those working outside the educational system with those who have been failed by that system, on the need to challenge and change its organisational, curricular and service paradigms, 'the education mainstream has largely ignored the discussion, and the (often vehement) critiques of those operating on its margins' (1999a). He continues that 'in general, the schooling system has argued that what is needed is more schooling. The voices outside of schools argue that more of what has failed is not the answer and that other approaches and relationships are required, in which school is a central but networked player' (1999a). Yet, he also uses the practice of claiming nodal points of common conceptualisation and language with representatives of the state policy-making mechanism and the thrust of state policy on education in a manner that seeks to membership individual actors and practices: 'the idea that it is okay to fail because you, your family or your community are in some way defective is unsustainable, and our service paradigms should not encourage it. Rather, as Stack (Chief Inspector, Department of Education and Science) has argued, and is embedded in the Green Paper on *Adult Education in an Era of Lifelong Learning* (1998), it is intended to promote participatory democracy' (1999a). Stokes's conceptualisation of Youthreach provision resonates with Fagan (1995). But even his oppositional discourse is more strategic, and he seeks to engage much more with existing thinking and practice in relation to provision for the 'distant other' by selectively maximising the extent of common understanding.

How widely dispersed these understandings might be is unclear, and even within Youthreach programmes their dominion may not be so secure. The background/experience of Youthreach centre co-ordinators in guidance, counselling, social work and youth and community work suggests a fertile and receptive habitus for understandings of young people in society that range beyond those of fitting them for the available employment opportunities. Yet the prior area of expertise of general staff follows a more skill/craft based pattern – carpentry, metalwork, office skills, computing, hairdressing – which could be expected to be sympathetic to the normality of preparing young people for the instrumental demands of the workplace. The 'deficit' text is also difficult to avoid and can be obligatory for programme maintenance in justifying staffing for special needs in relation to literacy, numeracy, counselling and advocacy. This tension may be more easily managed in oppositional discourse. This is because of the manner of which oppositional discourse foregrounds the deficiencies of the mainstream system while still acknowledging the gaps in the education, skill development, personal formation and social and cultural orientations of the young people involved.

Employability, as textualised within TSW studies, remained unaffected by these discordant and counter texts treating them more with non-recognition than explicit denial. The robustness of the textualisation of employability by TSW studies, with the life chances theme usurped by those of labour force needs and national efficiency, in the face of challenges from within and without is indicated in the NESC (1993) report *Education and Training Policies for Economic and Social Development*. In classifying education and training research in Ireland in terms of international developments and perspectives the report found it possible to be inclusive without going beyond the themes of equity/efficiency in state funding of education, the private and social returns on education considered as an investment, and the research areas of manpower planning and evaluation studies of training and retraining programmes. Significantly, the NESC report endorsed TSW themes without finding it necessary to define it as a distinct field of study. It demonstrated the consequences for employability of participating in a relationship of coalition/co-optation with the themes of national productivity, competitiveness and higher order skills of the human capital and mercantile paradigms.

In the NESC report we find a recurrence of the core theme of the employability paradigm – the capacities of those deemed to be most vulnerable to unemployment. By way of an overarching observation on how policies designed to enhance economic development and employment performance might be identified, the NESC remarked on how 'little comparative policy analysis of the Irish education and training system' and how 'little evidence of, or discussion about its comparative performance' there had been (p. 22). It pointed to what it referred to as 'a growing scepticism of commonly-used criteria of educational performance (relative quality of a country's graduates, average teacher/pupil ratio) and an increasing recognition that *the attainment levels of the lower-to-middle ability stratum, i.e. the generality of pupils* is the key criterion' (p. 23). It gave an example from the US of how it can be deceptive to dwell on the performance of those at the advanced levels of education and quotes the US report to the effect that 'vast numbers of our students fail to meet the educational requirements of the workplace … many young people's skills are insufficient to qualify them for entry level jobs' (p. 23).

This was reinforced in its endorsement of the 'institutional' analysis of the relationship between education and training systems and economic and industrial structures popularised in Finegold and Soskice's (1988) critique of British manufacturing as trapped in a 'low skills equilibrium' defined as a 'self-reinforcing network of societal and state institutions which interact to stifle the demand for improvements in skill levels'. The NESC considered aspects of the 'institutional' approach to have a 'telling parallel' (p. 29) in a review of past economic and industrial training policy and performance in Ireland. In acknowledging the meaningfulness of the 'institutional' approach for consideration of the education and labour market relationship in Ireland it commended the manner in which it operated 'to analyse critically the adequacy of education and training systems as they effect the *lower-to-middle range of attainment* students' (p. 33) and its focus on the skill and employment needs of the majority of pupils, especially those from the lower socio-economic groups. It acknowledges that there were serious problems affecting the education and labour market experience of such categories of school leavers. Yet it also insisted on accommodating what it referred to as the 'equity perspective', arguing that it was as important 'to analyse how the mainstream system affects them as to examine how best to increase their participation in the higher levels of the educational system' (p. 33).

In this textualisation of education and training issues, employability as a paradigm within the LEM domain is realised in the analysis of the 'distant other' segment of the labour force conceptualised/thematised in terms of equity. With the growing emphasis on the necessity for all entrants to the labour market to have at least some level of skill the 'distant other' becomes submerged among 'ordinary children' (McCulloch, 1998) – the low-to-middle range of attainment – and is open to conceptualisation in terms of human capital development and economic interest. The textualisation of government policy also stressed the changed nature of the labour market expectations in relation to this group since the 1960s (Kellaghan *et al.*, 1995). In the 1950s and 1960s the concern was that all those with talent would be given the opportunity to develop it for the well-being of the national economy. An unstated assumption was that those deemed to be without talent would find employment in unskilled and routine occupations. Increasingly, however, Kellaghan *et al.* argued that 'modern industry requires the entire labour force to be capable of adjusting to new technologies and of making informed decisions, and highly-skilled human intelligence becomes a nation's primary economic resource' (p. 6.)

The NESC report described the change in terms of the following contrast: 'while education and training policy in the 1960s was structured as a *response* to employment needs arising from economic growth, in the 1990s it is structured as a *contribution* to economic growth through human resource development' (p. 15). It is difficult to disentangle the relative significance of the equity and human capital strands in the development of such policy texts. What does seem clear is that the association with training and labour market studies forgrounded the social/economic interest and shaped conceptualisation and themes. The effect, in terms of the LEM domain, was that the concept of employability became at best a life chances issue within the context of the existing labour market structure. The morality of the LEM domain was excluded and there was no accommodation of the sociological or philosophical themes of interest, social structure (apart from stratification), ideology or benefit. The fact that employability was to remain distinct from sociological and cultural studies as well as from more specific areas of inquiry such as the feminist critique of work, youth studies and holistic life course analysis helps to explain the ease of its reorientation through co-optation by human capital/mercantile paradigms alongside its robustness in the face of less 'deficit' and more political and structuralist counter texts.

To educationally contextualise and further explain these patterns of resistance and surrender on the part of employability, it is necessary to return to the character of curriculum development as it developed from the 1970s.

Curriculum Development: Liberal Functionalism

As well as being the site of cultural production that realised employability, it was the curriculum development movement that continued to process, as educational knowledge, employability as it was textualised in relation to the curricular implications of expanding participation in post-primary schooling, European discourse and grant-led programmes, and TSW studies. As an academic field of study it might have been expected to be more amenable than policy-related and state-generated knowledge to engage with theory, critique and alternative perspectives, when processing existing orthodoxies on individual virtue and social order, of a kind that could have reconfigured employability's strengths and weaknesses of framing across its conceptual boundaries. This had the potential to reverse the character of its compatibility and resistance as a paradigm, making it less amenable to co-optation by human capital and mercantile paradigms and more open to incorporating some of the counter themes raised in relation to the civic functions of schooling, the political subjectivity of pupils, 'deficit' assumptions of schools and pupils, and specifications of labour market needs. The fact that this did not happen can be best explained by reference to the character of the curriculum development movement and the legitimatory basis of the knowledge that it successfully inserted as a curriculum text into Irish educational discourse.

When Professor John Coolahan delivered the Kathleen Quigley Memorial Lecture in 1990 he chose as his title 'Have we learned anything at all? Reflections on curriculum development in Ireland, 1972-1992' (Coolahan, 1990). As he explained, the period 1972-1992 was significant. In 1992 it was expected that there would be the first sitting of the Junior Certificate Examination, twenty years after the establishment of the first curriculum development unit in 1972. In his lecture he rightly applauded the work of the Irish Association for Curriculum Development (IACD) founded in 1971 which 'through good times and bad (had) kept curricular issues to the fore, generating ideas, disseminating ideas, promoting good practice, fostering teacher skill and confidence, influencing debate, publishing research and comment – in so many ways being a beacon for improved professionalism in education'. He listed a variety of books and reports broadly relating to the curriculum that had appeared during this period and identified a range of journals that gave prominence to curricular issues. Most indicative of the centrality that curriculum had attained in educational debate, and its penetration of the state, was the chronology of landmarks in the curriculum renewal movement that he was able to construct. There was scarcely a year that did not yield some innovation in terms of structures, programmes or publications.

It can be argued that the curriculum development movement of this era succeeded very quickly in having its discursive activity accepted not only as a text, as a recognisable strand of meaning-making about education, but as its dominant theorisation. In terms of quantity alone, this discursive activity was substantial and included guidelines, manuals, training exercises, teacher materials, dissemination activities and evaluations (see Crooks and McKernan, 1984; McNamara *et al.*, 1990). From these, two clear themes emerge – the construction of the curriculum to serve the diverse needs of pupils, and their preparation for life as adults and workers. These were made explicit in the 1977 policy statement of the IACD, 'Establishing Priorities for the Curriculum':

> Since children have different abilities, aptitudes and interests, no one programme can be suitable for all. The Association, therefore, promotes the concept of a comprehensive curriculum: that is, a new curriculum which has elements that are shared by all, but which allows for the development of all aspects of a child's personality and caters for different abilities ... social changes require that our pupils can cope with the pluralism of values and beliefs, particularly in such areas as the family and home, interpersonal relationships and moral decision-making. Technological changes require positive attitudes towards industry, the development of a wide variety of skills: scientific and manual and such competencies as initiative, personal responsibility and an enquiring mind (quoted in Crooks and McKernan, 1984, pp 24-25).

A number of performatives recur involving very specific recommendations for change in educational and classroom practices. These included the need to draw on principles of curriculum design other than the traditional disciplines and to move beyond the subject-based curriculum, the use of experiential and activity-based learning methods in place of frontal teaching, and the utilisation of forms of assessment other than terminal written examinations. The movement's membership was united through its focused purpose – the reform of the curriculum in terms of specified principles of individualisation and relevancy. Associations such as the IACD and the Educational Studies Association of Ireland, newsletters, pilot schools, training days, dissemination activities, evaluation exercises and publications, as well as their distinctive manifest functions, also supplied the associative function of identifying participants as members of a common curriculum movement. Identities as pioneering, oppositional agents served to further solidify the commonality of purpose of the members. Those members who were accepted as the representative authorities grew from within the movement and established their identities in this regard as authoritative on curriculum development. These included those involved in curriculum development centres, academic educationalists, educational administrators and school principals. Few of these could be said to have had any association with curriculum as a form of intervention or a mode of theorising before the emergence of the Irish curriculum development movement. For the most part, therefore, those accepted as authorities were established as such by the dynamics of the movement. This was an important element in the cultural homogeneity of the movement, in relation to the role of schooling in society.

Among the strengths of the curriculum development movement were the clarity of its discourse through the use of common-place concepts and non-technical language, their successful establishment as a text, and a clear identity-laden solidaristic membership both aware of itself as a social movement and strategically based throughout the educational system. It was also culturally and performatively compatible with the human capital and the emerging mercantile paradigm, most fundamentally in their sharing of the liberal functionalist understanding of society. Liberal functionalism assumes the obligation of social institutions, such as education, to adapt to the society in which they find themselves in the interests of stability, progress and change. A modernising version of traditional functionalism, it differs from it in its acceptance of levels of disagreement and conflict in modern complex and diverse societies and also in its acknowledgement of the interests of individuals as well as the needs of society. As Drudy and Lynch (1993) have pointed out, functionalism is not confined to sociological theory. It is a feature of our intellectual culture in the manner in which it supplies administrators, politicians, reformers and social movements with non-reflexive conceptualisations of how the world works.

The cultural compatibility of its textualisation of individual needs and social relevance with the dominant paradigm of the institution of education helps not only to explain the success of the curriculum development movement in its own terms but also the nature of its contribution to cultural production, in this instance in relation to employability. The curriculum development movement used two recurring legitimatory strategies grounded in liberal functionalism to establish the authority and validity of its discourse and, in particular, its performatives. These were periodicity, i.e. the designation of historical time as a particular phase having distinctive systemic characteristics and demands, and facticity, i.e. the inescapable reality of a phenomenon. These are ubiquitous throughout the discourse of the curriculum development movement and they can be discerned in the extracts from the IACD policy document quoted earlier. In these, appeals to facticity are to be found in the reification of differences in pupils' abilities, aptitudes, aspirations and motivations. Rather than being seen as social products they are accepted as inescapable realities that must be accommodated in the curriculum. Through this reification of differences in pupil achievement and adaptation, the issues of educability came to be conceptualised in terms of curricular/syllabus modification rather than of their aetiology and intervention. Through a periodisation of its historical time as characterised, above all, by change and, more specifically, by technological innovation and competing moral and cultural positions, and its attribution of facticity to it, it invalidated any critical questioning of what were treated as the inescapable demands of society. These legitimatory mechanisms were particularly effective in justifying performatives on diversification of the curriculum, the reconstruction of curriculum content, and innovation in the principles of curriculum organisation. The dominance of the vocationalism of the human capital and mercantile paradigms assisted in this regard. The overall contribution was to valorise activism rather than theorising, adaptation rather than reflection and pragmatism rather than moral reservation. Culturally, the common effect was to exclude any perspective, most likely from within the broad social science field, that would make explicit and open to question the functionalist nature of these legitimatory mechanisms of the discourse of the curriculum development movement.

This exclusion of the sociological perspective was essential for the stability of its legitimatory mechanisms of periodicity and facticity. Not surprisingly, what efforts were made to introduce themes of a sociological nature to the discourse were unsuccessful. One early critique of the conceptualisation underpinning the Humanities Curriculum of the CDVEC/Trinity College Curriculum Development Unit established the pattern and may well have served to immunise the discourse against the sociological perspective. The agent of this intervention was Professor F.X. Russo, an American academic and visiting professor at the School of Education, Trinity College Dublin. His address on the topic of social studies in the post-primary school curriculum was said to have generated considerable discussion when it was presented to the members of the IACD in 1973. It was later published under the title 'Ireland and the Social Studies: Irish Eyes Aren't

Smiling – They're Closed' in the association journal, *Compass* (Russo, 1973). Russo asserted the uniqueness of social studies as a coherent area for inclusion on the school curriculum with a contribution to make through its distinctive content, concepts, attitudes and methods to the formation of future citizens. Social studies, he argued, must be allowed their 'rightful place alongside that of the humanities and the sciences' and warned that 'Ireland cannot afford the luxury of ignoring the social studies by burying them in the humanities'. In responding, the director of the Humanities Curriculum project, J.A. Crooks (1973), argued, with some conviction in the circumstances, that the criticism was due to a problem with terminology, that what is termed social studies in North America is referred to as humanities in Britain and Ireland. Substantively, Crooks had no difficulty in demonstrating that the content and perspectives which Russo identified as distinctive to the social studies already featured in the Humanities Curriculum. These included understanding, skills and attitudes relating to the place of the individual within society and the treatment of highly controversial topics through discussion. He contended that 'what is being practised in the classroom is the same whether we name it Humanities or Social Studies' and, turning the intervention to advantage, declared that it was 'reassuring to feel that Professor Russo, writing from his experience of North American education should feel the need for the type of programme we are trying to implement here in Ireland'.

While Russo was concerned with social studies as an area of experience within the school curriculum rather than with the application of sociological perspectives to curriculum inquiry, the discourse of the curriculum development movement must have felt that it had been tested in this regard and not found wanting. In effect, Russo's characterisation of social studies was a diluted and truncated version of sociology from within the functionalist tradition. In fact, Russo's critique endorsed implicitly the two legitimatory mechanisms of periodicity and facticity in his representation of the distinct content and objectives of social studies. This exchange can be interpreted as an experience in cultural immunisation for the curriculum development discourse against the influence of sociological themes. In this interpretation, its exposure to sociology, in a diluted dose, had at once confirmed the validity of the curriculum development themes together with their textualisation, and diminished the potential impact of those of sociology. Whatever the significance of this episode, however, it anticipated the exclusion of sociological perspectives in general (O'Reilly, 1984) from curriculum development discourse and, in particular, any themes that it was in the nature of liberal functionalism to suppress, such as those relating to the partial and disadvantaging nature of school learning, knowledge and credentials as experienced by working-class pupils (Lynch, 1982).

One substantial textualisation on the curriculum did emerge independently of the dominant curriculum development discourse at the time which, though its penetration was very limited, merits the designation of a counter paradigm to employability in articulating the link between education and the world of adult life and work.

'Education for Development': A Counter Paradigm to Employability

This counter paradigm was realised through the North Mayo/Sligo Education for Development Project. This was one of the European-sponsored programmes on facilitating the transition from school to adult and working life which ran from 1979 to 1982. Callan's (1984) extensive evaluation report on the project not alone provides great detail on its nature and course but it explicitly seeks to illuminate the manner in which the project operated in conflict with more dominant texts. In fact, he considered its counter-cultural character to be the source of much of the implementation difficulties which it experienced. He identified '… at every level … a clash of ideological perspective between the perspectives of the people in the area as to their social, industrial and educational needs and the perspective of personnel from the Irish Foundation for Human Development who sponsored and directed the project'. From the minutes of seminars conducted with local interested bodies and selected economic and social experts, Callan was able to identify a distinct cleavage between how local industrialists and educationalists perceived their needs and held expectations as to how the project might change the existing situation in schools, and the aspirations of the sponsors and project leaders for the project in terms of the transition of young people from school to working life. The local expectations, which he characterised in terms of the 'efficiency' perspective and the 'job' philosophy, were consistent with employability. This described the thinking of those participants who perceived the problem in terms of making the existing arrangements between schools and work more efficient.

As Callan summarised it, the cultural framing of the local conceptualisation of the contribution of the school in the transition to working life restricted it to such topics as information on job opportunities, the development of skills required by industries and the demand for job creation. This was common to local parents and teachers, the general public, and industrialists. Since they did not question their underlying assumptions or orientations, the changes they aspired to were not radical in nature and included '… more expertise, better techniques, the establishment of better mechanisms and communication channels between existing bodies, organisations and institutions'.

The alternative perspective was put forward by representatives of the Irish Foundation for Human Development, the sponsors of the project. The evaluation report cites Dr Ivor Browne whose ideas on the need to find new ways of thinking about work, job creation and human development had been widely propagated at that time.

> We cannot find answers to this frightening problem while we continue to ask the wrong questions. The dilemma is made worse by the way in which we are construing reality … since the nation's wealth is produced by less than one-sixth of the population, the distribution of that wealth for the survival of all seems to be more relevant than job creation. We cannot have enough jobs. What will we do with our time? How will we live? We have to find alternatives for those ousted from jobs.

Browne argued that it was essential that we make 'an act of faith in the basic goodness of people'. He argued that if we could not ensure a job in the traditional sense for people, we could at least secure them in human dignity, anticipating that people '… will respond by engaging on their own initiative, in a wide variety of activities that are life enriching'. Listing the possibilities as gardening, food production, crafts, the arts, small industrial undertakings, and cultural activities, he concluded that 'the job is not the only way of life, it was not in the past and will not be in the future'. The oppositional nature of the thinking of the Irish Foundation for Human Development was synthesised by Callan as follows: 'their alternative ways of understanding work and its place in one's life is quite different from the dominant understanding of that concept, which equates "work" with the notion of a "job" for which one is paid.'

The project's programmes together with their pedagogies which operated in ten schools in the North Mayo/Sligo area were also innovative. The overall objective of the project was '… the development of the students' ability to learn', conceived in an integrated and holistic way involving intellectual, emotional, physical and spiritual capacities of the students. Three strands of activity were involved: orientation exercises which were preparatory in nature; imaging, providing access to a variety of ways of knowing including visual and auditory which would complement and stimulate verbal and linear processes; and movement, both as an expressive form and as a means of enhancing learning (Irish Foundation for Human Development, 1984). With regard to the success of the project in this regard, and more generally in communicating with schools and other interests in the area, Callan concluded: 'the story of this project is about good intentions but poorly communicated, good ideas but time ran out for satisfactory execution of them. It is also about mistrust, lack of clarity, non-creative contributions, and fear of taking risks.'

The project can be seen as part of a counter cultural movement that was more general than education in that it contained strands engaging psychiatry, lifestyle, ecology, meditation and self-knowledge, localism, sustainability and small-scale production. Many of these were later to emerge as more visible and influential sources of knowledge and social and political action. Education for Development did not share in this success. It remains a short-term educational experiment facilitated by a phase of high unemployment with its origins in civil society. The

Irish Foundation for Human Development, the project's sponsor, was a non-government body, in its own words (1984) 'concerned with study and action programmes relating to the essential nature of the individual, his relationships with other individuals, the environment and the community'. As Crooks and McKernan (1984) acknowledged, the project was distinctive in this regard and different from most other curriculum development projects in Ireland at that time which had their origins in local schools, curriculum development centres, education authorities or the state Department of Education.

There was support from academics such as Jim Callan, the evaluator of the project who argued that '… the project's underlying orientation is still valid. Radical alternatives to our schooling system are required which require tentative and exploratory work. This is what the Foundation basically embarked on. There is a value in it being further explored.' Its short cultural life, however, was signalled in 1984 when Crooks and McKernan reviewed curriculum development projects between 1970 and 1984. In characterising the Education for Development Project, they concentrated exclusively on its school programmes and pedagogies and made no mention of its distinctiveness as a text on the transition from school to working life. Its potential for Irish curriculum development discourse lay in its capacity to probematise its liberal functionalist assumptions about the obvious and proper relationship between schooling and the world of work, not merely by raising justice issues about the partiality of the relationship in terms of who benefits, but in its efforts to challenge the meaning attributed to constructs such as work, employment, socially-beneficial activity, and life-course development and fulfilment. This potential was not realised. The consequences for curriculum development discourse was its delayed and still restricted incorporation of such critical themes (Callan, 1995; Gleeson, 1998, 2000, 2004); for employability, thematic and textual resources of this nature would have allowed it to represent itself as a more obviously discordant understanding of schooling to the textual advances of the human capital and mercantile paradigms. Within the LEM domain, counter-texts such as those of Hannan, Kellaghan and Lewis, Fagan and Stokes might have found themselves incorporated in the repositioning and re-designation of the 'distant other'.

Employability: A Mutable Paradigm

As a paradigm, employability was prone to instability for both internal and external reasons. Such was the specific and middle-range nature of its position within the social structure – statuses, age-segments, school/society nexus – it would prove difficult to evade the influence of whatever institutional paradigms held sway in society. Human capital and mercantile paradigms would have included these aspects of social structure within their referents, and according as the latter expanded the co-optation of employability would have constituted an obvious means of strengthening its dominion. The process would have been self-confirming: co-optation deployed as a means of expanding its influence; enhanced orthodoxy and normalisation increasing its capacity and inclination to co-opt.

But employability was also vulnerable because of its internal structuration as a paradigm. The polyvalent nature of its conceptualisation of employability made it a ready target for intertextual activity. Deficit texts on individuals and schooling and productivity and efficiency texts on the labour force and the economy would have been drawn to it through these compatible meanings, and created a dynamic for its modification. The life chances theme of strict and relative employability was forced to engage with the systemic needs of the economy and compete for its positioning in the discourse. In this process, the obligation of society to improve the life chances of young people who had been unsuccessful in their competition for paid employment could be recast as a labour market, national productivity issue. The defining discourse of strict employability positioned it as the most vulnerable to reconceptualisation: the unemployable would become less understandable in LEM terms – deprived of work, status and material reward – and more so in relation to social order and stability. Specifically, employability's depiction of pupil deficits of disposition and skill as realities to be confronted rather than as products, at least in part, of society made its position within the LEM domain volatile and even problematic, readily truncated, as the responsibility of society for their predicament was easily submerged, to an issue of the life choices of individuals.

Even if curriculum development discourse had been less constrained by liberal functionalism it seems unlikely that it could have protected employability from co-optation. It could, however, have exposed the discordance of the penetration and made it more explicit, generated oppositional texts and, through losing the battle, left in place cultural resources to be deployed in future engagements between the meanings involved. Likewise, with the LEM domain, less in the gaze of liberal functionalism it might have demonstrated a receptivity to efforts at cultural production that were striving to structurally represent the status of the 'distant other' in terms other than their 'unemployability'. As it is, employability, in all its diversity of conceptualisation and looseness of framing, survives and, such is its mutable nature, continues to be deployed in texts that differ substantially from one another (e.g. NESC, 1999; *National Development Plan*, 1999; Kellaghan, 2002).

Chapter 9

Disadvantage: Texts, *Pastiche*, Consensus and Intervention

From the 1980s the 'distant other' came to be constituted in policy discourse and practice in terms of educational disadvantage. The terminal leaving non-beneficiary of educational expansion in the 1960s and the 'unemployable' school-leaver of the 1970s were replaced by the child whose educability was compromised because of socio-economic background. Disadvantage carved out a specific socio-economic semantic space for itself as the use of other signifiers, such as gender equity, ethnicity and disability, allowed it to be distinguished from those who suffered disadvantage in fully benefiting from education because of their sex, physical or mental disabilities, and membership of the Traveller Community. With disadvantage, the socio-economic focus of equality of educational opportunity during the 1960s re-entered Irish educational discourse. Indeed, as discourse and practice relating to disadvantage developed, it became evident that disadvantage did not even mean all of those who experience impediments in benefiting from education because of socio-economic factors, a quite widespread phenomenon in society even if one confines the analysis to the relative availability of economic resources to develop individual potential. To be disadvantaged came to be constructed, through the selection criteria of interventions, their objectives and character, the policy of targeting the most disadvantaged, and most explicitly from the manner in which 'poor', 'at-risk', 'marginalised', 'socially-excluded', 'underprivileged', even 'underclass' (Kellaghan *et al.*, 1995; Kellaghan, 2002) could be used interchangeably with disadvantage, as those who suffered the greatest socio-economic impediments to benefiting from schooling. It was these who were isolated for naming, theorisation and action when disadvantage was invoked.

This constitution of the 'distant other' and its sponsorship in educational policy is usually traced from Gemma Hussey's period as Minister for Education from 1982 to 1986 (Hussey, 1990). It is explicit in the *Programme for Action in Education 1984-1987* (1984). But it is the provision of special funding for some schools in deprived areas in Dublin, Cork and Limerick from 1984, however uneven and minimal it may have appeared at the time (Mackey, 1987), that most successfully initiated this textualisation of the 'distant other' as those most educationally disadvantaged who merited specific, targeted funding because of their socio-economic background. However, both socio-economic impediments to benefiting from education and dedicated funding were earlier thematised in the 1980 *White Paper on Educational Development.* This would have implications for the meaning of disadvantage, the social work focus of policy responses and the nature of the subjectivities cultivated and identities attracted to the discourse and practice of disadvantage intervention of a kind that were consistent with the construct of the 'distant other' and the 'discovery' of the deprived child from the 1960s.

The context was the growing attention to differences in life chances during the 1980s. There was a material basis to this in the high unemployment and emigration rates, and in the trade union activism and interest group protests and marches that followed cutbacks in government spending seeking to control the national finances of a country that was living beyond its means, according to a warning by its leader in 1980. Indeed, Gemma Hussey would later declare in interview (Cregan and Lodge, 2000) that the identification and sponsorship of the disadvantaged was meant as a means of ameliorating the effects of such cutbacks on those least capable economically of coping with them. Routinely viewed as a period of moral divisiveness in the light of the confrontational constitutional campaigns on abortion and divorce, the 1980s can be more positively interpreted as a time when differences on individual and collective rights that are central to the social order were revealed and asserted. Knowledge production relating to social mobility, poverty, literacy and educational access expanded and policy discourse and structures invoking moral themes of rights, social responsibility and equality of a kind that implicated educational experiences and resources developed. The less positive implications that followed for moral subjectivities, the public sphere and the individualisation of Irish society have been discussed in Part Two.

Despite the Irish tendency to see social class as a peculiarly 'English-problem', it had been found that social mobility rates in Ireland were more unequal than in countries such as France, Sweden and England. It was pointed out that the class position of most families had been established in the light of their ability to take advantage of the educational opportunities made available in the 1960s and 1970s and 'consequently to secure access to a favoured niche in the class system' (Breen *et al.,* 1990, p. 68). A major study on the extent and distribution of poverty, co-funded by the Combat Poverty Agency (CPA), the Economic and Social Research Institute (ESRI) and the European Community confirmed and extended Ó Cinnéide's (1972) 'rediscovery' of poverty at the 1971 Kilkenny Conference (Callan *et al.*, 1988). As has been noted earlier, while the ESRI researchers did not come down in favour of a single poverty line, 40, 50 or 60 per cent of average disposable income, the CPA expressed the opinion that anyone living on incomes below any of these three lines could be considered to be living in poverty. Their assertion that one-third of the Irish people was living in financial poverty received wide media coverage and continued to operate as a trope for inequality and restrictive socio-economic circumstances. This, in turn, the CPA linked with increasing unemployment since 1980, pointing out that one-third of all households at the 50 per cent poverty-line were headed by an unemployed person.

In contrast with the view expressed by the General Secretary of the Vocational Teachers' Association, Charles McCarthy (1960), unexceptional in its time, that the population of Ireland was 'almost universally literate; or more accurately … only the unteachable are illiterate', there was a growing recognition that Irish adults experienced problems with reading and writing in significant numbers. A Discussion Document of the Department of Education (1985) estimated that 18 per cent of adults required literacy tuition, 5 per cent on the basis that they were 'illiterate or nearly so' and 13 per cent because they were 'sub-literate'. The submerged voices and lived experiences of adults who were attempting to cope in life with literacy problems were being recorded (NALA Research and Development Sub-Committee, 1988). As well as providing training and support for the many local and largely voluntary literacy programmes, the National Adult Literacy Agency, founded in 1980, was successfully bringing both the magnitude of the problem and its inter-personal, economic and political implications to national prominence (O'Sullivan, 1989c). Clancy's six-yearly surveys of patterns of participation in higher education and the annual school-leavers' surveys, both of which were state-sponsored, commenced in 1980. Clancy's findings, first published in 1982, quickly established themselves as the most public and widely-quoted body of data from the Irish social sciences, featuring in newspaper editorials, letters' columns and articles, as well as in academic and policy discourse. It was Clancy's research, more than any other force, that revived and maintained the theme of social class/socio-economic impediments to benefiting from education within Irish cultural production. His socio-economic profiling of higher education students revealing their unrepresentative nature demonstrated, as did the advocacy of the women's movement, the power of percentages in raising questions of life chances.

While the annual school-leavers' surveys conducted by the ESRI were less widely-known, their data on patterns of transition from school to further education and training and the labour market informed policy-directed research (Breen, 1984; Hannan, 1986) and the interventions of the Youth Employment

Agency, established in 1982, targeting the employment opportunities of school leavers. Adults were also being included in discourse on educational opportunity. The Kenny Commission Report, *Lifelong Learning* (1984), drew attention to intergenerational inequalities in benefiting from education and the National Council for Educational Awards (1978, 1985) was advancing pioneering ideas on a progressive award structure for adult students who faced restrictions in progressing educationally because of the terminal nature of much of the certification of adult courses at that time.

This attention to life chances in knowledge production and policy discourse provided an entry point for LEM themes, such as the aetiology of, and moral responses to, differences in educability, that curriculum development had elided. By the 1980s, also, so much of the absences and restrictions that impeded paradigm formation within the LEM domain during the 1960s, and the full exploitation of the range of themes around the socio-economic focus of equality of educational opportunity available to cultural production at that time, were being rectified. Coolahan (1984a) has chartered the changing infrastructure of knowledge production within education at this time. Educational studies were expanding and diversifying within the universities and colleges of education and specialist appointments were being made in areas that included sociology. Research in the form of postgraduate theses and academic articles were introducing new concepts, theories and authorities to Irish thinking on education. The Educational Studies Association of Ireland (ESAI), established in 1976, through its conferences and publications, in particular *Irish Educational Studies*, facilitated communication and engagement among those circulating and negotiating these more variegated understandings of education. As well as providing a public sphere for cultural interchange and production around education, the ESAI also helped to establish for the participants similarities and differences among themselves which would provide the basis for varieties of association, differentiated in terms of shared understandings, and engaging with one another with differing degrees of frequency and intensity, of which the Curriculum Development Movement was to be the most coherent. Of particular relevance to the LEM domain was the fact that for the first time teacher education included the study of the sociology of education.

The production of sociological knowledge about Irish education was initially limited. In her review of developments in the sociology of education between 1966 and 1991, Drudy (1991) found that in her extensive bibliography, only 17 individuals had contributed more than a single entry. She also drew attention to the dominance of the empirical tradition and the relative lack of attention to theoretical issues and more diverse methodologies. With regard to areas of interest, however, she pointed out that the 'overriding concern north and south of the border (was) with equality of educational opportunity and the relationship of social background to educational participation and achievement'. This reflected the content of the most widely-used textbooks of the era, in particular Olive Banks's *The Sociology of Education*, first published in 1968. The broader range of theoretical perspectives and methodologies that later featured in sociology of education courses is well-captured in the first Irish textbook in the area, Sheelagh Drudy and Kathleen Lynch's *Schools and Society in Ireland* (1993). The overview of the texts on educability that follows reveals a diverse repertoire of theories and intervention strategies to which future teachers and educationalists would have been progressively exposed since the 1970s. This will provide a review of the resources available to those professionally involved in education for the textualisation of disadvantage once it became thematised in educational discourse in the 1980s, and gives an indication of the potential that was there for paradigm formation in relation to it.

The following are no more than brief sketches to allow the analysis of Irish understanding of disadvantage to proceed. Nonetheless, they should be sufficient to demonstrate the features of the texts and counter-texts on educability which will need to be drawn into the analysis of how educational disadvantage came to be culturally produced in Irish policy-related discourse. These include the internal variations they incorporated, the intertextual processes of confrontation, denial, repositioning and raiding that developed over time, and the political interests and processes involved.

Educability: Texts and Counter-Texts

Constitutional Limitation

This long-standing explanation of educability, which can be traced back to the studies on the heritability of genius in the latter half of the nineteenth century, continued as a point of reference and controversy, its reductionism proving to be both seductive and repulsive. This text would caution against interpreting raw figures on the differential representation of, for instance, socio-economic groups, at advanced levels of education as unrealised potential or as indicators of inequality. To do so, it would argue, is to ignore the limitations imposed by the human constitution on the capacity to benefit from education. It is this version, which proclaims the existence of individual variations in inherited educability, that the constitutional text persists and circulates most widely in the educational world and society at large. But the proposition also exists that ability is not evenly distributed throughout society. Educational failure, this asserts, among the children of those who have been economically unsuccessful in society should not surprise since their economic status indicates how much intellectual capacity they have to pass on to their children. In Jensen's words 'selective factors in social mobility and assortative mating have resulted in a genetic component in social class intelligence differences' (quoted in Eysenck, 1971, p. 26). In *The Bell Curve*, Herrnstein and Murray (1994) detected in American society the emergence of 'an increasingly isolated cognitive elite' merging with the affluent and resulting in 'a deteriorating quality of life for people at the bottom end of the cognitive ability distribution'. If unchecked, they predicted, 'these trends will lead the US towards something resembling a caste society, with the underclass mired even more firmly at the bottom and the cognitive elite even more firmly anchored at the top' (p. 509). The educational implication is to question the capacity of intervention programmes to 'overcome poor children's genetic limitations' (Zigler and Muenchow, 1992, p. 74).

In drawing implications for policy it is argued that while the state cannot be held responsible for one's genetic inheritance, it should nonetheless recognise differences in the capacity to cope with the mainstream curriculum, and devise appropriate programmes depending on developmental level, learning style and pattern of abilities. Also, the state should ensure that intelligent children in lower-achieving sub-groups within the population be identified, stimulated and challenged with a view to helping them achieve their potential (Jensen, 1969; Eysenck, 1971).

The environmentalist emphasis of sociology as well as the ideas and political actions of equality and civil rights campaigners from the 1960s proved an inhospitable climate for such ideas. In fact, what was frequently opposed was not merely the performatives of this discourse but the themes themselves, the argument being that such was their racist, sexist and elitist character they had no place in civilised debate. There was an explicit attempt to deny the entry of the constitutional text to discourse. The response from some of the key validators and producers of the constitutional text, such as those quoted earlier, is that they have been misrepresented, simplified and unscientifically demonised, an assertion also to be found in Pinker (2002). Much of the criticism of constitutional limitation as an explanation of differences in educability targets the construct 'intelligence', particularly in terms of its meaning and measurement. Widely read examples of this oppositional stance to the use of intelligence in educational explanation and practice such as Kamin's (1977) *The Science and Politics of IQ* and Gould's (1981) *The Mismeasure of Man* question the neurological basis of intelligence, its 'fixed' character, its measurability, its predictive capacity in spheres of life other than education, the validity of the nature *versus* nurture debate and the culture-fair status of IQ tests. Kamin concludes that to be 'trained to answer the kinds of questions asked by IQ tests ... requires both the opportunity and the willingness to accept the training regimen. To assert that those without opportunity or willingness have defective genes is not a conclusion of science. The social function of such an assertion is transparently obvious. The successful are very likely to believe it, including successful professors' (p. 226). Since the 1980s, Gardner's (1983) theory of multiple intelligences which challenges the reality of general intelligence and argues for the existence of a multiplicity of intelligences (originally seven: linguistic, logical-mathematical, spatial, bodily kinesthetic, musical, interpersonal, intrapersonal) has become a focal point of criticism of the application of traditional theories of intelligence in education.

Material Condition

In its basic version the material condition text links poverty with a lack of success in education. Where wealth is unequally distributed, it argues, pupils whose parents have fewest material resources are impeded in many ways from benefiting from education. Thus, even before birth, physical development is affected by the health of the mother. Inadequate or inappropriate diet and limited access to exercise and recreation hinders physical and intellectual development. In poor homes there are few educational materials, even books are in short supply and funds are not available for extra-curricular activities, additional tuition and educational travel. A less financially-based interpretation of material condition incorporates the quality of housing and health care. It stresses the mode of financial support within families and the extent to which the work of parents confers status and is self-enhancing. It also considers the availability of work for those leaving school. Where employment is available, older members of such families are likely to leave school early to supplement the family income. Compounding family poverty, schools in poor areas are said to face insurmountable difficulties in fund-raising and in obtaining voluntary contributions to invest in classroom materials and resources such as computers and musical instruments. Accordingly, poor pupils who come from educationally-limiting family backgrounds, usually attend schools that have fewer resources than schools that draw their pupils from better-off homes. The Plowden Report's characterisation of the typical Educational Priority Area school was a high profile example of a material condition text.

> They are quite untypical of schools in the rest of the country ... tiny playgrounds; gaunt looking buildings; often poor decorative conditions inside; narrow passages; dark rooms; unheated and cramped cloakrooms; unroofed outside lavatories; tiny staffrooms; inadequate storage space with consequent restriction on teaching materials and therefore methods; inadequate space for movement and PE; meals in classrooms; art on desks; music only to the discomfort of others in an echoing building; non-sound-proof partitions between classes; lack of small rooms for group work; lack of spare rooms for tuition of small groups; insufficient display space; attractive books kept unseen in cupboards for lack of space to lay them out; no privacy for parents waiting to see the head; sometimes the head and a secretary sharing the

same room; and, sometimes all around the engraved grime of generations ...' (Central Advisory Council for Education [England], 1967, pp 50-51).

As well as policies to combat poverty itself, educational interventions such as free education, grants for third-level education and for senior cycle post-primary level, and the more favorable funding of schools in poor areas are advocated within this text.

Personal 'Deficit'

According to the personal deficit' text the failure to benefit from school is due to pupils' abilities, values, beliefs and attitudes. Lacking appropriate dispositions and skills they come to schooling unable to benefit from it and therefore must be considered to be educationally disadvantaged. The application of Kluckhohn and Strodtbeck's scheme of value orientations to education and Bernstein's theory of linguistic codes encapsulates much of the content of this text. In the application of the value orientations schema, working-class pupils are said to be fatalistic, lacking in long-term planning, unable to forego immediate gratification and collectivist rather than individualist in approaching life (Banks, 1968). Bernstein (1961) in a widely-read article argued that the public language of the lower working class '... is likely to produce (from a formal educational point of view) deleterious effects, both cognitive and affective ...'. Thus, 'unlike the middle-class pupil, [the lower working-class pupil] lacks the understanding of basic concepts; neither is he orientated to building his experience upon those concepts. Insightful generalisation is difficult ... there is no continuity between the expectancies of the school and those of the child ...' all of which 'revealed the inadequacy of the lower working-class child's basic preparation'. Supplemented by physical and psychological characteristics, the academic accounts of educational disadvantage routinely carried lists of such 'deficiencies' (Gordon, 1968). A distinguishing feature of the personal 'deficit' text is the designation of the facticity of these 'deficiencies'. The cause of these disadvantages may well be in the pupils' culture or in the poverty of their family background, but the personal 'deficit' text stresses that for the school the real, immediate and pressing problem is that pupils are difficult to teach, motivate and even control. As Kellaghan and Greaney (1993) put it '... few would doubt that there are differences between children when they enter school in their ability to adapt to the work of the school, differences which are due, at least in part, to the varying familial experiences of the children. Whether or not the characteristics of some children and of some homes are regarded as deficient would seem to arise more from a valuation of the differences than from their recognition.'

The performatives of the personal 'deficit' text, therefore, target the presenting 'deficiencies' of pupils though in some versions schools are urged to campaign for social change and to be as accommodating and as adaptive as possible

(Gordon, 1968). Early intervention is recommended, and as the support of parents is essential, schools should do all that is possible to mobilise their participation and interest. Where intervention is unavailable or is unsuccessful, it is predicted that disadvantaged pupils are more likely to leave school early with few, if any, qualifications, fail to get a job, and develop anti-social behaviour. When the failure to benefit from schooling persists into the post-primary level, more specialised programmes and youth training are required to provide the skills and the personal attributes which will enhance job prospects. The counter-text derides this explanation of underachievement for blaming the pupils for their failure and for assessing them against the criteria of schooling as if these were the only valid measures of success. It goes on to assert that young people with few qualifications are unemployed not because they lack the necessary skills but because of inadequate occupational opportunities and the hiring practices of employers.

Cultural 'Deficit'

The cultural 'deficit' text argues that it is essential to acknowledge and respond to the realisation that the problem is larger than the 'deficiencies' of individual pupils. In some areas, it argues, the school system faces an inhospitable culture, a way of life that in its values, behaviour, organisation, personalities and role models acts against school goals. This takes the form of low participation in the political, civic, religious, economic and educational institutions of the wider society, an underdeveloped local social structure, families that are unstable and disorganised, a departure from the dominant values of society, a hostility to its police and other official agents, and personalities that are dependent and low in self-control. Pupils, it is argued, are reared to this culture and absorb its values. It becomes their world and they in turn represent it. Difficulties in motivating pupils, in maintaining discipline and in making education relevant for such pupils, therefore, must be confronted not as individual problems but rather as cultural ones. Associated with the culture of poverty thesis in the United States (Katz, 1989), it was given some prominence in Britain where it was identified with Keith Joseph as Secretary of State for Social Services (Robinson, 1976). The criticism that it is a fiction and that it distracts from the material and structural forces which produce inequality is easier to sustain in relation to such popularisations than to its original sources such as Harrington's (1962) *The Other America* which itself has been rebuked for playing a prime role in the politicisation of structural poverty in the US (Murray, 1994).

Culturally Discordant Schooling

This reaction against the 'deficit' texts argues that schools must shoulder much of the blame for the failure of pupils. Their codes of behaviour, their expectations of pupils' motivation and aspirations, their styles of speech, and above all, their formal curriculum, present a culture that is meaningless to many pupils. Schools ignore their pupils' abilities, tastes and preferences. Pupils therefore experience a discontinuity between home and school. This causes alienation from schooling which shows itself in absenteeism, early school leaving and apathy and, more dramatically and in extreme cases, in violence. To counteract this, schools are encouraged to accept as valid and significant the culture of the pupils which it should reflect in the activities of the school, particularly in the curriculum where items from the culture of the working class should find a place. In *Tinker, Tailor... the myth of cultural deprivation,* Keddie (1973) hoped that 'schools could become more flexible in their willingness to recognise and value the life experience that every child brings to school, and at the same time become more willing to examine and to justify what schooling could be about and what kind of life experiences children are being offered'. As a practical outcome of this change in emphasis she recommends '... a redirection of educational research away from attempting to formulate how to make children more like teachers. It would be more sensible to consider how to make teachers more bicultural, more like the children they teach ...'

The translation of this text into educational practice is to be found in the community-based syllabus of the Liverpool Educational Priority Area project under the directorship of Eric Midwinter (1972). This took the form of balancing the curriculum more in favour of the realities of the immediate environment, involving parents and local community, and the development by both teachers and pupils of a critical perspective on a range of social institutions, ideas and aspirations. As well as hoping in the long term for a higher level of social participation, the community curriculum was expected to confer other advantages: 'it is likely that the children will do as well or better in traditional subjects because they will be linked to their own experience. In realising that education is about himself and his community just as much as a remote middle-class world, the child will gain a sense of its worth and parents will more readily give their interest and support' (Halsey, 1972, p. 144). This text in turn has been criticised for romanticising disadvantaged lifestyles and trapping disadvantaged children in their social, economic and cultural background (Bantock, 1980).

Three generative questions arise in proposals that schools, in their operation and curriculum, should reflect the presenting culture of their pupils. Firstly, is it presumed that the culture provides a sufficient basis for a curriculum in the knowledge, skills and values which the pupils will need to contribute to and benefit from society? Secondly, is it being claimed that the culture provides a medium through which the skills, knowledge and values of mainstream culture can be effectively communicated? Or, thirdly, is it merely being proposed that illustrations from the culture be used to make an otherwise unaltered curriculum appear more immediate and in touch with the experience of the pupil? How these questions are responded to and further developed represent some of the sources of variation to be found within the text on culturally discordant schooling.

Political Economy

What distinguishes the Marxist-inspired political economy text is the primacy it attributes to the politico-economic context as the source of differences in benefiting from education. Its original reproductionist text, associated with Bowles and Gintis's (1976) *Schooling in Capitalist America*, proclaimed a deterministic vision of the link between education and the capitalist economic order. Relations of production were seen as the prime influence on education, with schools serving the interests of those who control production. The educational system supports the unequal society of which schools are a part. For unequal societies to reproduce themselves it was necessary that some pupils would fail. Privilege must be transmitted from parents to children to maintain the existing disparities in material resources, prestige and power. For Bowles and Gintis, socialisation throughout the process of education subverts the proclaimed ideal of equality of educational opportunity and functions to reproduce inherited position whereby working-class children get working-class jobs and middle-class children get middle-class jobs: 'different levels of education feed workers into different levels within the occupational structure, and, correspondingly, tend towards an internal organisation comparable to levels in the hierarchical division of labour ...' (p. 132).

For many reasons, which include streaming, teacher expectations and the hidden curriculum, and particularly because what counts as educational achievement is biased in favour of the middle class, certain pupils are deemed to be educationally less successful than others. Those who have power in society decide what should count as worthwhile knowledge and what schools should teach. The yardstick of educational success is said to be 'culture fair'. In fact, it is biased towards the middle classes. Through processes such as these, the identities of success and failure are products of the system itself. Pupils who suffer as a result are meant to see their failure as a consequence of their inability to do well in a system that gave them a fair chance. This is essential if society is to avoid dissent and political agitation. Bourdieu (1973) argued that of all the mechanisms that have been used throughout history to transmit power and privilege 'there surely does not exist one that is better concealed ... than that solution which the educational system provides by contributing to the reproduction of the structure of class relations and by concealing, by an apparently neutral attitude, the fact that it fills this function'. In particular, Bourdieu contends that this concealment is a requirement of societies 'which tend to refuse the most patent forms of hereditary transmission of power and privilege'.

Althusser (1971), the key theoretical influence on this reproductionist text on education, lists schools as crucial ideological state apparatuses, others being the family, law, church and unions, transmitting the required capitalist ideology. As a structural Marxist, Althusser stressed the force of existing social formations incorporating dominance and unequal power. This in turn was to be criticised because of its passive view of individuals, neglect of human agency and overall cultivation of a political hopelessness. Apple argued, 'certainly we must be honest about the ways power, knowledge, and interest are interrelated and made manifest, about how hegemony is economically and culturally maintained. But, we also must remember that the very sense of personal and collective futility that may come from such honesty is itself an aspect of an effective dominant culture' (1979, p. 161). Apple, in its place, proclaimed a resistance text in which he emphasised the existence of struggle in opposition to capitalist interests: 'the notion of reproduction can lead to an assumption that there is (perhaps can be) no significant resistance of power. This is not the case. The continuing struggle for economic rights by workers, the poor, women, blacks, native Americans, Latinos, and others, serves as a potent reminder of the possibility and actuality of concrete action' (p. 160).

The resistance text incorporated a politics of hope and a call for a return to a utopian vision in educational, social and political action. This called on teachers to function as transformative intellectuals, to become practitioners of critical pedagogy in the classroom creating new relationships of authority, public spheres of debate, and alliances with pupils in the creation of knowledge and identity. Teachers were invited to abandon their 'highly exclusionary and undemocratic' (Giroux, 1997, p. 111) professional position and form alliances with 'progressive social movements in an effort to create public spheres where the discourse of democracy can be debated and where the issues that arise in such contexts can be collectively acted on, in a political fashion if necessary'. In the extensive literature on critical pedagogy and the role of teachers as transformative intellectuals a number of disparate strands come together: a modernist commitment to justice and equality, Dewey's progressivism, the British school of Marxist cultural studies, Freirean liberation, a post-structuralist destabilisation of categories and a post-modernist acceptance of difference. This, in turn, has been criticised because of its vanguardism, its assumption that white male American academics are entitled to lead social change and the prediction that it is likely to create new forms of control and dependency (Ellsworth, 1989; Jóhannesson, 1992).

It might have been expected that, once educational disadvantage came to be thematised, these texts and counter-texts would find themselves drawn into the discourse to create a highly-systematised paradigm of disadvantage or, more likely, multiple paradigms. There could have been no predictability about the substantive outcome, such was the diversity of the texts as explanations of differences in educability. While some are compatible and invite coalitions and co-optations, others are incommensurable, the product of distinctive paradigms relating to society, the individual and social change. There are differences in what the 'problem' is considered to be, how it originates and what the possibilities are for intervention. Material conditions, culture and individual action are credited with varying powers of social formation and change. The role of schooling ranges over enslaver, redeemer and benign medium. Educational personnel are cast as concerned professionals, cultural dupes and collaborating activists. Human nature is variously viewed as rigid or pliable. There are differences in the cultural parameters of self-realisation and in what constitutes worthwhile knowledge. Visions of the ideal society include egalitarianism, equality opportunity in an unequal society and socio-economic allocation based on a matching of personal constitution to occupational role. It would have been impossible to envisage how this field of understanding might come to be structured, how the tapestry of the understandings of disadvantage would be woven, most particularly in terms of the relationship between the contributing texts. What could have been reasonably expected was an intertextual activity involving processes such as those of negotiation, transgression, denial, coalition and mutation. Not alone did this vibrant intertextuality of disadvantage not develop, but its absence went unrecognised as the focus of engagement moved to the mechanisms of intervention.

Cultural Production as *Pastiche*

There was to be extensive knowledge production relating to disadvantage as the bibliographies of Boldt and Devine (1998) and Murphy (2000) testify. But this has substantially concerned itself with intervention rather than understanding. While it is possible to excavate traces of different texts on disadvantage from many of these contributions, their focus is essentially on techniques for identifying and targeting those in need of intervention, assessments of the extent of the need, justifying state intervention and financial support, the theorisation of the processes of intervention, description and dissemination of existing practices, and evaluations. Boldt and Devine (1998) describe state policy in this regard: 'it should be noted that there is no policy initiative to clarify the precise meaning of educational disadvantage nor to explain its prevalence. Educational disadvantage is accepted as a problem and policies are aimed at tackling it.' As for academic and policy-related research, their review of this field of knowledge production over a decade is similar and fair: 'in the Republic of Ireland, most research on educational disadvantage has not been concerned with defining the term and finding explanations for the problem. Instead it is focused on identifying the extent of educational disadvantage, identifying factors which relate strongly to it, and proposing measures to address the perceived problem.'

While Boldt and Devine are not representative in making this implied criticism, they too find themselves induced into the characteristic silences and avoidances in line with the nature of their brief from the Combat Poverty Agency 'to undertake a literature review on educational disadvantage in Ireland and to draft a summary report of actions taken to address educational disadvantage over the past ten years'. From no more than their short representative selection of definitions of educational disadvantage from within the policy-related discourse of the state, corporatist bodies, advocacy groups and academic researchers, it is possible to detect the distinctive cultural form which the understanding of disadvantage has taken in both knowledge production and educational discourse. This can be best described as *pastiche*, a non-generative, consensual-driven mixing of traces of texts as distinct from an intertextuality that brings diverse paradigms into contact with one another to create an intersubjective dynamic. Thus, themes from many of the texts on educability are realised in these representative definitions, including poverty, limited financial means, economic factors, non-school experiences, inability to take advantage of opportunities, discontinuity between home and school, the inability of schools to meet the needs of disadvantaged children, and processes of credentialising individual achievement and attributes. In this manner, themes from many of the texts on educability are realised but, as *pastiche*, they remain depthless and untextualised as contestable understandings in their own right.

A prominent deployment of *pastiche* is to be found in the 1992 Green Paper, *Education for a Changing World*. In Chapter 2, on Equity and Access, it treats of socio-economic disadvantage alongside 'those suffering from particular difficulties or handicaps' (p. 45) including 'unfortunate emotional experiences, or ... general or specific learning difficulties' (p. 49). The Green Paper sees educational failure in terms of pupils 'needing particular care' and having 'particular educational needs', committing itself to the expansion of remedial teaching and psychological support (pp 49-50). It expresses concern for those 'students for whom the current curriculum at second level is unsuited' (p. 6) and proposes new courses 'attractive to a wide range of abilities' (p. 51). The Green Paper confines its analysis of material condition to financial need, recognising 'adverse socio-economic circumstances in the home and community' (p. 50), promises a review of the Higher Education Grants Scheme (p. 53) and proposes that 'all schools serving disadvantaged areas would receive a separately identified budget allocation' (p. 49). It tells us that students leave school early 'for a multiplicity of reasons relating to backgrounds from which they come, the value they and their families put on education, and the general support within the community for participation in education' (p. 59). The Home-School Liaison Project is designed to respond to these impediments.

The Green Paper is not clear, however, how the culture of the families involved is to be viewed and whether or not it merits recognition and attention as culture. This is in contrast to its recommended measures to improve the relevance of schooling for girls and Traveller children. These include the stipulations that 'the achievements and contribution of women to the country's economic, social and cultural life, past and present, must receive much more emphasis in all subjects' (p. 69), and that the 'unique culture' (p. 55) of Travellers is to be respected and material from it included in school books (p. 56). The Green Paper acknowledges that 'a complex set of factors – social, economic and cultural, as well as educational –' (p. 45) influences educational participation and it recommends 'integrated action and collaboration between education, health, social welfare, labour and training agencies' (p. 45). In adopting the form of *pastiche* rather than paradigm, this characterisation of the aetiology of disadvantage is rendered plausible, despite the potential tensions between the texts which it invokes, and survives in discourse without the dissonance, much less the disruption, that conflicting paragramatic engagement would provoke.

Pastiche is a term that has been used by some commentators on the post-modernist mixing of different styles, traditions or materials, be it in art, architecture, music, literature, etc. What they have to say about the implications for the character of representation, cultural production and human agency and understanding are suggestive for the theorisation of disadvantage, in particular the manner in which its textualisation since the 1980s has developed. Bringing educability texts into a relationship with one another has the potential to expand understanding of how pupils vary in benefiting from schooling. Allen (2000) has drawn attention to how the better examples of eclectic mixtures can bring different messages, be double-coded and ironic, capture the pluralist nature of meaning, and oppose any exclusivity of dogma. Starting from the plurality of explanations of educability in the 1992 Green Paper, the present author sought, in communicating with an informed general audience (O'Sullivan, 1994a), teachers (O'Sullivan, 1996c) and community workers (O'Sullivan, 1999a), to deconstruct the apparent dogma of their integration and reveal the suppressed intertextuality, thus releasing its generative dynamic of meaning-making. This was attempted in the belief that it would be both possible and productive to acknowledge the differences between texts, proceed to fine points of intersection and engagement and analyse the intertextuality of their circulation. It should not be expected that it would be in the nature of this exercise to produce a coherence of understanding inequality among those most involved in interventions to combat disadvantage (Zappone, 2002), though it should make a contribution to understanding the 'varied and opposing' 'mindsets' within schools, community groups and social service agencies in integrative approaches to tackling educational disadvantage (Cullen, 1998).

Seeking to exploit the generative potential of the mixing of educability texts confirmed that it is not in the nature of *pastiche* to facilitate this intertextuality.

This is because it brings no more than traces of texts, evocations rather than representations of them, together. The diversity of paradigm, ideology and advocacy within the knowledge production process that shapes these texts and their internal refinements are submerged. Their meaning is divorced from not only the political context but the overall social situation of their production and modification. Baudrillard's (1988, p. 166) use of the concept of simulacrum, following Plato, to refer to 'models of a real without origin or reality' is useful here in the manner in which it operates 'to deter every real process by its operational double, a metastable, programmatic, perfect descriptive machine which provides all the signs of the real and short-circuits all its vicissitudes' (p. 167). We can see its relevance in the filtering, shaping and editing experienced by educability texts in Irish discourse on disadvantage. This is the case even in relation to the author's outline sketches, let alone the complex bodies of knowledge which they represent. Personal and cultural 'deficit' and political economy texts provide the clearest illustrations. But with *pastiche* there is a further level of disengagement, in that it is a particular arrangement of simulacra of educability texts. This is what is agreed as reality in intersubjective engagement on educational disadvantage. As a text on educability in its own right, *pastiche* is accordingly characterised as immediate, depthless, ahistorical, reified, and performative. As such it operates, in Jameson's (1991, p. 17) words, as 'parody ... without a vocation ... the wearing of a linguistic mask, speech in a dead language ... blank parody, a statue with blind eyeballs'. With *pastiche* its users are not required to engage with the depth of educability texts, be it in relation to their production, complexity or contestation, which remain lost to intersubjectivity in cognitive history awaiting excavation.

An intersubjectivity that accepts simulacra in discourse dilutes the requirements for reaching not just understanding and communication but also agreement. For Habermas (1979, p. 3), the conditions of the 'intersubjective communality of mutual comprehension, shared knowledge, and reciprocal trust with one another' represent 'the fundamental norms of rational speech that we must always presuppose if we discourse at all' (Habermas, 1975, p. 110). To understand what is being communicated is not to agree with it, a point made by Fay (1987) in criticism of Habermas in this regard. What *pastiche* achieves by realising an arrangement of simulacra is to make the conditions for understanding and continued communication easier to attain. But it also operationally elides the distinction between understanding and agreement. Few are unwilling to engage with the discourse of *pastiche* and fewer still to process it cognitively in a manner that accepts its basic presuppositions. Rare examples would be those committed to the exclusive validity of a particular text or, relatedly, to a view of disadvantage as an impediment to the advancement of more appropriate conceptualisations. But once intersubjectivity has been established it can prove to be seductive. By not representing the contradictions and incommensurabilities of educability texts, *pastiche* provokes little dissonance that cannot be eased by negotiation, compromise or pragmatism. *Pastiche* well nigh enjoins agreement on those who accept its requirements for communication – the disengagement from the submerged complexities and contestations of educability texts.

In discourse on disadvantage, educability is accordingly spoken of less in dogmatic terms and more with matter-of-fact acceptance. There is an almost exhausted resignation (Allen, 2000) at having 'used' the available resources for understanding disadvantage. We find this reflected in the repeated assertion, more by way of a fall-back position, that disadvantage is a complex phenomenon with economic, social and cultural dimensions. There is discouragement to enquire further, and for the moment and in particular settings how disadvantage is to be understood is fixed, if only in the sense of deferring any explanation of how pupils come to be disadvantaged. A feature of this deferral is the use of other signifiers in place of disadvantage – at risk, excluded, poor, deprived, etc. – as the communication proceeds sideways rather than deeper into explanation. This, ironically, has the effect of dispersing (Derrida, 1978) the meaning of disadvantage even further as additional sets of explanatory texts become implicated, most likely also as *pastiche*.

Intervention

Pastiche is functional to the practice of intervening in disadvantage, particularly in the context of the diversity of personnel involved. As well as teachers, in differentiated roles, and parents, with the dispersing meaning of disadvantage the incumbents of roles in relation to training, social work, health, policing, housing, anti-drug and anti-poverty programmes, community and area development initiatives, etc. have come to be positioned as participants in combating disadvantage. Not alone are these personnel geographically dispersed but their paradigmatic formation in relation to disadvantage could also be expected to vary. If these human resources are to be mobilised, submerging difference and cultivating solidarity are essential. The cultural work that this requires is supplied by *pastiche*. This explains the need to resist engagement with the intertextuality that the invitation to confront the diverse texts on educability required. The appeal of *pastiche*, in facilitating consensus and a sense of common purpose, is captured in the objective of the National Research Project conducted in association with the National Forum on Primary Education and Educational Disadvantage (Gilligan, 2002). Its stated purpose was 'to build a way of thinking or to develop a conceptual framework that could direct action for achieving educational equality for the children of Ireland' (Zappone, 2002, p. 4). It was stressed that, in engaging with 'the reflected action (praxis) of those who were centrally involved in the process of promoting equality in children's education', 'the methods chosen were determined by our objective to facilitate a process that would produce *shared* understandings of the meaning of and requirements for equality in children's education ... we were there ... to invite participation and agreement – achieved through debate and consensus – on the most critical ingredients for a way of understanding equality in education' (p. 47). It recognised the potential of this achieved consensus for mobilising those involved in debate and action on disadvantage to higher associative forms of their relationship with one another beyond the collective level of a shared recognition of common meanings.

While it acknowledged the merit of collectivity in submerging personal interest and motivation, its aspirations for mobilisation were more ambitious: 'this "sticking together" yes has implications of community effort, solidarity across classes and other kinds of difference in terms of human identity, but ... if we can stick together in our ways of *thinking about what we're doing*, the effectiveness of our work I believe will take a quantum leap forward. In effect, if we can develop a shared understanding of what is meant by "achieving equality in children's education" it may release an energy that focuses and supports our navigation through the complex territory of building systems of engaging, inclusive and effective education for children in education' (Zappone, 2002). This primary intensity and orientation to action has become a feature of mobilisation around disadvantage. Examples include the Community Workers' Cooperative, the Working Class Access Network and the Network of Initial Teacher Educators Addressing Educational Disadvantage. Even at the atomistic level of association, *pastiche* maximises those who are likely to be successfully hailed by disadvantage. At the other extreme of mobilisation, of a kind that encompasses personal identity, it can induce an exclusionary perception of being at one with all those who are working to eliminate disadvantage in education and different from (unspecified) others who are perceived to be inactive in this regard.

Pastiche can accommodate a wide range of strategies of intervention. It is not in its character to be restrictive, or to suggest caution in proceeding with the establishment of new programmes. In endorsing activism, *pastiche* attracts both politicians who wish to see immediate responses to social problems and lobbyists who fear delaying lest public finances deteriorate or policy-makers are drawn to other concerns.

These features of the cultural production of disadvantage – avoidance of dissonance and contestation, deferral and dispersal in understanding disadvantage, the enjoining of agreement, the mobilisation of diverse participants, and the orientation to and facilitation of action – allowed intervention to be quickly foregrounded in discourse on disadvantage and to become the core of its textualisation. As programmes of intervention developed and expanded throughout the 1990s their existence and operation contributed to this textualisation. This contribution to the meaning of disadvantage is to be found in their performances, e.g. making submissions, consultation, information and dissemination exercises, the criteria for targeting and selecting those in need, the individuals and social configurations accepted as valid contributors to the interventions, and the nature of the changes that constituted the programme's objectives, the latter embodying the 'culture wars' between the mercantile and the modern described in Chapter 6.

The intervention programmes are extensive in volume and variety. In the words of the Minister for Education and Science, Noel Dempsey, in his opening address to the inaugural meeting of the Educational Disadvantage Forum (Educational Disadvantage Committee, 2003) in November 2002, they incorporate, 'a menu of programmes from preschool to life-long learning'. Their listing alone, in Murphy's (2000) diagrammatic representation, covers three pages and deals with Department of Education and Science initiatives, and those of other government departments, and tracks the pervasive contribution of European structural funds to their financing. In what is signified by their operation, they are consistent with and supportive of their cultural provenance in *pastiche*. The link between understanding and intervention in educational disadvantage is recognised by Kellaghan (2002): 'there is also general recognition that problems of disadvantage extend well beyond the school, and that the involvement of agencies and activities outside the education system is required'. He concludes, however, that the range of actions that this recognition has given rise to is probably as much 'a reflection of our lack of understanding of disadvantage and of inadequate conceptualisation of issues as it is a recognition of its complexity'. Indeed, if 'lack' and 'inadequate' were replaced with 'nature' in this quotation it could well serve as a synopsis of the overall line of interpretation in this chapter.

Andragogy, Community Action and Systems Theory

As the textualisation of intervention developed it can be seen to draw in additional themes from texts other than educability, such as those relating to the mobilisation of local resources and the administration and delivery of social services. The nodal point that facilitated their entry is the conceptualisation of intervention as service provision in response to the needs of deprived 'distant others' in which schools are but one among a wide range of providers. This has resulted in a greater variety in the agency of knowledge production about educational disadvantage and intervention beyond the traditional authority of teachers, inspectors and school-focused personnel. The shift is most obvious in relation to the largely unchallenged ability of teaching bodies up until the early 1990s, in particular the INTO, to influence policy discourse and public knowledge on the appropriate actions for correcting disadvantage of a kind that prescribed additional services and resources for the otherwise unaltered schools at their particular level of the educational system. Now, teachers are competing with others, such as those involved in lobbying and advocacy and non-school providers of intervention services, as to how disadvantage is to be understood and spoken of. Public examples of this dispersal of authority can be tracked in the positioning of written submissions and oral contributions in knowledge production about disadvantage from the 1993 National Education Convention (Coolahan, 1994) to the 2002 Educational Disadvantage Forum inaugural meeting (Educational Disadvantage Committee, 2003). In the reported discussion that followed the latter, it is now unremarkable to find calls for 'changing the mainstream' (p. 23) alongside teachers making the case for additional resources. While the power of those within the formal educational system is still substantial in this regard, as is evident from the membership of the Educational Disadvantage Committee, discourse on intervention now reflects the diversity of the paradigmatic formation of those who have been contributing to it, particularly since the 1990s. In fact, it is themes drawn from social service, social care, social work and community work discourse that now act as the basis for much of the textualisation on intervention. From this are isolated for attention themes characteristic of andragogy, community action and systems theory.

Andragogy is used to refer to the generative engagement with adults that acknowledges the validity of their prior experiential learning and their capacity for autonomous choice and decision-making that encompasses social, political and ideological commitment. This differs from the more descriptive understanding of andragogy as 'the art and science of helping adults learn' (Knowles, 1980, p. 43). It is also distinct from, though related to, the recognition of adults as learners and the inclusion of adulthood within the targeted age segments in programmes to combat educational disadvantage. Generative engagement can be expressed in the form of the development of adults in formal or informal learning programmes or as participants in the shaping and enactment of intervention programmes. In its collective manifestation, andragogy implicates local mobilisation, usually as a variety of community action, thus introducing additional themes of participation, empowerment, and subsidiarity in representing, understanding, and making decisions about specific categories of people and their areas. Taken together in discourse on disadvantage, andragogy and community action lean toward the standpoint position on knowledge creation, that those who experience disadvantage possess a privileged knowledge about it of a kind that cannot be gained through professional formation alone. Viewing society as a network of interacting systems derives from the likening of society, in classical sociology, to a biological organism that is subject to evolution, mutation and differentiation. The functions performed by individual systems for the overall social order, their inter-dependence, the manner in which they can act dysfunctionally in relation to each other, their internal coherence and boundaries, their structural imperatives and individual identities are but some of the issues that arise in adopting a systems approach to society. The work of Parsons, referred to in Chapter 1, continues to be the major point of reference in this regard.

Themes from andragogy, community action and systems theory are realised in the circulation of the dominant proposition of intervention discourse – that because of the complex interaction of social and economic forces in experiencing disadvantage, a multi-agency approach is required that incorporates the integration of services in a community setting (Cullen, 2000a). This is validated by reference to integrated service provision for children and families at risk in the US and, more recently, in Europe, mediated and expanded on in the Irish context by Cullen (1997, 2000b). Cullen uses the older advocacy of greater cooperation between agencies serving children and families experiencing difficulties (to be found in the 1960s in Ryan's 'Social Dynamite' discussed in Chapter 7) as a foil to emphasise the innovative meaning and implications of integration: 'there is a marked distinction between forms of integration that improve day-to-day communications in relation to individual service participants (simple cooperation) and forms of integration that are focused on achieving systems changes (systems partnerships) ... new integrative approaches are concerned with achieving a complex array of changes and not simply with the way existing services interact. Other distinctions relate to the types of integrative strategies and the different levels at which they operate' (Cullen, 1997, p. 9). Integrative strategies can range from networking, coordination and cooperation up to collaboration which 'requires the application of sophisticated organisational linkages involving the sharing of risks, the development of shared visions and the development of complex partnership relationships and processes' (p. 10). It is recommended that collaboration be developed between agencies at both administrative and service levels, within agencies, and between frontline workers and families. Initiatives that emerge through collaboration with parents and other community members are seen to contribute to community development processes, 'because they treat parents and children not simply as service receivers but as resources for planning and developing new responses' (p. 10).

Cullen recognises 'a growing expectation ... that integrated children's services need to be driven more at this community, service user level. They should provide new opportunities for service users, community members and marginalised people to directly participate in programme development and operation. This factor is now quite central to discussions about tackling social exclusion in Europe through improved education and social development programmes' (1997, p. 10).

This conceptualisation of intervention can be traced in its more proximate manifestations from the 1980s in the community-action focus of the CPA, in combating poverty, and of CORI in relation to educational disadvantage. It developed throughout the agreements between the government and the major social interests from the Programme for National Recovery 1987-1990, and exists rather tentatively in the Education Green Paper of 1992. It is explicit in the policy discourse of the state, including its corporatist structures: the *National Anti-Poverty Strategy* (1997), the *National Development Plan 2000-2006* (1999), the *Education (Welfare) Act* (2000), the National Economic and Social Forum Report *Early School Leavers* (2002), and the Educational Disadvantage Committee (2003).

Cullen (2000b) has contributed more complex understandings of andragogy (though he does not use the term), community action and social systems to policy discourse that begin to theorise intervention strategies and also reach back to the explanation of variations in educability in a manner that refuses the deferral of explanation in *pastiche*. In state policy on educational disadvantage, however, the discourse of intervention remains thematic and performative.

Communitarianism

Moving from tracing and describing to explaining the form that the cultural production of disadvantage has taken since the 1980s, it is tempting to consider if there might be a causal relationship between *pastiche* and intervention. Did one cause the other, and if so in what direction? Did the pressing urge to eradicate extreme manifestations of socio-economic disadvantage in education pragmatically necessitate the suspension of 'academic' disagreements about explanations of educability? Or did *pastiche* have another provenance and propel activists to devise interventions in the light of what they would have come to regard as a complex but unknowable, multi-factor explanation of disadvantage? It is doubtful if the question can be answered without retreating to some version of the position that *pastiche* and intervention exist in a symbiotic relationship, characterised by facilitation, reciprocation and need, to one another.

What seems more sustainable is the interpretation of both *pastiche* and intervention, in the overall cultural production of disadvantage since the 1980s, in terms of their compatibility with a broader set of meanings identifiable as communitarianism that gained in prominence around the same time. Features of understanding of disadvantage that are indicative of this include the avoidance of dissonance in understanding its nature, and in conceptualising and prescribing for intervention strategies in terms of the generative capacities of those who might otherwise have been treated as clients or victims, the centrality of the lifeworld of people and its immediate social context for bringing about change, and the collaboration between the state and its agencies and those of civil society. More macro in scope, communitarianism as a paradigm would have been positioned politically to co-opt the discourse on disadvantage. It would have been difficult for those involved in disadvantage discourse and intervention to resist since the effect of co-optation would have been to render the understanding of disadvantage consistent with EU social inclusion policies, the thrust of state policy-making through corporatism, described in terms of partnership, during the 1990s, and the political agendas of social democratic and 'third way' positions. Less obvious, because of its apparently 'unpeopled' character, was the influence of the mercantile paradigm of education which had rendered educational meanings susceptible to such co-optation. As we have seen in Chapter 6, this is indicated by the suppression of modernist themes in the textualisation of inequality in the manner in which unequal achievement was reconstituted as low-achieving 'distant others', social structure was realised as community, and action was valorised over understanding.

In Ireland, the most systematised manifestation of communitarianism is to be found, in its Christian and more radical variety, in the discourse of CORI on issues of justice, disadvantage, poverty and inequality in education. This, placed in its international and local secular context, will be the focus of the next chapter.

Chapter 10

(Christian) Communitarianism: Loose Framing, Merging and Mutation

Like disadvantage, communitarianism develops as a paradigm from the 1980s in the context of a growing public and policy attention, together with knowledge production, relating to issues of life chances, rights and obligations. Unlike it and employability, which formed around the intersection of schooling, production and life chances, communitarianism was more macro in its engagement of the social order. Like equality of educational opportunity, as it operated in the Ireland of the 1960s, it would function as an inclusive construct with quite accommodating (loosely-framed) boundaries of understanding. However, unlike the manner in which equality of educational opportunity had become the obligatory (over-determined) signifier for realising concerns about LEM issues, comunitarianism is not a term that is used with any frequency, if at all, in Ireland to describe an overall political position or a particular way of thinking about education. Yet, communitarian themes stretch back further in Irish cultural development within Catholic social teaching and in the forms of social and economic mobilisation shaped by it. Overall, communitarianism is consistent with the pre-reflexive, folk construct of fairness and does not generate dissonance, individually or culturally, in terms of it.

Communitarianism: Philosophy, Sociology, Politics

In describing a policy paradigm as communitarian one is mindful of the different understandings that it will evoke for anyone familiar with its use in general scholarship. Internationally three strands of communitarian thinking can be discerned. These can be differentiated between to the extent that their origins and focus are derived from philosophy, sociology or politics. The many points of common sentiment and principle will become evident from a brief outline of their key distinguishing features.

The roots of philosophical communitarianism can be traced to Greek thought. However, Hegel is often credited as the inspiration for contemporary communitarianism (Avineri and de-Shalit, 1992). His distinction between *Moralität*, the abstract or universal rules of morality, and *Sittlichkeit*, the ethical principles distinctive to a particular community, capture the core of the difference between communitarianism and liberalism widely debated since the 1980s. Like Hegel, communitarians argue that the understanding of morality to be found at the level of social attachment is the higher one and the only one capable of achieving genuine moral autonomy and freedom. A key premise among philosophical communitarians is that the self is constituted within a communal tradition (MacIntyre, 1981). This is in opposition to the image of the individual in liberal thought who chooses the value system he or she wishes to live by. For communitarians like Sandel (1984), this liberal notion of the 'unencumbered self' is a false one that in American society has resulted in fragmented identity and an absence of common purpose in political life. In a similar vein Lasch (1980) speaks of Western liberal culture producing individuals obsessed with themselves and America, in particular, succumbing to the 'culture of narcissism'.

While writers in the strand of philosophical communitarianism share a common focus on the obligations of people to the tradition that has nurtured them, there are differences in emphasis to be found in, for instance, what they accept as constituting a community and how they regard criticism within the tradition (Theobald and Snauwaert, 1995). For feminists, communitarianism has been described as a 'perilous ally' (Friedman, 1989). This is because, like communitarians, feminists reject the liberal view of the isolated self and its boundaries of social relationships but are suspicious of its absence of feminist consciousness and a commitment to resolving gender hierarchies found within traditions (Weiss, 1998). An overall concern of philosophical communitarianism is that the state under liberal influence is reduced to a 'procedural republic' (Sandel, 1984) rather than being constituted as a political community with common values and goals.

Sociological communitarianism can be identified in some of the classical writings in sociology. Tönnies (1855-1936) distinguished between *gemeinschaft*, usually translated as 'community' and referring to a form of social life routinely found in traditional societies in which relationships between people are face-to-face, intimate, personal and rounded, and *gesellschaft*, usually translated as 'association' in which social relationships are formal, contractual and one-dimensional. Tönnies greatly bemoaned the emergence of the latter with the spread of formal organisation and industrialisation. Durkheim (1858-1917), though he did not share Tönnies's romantic longings for traditional forms of social life, nonetheless recognised in his concept of 'anomie' or 'normlessness' that uprootedness, loss of identity and absence of a secure sense of social morality were among the undesirable implications of rapid social change.

In the more recent era, the concern to maintain communal ties was given prominence in a diagnosis of American life experience as 'total shipwreck' with the publication of Stein's (1960, p. 329) *The Eclipse of Community*. His fear that community ties had become inceasingly dispensible resulting in individuals becoming unduly dependent upon centralised authorities while personal loyalties weakened and decreased in range has since assumed a variety of manifestations up to Putnam's (2000) popular *Bowling Alone*. As countries experienced urbanisation, industrialisation and privatisation this concern to arrest the 'loss of community' became a common theme and fuelled an expansion and diversification in community-focused forms of discourse, mobilisation and action. The legacy of these developments is to be found in the extent to which community is deployed as a central organising category and principle in service provision in educational, health, social service, sporting, recreational and artistic domains, and in interventions in relation to economic, social and educational problems. Sociological communitarianism may no longer assume that communities are necessarily virtuous entities but the belief remains that engaging with that collective dimension of people's lives that is experienced as most meaningfully local and most immediately intimate constitutes the most appropriate and effective level of intervention. The robustness of this understanding is indicated by the diverse ideological positions that it can accommodate within the broad community organisation/development/action movement.

Political communitarianism is best known in Ireland through its linkage with what has been referred to as New Labour Third Way policies in Britain and, in particular, with Tony Blair's administration formed in 1997 (Blair, 1998). Its origins are in America in the writings of Amitai Etzioni and the activities of the Responsive Society platform (Burkitt and Ashton, 1996). Etzioni (1993, 1998) credits what he describes as the 'new communitarianism' of the 1990s with having taken communitarian ideals from the narrow confines of academic debate and introducing them to politicians, community leaders and the general public. It has represented itself as a 'third way' of thinking alongside the vocabulary and principles of liberals and conservatives. In Etzioni's (1998, p. xi) own words, the new communitarianism 'made the question of balance between individual rights and social responsibilities, between autonomy and the common good a major question'. It proclaimed the necessity of a theory of a good society to deal effectively with the twin dangers of 'a society where communal foundations are crumbling and … in which they have risen to the point that they block out individual freedoms'. The proposals of the Responsive Society platform are the most specific of all the varieties of communitarian thinking in applying principles to actual political issues of the day including marriage and the family, abortion, drug abuse and testing, spousal abuse, speeding and anti-social behaviour generally. It is for this reason that I refer to it as political communitarianism. The similarities with New Labour policies in Britain can be most clearly seen in Giddens's (1996a) *Beyond Left and Right*, described by Rawnsley (2001, p. 313) in his 'inside story of New Labour' as 'the quintessentially Blairite text' written by the 'guru of the Third Way'. In this, Giddens seeks to reconcile autonomy and interdependence in the various spheres of social life including the economic domain. His themes of repairing damaged solidarities, recognising the centrality of lifestyle politics, the role of generative politics – the politics of the public domain – in approaching problems of poverty and social exclusion, dialogic democracy as a means of democratising democracy, positive welfare, connecting autonomy with personal and collective responsibilities all resonate with those of the Responsive Society platform.

It is necessary to provide this sketch at the outset because the guiding understandings and meanings in Irish policy debate and activity in the LEM domain that are described here as communitarian make few explicit connections with these international bodies of thought, debate and social and political activity. Nor would those in Ireland whom one considers to embody these meanings in their discourse and action necessarily describe themselves as communitarian. None-the-less, there are common points of concern and perception, albeit in an unspecified fashion. In providing an outline of its more cosmopolitian meanings it should become clear why the use of communitarianism here is appropriate in this specific context for what is an exceptionally loosely-framed though pervasive paradigm.

Communitarianism in Ireland

Discourse and performance realising communitarianism and making it real as a feature of Irish understanding relating to the LEM domain is neither specific nor confined to education. Early manifestations are evident in Catholic social thought and action such as the principle of subsidiarity and whole community rather than class conflict approaches to mobilisation reflected in such organisations as Muintir na Tíre. At present, it can be discerned in the work of CORI and the CPA, in the broad community movement, particularly in what can be described as andagogical practices, in literacy advocacy and programmes, in poverty research and debate, in the structures of Area Management Development Ltd (ADM), in programmes agreed between the state and the social partners, in government policy such as the *National Anti-Poverty Strategy* and the *National Development Plan*, and in EU policies on poverty, social inclusion/exclusion and work. In these, the following communitarian themes are recognisable:

- Interdependence and co-responsibility, people are not unencumbered selves
- The inadequacy of free-market forces to meet the needs of all citizens
- The focus on specific vulnerable groups rather than society at large

- The state as distributor and facilitator rather than the agent of command redistribution
- The expectation of state commitment and financial support rather than direction
- The invigoration of the civic sphere
- Solidarity building, participation and dialogue
- Intervention at the most immediate units of public association and action
- The cultivation of human agency and anti-dependency
- Social inclusion/exclusion, the stakeholder society
- The necessity that people become generative forces in the formation of public policy.

Of its nature, communitarianism is not as specific or as easily recognised as the ideological extremes of free market or statist/socialist positions. Because it seeks a third way and middle space between these extremes, it can, without communicative disruption or cultural exclusion, accommodate a wide variety of understandings about the appropriate role of the state in combating inequality, a diversity of moral justifications for involvement/engagement/intervention, differences in the focus of intervention and shadings in human responsibility and agency. Examples include the distinction drawn between integrationist and oppositional tendencies in the relationships between community groups and the state (Curtin and Varley, 1995) and the fact that it has been found possible over a long period to continue to identify as many as ten varieties of what might be broadly described as community/local development (Lovett, 1989; Burgess, 1996). Particularly noteworthy is the manner in which the critical strand of community action, derived from a conflict view of society, that should be anathema to the principles of communitarianism, has come to be accommodated within it, albeit in a more diluted form than was manifested in the first European anti-poverty programme, the 1974-80 pilot schemes to combat poverty (National Committee on Pilot Schemes to Combat Poverty, 1980).

Apart from traces of radical critique of the role of the state in maintaining inequality, sources of unease about the functioning and intentions of the state also include a fear of co-optation generally, the domestication of feminist/radical tendencies, the substitution of volunteerism for funded services, the use of community agencies as a substitute for state employment creation, and the unwillingness to mainstream innovative local practices or to dilute centralist tendencies (Cullen, 1989; Donnison, 1991; Sabel, 1996; Connolly, B., 1997; Community Workers' Co-operative, 1998; Costello, 1999). Democracy, empowerment, decentralisation, anti-racism, Christian Communitarianism, social cohesion, feminism, liberation theology, redistribution and egalitarianism variously provide ideological support (Burgess, 1996; Community Workers Co-operative, 1998; CORI, 1997c; ADM, 1999). The focus of intervention spans employment opportunities, social services, housing, the environment, rural development, individual consciousness, and the needs of specific sub-groups differentiated by age, sex, ethnicity, disability, sexual orientation, poverty and educational disadvantage (Cullen, 1989; Commins, 1995; Curtin and Varley, 1995; ADM, 1999). A consideration of EU social policy would add further systemic and political variations (Kleinman, 2002).

The absence of a distinctive signification through language in these conceptualisations facilitates their fluidity and results in movement in the mapping of this sphere of knowledge that can evade the awareness of even the participants. In the absence of naming, change can remain hidden. This in turn has implications for the nature of the relationship between participants in the communitarian paradigm. Without a stable set of mechanisms for signifying and establishing commonality and difference, associative development is retarded and is required to rely on other more subtle forms of boundary indicators. Table 10.1 outlines the communitarian tropes that function to signal who is like oneself and collectively to identify like-minded people and distinguish them from those who would not share their communitarian understanding. These tropes include concepts/language, slogans that act to define membership and non-membership, approved authorities and texts, and characteristic social practices. It is of course open to others outside of communitarianism, with understandings and approaches that might be in clear conflict with it, to selectively appropriate these tropes. Inclusive social practices that acknowledge and cater for differences in family obligations, financial position, dietary needs and access have become increasingly universal to the point that they lose their discriminative function. Concepts and themes such as community, empowerment, partnership and participation are also used in texts that support projects that would be at odds with communitarianism. This 'raiding' of communitarian tropes, a practice occasionally recognised by the participants themselves (Connolly *et al.*, 1996), and their subsequent appropriation by non-members can further destabilise communitarianism as a coherent paradigm. In such circumstances it is difficult to be aware of who feels, understands or thinks like oneself, to acknowledge the membershipping of new recruits and to recognise the exiting of those who have become disengaged.

As a policy paradigm, communitarianism is exceptionally loosely framed in such dimensions as conceptualisation, language, themes and membership. A manifestation of this at EU level is to be found in the European Social Model and the *New Social Model*. These seem more secure in the knowledge of what they are against – neo-liberal, non-interventionist or EU regulation of markets – than what they are for, leaving considerable space for policy ambivalence and slippage in the porous, loosely-framed third-way position adopted (O'Hagan, 2002). The effects of this are evident when we look at the educational initiatives developed under the auspices of EU anti-poverty, social inclusion and employment objectives. What is most striking about these is how little they can reflect communitarian principles in their substance, as distinct from in the rationale and operational principles, however weakly inferred, of the European, National and Sub-National structures that generate, support and sustain them. This is most clearly illuminated by reference to the educational interventions funded through ADM. This represents a substantial area of educational activity. In 1998 there were 38 area-based partnerships and 33 community groups, as well as projects organised by a number of community/voluntary organisations which operate at a national/regional level. Data for 1997 and 1998 give some indication of the scale of their educational activities. There were 741 preventive education courses offered involving 34,000 young people, evenly divided between male and female. In terms of complementary education and training there were 1,420 courses involving almost 9,000 participants, substantially female. The most frequent courses offered were described as preparation/foundation, personal development, information technology, community development and financial management.

It is through these local interagency structures that what is known as the Local Development Programme was delivered. Officially, this was Sub-Programme Two of the Operational Programme for Local, Urban and Rural development (1994-1995) which itself is more fully designated as Integrated Development of Designated Disadvantaged and other Areas. The Chief Executive of ADM describes the principal objective of the programme as seeking 'to counter disadvantage through support for communities which make a collective effort to maximise the development potential of their areas, which are capable of sustained effort to implement a plan and which have committed an appropriate level of local rescources broadly defined to that process'. In this way, the local development programme hopes 'to accelerate local economic development and thereby increase employment, and to tackle exclusion and marginalisation resulting from long-term unemployment, poor educational attainment, poverty and demographic dependency' (Crooks, 1999). These are representative of themes from both the sociological and political strands of communitarianism realised through the programme's discourse and practice. They include enhancing participation, combating exclusion and dependency, utilising integrated approaches at associative levels that are most immediate and local, and developing structures of partnership rather than conflict between local people and state bodies and agencies. However, such is the loosely-framed nature of the communitarian paradigm that, while it is possible to detect communitarian themes in the representation and subjectivities that feature in the programme's educational initiatives, these diminish in the substance of the initiatives. The failure of the paradigm to infuse the character of the educational interventions through to their substance represents an example of unsuccessful/discordant expansion. This typifies a paradigm that is porous, breached and ill-defined in what it is and what

Table 10.1 Communitarian Tropes

| Concepts/Themes | | | | |
Valorisation of:	Negation of:	Texts	Authorities	Social Practices
Community	Fragmentation	Inclusivity	EU Social Policy	Consultation
Inclusion	Professional/ Bureaucratic Power	Poverty Action	National Anti-Poverty Strategy	Agency/Service Co-ordination
Dialogic	Competitive State Direction	Community Action	National Agreements/ Understandings/Social Partnerships	Reflective Practice
Participative Democracy	Monetarism	Environmentalism		Participative/Active Methods
Community Development as Process	Free Market	Sustainable Development	Selected academics: e.g. Freire, Lovett, Levitas	Area Meetings
Partnership	Enterprise	Option for the Poor		Community Participation
Working with, rather than for	Thatcherism	Liberation Theology		Submissions/Action Groups
Conscientisation	Individualism	Interculturalism		Estate Management
Empowerment		Andragogy/Gynagogy		Accommodating difference
Collective Change				

it is not. Thus, the content and objectives of the educational initiatives are rightly described by Crooks (1999) as preventive and compensatory.

At the same forum, a major ADM conference on partnerships in education in 1999, the head of the social inclusion unit of the Department of Education and Science sought to encapsulate the DES policy on social inclusion as increasing participation rates in schools and, 'where this strategy has failed, for second chance education for those who left school prematurely particularly those who left without any qualifications' (O'Brien, 1999). At this conference also, another communitarian theme, that of social cohesion, is interpreted in terms of employability by an official from the European Commission (Ní Chuirc, 1999). In describing the combating of unemployment as of paramount importance in EU policy, she contends that this does not in any sense diminish 'the overall priority accorded to economic and social cohesion'. In fact, she continued, 'the two go hand in hand. Increasing employment levels is one of the most effective ways of increasing economic and social cohesion within communities, between countries and across the union as a whole.' These are examples of how at such 'spectacles' as major conferences of this nature the meanings attached to signifiers such as social cohesion and social inclusion can be the object of 'negotiation', in this instance privileging economic signification (exclusion from paid work) over the social and economic. Even where this is never quite successful, in the sense of 'fixing' the meaning of social inclusion/exclusion, it nonetheless has the capacity to even further obfuscate a semantic field that is already unstable, variable and contested across European social policy (Levitas, 1998).

In the event, it is the objectives of enhancing educability and employability that are most evident in the educational initiatives of the ADM-sponsored programmes. This is systematically reflected across the full diversity of these programmes. These include:

- Preschool provision in urban and rural areas
- Supporting primary education in rural areas (literacy and special learning difficulties, networking smaller schools)
- Supplementing the work of schools in such areas as the arts, social skills and personal development, drug and alcohol abuse prevention
- Providing study centres, career advice, homework clubs, school-to-work transition schemes and parent support
- Responding to the educational needs of special groups such as poor attenders and early school leavers, deaf people, young offenders and Traveller children
- Promoting participation in third-level education among under-represented groups through scholarships, extra tuition and a broadening of the horizons of parents and pupils
- Literacy provision and educational guidance for adults.

Even at their most successful, the outcomes of these interventions are likely to be confined to enhancing the benefits to be derived from the educational system as it exists for those who are socially and economically most vulnerable, rather than the reconstruction of the educational system, and ultimately society, according to communitarian principles. This is not meant as a criticism of the ADM programme. What the example is used to illuminate is the difficulty in specifying performatives from 'third way' social and political positions and, more generally, the slippage that loosely-framed communitarianism is prone to from the point of entry of a theme to discourse and its embodiment in action.

As an intersubjective configuration that is variable in how it cognitively maps its world, in the language it uses to describe it, in the themes that it can accommodate, and in who it recognises as a fellow member, how can communitarianism claim any reality as a policy paradigm? An explanation must begin with the public knowledge about the LEM domain generated by the CMRS renamed in 1994 as CORI. This is referred to here as Christian Communitarianism.

Christian Communitarianism

Christian Communitarianism describes an approach to social policy (economic, cultural, political as well as educational) that emphasises the obligations of people to one another in their use of the world's resources, and grounds these obligations in the interpretation of Christian sources. In its construction of the cultural understanding of education it substantially represents the most visible and explicit manifestation of communitarianism available in Irish society. It gives coherence and focus, and potentially co-opts communitarian resources, such as themes, texts and agents, from other social and cultural spheres including economics, employment, literacy and welfare. Christian Communitarianism is most formally represented by the activities, both discourse and performance, of the CMRS/CORI and, in relation to education, by its Education Commission. Its clearest early statement of a communitarian position is to be found in *Local Education Committees. The Case for their Establishment and a Tentative Proposal* (CMRS, 1993a). In this it advocates what it describes as a transforming model of societal development. This it describes as taking its starting point from 'the systemic wholeness of society, that is a society where the individual units are interdependent and change in one part of society has implications for all the other parts and for the whole' (p. 3). It sees the relationship between the various elements of society as dynamic. That implies a pluralism that will emphasise 'communal rather than individualistic values and integration rather than fragmentation' (p. 3). A dominant concern in this model is the common good. This model is articulated against a background of rejecting authoritarian political structures and a liberal model of society. The liberal model is rejected because of its 'culture of individualism characterised by autonomy and self-fulfilment' (p. 3) which is seen to lead to a fragmentation of society. In this the pluralism that is valued 'is pluralism based on independent rather than interdependent units' (p. 3).

It specifies some of the key features of a society based on these principles of interdependency, communalism and the primacy of the common good, and uses these in its advocacy of the desirability of Local Education Committees. In this, many of Giddens's (1996a) themes of generative politics, the politics of the public domain, democratising democracy, reconstructing solidarity and collective responsibility recur:

> Adherence to this ... transforming model sees popular participation as the most significant element in social change and calls for new, more inclusive economic, political, cultural and social structures. It leads to an emphasis on more effective forms of devolution of power as a way of extending the democratisation of society and the emergence of the theme of solidarity as a way of counteracting the undue influence of lobby groups on decision making. The theme of solidarity is expressed in the development of community organisations through which local communities can become actors in the decisions that affect them rather than, as has often been the case, passive recipients of decisions made on their behalf (p. 3).

As this position paper on Local Education Committees points out, this advocacy of devolved decision making is in line with the principles of Roman Catholic teaching such as that of subsidiarity associated with the 1931 Papal Encyclical *Quadragesimo Anno*. According to this principle, policy decisions should be taken at the lowest practicable level to their point of influence and effect. However, the Christian Communitarianism of CMRS/CORI is more deeply rooted within the Judaeo-Christian tradition than this identification of political and sociological strands of communitarianism might suggest. A brief sketch of the evolution of the CMRS and, in particular, its Education Commission, will help to explain the nature of the Christian dimension in Christian Communitarianism.

Dargan (1992) has given an account of the first three decades of CMRS up to the 1990s. The CMRS had its origins in the pre-Vatican II 1950s with the organisation of male and female religious in the form of a conference in which 208 religious superiors were represented. He describes the early years of the conference as one of 'opening windows, with religious orders and congregations becoming aware of the world about them from a new perspective, becoming aware of each other and of the need to break out of their cocoons ... to see themselves more clearly as part of the church, the people of God'. The 1960s he regarded as a period of 'internal renewal and connection making'. The 1970s saw a 'corporate reading of the "sign of the times" in the light of the gospel' which drew religious closer to the formulation of policy but did so 'without formal overall vision'.

An example of the support structures promoted by the CMRS that might have been expected to assist with the formulation of this vision can be gleaned from their publication, *Ireland Today. Reflecting in the Light of the Gospel* (Healy and Reynolds, 1985). The approach is hesitant and concerned not to impose or prescribe. The authors describe the analysis as their own and not necessarily that of the Conference. They take their cue from the apostolic letter *Octogesima Adveniens* which urges 'Christian communities to analyse with objectivity the situation which is proper to their own country, to shed on it the light of the Gospel's unalterable word and to draw principles of reflection, norms of judgement and directives for action from the social teaching of the Church'. To this end, it gives an outline of aspects of Irish society from historical, economic, political and sociological perspectives which draws attention to issues such as tradition, identity, heritage and, in particular, provides an outline of inequalities and disparities in the distribution of income and in the political decision-making process. It then proceeds, in the spirit of *Octogesima Adveniens* to shed light on this reality by drawing on scriptural themes, which it feels resonate with these features of Irish life. In inviting reflection on Irish social reality in the light of scripture, the authors are careful to respect the process of personal and collective reflection and interpretation. They stress that the material they present is not exhaustive: 'no judgements are made on the present social reality. No conclusions are drawn. In line with our philosophy and methodology we do not give answers or directives.' Nonetheless, they believe that such reflection on the social reality of Irish life in the light of the gospel will 'challenge people to action' and to the formulation of 'an alternative vision of what Irish society could become' (p. 10).

At the 1986 Annual General Meeting of CMRS a common mission incorporating principles of justice, standing with the poor and social solidarity was agreed. Formal policy was articulated, and the orientation of the Justice Commission that had been formed in 1981, along with the other Commissions including Education which had been in place since the 1970s, was more clearly focused. This is the background to the point from which the contribution to paradigm formation by the Education Commission of the CMRS/CORI can be tracked.

The communitarian principles of interdependency, communalism and the primacy of the common good, proclaimed in the advocacy of Local Education Committees, recur in the discourse of the Educational Commission of CMRS/CORI. In this, their understanding of society and its appropriate development is shared with the political and sociological strands of the broad communitarian movement as it is known internationally. What distinguishes the communitarianism of CMRS/CORI as Christian is its philosophical location within the Judaeo-Christian tradition. It is to the sacred texts of this tradition and the more contemporary statements in Roman Catholic social thinking that the Education Commission turns in legitimating and communicating its understanding of its mission in the world and the values and priorities that characterise it.

The Education Commission describes its educational philosophy as 'inspired by the teaching and practice of Jesus, which … offers a genuine path to human growth and maturity'. This serves to realise a number of themes that systematically recur in the discourse of the Education Commission. Such a theme stresses its holistic view of the person and the need for education, accordingly, to take account of that wholeness. Brennan, in a contribution to *Staff Meeting Reflections. New syllabi, New learning?* (Brennan *et al.*, 1989), has elaborated on this understanding of being a person in the world and what the characteristics of an educational process based on this understanding might be. She identifies three features: the intergration of knowing and doing, the intergration of feeling, imagination and thought, and an intergration of the I and the We of culture and community. In elaborating on these she draws on the writings of Freire, Kolb, Ricoeur and Buber. On the intergration of knowing and doing she uses Freire's concept of praxis as 'the unity between practice and theory in which both are constructed, shaped and reshaped in constant movement from practice to theory, then back to new practice'. Thus, she sees knowledge as being developed through a process of reflecting on experience rather than through the transmission of the concepts contained in the syllabus. This latter approach she associates with the traditional educational separation of knowing and doing in which learning is seen to be a matter of transmitting ideas from teacher to taught. On the integration of feeling, imagination and thought, she draws on studies of experiential learning which stress the complementary nature of verbal and abstract modes of learning and those that are non-verbal and intuitive, and that 'concepts are developed not merely at the level of abstract thought but rather in a back and forth movement between action, images, narrative and concepts'.

The integration of the I into the We of community is developed through common action and common experience and through co-operative learning and participatory decision-making. It is realised when 'teachers and adult learners (while not ceasing to be professionals and specialists) provide models and opportunities for young people to learn to work and interact in a variety of roles: friend, peer, world citizen, employee', and 'when the past and future become truly ours: the past through an appropriation of our cultural heritage, the future through social responsibility for those yet unborn'.

Another theme that is drawn from and validated within the Judaeo-Christian tradition is the special concern for those who are poor, disadvantaged or suffering injustices. The psalms are quoted to this effect:

> Yahweh restores sight to the blind,
> Yahweh straightens the bent,
> Yahweh protects the stranger,
> He keeps the orphan and widow. (Psalms V.145)

So also is the New Testament where Jesus proclaims that the Christian message is:

> ... to bring the good news to the poor,
> to proclaim liberty to captives,
> and to the blind new sight,
> to set the down-trodden free. (Luke 4:8)

From this it is concluded that 'it seems clear that bringing the good news is about liberating poor people' (CORI, 1999). This is reflected in the vision statement of the Education Commission which states that, like the whole Conference, it 'stands with poor people and evaluates its orientations and formulates its policies and strategies from that perspective' (e.g. CORI, 1998b). This 'option for the poor', a common principle in post-Vatican II church teaching (Dorr, 1992), is thematised by the Education Commission by reference to contemporary church statements, not in terms of charity or remediation but rather as the obligation to 'address the structural causes of poverty and (to) take account of the collective advancement/development of peoples as well as their individual development'. Accordingly, education is cast as having a transformative potential, and the Education Commission commits itself to 'promoting genuine Christian education that is concerned with harmonious development of persons and the transformation of society' (CORI, 1999). The following extract from *Social Transformation and Lifelong Learning. Towards Policy on Adult and Community Education* (CORI, 1999, p. i) provides a comprehensive definition of Christian Communitarianism:

> The (education) commission is working on the basis of the holistic understanding of the human person. Education is thus seen as an effort to synthesise all aspects of human development – including the spiritual dimension – in an integrated and harmonious manner. Education also seeks to promote harmony and right relationships among people, God and the whole of creation. Humans must learn to live in harmony with the communities and the society of which they are a part. More importantly they must learn to become active agents in the development of these communities and of society. This means the ability to encounter others in their own otherness and not just as beings to be used and manipulated for oneself.

In summary, a number of specific themes follow from this understanding of people and their world in terms of the Christian tradition that systematically occur in the discourse of the Education Commission as it seeks to shape educational debate, participate in discussion and respond to issues and proposals. These include:

- the impact of educational practices and proposals on the life-world of those who are socially and economically disadvantaged
- unjust structures, as distinct from individual experiences, which maintain inequality
- social transformation through the empowerment of people, individually and collectively, within their community as a means of combating these unequal structures
- understanding the human person in an holistic manner with spiritual, cultural, affective, economic and political dimensions
- interdependence and the common good.

The textualisation of these themes, albeit in an uneven fashion, takes the form of a largely performative discourse. This constitutes the predominant substance of the body of knowledge produced by the Educational Commission. It is by this means that Christian Communitariansm experiences ideational expansion as a policy paradigm throughout the educational processes of society. But its nature as discourse and text also helps to explain its capacity for social expansion in the manner in which it facilitates the membershipping of others, both religious and secular. The detail of this body of knowledge is outlined here.

The Interests of the Disadvantaged

The most recognisable feature of the Education Commission's discourse on education is the manner in which it seeks to assess educational practice and policy proposals in terms of their likely impact on the life-world of those who are socially and economically disadvantaged. This has taken the form of dedicated publications dealing with educational experience in terms of inequality, disadvantage and poverty (CMRS, 1988, 1989a, 1992c; CORI, 1998b). More specifically, highlighting the interests of the poor and disadvantaged in educational practice and policy has realised a common set of themes that include committing education as an agent of social change (CMRS, 1989b; CORI, 1999); asserting the role of poverty in early leaving (CMRS, 1991c), educational under-achievement (CMRS, 1992c) and non-participation in third-level education (CORI, 1998a); the advocacy of lifelong learning for certification and social transformation (CORI, 1999); the representation of the disadvantaged on educational bodies, boards and committees (CMRS, 1993a); and the criticism of educational committees for their perceived lack of attention to inequality and disadvantage (CMRS, 1993b). Selection processes within education have been a common target for textualising the violation of the interests of the disadvantaged in education. These include school placement from the point of transition from primary to post-primary schooling, allocation to teaching groups differentiated in terms of some estimate of ability or attainment, the formal structures of assessment for the purpose of certifying educational attainment, and schemes such as the points system used to allocate places in third-level institutions.

In *Inequality in Schooling in Ireland: The Role of Selective Entry and Placement* (CMRS, 1989a) the extent to with children from different levels of the ability distribution and from different social backgrounds tend to find themselves with those who are similar to them in background and ability in different schools and, within schools, in different classes is documented. As well as being socially divisive, it is argued that this results in a widening of the gap in educational attainment which has the effect of worsening the plight of those who are already disadvantaged. A number of suggestions are made for the amelioration of these negative consequences such as the allocation of greater resources to those in the lower groupings. Overall, however, the thrust of this position paper is that homogeneous grouping needs to be confronted as an educational practice. It recommends the phasing out of streaming procedures, support for mixed-ability teaching, and the recognition in curriculum and examination reviews of the implications of the growing diversity of needs and aptitudes in post-primary schools. It urges school authorities in each area to come together to discuss the coordination of their respective admission policies with a view to investigating 'how they can jointly provide the best education for all the children of an area' (p. 26). To this end, they are encouraged to clarify the essential features of their provision so as to enable parents to make suitable decisions in selecting a post-primary school for their children. The position paper asserts 'the desirability of all schools catering for and welcoming the full range of student backgrounds and abilities and of avoiding practices which segregate students after they have been admitted' (p. 19).

These performatives are developed in the light of earlier empirical descriptions of the distribution of pupils of different attainment and background in different schools (CMRS, 1988). Here, also, and in later documents (CMRS, 1992c), we find the related concern with what is regarded as the undue competitiveness of the Irish educational system and the manner in which it is considered to consolidate disadvantage. Subsequently, in its response to the 1992 Green Paper on Education, (CMRS, 1993b), the Education Commission endorsed its suggestion that, to be eligible for state assistance, the admission policies of secondary schools should not discriminate on the basis of means, educational level or social background, and that provision should be made for a wide range of subject interests and ability levels.

The Education Commission had early and consistently expressed concern about selection and certification procedures at second level and, specifically, about the undue influence exerted by third-level entry requirements on post-primary schooling in terms of what was taught and how it was assessed (e.g. CMRS, 1989a, 1991a). In a conference organised by CORI on the topic of

Equality in Education. The Role of Assessment and Certification (CORI, 1998b) the Education Commission's position on the topic was set out by McCormack and Archer (1998). They regretted the absence of debate on what they suspected as a bias in favour of middle-class students in public examinations. They pointed to the greater capacity of middle-class families to negotiate the complexities of the assessment system. They were critical of how current assessment practices provide few, if any, opportunities for young people with leadership, cooperative or interpersonal skills to display their talents. They concluded that assessment and certification procedures were far from neutral and they regarded them as a contributory factor in early school leaving: 'The present system reinforces and accentuates the strong academic bias in second-level schooling … and it quickly becomes clear to students who are not strong academically, that their chances of experiencing success in this environment are limited.'

When the Commission on the Points System was established in 1997, the Education Commission's detailed consideration of the issue of third-level selection strategies gave special attention to the implications for those pupils who were less successful in the existing system and underrepresented in third-level institutions. In *The Points System. An Analysis and Review of some Alternatives* (CORI, 1998a) it makes a number of recommendations for action on third-level admission procedures. These include placing less reliance on Leaving Certificate results, increasing the number and variety of special access programmes, rationalising the colleges' approaches to special access, the accreditation of prior learning, a willingness to accept new forms of assessment, and a common policy on PLCs as an alternative pathway into higher education. It specifically recommended a new pathways pilot project for young people from disadvantaged backgrounds in which there would be a special allocation of 1,500 third-level places for such pupils who had successfully completed a third-level preparatory programme. It also recommended that the suggestion that there was a particularly high drop-out rate among students from disadvantaged backgrounds in third-level institutions be investigated.

In this manner we can see how the Education Commission, in seeking to consider the interests of the disadvantaged in the operation of patterns of assessment and selection, ideationally expands its text to engage the implications for such pupils of what constitutes appropriate school knowledge, its nature and value stratification at all levels and points of transition within the educational system.

Unjust Structures

The structural basis of inequality is regularly reaffirmed as a theme. This is represented as stratification based on the nature of paid employment, the associated differential valuing of varieties of knowledge and skill, and variations in wealth, privilege and power (CORI, 1998a, 1998b). Material poverty is given priority over issues of gender, ethnicity, special needs or disability (CORI, 1993b). Apart from this there is no elaboration on the structural dimension of inequality *per se*. Nor is it a social class analysis. In asserting the necessity for a 'greater equalisation of wealth, power and privilege in society' (CORI, 1998a, p. 45), it does not describe its position as egalitarianism. Apart from finding existing disparities in wealth and power unacceptable, it does not specify what degree of variation, if any, in this regard would be consistent with a just society. Elsewhere, the elimination of poverty is seen to require that society as a whole would begin 'to adopt or at least debate some aspects of an alternative vision of society' (McCormack and Archer, 1998). Nonetheless, it does describe the change that it is calling for as radical (CORI, 1997c, 1998a). Overall, the Education Commission does not address structure as a sociological issue, considering, for example its relationship with human agency or how it might be differentiated from the institutionalisation of practices and behaviours. The elaboration of the theme of unjust social structures requiring dismantling for the advancement of a just society takes the form of a number of strands of textualisation. These include pointing to the need for social change, and not educational change alone, distinguishing between individual and collective benefits of education, and specifying what distinct contributions schools and teachers might make to social change.

The Education Commission repeatedly calls for social change alongside educational change. In its response to the Green Paper on Education (CMRS, 1993b), the Education Commission warned that 'Education itself cannot be left to carry the burden of social change. If so, it will undoubtedly fail. Education can only be used successfully as a tool for social change when it is part of a wider and obvious movement by society as a whole to implement the same goals as those espoused by the education system' (p. 15). Yet, it equally reminds schools and teachers that confronting inequality requires more than helping disadvantaged pupils to perform better at school, achieve certification and gain paid employment. In setting out its educational philosophy in a publication aimed at influencing the agenda for the debate leading to an Education Act, it argued that 'debate about the purposes of education should not, in our view, be confined to considerations of individual advancement. The debate should also focus on the concept of collective advancement' (CMRS, 1991c, p. 4). It acknowledges the validity of mainstream and traditional educational aims such as those of cultural transmission, vocational preparation and personal improvement and advancement. However, it contends that 'education which seeks to promote the development of persons, communities and society is about much more than the provision of skills, knowledge and a sense of citizenship to individuals. It is also about the capacity to analyse and question the norms of society. The capacity for critical reflection … is essential if people are to be enabled to act collectively for justice in communities and in society' (p. 4). This aspiration of cultivating solidarity, co-responsibility and a commitment to the common good rather than sectoral interest among pupils is repeated in the discourse of the Education Commission. It also urges those in education to challenge the dominance of academic knowledge in the curriculum as well as in the selection process for third-level education, and to question the status differentials to be found within varieties of higher and post-Leaving Certificate education (McCormack and Archer, 1998; CORI, 1998a).

There is a further elaboration on how the educational system might contribute to collective advancement in the Education Commission's treatment of 'trail-blazing' educational initiatives, so described because of their pioneering efforts to give practical effect to a different vision of society (CORI, 1997c). It warns against confining oneself to simply 'doing good work' and, in taking the example of a programme for young people at risk of dropping out, it cautions against being satisfied with increased retention rates in the target schools. Rather, it urges that programmes 'would want to ensure that the assumptions, underlying a system that excludes young people, are challenged and that the lessons learnt in the initiative had a wider impact. Thus "Good Practice" developed would need to be disseminated and the implications for what happens in schools and in the system, as a whole, would need to be teased out' (p. 47). Similarly, it warns that not all such projects are counter-cultural and it goes on to specify some of the criteria of counter-cultural work in education. These include incorporating forms of education that are empowering, decision-making structures that involve the principles of partnership and participative democracy, enabling the participants to link local problems to broader socio-economic and political structures, and through modelling good practice and networking to facilitate connections with other programmes and with public policy. In concluding that it is difficult to meet these criteria within the confines of conventional schooling, and that such trail-blazing, counter-cultural initiatives are more likely to be concerned with community education, the Education Commission is engaging with its proposals on education for social transformation of which the conventional educational system would be one among a number of sectors. This will be discussed below. In the meantime, this textualisation of the role of education in confronting unjust social structures needs to be acknowledged.

Social Transformation through Community Education

As well as contending that schools should provide for more than the education of individuals, the Education Commission, from its earliest discourse and activities, advanced the proposition that education was not confined to schooling.

Previously, in Catholic social teaching of the pre-Vatican II era, particularly in how it was mediated in Ireland, this proposition would have been conceptualised in terms of the family, stressing its priority and autonomy as the first educator, and in terms of vocational/Catholic organisations and their charitable and social improvement projects. The principle of subsidiarity would have been invoked in defending both lower-order institutions against what was perceived as the potential encroachment of the state. The conference on 'Education for Family and Community Development' organised by the Education Commission in 1989, and published under that title later that year (CMRS, 1989b), signals a transition to a reconceptualisation of the collective dimension of social life in terms of the community rather than the parish, and to a view of social change that demanded a more radical and transformative rather than a remedial or compensatory approach. In McCormack's (1989) presentation at the conference, this transition is advocated in a textualisation that identifies the weaknesses of remedial and compensatory intervention strategies drawing on the social science literature of the era. These include the dominance of professionals and the cultivation of dependency among those defined as 'clients', *ad hoc* coping responses and measures, narrow understanding of the family as a unit of intervention, deficit assumptions of disadvantaged people and areas, and individualistic understandings of improvement and advancement. McCormack proposed a participatory approach which she described as having as its social purpose 'the empowerment of people and communities to shape their own situation and that of a future society'. The understanding of learning in this approach provides the core of what came to be proclaimed over the following decade as community education for social transformation.

> Here education occurs in the context of community development and social action which aim ultimately at creating structural and social change. In this sense the learning is essentially community-based and has political aims. These political aims are guided by the over-all principle of justice. They include the mobilisation of people to analyse their own needs as a community, to identify the structural causes at both local and societal levels which contribute to the community's problems and to devise action strategies at the appropriate levels in order to alleviate these problems.

As well as these themes of community-based learning, political aims, the empowerment of people, and social and political action, she goes on to emphasise the nature of the change for professionals and for the medium and focus of intervention. A participatory approach is described as 'one of working "with" rather than "for" people. The necessary skills and social tools are acquired in the context of the work itself … people learn to develop a deeper analysis of their situation, grow in self-esteem and confidence and begin to take more control over their lives. Families and communities are no longer the objects of professional intervention. Rather, a transaction between equals – people and professionals – is established in order to reach shared goals and to promote the development of complementary roles. Partnership, collaboration, networking are essential principles on which progress is built.' As for the associative level of social engagement and action, 'the characteristic style of the participatory approach is through small group, community groupings, regional and national networks rather than through bureaucratic processes or institutional procedures.' These themes are reaffirmed, expanded and more intensified than is usual in the textualisation of community education in a series of subsequent publications throughout the 1990s.

In an attempt to influence the agenda of the debate prior to the publication of the 1992 Green Paper on Education, the Education Commission called for greater prominence to be given to community education as understood in terms of collective as well as individual advancement, as a strategy in combating poverty, and in which schools cultivated communal values and acted in partnership with their communities (CMRS, 1991c). A year later in *Education and Poverty* (CMRS, 1992c) which sought to break the link between educational achievement and poverty, it proposed approaches from community education such as parental involvement, school-community linkages, interagency cooperation and community-originated social action, and outlined some of the empirical research evidence in support of the effectiveness of these approaches in combating disadvantage. A feature of this discourse is its construction of dualisms which allowed it to signify what it understood as partnership, participation, cooperation etc. by identifying what these are not, what they differ from, and what are their opposites. This specification of meaning by denial and exclusion is further grounded in reality by illuminations from programmes in the US, the UK and Ireland. This produces a more discriminating discourse, the effect of which is to strengthen the framing of what is and what is not understood or meant.

With the publication of the 1992 Green Paper on Education, and its offering of a specific text on community education, the Education Commission's discourse becomes more systematically oppositional (CMRS, 1993b). While acknowledging progress in advancing the standing of community education, it assesses its textualisation in the Green Paper as one of its 'most disappointing features' (p. 28). Proposals relating to home-school community links, making school facilities available to the community and second-chance education are applauded. This affirmation includes them within the performatives of community education as understood by the Education Commission. But it also highlights what in its view are omissions and deficiencies in the Green Paper's textualisation of community education as reflected in its conceptualisation and performatives. There are criticisms of the failure of the Green Paper to recognise the importance of the wider community, and not just parents, as a partner in all aspects of the life of the school including policy making, in its proposals relating to boards of management, and in the Green Paper's rejection of a local education structure. In having a text that it can judge to be an incomplete and partial understanding of community education, the Education Commission's communication of meaning in this regard improves in discrimination and specificity.

The Education Commission's developing text on community education is further elaborated in *Religious Congregations in Irish Education. A Role for the Future?* (CORI, 1997c) and, particularly and most extensively, in *Social Transformation and Lifelong Learning* (CORI, 1999). In this latter publication the Education Commission uses the 1998 Green Paper *Adult Education in an Era of Lifelong Learning* to continue its tactic of using a government publication as a foil for the construction and intensification of what it wishes to be meant by community education. When the Education Commission acknowledges the prominence given by the Adult Education Green Paper to participatory democracy, civil society and combating poverty, but criticises it for not reflecting these concerns in specific policy proposals, the Education Commission is participating in the negotiation of meaning. This instance of semantic positioning takes the form of asserting the inadequacy of merely allowing for the thematisation of these concerns in one's discourse without their subsequent textualisation in a form that yields performatives. But, as well as being critical of state textualisation for failing to follow up, in terms of recommendations for action, on declarations of support for specific ideas, we find new dimensions of community education being articulated in both of these CORI publications which in some instances avail of the semantic uncertainty and the subsequent definitional space provided by this act of contestation. These include civil society, co-optation, radical edge, the changing nature of work, counter-cultural critique, community education as an approach as well as a sector, and, though it is not named as such, andragogy. A further feature of this discourse which promotes the intensification of its text is its qualitative calibration of key themes through the setting out of criteria and specifications which are deemed to characterise community education and counter-cultural projects. In this manner, knowledge about community education is progressively driven forward by affirmation, denial, and exclusion, through expansion across educational practices and sites, and through a normalisation of what constitutes its policy applications.

Holistic Understanding of the Person

As we have seen earlier, the Education Commission describes the implications for a philosophy of education that follows from an holistic understanding of the human person. These include seeking to synthesise all aspects of human

which they belong' (CORI, 1997c, p. 38). It also requires that in acknowledging the 'systemic wholeness' and 'interdependence' of all parts of society, responsibility has to be taken for the impact that decisions concerning one part of an increasingly global society might have on another (CORI, 1999, p. 2). Interdependence and the common good experience the least textualisation of all the themes generated by the Education Commission. There is little by way of the implications for practice. In consequence, there is an absence of performatives or efforts to expand its dominion throughout the different spheres of education. Routinely, the Education Commission considers interdependence in the context of its advocacy of a wider participation in decision-making and of a community education approach to countering injustices in society. When it argues that greater participation and community involvement can be justified on other bases besides those of facilitating social transformation, it appeals to those of democratic rights and values (CORI, 1992c). While these can be consistent, even sympathetic, to communitarian values, they can also lean in the direction of individual rights and freedoms rather than the obligations of people to one another guided by the principle of advancing the common good. This adverts to the difference between arguing for a wider participation in educational decision-making as an expression of one's entitlement to have one's interests and positions proclaimed and heard, as distinct from engaging in the decision-making process in pursuit of supra-individual/sectional interests such as the common good.

Clear expressions of interdependency, as a moral obligation as distinct from an empirical sociological observation, are to be found in the Education Commission's aspiration to cultivate ecological balance and social solidarity through the direct promotion of the common good by a participative government (CORI, 1997c, 1999). There is also a recurring advocacy of a curriculum that cultivates communal values, and the rebuke that the 'competitiveness and individualism which characterise modern society have tended to subjugate communal and cooperative values' (CMRS, 1991c, p. 6). Similarly, reflecting its view of the systemic nature of society in the interdependence of its parts, the Education Commission is critical of the 'peculiarly detached view' taken by the Green Paper on Adult Education and its failure to stress the responsibilities of employers, trade unions and statutory agencies in the provision of adult learning opportunities (CORI, 1999, p. 9). Yet, the slippage in discourse from common good to sectional interests is difficult to avoid. This is the case even when the Education Commission is arguing for greater social power for those who are poor (CORI, 1997c), the involvement of parents in the policy process, and not just as resources to be used by schools (CMRS, 1991b), and a dilution in the influence of economic interests on the formulation of educational policy (CMRS, 1993b; CORI, 1999). In such instances, the discourse accommodates the understanding that the conditions for fair decision-making exist when all interested parties are capable of making their case with equal clarity, force and access to the independent decision making of the state, i.e. a pluralist rather than a communitarian politics.

Discursive Features

The dominating feature of the Education Commission's discourse is its efforts to intervene in educational policy through the specification of correct and incorrect educational practices. As a form of discourse, it moves quickly to produce what has become a predominantly performative text. The consequence is a foregoing of intensification of its core theological/social/political position as evidenced by the paucity of its conceptual analysis, linguistic refinement, engagement with contestation and legitimation in this regard. Indeed, such distinction and differentiation is more to be found in its performatives, in its applications in educational practice. We have seen this in the processes of affirmation, denial and exclusion as the Education Commission sought to 'fix' the meaning of community education for social transformation. Other examples include the introduction of the theme of co-optation through state funding as a threat to the radical edge of community education (CORI, 1997c), and the differentiation between the meanings of parental participation in education – as a resource to be used by schools or as partners in the construction of policy (CMRS, 1993b). The performative emphasis is even more in focus in later publications of the Education Commission (CORI, 1999) and reflected in lengthy recommendations for educational practice in the light of its vision of education. As a consequence, Christian Communitarianism, considered as a policy paradigm in education, has developed through expansion across processes, dimensions and levels of education considered in its widest sense rather than through intensification – the 'filling in' of the theoretical, conceptual and empirical detail of its guiding rationale and orientation to action.

As a discourse of assertion and advocacy, expressions of doubt, hesitancy, and expectations of difficulty or resistance are rare. The exceptions stand out. These include the acknowledgement of difficulties such as localism, failing to address developmental needs of individuals, and the absence of structures in community education contributing to a dissipation of energy (McCormack, 1989); uncertainty about the additive nature of the impact of parental and community participation in schools on educational achievement, and about the relative significance of characteristics of effective schools (CMRS, 1992c); identifying and engaging with possible objections to the partnership approach to combating educational disadvantage (CMRS, 1992c); questioning Boldt's inference that increased participation to Leaving Certificate level during the 1990s resulted in lower Leaving Certificate performance during that period (McCormack and Archer, 1998); and, relevant to the absence of intensification, recognising that despite advances in the application of theology to social change 'the theology of the alternative vision (the New Reign of God) is still poorly developed' (CORI, 1997c, p. 39).

Surprisingly absent as an impetus to intensification is any engagement with the international debate on communitarianism, and in particular with the criticisms it has evoked. Apart from the feminist suspicion that it ignores gender inequalities, a lack of clarity as to the parameters of community and the role of critique mentioned earlier, these criticisms include the fear of an overemphasis on obligation at the expense of personal rights, the exclusion implicit in the specification of community membership, lack of recognition of difference and the overall suspicion that it is no more than an ill-judged nostalgia for pre-modern living, a disguise for new forms of conservatism and an effort to re-establish traditional authorities. The failure of the Education Commission to address these concerns reflects the advocacy and proclamatory nature of its discourse. It is not meant as an academic exercise. Rather, it is political action to shape the subjectivities of people and the practices of the educational system. Because of this, in the absence of a counter text, there is no obvious reason for it to mount a defence by means of a justification of its position. Its experience of expansion, both of ideas and people, rather than intensification can be understood as a consequence of the political task it has set for itself.

Significant in this regard is the use of variegated discourse in the publications of the Education Commission. This developed throughout the 1990s, and is particularly pronounced in its consideration of the future role of religious congregations in Irish education (CORI, 1997c) and on the transformative potential of lifelong learning (CORI, 1999). Variegated discourse is produced when a text is reconstructed utilising different strategies of signification from the original but without any alteration to its meaning. Variegated discourse operates to counter the threat to persuasive communication posed by the proclamation and advocacy of uncompromising and unqualified principles such as giving primacy to the perspective of the disadvantaged, the use of education for social change, holism and interdependency. Once its initial sloganising power fades, persisting with a simple (as distinct from intense) text is likely to diminish its impact. It can appear as the same people saying the same thing using the same language. In fact, there is a considerable amount of repetition across the publications of the Education Commission in the form of paraphrasing or direct reproduction from earlier publications. This variety introduced in the Education Commission's discourse can be found in its language, imagery, textualisation, intertextuality and authorities.

The expanding vocabulary used by the Education Commission to realise its key concepts functions to confirm rather than extend existing meanings. While words like collaborative, collegial and cooperative have the capacity to signify difference and to establish graduation and variation in meaning, they are used to reproduce the dualisms – individual/collective, holistic/fragmented etc – of the text into which they are introduced. The effect is rhetorical: in this process, words are deprived of their capacity to signify a complex array of meanings. Similarly, a sociological world of good and evil forces is reproduced by an expanding repertoire of images – confronting bureaucracy, developing schools, resisting the threat of co-optation and refusing to compromise – all oppositional, evoking a will to action and a David and Goliath morality. A wider range of geographical and cultural contexts are introduced to illuminate the social and educational arrangements the Education Commission wishes to advocate. The insertion of details of community development projects, home/school schemes and school innovations from England, Scotland and the US into the text contributes to its performativity, and establishes its principles as practical, workable and enjoying wide credibility. The texts – community education, parent-school collaboration, sustainable development and school development – that conceptually support these projects are woven into the Education Commission's text with minimal independent impact on its meanings, in effect co-opting them as cultural resources. In this process, new authorities – Jackson, Lovett, Mayo, Kirby, the OECD – are appropriated along with their secular texts to add to those from its Christian tradition with the effect of diversifying its legitimating resources beyond its religious heritage.

Indeed, in discussing leadership strategies within congregations, the Education Commission (1997c, p. 63) speaks of the need 'to create images of an alternative which inspire and energise people to change' and goes on to quote Tsun-Yan Hsieh:

> What matters in making change happen is translating the central idea in a vision into key themes – memorable, meaningful and galvanising words and phrases – that will excite others to act quickly. This simple but distinctive language must capture the essence of what its vision compels an organisation to do differently … these themes capture 'what's new' at the heart of a vision.

In the light of its use of variegated discourse, it can be argued that the Education Commission already embodies this advice on the role of key signifiers in text construction as well as the need for their regular refurbishment and revivification.

Whether operating by individual design or structural force, a consequence of this tactic of communicating the Education Commission's vision is that it publicly creates it in an untheorised form. However, the fact that proclamation of principles quickly gives way to specification of correct educational practice, with little by way of intensification through the elaboration, justification, or extension of its guiding principles is deceptive. The Education Commission may have constructed a policy paradigm that was presented as conceptually simple but it has within the church, in the form of its teaching and individual scholarship, a vast resource that is available for clarification or legitimation without going beyond such topics as justice and inequality (Dorr, 1992) or culture and education (Gallagher, 1997) that are immediately relevant to its educational project. This is a latent resource by way of texts and intellectuals that is rarely mentioned by the Education Commission. Nonetheless, this field of knowledge is there to be appropriated, as happens occasionally: using Gallagher's process of cultural discernment to refine its concepts (CORI, 1997c); as a feature of its variegated discourse; or in the form of major spectacles such as conferences (CMRS, 1991d). This is a reflection of the network of associative forms that the intersubjectivity of Christian Communitarianism takes.

Associative Forms

At its most general, Christian Communitarianism is a shared meaning of those of similar religious beliefs. As such, they identify with the Christian religions and with those within the broad Judaeo-Christian tradition. Whatever differences in understanding or prescription in relation to education and society might exist within this collectivity, it remains a defining basis of commonality for its members which acknowledges the key similarities in worldview, and a predictability in the parameters of meaning and understanding that they bring to the interpretation of more specific social issues. By virtue of their religious identity there is an existing doxic basis for understanding and action. The Christian Communitarianism of CORI exists within the associative form of the Roman Catholic Church with its global bureaucratic structures and mechanisms for knowledge production and the establishment of orthodoxy. Christian Communitarianism may also be considered as part of the more diffuse social movement of communitarianism. The Education Commission is thus positioned at the intersection of church and social movement and can be regarded as a social movement organisation with its goal-directed formal organisation of offices and roles. It, in turn, is made up of other organisations in the form of its congregational members. The intensity and intimacy of primary association is reached at the level of religious communities, be they in the form of traditional convents and monasteries or single housing units.

The intersection and variety of the associative forms, in which those for whom Christian Communitarism is a meaningful basis for understanding and action find themselves, produces its own tensions. It would be wrong to regard all those within the Judaeo-Christian tradition or within the communitarian movement as being of one mind on religion and politics respectively. At all associative levels, Christian Communitarian subjectivities will constitute individual identities to varying degrees. For CORI, having organisations in the form of its congregational members within its own organisation raises problems with the degree of 'coupling' between its parts. Dargan (1992) has identified some of these features. These include the prior commitment of conference members to their own congregations, the transitional nature of membership of executives, working parties and commissions, and the fact that the member organisations of the conference are to a large extent autonomous and in no way bound by its decisions. The Education Commission has also identified discontinuities between the transformative innovations of individual religious and the corporate response of their congregations. It contends that while congregations are often supportive of such innovations 'it is not a sufficient indication of the congregation taking corporate ownership of the work or of the work becoming a fully integrated part of the congregation's overall mission' (CORI, 1997c, p. 57). Nor does a collective religious membership guarantee a homogenous policy response, as indicated by the tensions between the CMRS and the CMCSS, representing the secondary school managers, on the Education Commission's recommendations on abolishing selective entrance tests for secondary schools and on its endorsement of local education committees (Walshe, 1999).

The benefits for Christian Communitarianism in having an organisational base are spelled out by Dargan. Speaking of the CMRS in the totality of its activities, including those relating to education, he describes it as 'one clear voice among many and its aim is to bring about a more equitable society where no one is in want. Whether the conference speaks about unemployment, poverty, education, primary healthcare, evangelisation or the quality of life of members, the perspective is the same' (Dargan, 1992). But the associative forms through which Christian Communitarianism exists as a social phenomenon contribute more than a coherence in the public representation of its position. More fundamental to the existence of Christian Communitarianism as a policy paradigm is the viability of its social system. Though far from being homogeneous, Christian Communitarianism extends the plausibility structures grounded in a common religious world view that forms the cultural, conceptual, discursive and normative basis for meaningful social action and interaction. The fact that this interaction can be experienced at intimate, collective, bureaucratic and global levels, because of the variety of its associative forms, enhances its capacity for 'reality maintenance' among its members, ensuring in the words of Berger and Luckmann (1967, p. 167) 'a measure of symmetry between objective and subjective reality' for them. In this manner, Christian Communitarianism achieves the sanction of a viable social system. Through its continued existence, it experiences reification. Or to paraphrase Weber, the longer a view of life survives as a basis for social interaction the greater will be its legitimacy.

Membershipping and Subjectivities

For any group, its definition of the world is rarely without some forces of instability. Even when a belief system such as that of Christianity is accorded a doxic status among a collectivity of people, the implications that are drawn from its tenets for social practice may vary. Not all may feel, for instance, that poverty and disadvantage should have the primacy that Christian Communitarianism accords to them. And even if they agree that these constitute major social evils that Christian society should seek to eradicate, they may nonetheless differ in how the social and economic conditions are to be conceptualised and what the most appropriate policy response should be. CORI, as a formal organisation with its dedicated Education Commission, acts as a powerful definitional, interpretive and interpellative force in this regard. Its capacity for naming aspects of the educational process in terms of its interpretation of the Christian tradition both produces a consistent text for a Christian critique of educational policy and practice and draws those within the collectivity of Christianity into its use. This occurs through prior consultation with the religious involved in the particular aspect of education under consideration and through the systematic formulation and dissemination of its interpretations and prescriptions. The Education Commission's response to the Green Paper *Education for a Changing World* (1992) provides an example of the systematic nature of its knowledge production and interpellation of subjectivities. These include the following, in its own account of its response (CMRS, 1993b):

- *Towards An Agenda for the Debate on an Education Act* (CMRS, 1991c) was published shortly after it was announced that there was to be a Green Paper.
- Following the publication of the introduction to the Green Paper the *Initial Response to the Introduction to the Green Paper on Education* was issued (CMRS, 1992a).
- Within a few months of the publication of the full Green Paper in June 1992, *A Study Guide to the Green Paper on Education: Education for a Changing World* (CMRS, 1992b) was published.
- A section of a discussion paper entitled *Education and Poverty: Eliminating Disadvantage in the Primary School Years* (CMRS, 1992c), which had been in preparation, was rewritten in the light of some of the Green Paper's proposals.
- In 1993, the Commission published *Local Education Committees: A Case for their Establishment and a Tentative Proposal* (CMRS, 1993a) which dealt with one aspect of the Green Paper.

The Education Commission did not confine itself to knowledge production in its response to the Education Green Paper. Utilising the associative forms available to it within the CMRS, it drew others, in the first instance its members, into the Christian Communitarian text through the organisation of such events as the following:

- A special assembly of Major Religious Superiors was convened in October 1992 to discuss the Green Paper.

- Task forces were established by more that 60 religious congregations to deal with Green Paper issues, followed by a day conference for these groups organised by the Commission.
- Seminars were organised for CMRS Regional Associations and for individual congregations on the topic of 'Issues emerging from the Green Paper: Where do we stand?'
- Meetings were held with representatives of a number of organisations involved in Catholic Education.

In these social encounters, the Christian Communitarian text carries force and conviction. Its appeal to Christian texts and justice themes in church teaching highlights the shared normative base of the participants in Christianity. Their common beliefs about the world, the human person and values, and the authority of church documents provides the conditions for the successful interpellation of subjectivities.

As well as confirming its validity and constructing subjectivities among CORI members and otherwise sympathetic religious believers, the diverse associative forms which Christian Communitarian takes could be expected to enhance its capacity to extend its dominion. As a formal organisation with members throughout the country, CORI can claim a wide experiential base and argue for the validity of its propositions by claiming a privileged standpoint in knowing relevant aspects of the social world. The Education Commission (CORI, 1999, p. v) claims that 'because our members are living in 1,400 communities around Ireland we have first-hand experience of the relationship between education and poverty'. It points to the 'multiplicity of educational activities throughout the country' in which religious are involved and through which they work with individuals and groups at local level to improve the quality of their lives. CORI's religious members are represented as having a special capacity to understand and interpret the experiences of poor people.

As well as being a representative body, CORI is a social movement organisation which seeks to increase the visibility of its proposals, form alliances and generally insert itself into the state policy process. As well as organising conferences on topics relevant to its own mission, members of the Commission also participate in seminars organised by the major bodies involved in education. These are never represented as other than consensual encounters. In a brief mention of a conference organised in June 1998 in anticipation of the publication of the Adult Education Green Paper, a Professor of Social Inclusion is described as having delivered a 'very challenging keynote address' and an advisor on the Green and White papers is said to have responded to the discussions at the conference 'in a very thoughtful manner' (CORI, 1999, p. v). In the Education Commission's account of such interaction with those other than its members, dissent or disagreement of any variety, philosophical or pragmatic, do not routinely figure. While differences in perspective or emphasis are not explicitly excluded, the understanding is communicated that all are working from a common core of agreement.

As well as confirming its validity in constructing subjectivities among CORI members and otherwise receptive religious believers, the diverse associative forms which Christian Communitarianism takes could be expected to enhance its capacity to extend its dominion. The Education Commission is explicit in proclaiming its association with others beside the CORI membership: 'The Commission recognises that there are many who share with it values such as equity and justice in education, but do not do so from a Catholic or Christian perspective. Therefore, while maintaining its commitment to Christian values, the Commission seeks to dialogue and collaborate with all who seek to promote education that improves the quality of life for everyone in society' (CMRS, 1993b, p. 1). In this the Commission is reaching out to include a wider range of people beyond the Christian collectivity which forms the core membership with which it can claim some form of association because of religious beliefs. In this appeal, the basis of interpellation is a secular one derived from assumptions of a shared vision of education as an agent in the construction of a just society.

A feature of the membershipping practices employed by the Education Commission is that they tend not to have attracted opposition from those who would see its initiatives as a more subtle maintenance of religious beliefs in the areas of social theory and action, representing a continuation of the influence of religious, but with a more acceptable face. There is evidence of this suspicion in the group discussion that followed the 1989 conference on Education for Family and Community Development (CMRS, 1989b). It was reported that 'some participants distrusted the involvement of religious and of the CMRS in Community Education' due to what was described as the 'power-hold' of the Church throughout Irish life and its contribution to powerlessness and exclusion among the same groups whose cause it was now seeking to champion. The question was posed: 'is the Church's interest in community education not an expression of its desire to maintain its "power-hold" over communities or to recover lost ground?' (pp 84-85). In the same year, similar expressions of 'general concern and some scepticism' about the role of the church in community development were reported at a representative and wide-ranging conference on community work in Ireland organised by the Combat Poverty Agency, the Community Workers' Cooperative, and the Community and Youth Work Courses at St Patrick's College, Maynooth. There was said to be 'general agreement that the huge increase in church involvement in community work needs to be questioned. What is their agenda? Who are individual priests and nuns answerable to? Who do they represent? What does the "option for the poor" mean?' (Clarke, 1990). Recalling her involvement in community work around this time, Byrne (1995) claimed that 'the agenda of the church was being pushed in women's community groups and not just by religious sisters', and interpreted the emphasis on class and poverty by religious in these settings as 'a deliberate ploy to prevent solidarity being built between women on issues of common interest' such as access to free contraception, sexual and physical violence, etc.

Almost a decade later the relationship between community education and evangelisation remained a concern for the Education Commission, and they suggested that 'religious may not have done enough to explain to those with whom they were working that they shared their goals and that there was no "hidden agenda"', and they go on to endorse the practice of 'negotiated entry' and 'planned withdrawal' (CORI, 1997c, pp 54-55). Yet, such questioning or resistance, for what it is, of the Education Commission's efforts in forming alliances and claiming association and shared membership with others could well have been expected to be more assertive and even virulent in the light of the clerical scandals and accusations of abuse and mistreatment of children at the hands of religious personnel in childcare institutions made public from that time (e.g. Doyle, 1988; Raftery and O'Sullivan, 1999; see also Fuller, 2004).

The relative absence of resistance to the Education Commission's efforts to reach out beyond its Christian collectivity, to claim and establish association with others on the basis of secular commitments, can be explained in terms of a number of features of these efforts at social reconfiguration. While the normative basis of Christian Communitarianism is to be found within Christian texts, these are appropriated hermeneutically. Unlike the theocentric paradigm, which provided an integrated network of eternal truths and consequential directions for action requiring belief and adherence, in Christian Communitarianism the Christian tradition presents itself as a cultural inheritance that invites interpretation. For Gadamer, one of the most influential writers on hermeneutical method, 'this means that one cannot speak of "right" or "correct" interpretation, since no two interpreters, or even a single interpreter at different times of her or his life will confront a given text from within exactly the same horizon. As our historical horizons shift (as they continually do), so will our understanding of the meaning of a given text' (Surber, 1998, p. 60). This approach to interpretation serves to affirm the validity of the Christian tradition. But it also foregrounds the agency of those who would make their own of it, creatively engaging with it in the light of their own imagination, biography and historical context. It is a relationship in which 'the interpreter questions and is questioned by the text and its author' with the purpose of 'subtly persuading the cultural expression to yield its fullest meaning' (Sica, 1988, p. 86). The role of hermeneutical method in disarming suspicion of Christian Communitarianism as a project of evangelisation is ironic in the light of historical responses to it. For materialists such as Feuerbach and Marx, hermeneutics was condemned not only for misrecognising the real sources of cultural and historical change but also 'as conduits by which all the old religious and political superstitions attacked by the Enlightenment might be reintroduced' (Surber, 1998, p. 10). Indeed, somewhat over a hundred years later, Habermas objected to Gadamer's 'rehabilitation of authority and tradition'; as Sica wryly remarked, 'a Marxist of the Frankfurt type could hardly ally himself with any theory that had already won acclaim among the clergy' (Sica, 1988, p. 88).

This emphasis on interpretation rather than dogma is confirmed in the deployment of church teaching by the Education Commission. Overall, religious conceptualisation, language and legitimation are subdued and are not routinely used to ground, explain and validate aspects of its communitarian position – interdependence, integrated development, anti-individualism, holistic under-standing of the person – as well as its commitment to the poor and disadvantaged and the creation of a society in which their needs and interests would be accommodated. The social teaching of the Church in the form of papal encyclicals, messages and addresses, Vatican documents and the extensive commentaries and debates that these have generated (Dorr, 1992) represent an underused resource. This rarely penetrates the Christian Communitarian text while nonetheless being in line with it in its key orientations in relation to social justice. The consequence is a Christian Communitarian text that can accommodate in its interpretation the segregation of the sacred and the secular. While its theology of social action is explicit, there is nothing that is distinctly theological in its performatives. In its actual proposals for action as distinct from their *raison d'être* there is no evidence of a theological dimension. Support for its performatives does not require assenting to its Christian belief and inspiration. The Education Commission anticipates that articulating 'the theology of the alternative vision (the New Reign of God) … will involve a radical re-examination of some of our most fundamental assumptions about concepts that are central to this paper – justice, empowerment, community and education (with and without the adjective "Catholic")' (CORI, 1997c, pp 39-40). Yet, the absence of such an exercise in the intensification of Christian Communitarianism as a policy paradigm facilitates the successful assertion of associative status with others outside of the Christian collectivity, and the formation of tactical alliances on the basis of shared performatives. The downside in its successful reaching out beyond its Christian collectivity for Christian Communitarianism is that it mutates/merges to a form that is best described as (Christian) Communitarianism, to indicate its existence as a cultural form that for some is engaged with independently of, and for others derived from, religious belief.

(Christian) Communitarianism

(Christian) Communitarianism is made possible by the affinity that exists between the text of Christian Communitarianism as a policy paradigm within the LEM domain and the loosely-framed policy paradigm that we have identified at the outset as communitarianism. In terms of the structuration of paradigms, it hinges on the flexible boundaries of the latter and the theological/secular mutations of the former. In merging, (Christian) Communitarianism accommodates the communitarian themes together with their textualisation identified earlier in this chapter and recognisable in EU policy, and in national and sub-national structures associated with economic and social improvement. Indeed, given the loosely-framed nature of this communitarian paradigm, such that it is, it might not experience as discordant a more vigorous and explicit positioning of Christianity within (Christian) Communitarianism, be it in the form of its concepts, authorities or legitimation, once it stopped short of constituting its performatives as confessionally distinctive.

The most expanded manifestation of communitarianism in Irish culture is the (Christian) Communitarianism of the LEM domain. CORI's Education Commission continues to be the key source of its production and articulation. Without it, it is unlikely that it would be viable to speak of communitarianism in Irish culture. But (Christian) Communitarianism does benefit from the constitution of subjectivities however tentative or fluid in loosely-framed communitarianism which provides it with a constituency, beyond the core of its Christian collectivity, amenable to membershipping. It could be expected that those subjectivities that engaged with or were constituted through the weaker version of communitarianism would find themselves drawn to (Christian) Communitarianism because of its greater coherence. This would follow a process of recognising in (Christian) Communitarianism an aspect of themselves that had previously been less sharply defined and named. In terms of the construct of interpellation, they could be expected to be predisposed to assenting to the invitation of self-definition involved in being hailed by its text.

This movement of members and processes of merging are implicated with framing. As there will be acts of self-recognition in merging, so also will there be instances of non-recognition, denial and refusal. In the normal event, this sharpening of boundary definitions could be expected to result in more socially-critical and conflict-based versions of community work setting themselves apart from (Christian) Communitarianism with the potential to socially and culturally develop or experience rupture or diffusion. There were clear indications of paradigmatic activity around these themes in the case of critical community work during the 1970s, and into the 1990s with social-class and feminist varieties of andragogy/gynagogy. Yet, while such understandings and identities relating to inequality and social action persist, they can experience co-optation, depletion and isolation through the existence of versions and practices such as integrated service provision for those 'at risk', gender equity (to be discussed in the next chapter), and tactical subjectivities, that are accommodating of the communitarian themes of inclusion and partnership.

The numbers involved in this constituency of potential members for (Christian) Communitarianism are significant. Not alone do they hold out the possibility of the quantitative expansion of (Christian) Communitarianism, their social and political location is such that they promise to strengthen its dominion. They are distributed throughout the country in a diversity of programmes involving the state, be it in the form of government departments, statutory agencies or corporate bodies, and community, local and voluntary groups. If we interpret it more broadly in terms of these partnership arrangements, the call to community workers in 1990 '... to come together with common strategies and approaches ... to develop networks and alliances ... to build a social movement' (Clarke, 1990) is well on its way to being realised. This is manifested in the level of collective self-awareness, mobilisation and formal organisation evidenced by the steady flow of publications, programmes, submissions and conferences emanating from this sector of social and political activity, only some of which have been drawn on earlier in this chapter or are involved with education (Powell and Geoghegan, 2004).

Sometimes referred to as the community movement or the voluntary/ community pillar of society, it can helpfully be structurally characterised in terms of the 'knowledge class' of which it is a part. This helps to explain the susceptibility of its members to (Christian) Communitarianism. By 'knowledge class' Berger is referring to those 'whose occupations deal with the production and distribution of symbolic knowledge' (1987, p. 66). These include those employed in the education system, the communications media, counselling and guidance and the 'bureaucratic agencies planning for the putative non-material needs of the society (from racial amity to geriatric recreation)' (p. 67). He describes the knowledge class as anti-capitalist and ideologically to the left of the old middle class. This is because their privilege is based on educational credentials, which makes them antagonistic to achievement through the capitalist market system, and also because of the fact that they depend substantially for their livelihood on 'government payrolls or subsidies' (p. 69). The knowledge class has 'an interest in the distributive machinery of government, as against the production system' (p. 69) and, accordingly, in holding the state responsible for supporting anti-poverty and counter-disadvantage initiatives.

Self selection for these careers together with the professional preparation for them is also relevant. Indeed, for many such workers the texts of social inclusion, community action and andragogy can be key sources in the constitution of their personal as well as their professional identity.

But for educational policy, as for politics in general, the dynamics of paradigm formation around communitarian themes did not end there. An analysis of its diagnosis of and prescriptions for social and educational problems reveals why (Christian) Communitarianism might appeal to, or, at the very least, be less likely to invite opposition, from the more advantaged general population. It can be understood as distributive, in the sense of seeking to improve the educability and employability of those who are poor or with minimal life chances, without recourse to class conflict. It can appear as a 'win-win' discourse which proposes the incorporation of those on the margins into the mainstream of society and bringing the poor within the range of educational and income levels acceptable in a caring society, without diminishing the life chances, living standards and social position of the more privileged while holding off the threat of social instability from 'distant others' of whatever inscription. As such, (Christian) Communitarianism can be read as a text without threat to self interest that is not compromised by the accusation that it is either 'religious' or 'political'. This reading of (Christian) Communitarianism exemplifies how in appealing beyond those members for whom it is identity-forming it can exist in a more simple (as distinct from intense), almost sloganised form. It confirms how not all those attracted to a paradigm are assets to it. Loose framing, in which the absence of intensification of its core political position is central, facilitates what the authorities within (Christian) Communitarianism would diagnose as its mis-reading. Flawed fellow travellers they may be, but they are culturally compatible with the centrist nature of contemporary Irish politics, with its social-democratic type parties, coalition governments and corporatist approaches to policy-making. This is in the nature of the broad ideological space occupied by communitarianism between the extremes of right and left. Appropriated in this simplified form by the mercantile paradigm, it becomes instrumental in the regulation of the meaning of equality, as outlined in Chapter 6 on the culture wars between the mercantile and the modern.

This form and function of (Christian) Communitarianism differs significantly from the authorial intent of CORI's Education Commission. From their perspective this needs to be balanced against the expansion of those who have become subjectively engaged with it, albeit in this simplified form, and the possibility that it may indeed be having a mollifying effect on the individualism of the mercantile paradigm. Even in this simplified form, also, it remains a resource, both in terms of ideas and people, to be more authentically recruited to (Christian) Communitarianism through the on-going discourse and activities of its members, be they religious or secular in identity, who themselves remain a significant cultural force within the LEM domain.

Chapter 11

Gender Equity:
A Systematised Paradigm

After the theocentric paradigm, which, as we have seen, was dominant in official Irish educational policy commentaries up to the 1950s, the gender equity paradigm exemplifies the most complete set of features of a systematised paradigm to be found, not merely within the LEM domain, but in recent thought and action in Irish education. These include:

- an unambiguous guiding belief system
- explicit implications for action over a wide range of phenomena incorporated in the performatives of the discourse
- integration into the state apparatus through its structures and discourse
- instruments for articulating correct practice and guidelines
- mechanisms for monitoring behaviour and action, and for arbitrating on doubt, dissent, tension or threats be they in the form of individuals, events or counter texts
- arrangements for its reproduction over time.

This systematisation has been achieved despite a lack of intensification as indicated by its simple uncomplicated beliefs, verities/truths undisturbed by intellectual doubt, unelaborated conceptualisation and an undifferentiating use of language. As with the theocentric paradigm, which was similarly theoretically simple in its infusion of social policy, systematisation was made possible by their achievement of a doxic status. Because of this, comparisons with aspects of religious belief systems will be found to be illuminating and instructive.

The proposition that the Irish educational system has a 'gender problem' is a product of recent decades. Drudy (1991) concluded, in a review of developments in the sociology of education in Ireland between 1966 and 1991, that 'the relationship of gender and education was totally absent from published work on both sides of the border in the 1960s and 1970s'. The author's own experience in 1970 of seeking models and sources for the section on sexual inequalities in education as part of an undergraduate course on Education would further suggest that gender had yet to figure in any systematic way in the teaching of sociology or education in Irish third-level institutions at that time. The response of the students, experienced primary teachers taking a week-end degree course, to sexual differences in subject provision and choice, educational participation, occupational aspirations, classroom interaction and teacher expectancy effects, derived from Census Reports, the Department of Education Annual Reports, Irish manpower studies of the time and American classroom research, was more dutiful than engaged. Being thus able to set parameters of time and place to the conceptualisation of Irish education as a gendered phenomenon, it becomes all the more remarkable to record the normality achieved by this conceptualisation, and the sponsorship of gender as a category of concern, in the Irish educational policy process within no more than a decade or two. This chapter analyses the construction, sponsorship, dominion and dynamics of the gender equity paradigm by way of charting this achievement.

Construction

The base conceptualisation of the gender equity paradigm is most clearly articulated in the declaration on the elimination of discrimination against women adopted by the general assembly of the United Nations on 7 November, 1967. Not alone did Ireland vote for this declaration but the Report of the Commission on the Status of Women (1972) appealed to it by way of legitimating its analysis of gender equality and recommendations for action and legislative change, and its provisions in Article 10 on education were later used by the state to monitor Irish progress on gender equality in education (Department of Equality and Law Reform, 1997). The key concept of sameness of treatment is the central moral construct in Article 10. It sought to ensure:

- 'the *same* conditions for career and vocational guidance, for access to studies and for the achievement of diplomas in educational establishments of all categories …
- access to the *same* curricula, the *same* examinations, teaching staff with qualifications of the *same* standard and school premises and equipment of the *same* quality
- the elimination of any stereo-typed concept of the roles of men and women at all levels and in all forms of education by encouraging co-education and other types of education which will help to achieve this aim and, in particular, by the revision of textbooks and school programmes and the adaptation of teaching methods

- the *same* opportunities to benefit from scholarships and other study grants
- the *same* opportunities for access to programmes of continuing education, including adult and functional literacy programmes, particularly those aimed at reducing, at the earliest possible time, any gap in education existing between men and women
- the reduction of female drop-out rates and the organisation of programmes for girls and women who have left school prematurely
- the *same* opportunities to participate actively in sports and physical education.' (italics added)

Of the three provisions which do not specifically refer to sameness of treatment, it is implied in the two of them listed above, one requiring the elimination of stereo-typed concepts of male and female roles and the encouragement of co-education, the other advocating the reduction of female drop-out rates. Only one of the eight provisions, relating to access to information on the health and well-being of families including family planning, does not appear to target the disparity of provision between men and women in education.

As the 'sameness of treatment' construct entered Irish conceptualisation it immediately mutated to 'sameness of experience'. This is reflected in the recognition of the need for special treatment in the form of intervention programmes to ensure that female students would collectively experience the same curriculum, have the same aspirations and later experience the same levels and varieties of career, civic, political and cultural success in life as males. Throughout, the norms were those of male subject choice, career aspiration and life-course experience. None of this was made explicit, in line with the non-discordant nature of mutation. Such is the dominance of the 'sameness of experience' construct in conceptualising the issue of gender in equality discourse on Irish education that it can be realised by a number of signifiers that otherwise might be expected to have different meanings such as equity, equality, disadvantage and even feminism. These have been repeatedly used over the past three decades in Irish discourse on gender and education in an interchangeable fashion. This failure of the semantic field surrounding equality and gender to be more differentiated, despite the availability of a varied vocabulary that should have shaped and delineated separate and distinct meanings of gendered education, is a feature of the simplified (as opposed to intensified) nature of the gender equity paradigm. This can be attributed to the predominance of performatives in its texts and the failure of conceptual debate to disturb its unitary meaning of sameness of experience. To avoid any confusion in this regard gender equity is used here to more aptly represent the 'sameness of experience' construct.

Table 11.1 Thematic Stability and Expansion in the Gender Equity Paradigm, 1972-1993

Commission on the Status of Women (1972)	Second Commission on the Status of Women (1993)
Distinction between access to schooling and the nature of the schooling one receives	Legislating for gender equity and the establishment of structures for its promotion, implementation and monitoring
Sex role development in the home and school through role models and text books	The desirability, educationally and socially, of co-education
Female religious teaching orders and traditional approaches to women's role in society.	Recognising the expression of doubts about the benefits of co-education for girls
Role of career guidance in broadening the career aspirations of girls	Equality policy for all co-educational schools involving equal access to all subjects, in-service training for teachers on sexism in the classroom, non-sexist teaching materials, parent education programmes and the equitable distribution of roles in the management structures and organisation of the school
Low representation of women in the schools' inspectorate	The persisting lower representation of women in the schools' inspectorate and the need for the Department to adopt a more interventionist approach in its recruitment and employment practices
Disparity between the numbers of male and female principals	Gender equity as a feature of all preservice and inservice courses for teachers
Tracing the 'distinctions in treatment' (p. 205) later in life between males and females to segregated education	The elimination of sexism in textbooks, teaching materials and curriculum
Advocacy of co-education	The operation of the hidden curriculum in a way that reinforces a stereotyped thinking on boys' and girls' capabilities and appropriate behaviour
The initiation of a programme by the Department of Education to increase the number of girls taking maths and science subjects for	Advice for parents on the importance of the rationale of gender equity policies
	Awareness of gender equity issues among the members of interview boards for the position of school principal
	Education for life, relationships and parenting should be introduced for all pupils
	The equitable treatment of boys and girls in the allocation of facilities, time and expertise in the context of school sport
	A policy on departmental statistics that involves a breakdown by gender in order to effectively monitor the implementation of equality policy
	Pre-School Education
	The development of guidelines on the aims and activities of pre-school education incorporating a positive gender equality dimension

leaving cert level

Access by girls to apprenticeships

Diversification of subject choice by girls in vocational schools to include technically-orientated subjects

The desirability of increasing the lower representation of women on the VECs

Low participation of women in university and their concentration in a narrow range of faculties, particularly arts and social science

Primary Education

Prioritising the elimination of sex stereotyping and promoting equality for boys and girls when drawing up all aspects of the primary school curriculum

A balanced representation of the sexes on boards of management with compulsory minimum representation from each sex

Post-Primary Education

The sampling by first year pupils of a wide range of subjects in schools with the widest possible curriculum available

Equal access to the full range of technology subjects to Leaving Certificate level

Positive action programmes involving career guidance/counselling, targets and parent education initiatives, designed to promote the choice of non-traditional subjects by girls

Equal access to the Leaving Certificate Vocational Programme

At least 40% representation of either sex on post-primary schools boards of management

Ensuring gender equity in appointment and promotion procedures for teachers

Third-Level Education

Positive intervention measures, including active encouragement, open days, recruitment videos, career information, revision of text-books, positive role models, to encourage more women to take up non-traditional courses of study

The development and implementation of equal opportunity policies in relation to employment and promotions procedures

Facilitating access by adult women to third-level courses

Adult and Second-Chance Education

A strategy of adult education that responds to the actual and diverse needs of adult women returning to education and establishes linkages to further development and training opportunities

Sponsorship

From its introduction to Irish educational ideas in the early 1970s, gender equity has successfully realised a series of themes that have remained remarkably stable over the intervening years. A convenient illumination of this is a comparison of the educational themes generated by the two commissions on the status of women, the first reporting in 1972, the other in 1993. These are outlined in Table 11.1. Despite the more extensive treatment of education and gender equity in the 1993 Report, it contains no thematic additions to the 1972 Report apart from the acknowledgement of reservations about the benefits of co-education for girls and the related topic of the hidden curriculum. Rather, what has been experienced by the gender equity paradigm is its expansion throughout the educational system. While the 1972 Report contained no more than four recommendations and two suggestions, the 1993 Report, with minimal thematic change, lists 41 recommendations. Substantively, expansion is reflected in the manner in which the implications for practice are outlined in considerable detail, specifying what action needs to be taken in each of the different levels of education – pre-school, primary, post-primary, third-level, adult and second-chance education. It can be seen in the detail provided in the recommendations for interventions designed to achieve gender equity which have implications for classroom interaction, text-books, learning materials, the formal curriculum, the hidden curriculum of practices, attitudes, role models and hierarchies, parent behaviour, school management and staffing, and teacher formation.

Likewise, there are recommendations regarding legislative change, monitoring mechanisms and data collection. What has happened to the gender equity paradigm is that an unchanged principle of sameness of experience has been more rigorously applied to an increasingly wide range of legal, institutional, collective and individual features of education. In its reach and perception of its relevance, the penetration of the gender equity paradigm leaves no facet of educational life untouched, yet its message remains unchanged. In short, the performatives of its text have experienced expansion while its theorisation remains sparse.

The fact that gender equity was to achieve such a high level of systematisation despite a sparse theorisation can be explicated by reference to some features of its dominion in Irish society – its successful achievement of a doxic status for its core tenet, its incorporation within the liberal reformist ideology and strategies of the Irish women's movement and, relatedly, its penetration of the state to the depth of its corporatist structure.

Dominion

The concentration in the 1993 Report of the Second Commission on the Status of Women on performatives, on how, when and in which of its dimensions, gender equity in education should be advanced, suggests that the principle of gender equity itself had achieved, at least culturally, a general acceptance as a principle that acquired assent from all but the most disaffected and eccentric. All one finds of a legitimatory discourse is by way of asserting the career benefits for girls in opting for non-traditional subject choices. It is clear that the doxic status of gender equity had been established in Irish society. What is even more remarkable is that as early as the 1972 Report of the first Commission on the Status of Women, while it does employ a number of legitimatory strategies, they are of a largely non-intrusive nature and suggest that it did not anticipate any noteworthy dissent from its proclaimed principle of gender equity. The explanation of the non-discordant realisation of the principle of gender equity is to be found in the manner in which it was culturally produced through an expansion of an existing normative construct. The report used the universalistic concept of equality of educational opportunity as the stem concept and, in a process that can be likened to grafting, sought to include gender, along with social class and geography, within its semantic and categorical remit.

In its first paragraph on education, the report referred to the 1969 statement by the Minister for Education in a booklet for parents (Department of Education, 1969) on the centrality to the state of the social and educational objective of equality of opportunity, and sought its application to gender: 'he was not speaking specifically of the equality of educational opportunity between boys and girls but this equality clearly must come within the ambit of the general education objective' (p. 201). It went on to claim that 'it is probably true to say that there is, in general, broad agreement that women should have equal status as men, that they should have equal opportunity to develop their intellectual and other capabilities to the fullest extent and that they should be allowed to take their place on an equal footing with men in the economic, social and other aspects of the life of the country'. It sought, promptly and without fuss, to normalise this position by going on to assert that the problem is rather '… one of ensuring that this broad agreement is translated into practice' (p. 201). It denied credibility to any counter-positions by giving possible objections limited attention: in fact, it acknowledged and sought to counter only one possible objection, the argument that investment in the extended education of girls, relative to that of boys, would be largely a wasted investment because of the early termination of their careers by girls on marriage. Indeed, the only feature of the report that suggests that this was a path-breaking, innovative document is its general tone of hesitancy in making recommendations for practice. It is probably because of this that it sought to appeal to the United Nations declaration on the elimination of discrimination against women mentioned earlier and reminded its readers that Ireland had voted for this declaration.

It would appear that at that time gender equity was already well on its way to achieving a doxic status, putting it beyond serious contestation and from the point of view of its advocates requiring no further elaboration. An indication of the doxic standing achieved by gender equity is its successful inscription within democracy, the paradigm having no need for the themes of personal conscience or opting-out entitlements that would have prevailed even in the theocentric paradigm's dominion in education. An acceptance of gender equity became an obligation of democratic life. Such was the success of its inscription within democracy that, at times, it seemed to operate independently of other principles of equal opportunity as a distinct moral construct. Where this occurred, the semantic range of 'equality issues' or 'equality officers' within educational discourse could be so narrow as to be limited to gender equity. This limited meaning of equity is particularly pronounced in the 1992 Green Paper on Education which individualises social, economic and cultural inequalities in benefiting from education in terms of pupils 'at risk', 'needing particular care' and having 'particular educational needs' (Chapter 2). It exemplifies semantic raiding, followed by factioning and, periodically, dominance.

This cultural change was taking place within the context of more explicit and public political action seeking to advance the interests of women in Irish society. The dominant ideology and strategy of this activity helps to explain the nature of the dominion of the gender equity paradigm.

Commentaries on the emergence of the women's movement in Ireland in the 1970s (Fennell and Arnold, 1987; Mahon, 1995a; Connolly, L., 1997; Galligan, 1998) speak of how a disparate set of tactics, agendas, interests, ideologies and personalities quickly gave way to one dominant approach to advancing the cause of women in Irish society. That has been described as liberal reformist or state feminism. The Irish Women's Liberation Movement (IWLM) founded in Bewley's Café in 1970 included women of left-wing and nationalist beliefs, journalists and professionals. It organised a series of meetings and high-profile demonstrations, some of which, e.g. the 'contraceptive train' to Belfast in May 1971, were said to have 'alarmed both the moderate elements within the movement and ordinary women outside it' (Fennell and Arnold, 1987, p. 10). It can be described as incorporating two strands, 'a traditional, reformist, mainstream sector and a radical, autonomous sector' (Connolly, L., 1997) which were recognised within the movement from the beginning and differentiated between those who advocated feminism in its own right and those who wished to tackle the totality of injustices.

Disaffection over feminist ideology, tactics, identification with the left and the political situation in Northern Ireland led to resignations and the proliferation of single-issue groups and women-orientated services. Irish Women United (IWU) which lasted for 18 months between 1975 and 1977 brought together such left-wing groups as the Movement for a Socialist Republic, the Communist Party of Ireland, the Socialist Workers Movement, the Irish Republican Socialist Party and the International Lesbian Caucus. Described as 'the last radical feminist group to attempt a national profile' (Fennell and Arnold, 1987, p. 12), it diffused into a number of organisations including the first Rape Crisis Centre in 1977 and the first Women's Right to Choose Campaign in 1979.

The demands of the IWLM may appear modest in retrospect. In their manifesto *Chains or Change?*, published in 1971, they sought equal pay, equality before the law, equal education, contraception, justice for deserted wives, unmarried mothers and widows, and one house, one family. These proved to be controversial though even by the standards of the time they were politically non-radical. Yet, one of its more prominent members, Nuala Fennell, is reported to have charged that 'anyone who was not anti-American, anti-clerical, anti-government, anti-Irish Countrywomen's Association, anti-police and anti-man' (Mahon, 1995a) had no place in the IWLM. She favoured the approach of the National Organisation of Women (NOW) in the US, founded in 1966 in the wake of Friedan's *The Feminine Mystique*, which adopted a liberal feminist model of campaigning for equal rights for women in education, the family and in the law (Humm, 1992). AIM (Action, Inform, Motivate) was founded in January 1972 with the objective of improving 'the quality of life for women, while placing particular emphasis on the discrimination against women that exists under the Irish legal system'. Predominantly middle-class, it is described in a publication co-authored by Fennell herself as having 'politely, but persistently lobbied ministers … and patiently explained the terrible inequalities that existed in all areas of family law' (Fennell and Arnold, 1987, p. 19). Its achievements within a relatively short time span are testimony to its success. On the legislation front in a single year these included the Family Home Protection Act (1976) which prohibited the sale of the family home without the consent of both spouses, and the Family Law (Maintenance of Spouses and Children) Act (1976), which allowed for the legal barring of violent spouses from the family home (Galligan, 1998).

Also operating within existing state structures, the Irish Housewives' Association and the Association of Business and Professional Women had responded to a UN suggestion that non-governmental women's organisations lobby their respective governments to establish a national commission on the status of women. The Commission on the Status of Women (1972) grew out of their *ad hoc* committee on the subject. The Council for the Status of Women was in turn founded to monitor the implementation of the commission's recommendations (Connolly, L., 1997).

All of the accounts of the contemporary women's movement in Ireland recognise the diversity of activities, initiatives, advocacy and services which are inspired by feminism, broadly conceived. While these have the capacity to reshape the character of dominant feminist action in Ireland, at present this takes its rationale from the liberal reformist wing of the movement. This has succeeded in penetrating the state apparatus to such an extent that it justifies being referred to in terms of 'state feminism'. Stetson and Mazur (1995, p. 1) describe state feminism as 'the most striking consequence of over twenty-five years of women's movement activism ... that array of institutional arrangements inside democratic states devoted to women's policy questions ... with a potential of turning the state into an activist on behalf of feminist goals'. In their comparative study of state feminism they consider, as Irish examples, drawing on Mahon's (1995b) chapter, the activities of the Ministry of State for Women's Affairs set up in 1982 and the Joint Oireachtas Committee on Women's Rights, established in 1983. They also mention the Employment Equality Agency, 1977 and the Council for the Status of Women, 1973 (now the National Women's Council of Ireland). Their typology of state feminism is based on two criteria. These are *policy influence*, the extent to which women's policy structures contribute to feminist policy that promotes the status of women and undermines patterns of gender hierarchies, and *policy access*, the degree to which the same machinery facilitates access by feminists and women's advocacy organisations to the policy-making process. Ireland was rated low on both criteria. This was because certain topics such as divorce and abortion had been put off limits for the deliberation of these groups and the activities of the Minister of State for Women's Affairs, and the self-exclusion of many feminist groups who were described as refusing to participate in these structures because of their function within a patriarchal state. But this is not to deny the reality of state feminism as the dominant model of feminist action in Ireland. Rather, it parallels the argument of this chapter that the version of feminist action in education which was proclaimed and pursued through state activity was that of gender equity.

However paradoxically it may have appeared for feminists to seek to achieve their aims through state sponsorship, it is clear that there were advantages in working within state structures 'through positive cooperation ... rather than strident criticism' (Mahon and Morgan, 1999). The gender equity paradigm exemplifies this. In operating within the state its penetration was all the more effective and deep because of the corporatist structures and activities that were available to it in the form of national agreements between the 'social partners', consultative arrangements with the professional bodies within education, and the expanding engagement of interest groups within the policy-making process for education, as well as a centrally-regulated educational system that provided immediate, comprehensive and extended access to the formation of young people through curriculum change, targeted projects, policy initiatives and the orientations of their teachers.

Table 11.2 State Policy

Programme for Action in Education, 1984-1987	*Fianna Fáil and Labour Programme for a Partnership Government, 1993-1997*	*Education for a Changing World, Green Paper on Education, 1992*
A government commitment to develop a strategy to eliminate sexism in education by means of the following initiatives:	Gender Equity to be one of the main aims of educational policy together with affirmative action to include:	The promotion of gender equity in education by means of the following:
Raising the level of awareness among educators, parents and pupils in relation to traditional restrictions	Full curriculum choice for all students	A review of all teaching materials in schools and the withdrawal or adaptation of unsuitable materials
Nominating women to the selection boards for principals of national schools	Positive programme to encourage women to enter non-traditional labour markets	Ensuring that the full range of courses is available to students in second-level schools, irrespective of sex
Making teachers more aware of their role in eliminating sexism in education	Encouraging women to re-enter the labour force through adult education	Co-education to be encouraged as the norm
Making school managers and teachers aware of all aspects of sex differentiation within the school and in particular in relation to curricular provision	The promotion of women's studies in third-level education	Achieving a greater participation of women in all management levels in the Department of Education
Discussing with publishers the question of sexism/sex stereotyping in school textbooks	Encouraging women to participate in sport at all levels	Active gender equality policies in all educational institutions together with annual progress reports
Allocating responsibility to the Curriculum and Examinations Board for the monitoring of sexism and stereo-typing in the school curriculum	A comprehensive system of sex education at second level	Boards of Management including staff selection committees to aim towards a gender balance in their membership

Table 11.3 The Central State Apparatus

Higher Education Authority	Employment Equality Agency (1983)	Joint Oireachtas Committee on Women's Rights, *First Report, Education* (1984)
Charting our Education Future, White Paper on Education, 1995, made the Higher Education Authority responsible for monitoring and providing appropriate support at national level for the following policies:	Recommendations in the light of the findings of *Schooling and Sex roles* (Hannan *et al.*, 1983):	All new schools to be co-educational with pupils taught together in the same classroom and equality of subject availability and take up
Promoting equal opportunities, associated action programmes and procedures to prevent the sexual harassment of students and employees	The elimination of sex bias in texts	All aspects of equality and the elimination of sexism to be included in the preparation of students for the teaching profession
	The presentation of exam data broken down by sex	
	Ending segregation of exam scripts by the candidate's sex	Widening the subject availability to girls by means of cooperation within the educational system
Encouraging increased participation by women students in areas of study in which they have been traditionally underrepresented	Ensuring in-service training for teachers to promote equality of opportunity in subject allocation, provision and choice	Initiatives to ensure that girls will be able to benefit fully from training and apprenticeship schemes
All staff selection boards to be gender balanced	Establishing a 'small key group' with responsibility for an action programme to promote equality of opportunity between boys and girls within the educational system	
Encouraging and facilitating women to apply for senior academic and administrative positions	Pilot studies and supporting intervention programmes to increase the take up of practical subjects by female students	Better representation of women on all interview boards for vacancies for teachers in schools
Making arrangements to assist students with younger children		The extension of day-time classes for women

Assisting male and female teachers in identifying the links between adult sex role expectations and educational and occupational aspirations of pupils

Provide a comprehensive information programme for parents on the implications of subject choice for third-level courses and employment opportunities

That the Youth Employment Agency consider the implications of the report's findings for its policy on the sponsorship and funding of school-to-work transition schemes for boys and girls

Table 11.4 The Corporatist Structure

Programme for Competitiveness and Work, 1994	Association of Secondary Teachers Ireland, *Model Policy on Promotion of Gender Equity in Schools* (c. 1994)	Joint Managerial Body *Draft Working Document on Gender Equity*, 1999
Guidelines for teachers to be issued to promote equal opportunities for boys and girls	Schools to offer access to employment to male and female teachers on an equal basis recognising and utilising the different talents and capabilities and potential of both men and women at all levels and within all the activities of the school	Gender Equity means treating all people with respect at all times, and ensuring that there is no discrimination on the basis of gender or marital status. All staff are entitled to be treated equally and work in an atmosphere free from discrimination
Career Guidance programmes to be developed to encourage women to enter labour markets traditionally closed to them		
Action to be taken in the light of a current research project on gender equity in co-educational schools	Create school environment where boys and girls can enjoy equal access to the full range of curricular options, be given the same choices and guidance in terms of vocational and educational options and participate on an equal basis in the life and organisation of the school	Gender equity extends right across the spectrum of school life: *Staff* recruitment of staff, conditions of employment provision of training and (where applicable) promotion
A designated senior official in the Department of Education to be assigned responsibility for the promotion and implementation of gender equity policy in all areas of the educational system	Gender equity policy to be applied equally to single-sex schools in terms of policy for staff and for students	*Students* selection policy, participation in school activities and the code of behaviour
	Encouraging teacher awareness of gender issues in their method of teaching and in the roles and tasks they assign to students	*Curriculum* subject options, subject levels, extra-curricular cultural and physical activities, and other school-related activities

Tables 11.2, 11.3 and 11.4 chart the detail of the penetration of gender equity in state policy, among bodies within the central state apparatus and throughout the organisations engaged within is corporatist structure.

When we analyse the discourse of these bodies on gender issues we are presented with a thematisation that is seamless and unified in its realisation of gender equity as a guiding principle for changing a gendered educational system. Along with this unity in cultural meaning and imperatives, the discourse is highly prescriptive in articulating the implications for practice. This consistency and diffusion throughout state activity will appear remarkable only to those who succeed in suspending their engagement with the gender equity paradigm. Once it is perceived as a dimension of the democratic ideal it ceases to be surprising that it should have achieved such a level of political penetration.

During the period of this discourse, non-discursive textualisation from within the state in the form of intervention projects, promotional activities and dissemination exercises became more frequent and public (see Department of Equality and Law Reform, 1997). The FUTURES, GEAR and TENET projects are no more than high-profile examples. The Girls into Technology/FUTURES Project was co-funded by the Department of Education and the EU to broaden the subject choice of girls and involved the provision of information and awareness-raising materials for schools and the training of teachers in their use. GEAR (Gender Equity Action Research) comprised a research programme aimed at reducing imbalances in the educational experiences of boys and girls at primary level together with a subsequent resource pack to promote equal opportunities which included guidelines for teachers and a report of a working party on the elimination of sexism and sex-stereotyping in primary school textbooks and teaching materials. Within the framework of the EU TENET (Teacher Education Network) programme, five action research projects, under the general title of the Integration of Equal Opportunities in the Curriculum of Teacher Education were initiated in pre-service and in-service teacher education involving the teacher unions and teacher education bodies, with the aim of raising teacher awareness about gender inequalities in education and providing information and guidelines for action.

These communicated the meaning of gender equity through performance (Barthes, 1973) and rite (Durkheim, 1976[1912]) and in this manner succeeded in reaching a wider audience in education and beyond than would otherwise be accessible to the discursive activity of policy makers, the state and the corporatist sectors. In its penetration of social action it enhanced the normality of gender equity as the only thinkable principle of intervening in a gendered educational system and rendered unremarkable the provision of special treatment for female pupils in the pursuit of sameness of experience.

Gender equity succeeded in achieving this dominion by working through the state and in making liberal reformist demands in line with the dominant approach of the women's movement. It did so without the necessity of theorisation. In fact, in its discourse the theme of gender equity scarcely exists in its own right independently of the performatives in which it is embedded. As with the 1972 Report of the Commission on the Status of Women, the thrust has been to translate an indisputable principle into educational practice. The unquestionable status of gender equity is assumed throughout and any deviation by females from a sameness of aspiration, opportunity and attainment to that of males is responded to in a fashion that mirrors the treatment of deviations from other doxic positions: agency is only acknowledged in conformity. Indeed, in a manner reflective of the religious construct of an informed conscience, the 1993 report of the Second Commission on the Status of Women recommended positive intervention measures '… in order to overcome the cultural bias which militates against women making an informed choice' in relation to the take-up of non-traditional courses of study at third level (p. 281).

Because of this, the principle of gender equity did not require isolation and naming, much less defending. Having achieved the taken-for-granted status of doxa, and penetrated all levels of state activity as it relates to educational policy and practice, legitimation would have been assumed to be superfluous. In the absence of public dissent there was no need for the gender equity paradigm to reposition itself theoretically through a process of reconceptualising, differentiating and clarifying in a manner that would have advanced its intensification.

Systematisation

As the gender equity paradigm expanded it infused educational policy and practice at all levels and in all its aspects and, albeit sparsely theorised, it went on to assume many of the features of a system. These included monitoring mechanisms, dissemination exercises, and differentiated roles for the tasks of representation, advocacy, legitimation and membershipping, in fact many of the features of what Foucault (1980) refers to as 'regimes of truth'.

In seeking to translate its policy intentions into practice, monitoring and reporting procedures were extensively used. Even more important than their incidence was the form they took. A number of mechanisms operated. Bodies were established to report on progress in the implementation of recommendations, government departments were invited to give details of what action had been taken in relation to specific proposals, and the state itself reported on progress to international bodies such as the UN on the extent to which the provisions of inter-governmental agreements were being realised. The discursive character of the different mechanisms was similar: the recommendation/provision was listed without comment or elaboration and the reported action that had been taken in relation to its realisation was then described. These could be extensive with supportive descriptive, statistical and evaluative detail as in reports to inter-governmental organisations such as the EU or UN (Department of Equality and Law Reform, 1997) or more cryptic when the audience was local. The progress reports of the Women's Representative Committee, set up to monitor the progress in the implementation of the recommendations of the Commission on the Status of Women (1972), exemplifies the latter. This is typified by the following entry on co-education, identical in its 1976 and 1978 reports which reported the response from the Department of Education: 'The demand for co-education is growing and the Department of Education is prepared to meet this demand whenever it is practicable to do so. All teacher training is now mixed.' Be the reports extensive or cryptic, these monitoring mechanisms sought to assess the implementation of recommendations, not to question their underlying rationale. Their target was the orthodoxy of behaviour, not the orthodoxy itself which was further enhanced through remaining unquestioned.

A feature of these monitoring arrangements was their 'normalisation' of gender intervention in education as indicated by the setting of standards and criteria for appropriate practice in the form of targets and quotas. Working from the ideal of sameness of experience as proper practice, the intermediate phases in the realisation of the norm were calibrated and operationalised. In this manner a new set of behaviours and practices were isolated and named, and submitted to standardisation, measurement and surveillance (Foucault, 1979).

In the appropriate social contexts, usually characterised by educational policy-making activities and normative teacher professionalism, engagement with the gender equity paradigm was mandatory as proof of one's entitlement to participate. This is likely to have cultivated a public orthodoxy which disguised ambivalence and non-alignment with gender equity as well as more radical feminist interpretations. The doxic status of gender equity served to relegate any dissenting understandings to the limbo world of hidden, furtive, shameful and discrediting thought. Through a process of self-regulation as much as social control its effect was to maintain cultural silences alongside individual voice. Accordingly, it is rare to find disengagement from the gender equity paradigm in professional and policy-making contexts. Where there are attempts to modify or theorise its features they incorporate strategies designed to evade a disruption of communication and cultural exclusion. Examples include seeking to neutralise the attribution of idiosyncrasy, in an early questioning of the use of male norms of behaviour, choice and success in the gender equity paradigm (O'Sullivan, 1984b), and claiming nodal points of common meaning (Public Policy Institute of Ireland, 1993).

Beyond the sites of policy-making, questioning and dissent among teachers was more public and explicit, even in equal opportunities projects (Drudy *et al.*,

1991). Interventions designed to more comprehensively membership teachers to the gender equity paradigm were top-down and high-control. They exemplify what has been described as 'teacher-proofing' educational practice – seeking to determine the character of schooling independently of teacher agency. Gender equity was made an obligatory topic on all approved summer courses for primary teachers resulting in gender equity modules on such courses as horticulture and first aid. The content, methodology and resource material of these modules were prescribed by the Department of Education. In the Irish report to the UN in relation to its convention on the elimination of all forms of discrimination against women (Department of Equality and Law Reform, 1997) the degree of state direction in relation to these courses is explained:

> It is a requirement of the Department of Education that all approved summer courses for primary school teachers must cover the topic of gender equality either by way of a specific in-service module or by a permeation approach. This latter approach provides an opportunity for course participants to raise equality issues where they see relevance as well as allowing for discussion. Focused permeation implies some core sessions allied to a wide distribution of references supported by substantial research and not just casual asides.

The presenters of these modules – the teachers/trainers – were provided with specific directions on how to respond to itemised objections and alternative understandings of gender and education (Department of Education, 1996). These features are reflective of the legalism, prescriptiveness and low-trust membershipping practices within education and beyond of Roman Catholicism until recent decades (Inglis, 1998a; Kenny, 1997).

A consequence of these mechanisms for monitoring and membershipping was the creation of a number of roles with responsibilities for promoting gender equity within education. These included equality officers, teacher/trainers, school inspectors, education officers and project leaders and workers. At the very least, their subjectivities will not have remained unaffected by the texts they contributed to by way of discourse or performance. This in turn will have been confirmed by the public nature of these activities within the profession and by the membership checks that operate in the process of career advancement to the extent that they will inform their personal sense of identity. Nonetheless, as is argued later, a fluidity in the subjectivities and paradigm membership of these role incumbents is one of the more likely sites of change within the gender equity paradigm. Among these roles, those accorded the status of intellectual deserve special attention. This is because of their capacity to speak with authority on the truthfulness and validity of the paradigm's meanings.Yet, those best positioned to successfully challenge the gender equity paradigm, be it by way of questioning the existence of gendered education or in the form of more radical feminist critique, are intellectuals who can claim legitimacy for other understandings of how the construct of gender might be used to interrogate and change educational practice. The nature of knowledge production and legitimation on gender and education by intellectuals is therefore critical.

However, if we examine the research activity of independent academics and researchers on gender and education it is found that the major projects have been commissioned from within the state and its corporatist structure. This is the case with the path-breaking studies from the ESRI on gender and subject choice and later on co-education. *Schooling and Sex Roles* (Hannan *et al.*, 1983) had its origins in a proposal from the Women's Representative Committee resulting in a request from the Employment Equality Agency and the Department of Labour to study the contribution of curriculum differences to educational inequalities for girls. The study was co-sponsored by the Employment Equality Agency and the Departments of Labour and Education with financial support from the EEC of the time. *Coeducation and Gender Equality* (Hannan *et al.*, 1996) was requested by the Department of Labour '… to determine whether co-educational schools relative to single-sex schools, have negative effects on girls' educational achievement and personal and social development' (p. 5). A widely-quoted study on gender differences in promotional patterns within primary teaching (Kellaghan *et al.*, 1985) by the Educational Research Centre was commissioned by the INTO. The Educational Research Centre also, as part of the GEAR project, was requested and funded by the Department of Education to collect and analyse data relating to gender issues in Irish primary education (Lewis and Kellaghan, 1993). The effect of this pattern of knowledge production is that the major research studies on gender issues in education from the two independent social and educational research institutions in the country operated within the gender equity paradigm. Relatedly, in this process the gender equity paradigm acquired for itself paradigm intellectuals whose activity strongly determined the extent of its intensification and who functioned as agents of legitimation and arbitration. In fact, one of these studies (Hannan *et al.*, 1996) was itself a response to a threat to the doxic status of one of the beliefs of the gender equity paradigm, the superiority of co-education over single-sex schooling as a form of educational experience for young people. Since changes in the truth claims and truth-determining criteria of the gender equity paradigm in relation to co-education contribute to the only example of paradigm intensification that we can identify, it is instructive to trace this facet (albeit one of many) of the co-education text.

One of the earliest and most uncompromising arguments for co-education is to be found in the first report of the Joint Oireachtas Committee on Women's Rights (1984). It situated itself in the belief structure of the gender equity paradigm, demanding 'equality in the fullest sense with pupils of both sexes receiving the same education in the classroom and the same opportunities to use that education when they leave school'. An indication of the doxic status of this belief is provided by the manner in which they considered themselves to have established its truthfulness and in how they reacted to dissenting views. Members of the committee claimed to be in a position to speak for 'the people', projecting their own voice as no more than the manifestation of its collective understanding. The 'truth determining' mechanism was a populist one – if 'the people' believe it then it attests to its validity or facticity. Counter views were dismissed as being unworthy of cognitive response, and discrediting affective reservations were used to this end. These patterns of legitimating and discrediting definitions of reality are present in the following extract:

> The Joint Committee agrees that there is no sustainable rationale for the segregation of schools on the basis of sex and it sees the concept of co-education as the one which should be fostered and established on a nationwide basis. The members were alarmed at the obvious gulf that exists between the thinking of the Department of Education and parents. They know from their work throughout the country and from the submissions received from responsible groups that parents generally favour co-education, realising that it will be through such a system that their children will receive a broadly based education necessary to equip them for the changing and challenging conditions of the present day.

In 1983 Hannan *et al.* (p. 323) had found it necessary to 'sound a cautionary note' on the effects of co-education. While their all-Irish study did not support the pattern of 'polarisation effects' recorded at that time in British research in which girls preformed better academically in single-sex schools and were less sexually-stereotyped in their subject choices and social roles, they acknowledged that co-educational schools were more prevalent and longer established elsewhere. Since conclusive support for the Joint Committee's claims for co-education was not forthcoming from international research, a modification of the gender equity paradigm's legitimation of co-education was required. The consequence was a text on co-education in which the belief that it was the more desirable form of education, in the words of the 1992 Green Paper on Education (p. 71) to 'be encouraged as the norm', succeeded in persisting alongside concerns relating to the academic and social implications for girls emerging from international research. Distinction between belief and empirical research findings came to a head in Ireland with the dissemination of the findings of Hanafin's (1992) study of sixteen schools in the Limerick region which found that girls' examination performance was significantly better in single-sex than in co-educational schools. Within a year an exercise in arbitration was initiated when, as we have observed above, the Department of Education commissioned a study, subsequently published as *Coeducation and Gender Equality* (Hannan *et al.*, 1996) to examine the extent to which co-education relative to single-sex schooling might be having a detrimental effect on female pupils. There is no comparable example in Irish educational thought in which a threat to a definition of reality was responded to with such alacrity. Upon analysis, it emerged, however, that what was being judged was not the belief in the superiority of co-education over single-sex schooling as a basis for advancing gender equity, but rather the status of Hanafin's findings. In this, the policy that co-education should be the emerging form of school organisation does not appear to have been an issue. The purpose of the research for policy was to identify possible threats to gender equity within co-educational schools and where these were found to exist to suggest how they might be countered.

In pointing to the greater claim of *Coeducation and Gender Equality* to accurately reflect reality, the research appealed to the criteria that conferred validity within this kind of inquiry – empirical, positivistic, modelled on scientific method, a large-scale study capable of being generalised to the national population, and 'state of the art' statistical techniques to increase precision in identifying cause and effect and in discriminating between influences in a more exact fashion. These were also the truth-determining criteria that the state apparatus expected in their understanding of how the social sciences created knowledge about the educational system and how they expected them to contribute to the process of educational policy making. In the event, co-education was found to have a slight negative effect on girls' Junior Cert performance, no appreciable impact on their overall Leaving Cert performance or on their personal/social development, though co-education had clear negative effects on girls' mathematics performance.

The relationship between the belief in co-education and *Coeducation and Gender Equality* can be likened to the relationship found where theology and science are successfully fused. The latter is recognised as arbitrating on the 'facts' of the situation which in turn are integrated into belief structures that are not themselves subjected, or considered susceptible, to such empirical arbitration or consideration. Different truth-determining criteria are at work here which must be understood in terms of shifts in the truth claims of the gender equity paradigm's text on co-education. The Joint Oireachtas Committee on Women's Rights had asserted the superiority of co-education and advocated that all new schools be co-educational. According as international reservations about the benefits of co-education for girls had to be acknowledged a retrenched position took the form of an assumption, usually unstated, that co-education was the most appropriate basis from which to develop gender equity, particularly in its implications for the life course of women. *Coeducation and Gender Equality* assumed that co-education would increasingly be the norm according as schools amalgamated because of falling numbers. It did not seek to use its findings to arbitrate on the unequivocal populist legitimation of co-education or, in its more diluted version, that co-education represented the most appropriate starting point from which to advance gender equity. The study did not over-step the role allocated to it by the state to use empirical research, not to arbitrate on the relative merits of different forms of school organisation, but to identify how co-education (but not single-sex schooling) might more effectively advance the achievement of gender equity.

As with all research, *Coeducation and Gender Equality* is open to appropriation by diverse texts on co-education and, to distinguish between authorial intent and discursive formation (Popkewitz, 1998), one cannot predict what texts it will contribute to in the future. At present it has facilitated a modification of the legitimatory apparatus supporting co-education within the gender equity paradigm's text on co-education in which populism in a number of versions has been replaced by facticity derived from demographic and economic determinism, it no longer being a matter of what people *know* about co-education but rather what *is* or inevitably *will be* due to social and economic forces. As with the successful fusion of theology and science, the truth-determining criteria of faith/revelation are deemed to be distinctive from those of science and are agreed to address different kinds of questions: in producing the text on co-education, 'scientific' research is expected to resolve issues within the boundaries of possibility set by inexorable economic forces.

Systematised paradigms would normally be expected to embody many such examples of intensification as they counter oppositional or threatening interpretations of reality. However, as long as a paradigm can maintain its doxic status it is not obliged to engage in defensive theorisation of its position. This, of course, can change according as competing sites of knowledge creation gain legitimacy.

Coping with Counter-Texts

The establishment of undergraduate and postgraduate programmes on gender and women studies and associated research centres, as well as the activity of avowed feminist intellectuals, testifies to the availability of themes and texts that interpret the operation of a gendered society in terms other than gender equity. Critiques of the human subject, knowledge, language, interpretations of justice, and prescriptions for educational and social action, routine in feminist discourse, represent a reservoir of sources of comprehensive paradigmatic change. A number of applications of feminist perspectives to educational practice in Ireland represent an incipient textualisation in this regard. Feminist pedagogy and interpretations of adult and community education have questioned the individualist purpose of educational activity, the role of teacher/lecturer/facilitator as expert, definitions of worthwhile knowledge and the narrow range of the self acknowledged and made salient within the learning encounter, the absence of collective affiliation and the appropriateness of the assessment requirements of existing institutions for responding to personal knowledge (Fagan, 1991; Byrne, *et al.*, 1996; Connolly, B., 1997). An analysis of gender discourse among a group of girls in co-educational schools which adopted a feminist post-structuralist position disputed the assumptions of sex-role socialisation and internalisation that are a feature of gender equity and sought to centre analysis and action on the construction of gender in social relations (Ryan, 1997).

The survival of the gender equity paradigm alongside these alternative, often competing and potentially disruptive, texts may be partly explained by their failure to construct a public cultural existence for themselves of a kind that would realise meanings beyond the realms of private voice, circumscribed membership and catacombed worlds of sealed discursive communities. It must be also noted that many of these texts' prescriptions for practice – their performatives – can be accommodated within features of educational practice, e.g. holistic, dialogical and activity-based forms of learning, multiple intelligence theory and authentic assessment, that are not explicitly feminist. The contributors to this counter-textualisation recognise their exclusion and isolation. They remark on the persisting difficulty of bringing together the theoretical exploration of feminist researchers in the academy and the practical understandings of teachers (Ní Chárthaigh, 1998) and on how those who draw on assumptions other than gender equity such as feminist post-structuralism are most often left to do their own development on an individual basis because of the absence of teacher development programmes that draw on these texts (Ryan, 1997).

Yet, these feminists may well be underestimating the extent to which they are extending the interpretation of a gendered education particularly among those in policy, representational and membershipping roles within the gender equity paradigm. Because of its dominion, participation in the discourse of gender equity is obligatory for those who wish to participate in the policy-making process including those who are cognitively aware of, receptive to or actively engaged with alternative interpretations of a gendered society. In such a context, multiple membership and fluid subjectivities cannot be avoided. For some this may be regarded tactically as incrementalist in the pursuit of a more sophisticated and radical feminist vision (Ryan, 1997). Others will experience ambivalence. For many it is likely to be hidden or unknown. However slight, the consequence is an easing of the gender equity paradigm's framing of its membership, conceptualisation and themes. While, immediately, this involves minimal modification to the gender equity paradigm, together with some related features of its response to other counter-texts to be considered later, it does open up possibilities for more substantial change.

In the absence of an anti-feminist text that would seek to deny the existence of female inequality in education or indeed the phenomenon of a gendered educational system, the theme of male underachievement represents the greatest threat to the very foundational conceptualisations of the gender equity paradigm. The fact that males record lower levels of educational performance than females, be it measured as length of schooling or overall examination achievement, has been frequently noted in discourse on gender and education. Yet, as O'Connor (1998, pp 166-167) has pointed out, the failure to identify male underachievement as an educational problem requiring explanation '… is in stark contrast to attempts to explain class differences in attainment'. Rather, the discourse on gender differences in educational performance realises the theme of the failure of women to capitalise on their higher educational performance in their subsequent careers and not that of male disadvantage. Not surprisingly, therefore, the theory of the 'feminised primary school' which argued that gender differences in achievement were due to a largely female teaching profession maintaining a female ethos that was unsympathetic to male physicality, motoric activity and expressive style never achieved a cultural existence in Ireland (O'Sullivan, 1984a).

Another mechanism for coping with male underachievement that does not go as far as cultural exclusion is to thematise it as a more specific problem of male underachievement in languages. This allows its non-problematising, in contrast to concerns about female underachievement in some of the science and mathematical subjects, to be explained as an example of the low status of linguistic as opposed to scientific domains of knowledge in a patriarchal society (Lynch and Morgan, 1995). In recent years, male underachievement in Irish schools is beginning to be conceptualised as social and skill deficit, thematised as unemployability and textualised in terms of the human capital needs of a growing, high-tech economy (IBEC, 1999). This is in contrast to England where a pattern of early school leaving and lower examination results among males has been conceptualised as social pathology and thematised and progressively textualised as the construction of 'laddish', feckless masculinities (Epstein *et al.*, 1998). In neither instance of cultural production is male educational underachievement, relative to that of females, conceptualised as injustice, much less achieving a thematisation/textualisation in terms of rights. A rare attempt at such a thematisation, at the Gender Equality for 2000 and Beyond international conference held in Dublin in 1996, was resisted. When the conference rapporteur (Ní Chárthaigh, 1998) came to report on an intervention by one of the speakers in relation to male underachievement, she acknowledged its importance but continued: 'we must however be cautious here. The power relations between the sexes are not equal. In spite of their educational underachievement, men still hold power and wealth and we cannot assume that the consequences of educational behaviour are the same for boys and for girls.' This is an example of how a potential threat to a paradigm can not merely be negated but turned to advantage through its appropriation as a resource by means of its reinterpretation within the paradigm's conceptualisation and language.

If male underachievement threatened to disrupt the dominance of the theme of female inequality in discourse on gendered education, then the conceptualisation of the school curriculum as a gendered construct had a radicalising potential to introduce themes relating to knowledge and power that were routinely left unrealised by the gender equity paradigm. Within the gender equity paradigm the problem of the curriculum has been thematised in terms of role models, realising issues such as the representation of males and females and the visibility of women in materials and syllabi relating to science, history, art and literature etc. There has been a consistent and on-going textualisation of this in both academic and policy discourse (Department of Education, 1984a; McGowan, 1990) since gender inequality in education was first made an issue by the women's movement in the 1970s. In this form it has been faithful to the principle of sameness of experience. It was prescribed that male and female characters should be equally visible in texts and teaching materials, that the roles they occupied should encompass a similar range of functions, skills, competencies and personality traits, and should be seen to be similarly contributing to human achievement.

The epistemological critique of school knowledge, however equal its manifestation in the curriculum in terms of gender patterns of role allocation and visibility, more fundamentally argues that the knowledge selected for inclusion is itself a patriarchal construction. In this regard, Cullen's (1987) textualisation of the patriarchal curriculum was a unique cultural intervention in the Irish understanding of gender and education. Cullen argued that sexism in education cannot be said to derive solely from the sexist attitudes brought to it by students, teachers, parents and society at large and criticised the equality strategies which are based on this assumption. She was concerned with the implication that '… the actual knowledge taught and learned transcends sex and gender and is equally "female" and "male"'. This, she argued, is clearly not the case since the actual subject matter studied reflects the body of knowledge and theory passed on as part of our western intellectual inheritance which itself is '… for the most part based on the male experience and constructed within the framework of the patriarchal paradigm in human society'. In this the male is seen as '… the human norm and as the active agent in the activities which they rank as the highest human achievements, intellectual and artistic creativity, political, economic and social leadership and dominance'. Taking mainstream history as an example, she noted that successful feminist deconstruction '… would involve more than a simple process of adding on new information to the existing body. Major readjustments and reassessment of current judgements, rankings and periodisation will certainly follow.'

Similarly discordant with the gender equity paradigm was Ó Conaill's (1991) analysis, in a paper presented at the 1990 Educational Studies Association of Ireland Annual Conference, of the issue of girls' participation and achievement in science and technology subjects. Ó Conaill distinguished between 'girl friendly' and 'feminine' science interventions on the one hand and 'feminist' science on the other. Girl friendly/feminine science advocates teaching the existing scientific concepts and processes but using materials and examples and with a teaching style and classroom ethos designed to counteract its masculine image and make it more appealing to girls. Feminist science, he pointed out, in contrast, is not content 'to dally with the style of presentation or context of the knowledge'. It questions the epistemological nature of science itself, 'its view of the nature of objectivity, what constitutes evidence and the views it has of the status of scientific knowledge'. Ó Conaill specifically identified the opposition he was seeking to discredit and undermine in terms of its impact on educational policy: 'equal opportunity is a polite approach to gender inequality, it assuages the conscience of policy makers and inhibits the development of worthwhile counter-sexist initiatives.' While this is contributing to the same text as Cullen, Ó Conaill adopted a neo-marxist perspective as his macro-theory and placed patriarchal relations in that context in interpreting women's educational experience. He also adopted an anti-essentialist position on the category of women in society and sought to legitimate this understanding by reference to contemporary sociological writing in the radical and feminist traditions.

While the patriarchal curriculum is thematised in the major textbooks on education and society in Ireland, it is accorded no textualisation even on the scale attempted by Cullen and Ó Conaill. In fact, Cullen's exclusion from the intellectual discourse on gender and education invites study as a feature of 'the politics of footnoting' (Bensman, 1988). Lynch and Morgan (1995, p. 544) raised the theme as follows: 'achieving equality between the sexes in the curricular sphere is not merely a matter of getting women into science and technology, but of questioning the nature of the curriculum itself.' Similarly, Drudy and Lynch (1993, p. 196) observed that 'the problem (of female take up rates in Mathematics, Science and Technology) is not simply with women but with the way these fields of knowledge have developed in almost exclusively male hands'. But, in both of these instances the patriarchal curriculum is used to explain the alienation and detachment of girls from the more mathematical, scientific and technological subject areas, thus subsuming it within the theme of equity in subject choice. However, the discourse is macaronic in that it can be said to realise two texts. One representation remains within the gender equity paradigm and conceptualises the problem, as the Employment Equality Agency (1983) did, as capable of being resolved by making course material more interesting and relevant to girls, in effect arguing for 'girl friendly/feminine science' in Ó Conaill's categorisation. This would require no more than the additions and adjustments that Cullen deems to be inadequate. Yet the epistemological critique is also beginning to be textualised in references to '… the intrinsic nature of the knowledge and modes of thinking within the disciplines themselves' (Drudy and

Lynch, 1993, p. 196) and in a comment on the curriculum in general: 'the focus on stereotyped images and texts is only a tiny part of a much bigger problem. If the content of what is taught is patriarchal and class biased then having non-sexist images is a small part of the solution' (Drudy and Lynch, 1993, p. 182).

Macaronic discourse of this nature allows for the patriarchal curriculum to be constituted both as an impediment to female engagement and empathy and as a representation of partial culture and knowledge. The former can be accommodated within the gender equity paradigm by extending the sameness of experience principle to the domain of school knowledge and seeking to correct whatever epistemological impediments that are found to be experienced by male and female students in subject choice and attainment. The latter supersedes the gender equity paradigm by questioning the nature of western civilisation itself – seeing it, to paraphrase Rich (1979), as masculine subjectivity masquerading as objectivity – independently of how current pupils might react to or experience its manifestations in the shape of school knowledge. Macaronic discourse thus facilitates dual membership and non-dissonant engagement with both gender equity and more radical feminist interpretations of education. Without textualisation, the thematisation of the patriarchal curriculum both in the academic and policy context of knowledge production may serve to immunise the gender equity paradigm against its more disruptive potential. However, once a theme has gained a cultural foothold, in this instance focused around a substantive topic such as the curriculum, its development as a text becomes a more manageable intellectual and pedagogical exercise.

Intertextuality, Nodal Points and Change

While the penetration of these counter-texts, with their alternative understandings of what is entailed in gendered education and what will be required to change it, is slight, they nonetheless reveal a number of possibilities for change within the gender equity paradigm. These centre around the easing of the gender equity paradigm's framing of its membership, conceptualisation and themes. As with the infiltration of such texts as feminist pedagogy and feminist post-structuralism through tactical engagement, multiple paradigm membership and ambivalent subjectivities, macaronic discourse renders legitimate new ways of speaking about gendered education, provides access to authorities from within these counter-texts and helps to create nodal points of contact with other visions of how gendered education might be understood and countered.

The establishment of these nodal points and the nature and degree of expansion and intensification they facilitate will depend crucially on those who occupy key roles of advocacy, membershipping, monitoring and representation within the gender equity paradigm. These have the capacity to instigate change from within depending on how successful they are in drawing out the implications for schooling and teaching arising from the incorporation of texts other than gender equity such as those of post-structuralism, the epistemological critique of the curriculum and more radical feminist visions for social change. Much will depend on the accommodation reached between their identity as gender equity activists and aspects of their own subjectivities already aligned with these interpretations and understandings, as reflected in their engagement with macaronic discourse and their experience of fluid or multiple paradigm membership. But there are also challenges for feminist intellectuals, and none more so than in the need to textualise the feminist critique of school knowledge. Feminists who view these possibilities for change in tactical terms will no doubt recognise the dangers. Stressing difference can 'cellularise' women, dissipate the identity-base of feminism, retard mobilisation and 'balkanise' feminist politics, while macaronic discourse/fluid and multiple paradigm membership can become a permanent career position straddling domestication and redemption rather than a site of change. These need to be seen in the context of on-going debates on the competing claims of the ideals of assimilation and diversity, universalism and identity and the different interpretations of democratic life they demand (Young, 1990).

The intensification of the gender equity paradigm is one possible consequence of this blurring of its boundaries. Ambivalent identities, fluid subjectivities and multiple membershipping supply the dynamics for theoretical activity since the greater variety of concepts and themes that a paradigm is required to accommodate, the more elaborate will its understanding of a gendered education need to be. The mutation of its doxic status into an orthodoxy that increasingly demands legitimation can be expected. Seemingly ironic, it will be to its advantage that this will involve it validating its position in the light of counter-texts that it has introduced itself.

These issues will be discussed in the Epilogue in relation to the other paradigms at work within the LEM domain and in the macro-context of the mercantile paradigm of the institution of education. In the meantime, it needs to be acknowledged that the gender equity paradigm continues to enjoy dominion throughout the policy-making process, exemplifies the benefits for an understanding of education of being able to draw out specific material implications for educational policy and, within its own limits, must be regarded as exceptionally successful in its shaping of educational policy and practice.

Chapter 12

Travellers' Ethnicity and Egalitarianism: Generative and Integrative LEM Resources?

This final chapter dealing with cultural production relating to the intersection of life chances, education and morality represents a departure, both structurally and substantively, from what has gone before. The structuring features evident since the 1960s around the LEM domain – 'distant other', sponsorship and fairness – experience disruption, challenge or reconstitution in the cultural work relating to Travellers and education and in the knowledge production around egalitarianism as a social and educational objective. In this, 'distant others' become more agential and refuse official inscription, sponsorship is acquired more through political action than philanthropy, economic need or enlightened self-interest, and fairness, that abiding pre-reflexive moral construct in Irish social policy, is confronted by an intensified conceptualisation and textualisation of egalitarianism. Substantively, meanings are excavated that extend beyond distribution to encompass recognition, most obviously in relation to ethnicity and in terms of the scope of egalitarianism's remit. This is to connect with the debate on the politics of difference and recognition (Young, 1990; Taylor, 1992) but in a manner that stresses the interdependency of the so-called different varieties of justice, as reflected in the construct of life chances outlined at the beginning of this section. There, life chances was conceptualised not only in terms of access to material resources but also to those of a symbolic, psychological and political nature that empower people to name their world and their place in it, and to act collectively in the light of this, as well as to compete in the economic and status attainment process (O'Sullivan, 1993b).

But in a monolithic social order resistant to assertions of diversity such an inclusive realisation of life chances through education would be regarded as superfluous, indeed even subversive, while without it there would be little diversity of identity to be unrecognised or violated. Furthermore, we do not live in a world of finite, given and static identities awaiting assumption and recognition. Rather, identities variously experience rejection, modification and reclamation as well as assumption by individuals, and face denial and counter-definition as well as recognition by society. Identities are dynamic, and the successful assertion of one's sense of self and place in the world hinges, not just on access to diverse and empowering resources and a social order open to the redrawing of conventional boundaries establishing sameness and difference, but on the relationships of confrontation, fracture, opportunity and possibility between them. These features of identity politics are realised within the LEM domain, most notably through the cultural production of the relationship between Travellers and education.

Ethnicity, Travellers and Education

A particularly dynamic, intensified and explicit paradigmatic development within the LEM domain is evident in the theorising of the relationship between Travellers and education. Beginning with a conceptualisation of this relationship that drew from individual and cultural 'deficit' texts on educability in the 1960s, the discourse has shifted to one in which ethnicity is the central organising concept. In advancing the series of transitions involved in this development, the conceptualisation and textualisation has been explicitly sociological. Derived from the international texts on educability, often using similar categories to the ones outlined in Chapter 9 on Disadvantage, and on Freirean andragogy, multiculturalism, interculturalism and anti-racism, this has produced a vibrant disputation, contestation and a rare example of public recantation in Irish educational thought. The associative status of the participants has been diverse with an exceptional level of mobilisation and globalisation. The contributors to this discourse have been drawn from both the sedentary and nomadic cultures. What follows is an effort to describe some of these noteworthy and often distinctive features of cultural production within the LEM domain in terms of their paradigmatic processes and dimensions rather than a linear account of changing understandings of Travellers and education.

From 'Deficit' to Ethnicity

The 1963 Report of the Commission on Itinerancy outlined the overarching policy response at that time to what was perceived as the 'problem' of itinerants. In one of its terms of reference the assimilationist approach to Travellers, 'to promote their absorption into the general community' (p. 11), is clearly signalled.

The report was followed by individual and collective action among settled people which sought, in a spirit of Christian charity and fellowship, to 'rescue' Travellers from what was seen to be self-evidently a life of deprivation and squalor. Given the assumptions of this policy, that the settled way of life was the 'normal' civilised set of life circumstances to which Irish people could aspire, and to which Traveller children were entitled if they were to realise their full educational and social rights, the compensatory emphasis in the approach to the education of Travellers at that time was predictable. This compensatory approach is evident in the Report on the Provision of Educational Facilities for the Children of Itinerants (Department of Education, 1970). Arguing that 'the general aim (of the Department of Education) in regard to itinerants is to integrate them with the community', it recommended that 'voluntary organisations could continue to make a valuable contribution by providing the social training of children in preparation for attendance at school'. It conceived of Travellers' homes as lacking in 'facilities for reading, study, homework and normal play and recreational facilities', and proposed that interventions would need to contain 'some provisions for overcoming these disadvantages such as: (a) facilities similar to those provided in a normal home for social, cultural and physical activities; (b) help with homework, where necessary'. For parents, it urged the provision of adult education to help them 'understand what regular schooling can accomplish for their children'.

A version of the culture of poverty theory was explicitly applied to the way of life of Travellers around this time in one of the earliest sociological studies of Irish Travellers (McCarthy, 1972). This was used to consolidate the view within the settlement movement, where it was said to have been 'quoted widely', that Travellers were 'objects of charity whose life on the road was over and who, beneath the poverty, were exactly the same as other Irish men and women' (Gmelch, 1990). Less negative references to a distinctive way of life mentioning its positive features later followed in which themes of self-determination and choice between life on the road and settlement were introduced. Though Kenny (1997a) locates published work using the construct of ethnicity in the mid-1970s, she estimates that 'the ethnic status of Irish Travellers only became a matter of academic policy debate in the late 1980s' (p. 22). Yet, the thematising of ethnicity and its textualisation, particularly through the work of the Dublin Travellers Education and Development Group (DTEDG)/Pavee Point, in discourse from state, corporatist and civil society and professional sources suggest that the dominion of the ethnicity paradigm is substantial within the policy-making sector.

As the conceptualisation of Traveller children as deprived in the individual/ cultural 'deficit' discourse had yielded a compensatory performative, more appropriate implications for educational practice were drawn from the conceptualisation of the experience of Travellers in education in terms of their ethnicity. The affirmation of Traveller identity in the classroom, curriculum materials derived from Travellers' history, lore and culture, and modules on ethnicity and Travellers in teacher preparation programmes and in in-career development were proposed. Multiculturalism in education was itself found wanting because of the manner in which it was said to normalise the dominant culture, merely requiring that it reached out to minority cultures, and then only within schools with an ethnic mix. Interculturalism was proposed as an alternative strategy which would recognise the existence of racism in society at large and work through education towards an ethos of tolerance, mutual respect and affirmation in societies that recognised and celebrated their cultural diversity. These performatives are to be found throughout the 1990s in the policy proposals of the INTO (1992), the Green and White Papers on Education of 1992 and 1995, the Report on the National Education Convention (Coolahan, 1994), and the Task Force on the Travelling Community (Department of the Environment, 1995). Cremins (1997) has also drawn attention to the endorsement of intercultural education in the 1994 and 1995 international conferences on the topic hosted by the Department of Education, a policy that is being followed through in the development of the National Action Plan Against Racism (Department of Justice, Equality and Law Reform, 2002).

Associative Forms

The agents involved in advancing and expanding the shift to an ethnicity paradigm included academics, social activists, state officials, those professionally involved with Travellers and Travellers themselves. Few of those who voluntarily became involved with the life circumstances of Travellers could be described as detached. They brought or evolved explicit conceptualisations of Travellers and their way of life, contested the authoritative status of others, advanced various programmes of action and openly criticised impediments, in the shape of individuals, practices and ideas, to their own prescriptions. They associated with varying degrees of intensity, primacy, activism, exclusivity and confrontation. As well as this range of associative intensity, the number of configurations to have emerged in recent decades is considerable, as the following listing (derived from Rigal, 1989; Gmelch, 1990; INTO, 1992; Kenny, 1997a) demonstrates.

The Dublin Itinerant Settlement Committee (DISC) was formed in 1965 and this led to the Irish Council for Itinerant Settlement/Itinerant Settlement Movement (ISM) in 1969. In 1978 the DISC reformed as the Dublin Committee for Travelling People (DCTP) and the ISM became the National Council for Travelling People (NCTP). When the latter was disbanded in 1990 two groupings emerged, the Irish Traveller Movement (ITM) and the National Federation of Irish Travelling People (NFITP). The Association of Teachers of Travelling

People had as its founder and chairperson, Sr Colette Dwyer, who in 1973 had been appointed to the government-funded position of National Coordinator for Traveller Education under the aegis of NCTP. Among the many local groups with different life-spans to have emerged, a number recur in the official and academic discourse. These include the Navan Committee for Travellers, the Tallaght Committee for the Rights of Travellers, and Minceir Misli (Travellers Moving), a group formed after the urgings of Grattan Puxon, an English journalist of gypsy extraction, that Travellers seek change on their own behalf and not allow settled people to act as advocates for them. The DTEDG/Pavee Point, identified earlier as the most assertive in its advocacy of the ethnicity paradigm, was formed in 1985. This level of mobilisation and associative diversity is all the more remarkable when one considers the numerical representation of Travellers in Ireland. The Report of the Task Force on the Travelling Community (Department of the Environment, 1995) gives the 1994 figure of 4,083 families as the most recent estimate, while a number of Traveller activist sources (Collins, 1992; Mac Laughlin, 1995) put the total number in the region of 22,000 Travellers. If we are to believe Gmelch (1990), it was achieved from within a 'atomistic' social system, with no 'superordinate political structure' and a lack of 'lineages, clans, formal leaders (despite the public fiction of "tinker kings") and formalised mechanisms of social control'. She wonders how Travellers acquired the organisational skills needed and, quoting examples, she attributes significance to the influence of a few outsiders, in the case of Dublin Travellers, for instance, social workers with a commitment to change who adopted a community development rather than a casework approach.

Membershipping, Exiting, Factioning

These social configurations have represented distinct paradigms, as well as differences in conceptualisation, textualisation and performatives within the same paradigm. Assimilationist, sub-cultural and ethnicity paradigms are particularly visible. But differences can also be less clearly drawn. Thus, the INTO report *Travellers in Education* (1992) identified differences, on the basis of submissions received from them, between the ITM and the NFITP, as to the extent to which the 'concept of nomadism should determine the kind of education available to Traveller children' (p. 25) and whether or not 'it is in the interests of Travellers to designate them as a separate ethnic group in Irish society', the NFITP claiming that 'the majority of Travellers want to be regarded as Irish … take pride in their Irish heritage and have no interest in the concept of ethnicity' (pp 25-26). Yet, at the 1991 Conference, 'Irish Travellers: History, Culture, Society', attended by Travellers, sedentary people who work with them, and academics, only one speaker (McLoughlin, 1994) dissented from the ethnicity paradigm.

But the boundaries of the paradigm's membership can be less formally drawn and may be signalled by practice and discourse identified with a particular paradigm's tenets rather than collective association. An example is provided in McCarthy's (1994) refutation at the above conference of her influential application of the culture of poverty theory to Travellers 20 years after it had been initially advanced. She observed that 'it has done them a great disservice insofar as the theory has been used by certain people to discredit Travellers and to negate their separate cultural identity'. This, in turn, was welcomed by a community youth worker (Collins, 1994) with the DTEDG who used the opportunity to criticise the practice of 'experts' developing theories about Travellers without consultation and dialogue. Social integration was facilitated, however, as Collins acknowledged that 'it takes courage to admit that one has made mistakes', and at the same conference, Kenny (1994) conceded that McCarthy's original research was made to carry too much of the blame: 'it hardly caused, but rather was invoked as a rationale for the thinking of the dominant group, many of whom probably never read her work.'

This type of exiting/membershipping strategy at the informal level is frequent in policy paradigms but this was a uniquely public and theoretically explicit example. There are also recorded instances in the discourse on Travellers and education of new conceptualisations being disparaged in defence of existing understandings and strategies. Kenny (1997a, p. 113) quotes from the final report (1998) of the National Coordinator for Traveller Education, Sr Colette Dwyer: 'sometimes people who have returned from Third World countries ... seem to assume that the needs of the Travellers are identical with those of oppressed people ... abroad ... and to impose on a somewhat bewildered Traveller community their own philosophies.' Kenny interprets this to refer to groups such as Minceir Misli and the DTEDG/Pavee Point (whose Director, John O'Connell, had worked as a Columban Father in the Philippines) who proclaimed the ethnicity paradigm. In other instances those to whom a particular conceptualisation was attributed disputed its accuracy as a true reflection of their disposition towards Travellers and their life circumstances.

This was the experience of O'Connell (1992) who sought to identify the underlying assumptions about Travellers to be found in popular and official discourse. Using a set of categories that has much in common with similar efforts at classification in relation to class and gender (O'Sullivan, 1984a), he distinguishes between different models of Travellers – idealist, liberal humanist, social pathology, sub-culture of poverty, and human rights. He also theorised the construct of ethnicity in an effort to refute its association with 'the strange and exotic', and to confront the 'strong resistance and rebuttal' among settled people to its application to Travellers (O'Connell, 1994). He argues against biological and social essentialism, contending that ethnicity is not a 'natural' or 'immutable' entity but rather it 'refers primarily to the set of socio-cultural traits which define a shared identity' and 'is produced in historically specific contexts and … emerges, changes and adapts in meaning over time'. Kenny (1997a, p. 24) reports 'hostile' responses from the official and voluntary sectors to these attributions as to how they understood Travellers and their way of life. She observes that 'many practitioners and policy-makers maintained that they had no ideology, that these "models" caricatured much more subtle locally developed practices which met the needs of the moment'.

The manner in which multiculturalism was forced to give way to interculturalism as the sanctioned conceptualisation of policy discourse for managing ethnicity in education, provides us with another example of cultural work relevant to Travellers in action. It can be argued that multiculturalism accommodated diverse meanings, including all that is asserted in interculturalism, such as the celebration of diversity and the obligation to identify and challenge racism, including its institutionalisation within society (Haran and Tormey, 2002). But, in forcing a factioning of the meanings and, subsequently, texts of multiculturalism through the differentiation established through language, interculturalism not just appropriated what it deemed to be the more radical/ progressive interpretations from within multiculturalism, but it also positioned multiculturalism as the older, less modern, softer principle for dealing with cultural diversity. Semantically, this arguably was unnecessary, but as an exercise in cultural politics it was effective and tactical. No new meanings were added to intersubjectivity but interculturalism succeeded in foregrounding antiracism in discourse and, in contrast with the experience of equality of educational opportunity, forcing choices about paradigmatic positions and associations.

What distinguishes this paradigmatic interaction and communication – exiting/membershipping, confrontation, denial, factioning – is how discursive the message- sending procedures were and how difficult it seems to have been for any of the participants to claim paradigmatic neutrality. Position papers, submissions, seminars and publications carry conceptualisations and performatives that, either explicitly or through less academic terminology, signal well-framed paradigms with self-proclaimed/attributed members. And where there were blurred boundaries or fractured identities, these were often employed to facilitate progression in allegiance/dominance from one paradigm to the next.

Sedentary/Traveller Positionality

The growth in Traveller self-advocacy from a point in the 1960s when Travellers were spoken for or had their observations interpreted by professionals and sedentary activists has been routinely noted in the commentaries on the emergence of the Traveller movement (Rigal, 1989; Gmelch, 1990; Kenny, 1997a). Given this development, one would expect the positionality (sedentary/Traveller) of participants in discourse to be credited with significance in establishing the validity of knowledge creation about Travellers. Collins's (1994) critique of 'experts' who construct theories about Travellers without consultation or dialogue is an example. Mac Laughlin (1995, p. 82) diagnoses the work of Gramscian 'organic intellectuals', 'drawn from the ranks of the Travellers themselves ... articulating Traveller demands and, more importantly, raising the political and ethnic consciousness of the Traveller community, (as) arguably the single most important development in Irish Traveller culture in this century'. This is to ignore the role played by sedentary activists, as Kenny (1997b) points out, drawing attention to the prominence of the work of John O'Connell.

O'Connell (1992) describes the early work of the DTEDG from the 1980s when the perception of Travellers as an ethnic group was supported by 'some anthropologists and a small minority involved with Travellers'. Arguing that the question of identity had to be studied in terms of the concrete situation of Travellers, and that such questions cannot be answered by settled people, academic or otherwise, independently of Travellers, they sought to avoid the 'paternalistic relations of dependency' of earlier engagements between Travellers and settled people working with them. His description of the approaches adopted by the DTEDG reveals the influence of community activism, and andragogy with a strong Freirean lineage.

> We wanted to challenge the widespread racism, prejudice and discrimination towards Travellers. We also wanted to offer our skills in the support of Travellers in their struggle for justice and acceptance in Irish society ... we formed alliances with other groups and individuals who had a similar philosophy or were searching for new approaches. We decided to apply community work principles and methods ... undertaking an ongoing analysis of Travellers' living circumstances and marginal status in order to take collective action based on that. It also meant that Travellers themselves would have to be consulted and actively involved in all stages of the process in order to promote autonomy and self-reliance. We felt that a prerequisite for this was education, consciousness-raising and organisation ...

Further development of the significance of sedentary/Traveller positionality in the shaping of discourse and construction of knowledge, which draws on anti-colonial texts, is suggested in an analysis of the dynamics at work in the 1991 Conference 'Irish Travellers: History, Culture, Society'. Kenny (1994) describes the debate at the conference as a 'pull-push process': 'sedentary people pulled back, revealing the cultural terrain ... of the Travellers; and the Travellers pushed forward, claiming it. But did we yield it up? We showed ourselves to be caught up in a post-colonial dynamic – we, the power-holders, the sedentary people, still with a coloniser mind-set; the Travellers with a colonised one. Where the power lay was evident in the drift of the debate, for all our struggle, on both sides, to be free. The agenda of the sedentary dominated.' In order to understand and act more appropriately, Kenny recommends that 'we need to listen to Travellers, but this includes recognising the silencing of their traditions which their delegitimation has imposed: as an integral part of listening we must allow them opportunities to undo internal and internalised colonisation, we must return to them the space to come to terms with their experience and to find their voice'. The role of academic researchers is to 'serve the people, dialogue with Travellers and those working with Travellers in relation to our choice of topics and methods, and our research findings – not to pander to either practitioners or Travellers, but to do research which will, as appropriate, validate or challenge both groups'. This seems less an account of what happened at the conference and more an effort to prescribe good practice in relation to sedentary/Traveller positionality in the production of knowledge about Travellers.

There continue to be few Travellers who participate in academic debate, and those who do invoke specific texts in their discourse (Collins, 1992, 1994; McDonagh, 1994) are difficult to classify as either carriers or creators of these texts. The dynamics involved in the hailing of subjectivities through an engagement with texts, with its issues of authenticity, fragmentation, misrecognition, exploitation, or tactical engagement, seems to be a potential area for further exploration among those involved with the education of Travellers. Kenny's (1997a) adoption of discourse analysis and her increasing use of post-colonial concepts such as those of liminality and hybridity, has the potential to move the analysis of positionality and standpoint in knowledge production about Travellers further in this and related directions. As we have seen in Chapter 9, similar themes have been raised in relation to professionals working with the disadvantaged. But, unlike the experience of textualising socioeconomic impediments to educability, where there was an avoidance of the conflicting nature of texts in *pastiche*, the cultural production of Travellers' education in terms of ethnicity succeeded in proceeding through a theorised discourse of a kind that produced an intensified paradigm.

Intertextuality, Nodal Points and Change

While lived experience and Traveller identity inevitably enhance legitimacy, global appeals to legislative procedures and progressive principles and practices in other countries are prominent in the intensification of the ethnicity paradigm. The 1976 Race Relations Act in Britain has been regularly cited in support of the claim that Irish Travellers are a distinct ethnic group (Kenny, 1991; O'Connell, 1994). The conditions necessary to be regarded as an ethnic group under the 1976 Act were largely social, cultural and historical. They include self-definition, acknowledgement by others, shared history, common language and religion, and distinctive customs and practices. Irish Travellers argued that they satisfied these conditions. Council of Europe endorsement of intercultural education in the early 1980s, subsequent international conferences on the topic including two in Dublin, and authorities in the field of Traveller and Gypsy education at the European level have been used to situate and legitimate Irish advocacy in relation to Travellers and education, in particular its ethnicity paradigm, in a more global framework. As Gmelch (1990) puts it, 'Irish Travellers form a small minority within Ireland but as Traveller-Gypsies they have a potential collective strength of ten million.' She wonders, however, about the legitimatory and mobilisation benefits of globalisation since 'in England, the Travelling Community, composed of both Gypsies and Irish Travellers, is deeply factionised'. Far from strengthening the dominance of the ethnicity paradigm, in terms of numerical strength and orthodoxy, it could be that globalisation of the Traveller movement will destabilise its dominion through both the endorsement of less publicised subjectivities among Irish Travellers themselves and the introduction of new themes relevant to their ongoing exploration of identity and politics. A further dynamic has been introduced by the diversification of ethnicity through the greater cultural plurality of Irish society in recent years.

In reviewing the transition from a deprivation to an ethnicity paradigm over the past 40 years, a number of very visible features of paradigmatic change are evident. Expurgation, mutation, reconceptualisation, and factioning are all in evidence. Attributions of deprivation in the 1960s, used to stir the Christian conscience of fellow Irish people, allowed for the transition from the charity-motivated performatives of a culture of poverty text with its associated assimilationist policies and compensatory forms of educational intervention. The conceptualisation of a set of practices and dispositions as a distinctive way of life survived the rejection of poverty as its source. This collectivisation of identity, which spawned the themes of choice and self-determination, allowed for mutation through its reconceptualisation in terms of ethnicity. Successfully thematised and textualised, ethnicity yielded human rights and anti-racist performatives. Multiculturalism was forced to give way to interculturalism as the desired approach to the management of ethnicity in education.

What appears as a quantum leap in paradigmatic change in a few decades was in fact a highly skilled (though not necessarily knowing) achievement that used what it perceived as the most favourable elements (conceptualisations, signifiers, themes, performatives) in otherwise undesirable discourse to advance a more favoured paradigm. This is most visible and tactical in the case of the macaronic (at times, multiple) discourse of Sr Colette Dwyer, National Coordinator for Traveller Education, for much of the 1970s and 1980s, who succeeded in signaling, if not membership of, at least affinity with, a diversity of paradigms

institutional systems structured around equality'. She never quite spells out the implications for the political, civic and private spheres of her criticism of liberalism's 'prioritisation of freedom over equality'. Government action is expected: 'egalitarian policies will also require that the government intervenes in the market to ensure the redistribution of wealth, to protect rights and to ensure that there is equality in the distribution of power' (Lynch, 1994). While there are a number of similar suggestions as to what governments must do to achieve equality of condition, there is no mention of the political system necessary to allow governments the discretion to act in this way. Nor is it clear what vision of state action is assumed. Baker, however, who is favourably cited by Lynch on an ongoing basis, and who was also a founder member of the Equality Studies Centre, has produced a book-length argument for egalitarianism, *Arguing for Equality* (1987). In this he seeks to answer questions on the extent of state control, the degree of bureaucracy and the curbs on personal freedom in an egalitarian society, the limitations imposed by human nature on political change, the links between egalitarianism and socialism, and in general seeks to counter a wide range of objections to egalitarianism. But this makes scarcely any reference to education, and its themes have not been incorporated into Irish educational discourse. Also untextualised is the contribution, if any, that schools might make to facilitating the transition to an egalitarian society, as distinct from what would characterise schools when operating along egalitarian principles. These are potential sources of intensification for the egalitarian paradigm.

Because the production and insertion of egalitarianism into Irish educational discourse is an academic project, it possesses the intellectual resources necessary for intensification. But it is in a position to make its own choices as to how it is to develop, and it has not to date chosen to expand along these lines. There are no public challenges to its tenets that it might feel compelled to counter in the interests of its legitimacy. It can thus develop in whatever manner it is considered beneficial for its own project. It is not forced onto cultural battlegrounds of another's choosing. From its initial insertion into Irish educational discourse, egalitarianism has aspired to a substantively broader and more structural understanding of life chances than would have prevailed in Irish discourse on equality:

> within the liberal model, personal character and individual attributes, rather than public institutions or structures, become accountable for success or failure. Factors such as gender, social class, ethnicity, religion, race, disability or sexual orientation are examined, not in relational terms for their equality impact but rather in individualist, what Bourdieu (1973) called, 'atomistic terms'. The causes of inequality are sought within the attributes themselves rather than within the structures and institutions which order the relations within and between these attribute-bearing individuals (Lynch, 1996).

It has been along these lines that egalitarianism has developed in relation to education throughout the 1990s and to the present. In the process, further resources for its intensification have been drawn from egalitarian, feminist, and communication studies, as well as from sociology. No single source is seen as the origin of inequality in education. Depending on circumstances, it may be economic, political, socio-cultural or affective relations or some or all of these in interaction. This yields an approach to intensifying the egalitarian paradigm that embodies 'a pluri-disciplinary analytical framework that recognises the multivalent and interlocking character of student identities as relational subjects' (Lynch and Lodge, 2002, p. 6). The consequence for paradigm formation is the expansion of egalitarianism throughout the social order as additional and more complex sources of inequality are encompassed within it:

> Inequality is a distributive problem in so far as it is rooted in politico-economic
> systems in terms of patterns of ownership, control, distribution and consumption; it
> is a recognition problem insofar as it operates in culturally-based systems of
> recognition, non-recognition and mis-recognition; it is a representational problem in
> all contexts where power is enacted, in the realms of decision-making, and in
> systems of inclusion and exclusion in the exercise of power; and it is an affective
> matter when it pertains to relations of dependency and interdependency (Lynch and
> Lodge, 2002, p. 13).

Considered within the LEM domain, it positions itself as the master paradigm incorporating and aspiring to dominion over the cultural terrain of all the other LEM paradigms so far considered. Of the three requirements for an LEM paradigm to exist culturally – aspects of life chances, a basis for differentiation between beneficiaries and a moral dimension – only the latter is relatively under-developed, though its assertion is at the heart of egalitarianism. The variety and range in its coverage both of the resources, restraints and possibilities mediated by education and their beneficiaries and non-beneficiaries is comprehensive, and capable of further expansion as new sources of inequality are inevitably identified. Such is its political remit, it is in the nature of egalitarianism to be expansionist as a paradigm.

A key dynamic for further intensification within the egalitarian paradigm, more central than the textualisation of its political and moral dimensions, is the tension between its vanguardist and standpoint epistemology dimensions.

Vanguardist/Standpoint Tension: A Dynamic for Intensification?

The four variety model of equality – access, participation, outcome, condition – developed within the Equality Studies Centre is not merely a scheme for analysing issues of justice or a process by which certain understandings of justice held throughout society might be designated as inadequate or otherwise. Equality studies is described as an attempt 'to develop the intellectual apparatus which would both explain inequalities and offer an analysis of alternative futures both in the theoretical and the applied institutional sense. The aim is not simply to understand how to develop a classless society or a feminist one, rather how to create an egalitarian one' (Lynch, 1995). Over a series of works that embody sustained scholarly analysis, encompassing research findings, formalist conceptualisations and theories, argument and counter-argument, egalitarianism is presented as the only viable vision of social justice (Lynch, 1994, 1996, 1999a, 2000; Lynch and Lodge, 2002). The appeal is to the power and authority of modernist reason, possibility, hope and emancipation; not, for instance, to the hermeneutical analysis of sacred texts, the privileged voice of disadvantaged groups, populist sentiment or democratic process.

One could visualise egalitarianism being advanced from this vanguard position by means of proclamation, dissemination, mobilisation and alliances with a view to expanding its membership to the point at which it represents, at least, a critical mass in society. Lynch (2000) recognises the necessity for both the cultural and political expansion of egalitarianism: 'to achieve radical egalitarian change, we must develop a political culture which supports change; and the changes must be supported by the electorate ... this poses a serious challenge to political leaders, activists, educators and others committed to the ideal of creating a socially just society. It presents a challenge around ideology and ideas in the politics of change.' In a critique of approaches to inequality such as interpretative sociology and critical theory, which estimates the nature and extent of inequalities and the weaknesses of existing policies, Lynch (1995, 1999a) following Sayer (1995) advocates 'counterfactuals', clearly defined systematic outlines of alternative structures and social systems. Egalitarianism is meant to operate as such a 'counterfactual', inviting change in consciousness as part of the democratic process as it hails individuals and groups to its cultural interpretation of a just social order.

Standpoint epistemology is a central theme in Lynch's work on inequality. Indeed, she has argued, following Melucci (1996), that 'what people lack increasingly is the power to name their own world. One of the greatest exclusions today is exclusion from the power of naming' (Lynch, 2000). Standpoint on knowing the world is widely used in feminist theory and method as an argument for the perspective of women to be incorporated into the process of knowledge production (Harding, 1986; Hartsock, 1987) where it operates to different effect, including the relativisation of different perspectives and the privileging of that of the essentialised woman (Stanley and Wise, 1990). Its more generic form is to be found in the Marxist view that the perspective of the powerful is less likely to be reliable than that of the subordinated; in Lukács's (1971[1923]) characterisation, the proletariat possess a more dependable understanding of society than that of the bourgeoisie who benefit from their subordination (Maynard, 1998).

A collaborative paper by Lynch and O'Neill (1994) in which it is argued that middle-class academics colonise working-class inequalities for their own professional purpose provides an extended manifestation of this standpoint epistemology in operation. O'Neill is described in the paper as a working-class woman involved in community action and adult education who has participated with Lynch in a number of projects dealing with class, unemployment and poverty. O'Neill's (1992) account of how working-class women represent their lived experience, based on research conducted by working-class women themselves in a suburb of Dublin with a high welfare dependency, is used to argue that poverty and not culture is central to the explanation of educational inequalities. It is also drawn on to illuminate the issue at the heart of the paper – 'to explore the dilemmas posed by the analysis of working-class issues in education by professional sociologists'. Lynch and O'Neill wonder: 'by naming someone else's world for them are we robbing them of a voice? By speaking *for* people do we misrepresent their point of view? Can professional sociologists, no matter how well-intentioned or informed, give anything but an outsider's account of a working-class world?' They argue that 'the poverty which ensues from living on social welfare or low wages … is beyond the full comprehension of those who do not live it out daily'. The rendering of working-class standpoint in the article, however, is not uniform and realises a number of its representations:

> We are not suggesting here that there is some pure truth that exists about social class or that there is only one voice, that of the working-class itself; we are not saying that there is no role for the academic or the intellectual. We are not trying to substitute 'the lost figure of the colonised' (in this case the working-class) for intellectual analysis. What we are suggesting, at the very least, is that to avoid disassociating the reality of oppression from research analysis and theory, 'researchers have to learn how to put their knowledge and skills at the disposal of their research subjects, for them to use them in whatever ways they choose' (Oliver, 1992, p. 111).The agenda for research and theory must be set in dialogue with people themselves. It cannot be set with reference to the interests of professional sociologists alone.

> The first step which is required is that oppressed and exploited groups are in a position to name their own world, and fight their own struggles inside and outside education. They must find their own voice rather than have experts speaking 'at them', 'for them' or 'about them'. The social class experts have to hand back the voices they have territorialised; they have to let go.

Even in its mildest version, as a multiperspectival construction of reality, standpoint epistemology requires that disadvantaged or discriminated groups must participate in the production of knowledge about themselves, not only what constitutes the nature of their social, economic and political position but also how it might be redeemed. This is in contrast to presenting schemes, programmes or manifestoes to them as part of the political process be it at local, issue-based or party levels. This refers to the distinction between self-representation and democratic choice. Prescriptions for a just social order exist in tension with even the most diluted versions of standpoint epistemology, to say nothing of offering one's skills and knowledge to the oppressed to be deployed as they will.

While this is a potential source of intensification for the egalitarian paradigm, how it is engaged with could also destabilise it. All paradigms have doxic dimensions, yielding incorrigible positions in their defence. If these are compromised, the paradigm mutates, factions or even ruptures. With employability it is the link between paid work and life chances. For Christian Communitarianism it is the holding back of the materialist critique of the hermeneutics of sacred texts as the backdoor re-entry for religion in a rational society. For egalitarianism it is equality of condition. If this is opened up to the self-representation of disadvantaged and discriminated groups, it may give validity within the intersubjective community of egalitarianism to other understandings of equality along its continuum. At the individual level it has the capacity to create dissonance and the destabilisation of identities built around egalitarianism. For ideological, discursive and psychological reasons, therefore, a paradigm will seek to contain such threats. The principles of collaboration between intellectuals and grassroots activists may be extended only to such issues as strategy and not to the specification of what a vision of an ideal society might be. In this or some other manner, the possibility that as a result of such collaboration some other vision of justice might replace egalitarianism as the ideal social policy objective may be suppressed as a theme. Once egalitarianism is assumed to be an unquestioned good for the disadvantaged and discriminated, those who object to it, or are likely to oppose the implications of egalitarian policies, can be dismissed as acting out of self-interest and the domain assumptions of privileged positions.

It would seem that insofar as egalitarianism engages with the vanguardist/ standpoint tension, it does so in terms of such strategies of containment. In this, the role of the intellectual, intellectual activity and dialogue come to have meanings peculiar to the paradigm itself. Dialogue is foreclosed, its process and product, be they knowledge or social and political activism, circumscribed within the pursuit of egalitarianism. It is incapable of acknowledging the agency of sociologists or members of disadvantaged groups who might, for instance, dissent from the material analysis of educational opportunity or from egalitarian prescriptions on the basis of what they consider to be in the best interests of disadvantaged groups or society at large. Sociologists only attain validity when they work to advance the predetermined good of egalitarianism. If they dissent from this they are discredited as class thinkers or self-interested academics. This approach to knowledge production is consistent with dialogue in intellectual activity once one works within the assumptions of the egalitarian paradigm. Egalitarianism is limited in its manoeuverability in this regard by comparison with, for instance, Christian communitarianism. Unlike the sacred texts and religious beliefs of Christian communitarianism which are logically prior to its prescriptions, though not necessary if secularists are to be engaged in the pursuit of common goals, for egalitarianism its defining tenet is the desired end of its social mobilisation and action.

As exemplified by Lynch and O'Neill's (1994) article on the colonisation of social class in education, standpoint epistemology essentialises working-class experience of schooling, suppressing differences in how poor people both between and within themselves categorise, explain, evaluate and feel about their situation. This serves to elide any questioning of the authority of a member of the egalitarian paradigm to represent working-class life and relieves the egalitarian paradigm of the need to extend its legitimatory armoury to cope with working-class dissent from egalitarianism. If not instigated from within, it may well need counter-texts to provoke intensification along these lines. Yet, it is difficult to locate any public example of educational texts that explicitly position themselves in opposition to that of egalitarianism or even to any of its characteristic themes or performatives. In a specific commentary on 'The Colonisation of Social Class in Education', Tormey and Prendeville (2000) have pointed to the absence of a unitary working-class voice and the problems that follow in trying to accommodate a working-class standpoint into knowledge production – what happens when researchers and working-class subjects do not agree, as well as the potential for a derogation of moral responsibility in putting one's research skills at the disposal of some working-class people in a way that might have implications for other working-class people who differ from them in terms of gender, ethnicity, age, geography, substantive interpretation of their situation, and so on. A core issue 'is trying to identify which group of the working-class we should work with. We could choose to only dialogue with working-class people that we are likely to agree with. It may be that this is what Lynch has, perhaps unintentionally, done. This is problematic for all sorts of reasons. For a start it seems a bit too close to stacking one's research. Certainly it means ignoring the voices of some of the working-class' (p. 2).

Also relevant is Fagan's (1995) study of early school-leavers, a rare example of public discourse on Irish education that exclusively adopts the critical pedagogy text. This has much in common with egalitarianism. It includes a rejection of all the pre-political economy texts on educability and of economic determinism itself, an espousal of a communicative ethics which is sympathetic towards the 'epistemological privilege of the oppressed' (p. 160), and its advocacy of linkages between the struggles of early school-leavers and those of other groups seeking justice. Fagan, however, puts her trust in cultural politics on the basis that 'culture produces power, knowledge, subjectivities and identities ... Central to this is the understanding that social relations are as culturally as they are economically produced, and that rhetoric, ideology, and the articulations of the more egalitarian vision of society are as "real", as "material", and in certain instances may be as effective in emancipatory transformation as are the most material of economic changes' (p. 150). Yet, she is hesitant in suggesting tactics and refuses to prescribe for an ideal society. What she aspires to is 'a provisional political strategy that avoids the dangerous totalitarian clarity of a reified end, that is not messianic but yet contains a strategy of cultural production' (p. 150). She describes her text on the cultural politics of early school-levers as 'not complete'. But 'it is not complete because it should not be complete, but continuously open as a process of its own theory and practice. The political struggle for transformation can afford neither theoretical nor practical closure' (p. 168).

Fagan's critical pedagogy offered a mutated version of egalitarianism to Irish educational discourse and provided for shifting engagement, loyalties and subjectivities at their intersections. But, it did not connect directly with the egalitarian paradigm of Lynch and her associates. Nor did it address the Irish political, cultural or economic context, though its fieldwork was carried out in Ireland. While Lynch does not directly engage with Fagan's rendering of critical pedagogy on the issue of closure in political struggle, she has however repeatedly taken issue with American critical pedagogy, including that of Fagan, targeting, in particular, Giroux, Apple, McLaren and, more variably, Freire. Critical pedagogy, though applauded for holding out hope for educators in opposition to the deterministic fatalism of structural Marxism, is found wanting because of its over-reliance on the pedagogical relationship and the transformative capacity of teachers, its lack of connection with its political context and with marginalised people themselves, the absence of an explicit alternative social vision, and the failure to anticipate the potential among educational mediators for counter-resistance (Lynch, 1989, 1990, 1994, 1996, 1999a; Lynch and O'Riordan, 1998; Lynch and Lodge, 2002).

Egalitarianism could well persist and expand without intensifying around the legitimatory and knowledge production issues associated with the vanguardist/standpoint tension. But it is a tension that remains and recurs in egalitarian discourse most practically in Lynch's proposals relating to the establishment of Research Coalitions and Learning Partnerships in universities and research institutes with a view to incorporating a standpoint position into knowledge production and emancipatory action (Lynch, 1999b). It is argued that 'the only way in which people can exercise ongoing, systematic influence on naming their own world is by being centrally involved at all stages of the research process, including design, interpretation, and outcome-implementation'. If this is to happen:

> Procedures for Research Coalitions would need to be developed between research bodies, universities (and their departments) and communities and groups who are being researched. In addition, Learning Partnerships need to be established to enable researchers to learn (in the doing of research) about the role of experiential knowledge in understanding and, to enable marginalised people to name their own world in their own words. Finally, if knowledge is to have transformative potential at a structural as well as an ideological level, then Equality Action Plans need to be developed from the research findings.

In this regard, Lynch has acknowledged the diversity of understandings of inequality among disadvantaged and discriminated groups and the difficulty of academics being confronted by what for them are unacceptable interpretations held by those who have the benefit of the lived experience. In practice, this may well facilitate the stabilisation within egalitarian discourse of the status of dialogical learning popularised by Freire in the context of empowerment and emancipation. While Freire is routinely implicated in egalitarianism's dissatisfaction with critical pedagogy, his work is less systematically excluded or rejected than that of Giroux with whom he is most linked. On some occasions, Lynch (1999a) seems to hold out little hope for the full exploitation of the possibilities of dialogical learning, developed by Freire in non-formal learning settings initially in Brazil, within a state system of education. With O'Neill, she argues:

> The idea of developing pedagogical styles and curricula for the purposes of bringing about educational change is an appealing one to academics removed from the coal face of poverty and class attack. The political difficulties involved in achieving it however, within the state-controlled education systems of western bourgeois democracies, is self-evident to all but those who are wearing academic and political blindfolds (Lynch and O'Neill, 1994).

But she has also argued that 'while there is much written about the difficulties of translating Freirean principles of pedagogy into schools and classrooms, in the long run, the move in that direction is as inevitable as it is desirable, the reason being because of the change in the nature of authority relations in most Western countries from traditional authority to rational authority'; and later in the article contending that their application is not confined to schools and classrooms, that 'they are also crucial for the development of effective equality policies at regional, national or international level' (Lynch, 1996). Suitably integrated into the discursive practices and subjectivities of egalitarianism, it could well be a practice that would test its ability to confront its vanguardist/standpoint tensions, but with implications that are unpredictable and include the more intensified legitimation of its social vision and tenets, paradigmatic change and shifting membership.

Membershipping and Dominion

In signifying egalitarianism as equality of condition, its conceptualisation within the spectrum of meanings realised by the signifier 'equality' is promoted. Semantically, it is located in terms of the equality/inequality dualism, so that while equality of condition is said to be different from all the other three varieties of equality – access, participation, outcome – it enters into public understanding in a semantically non-discordant fashion through its conceptualisation along a continuum of equality. This eases its insertion into policy discourse, where linguistically it can appear as a variation of the mainstream concept of equality of educational opportunity. Even at the point of its cultural instantiation, therefore, egalitarianism remains a concept without a distinguishing signifier. It is known largely as the opposite to more liberal understandings of equality and, lacking a developed textualisation of the themes of political order, civil society, the role of the state, personal freedom and social and political change, it can appear as education reaching out to these spheres rather than as political ideology being applied. Nonetheless, in its engagement of the LEM domain, egalitarianism is the most comprehensive of the paradigms to emerge in Irish educational discourse in the range of the individual resources, structural relationships and social categories which it seeks to cover and to which its principles are meant to apply.

Egalitarianism, for Lynch (1994), demands 'adopting an holistic perspective on equality'. She draws attention to the manner in which 'discussion about equality is segmented into different camps' which she links with the approach to equality adopted: 'there is nothing impelling in the equal opportunities model requiring its protagonists to address all forms of inequality simultaneously. Yet, if we are to have a truly egalitarian education system, we must consider the needs of all underprivileged groups in the system, and not just address those which have the greatest lobbying power.' The egalitarian paradigm, therefore, 'hails' comprehensively, both in terms of culture and subjects. At first sight, it would appear that there is an extensive and varied constituency of meaning, both individually and collectively, in Ireland at present amenable to egalitarianism and open to self-definition on its terms. Lynch (2000) has drawn attention to the regular deployment of equality as a social principle in public discourse, the passing of two major pieces of legislation – the Employment Equality Act of 1998 and the Equal Status Act of 2000 –, the existence of a number of state bodies and agencies with an equality remit, and an increasing incidence of mobilisation and action around issues that involve distribution of resources, recognition and anti-discrimination, and power.

But Lynch also acknowledges the difficulty of successfully 'hailing' these equality activities, texts and subjectivities arising from their diversity of focus and interpretation of equality. Indeed, they may see themselves in competition with one another, may consider their self-interest lies in maintaining a narrow focus, or that society is likely to be more immediately and better served by adopting a more limited and realisable equality aspiration than that of egalitarianism (National Economic and Social Forum, 1996). For such reasons, egalitarianism may be variously experienced as discordant. It is also necessary to recognise that not all of those who describe themselves or their policies in terms of egalitarianism, do so in line with the principle of equality of condition. While it would be quite unrealistic to hope that this equality discourse and action could be substantially mobilised to a coordinated egalitarian politics, it does represent for the egalitarian paradigm the most immediate and necessary target of intertextual penetration and recruitment.

One might expect that egalitarianism would adapt in the face of such challenges and material opportunities, if not quite by modifying its key tenet of equality of condition, at least in how it represents and legitimates itself, particularly in what it might regard as the most likely nodal points of intersection with these diverse equality projects. The egalitarian paradigm has proved to be quite unadaptive in this regard, and the rare instances of this dynamic in its discourse, as it seeks to appeal to non-members and adopts strategic compromises to further its dominion within the enactment of policy, are worthy of note. In seeking to engage with non-members, it has shown a willingness to modify its conflict view of society and its suspicion of the deceptions of consensualist politics. While acknowledging that opposition to egalitarianism is inevitable due to the manner in which it threatens the interests of those who are already wealthy, have power and prestige, and generally benefit from the kinds of knowledge, skills and cultural capital currently rewarded in capitalist societies, Lynch (1996) eases towards a consensual 'win-win' text:

> ... what can be recognised and made more visible to existing elites and power holders in society is that the cost of inequality, politically, socially and economically is high. That is to say, while it may be unrealistic to expect privileged groups or individuals to support egalitarian aims, on the grounds of principle or on the grounds of compassion, what is possible is that they may come to support it on the basis of enlightened self-interest. Wastage of educational ability, poverty, unemployment, ethnic tensions, gender tensions, and other by-products of inequality create political and social instabilities and conflicts in a given society. These instabilities result in both direct costs and opportunity costs which are considerable. Such costs if enumerated and publicised could contribute to developing a commitment to equality even among those whose immediate self-interest may not be visibly served by equality of condition.

Another strategy of engagement with those who may feel threatened by the radical leap involved in setting egalitarian policy objectives for society, is to suggest that equality is not an 'all or nothing affair' (Baker, 1987, p.149). Lynch (1996) argues:

> Even if a given society does not adhere to the principle of equality of condition, a recognition of its importance does influence the way in which objectives are framed and targeted. For example, a move to promote greater equality in the distribution of income and wealth through the promotion of greater equality in taxation structures, would move society towards this objective; the introduction of systems and structures which promoted participatory democracy and decision-making would also help in the realisation of equality of condition.

This can act to blur the distinction between egalitarianism and the other three conceptions of equality since it may allow those who would, for instance, support no more than the elimination of the extremes and excesses in the distribution of power and wealth to regard themselves as having accommodated the egalitarian principle. At the cultural level, this would effectively immunise them from susceptibility to full-blown egalitarianism in their knowledge of the world. Baker (1987 p. 150) argues along the same lines as Lynch but recognises the strategic danger, that 'in declaring priorities that lower priorities will simply be forgotten'. While he argues that 'many egalitarian aims depend on the growth of a popular commitment to equality', he cautions that 'egalitarians should never allow current priorities to stifle the open discussion and endorsement of longer-term goals. Otherwise those will never be achieved at all.' However, the paradigmatic implications may run more deeply than performatives, such as the setting of social policy objectives, and are likely to be less easily cautioned against.

These are examples of boundary politics, as a paradigm's non-members are appealed to through an attenuation of what they are expected to experience as its discordant features. This may result in a permanent cultural shift within a paradigm, provide it with a more extensive or sophisticated legitimatory mechanism capable of coping with an additional range of doubts, resistance or counter-texts, or be no more than an example of liminal discourse – experimental, tentative, stretching and testing the limits of communication with non-members. Their rarity in egalitarian discourse suggests the latter. But these may well be examples of the boundary politics that could follow if, for instance, dialogue with equality activists in the contexts of Research Coalitions, Learning Partnerships and Equality Action Plans were to engage with such themes as the vanguardist/standpoint tension.

Egalitarianism is most likely a minority paradigm in terms of numbers. It is always possible to find students (though in fewer numbers) who are sympathetic to egalitarianism and associated educability texts such as that of political economy. But it is difficult to say if this ever proceeds beyond experimentation with ideas. It can equally be deceptive to accept as an indication of its dominion, the ease with which egalitarianism circulates in academic journals such as those of sociology and feminist studies. Because of the absence of a distinct signifier, and its high level of theorisation as a form of knowing, for egalitarians who are not politically active or familiar with the discourse their's can be an atomised cultural existence. For academics and activists, however, interaction at conferences, programme dissemination days and grant assessment exercises will act to reveal the paradigmatic allegiance of like-mind egalitarians. This recognition will be signalled back and forth through various sites of cultural production, in invitations to lecture, make presentations, act as collaborators, become involved in common projects and provide supportive testimonials, all of which will serve to cultivate among this group a more primary type (intimate, face-to-face, frequent contact) association providing emotional and moral support and allowing for comprehensive mutual knowledge. The institutional base of egalitarianism in the Equality Studies Centre, UCD, provides a site for engagement and collectivisation. Academically, it offers Postgraduate Diploma, Masters degree, non-graduate Certificate and PhD programmes. Over its first decade it has experienced a throughput of something in the region of 150 students (Lynch, 1999a). The Centre has also generated collaborative work between Lynch and other researchers/academics (Lynch and O'Riordan, 1998; Lynch and Lodge, 2002) and community activists (Lynch and O'Neill, 1994).

Egalitarianism is explicitly oppositional in the manner in which academics who have not committed themselves to equality of condition or emancipatory research are singled out for criticism. The work of those described as 'equality empiricists', preoccupied with realising 'the liberal goal of formal equality of opportunity rather than egalitarianism' is acknowledged to be motivated by 'the best of intentions' but, nonetheless, involving 'the oppressor writing "about the oppressed" from the distance of the universities and research institutes'. Sociologists who do not propose radical social change are accused of contenting themselves with no more than the 'analysis of oppression ... whether or not the exploititative conditions change is not in many professionals' view a sociological concern. This is seen as the job of lesser mortals than a full-time career sociologist!' One needs to go beyond analysis to be other than 'an intellectual parasite living off other people's miseries' (Lynch and O'Neill, 1994). This practice of identifying heretics is common to paradigms at different stages of their development and with various degrees of dominion, and serves to identify and explain to both insiders and outsiders the behaviour of deviants who have lost their way as well as the lack of enlightenment of those who have yet to see the truth. This is a high-risk discourse in terms of the expansion of one's membership and the enhancement of one's dominion. But for a minority paradigm such as egalitarianism is in Irish educational discourse, it is functional in the manner in which its oppositionalism cultivates solidarity, dedication and momentum, and above all a missionary identity as one who has been 'chosen' to champion a true and worthy, if minority, cause. This is a feature of egalitarianism's moral text which to date has been substantially constructed by means of expressions of outrage and anger and in the zealous tone of Lynch's discourse. This heightening of the exclusionary nature of egalitarianism may be a necessary condition for maintaining hope, energy and identity.

Visionary identities may prove to be a crucial resource for egalitarianism in the manner in which they promote an utopian stance, in relation to current educational realities, to think 'otherwise', and, in Merleau-Ponty's phrase, 'to take sides against the probable' (Young, 1977). The result in this regard may be less a matter of realising a future ideal society and more one of disrupting the doxic status of more specific but pivotal meanings within the existing social order. The most successful change of this nature has been in relation to the understanding of intelligence among educators and embodied within educational practices. Lynch's (1987) earliest work aimed to reveal and critique the assumptions of educational thought in Ireland. This included the cognitivist understanding of intelligence and its implications for equality in education. In contrast with the doxa of the time she argued that intelligence is not a singular entity but, rather, takes multiple forms, cannot be quantified in simple numerical terms as is implied by IQ tests and scores, is best seen as a quality of human behaviour, and is a product of experience. She drew validation from Gardner's (1983) work on multiple intelligences, and can be considered to have effectively introduced MI theory to Irish educational discourse (Lynch, 1992). MI theory was used in the Nagle-Rice Project, established in 1993 to commemorate the 150th anniversary of the death of Edmund Rice, with Anne Fleischmann as its director, to address the needs of students who appeared not to be benefiting from the traditional second-level curriculum and teaching methods (Feheney, 1998a). The MI project, Multiple Intelligences, Curriculum and Assessment Project, initiated in the Department of Education, University College, Cork, in 1995 developed the theory in the context of teachers' practices and classroom processes at both primary and second level (Doyle, 1999). The engagement throughout the educational system with the theory and application of MI was phenomenal, and invitations were received and presentations made both within and outside all levels of the formal educational system (Hyland, 2000). It would appear that MI theory had successfully 'hailed' otherwise diverse subjectivities and for equally diverse reasons – serving interests and needs, validating existing practices, providing legitimation of abilities in areas other than the linguistic and the logical-mathematical, and conceptualising and textualising previously unsignified and unvalidated thought. Research on the understanding of intelligence among teachers and the general public in Ireland (Fontes *et al.*, 1983) would have held out little hope for MI theory establishing itself in individual consciousness, discourse and practice. It would have appeared that such was the challenge to doxa in Lynch's early critique of the predominantly cognitivist understanding of intelligence that it would have disrupted intersubjective engagement and, ultimately, communication around the theme of intelligence. Yet, it was possible for Hanafin to propose the following at the 2002 Annual Conference of the Sociological Association of Ireland (SAI) without special pleading:

> The conception of intelligence (fixed, defined in narrow/logical-mathematical terms, and measurable by an IQ score) which underpins the educational system is largely invisible but very powerful. This hegemonic construct of intelligence is an agent of educational failure, exclusion and oppression. Droving and cloning are features of its agency. Learners are herded along well trodden droving paths, paths defined by the formal and hidden curriculum, assessment structures, and school organisational practices. The dominant mindset based on this construct of intelligence seeks to clone all learners to become like those who are deemed academically successful.

This is not to suggest that all those who engaged in MI discourse, or became involved in classroom-based projects derived from it, abandoned more mainstream conceptualisations of intelligence or, for that matter, that the communicative tolerance of SAI conferences is representative of Irish society. Nor should this be regarded as the main test of the intervention. It could be expected that there would be an inclination to avoid dissonance and maintain communication through attempting to accommodate both traditional and multiple understandings of intelligence. It is clear from the macaronic discourse of some teachers' accounts of the change they experienced through their involvement with the UCC MI project that such tensions existed for them. What is noteworthy is the change that occurred in the knowledge production process: the disruption of the boundaries between disciplines, and of the doxic status of intelligence, together with its legitimatory processes and authorities. It became difficult to speak of intelligence in the singular, those who routinely contributed to MI critiques of the educational system were largely drawn from disciplines other than psychology, and the first textbook on the sociology of education in Ireland contained a chapter on intelligence (Drudy and Lynch, 1993). The experience of the MI critique of intelligence is instructive in demonstrating what utopian discourse (that which challenges conventional understandings of what is or is not possible) does best – infiltrating a semantic field for the purpose of subverting it, in this instance, destabilising the meaning, classification and legitimation of intelligence. It might well be argued that this variety of cultural politics, a form of guerilla combat, both recognises the weaknesses and exploits the strengths of egalitarianism – a small but committed membership of intellectuals and activists with a knowledge of theory and practice that allows it to identify and target, for intertextual engagement and challenge, meanings sustaining the existing social order that are both strategic and vulnerable.

Epilogue to Part Three

This has been a wide-ranging section across a spectrum that includes comprehensive prescriptions for social change (egalitarianism), social and cultural indicators of difference and similarity (ethnicity), and individual needs in relation to contributing to production (employability) and benefiting from educational experience (disadvantage). The cultural production involved offers to society resources – categories, concepts and texts – that differ in their potential for dominion. The principles of distribution, recognition and representation, the classification of people, and educability and labour market competence are differently positioned within the social structure, and how these are understood will accordingly vary in their social and political reverberations.

This diversity of structural positioning and cultural dominion is always a possibility in engaging with middle-range social processes. As a sociological topic, how education is implicated in what people become in society is positioned between the macro (social, political and economic systems at national and global levels) and the micro (interactive, day-to-day engagement between people living their lives.) In developing these issues sociologically as well as culturally there is the option to theorise 'from above', in which systemic and supra-individual appeals predominate, or 'from below' when the human, immediate, personal and specific are given precedence. This can be ideologically driven by the desire for the advancement of social change, articulated in terms of the systemic implications of a specific issue, egalitarianism being an explicit manifestation. Or, as with gender equity, the approach can be more tactical and pragmatic, silently accommodating to the political system and working for improvements and benefits more likely to be immediately available and attainable without the appearance of adding new principles and values to the social system. Like ethnicity, (Christian) Communitarianism remains positioned within middle-range theorising, particularly in the manner in which communitarianism can be ideologically accommodated at the political centre while addressing the day-to-day life experiences of people. Disadvantage is firmly positioned at the interactive level in the manner in which it generates both discourse and action that represents it as a problem that is best engaged with by providing more co-ordinated services to those 'at risk'. Employability remains the most volatile, capable of being understood in terms of disadvantage, life-cycle and labour market transitions, and national effectiveness and international competitiveness.

After a half century of cultural production around such issues, what exists as substantive cultural resources to help Irish society to think about, communicate and act in relation to the intersection of life chances, education and morality, can be encompassed within the semantic field of equality, communitarianism and ethnicity.

Gender equity developed from the 1970s and represents the most immediate resuscitation of the construct of equality of educational opportunity from the truncated cultural production surrounding it in the postponed paradigms of the 1960s. This remains the most systematised paradigm within the LEM domain in Irish experience, incorporating an unambiguous belief system, explicit implications for action over a wide range of phenomena, integration into the state apparatus, together with instruments and mechanisms for the articulation of correct practices, the monitoring of behaviour and action, the arbitration of doubt and dissent, and for its reproduction over time. It might have been expected that this would have expanded to incorporate other bases of inequality such as social class, particularly in the light of the re-emergence in the 1980s as educational disadvantage of the socio-economic focus from the 'postponed' paradigm formation surrounding equality of educational opportunity in the 1960s. Too restricted in meaning (those least benefiting from education) and understanding (as *pastiche*), the nature of state discourse on disadvantage was not conducive to intertextuality of this nature. Employability, for its part, was allowed to remain too volatile in conceptualisation, too easily claimed as a labour market or national efficiency issue. For its part, the gender equity paradigm showed little inclination towards coalitions of this nature, perhaps recognising their threat to its dominion within the state by introducing the theme of difference.

At the 1996 conference Gender Equality for 2000 and Beyond, the rapporteur proposed a more complex and fluid classification of people. She recorded that 'the fundamental debate on whether gender equity requires emphasising "sameness" or valuing diversity arose in many contexts throughout the conference and it is clear that teachers require more complex approaches to this question in relation to the intersection of gender with social class, religion, race, ethnicity, disability' (Ní Chárthaigh, 1998, p. 5). More specifically, working-class feminist activists were also calling for dialogue on the intersection of class and gender identities in intellectual inquiry and political action (Dorgan and McDonnell, 1997). However, the price that gender equity paid for the clarity and doxa of its performatives was the dualism of its male/female construct, the semantic unity of the language of its objectives, its subdued incorporation of moral themes, at most inscribing itself within uncontestable democratic practices, and the exposure of female identity formation to the influence of mercantile subjectivities. What of its potential for intertextuality with egalitarianism? Egalitarianism, which seeks to excavate the moral issues around the purpose of educational intervention and force explicit confrontation between the positions thus revealed, is the most ambitious in its aspiration to become the master paradigm capable of subsuming all the others. While its core tenet of equality of economic condition has experienced cultural exclusion from the state policy-making apparatus, it nonetheless has the capacity to establish further nodal points of influence relating to conceptualisation, language, themes and identities with the gender equity paradigm. In particular, in distinguishing between equality objectives – equality of formal rights, opportunities and access, equality of participation, equality of outcome, and equality of condition – egalitarianism is capable of facilitating a more differentiating use of language within the gender equity paradigm. Indeed, given the success of feminist action on language and its use, it is remarkable that the existing linguistic resources of the gender equity paradigm have not been deployed more as a resource in its critique by those who would wish to force it to discriminate within the semantic field of its objectives. Much of this will depend on the identities and tactical subjectivities of those who occupy key roles of advocacy, membershipping, monitoring and representation within the gender equity paradigm.

The dynamics of paradigm formation around communitarian themes yields a number of versions that between them are capable of accommodating a wide middle-ground of meanings and people. Central to this is Christian Communitarianism which is used to describe the approach to social policy developed and propagated by CORI. This emphasises the obligations of people to one another in their use of the world's resources and grounds these obligations in the interpretation of sources from within the Christian tradition. This brings a structuring and membershipping capacity to an otherwise disparate and secular set of communitarian themes generated by the Combat Poverty Agency, the Community Development Movement, and andragogical practices in literacy and adult education programmes, and in EU-sponsored interventions in local development, partnerships and anti-poverty and social inclusion initiatives. Through a process of mutation/merging, (Christian) Communitarianism, a cultural form that for some is engaged with independently of and for others derived from religious belief, is produced. As (Christian) Communitarianism engages more widely with people in society, beyond those for whom such paradigms can be identity-forming, it can find its themes of solidarity, co-responsibility and interdependence resignified and textualised in simple sloganised discourse. Typically, a social morality is realised in aspirations to incorporate those on the margins into the mainstream of society and bring the poor within the range of educational and income levels acceptable in a caring society, but without diminishing the life chances, living standards and social position of the more privileged while holding off the threat to social stability that might follow from inaction in this regard.

As such, (Christian) Communitarianism can be appropriated by the mercantile paradigm as a text without threat to self-interest that is not compromised by the accusation that it is either 'religious' or 'political', an 'end of history' Irish-style. Though often described by government spokespersons as 'the only show in town', this remains the most obvious target for mobilisation and modification. In this, the Christian Communitarianism of CORI is well-positioned in terms of educational policy. While it prioritises the life word of the socially and economically disadvantaged, stresses unjust structures, advocates social transformation as a means of change, and incorporates an holistic understanding of the person, as well as being persistent and coherent, it continues to maintain nodal points of common engagement with current partnership discourse and practice. At the societal level, its success will hinge on the emergence of a critical reflexivity towards the mercantile paradigm, a more dialogical and generative rather than populist role for the state, and the politics of solidarity building.

The concentrated focus of the cultural production of Travellers' ethnicity mirrors that of gender equity. There is much to learn from Travellers' refusal of society's inscription, and their assertion of difference on their own terms as ethnicity. These include the skilled and tactical reconceptualisation of Travellers, a vibrant and differentiating discursive communication, exceptional levels of mobilisation and globalisation, explicit exiting and membershipping, contested authoritative status, and a reflexivity towards its own modes of knowledge production, even about itself. These are rendered all the most distinctive when set against the refusal of the opportunities to intensify equality of educational opportunity in the 1960s, the instability of employability, the suspension of disagreement around disadvantage, the loosely-framed (Christian) Communitarianism, and the unelaborated conceptualisation and undifferentiated use of language in an otherwise systematised gender equity paradigm. As with gender equity, Travellers' ethnicity has not to date indicated an inclination to engage with egalitarianism. Perhaps its exclusivity of focus and mobilisation has been a contributory factor, if not a necessary condition, for the successful cultural production of Travellers' life chances and education in terms of ethnicity. However, a further dynamic will be introduced as newer ethnic groups become a feature of Irish educational policy-making.

Any cultural intervention in relation to the LEM domain will need to take account of the three structuring features that pertain to it – 'distant other', sponsorship and fairness. These were initially identified during the 1960s in the failure of equality of educational opportunity to supplant them through conceptualisation and signification. Since then, and it seems unlikely that they had no prior existence, all or some of these features have been implicated in every policy paradigm identified in this section. The 'distant other' experienced signification as the non-beneficiary of educational expansion in the 1960s, the deprived premodern 'itinerant' child, the 'unemployable' school-leaver and, since the 1980s, the disadvantaged of state educational policy and of communitarianism. Socially, in traditional societies it could be expected that the orientation to pity, help, or champion would be directed towards those positioned at a sufficient remove from oneself not to destabilise status and power relationships. Relatedly, it might be argued that the 'distant other' is a construction that functions to regulate the effects of dispositions, be they elemental or social, such as pity and guilt on social structure.

Sponsorship, described as a process by which society manages mobility opportunities, began to operate more at a collective level after the 1960s. This became institutionalised into the political process where it interacts with pluralist representation and advocacy. Examples would include the National Adult Literacy Agency, the Combat Poverty Agency, and the specification of particular categories – gender, marital status, family status, etc. – in the Equal Status Act, 2000. What is important to recognise in this regard is that the sponsorship process does not leave the sponsored unaffected or static as a category of concern. In the case of the politics of disability, which has not been addressed substantively in this book, authoritative, advocative and interventionist subjectivities often fluctuate and overlap in discourse, and in the process new syndromes, taxonomies and pedagogies are successfully introduced. Even Travellers, who refused the definition as premodern and deprived by philanthropic sponsors, could be said to have exchanged them for other sponsors who introduced them to concepts of ethnicity. Sponsors for their part are not without specific benefit. The Christian Communitarianism of CORI provided the church with a new authoritative discourse, mirroring the experience of the state after *Investment in Education*, at a time when its prescriptions for public life were facing challenge and delegitimation.

The relationship between 'distant others' and their sponsors raises enduring issues, such as those of otherness and alterity, that have been widely debated in a different context in post-colonial studies (Bhabha, 1995[1985]; Parry, 1987; Spivak, 1988). These include the consideration of the 'distant other' as the construction and constitution of the sponsor, an effect of its interests, and the resulting epistemic violence done to the muted subject, who accepts or rejects but does not create its subjectivity. To these can be added second order effects when sponsors seek to engage reflexively with such issues and correct for past errors – atoning for guilt, adopting nativist positions, hesitancy in engagement, use of a coded terminology and the renouncing of expertise, in general a transition from epistemic violence to privileging. Clearly, there is a need to move beyond this dualism.

The abiding relevance of fairness in engaging with LEM issues is indicative of how little development there has been in relation to the moral dimension of the intersection between life chances and education. The vagueness of fairness allows it to accommodate a diversity of moral imperatives but within the less demanding, softer understanding of justice. Baker (1987) uses the synonyms of impartiality and reasonableness. Theoretically it is quite valid for him to argue that 'being such a loose and flexible idea, it seems wise not to place too much weight on it' (p. 156). Yet, its place within Irish intersubjectivity relating to the LEM domain and beyond is such that it carries very practical implications for the moral appeal and acceptability of justifications for prescriptions for educational change. With communitarianism, its variety of forms is not unrelated to the flexible interpretations and uses that fairness will allow. Disadvantage operates within its terms, the salience of life chances and difference during the 1980s having failed to yield a social ethic as the 1990s progressed. Egalitarianism, as equality of condition, continues to be constituted as utopian by the moral and performative (in)tolerance of fairness. Its most tactical, though not necessarily knowing, deployment is exemplified by gender equity's success in having 'sameness of experience' between men and women (mutated from 'sameness of treatment'), accepted in public life as an unremarkable principle of a democratic society. It persisted with this from the use of equality of educational opportunity as the stem concept for gender equity and in its integration within the reformist ideology of the women's movement. Working within the tolerance spectrum of fairness, and eschewing such elaboration of objectives that less equity-based understandings of a gendered education would suggest, conferred benefits in the achievement of policy objectives within the parameters of the mercantile paradigm.

The persistence of these three structural features, but particularly those of 'distant other' and fairness, raise a number of questions in relation to mental constructs and their signification identified earlier on the function of language in the construction of meaning. All three address core systemic issues relating to how society deals with diversity among people, differentiation of roles and duties, and the norms governing these in relation to stability and change. Yet, none of them come to us as prenamed features of social life or moral principles. Could this be an example of unsignified, or loosely-signified, unencoded thought, used by but not linguistically known to people, and maintained as a feature of Fodor's (1976) 'internal representational system', an 'inner code', the product of a universal conceptual endowment or a more culturally-specific learned conceptualisation? Insofar as the operation of the three constructs can be inferred, they appear as innate and instinctive, unreflexively reactive and intuitive. Yet, their provenance in society and culture, rather than in a universal human inheritance, is suggested by the pattern of their association and its functionalist instantiation as pre-reflexive folk constructs at a time of change in Irish society. This untheorised loosely-framed set of LEM resources remained resistant to modification by equality of educational opportunity throughout the 1960s. Subsequently, in the LEM paradigms considered in this section, there is evidence of the so-called scientific concepts and spontaneous concepts, to employ Vygotsky's characterisation, reaching accommodations. But the dynamics in this and the subsequent status of these spontaneous concepts are less clear. What does seem sustainable is that unencoded thought continues to act as a structuring force in the production of meaning, and that it is unlikely to be peculiar to the LEM domain of life. This gives some indication of the complexity of the cultural terrain that the public sphere has to engage with, and incorporate within its intersubjective circulation of political meanings, if there is to be public engagement with the reconstruction that continues to be experienced by education as an institution within Irish society. This will be developed in the Conclusion.

Part Four

The Micro-Politics of Policy Paradigms:
Concepts, Agents and Texts

Having commenced with the institution of education in Part Two in terms of the changing nature of its cultural construction, we progressed to more middle-range processes in Part Three. There, we saw how education is implicated, in its mediation of resources, restraints and possibilities, in the character of a person's life course, in the sense of what one becomes in terms of identity, social and material status and power. This final section sharpens the focus further. It selects three analytical components of policy paradigms – concepts, agents and texts – for special attention. These, of course, have all been implicated in the transition from a theocentric to a mercantile paradigm of the institution of education and across the wide range of paradigms considered within the LEM domain, and as such have been studied in terms of their role in these transitions and constructions. Here they are addressed in some detail in terms of their contribution to cultural politics in their own right.

Chapter 13 deals with the functioning of conceptualisation within cultural politics. This is firstly explored by means of case studies of the construct of children and childhood during the 1960s and 1970s, a defining period of activity in this regard in Ireland. These include the changed constructions of childhood represented in the imaging of the primary school pupil in the New Primary School Curriculum in 1971 and its interplay with existing constructions in subsequent pedagogies. There then follows an examination of the interaction between historically- and institutionally-embedded meanings, the discourse and ideology of child advocacy organisations, and the experiential constraints and leanings of childcare personnel in how children, in what was then the Industrial and Reformatory School System, were to be understood and catered for. These will demonstrate how at the most basic level of how a phenomenon is to be conceptualised, political interests and activities are involved in its inheritance, maintenance, (re)construction and denial.

Chapter 14 turns to the contribution of human agents to cultural change in education, encompassing developments in adult education, educational funding and the role of the Roman Catholic Church in Irish education. Apart from the substantive changes involved, this facilitates the analysis of conditions under which social actors become forces for change and succeed in becoming agents rather than conduits in the flow of cultural politics. The twin constructs of 'cultural stranger' and 'cultural contrarian', referring to a relationship of distance, independence and otherness between social actors and the culture, is given particular attention in this regard.

Adult education, which provides the substance for Chapter 15, has up to recent times operated on the margins of the mainstream educational system, with erratic and minimal attention from the state. Largely a product of individual commitment and initiative, as a particular field of knowledge production it has the virtue for analysts of recognisable temporal, organisational and thematic boundaries. From the 1960s it is possible to identify efforts to textualise adult education as a component of the overall educational system that find their most tangible expression in 1969 with the formation of Aontas, the National Association of Adult Education, and the establishment of the Murphy Committee which reported in 1970 and 1973. It is from this point that the development of meaning and knowledge surrounding the phenomenon of adult learning and the discursive and non-discursive activities that sought to establish adult education as a meaningful construct and practice are traced. This includes the isolation and conceptualisation of phenomena that form the basis for textualising adult education, the producers of this knowledge, its recurring themes, and the theorisation through which its intellectuals have sought to interpret what has come to be known as adult education. Throughout, there will be a focus on seeking to interpret the sense of both stability and change that pervades adult education as a field of knowledge.

Overall, in this section, a number of features of cultural politics are explored: the ubiquity and pivotal role of conceptualisation, the variable nature of human agency, and the principles of formation that guide the production of what is known as a particular educational sector.

Chapter 13

Conceptualising Children and Childhoods

In this chapter, the functioning of conceptualisation within cultural politics is explored by means of case studies of the constructs of children and childhoods. The focus here is on a defining period of activity in this regard in Ireland when childhood became more salient, child development more explicitly and theoretically acknowledged within the life-course, and the concept of the deprived child was successfully inserted into public discourse. The 1960s and 1970s saw a considerable amount of cultural work around the meaning of childhood. While this took the form of a patterned shift of understanding in discourse about childhood in newspapers, magazines, radio and educational debate, it was only a social movement in the loosest sense. Within this site of recognisable change in the conceptualisation of childhood, however, there did exist a specific child-advocacy movement that sought to champion the needs of particularly neglected or 'invisible' categories of children, most notably those in child-care institutions. This provides the social and cultural context for the two case studies selected, and the analysis moves back and forth between case study and context to facilitate grounding and illumination in demonstrating the formation and functions of conceptualisation.

Both general and specific manifestations of this cultural change in defining childhood are represented in the two case studies selected: the changed construction of childhood represented in the imaging of the primary school pupil incorporated in the New Primary School Curriculum of 1971 and its interplay with existing constructions in the subsequent pedagogy; and the interaction between historical and institutionally-embedded meanings, the discourse and ideology of child-advocacy organisations, and the experiential constraints and leanings of child-care personnel in how children in what was then the Industrial and Reformatory School System were to be understood and catered for.

Taken together, the effect is to demonstrate how conceptualisations of childhood can be inherited in institutional practices, implicated in pedagogy and curriculum organisation, functional in boundary maintenance, and how the advocacy of other 'children' and 'childhoods' in opposition to those that prevail set in motion various forms of resistance, adaptation and coping. It demonstrates that at the most basic level of how a phenomenon is conceptualised, political interests and activity are involved in its inheritance, maintenance, (re)construction and denial.

The Child as an Agent of Learning

The introduction in 1971 of what came to be known as the New Primary School Curriculum (Department of Education, 1971) had the potential to have the greatest import for the lives of Irish children, not alone in the changes in pedagogy and curriculum that it introduced but more fundamentally for the conceptualisation of childhood that it embodied.

In line with both the content and spirit of the Plowden Report (Central Advisory Council for Education [England], 1967), the New Curriculum was meant to facilitate a greater flexibility and child-centredness in learning and curriculum organisation. In the sections on Aims and Functions and on The Structure of the Curriculum the following recognisable sentiments concerning child development, learning and curriculum organisation appear:

> Throughout the more progressive primary schools children now play a much more active role in their own education ... The basic skills are acquired not so much through class teaching as through individual and group activity, each child progressing at his own natural rate, each at the different stages of his advancement, being allowed full scope to express his own personality and experience the joy of discovery, each being led to consult a variety of appropriate reading material ... (p. 16)

> ... when he tackles problems as an individual he develops self-reliance and independence. At other times, when he works as a member of a group or of a class he learns the value of co-operation and his social development is fostered. (p. 18)

> The teacher is no longer regarded as one who merely imparts information but rather as one who provides suitable learning situations and who guides and stimulates the child in his pursuit of knowledge. (p. 18)

> ... the curriculum should be sufficiently flexible to allow each child to progress at an appropriate pace and to achieve satisfaction and success at his own level. (p. 19)

> ... the young child is not conscious of subject barriers ... the curriculum should reflect this attitude of the child and be seen as an integral whole rather than as a logical structure containing conveniently differentiated parts. (p. 19)

In fact, the New Curriculum was the end product of a process that predated the publication of the Plowden Report. Specifically, it originated from a steering committee established within the Department of Education in 1966 to advise on the primary education aspects of a proposed White Paper. Séamas de Buitléar (1969), who was to be one of the key architects of the New Curriculum, explained that the committee had come to the view that it was more appropriate to build a new curriculum from first principles rather than seek to make adjustments to the older programme. Coolahan (1989) recognised the influence of Piaget and the Plowden Report in the following criticism of the existing programme in the committee's unpublished report.

> (it) tends to treat children as if they were identical, environment as if it were irrelevant, and subject content as if it were easily defined. Its greatest fault, perhaps, is that it fails to look on education as a trail of discovery, enrichment and understanding for the growing child, and sees it instead as a logical structure containing conveniently differentiated parts which may be imposed by adults on children.

While for some teachers, according to de Buitléar (1969), the New Curriculum merely acknowledged and put the seal of approval on their existing practices in expanding and pushing out the boundaries of the old programme, for many the success of the proposed innovation required changes in their approaches to pedagogy and curriculum. For all, a view of childhood that differed from traditional understandings of children and their place in Irish society was demanded. Both the Teacher's Handbook (Department of Education, 1971) and de Buitléar's (1969) rationale for the new programme placed it within a theocentric framework of human development, purpose and destiny. Yet, the imaging of childhood throughout the Teacher's Handbook realised a number of novel and potentially discordant themes:

- that children should be active rather than passive in the learning process
- the recognition of a unique personhood awaiting to avail of this opportunity for activism
- an autonomy in selecting opportunities for learning, in personal change and in adopting personal viewpoints and dispositions
- a view of childhood incorporating different and sequenced phases of development, by implication essentialist in that they are seen to follow from the nature of childhood
- a diversity of personality that involves emotional and social as well as moral and cognitive dimensions
- an entitlement to a more symmetrical communicative relationship with representatives of the adult world.

Little of this conflict in the conceptualisation of childhood between the New Curriculum and the culture into which it was being inserted attracted attention, and the New Curriculum was welcomed by all involved in primary education including managerial bodies, colleges of education and the INTO, creating in Coolahan's (1989) words 'a considerable buzz of excitement'.

Teacher Subjectivities and Pedagogies

Conflict over how childhood was to be understood did, however, surface in a study conducted by the author within the decade in which the New Curriculum was introduced, where it appeared to be implicated in how aspects of the new pedagogy were being incorporated into the classroom practices of teachers. The study, in June 1978, of 153 teachers (response rate 83 per cent) in 21 primary schools throughout Cork City, sought to link the subjectivities of teachers with their classroom practices. Three aspects are relevant here: the differential implementation of the various aspects of 'progressive' teaching style embodied in the New Curriculum; the internal structure of the teacher-reported classroom behaviours; and the variation in teaching style according to demographic, professional and contextual variables (O'Sullivan, 1980a).

In a closed questionnaire teachers were requested to locate their classroom practices on a seven-point scale between two behavioural poles, as follows:

Learning is predominantly by discovery techniques	1	2	3	4	5	6	7	There is little use of discovery techniques

Behavioural poles for ten aspects of teaching style were selected from the Teacher's Handbook quoted from above and from such sources as Adams (1970), Bennett & Jordan (1975) and Bennett (1976).

The teachers' descriptions of their classroom behaviour are summarised in Fig. 13.1. The order of the ten aspects of teaching style is based on the mean rating for each item. While the range of the means is small, it nevertheless follows a coherent pattern. It suggests that while teachers saw themselves as incorporating certain emphases of the New Curriculum, such as creativity/co-operation, in their teaching, the more an aspect of teaching style impinged on their overseeing and control of the motivation, direction and content of pupil learning, the less likely it was to be implemented. This restriction of pupil self-direction was also in evidence in an earlier study, in which principals reported that activity and discovery methods were the least likely of four aspects of the New Curriculum to be implemented to a high degree (Fontes and Kellaghan, 1977).

Fig. 13.1 Teacher Scores on Specified Aspects of Teaching Style, Ordered According to Mean Score

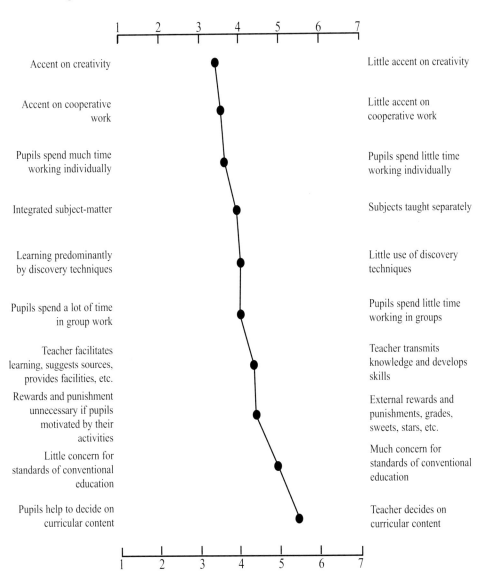

Factor analysis was then used to chart the manner in which the ten teacher behaviours related to one another in classroom life and, in this way, to identify the main dimensions of teaching style as reported by the teachers themselves. A varimax rotation identified five factors which accounted for 75 per cent of the variance in the responses. Details of these factors are contained in Table 13.I.

Factor 1 is heavily loaded by the degree of pupil/teacher curriculum control and concern for standards, and the use of intrinsic/extrinsic rewards. It can be best described as 'pupil-centredness' and alone accounts for almost one-third of the variation in the responses. Factor 2 is immediately identifiable as a co-operative/creative emphasis, and accounts, for instance, for two-thirds of the variation in 'accent on co-operative work'. Factor 3 accounts for half of the variation in 'learning by discovery' and about one-third in 'teacher-facilitated learning'. It can most appropriately be labelled 'discovery learning'. A 'group learning' factor, Factor 4 is heavily loaded by 'group learning' and (negatively) by individual learning, while Factor 5 is a 'curriculum integration' factor. It accounts for almost all of the explained variation in the integrated/subject-based curriculum variable.

Table 13.1 Dimensions of Teaching Style: Varimax Factor Loadings

Variables	*Factor Loadings*					
	1	*2*	*3*	*4*	*5*	h_2*
Integrated/subject-based curriculum	06	14	20	09	59	42
Pupil curricular control	52	00	21	-07	30	41
Learning by discovery	21	16	70	18	28	68
Teacher facilitated learning	26	26	58	-02	16	51
Concern for standards of conventional education	50	02	25	20	01	35
Intrinsic/extrinsic rewards	51	17	03	-17	00	32
Accent on cooperation	26	81	05	03	28	81
Accent on creativity	-02	64	32	03	00	51
Group work	16	26	22	59	32	60
Individual work	11	05	00	-61	01	39
Percentage variance accounted for	31.6	14.2	11.7	9.2	8.1	

Total variance accounted for: 74.9%
*The h_2 value refers to the proportion of the variation in each classroom behaviour that is accounted for by the five common factors.

An interesting feature of the teachers' descriptions of their classroom behaviour was the manner in which 'discovery learning' emerged as a relatively autonomous dimension in addition to the major dimension of 'pupil-centredness'. The fact that teachers in describing their classroom behaviour distinguished in this manner between 'discovery learning' and 'pupil-centredness' facilities further elaboration on teacher resistance to pupil self-direction. Given the low level of implementation of classroom behaviours characterised by the 'pupil-centredness' factor, a syndrome of resistance was indicated which needed to be explained.

Control of Pupil Learning and Motivation

Material restrictions imposed on teachers by large classes and inadequate resources seemed an obvious starting point in seeking to explain the reluctance of teachers to concede more control of pupil learning and motivation. The INTO had repeatedly argued that smaller classes were essential for the successful implementation of the New Curriculum and, in a survey of its members concerning the New Curriculum in 1975, 83 per cent considered class size to be a source of difficulty in teaching, and a similar percentage felt that the New Curriculum could be most satisfactorily implemented with a class of less than twenty-five (INTO, 1976). Yet, no significant difference was found in any of the five dimensions of teaching style between classes of varying sizes. Professional relationships with secondary teachers proved to be a more plausible source of resistance. At the time of its introduction a number of groups had pointed to the lack of alignment between the New Curriculum and the junior cycle post-primary programme, and to the failure to liaise with post-primary school interests (Coolahan, 1989).

Specific concerns had been expressed by secondary teachers at the low levels of attainment in the basic skills among a significant number entering their schools (Coolahan, 1984c), and frequently by implication, and at times quite explicitly, the New Curriculum was criticised as the cause of this perceived deterioration. Studies which recorded inadequate levels of reading and mathematical ability among first-year post-primary school pupils gave substance to these anxieties (Swan, 1976; Kellaghan *et al.*, 1976). It was arguable that teachers' perceptions of deteriorating standards of literacy and numeracy were primarily the consequence of the changing character of post-primary school entrants. Whereas terminal leaving from primary school had become minimal, up to the late 1960s 15 per cent of primary school leavers in Ireland terminated full-time schooling, and in some areas the figure exceeded 20 per cent (Rudd, 1972). The fact that this category of pupils, characterised by educational delay (O'Sullivan, 1973) and recording low levels of achievement on intelligence tests (Kellaghan and Greaney, 1970), now constituted a significant proportion of post-primary school entrants did not appear to have diverted attention from the New Curriculum as a source of the perceived deterioration in standards. The sensitivity on the part of primary teachers concerning educational standards remained, and in terms of teaching style may well have taken the form of a reluctance to permit pupil self-direction in learning, motivation or content choice which might endanger the formation and conservation of basic skills.

Professional judgement based on a considered assessment of the implications of aspects of the New Curriculum for standards in the basic skills, as well as less reflexive reactions in the light of individual psychology and implicit theories of teaching could also have been involved. The broad role of teacher formation in this is suggested by the findings. From the early 1960s the content of primary teacher preparation programmes, traditionally prescriptive in approach, had seen the infusion of courses in psychology, sociology, philosophy and curriculum studies (Coolahan, 1984a). It was teachers who would have experienced these innovations in teacher formation (those less than thirty years) who reported the greatest use of 'discovery learning'.

These influences on teaching styles – material constraints and resources, professional sensitivities and formation, and personal psychology – are not discrete. Nor is it necessary to seek to diminish their significance to argue that the cultural understanding of childhood to which the teachers in this study would have been variously exposed is implicated in how they mediated the pedagogical and curricular principles of the New Curriculum into their classroom practices. At that time, Akenson (1975), in conceptualising the Irish educational system as a mirror of the culture in which it is located, interpreted low levels of educational expenditure as an indication of the low status of the child in Irish society. He argued that despite the 'stereotyped image of the warm supportive Irish family' (p. 89) the anthropological work of Arensberg & Kimball (1940) – carried out in an isolated area of County Clare in the 1930s – highlighted the gerontocratic character of the Irish family, in which economic and social power was maintained by parents well into their old age. Even at the time of his writing, Akenson's interpretations demanded considerable refinement and development in the light of, for instance, social and economic change in rural Ireland (Hannan, 1972), changes in the Irish farm family (Hannan and Katsiaouni, 1977) and processes of industrialisation and urbanisation (Humphreys, 1966). A more critical reading of anthropological studies of childhood and interpersonal relationships in Irish families to allow for ethnocentrism in their interpretation of the position and valuing of children (Curtin and Varley, 1984) is also required. Nonetheless, Akenson's attention to the cultural definition of childhood in seeking to understand aspects of Irish educational policy and practice was particularly apposite.

Conflicting Childhoods

Two related aspects of childhood in Irish society can contribute to our understanding of the resistance to child-centredness recorded in this study: an ultra-protectionist orientation towards children, and the diffusion of a Catholic viewpoint throughout educational and child-caring agencies in which children were ascribed a passive role in their development. An unwarranted interpretation of these understandings of children's needs and nature has been the contention that the Irish primary teacher displayed authoritarian leanings. A number of commentators (McCarthy, 1968; Chubb, 1970) regarded the primary teacher as a key figure in the cultivation of deference to authority figures, particularly religious, and traced this to their rural and socially narrow origins, and to the authoritarian character of their religious-controlled post-primary schooling and teacher training. A less sinister interpretation of Irish teachers' orientations towards childhood would see them as not specifically authoritarian in the context of their time, and more fundamentally guided by their obligations to their pupils in the light of their understanding of their religious, social and cultural needs.

The ultra-protectionist orientation towards children reflected a general paternalism in social, moral and religious affairs that pervaded Irish society up to the 1960s. It thought of childhood in terms of vulnerability and susceptibility to undesirable influences, and is likely to have its origins in a consciousness moulded by discourse and controversy concerning moral, political and religious formation during childhood, both in the family and educational system. It was a point of view which, far from devaluing childhood as a period of formation, implicitly accorded it the significance for adult behaviour, as does modern psychology. In fact, in its alertness to the manipulatory potential of schooling, this view of the child has curious parallels with conflict and Marxist perspectives in educational analysis which interpret the provision and spread of public education as a form of social control in capitalist societies. One has only to glance at the main issues in Irish educational historiography – religious instruction and interpretation, secular education, church/state control, national identity and language revival – to realise how central and sensitive the school-based formation of identity, commitment and world view have been (Titley, 1979). In the Catholic understanding of childhood, the realities of original sin and temptation, the frailty of human nature, to say nothing of the encroachment of the devil, were such that they placed ultimate responsibility on those with authority over children to ensure that they were suitably alerted to and protected from such threats to the pursuit of their eternal salvation.

Catholic thinking influential within the educational system conflicted in its key elements with the developmental approach to childhood underpinning child-centred education. In the traditional Irish Catholic view the child was passive: 'formation', 'instilling' and 'inculcating' dominated its rhetoric. In his *Manual of Social Ethics*, Kavanagh (1966) quotes a Papal Encyclical in which children are characterised as having been received from God by parents 'not only to be employed for their own advantage or for that of an earthly commonwealth, but to be restored to God with interest on the day of reckoning' (p. 39), and in another

Encyclical as 'something of the father, a sort of extension of the father's personality; so that properly speaking, they do not enter or become members of a civil society directly of themselves, but through the family in which they were born' (p. 92). In contrast, the developmental view conceived of children as passing through successive stages of personal growth, which were distinguished by particular tasks to be accomplished and needs to be satisfied if they were to develop to maturity and attain their full potential as persons. This would lean in some of its manifestations towards the 'horticultural' view of child development which variously essentialised human nature and demanded an environment with which pupils would interact in the realisation of their unique self and potential (Bernstein and Davies, 1969; Sugrue, 1997).

As we shall see in the section that follows on child advocacy, the overriding fear that undesirable and irreversible patterns might be established during childhood, both supported by and in turn legitimating the controlled adult-centred socialisation of children, came to be replaced from the 1960s in policy discourse pertaining to children by a view of childhood in which stress was placed on children's best interests and the need to provide a suitable environment in which their capacities might flourish. The syndrome of resistance to such aspects of pupil-centredness as intrinsic motivation and individualised standards and content recorded during the 1970s suggests the residual influence of these earlier cultural definitions of childhood. In terms of teacher subjectivities and the intersubjective contexts they inhabit, it represents an instructive case study of how the impact of conceptualisation, in all probability mediated through interacting individual and professional subjectivities, can influence something as tangible as the classroom behaviour of teachers. But the child as an agent of learning was not the only new childhood introduced to Irish understanding at this time. What the era also experienced from that time, through the championing by the child-advocacy movement of 'invisible' childhoods in institutionalised settings, was the successful construction and insertion into policy discourse of the deprived child.

Childhood and its Advocates

To socially situate the rise of child advocacy in Ireland during the 1960s and 1970s it is necessary to consider both indigenous and cosmopolitan developments, and in particular the process of selection and filtration that operated on external ideas and innovations as they were introduced to Irish debate and consciousness. Not all facets of international child advocacy were made visible in Ireland; what did appear was filtered through key legitimating groups in Irish society and through a social structure receptive to particular features of the human condition. Overviews of child advocacy elsewhere had identified such areas of concern as the rights of children undergoing psychological treatment, in alternative family life styles, and in an educational system that attempts to form their intellect and personality, as well as the problems posed for child advocacy by the invisibility of child-rearing in the isolated nuclear family (O'Sullivan, 1980b). In Ireland what was made available for debate reflected generally the professional interests and concerns of primary and pre-school teachers and specifically those of social workers, and the religious-inspired ideals of church personnel involved in social service provision in a society becoming increasingly alerted to the 'life chances' of individuals. The main themes of child advocacy were to be the importance of childhood within a sequence of developmental stages, children's entitlements in the light of this, and most distinctively the needs of deprived children and children 'at risk'.

As elsewhere, demographic changes had made childhood more salient. But while fewer children in other western countries had made childhood more 'precious' and improved child-related services such as education less of an economic burden, in Ireland rising birth rates and increasing child immigration, together with rapid enrolment increases, strained existing services, particularly education (Tussing, 1978). Throughout the 1970s, economists responding to this situation were to support what primary and pre-school teachers had been arguing for – the favouring of the earlier stages of the educational system in the allocation of scarce resources. This economist support was to culminate in the recommendation of the National Economic and Social Council (1976) that preference be given to the compulsory education age group in educational investment, and in the much-publicised and even stronger conclusion from an Economic and Social Research Institute Report (Tussing, 1978) that scarce resources available to education should be reserved for those aspects of schooling – defined as the years of compulsory attendance – which benefit society rather than the individual learner. Primary teachers, traditionally attracting less funding than other sectors, found their claims considerably encouraged and enhanced by this support: with the emergence of the Human Capital paradigm, as we have seen, economists and economic discourse had come to carry considerable legitimacy in educational analysis.

Similarly supportive, though in a less direct way, was the extensive media coverage given to the claim of the diffuse group of pre-school teachers, organisers and leaders that pre-school children be considered a legitimate educational category (Douglas, 1994). If childhood was becoming more salient and the earlier stages of schooling more favoured for educational investment, the needs of deprived children were to be given particular recognition and attention. Primary teachers were being introduced to the phenomenon of educationally disadvantaged children, some through Summer School contact with Headstart programmes in the United States, from the concept of positive discrimination enunciated by the English Plowden Report of 1967, *Children and their Primary*

Schools, and particularly from the high-profile and ground-breaking Rutland Street pre-school intervention programme for disadvantaged children (Ó hUallacháin and Kellaghan, 1969; Kellaghan and Ó hUallacháin, 1973). Those involved in the training of social workers and others in social service provision had a more direct and immediate interest in alerting the public to the existence of more general deprivation. As one sociologist was to complain: 'Each year, our universities are turning out trained social workers and social scientists, the majority of them for export. Do social problems exist only in England? Or are we content to spend our money on social welfare benefits rather than on real social welfare?' (Ryan, 1967b). In their academic training, also, these social workers became familiar with the UK social welfare system with its concepts of personal rights and entitlements. For religions personnel involved in Catholic social services, the post-Vatican II 'Option for the Poor' produced a shift from thinking of service provision for the needy to advocacy and social action for the deprived and disadvantaged. The 1971 Kilkenny conference on poverty organised by the Catholic Bishops' Council on Social Welfare, at which Ó Cinnéide's (1972) estimation that as many as 30 per cent of Irish people could be living in poverty was given prominence, is routinely taken to be the point at which the modern awareness of poverty in Irish society began.

Neither the efforts of teachers, social workers nor religious personnel in directing attention to poverty and deprivation, the special needs of 'vulnerable' children, and society's moral obligations to them would have succeeded to the extent that they did, were it not for the receptivity of the social system at that time to such exhortations. In Irish society in the 1960s, the existence of individual differences in capacity, disposition, perspective and belief was coming to be acknowledged in educational, political, social and religious spheres. These would have been previously submerged within the collective categories and identities of family, kinship, community, party, religion and nation. There was also a greater willingness to acknowledge defects in Irish society, associated perhaps with the confidence that comes from industrialisation, increased prosperity and state activism in social and economic spheres. But most of all the willingness to attend to significant and questionable variations in children's 'life chances', has to be seen in terms of the tipping of the balance towards class rather than status (Weber, 1972[1922]) in the consideration of the life experiences of Irish children. From the 1960s industrial development had highlighted class-based attributes – basic skills such as literacy and numeracy, marketable skills such as technical expertise, and paper qualifications for an increasingly credentialising job market. This was in contrast to the status attributes of a relatively fixed social system in which ascriptive characteristics such as family background, kinship and school-related networks and inheritance featured widely in social reproduction, and in which emigration provided the safety valve for the release of 'failures', dissidents and the non-inheriting. It was in this environment of a heightened salience of childhood and an alertness to differential 'life chances' that childhood advocacy emerged and flourished.

The most public target of the child advocacy movement, and the one used here as the second case study in the politics of conceptualisation, was the plight of children and the nature of childhood in the Industrial and Reformatory School System, as it was then known. Its most relevant success – the thematising of the deprived child, constructed around a failure to cater for the developmental needs of children – is traced against the cultural and material legacy it challenged. But its most abiding achievement would be the establishment of the deprived, 'invisible' child in institutional care as the prototype 'distant other' for the period under consideration, the various inscriptions on which, as we have seen in Part Three, continue to play such a role in the identification of those in need of sponsorship for intervention in relation to life chances, education and morality.

Institutionalised Childhoods

In its final stages of contraction when the Kennedy Report on the Industrial and Reformatory School System was published in 1970, it consisted of 29 schools, certified for 3,750 pupils but then catering for some 2,000 pupils, predominantly in Industrial Schools (Committee on Reformatory and Industrial Schools, 1970, p. 2). It is Industrial Schools and their pupils that are largely or concern here. However, in the case of a number of Industrial Schools for senior boys there was overlap between the systems. Their pupils covered a wide age-range, from a few months to nineteen years, but they were mainly within the compulsory school attendance age-range. The majority had been placed by the Courts, for reasons of lack of proper guardianship, school non-attendance or indictable offences. About a quarter had been placed by local health authorities due to broken homes, bereavement or prolonged illness in their families. A small percentage were placed voluntarily, by parents or guardians (Appendix E).

In championing the case of these pupils, the child advocacy movement was engaging with conceptualisations of children and institutionalised childhoods embodied in the system's assumptions, practices and structures that had been evolving for nearly a century. As well as drawing on existing sources in charting this engagement, use is also made of findings from a study conducted by the author in a senior boys industrial school in the early 1970s, hereafter referred to as the Research School (O'Sullivan, 1979). This requires a brief account of developments prior to the 1960s.

In the extension of the Industrial School System to Ireland in the second half of the nineteenth century, the social risk perceived in certain kinds of childhoods prevailed. The 'discovery' of vagrancy and destitution as pre-delinquent had been seen as a matter of public concern (Commission of Inquiry into the Reformatory and Industrial Schools System [Cussen Report], 1936, p. 7) and the Industrial School System, designed to prevent juvenile and adult crime through anticipatory intervention among those deemed to constitute a social risk, was introduced to Ireland in 1868. The assumptions of 'social risk' are most apparent in the justification of the system by the Lord Chancellor to the Statistical and Social Inquiry Society of Ireland in 1870 (O'Hagan, 1870). The Industrial School system, he hoped, would prevent those 'who are cast abroad as waifs and strays on the world … from developing into the criminal preying upon society whilst he is at large, and becoming a burden to it when it is forced to pay for his punishment'. He spoke of such a system, 'giving so many useful citizens to the State – so many immortal souls to heaven' and rescuing thousands 'from lives of penury and sin' who would have 'lived and died in crime and misery – enemies of God and man'.

We find nothing in this of the 'innocence' (Ariès, 1962) of childhood, nothing of the moral indignation at the exposure of children to the experience of destitution and vice. What had to be guarded against were the consequences of such exposure in terms of increased crime rates. Its concern was for society and, it could be argued, for certain social groups, rather than for individual welfare. Child-care intervention was seen in the same vein as was education for the working classes in the nineteenth century – as a means of social control rather than of individual fulfilment. Moreover, if we look at the nature of the information about pupils considered worthy of attention in the Research School records and at the manner of its recording, we find little recognition of the reality of individual differences. The necessity to place the child in a series of administrative categories – reason for committal, length of committal and religion – is predominant in the information made available to the school and recorded in the school register. Personalised information is confined to educational standard and physical characteristics. Similarly, in the school diary differentiation of pupils in terms of background, experience and personal attributes is rare and in the instances where a pupil's response to the school is recorded there appeared an almost total failure to appreciate either the predictability of a differentiated response among the pupil body or its aetiology in the individuality of the pupil.

With those labelled as a social risk perceived as a collective phenomenon, as an identifiable childhood, the solution of segregation and training was formulated in a global fashion, stressing the overall experience of the child-care institution and its impact on the formation of the child (Jones, 1968). From the Research School Records, Department of Education Annual Reports and the Cussen Report (1936) on the Industrial and Reformatory School System, it would appear that a tripartite programme of physical care, literary and manual instruction and moral formation, undifferentiated either within the schools or, indeed, between industrial and reformatory schools, was considered to be multi-functional and to constitute a suitable training, not alone for those who had come into care due to poverty or desertion, but also for those who had committed a variety of offences. An over-riding faith in the efficacy of this programme pervaded the Research School records and is particularly in evidence in commentaries on the careers and fortunes of ex-pupils. Such was the confidence in school effects that a system of vocational placement and foster-care does not appear to have been considered before the promptings of the Cussen Report (1936). The impression is given that vocational success and adjustment to the outside world are to be expected, and there is more than a hint of indignation in the recording of unfavourable reports on ex-pupils, as for instance in the case of the pupil who was said to be 'not doing well': 'He is selling papers on the streets of (a small Irish town)'.

This view of the child-care institution as an effective agent of socialisation is itself a reflection of a belief in the critical role of education in social and political formation which remained unchallenged up until the 1960s (O'Sullivan, 1972b). Indeed, a central feature of the segregation and training model of child care intervention is a curious merging of sociologistic and psychologistic faiths: children once removed from potentially corrupting circumstances will develop within the environment of the institution such personality traits as will insulate them against these and similar corrupting forces on their release. The impact of environment on personality and the resistance of personality to environment are at once affirmed.

In both 'social risk' and 'segregation and training' conceptualisations the perspective is that of the system rather than the child. The child is seen as a potential threat to society rather than someone with needs and rights. The child-centred theme in the organisation of child care and the treatment of childhood and adolescence as particular phases of social, emotional and cognitive development are scarcely in evidence before the Cussen Report and had to wait until the 1960s before they were to attain a fuller recognition. The suggestion that children in care have been denied life circumstances to which they could justifiably make claim is similarly rare in the early years of the system.

A fundamental change of emphasis with regard to neglected, orphaned and illegitimate children is to be found in the Cussen Report of 1936. Throughout its deliberations the possibility of such children drifting into crime and thus posing a potential threat to society was not as explicit as it had been in the nineteenth century. Exhortations to protect society from the children of the 'perishing and dangerous classes' were conspicuously absent. While the obvious social benefits for society of an adequate childcare system were not minimised, the individual child's welfare was recognised more than heretofore. The focusing of attention on the child seems to have coincided with a similar turning point in the treatment of young offenders in England (Ford, 1975). This indication of a change of emphasis apart, however, the Cussen Report in its acceptance both of institutionalised childhood and of a narrow understanding of its requirements failed to anticipate two primary features of the developmental conceptualisation of children and of how childhood should be experienced.

A disenchantment with institutionalisation as a form of intervention is evident in the recommendation of such alternatives as adoption and boarding out in both the Briscoe Report of the Commission on Mental Handicap (1965) and of the Henchy Report of the Commission on Mental Illness (1966). By 1970, developmentalism's antipathy to institutionalisation can be seen to permeate the first major recommendation of the Kennedy Report on the Industrial and Reformatory School System: 'The committal or admission of children to Residential Care should be considered only when there is no satisfactory alternative' (p. 6). In the same sequence of reports there is a departure from the narrow conception of care in terms of physical needs to encompass psychological and emotional dimensions of developmental tasks. In particular, the Briscoe Report argued that many institutionalised children fail to realise their potential through 'loss of firm ties of affection, lack of stimulation and absence of suitable adults to provide a feeling of security' (p. 124), while the Kennedy Report asserted the need to 'reorientate our thinking' so as to lay 'primary emphasis' on 'the child's needs to enable him to develop into maturity and to adjust himself satisfactorily to … society' (12). In its emphasis on security and emotional attachment during childhood and in its antipathy to institutionalised childhood, the developmental assumptions of intervening in the experience of childhood reflect the climate of thought on child care popularised by Bowlby's (1953) *Child Care and the Growth of Love*.

While the adoption of a developmental model of child-care intervention in official reports indicated a recognition of the multi-faceted needs of the child in care and served to firmly establish the child at the centre of attention and concern, it was the emergence of child-advocacy associations such as CARE (Campaign for the Care of Deprived Children), established at the end of 1970 (CARE, 1972) and specifically dedicated to children in care, that most successfully proclaimed the failure to cater for these developmental needs as constituting deprivation. This application of changing interpretations of equality to the life circumstances of children who come into care, mediated to the public through conferences, publications and considerable media coverage, was to be a primary source of the 'discovery' of the deprived child in Ireland.

Child Advocacy: Discourse, Ideology and Policy Formulation

It was at this stage of cultural change that the child advocacy movement entered as a participant and engaged with the conceptualisations of childhood embedded in the organisation and practices of child-care institutions. But as the cultural definition of children in care had not been static, pliable or a *tabula rasa* awaiting structuration, neither was the child advocacy movement politically innocent. Its mobilisation, tactics and approach to policy change enhanced its effectiveness in pursuing its objectives. Most notably, its discourse was slogan-based, issue-centred and grounded in expert legitimation, its ideology was liberal reformist, and it followed a social planning approach to policy formulation. This had implications for the manner in which it engaged with the conceptualisations of childhood and childcare intervention circulating in the structures, practices and personnel within the Industrial and Reformatory School System and among the general public at that time.

The manner in which child advocates presented their ideas, be it in recruitment, diffusion of their policies, or campaigning for change, displayed some key features of a slogan system. Social commitment took precedence over the intellectual elaboration and justification of their proposals. The emphasis was on action and achieving change rather than on attempting to anticipate what the limitations, contradictions and broad social implications of the proposed innovations might be. Much of the advocacy was grounded on a number of principles or appeals of a high moral loading which were considered self-evident, beyond dispute, and not demanding justification to anyone socially alert and concerned. *Children Deprived* (CARE, 1972) appealed to such sources as the Proclamation of Independence, 1916 ('cherishing all the children of the nation equally'), and the United Nations Declaration of the Rights of the Child, 1959 ('the best interests of the child shall be the paramount consideration'). The editorial of the initial Children First Newsletter in 1975 proclaimed: 'our basic objective is (surely?) unobjectionable – to champion the rights of each child in the state to maximum protection, security and happiness' (O'Sullivan, 1980b). By means of uncontentious appeals of this nature many diverse viewpoints were capable of being attracted to and accommodated within child advocacy organisations. For the existing members, slogans helped to confirm the rationale of their participation and enhance solidarity.

The more slogans are interpreted within the organisation, the more consensus is endangered and the stability of the organisation threatened. Yet, if an organisation is to attain any credibility as an agent of change it must offer some proposals concerning the day-to-day operations of, in this case, services and laws relating to children. This, as Apple (1978) points out, is a tenuous balance for 'if it (the slogan system) is too broad it has little power to give tactical guidance to the people who fit under it. If it is too specific, it risks alienating a large portion of its original adherents who disagree with some of the concrete suggestions.' In the case of CARE and Children First, this balance was maintained by centering the practical extension of their slogans on such general child-related issues as institutionalisation, secure units, age of criminal responsibility, judicial arrangements for dealing with children, and disorganised, uncoordinated and underdeveloped children's and family services. A wide leap was made from slogan to issue, avoiding in the process a full theoretical elaboration of the slogan and a consideration of the practical problems such an elaboration might present at the implementation stage. Indeed, the link between the relevant slogan and the stance on specific issues was often slight. Rather, the rationale of the proposed innovations owed more to contemporary child-related developments in other countries, the child development conventions of their time and practitioner wisdom. This reflected the emergence of expert, credentialised knowledge as the basis of legitimation within the discourse.

In presenting their slogans or issue-centred proposals or objections to the public, the child advocates of the 1970s differed in the legitimation of their activities from their predecessors. Those bodies which had previously campaigned for changes in children's services possessed many of the characteristics of Platt's (1969) 'child savers' – missionary ethos and middle-class background – as well as the local religious dimensions which reflected the predominance of Catholic religious in the ownership and staffing of child care institutions. This non-governmental level of response to social problems, be it individualistic, charitable or religious, was very much in tune with Catholic teaching and, in particular, with the principle of subsidiarity; and in its practices would have been guided by its understandings of human nature and destiny. While the credibility of those with a vocation, natural talent or long experience in childcare and the acceptability of concerned pronouncements from religious on children's issues persisted, the professionalisation of human caring and the pressure for visibility, recognition and employment opportunities among social workers and psychologists was to ground child advocacy on secular humanistic appeals and expert knowledge. It was in this sense that the slogan-based, issue-centred approach functioned not merely as child advocacy but also as a legitimation of the emergence of lay, university-trained, human caring personnel as its most salient and authoritative advocates. Practitioner wisdom and Catholic-inspired moral exhortations continued to influence, though in a less direct way: the sensitivity in publications such as *Children Deprived* (CARE, 1972) regarding the interest groups and traditions associated with these perspectives was most apparent in discussions concerning adoption, the training of child-care personnel and the co-ordination of private religious-controlled children's homes. Whatever the interaction, the discourse of child advocacy as the 1970s progressed – its ideals, categories, language and appeals – increasingly reflected the content of the sanctioned and certified bodies of knowledge which set social workers and psychologists apart from others speaking on behalf of children.

Ideologically, the child advocacy movement was sympathetic to the leanings of Irish society on social issues at that time in its liberal reformist mediation of international thinking on children's rights. Social problems tended to be defined and explored in isolation from one another and from broad social phenomena such as power, control, and the distribution of material resources. When suggested, solutions were accordingly piecemeal, involving reforms in relation to the presenting problems and grounded on the assumptions that social conditions in one sector of society can be improved without impinging on other sectors. So it was with the advocacy of children's rights. The concern was for the children of other people such as children 'at risk', in care or adopted children, without any apparent recognition of the implications which the proposed innovations or principles cited might have for the power relationships between the age groups in society at large.

The innovations proposed by child advocates followed a social planning model in which expert specialists identified problems of particular individuals, families or communities and prescribed forms of intervention which demanded legislative change, the establishment of new institutions or bureaucratic structures, or the participation of further specialists. This involved doing something 'for' rather than 'with' people, and is premised on the assumption that the child advocates' expert or informed perception of the reality of the target group's social context is the most effective basis for social planning. For example, there was a repeated demand for the replacement of formal court proceedings for juveniles by a children's/family hearing system in which the trappings of the judicial system would be reduced to a minimum. Yet, what little evidence exists on children's constructions of their court appearances at that time suggests that it was the power of the police witness and not the archaic language and ritual that was perceived as offensive; and under the proposed de-formalisation of the legal processing of children it was generally proposed that police be allowed greater discretion in initiating formal charges, which in effect, would give more power to the police than that which was already perceived as unfair (O'Sullivan, 1977).

In fact, no official consideration of child care in Ireland in that era has recorded attempts to understand how the children themselves interpreted what was happening to them or how their parents perceived the experience of having their children brought into care. Viewing the child as subject rather than object is confined to a few academic studies (O'Connor, 1971; O'Sullivan, 1977, 1978). Elsewhere, excluding those targeted by social policy from the planning process was being criticised on the basis of it being a violation of democratic principles and likely to detract from the adequacy of the policy in its formulation and implementation (Coleman, 1976). Yet, their exclusion at that time in Ireland was consistent with, and perhaps even necessary for, the emergence of the expert legitimation of knowledge and practice in child care. Likewise, suggesting that 'victims' or 'clients' should have a role in policy formulation would not have enhanced the credibility of child advocates among state policy-makers.

Cultural Lag

The fact that child-care definitions in official reports or social movements change is no indication that child-care practices will be harmoniously modified in line with the changed conceptualisations of childhood and intervention. Indeed, the phenomenon of cultural lag is reasonably predictable in organisations such as child-care institutions. Sometimes the maintenance of institutionalised conceptualisations is disguised through a change in language and terminology. In Britain at that time, the tendency to re-label penal facilities without any accompanying change in practice was highlighted by May (1971) who also distinguished between 'rhetoric' and 'reality' in the operation of the children's panels in Scotland (May, 1977).

The discourse of the Department of Justice in setting up Loughan House as a secure unit suggested a modification of the segregation and training model, with the training element being replaced by 'treatment'; the juvenile offenders involved were considered to be maladjusted and in need of specialised help, as in the case of physical illness, to cure the underlying 'disease' of which the delinquent act is merely the presenting symptom. Given certain aspects of the reality of Loughan House, however – in particular, the employment of prison officers – it seems reasonable to conclude that here also 'the vocabulary of therapy (was being) exploited to serve a public relations function' (Allen, 1959). In the case of the Research School we find that into the 1970s, at a time when children in care were being officially defined in terms of their individuality and developmental needs, the information about pupils which was considered sufficiently important to be officially recorded and made available to it still reflected the understanding of children coming into care as a social risk and threat to society.

This information fell into two principal categories – that of home background and institutional deviant career. Information relating to at least one aspect of the home background was provided in the case of 47 per cent of the pupils, and information concerning at least one aspect of the pupil's institutional/deviant career was made available in 35 per cent of the cases. In a breakdown of the particular aspects of home background for which information was made available to the school, it emerged that material characteristics were most frequently recorded, family size, parental income and physical conditions of the home being recorded for about one-third of the pupils. By contrast, information about other members of the family was infrequently recorded, information concerning fathers, mothers and siblings having been made known in 10 per cent, 5 per cent and 6 per cent of the cases, respectively. This information consisted of short comments such as 'Father unemployed for health reasons', 'Mother idle and dissolute character' and 'Both brothers have criminal records'. In the case of institutional/deviant career, the nature and extent of the damage involved in the offence for which pupils had been committed to the Research School were the most frequently recorded. 'Spent money on luxuries', 'Easter eggs (value: equivalent of c.€8) stolen from supermarket; eaten or destroyed', and 'Stole drink, bicycle and clothes (to the equivalent value of c.€40)' are typical examples.

What is most striking about the information supplied to the school, apart from its paucity, is the neglect of the pupil as a developing individual with social, cognitive and emotional needs and dispositions. There is, for instance, no recorded instance of a report from a psychologist, social worker, priest or teacher, in connection with any of these pupils, the information concerning home background provides little insight into the quality of family life in the pupils' homes, and the documentation relating to the institutional/deviant career of the pupils appears more concerned with the damage done to society than with the individual involved and the circumstances of his actions.

The nature and the content of pupil records were not anomalies or curiosities, in that they reflected earlier understandings of children in care. But in the specific instance of the Research School their continued use was organisationally meaningful, and more than an instance of disinterested cultural lag, in its relationship to the boundary maintenance problems of the school staff, particularly those arising from the activities of the child advocacy movement. As we shall see it makes good organisational sense (Garfinkel, 1967) not to know too much about pupils, and particularly not to have what is known given a legitimacy, permanence, and transferability through official recording (Wheeler, 1969), in that it permits greater subjectivity in the categorisation of the pupil, with its attendant flexibility in goal setting, the definition of school function and the handling of prescriptions from external sources.

Conceptualisation as Boundary Maintenance

Increasingly, as the 1960s progressed, the staff of the Research School were to find themselves the victims of social and cultural change. Though the professionalisation of human caring had been expanding, resulting in the outflow of social workers, in particular, from the universities, staff training for those in the Industrial and Reformatory School System lagged considerably behind. Indeed, such was the situation that those who came nearest to accepted professional competence in the area of child care were, in the main, working outside of the Industrial and Reformatory School System and active in the child advocacy movement. Whereas regular school systems and their personnel can be, and frequently are, subjected to demands and prescriptions from external organisations and individuals, the situation whereby professionalism in the activity under discussion is more a feature of the external pressure groups is quite unique and, when it occurs, cannot but enhance the legitimacy of these pressure groups to comment and prescribe. While the legitimacy of external pressure groups was being enhanced in this manner, that of the schools' staff, almost totally religious, was being undermined by the questioning of the role of religious in education generally, but particularly in child care (Kennedy, 1971).

There had been a considerable decline in numbers admitted to industrial schools, particularly since 1950, though those committed because of an indictable offence had increased their representation and had come to be concentrated in three schools, the Research School included (O'Connor, 1963). Having been established to cater for 'waifs and strays', the Research School now found itself in the role of junior reformatory. The child advocacy movement, speaking from its legitimated position, was highly critical of this mixing of 'offenders' and 'non-offenders' and the school was to be the object of repeated reprimands for its failure to segregate the two categories of pupils. Other frequent criticisms related to its isolated location, institutional nature and inadequate staffing and facilities. And this was occurring at a time when the future of the Research School was being discussed at parliamentary level and by the religious congregation responsible for it. One feature of the response of the school staff in coping with this invasiveness of external forces was to deploy the conceptualisation of the children coming into their care as a boundary maintenance mechanism.

The paucity of information made available to the Research School concerning the pupils' backgrounds and personalities and the absence of professional reports and assessments from psychologists and social workers has been noted. Nor was it known how pupils came to be categorised as 'indictable offenders', 'lacking in proper guardianship' and 'school non-attenders'; my own analysis failed to identify any meaningful differences between the categories in terms of age, socio-economic background, family size, stability and structure, educational progress and previous court appearance (O'Sullivan, 1977). In short, there was nothing in the information about pupils conveyed to the Research School which demanded acceptance by the staff as legitimated categorisation, be it on the basis of professional or legislative authority.

Davies (1973) has pointed out that 'in the absence of sufficient agreed objective information about their (children's) attributes, and the attributes of knowledge and effective learning situations, beliefs or values about all of these things assume a greatly magnified importance'. In their everyday characterisation of the pupils, the staff, apparently unreflexively, alternated in their appeal to two variants of deprivation – one normal, the other pathological. On the one hand, the child was seen as someone who has been removed from an unfavourable environment. If he has been charged with an indictable offence, the parents and the environment they created were blamed; he was seen as lacking in culpability, having reacted in a predictable manner to his environment. Above all, he was considered to have suffered no psychological damage; he was a 'normal child', no different from any other except in relation to the background from which he had been removed. On the other hand, the child's deprivation was seen in distinctly pathological terms. Whatever their origin – the role of parents was not highlighted – the child was considered to possess distinctly deviant traits that must be guarded against. He was seen as abnormally self-protective and to this end was devious, cunning and untrustworthy. A feature of the use of these variants was the reluctance by the staff to differentiate *within* the pupil body in these terms. Whatever variant was appealed to in interaction was applied to the pupils as a group, as identifiable childhoods, though individual pupils were used to explain or substantiate particular facets of the variant.

In one of the institutions studied by Strauss *et al.* (1964, p. 353), they recorded that among staff with no psychiatric training 'lay philosophies predominated and were accommodated to institutional conditions'. In the case of the Research School staff, their ambivalence in the definition of the pupil population as either normal or pathological needs to be seen in the light of external pressures and criticisms and in relation to the holding operation being performed by a staff awaiting a formal declaration on the future of the school. Some relevant variables are listed in Table 13.2. These related to the perceptions of the staff concerning government and congregational plans for the Research School, the role of the congregation in child care, and their attitudes and response to the prescriptions of the child advocacy movement. The nature of these perceptions and attitudes was quite variable and complex and can only be represented in global terms. Perceptions of government and congregational plans for the school are presented as anticipating either closure or development. Perceptions of the role of the congregation in child care yield three possibilities: provision for non-offenders only, the rehabilitation of delinquents or a withdrawal from child care entirely. The categorisation used to describe reactions to the child advocacy movement was devised by setting Litwak and Meyer's (1965) open, swinging and locked door approaches to community linkages in the context of Berger and Luckmann's (1967) analysis of social responses to alternative definitions of reality.

A central and recurring theme throughout these variables was that of boundary maintenance, both in relation to congregation and school: the relationship between the vocation of the staff and the nature of child care; the implications of government investment in school redevelopment for congregational control; and the inevitability of having to incorporate other than congregational members in the work of the school if the recommendations of the child advocacy movement, particularly with regard to specialised staff, were to be accepted. Discussions with members of the congregation and a consideration of its history suggested that these boundary maintenance problems were part of a wider concern for the identity of the congregation at a time of considerable educational change in Ireland.

Table 13.3 lists some of the combinations of variables which appeared to be associated with normal and pathological perceptions of the pupils. In general it can be seen that normal perceptions of pupils were associated with redevelopment plans for the Research School by the congregation and/or the government, linked to a 'non-offender only' definition of congregational role. The most frequently recorded combination associated with the pathological perception was congregational and governmental closure plans linked to a 'non-offender only' definition of congregational role. Pattern F was very rare, though some staff appeared to accept a role for the congregation in the area of delinquency treatment, and where this was linked to redevelopment plans the pathological model was dominant. Reaction to the prescriptions of the child advocacy movement was typically one of nihilation: the validity of the prescriptions was challenged by pointing to their non-practitioner origin ('well-meaning do-gooders'; 'theoretical psychologists'; 'people who have no knowledge of what it's really like here', etc.), though they could be used with varying degrees of filtration and openness to handle undesired discrepancies between perceived congregational and governmental plans for the school. Generally, when closure rather than redevelopment was desired, as in pattern E, the validity of external prescriptions was accepted and marshalled in support, whereas when the opposite was desired, as in patterns B and C, staff use of external prescriptions was more guarded and selective.

A very frequent instance of nihilation as a response was the dismissing of the 'failure to segregate "offenders" and "non-offenders"' criticism of the child advocacy movement by proclaiming the homogeneity of the pupil population. The actual definition employed, be it normal or pathological, depended on the accompanying criticism, the pupils' 'normality' being stressed in denying the need for specialised psychological/psychiatric staff, while their pathological nature was emphasised to highlight the naïvety of arguing for the employment of house-mothers or a sexually-mixed pupil population. What the findings suggest, is the existence of an ambivalence, subject to situational fluctuations, among staff in the definition and explanation of the personalities and behaviour of the pupils in the school of a kind that facilitated tactical, defensive and stabilising responses to challenges and tensions relating to vocation, congregational role, institutional function and organisational change, in the form of shifting conceptualisations of the children in their care. In the event, it provided no more than temporary respite and stability. The closure of the Research School in 1974 and the dismantling of the Industrial and Reformatory School System signalled the coming to fruition of the criticism of institutionalised childhood in the policy reports of the 1960s and 1970s, and of their dissemination and popularisation through the work of the child-advocacy movement.

Table 13.2 Variables Relevant to Staff Adoption of Normal/Pathological Variants of Pupils as Deprived Children

Perception of Congregation's most likely decision on the future of the Research School	Perception of government's plans for Research School	Perception of Congregation's role in child care	Reactions to child advocacy movement's prescriptions
Closure in the near future	Closure in the near future	Non-offender only	Openness
Redevelopment with the aid of government investment	Investment and redevelopment	Delinquency treatment only	Filtration
		No role in either area	Nihilation

Table 13.3 Clusters of Variables Associated with Staff Adoption of Normal/Pathological Variants of Pupils as Deprived Children

	Perception of Congregation's most likely decision on the future of the Research School	Perception of government's plans for Research School	Perception of Congregation's role in child care	Reactions to child advocacy movement's prescriptions
Normal perception of pupils	A. Redevelopment	Redevelopment	Non-offender only	Nihilation
	B. Redevelopment	Closure	Non-offender only	Filtration
	C. Closure	Redevelopment	Non-offender only	Filtration
Pathological perception of pupils	D. Closure	Closure	Non-offender only	Nihilation
	E. Closure	Redevelopment	Non-offender only	Openness
	F. Redevelopment	Redevelopment	Delinquency Treatment	Openness

Conceptualisation in Cultural Politics

What this chapter demonstrates is the ubiquity of conceptualisation in how we make sense of the world, communicate with one another about it, and act collectively in its maintenance or modification. Though confined to children and childhood, to no more than the specific manifestations or experiences of a life segment, we have found the analysis ranging across education, pedagogy and curriculum, the rationale, organisation and programmes within child care, social movements addressing issues of entitlement and best interests, the claims of professionalising occupations, and the boundary maintenance practices of child-care personnel in organisational settings. What the chapter relatedly illuminates in this diversity of manifestations of conceptualisation is how pivotal it is in cultural politics. Be it in efforts to change teaching styles and curriculum organisation, how the state caters for those committed to its care, or what knowledge is most valid, how children and childhood are to be conceptualised was established as the cultural terrain on which opposing interests, encompassing religion, professionalising groups, educational progressives and the state, joined battle.

There are tactical reasons for this centrality in the immediate engagement between the opposing forces. To change how we conceptualise children is to reconfigure the power/knowledge relationship between those who work with them, and claim authority to act on their behalf, and to speak about their needs. But the centrality of conceptualisation in cultural politics is more structurally explained by its foundational position within a policy paradigm, which as we have seen can usually be described in terms of conceptualisation. Conceptualisation is ubiquitous and pivotal in cultural politics precisely for the reason that how we define and classify phenomena is implicated in how we believe the world to be or ought to be. Thus, as we have seen in this chapter at the most basic level of how children and childhood is conceptualised, political interests and activity are involved in its inheritance, maintenance, (re)construction and denial.

Chapter 14

Human Agency: Cultural Strangers and Cultural Contrarians

In considering the contribution of human agents to cultural change in education, principles of educational funding, developments in the education of adults and the role of the Roman Catholic church in Irish education are encompassed. Apart from the substantive changes outlined, this facilitates the analysis of the conditions under which social actors become forces for change and succeed in becoming agents rather than conduits in the flow of cultural politics. In this analysis, cultural unorthodoxy, characterised by alienation, distance, independence or otherness, is given particular attention. Two constructs are deployed throughout – cultural strangers and contrarians.

Non-indigenous commentators are conceptualised as cultural strangers. By the fact of their location within a different culture, cultural strangers bring with them a set of expectations, categories of knowledge and interpretations that are likely to differ from those of the indigenous culture. The perils of being a cultural stranger are well known. In making sense of another society there is the inevitable temptation to interpret the new culture in terms of the assumptions and logic of one's own culture. This can take the form of using culture-bound tests, misinterpreting symbols and practices and making inappropriate assessments. Yet, within this weakness lies the peculiar function of the cultural stranger as an agent for illuminating a culture to its participants. As Bourdieu (1988, p. xi) puts it, the uncompromisingly alien view of the cultural stranger can challenge us to 'exoticise the domestic' by disrupting our 'relation of intimacy with modes of life and thought which remain opaque ... because they are too familiar'. Benignly, this can help people to see their culture and their relationship to it more clearly and fully. More threateningly, it can disrupt the certainties which legitimate power relationships and in turn provoke resistance and mobilisation.

Cultural contrarians describe those who, while indigenous to a culture, nonetheless think otherwise in some significant regard. Be it through distinctive features of their personal and intellectual formation or the product of reflexive engagement with their cultural inheritance, they come to think, feel or imagine in a manner that is discordant with the general or specific social context in which they operate. They are liable to be dismissed as disaffected, disloyal or disgruntled. Yet, they can be a dynamic for change with the capacity to be culturally innovative or restorationist. In general discourse, the journalists John Waters (1997, 2004) and Desmond Fennell (1993; see also Quinn, 2001) are representative. In sociological terms, cultural contrarians invalidate the construct of cultural dupe, used to refer to the theorised dominance of culture to the exclusion of human agency in individual habitus.

We begin with the cultural stranger A. Dale Tussing and his interventions in Irish thinking on educational funding, followed by the cultural contrarian Alfred O'Rahilly and his influence on how we think about the interface of adulthood and education, and finally, the interacting contributions of cultural strangers and contrarians to the changing status of the theocentric paradigm in Irish educational policy.

A. Dale Tussing and the Principles of Educational Funding

A. Dale Tussing, Professor of Economics at Syracuse University, New York, published *Irish Educational Expenditures – Past, Present and Future* in 1978. This was based on research carried out during a fifteen-month period as Visiting Research Professor of Economics at the Economic and Social Research Institute in Dublin over 1975/1976. Before this visit, and subsequently, Tussing made many extensive visits to Ireland.

At one level Tussing's analysis of educational expenditure in the Republic of Ireland was non-controversial and within the mainstream commercial text on education. He highlighted the extent and depth of the Irish system of schooling, more developed, he pointed out, than would have been expected given Irish income levels, industrial structure and degree of urbanisation. He gave as examples, universal participation at primary level, very nearly so at junior cycle and the rates for senior cycle higher than in many richer countries. Looking back into the historical origins of the system in the eighteenth and early nineteenth century, he wondered how this could be, given that at that time Ireland was 'a poor country from all accounts, whose main economic activity was non-commercial agriculture, and whose housing conditions, infant mortality rate and cash incomes were among the worst in Europe'. And locating his analysis in the 1970s: 'how can Ireland, by a long chalk the poorest country in the EEC, afford such a highly developed system' (p. 54).

His research, however, led him to conclude that the factors which made such educational provision possible – spartan schools, large classes, poorly paid teachers, Catholic Church investment, members of religious orders redirecting their salaries back into the schools or providing services without pay, and the low scientific and technical content of the curriculum – were fading or totally disappearing, leaving Ireland with a highly-developed and expensive school system. And this, he pointed out, was coinciding with a growth in enrolments that was unprecedented in recent decades. He predicted that second-level total public expenditures, adjusted for inflation, would almost double in the period 1974 to 1986 and that during the same period third-level expenditures would more than double. Tussing was fearful that little would be done or said about these enrolment and budgetary pressures until a crisis situation had been reached. If this was allowed to happen he warned that parents, particularly those who were poor or disadvantaged, would experience the crisis in the form of overcrowded classes, temporary classrooms and a lack of sufficient school places. For this reason he urged 'a major national debate on educational priorities' (p. 173).

Public/Private Benefit

As a contribution to this debate Tussing suggested a particular approach which, in its principles and policy implications, sought to expand the commercial text on education. It was this departure from conventional thinking which gave the report its controversial and culturally disruptive dimension. He recommended that education be treated as a 'quasi-public good' with both public and private characteristics. Where its principal beneficiaries are individual pupils, through cultural and social formation or enhanced life-long earnings, education can be said to be private. Education is a public good in that political, social and economic life requires a certain minimum educational standard which he deemed to be roughly equivalent to the years of compulsory schooling.

Where resources are scarce, Tussing proposed that they be reserved for those aspects of schooling which benefit society and, in particular, Irish society and its less-advantaged members. Translated into a fees and financing policy, this would result in students at third-level institutions paying, by means of a loan scheme, the full economic cost of their education. At senior cycle post-primary level, Tussing suggested a number of possible ways of making parents more financially accountable for the education of their children – the abolition of all or some of the schemes of state subvention to schools or the treatment of state financing of education at this level as personal income and thus liable to income tax. Directly or indirectly, these would have resulted in a repeal of the free education scheme introduced slightly more than a decade earlier.

In terms of policy options, Tussing was attempting to put on the agenda a proposal that had not been seriously entertained in any public way since free education has been debated within the Department of Education. A senior civil servant of the time has recalled how he attempted to convince the Minister, Donagh O'Malley, of the desirability of setting a means test in relation to free senior-cycle post-primary schooling. Mr O'Malley is said to have responded that, having discussed the matter with the Taoiseach, there would be no means test. In retrospect, the same civil servant was of the view that the free nature of the scheme captured the imagination of the public (O'Connor 1986: 153). There is a sense, in fact, in which free education became a cultural icon, suggestive of change and optimism, reflective of openness and opportunity and symbolising a new departure in Irish society which had recently celebrated the fiftieth anniversary of the insurrection of 1916. To suggest any dismantling of the scheme, as Tussing was doing, was quite literally iconoclastic. However compelling Tussing's arguments might have been, public political endorsement for such a dismantling of the free education scheme would have done untold damage in terms of popular support.

While it may be the case, as Tussing (1983) later recollected, that 'Ministers and civil servants rejected the notion of a crisis at the time', there is reason to believe they concurred with the key aspects of Tussing's analysis and perhaps even with the thrust of his approach to the resolution of rising educational costs. At the very least, the view that for many parents free post-primary education was a windfall, and that such parents could and would contribute towards their children's education, seems to have been taken seriously in estimating the likely political reaction to the economies applied to educational funding in the early 1980s. These initiatives, taken in 1982 by the Minister for Education, were intended to reduce the projected 1983 expenditure on education by 2 per cent. Some of the more significant financial savings were to be accounted for by an increase in teacher/pupil ratios at second level of approximately 5 per cent together with a reduction of ex-quota teachers, the introduction of school transport charges for secondary school students where parents did not qualify for free medical care and a reduction in the capital budget (NESC, 1983).

As the crisis which Tussing had predicted began to put pressure on schools through these cutbacks of finance and personnel, schools began to rely increasingly on voluntary contributions from parents to make good the deficit. *De facto*, the free education scheme was seriously eroded, but indirectly as a consequence of government cutbacks and the damage-limitation reactions of schools rather than as a result of any public change in fees policy for second-level schooling.

Undoing the free-education initiative and introducing a fees policy for second-level schooling were excluded as themes in state discourse on education. Tussing may have strengthened the hand of state policy makers in introducing economies but not to the point of being able to communicate publicly in terms of the erosion of free education that was nonetheless forced on schools as a result of these economies.

State Discourse

In the context of third-level education, *Irish Educational Expenditures* made it possible for politically sensitive proposals to be highlighted without any indigenous body or person claiming responsibility for them. Even the very act of identifying an option in public debate implies some level of support, if only in the sense that it has been considered worthy of attention to the exclusion of other more dormant issues. The thematising of a number of possibilities or proposals relating to the financing of education and the degree and nature of financial support for individual students was to follow in a series of publications from within the central state apparatus.

In 1978, the same year that *Irish Educational Expenditures* was published, the government presented its Green Paper *Development for Full Employment*. This raised the possibility of an increase in the fees charged by third-level institutions. The 1979 White Paper, *Programme for National Development 1978-1981*, set out the government's decisions on the matters raised in the Green Paper. Of the four paragraphs dealing with education in the White Paper, three concerned the optimum use of resources and, in particular, the options relating to a fees policy for third-level institutions: '... the government feel that third-level institutions should be moving towards a situation where they would collect a greater proportion of their income in fees ...' (p. 86). These considerations are representative of the commercial text on education and fit conventionally within its contribution to the structuring of the mercantile paradigm. The conceptualisation of educational provision in terms of 'resources', and the establishment of their 'optimum use' as a prime systemic virtue are indicative of this. Above all, we find the almost total dominance of financial considerations in the treatment of education in the 1979 White Paper.

The *White Paper on Educational Development* followed in 1980 and, much to Tussing's (1981) annoyance, failed to pursue this question of the balance to be struck between student fees and subsidies from the exchequer in the funding of third-level institutions. The subject of direct grants to third-level institutions was ignored, he argued, '... despite their far greater budgetary weight, despite their prominence in the 1979 White Paper, and despite the public discussion of them'. He recalled that while *Irish Educational Expenditures* had called for a public debate on the financing of education, 'the current Minister for Education shrinks from such a debate, which, however, goes on without him'. In fact, Tussing's thematising of the private/public nature of the functions and benefits of schooling was to find its way into the 1980 White Paper in the recorded view of the Higher Education Authority 'that benefits accruing to individual students should be taken into account when policy decisions are made in relation to student support' (p. 79).

This added a new theme to the commercial text on schooling as represented by the 1978 Green Paper and the 1979 White Paper. It was to be given greater prominence, expanded in its representation and logic and made more propositional in its communication by the government advisory body, the National Economic and Social Council, in its *Economic and Social Policy in 1983: Aims and Recommendations*. The Council '... suggested that the method of financing third-level education should be reconsidered due to the regressive distributional implications of providing courses to students at fees which are equivalent to less than one quarter of the total cost. While the council recognises that aspects of higher education can contribute to social and economic development, it believes that the costs of third level education should be financed more than they are at present by the recipients who gain substantial financial benefits as a result' (NESC, 1983, p. 30).

In the government's *Programme for Action in Education 1984-1987* in 1984 we find the state's articulation of the commercial text on education structured in terms of Tussing's concepts. The theme of private benefit had been incorporated into the analysis as had a recognition of the need to prioritise between the claims on public funding of the different levels of the educational system.

> Given that there must be a severe restriction on the amount of funds available for overall public spending, it is important to consider the provisions for third-level education relative to those for primary and second-level education and, particularly, to the needs of those in the compulsory education period ... (and) the extent to which individuals who will derive economic benefit from third-level education should themselves pay for their own education either while partaking of it or later in life (p. 28).

In communicating these views, however, the programme is less propositional and more oblique in presentation than either the NESC or Tussing. Throughout the section of the financing of higher education anonymous attribution – e.g. 'there is an argument', 'some important questions of principle arise', 'account must be taken of' – make it possible for politically sensitive ideas to be integrated into educational discourse without political risk. This use of cultural strangers allows the response to ideas to be gauged where no public consultative procedure exists or where to utilise such a procedure would require a more explicit addition of a theme to policy-making discourse.

Equity, Elitism and Stratification

Apart from succeeding in expanding the range of themes in the commercial text on education, Tussing also managed to introduce considerations of principle and values, in particular the question of equity and the distribution of scarce resources in relation to the funding on education. In a number of subsequent contributions to Irish educational debate, Tussing broadened these to encompass a series of sociological themes including that of stratification of schools along class lines.

In a symposium on the 1980 *White Paper on Educational Development*, Tussing (1981) observed that 'a major issue concerning the Irish system of education, one not discussed in the White Paper and rarely mentioned in public discussion, is the extent to which the structure of that system serves to separate and divide people rather than to bring them together'. In this regard he pointed to class stratification at second-level education, drawing attention to the clientele and funding arrangements in fee-charging and free secondary schools, in comprehensive and community schools and in vocational schools. Tussing went on to argue that this view of Irish education exposes only the 'grossest' manifestations of stratification in second-level schooling and ignores 'the subtle differences within the various categories, e.g. as between Presentation and Christian Brothers schools on the one hand and Loreto and Dominican schools on the other, or as between the prestigious Dublin Protestant schools and some of the more plebian Protestant schools around the country'.

Tussing returned to the principles which guide state funding of education in an address to the Irish Vocational Education Association in 1983. He elaborated on what he considered to be the implications of such a divided educational system for grant aid to schools:

> I have to question continued large scale state aid to fee-charging secondary schools ... This support of fee-charging second-level schools, through capitulation grants and payment of incremental teacher salaries, constitutes a device by which the state contributes to the perpetuation of elitism and class stratification through the school system ... In my opinion, no further cuts in second-level finance in the free sector are appropriate before there are significant reductions in state support to the fee sector.

Sponsorship

In drawing attention to the issues of social stratification in second-level schooling and equity in educational funding, and given the nature of his critique and proposals, Tussing's arguments were congruent with the interests of the vocational education sector. This strand of post-primary education attracted a disproportionate number of children from manual worker and small farmer backgrounds. It enjoyed less status than the more academic secondary sector, and had traditionally led to, at most, skilled manual work, being unable until 1967 to prepare students for the Leaving Certificate Examinations which provided access to university and white collar/professional occupations.

Having such weighty analysis from a scholarly source available to them enhanced the power of advocacy of representatives of the vocational educational system and of its umbrella body, the Irish Vocational Education Association. What happened had occurred in a less focused and personalised manner with *Investment in Education*. It was possible to argue that here was an independent academic who had looked dispassionately at the Irish educational system and came to the conclusion that the vocational schools, which accepted all comers, should be given favourable consideration in educational funding. Even more than that, Tussing was drawing attention to the function of schooling in confirming class structure and elitism in Irish society. Academics and politicians had in the past written and spoken in support of expansion, investment and more favourable treatment for the vocational system, and generally decried its lower status within the post-primary sector (Randles, 1975). By introducing themes of equity and social justice Tussing contributed a sharp comparative and moral dimension to the analysis of post-primary schooling. While such themes had indeed been a feature of sociological analysis of Irish education, Tussing enjoyed a particular success in having equity and social justice accepted as themes within the policy community. As an economist, with its value-free connotations, Tussing achieved a level of acceptance in discourse for what, had it come from a sociologist, would have risked dismissal as ideological, as the exchange between Brendan Walsh and the authors of *Understanding Contemporary Ireland* (Breen *et al.*, 1990) illuminates (Walsh *et al.*, 1991).

Support for vocational schooling was not routinely accompanied by such an interpretation of the elitist function of schooling and the principles of educational funding. It would have been accepted in providing financial support for schools that the state should take no interest in the admissions policy or whether the school was fee paying or not. Changes in level of grants or the introduction of new types of grants, such as those for school building or equipment, were devoid of considerations of principle and seemed to owe their origin to educational developments and to economic or political considerations. The ideological debates on these issues in countries such as the United States and England involved sharply-divided points of view on what in Ireland did not seem to constitute a meaningful issue. Such moral themes were outside the Irish paradigms governing the funding of schooling.

As a cultural stranger, Tussing had found an indigenous sponsor in the vocational system, essential if he was to avoid the cultural exclusion described later in this chapter. Such sponsorship served to vouch for his ideas, proclaim them as meaningful and defuse any accusation concerning their 'alien' status. It also acted as a means by which they would be introduced to Irish educational discourse in the context of schools, teachers, administrators and the media. In fact, one can think of no other publication on Irish education that received the level of attention and publicity that *Irish Educational Expenditures – Past, Present and Future* did on the Late Late Show. The minor changes that followed in the funding of schools, such as the withdrawal of the capitation grant of £31 per pupil from the fee-charging secondary schools under the terms of the 1986 Budget (Breen *et al.*, 1990) were less significant in the overall context of Irish thinking than the fact that the financing of education came to be recognised as a topic about which there could be disputes of principle and values.

Cultural Strangers and Change

In the contrasting responses of state educational planners and the vocational system to Tussing's analysis, the relationship between cultural strangers, indigenous sponsor and policy paradigm is further illuminated. Tussing may have breached Irish paradigms in relation to the principles of social justice which he felt should govern the funding of the different post-primary sectors. But he stopped short of thematising a factor fundamental to and underpinning the differential status between the vocational and secondary sectors – the social stratification of the knowledge and skill they were entrusted to transmit. It was not part of Tussing's argument that the superior social evaluation of the academic and systematised knowledge of the secondary school should be made problematic. This restriction of the paradigmatic confrontation involved in Tussing's analysis is likely to have helped in making it possible for the representatives of the vocational system to support Tussing's ideas without having them dismissed as outlandish or as a distraction, the response typically anticipated by those who seek to breach paradigms (Maguire, 1988).

By way of contrast, despite being an economist with its value-free connotations, and even though he operated within the commercial text on schooling seeking better value for state funding, Tussing created problems for the state educational planners. For the state educational planners to publicly endorse Tussing's interpretating of the individual's responsibility for financing post-compulsory schooling, even though they may well have recognised its validity, would have been to violate a social and educational icon – the free education scheme. It is clear that not all elements of a paradigm are invested with equal meaning and significance. Here we gain an insight into the qualitative differences involved in paradigmatic shifts and the conditions which make such change possible.

Tussing demonstrated how policy paradigms can be penetrated. He succeeded, in relation to the funding of education, in making public existing assumptions (the unnecessity of guiding principles), advanced a reconceptualisation of the benefits of schooling (private/public), suggested principles for guiding funding decisions, proposed values of equity and justice, and added stratification and elitism to the terminology of concern in educational discourse. For this to be successful, his reception into Irish educational discourse was pivotal, be it through overt sponsorship or more covertly through unattributed intertextual invocation and retrieval. For his part, only in relation to the violation of the iconic status of free education could Tussing be said to have compromised the validity and legitimacy of the advocacy of potential sponsors. Otherwise, Tussing operated within the commercial text on education, avoided characteristic sociological themes such as stratified knowledge, and benefited from the value-free connotations of the economist and the independent status of an external authority.

Alfred O'Rahilly and the Education of Adults

While University College Cork had been involved in the provision of extramural lectures and tutorial classes for workers since the early years of the century, the establishment of the Diploma in Social and Economic Science in 1946 was a major step in the formalisation of its provision for adult learners. At the inaugural conferring of the Diploma in 1948, Alfred O'Rahilly, the President of the College and the prime mover in the provision of the course, declared:

> This is a very important day in the history of the College. It marks the first occasion since the establishment of the College one hundred years ago, that workers were allowed to attend a complete course here. I want to congratulate the workers who have completed two years study in the College and the School of Commerce. I consider it a great honour and privilege to award the Diploma to them today. I hope many others will follow their example. The door is now open (quoted in Ó Murchú, 1989, p. 29).

Like all university presidents on such occasions, O'Rahilly was sending out signals to a number of interests: to other colleges by way of encouragement to commit themselves more to adult education; by way of a broadside against those within UCC who had opposed his earlier initiatives in bringing workers onto the campus; and as a declaration of his intent to expand and develop the adult education diploma programme.

Cultural Contrarian

Though O'Rahilly had the support and indeed involvement of others within UCC for his adult education initiatives, his violation of some of the assumptions of university education at that time were becoming more explicit. Extension lectures, even on a regular basis, were consistent with the notion of personal self-improvement which did not disrupt the certainties and hierarchies of the class and knowledge structures. Even specific diploma courses for particular varieties of technical work were reconcilable with the UCC Governing Body's aim, in a 1910 document on extension lectures, 'to extend, as far as possible, the sphere of usefulness of the College throughout Munster' (quoted in Ó Murchú, 1989), and operated in the tradition of the mechanics institutes seeking to produce more efficient, disciplined and productive workers. The Diploma in Social and

Economic Science, however, was different. It was targeting trade unionists as a category and seeking what in later times could have been interpreted as a form of empowerment for citizenship, both within the context of industrial relations and beyond it politically. At that same inaugural conferring in 1948, O'Rahilly specified some of the objectives of the course:

> There is no doubt that a student who has successfully pursued this course will have a grasp of the big ideological issues confronting the world today. He will understand company and banking statements, he will be familiar with the statistical abstract and the trade journal, he will not be frightened by economic jargon. He will have learned the rules of debate and the conduct of meetings. He will know about filing systems, minutes and account books. He will have knowledge of the history of principles of trade unions. He will be familiar with the Industrial Relations Act and similar legislation. And he ought to have increased facility in speaking and writing on these subjects (quoted in Gaughan, 1986, p. 98).

Of the economic conferences, a precursor of the diploma courses and attended largely by workers and students from the Faculty of Commerce, O'Rahilly had this to say:

> It is expected that the intimate personal knowledge which the workers have of social and economic problems will throw light on the studies of the Faculty of Commerce, and will save the students from the limitations of mere book knowledge. Perhaps, too, the association of students and workmen will render possible many systematic enquiries and social investigations which at present are largely neglected in Ireland. And in any case it will serve to foster the spirit of brotherhood and nationality between Irishmen of all classes and creeds (quoted in Gaughan, 1986, p. 95).

This republican questioning of the class structure, the elevation of the lived and experiential knowledge of workers in the context of university learning, and seeking to cultivate in them the knowledge, skills and self-confidence required for political participation, deviated too radically from the conventional elitism of the university and the class and knowledge hierarchies on which it was based, not to have been experienced as threatening within the university. Awarding the diploma (albeit college rather than university in status) with all the pomp and ceremony of an academic conferring would have focused the challenge and accentuated the violation of university verities. It does not surprise, therefore, to find Murphy in his history of the College recalling 'the brutally caustic comment, made only half in jest, of one of the College's professorial "characters", long since dead: "I'm not sure if I agree with this idea of O'Rahilly's. It's trying to make Jack as good as his master – and he isn't, damn him!"' (Murphy, 1995, p. 255). Murphy estimates that such disapproving academics were in a minority at that time and attributes their reservation about using College resources for other than 'real' students to class prejudice and snobbishness.

Murphy may well be unduly benign in his estimation of the extent of this opposition and unduly individualistic and insufficiently structural in its interpretation. Gaughan, describing the organisation of the economic conferences of three decades earlier, held during the winter months of 1915-16, and organised by O'Rahilly and Timothy A. Smiddy, Professor of Economics and Dean of the Faculty of Commerce, describes a different level of support: 'apart from Alfred and Smiddy no other member of the College staff showed any interest in the project and most were strongly opposed to it, as they considered that UCC should have nothing to do with persons, especially workers, who were not students of the College' (Gaughan, 1986, p. 94). A half-century after these extension lectures, and two decades after the launch of the Diploma in Social and Economic Science, we continue to find evidence in the report of the Commission on Higher Education 1960-67 (1967) of antipathy to university engagement with un-matriculated students and to the expansion of the certified learning of the university beyond the minority who could afford to be in full-time day attendance.

With regard to adult education, the Commission acknowledged that there existed a number of objections to the involvement of the university in this area, e.g. the 'diversion of funds from other pressing needs, the general nature and level of the courses, the attachment of university qualifications to courses that are not really university courses' (p. 659). On the other hand, the Commission pointed out that these courses did not absorb a very large amount of College funds or staff time, they had established themselves as part of the tradition of the NUI colleges, and they served as a link between the universities and the community generally. However, they recommended that the proposed new colleges (to teach to pass degree level) should supply the demand for such courses either by themselves or in conjunction with Vocational Education Committees, thus making 'university participation less necessary' (p. 659).

The attitude of the Commission to part-time degree courses was similar. In the evidence it received it identified two trends: an acknowledgement of the need for evening degree courses on the one hand and, on the other, 'severe criticism of the award of degrees from part-time courses and of the organisation of evening degree courses and their effects on the standards of degrees' (p. 660). Examples of the latter include the following:

> Board of TCD (in a memorandum of Professor Basil Chubb). It is doubtful whether evening degrees or diplomas are desirable at all; young people can get the full benefits of a university education only through full-time attendance, either prior to employment or during employment by release from normal duties (p. 661).

> Association of Secondary Teachers, Ireland: to profit fully from university education, a student must be a full-time student; a candidate for a primary degree should be a full-time student, and diplomas and certificates should be substituted for the so-called evening degrees (p. 661).

Professor R. Dudley Edwards, UCD: it seems likely that such courses (i.e. evening degree courses) accentuate existing tendencies at pass degree levels towards lower grades and routine work which, without a tutorial system, could leave its recipients without any real awareness of the nature of higher education (p. 662).

UCD Academic Staff Association: many of these evening students have ability but evening classes as a whole have tended to lower the standards of the general degree, through the final examination which day and evening students take in common (p. 662).

The deeply sedimented and disguised origins of these sentiments in university elitism can be gauged from the otherwise innovative record of some of the sources of these views: Professor Chubb is recognised as a pioneer of political studies in Ireland and Professor Dudley Edwards as a moderniser of Irish historiography. Other submissions sought to refute these negative arguments. But the Commission concluded that part-time degree courses were not appropriate in a university where they raise 'problems of principle and organisation' (p. 665), and recommended that responsibility for this kind of provision should be allocated to the sub-university new colleges. It envisaged that as well as offering evening, weekend and vacation courses these new colleges would also introduce correspondence, radio and television courses. The Commission concluded:

They (the new colleges) need not feel as apparently many in the universities now feel, that they were offering a substitute, however necessary and desirable, for the full-time course; on the contrary, they would be meeting a real need in a distinct and special way, and would have opportunities for experimenting with new forms of teaching and curricular organisation (p. 663).

It would appear that the Commission had no objection to, and indeed welcomed, innovations in higher education provision, access, teaching and learning, but only so long as such experimentation did not impinge on the universities and that their assumptions about their appropriate clientele, knowledge, learning and formation remained exempt from scrutiny and change. This appears to have been the consensual view of the Commission in that of the many reservations appended to the Report none addressed such issues.

This provides us with a measure of how out of keeping O'Rahilly was with the thinking of his time on the role of universities in society, and is suggestive of the opposition, both latent and explicit, that he had to face down in advocating and introducing his adult education initiatives. As with any attempt to assess the role of agents in cultural change, O'Rahilly must be considered in terms of the interaction of the individual, the social and the cultural. All components of social action – individual psychology, the group and collective context, and world views and ideologies – are vividly represented in O'Rahilly's career and have been extensively documented. O'Rahilly was committed to the reconstruction of Irish society according to the principles of Roman Catholic social teaching and was a leader of the Roman Catholic social movement of the 1930s and 1940s. His personal psychology is no less significant in understanding his success as an innovator in university-based adult education, most particularly in conquering opposition, cultivating loyalty and breaching the cultural understandings relating to university education, social action and adults. For this reason, a somewhat extended summary of his background, formative experience and diverse academic, political and religious career, which draws substantially on Gaughan's multi-volume biography, in particular those dealing with his academic (1986) and public life (1989), should prove to be a productive point of entry for our analysis of his influence in adult education.

Formation and Career

Alfred O'Rahilly was born in Listowel, Co. Kerry on 19 September, 1884, the eighth child in a family of fifteen. Educated locally until the age of twelve, he entered Blackrock College where he showed considerable academic promise and performed with distinction in public examinations. After his formal request for admission to the Society of Jesus, he entered the novitiate at Tullabeg in 1901 and transferred to University College, at St Stephen's Green, in 1905. He took his BA degree in Mathematical Physics and Experimental Physics with First Class Honours and first place in the examination which was open to all colleges affiliated to the Royal University. To this he added the MA, with a studentship and gold medal, in the same subjects in the following year. Three years at St Mary's Hall, Stoneyhurst, followed. There, O'Rahilly studied mathematical and experimental physics though his main preoccupation seems to have been the courses in scholastic philosophy and natural science. After two years as a member of the community of St Ignatius's House of Studies, Lower Leeson Street, Dublin, he commenced on the last stage of his preparation for the priesthood in 1913 when he joined the first-year theology course at Milltown Park. He departed from Milltown in May 1914. Two years later, in 1916 he married his first cousin, Agnes O'Donoghue, despite the efforts of both families to dissuade them.

In October 1914, O'Rahilly was appointed as assistant lecturer in the Department of Mathematics and Mathematical Physics at UCC, becoming Professor of Mathematical Physics in 1917. He was appointed Registrar in 1920 and held that position until his appointment as President in 1943. Among his institutional achievements at UCC, apart from his adult education initiatives, can be listed his founding of the Electrical Engineering Department, his sponsorship of the College Library, his establishment of Cork University Press and the improvement of student facilities. His publications were wide-ranging and extensive, the full bibliography running to some 40 pages. The most ambitious of his scientific works on electro-magnetics, which attracted the award of DSc from the National University of Ireland, was published by Cork University Press in 1938. The National University of Ireland also conferred upon him the honorary degree of DLitt in recognition of his published work in such areas as economic and social questions in 1939. He was also to write on Christology and religious issues. In his last conferring speech as President of UCC he took pride in proclaiming that he had never lived in academic isolation and that he had taken part in national and social life. His association with the Sinn Féin movement led to membership of Cork Corporation, internment on Spike Island in 1921 and election to the Dáil as one of the members for Cork city after the ratification of the Anglo-Irish Treaty by Dáil Éireann. He was associated with Labour movements at home and abroad, acting as government representative at international conferences, as arbitration board member and as a mediator in Labour disputes. As well as serving on government commissions on banking and vocational organisation, he contributed to debates on issues as diverse as the Constitution, the burning of Cork city, wheat growing and flour milling, the shroud of Turin, labour relations, poverty and property rights, education, and the stigmata of Thérèse Neumann. In this context, one admirer was to remark that O'Rahilly 'advanced on all fronts with his quill drawn' (quoted in Gaughan, 1986, p. 243).

On retiring from UCC in 1954 he went to live in Blackrock College, Dublin, his wife having died in 1953. He was ordained a priest in 1955 and, continuing to write and lecture, he died on 2 August 1969, just short of his 85th birthday. The strength of his personality can be gauged from the contradictory human responses he evoked, having been variously described as arrogant, a boorish devil, Machiavellian, a genius, and the greatest Kerryman of them all (Ó Fathaigh and O'Sullivan, 2000). At his most bland, O'Rahilly can be said to have been self-willed and determined, managing to fit at least three careers – academic, Catholic apologist and civil activist – into one life.

Educational Intervention

The four diploma courses instituted by O'Rahilly – the Diploma in Social and Economic Science, the Diploma in Social and Rural Science, the Diploma in Social Study, and the Diploma in Social and Domestic Science – represented the public face of his adult education achievements. He also put enduring structures in place for the identification of needs and the delivery of learning opportunities for adults – the establishment of an Adult Education Committee and an Adult Education Department at University College Cork and the formalisation of cooperative linkages with local labour and rural associations and statutory bodies. In terms of administration and delivery alone, there was much that was innovative in these programmes and structures.

The twenty-four students conferred with the Diploma in Social and Economic Science in 1948 had studied Sociology and Economics at UCC on Wednesday afternoons, and Accounting, Secretarial and Business Practice and Modern Social Organisation at the School of Commerce on Monday and Friday evenings, seven-and-a-half hours in all. As Ó Murchú (1989) has pointed out, it incorporated many novel features including paid educational leave, negotiated with the Cork Chamber of Commerce, a broad funding base drawing on UCC, the City of Cork Vocational Education Committee, and Cork Corporation, and the provision of learning resources in the form of texts and manuals.

The outreach approach of the Adult Education Department formalised the College's proactive role in providing adult education for its hinterland. This outreach tradition incorporated widely-dispersed geographical out-centres for the provision of adult education diploma courses and the identification of target groups. Rather than wait for the demand for adult education to manifest itself, the College set about constructing programmes to meet the perceived needs of specific groups in locations far removed from the College. The role of Adult Education Department staff as boundary personnel representing the College to the community and the community to College continues to be a crucial element of this outreach provision. The benefits of co-sponsorship of programmes were also recognised – the partnership with the trade unions and the rural groups aided recruitment of students, and the association with the Vocational Education Committees and Agricultural Committees provided the resources in the form of centres and teachers.

The effect of the university's involvement on the public perception of adult education is inestimable. This is heightened by the realisation that this involvement occurred in an era when universities were a good deal more remote from the lives of ordinary people than they are at present, and when there was little by way of government, moral or financial encouragement to respond to the needs of the community. The perception of adult education as serious endeavour rather than discretionary practice must surely have been enhanced by it being seen as worthy of university initiative, even if the non-vocational status of the diploma (no material gain being intended to the participants) failed to challenge the absence of opportunities for adults to gain educational credentials.

However, in these developments there was a failure to treat adult education as an aspect of education worthy of research and teaching in its own right. This may well be traced to O'Rahilly's perception of the role of adult education in society. He seemed to be less concerned with adult education as a process or as a right and more attracted by the nature of the learning that the provision of adult education made possible. The emphasis was on message rather than on medium, on a social project rather than on an organic level of the educational system. The Adult Education Department, accordingly, was to be delivery-based and an administrative structure rather than being committed to research and teaching on the processes of adult programmes and learning.

Roman Catholic Social Teaching

What vision of society, strategy for change and the role of adult education in this strategy informed O'Rahilly's adult education initiatives? O'Rahilly was far from reticent on this point: he saw his social project in adult education as a means by which the reconstruction of Irish society according to Roman Catholic social principles could be advanced. Putti (1987) argued that at their broadest these principles involved a commitment to such basic values as human dignity, human rights, the right to a free and responsible life, the common good, by which was meant the welfare of all but giving priority at the same time to the individual rather than the State, and the importance of human community. However, even in an analysis confined to the past hundred years, it is possible to discern changes of emphasis in the understanding, interpretation or application of these values in the church's social teaching. These variations have been said to derive from the personalities of individual Popes, changing social, economic and political circumstances and the needs of the church.

A number of O'Rahilly's contributions to the University and Labour series published by Cork University Press – *Aquinas versus Marx, Moral Principles*, and *Social Principles* – all published in 1948 give a direct insight into the ideological content of his courses. In these publications there are a number of recurring themes: a desire to restrict the encroachment of the state into people's lives; an anxiety about the concentration of political power in the hands of the few; an advocacy of a greater diffusion of property; the assertion that the just wage be seen in terms of a family wage; and the necessity for an element of partnership to pervade the employer/employee relationship. In justifying these demands, O'Rahilly quotes widely from St Thomas Aquinas and the Papal Encyclicals *Rerum Novarum* (1891) and *Quadragesimo Anno* (1931) from which the principles of subsidiarity and vocational organisation entered the conceptualisation of the Roman Catholic Social Movement. The influence of socially progressive church teaching is obvious. While there is a desire to protect workers from the excesses of capitalism, the approach to the existing social order is reformist rather than radical in terms of its understanding of distributive and recognitive justice. Paradoxically, many of its criticisms of western capitalism have much in common with socialism, though there was a distinct hostility towards that ideology. Versions of existing social institutions such as trade unions, political parties, mutual aid societies and professional associations based on Roman Catholic social teaching were recommended.

The stridency to be found in O'Rahilly's writings helps us to understand his perception of the role of adult education in his strategy for social change: 'the alternative to Rome is Moscow' (1948a, p. 71); 'once more men are facing the great decision: Christ or Caesar' (1948b, p. 49); 'more fortunate in this country, we must yet beware lest this secularist naturalist view creep into our education' (1948b, p. 30); 'it is time for humanity to assert itself against this agnostic dogmatism masquerading as science' (1948b, p. 20). O'Rahilly saw himself protecting the Irish people against such 'alien' and 'false' ideologies as secularism, liberalism, socialism and communism. His ideology of adult education can be classified as a non-radical emancipatory variety of redemption, the broader context of which will be described in the next chapter.

Programme Content, Values and Principles

This model of change through adult education forms the central point of departure and reference in O'Rahilly's approach to specifying what students should learn. This had the merit of making explicit the values that informed his programmes, which he would characterise as foregoing the progressive appeal of individualised felt-needs, and eschewing a spurious student-centred, value-free rhetoric. At the 1948 conferring, he reminded the successful diplomates in Social and Economic Science:

> The idea that trade unions could be neutral, that their members and officials could or did avoid a stand on fundamental issues is either delusion or hypocrisy. You who have participated in the course make no such deceitful pretence of being neutral. We make free profession of the christian values and social principles that are embodied in the Papal Encyclicals and our Constitution (quoted in Cathcart, 1989).

In fact, denouncing the 'humbug of neutrality' was a common theme of O'Rahilly through which he argued that all educational programmes, including non-denominational ones, incorporated a philosophy of education:

> A university is not a general store whence immature youths may arbitrarily select any philosophy of life they choose or have imposed on them. We in this College stand for the philosophy which is enshrined in our Constitution and for the religious ideals of our people. And we are quite unperturbed if we are daubed 'sectarian' by that small clique which is trying to beguile us into the 'common front' which in other countries has been a prelude to communism (quoted in Cathcart, 1989).

The underside of being forthright about values was the prescriptiveness in the identification of student needs/entitlements and, in consequence, the institutionally-led determination of the content of the diploma courses. Yet, at that time, its pre-planned curriculum, class-bound pedagogy and formal examination would have been consistent with the ethos of a mainstream education institution such as a university.

O'Rahilly's diploma courses were presented as role-based and this can be a source of deception. The demands of social and economic roles – worker, farmer, home-maker, citizen – consistent with Roman Catholic social teaching informed the selection of knowledge and skills deemed appropriate for transmission to participants in the programmes. This content reflected the role-prescriptions of an ideal Roman Catholic social order. Role-based adult education programmes are usually understood to be underscored by individualism and social consensus and equilibrium. O'Rahilly's programmes do not quite fit this neat characterisation. Certainly, there is no evidence from them of a view that Irish society was characterised by domination and exploitation and was destined to suffer from class tensions and antagonism as long as wealth and the means of production were predominantly in the hands of the few. The perception of society as constituting social classes in an inevitable confrontation because of their conflicting interests did not figure in O'Rahilly's programmes. Nor did a desire to encourage a questioning of the social and economic position of women. O'Rahilly would have subscribed to the principle of vocational organisation proclaimed in the following terms by Fr John Hayes, the founder of Muintir na Tíre in 1931, itself an application of this principle in rural Ireland:

> We are endeavouring to unite the rural communities of Ireland on the Leo XIII principle that there must exist friendly relations between master and man; that it is a mistake to assume that class is naturally hostile to class, and that the well-to-do and working men are intended by nature to live in mutual conflict. This new rural organisation we are launching, in the name of God, intends to unite in one body the rural workers of the country, not for the purpose of attacking any one section of the community, but to give to agricultural workers in Ireland their due and proper place (quoted in Rynne, 1960, pp107-108).

This consensual approach to social roles distinguishes O'Rahilly's programmes from others at the emancipatory end of the redemptive spectrum where the conflict view of society predominates. Yet, it needs to be kept in mind that the Roman Catholic consensual view of society was an ideal rather than a description of existing reality. In this regard, O'Rahilly would have been more familiar than most with industrial conflict through his work in the area of industrial relations, conciliation and mediation. In holding open the possibility of creating a consensual and equitable society, Roman Catholic social teaching has parallels in other ideologies, such as those of socialism and feminism, which incorporate an ideal vision of society to be aspired to and worked towards. Even for Marx, conflict was not inevitable given the appropriate political and economic order.

O'Rahilly's programmes were more collectivist than individualist in orientation. They contained strong elements of collective mobilisation and this was particularly evident in the impact of the programmes on the formation of cooperatives and group water schemes. And even in relation to the development of individual skills and talents, it was assumed that the influence of those students who had benefited individually from the programmes would, as leaders and opinion formers, be a collective one. The minority was being educated to contribute to the community. There was no sense in which it was being educated for social mobility or for cultural uprooting.

Penetration and Change

O'Rahilly's influence on adult education can be discerned at a number of levels. At the individual level, he influenced others who went on to play a formative role in Irish adult education. These included leaders and change agents, not just in university-based adult education but at national policy level and in communities and voluntary associations. Organisationally, he established structures such as adult education committees and departments which served as models for similar structures elsewhere in the country. These formed the links between providers and their constituencies. Culturally, O'Rahilly paved the way for the principle of lifelong learning and for a broadening of access to university by bringing workers onto the campus and forcing a redefinition of a university student. Most significant in terms of cultural politics was O'Rahilly's success in putting redemptive adult education programmes, with such emancipatory features as a high degree of closure in terms of truth and social transformation and totalising penetration and change, in place within a university setting.

O'Rahilly's psychology, his role as University President and public figure, the religious culture of the time, and his religious conviction are crucial in understanding his success as a 'cultural worker' in the transformation of meanings attached to learning, education, social action and adults. His resources as an agent of cultural change in adult education included a forceful personality not given to self-doubt, religious certainty, positions of university power over a long period, and proclaiming a view of education in line with the theocentric doxa of his era. It is difficult to imagine O'Rahilly being so successful with his adult education initiatives in the absence of any one of these resources. And as they had operated in unison so also did they change.

Within a decade of O'Rahilly's retirement from UCC in 1954, the theocentric paradigm of education was being challenged. When he died in 1969, the Murphy Committee, under the leadership of a former outreach worker from the Department of Adult Education at UCC, was proceeding to establish a more diverse understanding of adult education, placing it within the context of an international discourse with social, psychological, and philosophical dimensions. Within UCC, the confessional character of the programmes changed without ceremony or resistance as new staff in Sociology and Economics developed programmes of study in keeping with the distinctive ideologies of their disciplines at that time. It was the orthodoxy of prescribed programmes and summative evaluation that was slowest to change. This illuminates not merely the vulnerability of religious beliefs during a period of modernisation but, more significantly, the capacity of secular beliefs to disguise their existence, let alone resist penetration, as ideologies in eras of religious critique. Adult education provision at UCC was to experience enormous expansion in student numbers, programmes, centres and catchment areas over the remaining decades of the century. In the absence of O'Rahilly and a cultural context receptive to Catholic social teaching, the UCC programmes contracted to less closed forms of redemptive learning. Emancipation was ruptured and replaced by empowerment as a programme objective and as a rationale in programme initiation through community partnerships and negotiated learning (Ó Fathaigh and O'Sullivan, 2000).

In terms of cultural politics, what O'Rahilly achieved was to establish an understanding of university adult education as a form of learning committed to social change. Its legacy is to be found in the acceptance within universities of the 'social mission' of their adult education provision and is specifically reflected in the location of many of their programmes at the socially critical end of the redemptive spectrum. It is ironic that currently the purest descendants of O'Rahilly's Roman Catholic reconstructionist adult education project are to be found in programmes with a similarly totalising and closed redemptive intent but derived from feminist and egalitarian principles. And that were O'Rahilly alive today and working alongside groups such as CORI seeking to advance contemporary church teaching on social justice, he would find himself located much nearer the substance, as well as the form, of these newer varieties of emancipatory adult education.

Cultural Strangers and Contrarians: Education, Church and Religion

Researchers with an interest in the relationship between religion and education are frequently attracted to Ireland because of the distinctive and extensive role of the churches in the Irish educational system. Even those whose interests are more general, or are not specific to church/state relationships in education, are unlikely to be able to avoid consideration of the implications for their particular area of enquiry of the position of religion in the Irish educational system. These include visiting sociologists, historians, political scientists, anthropologists as well as educationists. It should come as no great surprise, therefore, that there exists many references to and commentaries on the role of the churches, and most particularly the Roman Catholic church, in Irish education in the writings of cultural strangers. Cultural contrarians have traditionally been fewer in number and more restrained in their challenges on the place of the church and religion in Irish education, most obviously at the beginning of the period under consideration when the theocentric paradigm benefited from its doxic defences. Yet, even then there were those who thought the unthinkable and were willing to say the unsayable. The exceptional resilience of the Dalkey School Project Association, in their efforts from the mid-1970s to establish a multi-denominational option within the national school system, stands out and has been referred to earlier in Chapter 6. Here, we draw from other cultural contrarians whose efforts to change the thinking and practice at the interface at church, religion and education have been less visible and sustained within Irish education. Three themes, realised and variously textualised in the critical commentaries of cultural strangers and contrarians taken together, are selected for analysis.

The managerial theme addresses what is criticised as the excessive involvement of the church in the ownership and management of Irish schools, and raises questions concerning the mission of religious personnel, the career opportunities of lay teachers, the entitlement of lay people to be more centrally involved in the management of schools, and the state's capacity to pursue policy changes in the interests of the common good. The politico-social theme configures and questions the impact of a school system, operating according to Catholic social and moral teaching, in terms of its consequences for society in such areas as the social well-being and mental health of citizens, the ideological independence of legislators, and the civic values and democratic practices of society. The secular rights theme raises issues of the entitlement of citizens to freedom from exposure to religious influences in schools, expressed either in terms of the parents acting on behalf of their children or of children themselves in their own right. This seeks to enter concerns about religious indoctrination to Irish thinking on school processes and effects. These are generally hierarchically inclusive in their textualisation. Both secular rights and politico-social critiques employ the managerial theme to support their arguments, to which the secular rights discourse adds the resources of the politico-social theme. What follows are representative of efforts by cultural strangers and contrarians to circulate these themes within Irish intersubjectivity on education.

Managerial

In *The Lay Teacher* Patrick Duffy (1967), writing from an American academic background, surveyed the teaching personnel in primary and secondary schools in Ireland. He set out to determine whether the prominence of religious in Irish education '… relegates the lay primary teacher to rural schools of lesser enrolments' and '… restricts the employment of lay secondary teachers' (p. xv). His conclusions in relation to both of these propositions were in the affirmative. Drawing on official and other published sources, Duffy asserted that 'priests, brothers and sisters are now occupying teaching positions that could be filled by the laity'. The alternative for the lay teacher was 'either employment in areas other than education, or emigration' (p. 92). The situation was such, he argued, that the desire to leave the profession was strong while the incentive to enter the profession, especially for the more intelligent and more progressive, was weakened.

The sentiments expressed by Dr James Good (1970), diocesan priest and lecturer at University College Cork, in an address to a conference of priests in 1969 were typical of his many observations on the role of the church in education at this time. Lay secondary teachers, he argued, may well be forgiven if they 'look askance' at a situation which, with expanding secondary education and a reduction in vocations, involves 'control of too many schools by too few religious'. He advocated that the church 'should gradually induce the secular power to take over the service and run it. And then she should pull out.' Dr Good went on to argue, in a manner similar to Duffy, on the implications of the religious vocation for the chuch's involvement in education:

> There are times when the takeover is little more than a reminder that the church's task is done, and that the service in question can now be effectively provided by the secular arm. A refusal to leave in the circumstances would show, on the part of the church, a lack of realism, as well as a suggestion of inordinate attachment to worldly power.

Similarly, the absence of promotional opportunities for lay teachers, and its implications for recruitment, also raised by Duffy, was decried by Seán O'Connor (1968), then Assistant Secretary in the Department of Education, in a rare event, the publication by a senior civil servant under his own name of an article outlining his views on educational policy:

> The lay secondary teacher remains always the hired man. His responsibility ends at the classroom door. He is consulted with, of course, because he may have something of value to offer, but he is never part of the decision-making. If he wants authority so that he may innovate, experiment, he must go elsewhere … It is a frustrating situation for the good teacher. Is the situation responsible, at least in part, for keeping the high-class graduate out of education?

In considering the implications of the changed arrangements for the capital funding of school building, O'Connor drew attention to the advantaged position of the church in the provision of secondary education:

> Since 1963 the situation has changed. Now the state will give 100 percent grant on approved building costs, 70 per cent as outright gift and 30 percent as loan repayable over fifteen years … Strangely enough the effect of the state assistance has been to freeze out the lay man altogether. At £400 a pupil-place, £100,000 will build a school for 250 pupils – a modest enough target. The amount of the repayable loan is £30,000, too much for any lay teacher, however ambitious, so that, in effect, the church has been given a monopoly in relation to secondary schools for Catholic pupils.

He went on to advance one of the most celebrated and derided policy aspirations on the role of the church in Irish education: 'no one wants to push the religious out of education; that would be disastrous, in my opinion. But I want them in as partners not always as masters.' Branded as 'nationalisation by stealth' by the Executive of the Teaching Brothers' Association (1968), it was Dr Good (1970) who again cautioned realism: 'I think we would be foolish if we did not read the sign of the times, and perhaps even the writing on the wall.'

Politico-Social

In *A Mirror to Kathleen's Face* (Akenson, 1975) and *Church, State and the Control of Schooling in Ireland 1900-1944* (Titley, 1983a), two Canadian professors portrayed the church's role in Irish education as coercive, antidemocratic, authoritarian and manipulative. For Titley, who was Irish-born and educated, there were other reasons for the church's involvement in education, besides its espoused spiritual objective of saving souls. 'The reasons have to do with the continued existence of the church as an institution and the perpetuation of its influence in society' (p. 143). These included recruitment of personnel for the church at home and abroad, the cultivation of an unquestioning laity and a loyal cadre of future political leaders who could be relied on to adhere to rather than query church teaching in the enactment of legislation. Explaining the absence of contestation, the fact that the Irish laity granted the church 'a licence for their activities', Akenson (p. 108) writes that 'this is understandable, for most Irish men were the product of the church's educational system and therefore had been indoctrinated during childhood years with the very ideas and assumptions upon which the clergy's actions were based'. His interpretation of the manipulative role of the church is more intertextual than that of Titley. Akenson sees church suspicion of state involvement, of progressive education and of ideas relating to the natural goodness of children as paralleling the cultural contours of Irish society. He concludes that the real triumph of the Catholic church in the field of education was not so much that it gained such extensive control over the process of schooling but rather that 'its hegemony was won not by the repression of popular sentiment but by articulating ideas and attitudes compatible with the popular will' (p. 108). In the conceptualisations of Akenson and Titley there would be a scepticism about the view that the church was no more than an organisation serving the needs of those who, because of voluntary commitment, constituted its members and, as such, proclaimed its views on social and political issues like other interest groups in a context of pluralist decision-making.

Secular Rights

David Alvey, a founding member of the Campaign to Separate Church and State, published *Irish Education: The Case for Secular Reform* in 1991, with the aim of promoting 'clear thinking on a sometimes complicated subject in good time for the debate on an Education Act' (p. 8). Referring to the rights and duties of parents outlined in the Constitution, he contended that the state was nonetheless 'under no legal obligation to help particular parents, whose beliefs do not fit neatly into the two major categories allowed for in education, to meet their duties or assert their rights. That is a central question that needs to be addressed in legislation' (p. 8). He provides testimonies from parents who, because of their religious beliefs or preferences in relation to religious formation for their children, experienced difficulties with denominational features of the Irish educational system. He highlighted the difficulty of keeping secular and religious instruction separate following the introduction of the 1971 Primary School Curriculum which advocated integrating aspects of subjects from across the range of the curriculum. Furthermore, a 'more solid indication of the interweaving of secular and religious ideas is to be found in primary school textbooks, even in textbooks issued by the Department of Education' (p. 38). Citing such examples as 'the May altar', 'going to Mass', 'the Virgin Mary', 'the True Cross', and the work of priests or ministers of religion who 'lead us to God', he concludes that 'the assumptions underlying many of these textbook references is that the children reading them share the same religious faith. They also treat matters of faith as factual' (p. 39). In his proposals for reform he concludes:

> It should be specifically stated in an Education Act that it is the duty of the Minister to ensure that sufficient schooling is available to enable parents to avail themselves of their constitutional right of conscience. This can be done by sponsoring public schools which respect freedom of conscience; by subsidising voluntary schools on these lines; and by placing statutory obligations on denominational schools.

Alvey addresses the vindication of secular rights in terms of the rights of parents who in conscience decide that it is in the best interests of their children that they be protected from exposure to religious formation. Desmond M. Clarke, then a lecturer (currently Professor) in the Department of Philosophy at University College Cork, in his essays in political philosophy, *Church and State* (1985), distinguishes between adults and children in this regard and seeks to vindicate the latter's right to protection from religious 'indoctrination', meaning 'causally determining the beliefs of another through non-rational procedures' (p. 215). In acknowledging that the Constitution recognises that parents have fundamental rights in determining the education of their minor children, he points out that 'it is not explicit on how these rights may have to yield to the rights of children' (p. 214). Having reviewed relevant US court decisions which confronted the issue of a potential conflict between parents' rights and children's rights, he concluded that:

> ... likewise, the constitutional guarantees of freedom of conscience and religious freedom of the Irish Constitution should protect Irish children from the probable effects of a system of education which leaves them subject, with the parents' consent in most cases, to the systematic indoctrination of the churches (p. 221).

Clarke diagnoses more activist implications for the state in the light of the recognition of such children's rights and the state's principle of religious neutrality:

> If this principle is impartially applied to the early education of school-age children, it implies that the civil authorities should be strictly neutral with respect to religious teaching. It should not finance any religious indoctrination. Instead, it should actively defend the liberties of young citizens against all those who might, in good faith or otherwise, conspire to determine the religious beliefs of individuals in the hope of realising what, according to their own theological beliefs, is the salvation of individual 'souls' (p. 226).

Reception, Sponsorship and Penetration

The cultural contrarians, O'Connor and Good, along with the cultural stranger Duffy, evoked the characteristic reactions to those who challenge doxa – incredulous, censorious, derisive, hurt and offended. Personal communications from the parties involved report a threat to boycott the school textbooks of Fallons, the publishers of *The Lay Teacher*, and a perplexed perception of Dr Good as a destabilising force within the Irish church. As the 'rationalisation by stealth' jibe suggested, Seán O'Connor would find himself established as the *bette noir* of religious authorities in relation to educational planning. But, as we have seen in previous chapters, social change was on the side of those who argued that the involvement of religious in the work of Irish schools was excessive. The diagnosis of the FIRE Report in 1973, on the need for rationalisation and an acceptance of greater lay involvement and state activism, would within a decade become widely accepted within the church, and not merely in the pragmatics of school rationalisation (Walsh, 1999) but in recognition of the church's dependency on lay teachers in evangelisation (CMRS, 1986), and in time even in the trusteeship of Catholic voluntary secondary schools (CORI, 1996, 1997b).

In contrast, while the secular rights theme circulates in Irish intersubjectivity on education (Coolahan, 1994), its textualisation remains minimal and even covert, accommodated in the multi-denominational schools of *Educate Together*, incorporated within such constructs as 'those of all religions and none', and submerged within the, consequently strained, semantic remit of multi-denominationalism. But it is Alvey's thematisation of parents' rights to exclude their children from exposure to religious experience in schools that is routine in discourse. Clarke's assertion of children's rights to protection from religious formation during their early schooling, with its potential to conflict with the rights of parents and, indeed, application to other substantive varieties of formation, remains largely unthematised in policy discourse. This must surprise in a context in which the Association of Irish Humanists can claim that they are Ireland's largest 'ethical minority' on the basis of the 2002 Census figures on religion, 138,300 alone declaring themselves as having no religion, in comparison with Church of Ireland (115,600) and Presbyterian (20,600) memberships (McGarry, 2004). Thus, it would appear that alongside the modernist unease with religion, outlined in Chapter 6, there co-exists a residual traditionalist fearfulness of the textualisation of its denial in Irish public discourse at large.

More might have reasonably been expected from the cultural strangers. In terms of explicit presence in policy discourse, one must conclude that their impact on policy paradigms relating to the church/state relationship and the role of religion in Irish education appears slight, marginal and non-invasive. In this regard they lacked sponsorship, through validation and incorporation into their discourse by established participants within the policy process. Why were they not used more as cultural resources in the manner of the OECD involvement in *Investment in Education* and Tussing on educational funding, their virtues as cultural strangers emphasised – independence, expert knowledge, comparative perspective, etc. – to boost the legitimacy and urgency of their critiques of Irish education, and to be positioned as external consultants validating the diagnosis of the indigenous practitioners?

Academically, doubts had been raised about the validity of some of the conclusions of these cultural strangers. Duffy, in particular, appeared vulnerable. He failed to cite sources for some critical data. These included the numbers of teachers who, once trained, never embarked on teaching, and the numbers of lay teachers who left the profession for reasons other than death, retirement or marriage. Likewise, he ignored the publicly controlled vocational system as a source of employment for lay teachers (Kellaghan, 1968). Of Titley's analysis it was said that 'systematic historical analysis and interpretation are often sacrificed to an over-dwelling on the undeniable inadequacies and inconsistencies of Irish education' (Byrne, 1985). Akenson's study, though essentially a sociological one, seemed unfamiliar with contemporary sociological research on Irish society (O'Sullivan, 1980a). Yet, these criticisms, particularly in the case of Akenson and Titley, were no more than would be expected in the routine scholarly process. What seemed a more important consideration than the actual scholarly quality of these analyses of Irish education was the apparent disposition of the cultural strangers to Irish society and culture and, more particularly, the possibility that a hostility to the indigenous culture could be inferred by those who would wish to discount their interrogation in native policy paradigms.

Titley's observations on the Irish educational scene were blunt: the Irish classroom had only recently become 'a less brutal and terrifying place to be' (Titley, 1983b), the study of Irish education had 'largely escaped the attention of serious scholarship' (Titley, 1983b) and 'the writing of Irish educational history was moribund, amateurish and narrow, both in scope and sympathy' (Titley, 1979). In this, Titley was open to the accusation of offering no evidence in support of his damning description of Irish classrooms and of ignoring or devaluing established publications such as the *Irish Journal of Education* and *Irish Educational Studies*, the conferences and activities of the Educational Studies Association of Ireland, to which Titley himself had contributed, and an extensive range of postgraduate research. Both Duffy and Akenson, in acknowledging the help of Irish people in conducting their research, implied an image of Irish society as narrow, conspiratorial and vindictive by declaring an unwillingness to name them lest being associated with the controversial nature of their findings might compromise their reputations and careers. Akenson portrayed the church as a conservative force in Irish society, parochial in outlook, fearful of the state, narrow and restrictive in its emphasis on sexuality, triumphant, sectarian and insensitive towards the minority Protestant churches, and a contributor to a series of social and personal ills ranging from a high incidence of psychiatric illness to a low prioritising of the needs of children. Yet, even as this characterisation of the church's contribution to Irish society was published, criticism of inadequate government action by church leaders and agencies in relation to poverty and inequality in Irish society was already a common feature of public debate. This is epitomised in the 1977 Joint Pastoral Letter of the Irish Bishops *The Work of Justice* which, according to one radical political activist, contained 'some of the most astonishingly radical pronouncements on justice and society that I have ever come across in Episcopal pronouncements ... well beyond – indeed totally at variance with – the thinking of the two largest Irish political parties' (Ryan, 1985).

Potential sponsors who might have considered using their organisations, conferences or publications to provide a point of penetration to these cultural strangers would have been vulnerable to the 'discourse of derision' (Ball, 1990, p. 31). For a potential sponsor to expose itself in this manner would be to weaken its credibility within the policy-making community. For teachers' organisations this was a sensitive issue since it was only during the 1970s that they came to be considered by the state as full partners in educational policy-making. Furthermore, secondary teachers benefited from their association with the church and the private nature and high status of their schools. They were not given to broad critical analysis of the power of the church in education. They approached each issue –

rationalisation, comprehensive schools, community schools, deeds of trust, promotional opportunities, etc. – in pragmatic terms, acting to defend and advance the best interests of their members, rarely allowing themselves to be drawn into strictly ideological battles with the church (Barry, 1989; O'Flaherty, 1992).

In the report of the Primary Education Review Body (1990) on which all teaching organisations and the National Parents' Council were represented, it was necessary for the representative of the Teachers' Union of Ireland to append a minority report to advance the view of church control of schooling as undemocratic, in effect a mild version of the politico-social criticism to be found in Akenson's and Titley's analyses. But even in this minority report there is no appeal to the writings of any of the cultural strangers considered here. The public self-representation of the multi-denominational school movement, Educate Together, has always been consistently in terms of its 1990 Charter, to equally accommodate and respect pupils of all social, cultural and religious backgrounds. It does not criticise denominational education or, directly, the power of the church in Irish education. Rather, it asserts its right to the conditions to enable it to develop its schools in line with freely-expressed parental preferences. The Campaign to Separate Church and State would have been a likely sponsor but it has a limited ability to penetrate public consciousness or to project its perspectives into the policy-making process. In consequence, references to Duffy, Akenson and Titley are most likely to be found among sympathetic academic researchers (Clarke, 1985; Inglis, 1998a) politically marginalised social critics (Browne, 1986) or by one another (Titley, 1979, 1983b).

It seemed as if discourse on church, religion and education operated within distinct domains, largely segmented, generated and participated in by different individuals, conducted in distinct social arenas and pursuing divergent objectives. The cultural strangers operated within the academic domain on the church's role in education. They were scholars who made their analysis public through publication in academic journals and books, and their orientation was to critique. In contrast, the indigenous discourse was more within the practitioner domain, participated in by chalk-face personnel and their representatives and spokespersons. It was conducted at conferences, study days, public speeches and pronouncements and in professional and church-related publications, and was geared towards policy analysis and formulation and educational practice. It was this indigenous discourse rather than that of the cultural strangers which had an impact on the structuring of Irish consciousness about the position of the church and religion in Irish education, of which the round of discussion documents, submissions, conventions, conferences and policy statements during the 1990s is a well-documented manifestation (Coolahan, 1994; Walshe, 1999).

A more intertextual interpretation would suggest that the threat of the cultural strangers and contrarians taken together acted as an impulse to church personnel to rework the rationale for their involvement in education and the form that this involvement should take. This would be to take the line that it could reasonably be argued that, whatever about the absence of sponsorship, the church must nonetheless have feared that the critiques might penetrate and take root in Irish consciousness. According to this interpretation, paradigmatic contraction would be partly explained as a coping response to threat: in the case of the church's participation in the provision of education the relevant paradigm retreated to a more secure and sustainable position – that of a representative organisation catering for the spiritual and pastoral needs of its members. This would constitute a form of cultural co-optation, an integration within one's cultural assumptions of external features that might, if not accommodated, be experienced as confrontational and threatening. It is possible to overstate the calculation of the church. As shapers of a culture, influential church personnel will themselves have been shaped in their thinking by local material circumstances, by thinkers from within the church itself, as well as by the same kind of modernist ideas that would have informed the critiques of the cultural strangers and contrarians (Fuller, 2004).

Whatever the degree of its strategic awareness, the church's participation in these cultural changes had implications for stability and change in its power relationships. In the marginalisation or co-optation of the managerial, politico-social and secular rights themes of the challenging cultural strangers and contrarians, church personnel maintained more control over the pace and direction of critical changes affecting their role in Irish education. In this way the paradigmatic change that occurred was coordinated with the involvement and initiative of the church. The nature of the change, thus managed, was accordingly less threatening to church interests than it otherwise might have been. To follow the logic of this interpretation is to suggest a paradox. If the cultural strangers and contrarians did indeed move the church to redefine its role in education in a manner that maximised its hold on power in Irish education in the face of depleted human resources and social and cultural change, their contribution to social change may have been ultimately stabilising rather than disruptive.

Human Agency and Educational Change

The examples of human agency described in this chapter, be they in the activities of cultural strangers or contrarians, derive their dynamic from the sense of distance, incomprehension, lack of integration or alienation experienced by actors in relation to the cultural space in which they find themselves. What this demonstrates is that not all such actors are equally positioned to influence educational policy; nor do those who are effective in this regard contribute to the policy process in the same manner. We have seen the challenging of doxa in the questioning of cognitions, feelings and values that are scarcely recognised as such so embedded are they in routine and normative understandings. Participants in the policy process have been seen to benefit in having their advocacy legitimated by those who carry the status of independent experts. Policy-makers cite or invoke culturally discordant agents as a means of testing, at a remove, public opinion on sensitive issues. New themes have been added to policy discourse as a result of the intervention of cultural strangers and contrarians.

Cultural strangers benefit from attributions of independence, expertise and a global perspective. But they can equally be marginalised and delegitimated by reference to their 'alien' status. In consequence, they need to build idiosyncrasy credit to allow their differences to be more positively regarded and to be beneficial to indigenous sponsors. Cultural contrarians can be similarly marginalised – as disaffected locals etc. – but their continuity within the state allows them the space to membership and mobilise. Their success will vary according to their positioning and resources in terms of their persistence, power and the extent to which they are otherwise culturally integrated.

Taken together with the efforts at cultural intervention described earlier, what the examples in this chapter demonstrate is that the reconciliation of the relative influence of culture and human agency is not simply a matter of striking a balance between them. The structural instability of the 1950s and the social and cultural changes of the 1960s all offered opportunities to participants that were specific to their time to assert their influence, in relation to state activism in education and the interface of church, religion and education. But more than merely availing of opportunities that present themselves, it has also been shown that it is possible to create them from the resources at hand. This is exemplified in the reconfiguration of the place of adults in education from within the certainties of the theocentric paradigm, the deployment of equality of educational opportunity in advancing gender equity, the expansion of the commercial text on education to include themes of social principle and justice, and the reconceptualisation of the relationship between Travellers and education in terms of ethnicity. Even the apparently marginalised critics, it can be argued, who challenged the doxa of church power in education during the 1960s were not without impact. People are indeed dependent on the inherited circumstances of their interaction. Yet, even when structural fractures and cultural instabilities do not present themselves, the creativity of human agents in intervening in culturally innovative ways remains a potential for change.

Chapter 15

Textualising Adult Education: Constructing a Field of Knowledge and Practice

As we have seen in the schematisation of the construct of policy paradigm, texts represent the instantiation of a policy paradigm, the strand of meaning-making derived from its characteristic themes and concepts. Different levels of selectivity are involved including the isolation of a particular feature of the policy process for attention, and the extracting of lines of coherence from within the diffuse, shifting and complex realm of cultural production. In addressing the textualisation of adult education in this chapter, however, no single text is privileged over another, nor does it involve a working back from some recognisable policy issues in the form of charting the manner in which they came to be constituted and constructed. Rather, the focus here is on the totality of knowledge production in one field – that of adult learning in its implication with the institution of education. In this, it will be possible to diagnose the work of paradigms in formation, emergence, dominion and demise, but the purpose of the case study is not to pursue this line of inquiry. The intention of the chapter is to reconstruct how the manifestations of adult learning have been isolated for attention and conceptualisation, the change and level of integration they experienced, the agents involved in this production, the themes and texts they generated, and the extent to which as a field of knowledge and practice it has been theorised and made recognisable and understandable.

Comparatively, what the approach acknowledges is that across different sites of knowledge production there will be variations in the theoretical and ideological resources, in personnel and their identities and intellectual formation, and in the social, economic and technological forces that come into play in giving a field of knowledge its distinctive contours. Relevant issues in this regard in adult education include the on-going re-interpretations of the classic question, 'what knowledge is of most worth?' (Grace, 1999), what contribution should it make to a nation state (Courtney, 1994), and techniques of mobilisation on the part of discourse communities (Edwards, 2001). Theoretical issues also arise in relation to the surveillance and shaping of policy discourse. In Ireland, adult education has for long operated on the margins of the mainstream system, and accordingly been culturally constructed less in the gaze of the state, teachers' associations and, in the modern era, the church. How distinctive and individualistic as an exercise in knowledge production has this been, or does it reveal an underlying coherence, and if so what is its source? In this regard, academic and practitioner experience in adult education over many years suggested that one should seek throughout to excavate beneath the flow of detail, processes and agents in the textualisation of adult education, specifically remaining open to the possibility that the field of adult education might yield up underlying regulative patterns along the lines interpreted in structuralist studies of myths, folk-tales and literary works, etc. referred to in Chapter 2.

Adults as Learners

From the 1960s it is possible to identify efforts to textualise adult education as a component of the overall educational system that find their most tangible expressions in 1969 with the formation of AONTAS, the National Association of Adult Education, and the establishment of the Murphy Committee which reported on an interim basis in 1970, and published its final report in 1973. It is from this point that an attempt is made here to trace the development of meaning and knowledge surrounding the phenomenon of adult learning and the discursive and non-discursive activities that sought to establish adult education as a meaningful construct and practice.

The acknowledgement that adults learn by way of direct instruction, imitation or adaptation is probably as old as history. In modern accounts of the Irish experience of providing learning opportunities for adults, developments dating from the nineteenth century such as the Mechanics Institutes, the Provincial Lecture Series of the Royal Dublin Society, the GAA and the Gaelic League, local social and scientific associations, and Horace Plunkett's Cooperative Movement are most frequently mentioned, and illuminate the diversity of provision and content involved. In the last century the formation of the United Irishwomen in 1910, later the ICA, Muintir na Tíre in 1931, Alfred O'Rahilly's university extramural programmes and the work of the People's College from the 1940s, and the pioneering work of the Agricultural Advisory Service have all been variously recognised as examples of more recent efforts to acknowledge and respond to the capacity of adults to change, develop and improve themselves and their society

(O'Sullivan, 1989c). All of these organisations, programmes and individuals have been involved in cultural production related to adult education. But apart from maintaining the understanding that adults can change, and asserting that individual change can be the dynamic for collective change, the predominant product of their meaning-making centred around the social, economic, industrial, political, and cultural objectives they were seeking to attain. Their textualisation related to the technical and moral improvement of workers, anti-colonialism and gaelicisation, the benefits of cooperativism, rural revitalisation, catholic social reconstructionism and trade unionism. There are few instances – the activities of the Agricultural Advisory Service have been singled out in this regard in the 1970 interim Murphy report – in which we find a theorisation of the adult learning process, the requirements of adult as learners, and techniques of communication and instruction. Overall, it is difficult to detect a sense that it is culturally permissable to communicate about adult education as an object in its own right, as a learning process that exists semantically independently of the social projects which deployed it as a medium for the realisation of their goals.

An overview of the definitions of adult education provided in the two Murphy Reports and the subsequent Kenny Report of 1984 suggest the existence of a consistent and developing discourse constructing the meaning of adult education and a distinctive body of knowledge surrounding it:

> It is all the educational activity engaged in by people who have broken with full-time continuous education (Interim Murphy Report, 1970, p. 10).

> The provision and utilisation of facilities whereby those who are no longer participants in the full-time school system may learn whatever they need to learn at any period of their lives (Final Murphy Report, 1973, p. 1).

> Adult education includes all systematic learning by adults which contributes to their development as individuals and as members of a community and of society apart from full-time instruction received by persons as part of their uninterrupted initial education and training. It may be formal education which takes place in institutions, e.g. training centres, schools, colleges, institutes and universities; or non-formal education, which is any other systematic form of learning, including self-directed learning (Kenny Report, 1984, p. 9).

This broad and inclusive definition of adult education was being explicitly advanced by the Murphy Committee with a view to challenging and changing existing understandings of adult education:

> Adult education in this country is usually considered as a process of classes for adults in schoolrooms but the Committee considered that this is too narrow a view, and that other activities which impart knowledge to adults in a less formal way may be even more important (Interim Murphy Report, 1970, p. 10).

It was mainly because of this 'expansion of its concept of what adult education is' (p. 11) that the committee decided to issue an interim report in the hope of generating excitement and engaging the attention of the public. The low response rate from some of the groups invited to make submissions to the committee (Table 15.1) would be unthinkable nowadays. Non-response rates of 29 per cent from vocational education committees, 55 per cent from church-related bodies and church leaders, and 73 per cent from trade unions, professional associations and employer bodies suggest a precarious, fragile and limited understanding of adult education at that time.

Table 15.1 Percentage response from various groups invited to make submissions to the Murphy Committee (from Interim Murphy Report, 1970, Appendix A, p. 56)

Percentage	*Response*
Farming and Rural Organisations	100
Universities	100
County Committees of Agriculture	85
Government Departments	77
Vocational Education Committees	71
County Development Teams	57
Trade Associations	53
Church-related Bodies and Church Leaders	45
Trade Unions, Professional Associations and Employer Bodies	27
Chamber of Commerce and Junior Chambers of Commerce	7
Others	52

Accordingly, this intervention of the Murphy Committee could be read as an effort to select and isolate a broad range of adult learning experiences from their background and context and fuse them together to be collectively signified as adult education. As well as advancing adult education as a practice, the Murphy Committee was seeking to extend its meaning and to culturally reconstitute it as a category of the educational process. In this sense, the Murphy Committee was both culturally innovative and interventionist. It was offering a reconstituted construct as an object for textualisation.

This broad definition of adult education was maintained in the final Murphy Report. In speaking of the 'provision and utilisation of facilities' the Committee was seeking to include independent study, experiential learning and community development within its definition of adult education. The Kenny Report was more expansive and specific in its definition and explicitly included self-directed learning. The inclusion of self-directed learning represented a departure from the final Murphy Report which disqualified it because it was deemed to lack the guidance by another person required to be characterised as adult education, as distinct from adult learning. This apart, the three definitions can be regarded as progressively extended significations of a single construct of adult education. This impression of a linear expansion of understanding and knowledge in relation to adult education is further communicated by the repetition and continuous confirmation of the last of these definitions in all the main policy documents on education up to 2000, including the 1980 White Paper on Educational Development, and both sets of Green and White Papers on Education and Adult Education. From this it might seem reasonable to assume that the early Murphy Reports had been the impetus and intellectual source for the cultivation of how adult education was to be subsequently understood and known. The reality was to be more dynamic, revealing change and diversity alongside stability and structure.

Isolation and Conceptualisation of Adult Learning Activities

The primary cultural function of the Murphy Reports had been the identification of all forms of systematic learning among those who had broken with full-time initial education as the object of attention and the site for textualising the theme of adult education. The Interim Murphy Report had listed some 90 agencies and bodies engaged directly or indirectly in adult education. The diversity of the learning activities it was seeking to bring within its semantic remit is indicated by the inclusion, along with universities and vocational education committees, of such bodies as the Irish Creamery Managers Association, the Irish Wild Bird Conservancy, the National Film Institute and the Catholic Marriage Advisory Council. In Table 15.2 this broad field of adult learning is represented in terms of five content areas as they existed in the 1970s. It was the extent of their provision, visibility and engagement with people's lives, and the degree of conceptualisation as forms of adult learning and collective classification as adult education that they achieved, that represents and characterises the first phase of textualisation of adult education.

Personal Learning

Personal learning in the form of self-development, hobby and recreational courses influenced the meaning which many people gave to the concept of adult education at that time. This can be attributed to the popularity of the evening classes provided by the Vocational Education Committees throughout the country. The range of active and conceptual subjects available through these classes was extensive with routine programmes offering as many as 30 different courses (Daly, 1978) on languages, musical instruments, artistic topics, sports, etc. Short university extramural courses, classes provided by such agencies as the People's College and The Dublin Institute of Adult Education, as well as Radio Telefís Éireann programmes (Moody, 1979), supplemented the provision of the VECs. Although experiences in non-formal learning are elusive and less systematised than formal classes it is clear from Ó Buachalla's (1978) study of non-formal learning agencies in County Clare and from national directories of adult education agencies (AONTAS, 1980) that a very wide range of opportunities for personal and cultural development was available independently of the formal educational system in local communities.

Social Learning

Civic and community courses on leadership, communication, organisational skills, and social action and initiative represented the unique contribution of rural groups such as Muintir na Tíre and Macra na Feirme. The extramural diploma courses of the universities in Cork, Galway, Dublin and Maynooth came to be major contributors to this area. Family-based courses also experienced growth. As well as the VEC courses in the domestic arts and skills such as dress-making, interior decorating, woodwork and cooking, these included the non-formal and formal work of marriage advisory councils, family study groups and radio and television. There appeared to be a developing interest in courses on parenting and on child and adolescent development (Clarke, 1977; Advisory Committee on Educational Broadcasting, 1979).

Table 15.2 Varieties of Provision for Adult Learning in the 1970s

	Personal	*Social*	*Vocational*	*Certificated*	*Special Needs*
Content/ Orientation	Active and conceptual courses of a self-development, hobby/ recreational nature	Social, political and economic studies, local development, leadership, family life and parenting courses	Largely in-service courses, not generally leading to marketable qualifications	Re-entry to second- and third-level educational programmes	Basic and social skills, sheltered training, consciousness raising.
Providers	Vocational education committees (second-level schools and regional technical colleges). Institutions such as The People's College, Dublin Institute of Adult Education. Radio Telefís Éireann. Sporting and cultural organisations.	Muintir na Tíre. Marriage Advisory Councils. University extramurals. Radio Telefís Éireann. Institutions such as The People's College, Dublin Institute of Adult Education.	AnCo. Irish Management Institute. ACOT Trade Unions. College of Industrial Relations. Third-level colleges.	Second- and third-level education institutions. Correspondence colleges. Professional bodies.	Literacy schemes. National Rehabilitation Institute. Prison Service. Compensatory schemes. Advocacy and Activist groups representing minorities and the disadvantaged.

Vocational Learning

This refers to inservice and retraining courses for particular occupations which, though they may be marketable in occupational mobility, did not lead to entry qualifications to skilled or professional occupations. Courses for those employed in agriculture, industry, public service, management and trade unions were provided by statutory and private agencies. An impressive array of courses was available, some employing television and correspondence techniques and outreach centres. While there are instances of favourable comparisons with provision in other countries (National Economic and Social Council, 1982) and high participation rates (Irish National Teachers' Organisation, 1980), it was being consistently argued by a variety of sources that vocational learning needed considerable coordination, development and expansion in order to meet the requirements of such specific occupations as teaching (*White Paper on Educational Development*, 1980), management (European Foundation for Management Development, 1978), and industry (Whelan and Walsh, 1977).

Certificated Learning

Educational programmes for adults leading to certification through full-time or part-time re-entry to second- or third-level education were not as developed as other types of adult learning. Learning opportunities for adults were not included in the expansionist policies of the 1960s. As we have seen in the previous chapter, the Commission on Higher Education 1960-1967 gave a grudging and temporary acceptance to even extramural studies in universities. With regard to evening and part-time degree courses, a sense of threat among interest groups and undue caution about standards were evident in submissions from graduate professions and some university staff to the Commission with the result that it was the proposed new colleges (to teach to pass degree level) that were recommended to experiment with flexible arrangements for part-time university courses. Mac Gréil's (1974) study of the educational standards of the adult population of greater Dublin in 1972-1973 estimated that 6 per cent of the respondents were beyond 21 years of age when they completed their post-primary education, and suggested that this group had probably availed of correspondence courses or other forms of alternative provision. A number of arrangements had been made for adults returning to second-level education (Feehan, 1979) and the universities of Cork, Dublin and Galway made degree courses available through evening and weekend lectures. This was the weakest element of adult learning provision. A study of new full-time entrants to third-level education institutions in 1980 showed that less than 8 per cent were aged 20 or over at the time of entry and 1.3 per cent were aged 26 or over (Clancy, 1982, p. 17). A comparison of trainee teachers in the Irish Republic and Northern Ireland (Dunn and Morgan, 1979) was revealing – no student among the Irish Republic respondents was aged 26 or more, but 7.1 per cent were in that age category in Northern Ireland. In fact there were indications of a reduction in the number of full-time students over the age of 21 in third-level institutions (Hanratty, 1982) and of a more restricted range of university degrees on offer on a part-time basis (Hanratty, 1973) since the mid-1960s. The National Council for Educational Awards (1978) appears to have been more prescient than most in its attention to mature students, and impediments to adults to gain educational and professional qualifications such as inadequate grants, selection criteria, and the absence of special programmes were beginning to enter the discourse (Maloney, 1980).

Special Needs Learning

A number of areas of special needs were identified by the Interim Murphy Report that required tailored and targeted programmes. It identified such groups as those living in poverty, functional illiterates, unattached youths, the unemployed, the aged and those about to retire, itinerants (in line with the terminology of the time) and prisoners. It recommended that programmes to meet the needs of such groups who were unlikely to be in a position to organise or seek out learning opportunities on their own behalf should become a priority in a national adult education programme.

In 1975 the Robins Report on the training and employment of the handicapped (Department of Health, 1975), estimated that 15,000 of the 100,000 adult handicapped people (mental and physical) could benefit from preparation for employment, and the responsibility for vocational training and employment services was allocated to the National Rehabilitation Board. The experience of providing these courses helped to identify further needs in the area of social and literacy skills (Hastings *et al.*, 1978). In 1965, the Commission of Inquiry on Mental Handicap had argued for adult education for mildly handicapped persons, particularly in the area of oral expression, reading, writing and simple calculation. While some provision of this nature was being made in the training centres and workshops of the Rehabilitation Institute and the Cork Polio and General Aftercare Association, a report to the National Economic and Social Council concluded that education for social and interpersonal skills remained an important area of need for adult handicapped persons (Faughnan and O'Connor, 1980).

Throughout the 1970s, the education and training of prisoners assumed a more central position in the Department of Justice Annual Reports on prisons and places of detention. A coordinator of education was appointed in 1975 and greater emphasis was being placed on modern technical training to AnCo standards, community-based projects and social and basic education. The number of full-time teacher equivalents provided through the VECs almost doubled to 60 between

1978 and 1981. Yet, to place these developments in context, in 1981 when a daily average of 1,196 people were in custody, only 72 inmates commenced a course of industrial training (Mac Gréil, 1980; Department of Justice, 1981).

The Interim Murphy Report, as we have seen, identified functional illiteracy as an area of special need demanding intervention. It made a point of asserting that functional illiteracy was not absolute illiteracy. It defined functional illiteracy as the 'inability to cope with the ordinary functions of living which require a knowledge of reading and writing ... manifested by an inability to read advertisements, warning signs, notices, or to write letters and to complete forms' (p. 19). This diagnosis of a literacy problem, however circumscribed, was greeted with considerable disbelief at the time. This should not altogether surprise. As we have seen in Chapter 9, no more than ten years earlier a well-placed educational source had claimed that in Ireland only the unteachable were illiterate. Problems of literacy were to be identified among people with disabilities, prisoners and Travellers, but it was also becoming clear that they were not confined to such groups (O'Doherty, 1977). Literacy schemes began on the initiative of individual volunteers leading to the formation of the National Adult Literacy Agency in 1980.

Approaches to provision for the unemployed and the generally disadvantaged sought to help people to manage their return to the world of work or to cope with unemployment and low wages. Topics covered on these courses included job-search and interview skills, setting up your own business, establishing workers' cooperatives, budgeting, and knowing your social welfare entitlements (Toner, 1979; O'Connor and Kelly, 1980). A radical departure was indicated by the schemes in the first European-sponsored anti-poverty programme which set as their objectives the raising of consciousness about inequality, the cultivation of solidarity, and the facilitation of social action among disadvantaged groups (National Committee on Pilot Schemes to Combat Poverty, 1980).

An indication of the relative size of these five varieties of adult learning provision is given in Table 15.3 which is reworked from Farrell's (1982) content analysis of a 100 programmes offering almost 10,000 courses in 1980-1981. The insignificance of the certificated and special needs offerings is probably overstated: many of the special needs courses were outside the mainstream of adult learning providers and some of the professional and vocational courses could, more appropriately, be considered as certificated provision. Nevertheless, it is a good indicator of the relative weakness of certificated and special needs provision at that time.

Table 15.3 Adult Learning Courses Offered in 1980-1981. N: 9,652
[Derived from data collected by Farrell, 1982]

Courses	*Percentage of Courses*
Personal	**Total 35.4**
Personal interests/hobbies	9.9
Crafts	6.0
Fine Arts	5.6
Physical fitness/Sport	4.9
Irish language, culture and heritage	4.7
Languages	4.3
Social	**Total 21.95**
Home management	7.2
Home maintenance	6.5
Community/Social studies	3.7
Religious studies	2.1
Family life	1.7
Preschool playgroups	0.7
Women's studies	0.04
Third World studies	0.01
Vocational	**Total 38.6**
Farm/Agricultural education	17.9
Professional and vocational courses	14.9
Business and Commercial studies	5.8
Certificated	**Total 2.95**
Leaving, Intermediate, Group Cert.	2.9
Training for adult educators	0.05
Special Needs	**Total 1.1**
Basic/Second chance education	1.1

The near invisibility of women's studies and the low percentage of courses described as community/social studies should also be noted as a foil to future expansion of these areas. Obviously, courses on offer need not mirror the numbers which actually attend. But Farrell's research does allow us to gain a synoptic view of how adult learning was representing itself experientially at that time and what it was making available as the objects for conceptualisation in the cultural production of adult education.

Permanent/Lifelong Education

As well as seeking to classify these diverse adult learning activities as adult education, the Murphy Reports also sought to confirm its educational status by integrating it as a new category of education within the established educational system. In this, it drew from the over-arching construct of permanent education.

The Interim Murphy Report argued that any report on adult education needed to take into account the concept of permanent education which, it explained, was becoming widely accepted in continental Europe, Great Britain and the US. It pointed out that permanent education was not identical with adult education. Rather, it was a 'new integrating concept comprising the whole spectrum of educational activity from nursery school to educational institutions attended in the "third age"' (p. 11). While both Interim and Final Murphy Reports were drawing on the Council of Europe's conceptualisation and definition of permanent education in this regard, they used the term interchangeably with that of lifelong education. The Final Murphy Report acknowledged that the concept of permanent education would necessitate changes of attitude to policy among planners and participants in the educational system if 'the spread of the educational process over the whole of human life' (p. 18) was to be achieved. The 'absurdity of cramming into a few years of childhood and youth, often in unfavourable conditions, so much information and skills that could more satisfactorily be spread over a whole lifetime, to the greater good of the individual and the community' (p. 18), though evident to some people, was a novel idea that had not been debated in Ireland to any great extent. It encouraged debate among educationalists on this new principle of education, and interpreted as indicators of an emergence of an understanding and limited acceptance of the concept of permanent education, a number of developments in Irish education generally at that time. These included preschool intervention programmes, the introduction of comprehensive schooling, the commitment to provision for adult education in the community school concept, the innovative work of government departments such as Agricultural and Fisheries, Health and Labour in recognising and responding to the learning needs of adults, the creation of training and adult education units by trade unions, employers and commercial organisations, and the growth of voluntary organisations highlighting new needs and demands among adults.

While the Final Murphy Report may have been unduly sanguine in interpreting these developments as indicators of the emergence of permanent education within Irish understanding and practice in education, it was nonetheless uncompromising and explicit in acknowledging that the realisation of permanent education would 'mean a complete change, indeed revolution, in the present Irish system of education' (p. 21). It would require:

- the end of rote learning and the assembly and memorising of facts and pieces of information
- knowing where and how to secure, utilise and integrate knowledge
- a carefully planned approach to the elimination of functional illiteracy
- less passivity and immobility among students
- more activity and variety in learning methodologies
- an integration of the new educational institutions and approaches with the mass media and the family
- the end of specialisation as an outcome of education.

In the event, permanent education and lifelong education never achieved more than the status of empty signifiers, occasionally deployed to refer to the fact of ongoing learning throughout the life cycle and on other occasions more narrowly to the inclusive understanding of adult education propagated by the Murphy Reports. A decade later, the Kenny Commission's Report, *Lifelong Learning* (1984), was forced to conclude that the Murphy Report's hope that this principle of education would be debated had been realised only to 'limited extent' (p. 38). It also proclaimed the principles of permanent education and lifelong education and, in its first recommendation, advocated that 'the government should publicly commit itself to the implementation of permanent education as a national objective' (p. 41). Once again, there was a call for the propagation of the principles of permanent and lifelong education throughout the country as a basis for national debate about our educational future. Taking stock of the situation in the late 1980s, Cathcart (1989), a member of the Kenny Commission and very much identified with the principles of permanent and lifelong education, concluded that it was the 'narrower sectional demand which won universal acceptance among adult educators' (p. 130). He saw as evidence of this the philosophy of action declared by AONTAS, 'a parliament of the organisations and individuals concerned with adult education in the Republic of Ireland' (p. 130) which he interpreted as being entirely concerned with the promotion of the educational interests of individual adults and not with the broader perspective drawn from permanent education.

Irrespective of the relative merits of adopting the broader or sectoral perspective on the positioning of adult education within the overall educational system, this absence of debate is germane to the conceptualisation of adult learning activities. It is indicative of the limited stock of knowledge of a theorised nature available to describe, situate, contrast, extend or critique what adult educators had chosen to make the object of their attention. There were few intellectual resources which those who wished to communicate about adult education could draw on: the provision of adult education and its advocacy circumscribed what and how people knew about it; and its conceptualisation was dependent on constructs, often derived from other bodies of knowledge, which advocates and practitioners of specific varieties of adult learning introduced to the discourse.

When lifelong learning was again advanced in the mid-1990s in the context of adult learning, the inclusive understanding of adult education which the Murphy Reports had sought to advance was no longer viable, and indeed had not been for over a decade. From the 1980s onwards, at various points of departure, the five varieties of adult learning that had been made the objects of conceptualisation and understanding in adult education in the 1970s had developed materially and conceptually in directions that disallowed the use of adult education as a signifier except with the narrowest of meanings.

Reconceptualisation of Adult Learning Activities

Materially and conceptually, a new configuration of adult learning activities emerged in the 1980s. Adult learning activities came to be set apart from one another in terms of origination, provider, location, determination of content, targeted learners and funding basis, and distinguished by a new set of signifiers. The contemporary categories of literacy education, community education, women's education, second-chance and continuing education can be traced from this time. This classification of adult learning is distinctively a product of the 1980s but it did not arise *ab initio* at this time. It developed largely from a reconceptualisation and material expansion of dimensions and features of the largely content-driven categories of the 1970s. In this reconceptualisation, each category exists within an overall system of classification in which the meaning of each category, and its adult learning referent, is determined by the conventions of their differentiation from one another. Accordingly, the language by which their distinctiveness is designated has meaning only within their overall system of signification, and any modification of meaning will create reverberations throughout the system.

Literacy Education

Within this system of classification, literacy education was the first to set itself apart as a distinct category of adult learning. NALA, formed in 1980, received its first government grant to establish a secretariat in 1984. In the early 1980s, a NALA survey recorded the existence of about 40 literacy schemes serving 1,200 students and involving almost as many voluntary tutors throughout the country (Kennedy, 1982). NALA (1981) also estimated at that time that many more in need of help did not come forward due to sensitivity and inadequate publicity. Since then there has been a greater recognition of the extent of the problem, literacy schemes have greatly expanded, and the area has attracted considerable investment, particularly in recent years. In the mid-1980s, a Department of Education Discussion Document used the arbitrary figure of 18% of the adult population requiring literacy tuition (5 per cent illiterate or nearly so, 13 per cent sub-literate) as the basis for its recommendations (Department of Education, 1985). As Du Vivier (1991) was subsequently to observe, the extent of the literacy problem in Ireland had been difficult to quantify and existing estimates of need varied in the light of definitions and methods used. In its survey of 1994/95, NALA received responses from 72 schemes catering for over 4,000 students and staffed mainly by voluntary tutors. This survey estimated that this represented less than 1 per cent of adults with literacy difficulties affecting them in their daily lives (Bailey and Coleman, 1998).

The extent and depth of the adult literacy problem was brought into sharp public focus by the publication of the Irish results from the OECD International Adult Literacy Survey which found that about a quarter of the adult population (16-64 years) was unable to achieve higher than level one on a five-level literacy scale (Morgan *et al.*, 1997). The 1998 Green Paper announced a multi-faceted national adult literacy programme incorporating statutory/voluntary co-operation, enhancement of literacy tutor training, user-friendly provision and guidance. There has been a significant increase in government funding and the 2000 White Paper promised further development of the programme. At that time, NALA estimated that there were 125 schemes with some 15,000 students staffed by 4,200 tutors of whom 3,400 were voluntary (personal communication).

Community Education

As the 1970s progressed there was a notable tendency to conceptualise social learning, incorporating leadership courses, social and political studies, and family and parenting courses, as community education. Some programmes, encouraged by the emergence of community schools, began to describe their total adult learning provision as community education. The conceptualisation of localities as communities stretches further back in Ireland, particularly in rural areas, where the preferred base of mobilisation was the whole community, in opposition to the conflict-based class analysis of society and social action, advanced by Catholic social teaching. Muintir na Tíre founded by Canon Hayes is the clearest manifestation of this form of collective action. Community education as it emerged in the 1970s made few efforts to connect with this legacy, and in some instances there has been an explicit repudiation of it as 'radical conservatism', the combination of 'high levels of enthusiasm' with 'varied dosages of rural fundamentalism, nationalism, catholicism and sexism' (Collins and Ryan, 1996). The popularity of community as a construct, and its growing use at this time, owed more to urbanisation, fears about the eclipse of community, and the activities of individuals and models of practice associated with the community development dimension of urban disadvantage programmes in Great Britain during the 1970s (Robinson, 1976). As many writers, in contexts quite disparate from rural Ireland and Catholic social action, have pointed out, community evokes virtue, goodness and inclusivity that act as barriers to the critique of the use of the construct, foreclosing on debate and operating in Brookfield's (1983, p. 60) words as a 'premature ultimate'.

Beyond the relabelling of specific content areas and total programmes of adult learning provision, the precursor of the contemporary meaning of community education was the European-funded pilot schemes to combat poverty in the 1970s. What distinguished these schemes was their adoption of an explicit class analysis of society, from which conflict, disparities of power, and exploitation and its mis-recognition became the basis of intervention, be it in terms of the mobilisation of particularly vulnerable groups of workers, consciousness raising, and forcing the revelation of previously disguised power bases and their partiality. Much diluted and non-social class based versions are to be found in the local approaches to poverty in the *National Anti-Poverty Strategy* (1997), in a series of EU-driven initiatives in urban and rural areas, and in the 2000 Adult Education White Paper's inclusion of the work of the area-based partnerships with such groups as Travellers, people with disabilities, rural smallholders and the elderly. However, it is the concept of gender that has come to dominate the manner in which community education has come to be understood and set apart from other forms of adult learning.

Women's Education

The 2000 White Paper describes the development of community education in the following terms:

> Community education has evolved in Ireland in recent years as an ideologically-driven, highly-innovative and large-scale adult education provision consisting mainly of self-directed women's groups. These groups have been central in the defining character of community education in Ireland and merit particular recognition for their contribution to date. Such groups began to emerge in the early 1980s in Ireland, mostly in urban working-class areas, badly affected by high rates of unemployment and dealing with high levels of youth dependency (p. 111).

As we shall later see, this is a much-contested terrain in which social actors variously positioned within adult education, local development, poverty action and the academy offer diverse and often contradictory accounts of how these women's groups are to be conceptualised and explained. The early research on this phenomenon refers to it as daytime adult education (Inglis and Bassett, 1988; Inglis *et al.*, 1993) but the terms locally based women's groups, women's self-help groups, and autonomous women's groups have come to be used interchangeably (Costello, 1999). From these and other sources (Rath, 1999) it is possible to chart their material development, in terms of numbers and activities, as objects made available to social actors for conceptualisation. At the beginning of the 1980s it was estimated that about six such groups existed. A decade later this had increased to something in excess of 100, and at the end of the 1990s a figure of 1,000 was proposed. The first national survey described the main objective of the groups as the provision of 'cheap, open-access courses, based on shared, self-directed learning, principally directed towards women in the home' (Inglis *et al.*, 1993). The following are some typical objectives given by the groups for their establishment:

- 'To provide daytime courses for women confined to the home
- To give women confidence, dignity, and a feeling of self-worth and a realisation of their full potential
- To help alleviate loneliness and isolation of young mothers in the housing estate by getting them together and making acquaintances
- To run courses to raise the awareness of people about their own personal development …
- To find a better quality of life for ourselves. To promote skills and self-awareness, assertiveness and leadership …
- These courses encourage personal development for women and encourage participation of women in their community …
- The group was set up in the beginning just as a social group …
- People wanted education that reflected their own needs. To provide locally based morning-time courses at a reasonable cost' (pp19-21).

Of the first aim or objective mentioned, 45 per cent listed overcoming isolation, providing support, information, counselling and awareness, 40 per cent mentioned the provision of cheap classes/courses, and 15 per cent mentioned service to the community. The authors summarise the groups as follows:

> Daytime education groups are for the most part run by women for women. Yet they are not women's groups in that their aims and objectives tend to be educational rather than political. Initially not all would have had the express purpose of raising consciousness about, and changing the position, role and power of women in Irish society. Their aims were generally more immediate and practical. Furthermore, the membership of many groups was open to women and men. However, through the process of education, many women developed strong political consciousness in relation to their roles and position as women in Irish society (p. 11).

Reviewing a series of studies of these groups up to the end of the 1990s, Costello (1999) lists an unchanged range of activities apart from the addition of work-related skills. She identifies four categories of educational courses in demand:

- Personal development
- Confidence building, creative writing, aromatherapy, reflexology
- Practical skills for family maintenance: cookery, first-aid, parenting, health, literacy and numeracy
- Return to work skills: job search skills, paper skills, information technology, tourism training.

In terms of funding, 40 per cent was allocated to personal development activities, 17 per cent to crafts, and 16 per cent to parenting in 1995 (Dolphin and Mulvey, 1997).

It is clear that there has been much movement in what is meant by community education since the 1970s when it initially represented no more than a relabelling of courses and programmes. From that point when community education had a wide range and inclusive set of referents, it progressed through a series of stages to signify a more selective set of meanings. This involved the foregrounding of gender and the inclusion of independence, self-direction and the absence of hierarchy. But it also submerged class, the involvement of religious personnel and statutory bodies, and any indicator or even the search for indicators which might contradict the principles of feminist methodology. Community education thus came to mean not necessarily the practices of women's groups but an idealised feminist version of what such groups should be like. This was facilitated by the conceptual flexibility of such related developments as multi-purpose learning programmes in disadvantaged communities, second-chance education, education and training initiatives and area-based interagency educational activities which proved to be sufficiently pliable to adjust semantically according as community education carved out its own space in the overall system of meanings relating to these phenomena. In this sense, as a linguistic signifier community education came to act as a constructor of meaning and not as a mere reflector of actual practice. The implication of this reconfiguration of meaning for the conceptualisation of other learning activities engaged in by adult women is the disruption of the category of women's education.

Learning programmes for middle-class women, those of higher educational levels, in more formal academic settings, or with an IT, technological or scientific content are left with the ongoing tension as to how they are to be classified: if not gender, which of their other dimensions – content, learning setting, pedagogical mode, academic level, rationale – are to be made the basis for establishing difference and commonality in the construction of boundaries between themselves and other adult learning activities? These processes relate to questions of conceptualisation and the role of language in establishing and destabilising meanings in relation to community education and women's education. It is to say nothing as yet about the textualisation of the activities of women's groups in terms of the approaches and assumptions of their methodologies, politicisation and feminist orientation.

Second-Chance Education

Second-chance education takes as the object of conceptualisation disadvantaged adults who return to the mainstream educational system. Their disadvantaged status may be derived from their current labour market positioning or from the extent of their initial level of educational attainment. During an era of stable educational opportunity these would be expected to correlate with one another. But given the dramatic expansion in educational participation in Ireland since the 1960s many occupationally successful adults possess what by modern standards would be regarded as no more than moderate levels of education. Both the 1998 Green Paper and the 2000 White Paper devote much space to statistically detailing Ireland's low international ranking in relation to age-based differentials in educational attainment, and recognise that upgrading overall educational levels will require substantial adult re-entry to the formal educational system. However this broadened the category of disadvantage and those in need of second-chance education, the priorities for policy set by the White Paper refocused the conceptualisation of second-chance education. The White Paper announced a Back to Education Initiative (BTEI) providing for a significant expansion of part-time options under Youthreach/Traveller, Vocational Training Opportunities Schemes and Post-Leaving Cert courses. In this, there was to be a particular emphasis on promoting a return to learning for those in the population with less than upper second-level education. The White Paper had identified, among its top priorities, the large number of Irish adults (1.1 million aged 15-64) who had not completed upper second-level education, of whom 529,600 had not completed lower second-level. Its policy on the funding of part-time mature students in higher education was to 'positively discriminate in favour of the most deserving groups economically; reach the most educationally disadvantaged sector within the mature student population and respond in a very tangible way to the educational needs of those with the lowest incomes' (p. 146). The effect was to conceptualise second-chance education as a remedial and compensatory rather than an upgrading or uplifting form of adult learning.

This construct of second-chance education is of comparatively recent origin. As we have seen, in reviewing adult learning patterns in the 1970s, it was rare at that time for adults to return as full-time students to the mainstream educational system, be it at second or third level, after they had broken with full-time education. Conceptually, such was the association of adult education with the evening class and non-accreditated learning, that such adult re-entry was slow to be understood in terms of adult education. Even evening programmes leading to university degrees were more routinely seen as a form of university education rather than as adult education. Both Murphy Reports were supportive of changes and innovations likely to increase adult access to third-level education. They considered distance education and Open University-type provision, and the Final Murphy Report recommended the expansion of evening courses in the institutes of higher education, and the possibility for adults to 'acquire higher educational awards through the accumulation of credits over a period of time' (p. 40). But it was the representation of adult re-entry to the mainstream educational system by the Kenny Report in terms of equal opportunity and inter-generational inequality that was to establish the distinctiveness of second-chance education from the construct of the mature student.

The Kenny Report pointed to the failure of the expansion of the formal educational system since the 1960s to have any significant impact on the disparities in participation between the different social groups in post-compulsory education. In the interests of increasing the participation in higher education of less advantaged adults it recommended that entrance criteria should give credit for work and life experience as well as academic attainment. It also identified the existence of inter-generational inequality resulting from the increased educational opportunities available to those educated since the 1960s. It targeted the needs of the third of the adult population who had left school at or before the age of 14, those who were 'most likely to have had no experience of continuing education and to have experienced or be experiencing unemployment' (p. 32). It recommended that 'in equity and in the interests of the economy and social stability, they must be encouraged to participate in education and provided with more opportunities to do so' (p. 32). To this end, the Kenny Report recommended the removal of the restrictions in the unemployment benefit system on participation in education by the unemployed, and to facilitate this it advised that educational innovations in other countries involving such changes to the social welfare code should be studied.

Second-chance education achieved a material presence with the establishment of the Educational Opportunities Scheme on an experimental basis in 1986. This allowed for those who were in receipt of unemployment benefit for more than a year and who were over 25 years of age to pursue a one-year full-time education course without loss of benefit (Goulding *et al.*, 1987). Three centres had been planned, Tallaght, Limerick and Donegal but the latter never materialised. Reconstituted as the Vocational Training Opportunities Scheme (VTOS) it attracted European social funding from 1989, broadened its qualifying conditions, and became a national programme enjoying extensive participation and success.

Participants receive a training allowance in lieu of social welfare entitlements and travel and meal allowances are also paid. Participants take a one or two year full-time course depending on need and previous educational achievement. These can vary from literacy work to certified courses up to Leaving Certificate and Post-Leaving Certificate levels (Keogh and Downes, 1998).

Continuing Education

The Universities Act 1997 commits universities to 'facilitate lifelong learning through the provision of adult and continuing education'. The distinction between adult and continuing education in the provision of learning opportunities for adults returning to education is a product of developments in higher education, particularly in the 1990s. As Ó Murchú (1986) predicted in his study of adult education in the universities, a new type of educational provision for adults developed alongside the traditional extramural programmes in adult education which in the process became ring-fenced as adult education. These newer programmes, referred to as continuing education, distinguish themselves from adult education in their rationale, content, clientele and certification. Adult education was open access, public service in orientation, and uncredentialised at university level. Continuing education was vocationally based and was expected to be at least self-financing. At UCC, for instance, this expansion of provision for adults was acknowledged in the reconstitution of the Department of Adult Education as the Centre for Adult and Continuing Education in the early 1990s. Alongside its adult education provision, it developed continuing education courses initially in Credit Union Studies, Corporate Direction, Management Practice, Personnel Management, Safety, Health and Welfare, and Food Science and Technology. This expansion of provision is reflected in its growth of student numbers at that time – from some 800 to over 2,000 students during the first half of the 1990s (Centre for Adult and Continuing Education, 1996). Many of these developments in continuing education related to newly credentialised vocational roles and specialisations. But, as elsewhere, profession-specific postgraduate education provided by individual academic departments, such as Medicine, Law, Engineering, Management, and Education, came to be conceptualised as continuing education. This reflected the fact of the growth of knowledge in these areas and the realisation that in other jurisdictions such continuing education was mandatory for specific professions.

The development of continuing education was greatly supported by policy-related reports on education and training in the 1990s. Even in the early 1990s when few skills shortages were being reported by industrialists, the Culliton Report of 1992 took the view that the perception of many managers that there was not a skills shortage 'may itself be part of the skills problem facing Irish industry' (p. 54). It concluded:

The real skills gap is not measured by the absence of people to do a particular job or even necessarily by asking people what training they need. The real skills gap is the one which exists between skill levels in firms in Ireland and that of best practice firms in competitor countries. In this respect the evidence suggests that Ireland has a significant real skills gap in many areas (p. 54).

It went on to specify the deficient nature of provision for continuing education in Irish industry. In a typical year only one in every two employees received any training on an annual basis, and only one in five received off-the-job training which had an average duration of one day per person per annum. This was significantly lower than in more advanced countries and the duration was about half as long. About one in three managers received off-the-job training compared with one in two in more advanced countries. Only one in five of Irish managers received more than four days training off-the-job each year.

The 1998 Green Paper captured the sentiments of a number of reports of the late 1990s on human resource development, skill needs and deficiencies, manpower forecasting, and information technology. It argued that:

A context of ever more rapidly changing technology not only reduces the possibility of a 'job for life' but, perhaps even more, reduces the likelihood of a 'skill for life'. The well-educated and flexible workforce which has been a central part of Ireland's current economic growth is itself a wasting asset, unless renewed on an ongoing basis through a continuous drive to upgrade and re-skill (p. 32).

It prescribed a strengthening of the interaction between education and training institutions and the world of work, greater flexibility of provision in terms of timing, access routes, progression pathways, and modularisation and more flexible certification systems involving the accreditation of prior learning and work-based experience. It predicted that 'as the demand for ongoing or continuing education grows in the future, educational institutions will look to "accompanying" the student through their work life cycle rather than merely preparing them for it' (p. 33).

In the process, the semantic range of continuing education expanded and continues to do so. This is facilitated by the growing credentialisation of all forms of planned employee learning, and by the longstanding tradition in Irish discourse on adult learning of not making a meaningful distinction between education and training. From the 2000 White Paper it would appear that continuing education was well on its way to meaning all forms of enhancing employee/worker efficiency, in all types of occupations and at all levels, apart from the compensatory provision in second chance education geared towards labour-market entry and re-entry.

Adult Education: Compensation or Andragogy?

It needs to be stressed that these five constructs of adult learning are social products. They result from being identified, set apart and distinguished from the overall material and conceptual environment of adult learning. There is nothing pre-determined or natural or obvious about these conceptualisations. The objects they classify could have been otherwise classified. This is borne out by a comparison with the 1970s which reveals how the semantic field of adult learning shifted over a decade to one in which particular forms of learning took on distinct identities. In the transition, social learning experienced a disruption of conceptualisation involving a process of conceptual mutation and appropriation and isolation of its objects. Vocational learning gained in coherence and rationale, and its objects expanded in their materiality. The certificated learning of the mainstream educational system lost its privileged position according as non-institutionalised forms of learning became increasingly credentialised. Despite its continued material presence, personal learning is approaching conceptual extinction. The Green Paper gives a figure of almost 140,000 adults attending self-financing, part-time courses in the VEC and community/comprehensive sector alone (pp 52-53). The Green Paper describes this as 'a valued tradition in terms of its contribution to general personal, social and overall cultural well-being', one that deserves 'to be celebrated and sustained' (p. 91).

The White Paper recognises this countrywide network of schools and teachers as an adult learning infrastructure which, 'if adequately and appropriately resourced, has a major role to play in enhancing the learning opportunities of the adult population' (p. 103). In this regard, the White Paper seems willing to support the expansion of this type of provision. But, even more so than in the Green Paper, it is unclear as to how it is to be spoken about or, indeed, what it is. Personal learning begins to make contact with their understanding of adult education only when it is spoken of in terms of how it is likely to develop in new ways that would involve adults other than the educationally successful students who predominate among its participants at present. This under-representation of the disadvantaged in personal learning is the only criticism of this type of provision that is mentioned by either the Green or White Papers.

The understanding of adult education as something to be used to compensate, remediate, or upgrade is to be seen in the manner in which since the 1970s the interventionism of special needs learning has come to dominate and provide some sense of a unifying rationale in an otherwise fragmented conceptualisation of adult learning. Fleming (1996) recognised this transition in his criticism of the absence of a philosophy of adult education in the 1995 Education White Paper:

> Without this vision of what adult learning really involves, adult education becomes a sort of remedy for what was missed the first time on the educational merry-go-round. The implication of the White Paper is that anything that is not remedial is a luxury and not essential. There has to be an acceptance that lifelong learning is not just a catch-up on lost or missed opportunities and not only justifiable as good for

getting a job. It is the essential precondition for the health of our culture, the development of citizenship and the survival of democracy.

Asserting the distinctiveness of adult education and the necessity to understand it in a manner that is different from childhood or adolescent learning, reflects a sentiment that is to be found throughout adult education practitioners. Andragogy is rarely if ever used but its meanings, of which there is a broad spectrum, recur largely at the pre-theoretical level of adult education discourse. It suggests the existence of a meaning awaiting conceptualisation, but particularly naming and textualisation. Andragogy, in the tradition of Knowles (1980), referring to patterns of learning that are experientially distinctive to adults, is captured in Bane's (1995) description of the adult approach to education:

> It is as concerned with learning as it is with teaching. It operates on principles of equality and respect, where knowledge is shared, not transmitted, where who you are is infinitely more important that where you come from, where there is more interest in facilitation than in control and where we tread softly lest we tread on your dreams.

The ideological understanding of andragogy (Jarvis, 1995), also evident in Bane's description, is pushed further by Fleming (1996) in seeking to establish the distinctiveness of adult education in terms of its philosophy:

> Adult learning is participatory, critically reflexive, open to new ideas and changing frames of reference. It has a vision of learners engaged in dialogic participatory discourse, collectively seeking ways of changing themselves and society so that all systems, organisations and individuals respond to the needs of others.

As he puts it in relation to the Education White Paper, while it may be appropriate to teach children respect for and appreciation of the values which have traditionally shaped our society and culture, for adults the task is to be 'critical and active remakers of culture and society'. Both understandings of the distinctiveness of adult education are merely different shadings of andragogy, and are the products of writers with a long and deep commitment to adult education practice and reflection. But, for whatever reasons, a pattern of signals and sentiments, widespread but particularly strong among those within the community education movement, which appeared to invite such a conceptualisation as a rationale for the unification of adult education, has not to date been realised.

Lifelong Learning

From the mid-1990s lifelong learning achieved greater prominence as a way of accommodating developments in adult learning. This was in contrast to the disenchantment with the concept and the manner of its application in national systems of education that was evident into the 1990s (Rubenson and Field, 1987).

Lifelong learning was now proposed as one of the main lines of attack on a range of pressing problems, as 'a precondition for economic advance, democracy, social cohesion and personal growth' (Chapman and Aspin, 1997), becoming 'a central feature of the agenda for educational change in Europe' among the 'major international fora of opinion and strategic decision-making' (Coolahan, 1996b). The renewed interest is to be found among such international bodies as the OECD which published its *Lifelong Learning for All* in 1996, a year that was designated by the European Union as the European Year of Lifelong Learning, the Minister for Education, Niamh Bhreathnach, having made lifelong learning one of her main policy themes during the Irish Presidency of the European Community (Coolahan, 1996a). A number of European national governments also published policy documents incorporating the concept of lifelong learning (Chapman and Aspin, 1997). A major national conference was held in Dublin to coincide with the year of lifelong learning (Coolahan, 1996a), and its impact on policy is to be found in its use as the master concept in both Green and White Papers on Adult Education.

This reintroduction of lifelong learning to Irish educational policy seems set to follow a different course to what had been experienced following the dissemination and popularisation of the concept in the Murphy Reports and later in the Kenny Report. Unlike these earlier uses of permanent or lifelong education which, as Cathcart (1989) astutely observed, came to mean no more than an acknowledgement of the fact of ongoing learning through a sequence of distinct sectors of education or more frequently as a substitute for adult education itself, this newer use of lifelong learning has been more faithful to the original idea of lifelong learning as the master principle for all education. Not alone does this not require a sense of what is distinctive about adult education, it should actively discourage such efforts at what would be regarded as the fragmentation of the very construct of lifelong learning itself. For the Green Paper:

> Shifting the adult education debate into a lifelong learning framework raises issues of the relationship between the different levels of education, the transitions between these levels and the ease of transfer between work and education. As stated above, a concern with learning through the life cycle also raises questions concerning the quality of the school experience in learning how to learn, as well as raising the issue of increased expenditure on education through the life cycle (p. 19).

Both Green and White Papers on Adult Education were pragmatic documents in this regard. They struck a balance between the more visionary ideal of lifelong learning as the overarching principle of education and the need to give the status and coherence of a sector of education to adult education in its own right. This was followed through in the White Paper which maintained the primacy of lifelong learning as the master concept by attempting to integrate the diverse forms of adult learning within a system rather than a concept of adult education:

The challenge is to provide a structure that can provide a coordinating and formalising framework ... the lifelong and lifewide dimension of the adult education agenda implies an intimidating diversity of providers with associated differences in ideologies, methodologies, outcomes and constituencies. It is clearly imperative that this multiple-sourced provision is integrated and coordinated (p. 184).

To this end, the White Paper made a number of proposals designed to give the diverse field of adult learning the characteristics of a system of education. These included a commitment to establishing a National Adult Learning Council as an Executive Agency of the Department of Education and Science with responsibility for coordination, liaison, policy advice, monitoring, quality, staff development and research, and with the possibility of becoming a funding and administration body. At local level, the task of planning, managing and developing adult education was to be allocated to 33 Local Adult Learning Boards. A National Adult Guidance and Counselling Service was to be established. Priority was to be given to developing processes for accrediting those forms of learning that currently fall outside the domains of the mainstream certification agencies within the context of a national qualifications framework. In terms of personnel, a further 35 adult education organisers were to be appointed to undertake the additional work arising from the planned expansion of provision, the role of the Local Adult Learning Boards, and the expanding provision for adult learning in community, comprehensive and secondary schools. In moving to professionalising adult education, the White Paper accepted the Green Paper's recommendations that a recognised qualification for the teaching and practice of adult education be developed, that provision be made for inservice training and career progression, and that a forum for practitioners of adult and community education be established.

By integrating the diverse forms of adult learning materially rather than conceptually, within a system rather than a principle of education, the primacy of lifelong learning was maintained. The challenge of envisioning a meaning for adult education was avoided by concentrating on developing it as a sector of education. This allowed for the incorporation of andragogical themes such as education for consciousness raising, citizenship, civil society, and empowerment within an overall framework of lifelong learning. In the absence of a distinctive concept of adult education, it is its materiality as a system that is foregrounded as a basis for thinking about it. In this construction of meaning about learning during the adult years and throughout the life cycle, adult education does not exist in its own right, as distinct from specific kinds of adult learning, in any philosophical, sociological or psychological sense apart from its materiality as a structure of educational provision for adults.

The Producers of Adult Education Knowledge

At this point it is appropriate to turn to the producers of knowledge about adult education. This serves as a link between what has been covered so far – the isolation and conceptualisation of activities that form the basis for textualising adult education – and what is to follow in terms of the themes, texts and paradigms that constitute what has come to be known about adult education. It refers us back to the agents involved in the classification and re-classification of adult learning and helps to explain how these categories of distinctiveness and difference came to be constructed. Looking forward, identifying those who were to produce our current stock of knowledge about adult education will clarify the character and mode of production of this knowledge. Two distinguishing interlinked features emerge: the primacy of the provision of adult education as distinct from discourse about it in the signification of adult education, and the role of individuals (by contrast with the state, social movements, or political groupings) in making available these opportunities for adult learning and constructing a discourse about them. The pre-eminence of provision is due to the untheorised nature of discourse about adult education. As we have seen, it was what was isolated with no more than the received cultural categories of adulthood and learning that provided the objects for conceptualising adult education. To be a skilled participant in communication about adult education required little by way of interpretation beyond these rudimentary cultural categories. Therefore, it is those who provide, publicise and participate in adult learning programmes who are the major forces in establishing what is meant by adult education.

Individual Initiative

It is widely recognised that adult education provision in Ireland relied for long on the interest and initiative of voluntary organisations, religious groups and particular sectors within the educational system. What has not been sufficiently stressed is that it was individuals within these bodies who were the primary movers. A collective commitment to adult education was slow to develop. To a large extent this remained the situation well into the 1980s. Even within statutory bodies such as the VECs, the nature and extent of adult education provision depended very much on the level of interest and commitment on the part of a particular CEO, VEC committee member, school principal or individual member of a school's staff. It was most strikingly the case with literacy programmes, and in the community sector the early innovators were religious personnel dealing with vulnerable groups, and women with experience in the self-help groups of the women's movement. In the 1960s and 1970s, these innovators were distinguished by their commitment to the idea of change through adult education, be it in rural life, family, community, religious and civic activity. A number of these were to come together to form AONTAS, the National Association of Adult Education, in 1969. Some have written about their early experiences, their organisations which in some cases they helped to form, and their contemporaries (Carey, 1979; McDwyer, 1982). Their sense of commitment, missionary zeal and isolation is palpable. What they shared was a conviction that adult education was important in its own right to the extent that it is possible to detect an incipient social movement at this time. But with the fragmentation of adult learning provision from the 1980s onwards, this dissipated as a limited pool of activists went their different ways in pursuit of literacy, second chance and day-time women's programmes initially. The collectivisation of like-minded and committed individuals during the 1960s and 1970s, epitomised by the formation of AONTAS, was to be restricted as the process of mobilisation beyond atomised association was embarked upon again around these distinct forms of adult learning.

The emphasis in the adult education Green Paper on the manner in which the membership of AONTAS shifted from a predominantly statutory to a more diversified base incorporating voluntary organisations acts to obscure this atomised nature of adult education activism. More significantly, it disguises the manner in which these innovative individuals only in a very minimal sense could be said to be acting as delegates for the bodies they represented. The reality was that the resources of these bodies, in terms of their facilities, personnel and bureaucratic location, were mobilised for the promotion and advancement of their adult education visions. Though from a somewhat earlier era Alfred O'Rahilly, as President of University College Cork in the 1940s and 1950s, epitomises this pattern of innovation. As we have seen in the previous chapter, he was in no sense representative of academic thinking at that time on access to the knowledge and resources of the university in his championing of workers' tutorial classes which eventually led in the 1940s to diploma courses in social, economic and rural studies. It is only as the 1980s progressed, but particularly in the 1990s, that it is possible to identify distinct social configurations, incorporating collectivist, exclusionary and bureaucratic associations, operating as interest groups and pressure groups – government departments and state agencies, educational institutions, employer and business associations, farming and rural organisations and the feminist and community movements.

State Inactivism

The foil to individual initiative and activism in promoting adult learning opportunities has been the remoteness of the state from adult education. In his foreword to the adult education Green Paper in 1998, the Minister of State, Willie O'Dea, acknowledged as much when he admitted that it was 'a sector which has received inadequate attention up to this point' (p. 3). Over the years, commentators on government policy on adult education have variously criticised it for its dismissive attitude, its marginalisation of the sector, its lack of understanding of the distinctiveness of adult learning, and its incoherence. Not alone did adult education not benefit from the greater investment in education from the 1960s, but, as is epitomised by the sentiments of the Commission on Higher Education 1960-67, it had difficulty being accepted within the state sector as legitimate education. The excellent Murphy Reports of the 1970s signalled new hope of state interest in adult education and their efforts to popularise the proposition, that learning was a lifelong process, diverse in content and to be found in formal and non-formal settings, seemed to be having an impact. Following on the establishment of AnCo, the national training authority, in 1967, the Community School document of 1970 incorporated a specific commitment to adult education provision. The Health Education Bureau was established in 1978, the same year that the NCEA (1978) issued its discussion document on award structures for recurrent education.

In 1979 ACOT, the agricultural training authority, was established and fifteen adult education organisers were appointed to examine existing provision of adult education courses and facilities, and to liaise with other interested parties to identify the educational needs of adults in their areas. Despite this, the commitment of the White Paper on Education Development (1980) was muted and promised no more than that adult education activities would be developed 'as resources allow' (p. 94). The stringent guidelines on fees that followed in the early 1980s were low points in state commitment to adult education. In April 1980 it was announced that all adult education class fees were to be increased by 40 per cent from the 1980/81 session. The circular directed that adult education fees must 'at least cover all the cost in maintaining and providing these courses, i.e. costs of instruction, heating, lighting, class materials, advertising, etc.' This was objected to by the President of AONTAS, Seamus O'Grady, at its 1980 Conference (O'Grady, 1980). A further circular in 1982 set minimum fees for different categories of courses, and this in turn was criticised as undue centralisation by the AONTAS President at its 1982 AGM (O'Grady, 1982). Carey (1981) drew attention to the fact that directly or indirectly adult education was the concern of at least nine government departments and in the absence of an inter-departmental committee there were signs of a lack of coordination, particularly in relation to funding. If this seemed to confirm the marginal status of adult education in the critical domain of state funding, worse was to follow in the *Programme for Action in Education 1984-1987*. Of this, Tom Inglis (1989), Director of AONTAS, was to complain: 'Not alone is there no chapter on adult education; not alone is there no section on adult education; not alone is there not one recommendation in relation to adult education; but the words "adult education" never occur once in the whole document.'

During the 1990s much faith was placed in the government's proposal to publish the Green Paper on Education as a preamble to substantial change and legislation. Expectations were positive in the light of the prioritising of training for young unemployed adults, literacy and second chance programmes in the Programme for Economic and Social Progress agreed with the major interest groups in 1991. These commitments were maintained in similar corporatist-type agreements and in the programmes of coalition governments during the 1990s. Yet, official thinking on adult education remained depressingly narrow and even regressive. In all, there was an uncertainty as to what adult education was and what was distinctive about it as a mode of learning. The Green Paper *Education for a Changing World* (1992) linked it in the same chapter with sport reviving fears of a revisitation of adult education as a discretionary activity. The White Paper *Charting Our Education Future* (1995) seemed to differentiate between 'adult education', 'continuing education', and 'training', and sought to resolve the confusion by subsuming it all under further education. The report of the steering committee on the future development of higher education (Higher Education Authority, 1995) was more explicit about these sub-divisions but while it applauded the contribution of the sector to the formation of technical skills, it concluded that the cultivation of social and communary skills did not for the most part merit support through the Higher Education budget.

A more positive indication of government policy has been its response to the certification demands of adult learners (Kelly, 1994) and its recognition of the need to provide a progressive avenue of certification from local community-based courses up to degree level. A national certification authority, TEASTAS, had been established by the Minister for Education in 1995, and the Qualifications (Education and Training) Act (1999) provided for the establishment of a National Qualifications Authority of Ireland with two councils overseeing education and training awards in higher education (HETAC) and further education (FETAC). This, according to the 2000 Adult Education White paper (p. 58), was meant to 'provide a transparent and progressive ladder of qualifications, whereby the learner can negotiate a certificated learning route *via* a combination of providers from foundation level to degree'. The university sector, for its part, as we have seen, is obliged by the Universities Act (1997) to make provision for adult and continuing education. In the 1998 Green Paper on Adult Education there was a state commitment to lifelong learning guided by the policy objectives of tackling poverty and exclusion, developing the skill pool available to the economy, and enhancing the quality of social, cultural and intellectual life. There was a resolution to redress the neglect of the sector in the past, and these commitments are maintained in the 2000 White Paper which identifies six priority areas: consciousness-raising, citizenship, cohesion, competitiveness, cultural development and community building.

Intellectuals

Intellectual interest in adult education as an object of study is of very recent origin in Ireland. Within the universities, adult education departments have traditionally been administrative rather than academic units, though this is no longer the case in relation to the National University of Ireland, Maynooth, and University College, Cork. This academic neglect of adult education until recent decades is reflected in the fact that a bibliography of empirical educational research carried out between 1960 and 1980, excluding unpublished theses, contained no research on adult education (Alvarez, 1981). On the other hand, the increased attention to the area is reflected in the Register of Theses on Educational Topics in Universities in Ireland (Educational Studies Association of Ireland, 1982) and in its subsequent annual supplements. While only one thesis on adult education was written prior to 1973, and that was completed in 1924, nowadays theses on the topic have become common-place. Articles and chapters on adult education appear in academic journals and edited collections. Yet, it still remains a minority research focus: few active researchers would describe it as their primary research interest and it cannot always claim a place in studies of the educational system.

The nature of intellectual engagement with adult education parallels the pattern of individual/collective activism in the promotion of learning opportunities for adults. As a member of the Murphy Committee, Carey, who had studied adult education in the US, was well-placed along with those who acted as research officers to the committee to bring existing theories and conceptualisations relevant to adult education to bear on the deliberations of the committee and the discourse of their reports. Both Murphy Reports were very supportive of research. AONTAS had also recognised the importance of research in adult education from its inception. In 1974, it established a research and development sub-committee with the aid of commercial sponsorship and appointed a research fellow, Maria Slowey, to conduct research on the structure and meaning of women's participation in adult education. Having fallen into abeyance for some years, the sub-committee was reconstituted in 1984, drawing its members from a variety of institutional settings and disciplinary traditions.

During this period the nature of the intellectual consideration of adult education changes, and this can be discerned in the work of the sub-committee, most particularly its 1986 report, *Priority Areas in Adult Education* (AONTAS Research, Planning and Development Sub-Committee, 1986), which decided to prioritise four areas of adult education responses to the underprivileged – the unemployed and unwaged, women, adult basic education, and rural community development. From the 1980s what theorisation of adult education has occurred has been substantially conducted by intellectuals representing specific social movements such as those of feminism and anti-poverty and social exclusion.

Whereas earlier those who occupied the role of intellectual were concerned to advance and expand adult education provision, since the 1980s they have been drawn from those within adult education who valorise particular kinds of adult learning over others as mechanisms for the advance of specific kinds of social change, and from those of other substantive and academic backgrounds who are attracted to it because of its ideological potential. There are few intellectuals who address adult education as an object of study in its own right, apart from its potential for advancing the objectives of social movements, or because of the scholarly issues that it raises.

Adult Education Participants

The adult students themselves contribute to how education is understood, but they do so within received boundaries. By their physical presence they constitute the materiality of adult education and in that sense they have an input into the relative prominence or invisibility of different kinds of adult education. But they are not agents of its conceptualisation and interpretation. The nature of adult education programmes and course content have traditionally been determined by providers on the basis of past experience and perceptions of demand. A bureaucratic model of provision co-existed with a discourse on the concepts of real and felt needs among potential clients (Carey, 1974; Rouine, 1976). In his study in the west of Ireland, Irvine (1974) concluded that decisions on course offerings were taken by committees within the sponsoring bodies, describing the process as 'rather undemocratic' (p. 261). And Clarke (1977) found only one example of self-management in her national study of adult education provided by religious orders. While bureaucratic exclusion of adult learners has eased with the practice of consultation and negotiation between providers and client groups in determining the content of adult learning programmes (Forde, 1996), ideological exclusion restricts the contribution of adult learners to the public understanding of their learning. When academic studies seek to elicit the views of participants in adult learning programmes or where evaluative or publicity material records their experiences, they are processed through the conceptual schemes or ideological filters of the authors. Sometimes those with recent experience of adult learning programmes get to contribute directly to intellectual discourse in the form of conferences, journals or edited collections. But it is those who prove themselves to be competent enunciators of approved texts who seem to be invited. To again invoke Gramsci (1971) on the status of intellectual, all adult learners will have some understanding of what is happening to them but only the understandings of some are given exposure and legitimacy.

Themes and Their Textualisation

Despite the conceptual re-shaping of the area, and the many social and ideological changes over the period, the themes of adult education discourse appear not to have changed greatly since the 1970s. As the detail of Table 15.4 makes clear, the focus has been on issues of provision, participation and benefit. Table 15.4 draws on three sources, representing each of the last three decades, to illuminate the strong performative character of adult education discourse. The themes representing the final Murphy Report (1973) are drawn from the totality of its recommendations. The Kenny Report, *Lifelong Learning* (1984), provided a summary of what an analysis of the submissions made to it identified as the major impediments to the development of adult education at that time. The Irish research for the Euro-Delphi study invited 'selected samples of knowledgeable individuals' (Murphy, 1996) to give their understanding of adult learning needs and the challenges and issues confronting them. Represented, therefore, are members of a government-appointed committee of inquiry into adult education, groups and individuals who made submissions to a later commission, and a selection of policy-makers, practitioners, researchers and educational commentators representing different areas of adult learning.

The appearance of an over-arching consensus reflects the practitioner-basis of the discourse and disguises difference. Those who are involved in the advocacy and development of adult education, for whatever purpose, will seek to maximise the opportunities for their favoured form of adult learning and to motivate adults to avail of these opportunities, and will require a sense of common purpose and perceived benefit to maintain their commitment and collective engagement. It should not surprise, therefore, that over the three decades covered in Table 15.4 certain themes recur: the importance of adult education; its social function and entitlement to expansion and greater funding; guidance and counselling; fears of co-optation; systematisation, accreditation and professionalisation; and legislation. Some of the differences over the period are revealed in the language: access rather than participation signifies the existence of systemic and cultural impediments to participation rather than personal motivation, and reflects the more explicit recognition of disparities of power involved in educational processes including curriculum and ethos as well as the more obvious spheres of certification and entry requirements. The greater prominence of accreditation in more recent times also acknowledges the links between certified knowledge, power and opportunity.

Table 15.4 Themes in Irish Adult Education Discourse

Murphy Report (1973)	Lifelong Learning (1984, pp.67-68)	Euro-Delphi Study: Ireland (1995) (Murphy, 1996)
• 'Urgency and importance' of adult education to be recognised by all. • Vocational/economic, personal development, remedial and political roles for adult education. • Inadequate provision and resources. • Accredited programmes/professional qualifications. • The need for government policy and legislation. • Professional training for adult educators. • Provision of guidance and counselling. • The establishment of national and local structures for the development of adult education. • Prioritising of research on functional literacy, motivation to participate, poverty and adult education, techniques of adult education and community development, and the methodology of adult education, with a special emphasis on radio and television provision.	• Perception of adult education as 'a relatively minor adjunct' to second- and third-level education. • Subordinate position in resource allocation. • Tutor training, supply and remuneration. • Absence of adult guidance and counselling. • More flexible access to the mainstream educational system. • Limited opportunities for day-time classes. • More discretionary powers for local decision-making bodies. • Perception among non-statutory providers that their contribution is undervalued. • Need for greater funding of non-statutory provision without a surrendering of independence.	• The importance and necessity of adult education. • The mission of adult education in combating inequality and exclusion. • The need for legislation. • The importance of consultation, participation and partnership. • Easier access to relevant, accredited education. • Accredited training for adult educators. • Reduction in bureaucracy.

Redemption

The main differences in the discourse are revealed with the textualisation of these themes in relation to the different kinds of adult learning which emerged from the 1960s. Yet, despite the differences in their substantive objectives, they share a common ideological orientation to redemption. This is exemplified by the assumption on the part of providers/advocates that they know what adults need and how they ought to change so as to reposition them according to some vision of their essentialised and rightful relationship to society/world/cosmos. Redemption is used somewhat differently by Shilling (1993) and Popkewitz (1998). It is very explicit in literacy, second chance and community education programmes but, on inspection, it is also true of continuing education and earlier varieties of adult education. Two quotations, almost three decades apart, characterise redemptive ideology:

> A recurring observation in many of the submissions was 'to get the people to appreciate the need for and value of adult education'. Unless the need is felt, the effort will not be made. We would accept as a priority, appreciation programmes in adult education itself, i.e. programmes designed to excite people to want what they need (Interim Murphy Report, 1970, p. 13).

> This question (what is needed for women to move beyond personal development) would have addressed the issue much better, if it had asked what is needed to politicise personal development education for women and prevent it becoming an exercise focused solely on personal symptoms, spirituality and individual healing? My immediate answer to this question ... is that we need feminist/politicised facilitators who are able to incorporate social analysis, radical politics and feminism into course content which is also capable of meeting the felt and expressed needs of many women for a focus on their personal and domestic lives (Ryan, 1999).

These quotations serve to reveal some of the distinctive features of redemption in adult education discourse. There is a vanguardism (the assumption of knowledge, obligation and duty) in identifying targets for redemption and specifying their needs. It is non-reflexive in relation to what constitutes redemption. The agency of its recipients is acknowledged only in conformity, and the refusal of redemption is explained in terms of misrecognition or structural resistance.

Table 15.5 outlines some of the forms which redemption has taken in Irish adult education discourse. The first two varieties of redemptive discourse have existed since the 1970s. Firstly, there is the objective of providing for personal improvement through role education. Its rationale is to develop more knowledgeable, happier, fulfilled individuals who would contribute to a better society by their greater efficiency, consideration and sensitivity in the enactment of their social roles, be they civic, social, occupational or personal. This reflects a broad satisfaction with the structure of society and seems to assume that whatever improvements are required are capable of being effected by better role performance by individuals, rather than by changes in role definitions or in the relationships between roles. Even with new work demands and arrangements, the assumption remains that the individual's self-fulfilment and society's needs are essentially complementary and compatible. Secondly, there is the aspiration to foster individual adjustment to social and technological change. The intention is to help people to cope with the phenomenon of change, and particularly with periods of accelerated technological change, and with temporary phases of unemployment by forming adjustable, mobile and trainable persons. Change is seen to be inevitable and, once the necessary adjustments are made, benign and representing progress. Contemporary versions stress the need to establish or maintain competitive advantage in international trading and attractiveness to investment, and social cohesion and community integration and responsiveness. Active reflection is not expected and the main requirement of people is that they would rise to the challenge of change and modify and adjust to reap the potential benefits.

While these themes of role performance and adaptability are ongoing in adult education discourse, during the 1980s more socially critically perspectives were introduced and the need to broaden the nature of reflection to encompass a consideration of ideology, stratification and power was recognised by a number of researchers and practitioners involved in adult learning (O'Sullivan, 1980d, 1982; AONTAS Research, Planning and Development Sub-Committee, 1986). The inspiration for this change of perspective can be traced to the writings of Freire and later those of Mezirow, to the social criticism of the women's movement and to European social theorists such as Habermas and Bourdieu. This influence is to be found in two new forms of redemptive discourse – empowerment and emancipation. Empowerment seeks to put people in control of their lives by removing whatever is limiting them from becoming makers of their own future, individually and collectively. This can take the form of self-analysis and social analysis, changing one's personal beliefs and interpretations which act against one's true interests, and generally removing whatever impediments there are to one's capacity for personal and social change. Included are interpretations of Freire's conscientisation and Mezirow's perspective transformation which confined themselves to personal change or, where they aspire to collective change, fall short of seeking to advance specific political solutions. Emancipation is not necessarily radical in the conventional sociopolitical sense. It differs from empowerment as a form of redemption in its dualist interpretation of social conditions and the specificity of its political solutions. Nor are all programmes in adult education advocating radical change emancipatory in this sense. CORI's discourse, for instance, on social transformation positions the participants in transformative programmes as agents in determining the nature of the

Table 15.5 Features of Redemption in Irish Adult Education Discourse

Varieties	Role Education	Adaptability to change	Empowerment	Emancipation
	Enabling people to enact their social roles in a more functional manner.	Coping with and adapting to social and technological change.	Putting people in control of their lives.	Designated social and political transformation.
Manifestations	Parenting, citizenship, family, occupational learning, etc. Later: Time/Stress management, and work/home balance programmes.	Upgrading and reskilling for workers; training for new work practices; adaptation to social change. Later: training for national competitiveness.	Social and personal development programmes; some adult education programmes for social change; some applications of Freire's and Mezirow's theories.	Anti-colonial, Catholic social reconstructionist, feminist and egalitarian programmes.
Vanguardism	Functionally conservative. Later: Liberal functionalist/ Human Resource management.	Regulated modernisers, guardians of tradition. Later: technical/competitive rationalities.	Assumption of skill and knowledge in critical analysis.	Ideologically initiated and possessors of truth.
Closure	Limited regulation of learning; space for learner agency in accessing knowledge. Later: more interventionist and regulative.	More politically explicit, but eclectic. Later: more systematised.	Specific in the identification of the targets for empowerment.	Totalising political ideologies.

transformation. The clearest example of emancipatory discourse in recent times is to be found in feminist texts. Earlier manifestations would have been O'Rahilly's Catholic social reconstructionism and, further back, the de-anglicisation efforts of the Gaelic League. All of these would qualify as emancipatory because of the incorrigibility of their social diagnosis and the inviolability of their prescriptions for change.

Need/Entitlement

While these varieties of redemption differ in their political and ideological substance, they share a similar relationship, characterised by vanguardism, limited reflexivity, and circumscribed student agency, within adult education between provider and participant. There is a consistent desire, of a kind that would be interpreted in the tradition of Nietzsche and Foucault as a 'will to power', to re-engage with adults who are beyond the influence of initial education for the purpose of changing them in ways that they have yet to recognise as beneficial. This subordination of the agency of the adult learner was not a problem for the form of adult education operating in the 1970s when expert knowledge and the goodness of education went unquestioned. It runs counter, however, to the expressed principles of some forms of redemption such as those which espouse more populist, participative and egalitarian approaches to learning, its content and authorities, and in the process valorise student autonomy, personal empowerment and self-direction. This is discursively reconciled by means of the need/entitlement construct. In this, need refers to a personal deficiency, the absence of something which requires to be put right to establish an equilibrium. Entitlement establishes one's right to have the need satisfied and the obligation of others to make this possible. Whereas need refers to a condition of the individual, entitlement invokes a moral community with responsibilities to one another. In more socially static forms of redemption, the individual need (for learning, training, literacy, etc.) generates and justifies the entitlement. In more socially transformative forms of redemption, the need is identified, in the context of the moral entitlement to a different kind of society, in relation to impediments to its realisation in the personal psychology, consciousness and structural position of its proposed beneficiaries. A number of examples from throughout the period under review will help to illuminate the deployment of the need/entitlement construct in adult education discourse.

The final report of the Murphy Committee identified needs in relation to agricultural, industrial, commercial, social and religious roles, e.g. remedial and 'topping up' education, day release courses, vocational training, courses in trade union organisation and industrial relations, political education, education for leisure and education for christian values. The more static version is to be found in the interim report. In its view, education should initially aim at enabling the poor 'to live better, in their domestic economy, even within their low-income situation' (p. 20), and later to provide a means of improvement for individual poor people. For housewives, educational activity was seen as a means of ameliorating the unnecessary hard routine characterised by budgetary problems and confinement to the home (p. 21). A more dynamic view of the needs/entitlements of poverty groups is to be found in the final Murphy report (pp 80-82) where the emphasis is on the exploration of conditions which facilitate and sustain poverty and related social problems, though it does appear to confine its explanatory perspective primarily to the growth of bureaucracy. In both reports, however, a consensus view of role prevails in which what is expected of individuals in social positions is considered to be settled and beyond dispute, and therefore not demanding critical reflection. For instance, Irish values, beliefs and culture are assumed to be homogenous and are presented throughout both reports as the 'given', established yardstick for evaluating innovation and change, rather than being acknowledged as suitable objects for analysis, justification and possible modification. In more recent years, role needs are more likely to be articulated in terms of the discourse of liberal functionalism and human resource development.

Needs/entitlements in relation to adaptability are outlined throughout the final Murphy Report. The following example from the Report anticipates a similar diagnosis to be found in adult education discourse almost three decades later: 'the adaptability needed to develop one's true potential, especially in a rapidly changing society, most be nurtured throughout one's lifetime by systematic adult education' (p. 4). The Murphy Reports are more openly selective in preparing individuals to interpret, evaluate and actively determine their response to change. New ideas, particularly those emanating from the mass media (Interim Report, p. 13; Final Report, pp 23 and 74) and from a 'Europe committed to economic and merely human objectives' (Final Report, p. 20) are considered to demand critical orientation. Yet, adults 'should be able to see and grasp' the opportunities produced by technological advances (Interim Report, p.13) and provided with 'programmes of liberal education which may help to avoid the dehumanising effects of repetitive manipulation of products and machines' (Final Report, p. 73). While the 2000 White Paper construes lifelong learning more comprehensively, increasingly since the mid-1990s lifelong learning needs have come to be invoked more systematically in policy discourse on the maintenance of Irish economic success, both in terms of productivity and attractiveness to multinational investment (Joint Committee on Lifelong Learning, 2001).

In welcoming the emphasis in the adult education Green Paper on community education as an empowering process, CORI (1999, p. 30) explains that 'as a result of its focus on collective advancement, community education tends to be a very participative process in which the empowerment of individuals, families and communities is an important guiding principle'. It quotes with approval the following summary of an approach to education where empowerment is central:

> This approach means working with rather than for people to develop their innate skills and capacities in order to enable them to gain a greater measure of control over their lives; it means affirmation and reinforcement of their belief in themselves and in their own worth. It means facilitating the process by means of which people develop their ability, will, and confidence to manage their own affairs; it means respecting their way of doing things without attempting to impose solutions (Paz, 1990, p. ix).

Connolly (1996) specifies the needs/entitlements relating to emancipatory learning among 'women who are oppressed in a uniquely personal, political and social way' but who 'identify their need for a particular, narrowly-focused personal development programme to overcome the personal powerlessness endemic to their experience in this patriarchal capitalist society'. Pointing out that 'some do not make the transition from personal empowerment to collective action', she continues:

> When the emancipatory learning process is foremost, the outcomes are different. The role of adult educators in this context is to facilitate the process. The adult educators have to subscribe to the full meaning of adult education. Their role is ultimately to bring about emancipatory social change. When the adult educators fully understand this through their own emancipatory learning, then they can implement it.

> Community development without the essential element of emancipatory learning domesticates the activists and subverts the possibility of radical social change. Emancipatory learning is mediated through the agency of adult educators who have undergone an emancipatory learning process, themselves.

The need/entitlement construct operates not alone rhetorically, but also at the level of socially reconstructing the subjectivities of the participants in the adult learning process. It directs attention to participants and appears to allocate a central position to their requirements in programme planning. Discourse in prospectuses, official reports and theoretical accounts can appear as student-centred. But there is limited reflexivity in relation to the paradigms of social change which inform the specification of learner needs/entitlements. The value judgements and social interpretations implicit in the paradigm thus remain concealed, unexplicated or unchallenged by counter texts. In this manner they acquire the robustness of taken-for-granted constructs, and the associated individual needs/entitlements assume an existence and plausability of their own. At a legitimatory level, this justifies the distribution of knowledge and the formation of subjectivities: the issue of who is to be given access to different forms of educational experience becomes a technical problem of need assessment while the ideological contradictions go unrecognised. In the process, vanguardism is variously reconstituted as visionary, philanthropy, social service, enlightenment, commitment, or liberation.

Theorising Adult Education

Even the most basic theorisation of Irish adult education would have revealed the operation of these varieties of redemption together with their associated needs/ entitlements, forced their greater explication, and made them the object of discourse. Exploring the world of concepts, interpretations and legitimations in a body of thought beyond its immediate application in the form of 'recipe knowledge' is the distinctive task of intellectuals. Yet the limited number of intellectuals involved in the task of producing adult education knowledge only partly explains the absence of a theoretical discourse in the field. More significant is the manner in which those who seem to be best positioned, because of academic background and position, deployed their intellectual resources. Intellectuals themselves became caught up in the professional orientation of much of adult education discourse with its emphasis on provision, advocacy and operational issues. Even where intellectual discourse incorporated conceptual and ideological critique, it tended to be employed to advance particular varieties of redemption. In all, this yields a performative discourse in which the implications for practice predominate. The result has been a number of erratic and unsuccessful efforts at thematisation and a circumscribed theorisation of a limited number of texts within the field. This has already been signalled in the failure to conceptualise adult education other than holistically, as all the education engaged in by adults, or materially, as a sector of educational provision.

The hopes and aspirations among the small number of those positioned as intellectuals within adult education that a theoretical discourse could be developed from the developing system of provision and advocacy had been positive. Cathcart (1989) recalled the hope that once adult education ceased to be confessional and Roman Catholic in orientation, it would see the end of restrictiveness and ideological intrusion on the content of adult learning engagements. Henceforth, he believed, the articulation of the purpose of adult education would be openly contested rather than dogmatically controlled.

> Dissident opinion had no longer to be muted for fear of the consequences of its public expression; the period of 'mind you I said nothing' was over. Courses in sensitive areas of the adult education curriculum could be the occasions of fruitful and critical surveys of the diversity of approaches rather than presentations of dogmatic exposition.

Though formulated as late as the mid-1980s, the agenda for theoretical inquiry into adult education in terms of its concepts and meaning, set out by the Research,

Planning and Development Sub-Committee of AONTAS (1986), was ambitious for its time. It proclaimed the need for 'a firm theoretical foundation – a set of well argued propositions which will help delineate and classify the different types of adult learning and the specific contribution which each of these make to Irish society' (p. 31). It pointed out that certain concepts used to describe various activities such as functional literacy, daytime provision, consciousness raising, education for life, community education, second chance learning, etc. had become the taken-for-granted language of the adult educator. While it acknowledged that this was of benefit in mobilisation, advocacy and fund-raising, it cautioned that 'rhetoric can often hide important questions':

> it becomes difficult to ask questions about the role of adult education in these areas. For instance, it is difficult to be against community education – in fact it is difficult to be against anything with the prefix community ... This is part of the problem when the language of adult education becomes 'household words'. It becomes difficult to raise critical questions about what is worthwhile in adult education (p. 29).

The priorities for research established by the Final Murphy Report in 1973 reflected the interests and concerns of the practitioner/provider base which for the most part generated them, and, as we have seen, continue to resonate thematically in adult education discourse up to the present. In this context the concerns are understandable. Who attends and why? What difficulties do students have and why do they drop out? How are adults to be made aware of the existence and benefits of adult education? What are the accreditation needs of adult students? What learning and assessment arrangements best suit adults? Understandably, the earliest academic studies of Irish adult education were empirical inquiries into participation and motivation, all conducted in the late 1970s (Daly, 1978; Slowey, 1979; O'Sullivan, 1981). The author's own study of students taking the UCC Diploma in Social Study throughout Munster, however, was primarily concerned with the impact of the course on the personal, social and political lives of the students. It was also framed within a theory of personal change that integrated the symbolic interactionism of traditional socialisation theory, the constructionism of Berger and Luckmann and the critical edge of Freire's conscientisation. There was much in the findings of the study that invited a consideration of the function of adult education in Irish society. As well as preporting a sense of instrumental (skills and knowledge) and personal empowerment, the students believed that they had changed politically: they had come to adopt a more critical perception of Irish society – more inequality and social domination than they had previously perceived – and their sense of social and political efficacy, particularly when acting collectively, had increased. But it was the 'facts' in the study, rather than their sociological, philosophical and political elaboration, that engaged the consciousness of adult educators at that time.

This delineation of what was to be developed as adult education knowledge is further reflected some years later when the Kenny Report in 1984 bemoaned 'a dearth of statistical data on adult education in Ireland' (p. x). In the absence of an audience there was no obvious forum for theorising adult education. It was necessary to publish 'Socialisation, Social Change and Ideology in Adult Education' (O'Sullivan, 1980d), which added Bourdieu's emerging writing on education to the perspectives mentioned earlier, in the National Institute of Adult Education, England and Wales journal *Adult Education*, where it was admittedly still novel to suggest that contemporary French social theory might have a relevance for adult education. Nor was an effort to begin with the existing discourse and practice of adult education, and seek to excavate the models of social change and legitimatory constructs and techniques embedded in it, any more successful. The *AONTAS Review* published the author's 'Adult Education, Social Change and the Interpretive Model' in 1983 with a private caution that it was unlikely to be of interest to many of its readers.

Wilson's (1985) attempt to seek a forum for the application of Gramsci's ideas at the 1985 AONTAS conference on community education in Cork was only marginally more successful. Coming from the background of the Ulster People's College in Belfast, he was openly confrontational in challenging some of the uncritical approaches to community education presented at the conference, and this generated considerable interest in and requests for information on Gramsci's writings at the time. However, despite a spirited and accessible account of Gramsci's theory of hegemony, and how it might translate into a theory of adult education for social transformation by helping the participants to discover the ideological nature of their common-sense understanding of the world, it never succeeded in becoming a feature of Irish adult education discourse. The fate of Gramsci in Irish adult education thought is a further illumination of the failure of theoretical themes to establish themselves and develop as texts.

Fleming, initially in the AONTAS Research, Planning and Development Sub-Committee Report (1986) *Priority Areas in Adult Education*, and later in various contexts including a further AONTAS report, *For Adults Only: A case for adult education in Ireland* (Bassett *et al.*, 1989), sought to introduce an aspect of the theories of Jürgen Habermas as a means of reconceptualising adult education activities and objectives. Habermas, a major representative of the neo-Marxist tradition associated with the critical theory of the Frankfurt School, was concerned with the manner in which human freedom had been restricted by various forms of repression and domination, and sought to identify what needed to be done to create a just and democratic society. Fleming drew on Habermas's theory of human interests, and the knowledge they generate, to classify adult education courses: technical, practical and emancipatory knowledge derived respectively from the orientation to control and regulate the world, to understand it, and to attain freedom from delusions about it. While Fleming was concerned that the technical kind of learning was dominant in the existing meaning and practice of Irish adult education, and that the aim of understanding one's place in the world was undervalued, the main focus of his application of Habermas was to establish the objective of emancipatory learning as an integral part of Irish adult education discourse and practice. Without it, he doubted if it would be valid to speak of adult education at all: 'to merit the title adult education, a programme or course has to provide opportunities for all three kinds of learning to take place, especially emancipatory learning' (Bassett *et al.*, 1989, p. 33). Fleming expanded on the implications of adopting emancipatory learning as an objective in adult education programmes. It would involve helping learners to recognise the unreflective manner in which their understanding of the world had been shaped by political, religious, psychological and cultural forces, and would seek to facilitate a critical review of these forces and the frameworks of meaning and interpretation through which their influence operates. He offered the practices and ideas of Freire, Lovett and Mezirow as examples of emancipatory adult learning.

Fleming's intervention proved to be successful in adding technical, practical and, in particular, emancipatory learning to the repertoire of concepts employed in Irish adult education discourse. But its contribution to adult education thought was a further reified and normative typology rather than a critique of the classification and objectives of adult education in the light of Habermas's thought. There was neither elaboration nor disputation. Even the reservations expressed by avowedly sympathetic commentators on Habermas's theory of cognitive interests, such as the plausibility of the orientation to critical enquiry as a deep-rooted anthropological thrust alongside those of control and understanding, as well as linguistic, conceptual and methodological issues (McCarthy, 1988), remained hidden, as did the contested nature of Habermas's theory of society and social change. Nor is there any evidence that the many other possibilities for adult education thought in Habermas's voluminous writings, other than on knowledge and human interest, such as those on language, communication and legitimation crisis, were mined for new and challenging ways of analysing the practice of Irish adult education. Some use has been made of Habermas's writings on communication, the conditions for its maintenance and use in establishing rationally-derived agreement between people, in particular his construct of 'ideal speech situation' (O'Sullivan, 1993b; Mezirow, 1996). A more critical contextualisation of Habermas's belief in the capacity for symmetrical communication to erode the delusions and myths holding unequal structures in position is to be found in Inglis's (1997) critique of the absence of a debate about power itself in programmes which claim as their objective the empowerment of their learners. Yet, at best these constitute examples of erratic and unrelated thematisation rather than the emergence over time of a coherent text.

The editors of *Radical Learning for Liberation* (Connolly *et al.*, 1996), which included Fleming himself, correctly identified the circumscribed character of Irish adult education knowledge when they observed that 'writing, reading, thinking and research' are among the areas of adult education 'often pushed down the agendas of our meetings and frequently even out of our discourse'. But their explanation in terms of the priorities forced on adult educators because of their limited resources and policy recognition only partly captures the forces involved. This becomes even more evident with a more sustained production of knowledge about transformative adult education (CMRS, 1992c; CORI, 1997c, 1999), feminist adult learning (Fagan, 1991; Byrne *et al.*, 1996; Connolly, B., 1996, 1997, 1999; Byrne and Lyons, 1999; Ryan, 1999) and adult literacy programmes (NALA Research and Development Sub-Committee, 1988; du Vivier, 1991; Morgan *et al.*, 1997; Bailey and Coleman, 1998) particularly throughout the 1990s.

More than a circumstantial omission, the regulation of knowledge production in adult education discourse is a constituent feature of Irish adult education practice. The orientation to redemption in Irish adult education discourse and practice sets horizons on the pursuit of knowledge. This is not necessarily a matter of explicit censorship. Doxic-like, it is more likely to operate from a conviction that core objectives and principles are valid, settled and established, and do not constitute a productive theme for discourse. To suggest otherwise would be interpreted as a distraction, academicism or reactionary. There are substantial and procedural variations in the light of the variety of redemption involved, and the nature of its closure and vanguard. But the overall pattern is for discourse to follow along predictable textual lines. This takes the form of a 'theoretical glass ceiling' on discourse which excludes whatever might challenge or disrupt key verities. Accordingly, the vast edifice of social, cultural and political theory, and more specifically adult education thought, is only drawn on, if at all, in support of received, established and accepted positions. There continues to be a built-in privileging of 'fact gathering', be it through quantitative or qualitative methodologies, to be used in advocacy, fund-raising, and in programme planning, delivery and assessment.

In a more pluralist site of knowledge production what would experience exclusion in one text might be expected to be foregrounded in the form of a counter-text. This has not been the experience of the transformative, literacy and feminist texts in Irish adult education. Nor do they address one another. Indeed the CMRS/CORI representation of inequality, empowerment and social transformation explicitly excludes a gender reading of the social condition, prescriptions for change and social objectives involved. Its questioning of how the understanding of literacy is constructed in the Adult Education Green Paper (CORI, 1999) is exceptional and provides a mere glimpse of what is missing by way of integrating, contesting and interlocking meanings between the texts. The feminist text contains critiques of some of the dominant approaches within community education and personal development programmes, including Freirean conscientisation and critical reflection, humanist group work, and mainstream psychological approaches to counselling (Connolly, B., 1996, 1997, 1999; Ryan, 1999). It proclaims the view that, as places where people explore feelings and desires, personal development courses 'need to be actively colonised by feminists acting outside of liberal humanist and religious discourses, because otherwise they will have anti-feminist effects' (Ryan, 1999). Yet, it does not engage directly with the discourse of CORI on empowerment and social transformation where some of these approaches feature.

The failure of these three texts to experience any significant intertextuality that transgresses or even contests has already been demonstrated in relation to social transformation in the section on CORI's Christian Communitarianism in Chapter 10. Here, the theorised nature of the feminist adult education text facilitates its further illumination. As we have seen, early forms of redemption did not enter Irish adult education discourse from a theoretical position but rather from an urge to action in the servicing of needs that were seen to be self-evidently valid. Even empowerment relied for long on no more than a number of key concepts and quotations from Freire to provide a legitimatory discourse for what were popular concepts in the civil rights, women's and community movements such as false consciousness, consciousness raising and praxis. Feminist discourse on Irish adult education is distinguished from other forms of redemptive adult education in the diversity of the theoretical perspectives which it introduces and in its deployment, in furthering the liberation of women, of complex and contested views and interpretations from international scholarship on the self, society, the position of women, change, learning and pedagogy. In this sense, feminist adult education is the only manifestation of theorised adult education texts in the Irish experience. As such, it does generate an intertextuality in its theoretical, conceptual and political diversity, but it is one which it operates to regulate and to control.

Other texts are used as points of departure, negatively or positively. The absence of a monolithic feminism is acknowledged and the tensions between psychologistic, liberal, radical, Marxist, and post-structuralist positions are recognised. But these are prematurely resolved by interpreting them segmentally, as focusing on different systems of women's oppression, or tactically, as incrementally building on one another in political mobilisation and action. Unredeemable texts remain the 'other' and do not get to speak for themselves in the absence of a counter-text. In the feminist text they are represented in a manner that serves the interest of the host text and domesticates their most challenging meanings. For instance, while the challenges of post-structuralism for dogma, conviction and dualisms are mentioned, they are not incorporated into the prescriptions of the text for feminist educational practice, where truth and error, certainty and delusion, liberation and domestication, and the enlightened and unenlightened recur in its representation of meaning, subjectivity and action. Where the feminist text treats of student resistance to feminist pedagogy or political agenda, it is explained in terms of the flawed or compromised nature of their emotional and rational responses. This is in contrast to the representation of those students who profess themselves to enjoy and benefit from, and adopt the interpretations of such courses. These are deemed to be taking control of their lives and opening up to the truth of their personal and political situation. Where adult educators are only willing to acknowledge the agency of students when they display conformity with their views and approaches we are observing the intolerance of difference that derives from the certainty of doxa.

The nearer one gets to the emancipatory end of the redemptive spectrum, the greater the incomprehension in the face of difference. This regulation of intertextuality explains not only subordinated voices of Irish adult education discourse but also its self-imposed restraints on its own development. This is not a matter of expecting adult education knowledge to be produced outside of ideology. Rather, it is to highlight the sphere of ambivalence, contingency and fragmentation in adult education engagements, such as has been revealed in post-modern and post-structural scholarship, including the work of feminist educators (Pitt, 1997; Roman and Eyre, 1997; Hughes, 2000) that is foreclosed in adopting a redemptive ideology. This is illuminated in a rare outsider analysis of an adult education programme – a study of women's groups by feminists who are not within the adult education tradition (O'Donovan and Ward, 1999) – where we find a greater leaning towards difference than deficit in explaining the responses of those women who remain unpoliticised and unfeminised, less closure on the social implications of feminism, limited vanguardist assumptions, and less selectivity in the acknowledgement of the agency of the participants. In this they appear sensitive to the dilemmas represented by the 'resistant' student for post-structuralist feminist adult educators. In Hughes's (2000) account:

> … the perplexity many of us experience at such resistance draws attention to a key disjunction in any emancipatory project. This is the way that liberation and subjugation go hand in hand. Our concern at learners' resistances to the knowledge we offer rests in our belief in the legitimacy of our projects. We actually do believe we have 'better' knowledge at least some, if not most, of the time. In liberating the resistant learner, nonetheless, the danger is that we may seek to subjugate their preferred or prior ways of knowing. As educators, we are appropriators of the subject even though we might prefer to think of ourselves as relatively benign ones.

According to Hughes, this calls for an acknowledgement by adult educators of the tensions that resistance exposes in liberatory discourse:

One core tension relates to the truth claims contained therein. One of the challenges that poststructuralism offers those of an emancipatory persuasion is a challenge to truth-claims ... Feminism, for example, is based on a truth narrative that men oppress women. Poststructuralism suggests that this is not always the case. Feminism contains within it the unitary category 'woman' as its founding subject. Poststructuralism suggests there is no founding subject but that identities are constituted within discourses. Feminism promises a better world by following the 'feminist' way or, of course, ways. Poststructuralism questions the possibility of this. There may simply be different worlds in which women and men live.

Inglis's (1997) article on the nature of power in debate and practice relating to empowerment and emancipation in adult education at times moves outside the safety net of textual certainty. He hovers between empowerment and emancipation as understood here. However, his representation of empowerment is limiting and domesticates its potential in discourse and practice in a similar fashion to the regulative practices of the feminist texts. But he does acknowledge that adult educators committed to emancipatory learning may have 'become caught up in the contradictions of the post-modern era':

> On the one hand, they are constrained by Foucauldian pessimism which binds their discourse and the search for truth into an endlessly evolving politics of power in which they implement discipline and order. On the other hand, adult educators can be enthused by Habermasian optimism, namely that power and its colonising effects on the life world can be overcome; that it is possible to reach a just, free and equal society through rational communication.

He does not attempt to resolve this contradiction and argues that we understand our lives between these two extremes. Emancipation, he feels, may well involve 'a continual juggling between the two'. The central theme of his article is that the involvement in this process of those who are selected for emancipation from oppression must be facilitated by providing them with an accessible theoretical framework which would enable them to see how power is implicated not only in their personal, social and political condition but also in their engagements with educational institutions, learning programmes and teachers. It is not clear, however, if he intends emancipatory education and educators to be exempted. Having come to the conclusion, after two decades of involvement in socially-critical adult education, that the very opposite is essential, the author's own efforts at self-interrogation led him to construct a framework to facilitate reflexivity among providers and teachers who would seek to change others or society, according to whatever ideology (O'Sullivan, 1993b). It argued that it was incumbent on those who operated with such a 'will to power' to include themselves within their analysis of power (O'Sullivan, 1994b).

But in such situations, theorists tend to be unwilling to turn their theories on themselves. It is not in the interests of redemptive adult education to encourage the 'juggling' of meaning that Inglis speaks of; rather, it is in its nature to regulate it together with any conceptual framework that invites it. It is the discourse that would represent the efforts to understand the contradictions and tensions of the contemporary world, of which working through the tensions between the Foucauldian drive to discipline and the Habermasian faith in rational communication is just one example, that is absent from Irish adult education. And this is set to persist as long as redemption continues to be a constitutive force in Irish adult education. It is ironic and regrettable that this has been illuminated in relation to feminist adult education which, as a sphere of knowledge production, is almost alone in Ireland in engaging with many of the texts that would be expected to contribute to a more complex intertextual discourse on Irish adult education. It is true that the numbers involved remain a key factor, but the few who are producing theorised adult education knowledge do so within the constraints imposed by a redemptive orientation of the emancipatory variety.

Adult Education Knowledge: Interrogating Structures

It is possible to periodise the textualisation of adult education with less violence to historical development than other areas of education which carry more invasively the cultural legacy of history. Historicising adult education, in the sense of interpreting its understandings and development in the light of particular phases of social, economic and cultural change, is an obvious basis for differentiating within the processes and substance of its knowledge production. However, this study has found it more penetrating to inform the scrutiny of the identification and naming of patterns in the textualisation of adult education by such structural approaches as those used in the study of myth, folk-tales and literary works in the writings of Lévi-Strauss (1969[1949]), Propp (1958[1928]) and Barthes (1970), respectively.

In seeking out the deep structure of myth, the narrative structure of folk-tales, or the codes which regulate the sequence of events, the meaning of situations and the evocation of the cultural assumptions of the readers of literary works, there is a common effort to get behind the content and substance of these forms of cultural production. The textualisation of adult education cannot be said to have a plot, situations or characters in the strictly narrative sense as components of a tale. Yet, it does have human actors, relating to one another in concrete settings seeking a resolution of the conflicts that arise in relation to whatever manifestations of adult learning they attempt to conceptualise and develop. The merit of these broad structural approaches is their invitation to find some sense of underlying order in the diverse agents, conceptualisations and programmes that represent the public face of adult education. This is particularly useful with adult education as an antidote to its pervasive sense of mission, immediacy, individual idealism, self-direction and earnestness. While the phases of development identified in the textualisation of adult education since the 1960s are explicable in terms of social, economic and cultural change in Irish society, a more revealing analysis is achieved by foregrounding the dualisms, in particular that of change/stability, that underpin it.

We have seen how the conceptualisation of manifestations of adult learning changes after the 1970s together with their associated objectives. What is known as adult education appears substantially as a voluntaristic production, dependent on the commitment, advocacy and activism of individuals – educators, intellectuals as well as students – and resists integration and coordination. The state is only erratically involved – seeking to exert some leverage through the appointment of committees of inquiry and taking action in relation to the consumption of resources – until the mid-1990s when it comes to acknowledge adult education as a necessary investment in pursuit of national cohesion, productivity and competitiveness. Yet, there is a stability in its characteristic themes in the form of complaints, anxieties, demands and aspirations, that share a common ideological orientation to redemption, legitimated by means of the construct of need/entitlement. As with Durkheim's (1952[1897]) classic study of suicide, which demonstrated how what appears as the most individualistic of choices in social action nonetheless followed distinct patterns of variations in its occurrence, the production of adult education knowledge over the past half-century in Ireland reveals sameness within diversity, structure amid individuality, and change alongside stability. And because it is a relatively untheorised field of knowledge production with limited reflexivity, it currently lacks the capacity and orientation to reveal and further explicate its structures. Such an agenda, addressing issues that include the subjectivities attracted to adult education, the political economy of its material base, and the political possibilities for its destabilisation and reconstruction offers a fascinating challenge to adult educators.

Epilogue to Part Four

Following the macro issues of cultural transformation in Part Two and the middle-range processes, by which education is implicated in what people become, in Part Three, this final section sharpened the focus further. The three analytical components of policy paradigms – concepts, agents and texts – it selected for attention have already been implicated in the transition from a theocentric to a mercantile paradigm of the institution of education and across the wide range of paradigms considered within the LEM domain, and as such have been studied in terms of their role in these transitions and reconstructions. In addressing them in some detail in terms of their contribution to cultural politics in their own right – the ubiquity and pivotal role of conceptualisation, the variable and creative nature of human agency, and the principles of formation that guide the production of what is known as a particular educational sector – the 'tool box' function of theoretical systems is modelled in relation to the construct of policy paradigm. Mirroring the mechanisms of its construction – the theorist as *bricoleur* using and adapting the resources at hand, the modification of existing concepts to suit particularistic situations, and the 'raiding' of theoretical positions without conceding allegiance – this demonstrates how aspects of the schematisation of policy paradigm can be appropriated as stand-alone constructs in the study of cultural politics or as resources for conceptually expanding previously 'glossed' dimensions of more socially- or behaviourally-based policy studies. Extrapolating from the substantive and analytical features of the micro-politics of policy paradigms considered in this section provides some illumination of this potential.

Since the cultural work around children and childhoods in the 1960s and 1970s, there has been a dramatic transformation in the public attention to childhood. The nature and extent of this is such that it is valid to speak of the emergence of a 'new protectionism'. Since the 1980s, this has been instigated by an unprecedented level of public revelations and media interest relating to 'childhood adversity' (Ferguson *et al.*, 1993), but in particular to what has come to be described as 'child abuse'. Efforts to understand the processes by which 'child abuse' became constructed as a social problem, and the technologies of control including investigation and protection that developed in the light of this, have drawn on a number of dimensions of social change used at various points in this study – the detraditionalisation of authority and trust, a heightened awareness of risk and the limitations of expert knowledge. A vivid feature of the context for these transformations is identified by Ferguson (1996) as 'the impact of a series of scandals and child abuse inquiries which have come to surround every aspect of the child care and protection system – from failures to identify and manage all forms of child abuse within the family ... by Catholic priests ... to the abuse of children in care, and public knowledge of the fact that the safety of children cannot even be guaranteed by removing them from high-risk home situations'.

While contributors to this analysis, to take Ferguson as an example, speak in terms of 'discursive space' and 'the structure of meaning', they do so without fully exploiting the possibilities available to them for their more diversified and discriminating use. Thorpe's (1997) essay review on 'Regulating Late Modern Child Rearing in Ireland', instigated by Ferguson and McNamara's (1996) edited collection *Protecting Irish Children: Investigation, Potential and Welfare*, points in this direction. He describes 'child protection' as an identifiable way of doing social welfare work which includes 'a new social work vocabulary embedded in a discourse which is only very rarely questioned'. He speaks of the irony of child welfare practitioners apparently aware of this, as in transforming 'moral categories into objectifying discourses', but unable to consciously articulate it. Thorpe's application of Baudrillard's writing on the merging of the signified and the sign to demonstrate how the word 'abuse' has become detached from its original use, and in a process of intertextuality (although he does not use the term) takes on new meanings including dissatisfaction with governments and the unaccountable power of the church, is suggestive of some of the resources from cultural politics that could 're-tool' child care practitioners in their self-reflexivity. This is also true of studies of 'ordinary children' which unfortunately tend to be obscured by the focus on high-profile abuse cases. Examples include Devine's (2000) attention to the negotiation of power in the relationships between children and schools, and Deegan's (2002) rethinking of the 'epistemologies of research', in which he draws on Foucault and Popkewitz, in adopting a 'policy-as-discourse methodology' in the study of early childhood discourse in state and policy frameworks on children and families.

Childhood is only one site of application for the study of conceptualisation. Bound up as it is with the other epistemic building blocks of thought, language, signification and intersubjectivity, as well as with the ongoing dynamics of meaning-making such as nodal points of engagement, raiding and appropriation in intertextuality, conceptualisation is ubiquitous in cultural politics. Be it in seeking to establish new educational goals, explaining differences in educational achievement, changing the curriculum, monitoring teacher performance, or identifying new pupil psychologies, it is no exaggeration to say that wherever education is thought of, spoken about and contested issues of conceptualisation are being invoked.

Another central question is that of human agency, which was addressed initially in relation to the field of cultural politics itself and the space it allowed for the actions of individuals and their creative impact on the policy process. In responding to the implications of placing culture at the centre of the analysis, the orientation adopted recognised the ontological depth of society, the analytical separateness of its individual, social and cultural layers, and the emergent qualities that are distinctive and innovative at each level. But, as well as those who would commence with culture, as here, this is also relevant to those who, having centred the economy, social processes or individual psychologies in explaining policy change, come to culture by way of expansion or contextualisation. Whatever the starting point, adopting a 'deep', analytically-separable model of society facilitates a more differentiated explanatory access to the dynamics involved within the policy process.

Apart from historical studies, particularly where archival material is being used, it has not been common in studies of Irish educational policy to treat individual participants in the policy process as forces in their own right as distinct from the positions they occupy as, for instance, politicians, civil servants, or representatives of parents, teachers and management. Something of this is to be found in Gemma Hussey's (1990) diaries and Seán O'Connor's (1986) memoirs, the attribution of negative attitudes to multi-denominational schools to named senior policy figures in education (Hyland, 1989), in the contributions of named educational advisors and academics to the various drafts of the 1992 Green Paper (Walshe, 1999) and in Sugrue's (2004) study of the construction of the Revised Primary School Curriculum.

By centering the issue of human agency around the activities of cultural strangers and contrarians, there is a foregrounding of the basis of their dynamic, as incomprehension, lack of integration or alienation, in the character of their relationship with culture. It also allowed the analysis to move beyond issues of substantive contributions to differentiate between the functions that human agents can perform within the policy process, and to seek to distinguish between human agency and influence (as initiators as distinct from carriers) in a manner that acknowledges the diversity and fluidity of the self in the multiple subject positions that an individual can occupy. We have tracked examples of doxa being challenged, legitimacy being enhanced, the politically-safe testing of public tolerance, and thematic additions. But this no more than touches on the possibilities for the study of the contribution of human agents to the educational policy process that, nonetheless, is constrained by the smallness of the pool of potential subjects and the primary nature of their relationship with those who would become their analysts/interpreters.

When set alongside concepts and agents, exploring the manner in which adult education has been textualised suggests a different kind of application for the conceptual resources provided by the construct of policy paradigm. This involved isolating manifestations of adult learning from their background and signifying them through conceptualisation as different kinds of adult education, tracking the change and level of integration they experienced, and identifying the agents involved. However complicated it may be in starting from a specific policy issue and seeking to identify the processes of meaning-making involved, in terms of its constitution and effects, it is on a different scale from where the focus is on the knowledge production in one field of educational activity of a kind that establishes its positioning as an educational sector. Yet, because this aspires to address a totality rather than an aspect, it facilitates consideration of whatever structuring principles might be operating as well as suggesting comparative inquiries across educational issues, sectors and systems.

The knowledge field defined in terms of special needs, learning support and disability is an obvious target for inquiry, given the extent of change and contestation in conceptualisation, language, texts and authorities it seems to have experienced in recent years. Like adult education, because of its traditionally more marginal position within the educational system it should be possible to establish temporal and intellectual boundaries and points of calibration in its construction. Unlike adult education, but facilitating its analysis, it has experienced its fair share of public and discursive disputes of a kind that engage issues of conceptualisation, legitimacy, classification and intervention all with the capacity to have real material consequences for the sector involved.

Comparatively across paradigms, a number of distinctive features have been identified throughout the study. These include the systematisation of gender equity, the polyvalent conceptualisation of employability, the vibrant and differentiating discursive activity around Travellers' ethnicity, and the deferral and dispersal of the meaning of disadvantage in *pastiche*. Comparative studies across systems of education are more complex. Not alone can it be expected that there would be variations in the theoretical and ideological resources, in personnel and their identities and intellectual formation, and in the social, economic and technological forces that come into play in giving a field of knowledge its distinctive contours, but the basic epistemic building blocks of concepts and language are also likely to diverge. But while challenging, this is a complexity that enhances the illumination of the educational systems drawn into comparison.

However configured or applied, this exploration of aspects of the micro-politics of policy paradigms models the viability of its 'toolbox' function. To engage with the construct of policy paradigm in this selective fashion brings with it the tension between theoretical eclecticism and depth of analysis, with the potential slippage into *pastiche*. The upside is the cultural sensitising and resourcing of educational policy studies.

Conclusion

A Continuing Project

These final pages conclude the book, but the explication of its content continues. Like all interpretations it is partial, situated and should invite revision and elaboration. What has been written of the cultural politics of Irish education bears the influence of subjective forces, intellectual biographies and theoretical frameworks. Reality is always open to being otherwise construed. The author hopes to continue to participate in this further explication of the cultural politics of Irish education and that others will be attracted to it. This conclusion is transitional, linking the interpretations of the book with what might follow at another time and from a variety of commentators. In this vein, some omissions are identified, possibilities for further research are suggested, both in relation to substantive policy issues and the theoretical development of the construct of policy paradigm, and connections are drawn between dimensions from across the sections which have implications for a more public awareness of, engagement with and control of, the strategies of meaning-making in education and their impact and functioning in shaping educational policy and practice.

Since this did not aspire to being a comprehensive treatment of the cultural politics of Irish education – impossible, given the half-century coverage and the detailed analysis in parts – there are obvious omissions that invite further analysis in terms of the construct of policy paradigm. Early years and third-level education received no more than passing reference in advancing the consideration of other topics. The attention paid to cultural nationalism and the Irish language in the reconstruction of the institution of education only marginally begins to correct its neglect in educational policy studies. The cultural politics of educational disability awaits configuration as a research issue, despite the availability of resources – classifications, mobilisation, authorities, legitimation, interventions – pertaining to paradigm formation and contestation, and requires a full-length study in its own right.

Many specific possibilities for research follow from the substantive issues analysed throughout the book. The following are no more than representative of the four sections of the study.

- The recognition of intertextuality as a recurring and central feature of meaning-making in education and the further adaptation of its conceptualisation and language for use in educational inquiry.
- A more elaborate calibration of mutation, to take account of its different manifestations in this study, that may require a new and diversified conceptualisation. It would be revealing to inquire if mutation is as prevalent in the processes of cultural change in other educational systems and to pursue this comparatively in terms of the variable and situated dynamics of educational change.
- The place of culture in educational change was privileged only as a research issue and the schematisation of the construct of policy paradigm was offered,

in its totality or as a 'toolbox' to be drawn from, to researchers who would approach the explanation of educational change from different entry points. It is likely that such a use would suggest further modifications to its schematisation. As it stands, policy paradigm is an integrated theoretical construct, albeit one that privileges culture in its conceptual elaboration. An even more ambitious undertaking would be to expand, to a degree commensurate with that of culture, its psychological, social, political and economic dimensions.

- The monitoring of the mercantile transformation of education as an on-going process and the consideration of the possibilities for its reformulation and reconstruction in terms of social, moral and generative principles.
- An explanation of the relationship between managerialism and corporatism that includes the Higher Education Authority, the new structures dealing with examinations and special education and the Teaching Council.
- Recording instances of resistance to the mercantile paradigm and the management of dissent.
- A rethinking of schooling and religious belief that refuses the modernist dualism of faith and reason, and works towards a post-modern conceptualisation of how religious education might accommodate diversity without limiting formation to a cognitivist engagement with children.
- A more accessible representation of structure as a construct in sociological accounts of inequality and power within the LEM domain that connects more with middle-range and micro interventions.
- The production of a post-deficit sociological discourse on disadvantage/ socioeconomic inequalities in educational performance that moves beyond the deficit/difference dualism and its associated labelling (and disparaging) of theories and theorists.
- An analysis of the meaning and functioning of multiculturalism in discourse – as an empirical reality, political project, mechanism for detraditionalisation, badge/trope of modernity, etc.?
- An examination of the new protectionism, particularly as it affects 'ordinary children', and the functioning of new protectionist discourse as a substitute in solidarity building and moral deliberation.
- A specification of the possibilities for andragogy in adult education that recognise its potential for a generative politics of civil society and the public sphere.

The primary objective of the study was to reveal the relationship between understanding and action in Irish education and to facilitate its incorporation into the public sphere of political deliberation about educational policy. Too often 'glossed' as conceptually and procedurally uncomplicated, the construct of policy paradigm was developed and applied to aspects of Irish educational policy over half a century, to supply and model a theoretical literacy through which the cultural politics of Irish education could be prised open to the depths of its dimensions and mechanisms and exposed to public scrutiny. Apart from the theorising of the construct of policy paradigm and its application, a number of linked topics that arose across the sections are relevant to this objective of revitalising the public sphere. These include the possibilities for the role of the state in policy-making in the context of a mercantile politics and its alternatives, the contributions of intellectuals, and the specification of an andragogical role for adult education.

Drawing on the linkages between policy formulation and implementation in the relationship between state and society, managerial populism was used to differentiate and extend the 'pragmatic gradualism' that Coolahan (1989) diagnoses in the state's advancement of educational change. It is true that in the implementation of educational policy, the state could not operate by centralised diktat, though its scope for action tends to be variable and underestimated, and the power of the church and the teacher associations too often offered to it as a defence against the accusation of caution and inactivity. There were other restrictions on policy formulation apart from self-censorship in anticipation of implementation difficulties. And there were, and continue to be, alternatives both to populism and to the statist interventionism that critics prescribe (Girvin, 1989; Breen *et al.*, 1990).

Rather than an interpretation of what the people want, the state's engagement with society could aspire to being more dialogical and generative. Generative dialogue between state and society lies outside the interest group/corporatist spectrum. In shaping educational policy, it differs from the sequence of state/corporatist production of Green Paper/Discussion Document followed by submissions and consultations seeking reconciliation of the greatest public accord and manageability. It also differs from the OECD expert group model of constructing country or sectoral commentaries on educational systems in terms of contemporary best practice. Generative dialogue involves more than what people want, prefer or are willing as taxpayers to fund. It demands more than the invitation of tactical responses from an increasing range of interest groups, incorporated within state structures or otherwise, and an attempt to reach an accommodation between them, even where the state itself acts as a committed participant as well as in adjudication. The normative and widely-publicised OECD reports, for their part, are too performative and unreflexive to be generative, and far from cultivating reflexivity and dialogue in society at large they tend to be selectively trawled for supportive resources by indigenous interests.

The state in generative dialogue does not invite responses to given meanings. Rather, it seeks to cultivate widely the conditions for the production of meaning.

This is a slow and challenging process to maintain as well as to establish. In this, it is likely that gradualism would continue to be a constituent feature, not in terms of changing the system a little at a time as allowed by popular sentiment, but of cultivating a public understanding of the diversity, complexity and ambivalence of possible educational futures. Setting, and indeed costing, targets could well continue to have a place in policy making but it would also be by way of seeking to calibrate the quality of the generative process and the status of the public sphere, for which the varieties of qualitative change identified in policy paradigms are suggestive. This cannot develop in a vacuum and has to be a feature of the general democratic politics of the public sphere, the conditions of which in Ireland have not been supportive of generative dialogue. If the state, and specifically the Department of Education and Science, is to be excused for its populism, it is because it has never been encouraged to think more innovatively about its relationship with society, and has only been offered statism as an alternative.

Because it tends to be used with different referents, in speaking of the public sphere, this study distinguishes between three interrelated understandings/ dimensions – social, juridical and cultural – the latter being the primary focus of this analysis. The social arena of public discourse about the polity encompasses parliaments, assemblies, conventions, mass media and the associations of civil society. In these settings, ideas are meant to be put forward, subjected to public scrutiny and succeed or fail to convince in their impact on legislation on the basis of what McCarthy (1988, p. 306) describes, in his treatment of Habermas's 'ideal speech situation', as 'the force of the better argument'. The juridical public sphere refers to the state's jurisdiction of binding normativity, those behaviours, practices and locations which are regulated by state law as a matter of public concern, as distinct from the private sphere which is designated as being of no 'interest' to the state, or of being immune from state intrusion. This refers to the classic mechanism for resolving normative conflicts which emerged in response to the religious wars of the seventeenth century, the private sphere of diversity and the public sphere of difference – blind law and universal citizenship (Joppke, 2004). The cultural dimension of the public sphere criss-crosses these two in the manner in which it facilitates the intersubjectivity of political intertextuality through which meanings pertaining to the processes and direction of the polity circulate and interact. It is this public sphere that, as has been argued earlier, needs to be more accommodating, dense and diverse as a requirement for a generative dialogue about educational policy between state and society. In this process, the state must be called upon to act as an animateur as well as a participant. This is no easy task and can anticipate opposition.

Such was Young's (1996) experience when she proposed an expanded conception of democratic communication in which other speaking styles besides critical argument such as greeting, rhetoric and story-telling are recognised as contributing to political discourse. In this, she was seeking to counter the 'devaluation and silencing' that is produced by the norms of discussion-based democracy. These norms, she argues,

> ... privilege speech that is formal and general. Speech that proceeds from premise to conclusion in an orderly fashion ... speech that is dispassionate and disembodied. They tend to presuppose an opposition between mind and body, reason and emotion. They tend falsely to identify objectivity with calm and absence of emotional expression. Thus, expressions of anger, hurt, and passionate concern discount the claims and reasons they accompany. Similarly, the entrance of the body into speech – in wide gestures, movements of nervousness or body expressions of emotion – are signs of weakness that cancel out one's assertions or reveal one's lack of objectivity and control.

As the engagement with these ideas by Benhabib (1996) and Cohen (1996) demonstrates, even for sympathetic commentators this represents a step too far from Habermasian rationality, on the basis that it constitutes an inadequate mechanism for normative justification and supplying the rules for a politics of binding decision-making. On this basis also, one could reasonably expect that the proposition that the public sphere be reconstituted, not only as an intersubjective space in which substantive ideas collide, but in which other mechanisms of truth-seeking besides rationality are accommodated, would face even greater incredulity and opposition as a practical or even desirable possibility. Yet, it needs to be an objective of democratic politics to maximise the circulation within the public sphere of what is currently relegated to the private sphere. Privatisation continues to be a compelling strategy for dealing with received belief in a discussion-based politics (Barry, 2001). But it requires continuing revisitation in the light of the escalating assertion and acknowledgement of diversity where it is in danger of yielding an expanding sphere of private worlds and a diminished public coming-together of minds, hearts, bodies and spirits in common purpose and morality, with an even further fragmentation of identities and solidarities. Theorising these issues has yielded quite exciting possibilities. An example is Cohen's (1996) notion of a differentiated public sphere, involving different types of 'public', a quite different proposition to interest-group pluralism or even a deliberative democratic politics, which invites inquiry into the 'different constraints constitutive of specific discursive rules in specific institutional domains'. This is particularly pertinent to the construction of an affirmative post-modern public sphere, in which space is found for procedural as well as substantive differences incorporating a destabilisation of such dualisms as faith/reason as well as that of public/private itself.

However complex and contestable the theorisation of possibilities for a public sphere, efforts to expand, diversify and deepen it can only begin in terms of its current status in Irish society. This is to recognise that such a project as the facilitation by the state, in generative dialogue with society, of public engagement with the cultural politics of education, since it requires such a revitalised public sphere, is forced to begin from a weak base. The inadequacy of the public sphere has been captured by O'Carroll (1991) in the context of the Abortion Referendum Debate of 1983:

> ...the argument was tightly locked into the occasion with no room for manœuvre, and protagonists found themselves reduced to declaiming their truths or abusing their opponents. This tendency is also an example of a consequence of the failure to externalise thought ... Ideas are seldom if ever used apart from the concrete occasions to which they refer. The result of this tendency is a limitation of the growth of the public sphere in many domains.

This characterisation was not distinctive to the moral debates of the 1980s. The patterned regulation of themes, the obfuscation and submersion of meanings, the disrupted sending and reception of signs, truncated communication, inadequate reflexivity, and the failure of subjectivities to connect are recurring features of Irish public discourse. These constitutive features are to be distinguished from such tactical practices as, for example, the avoidance of the more challenging of an opposition's arguments. The influence of debating discourse – confrontational, produced it is assumed by a unitary integrated subject, competitive, psychologically-laden, audience- if not entertainment-directed, zero-sum validity games – is evident, and indeed invites a post-colonial interpretation. Whatever its provenance, in areas within the media such as opinion columns, where meanings circulate most formally as ideas and are potentially more accessible, the contribution to the public sphere tends to be more by way of the disruption of meanings than in the expansion of understanding. Investigative journalism, often celebrated as public service, can have too much of populist exposé about it, an exercise in identifying 'men (and women) behaving badly' within a comfort zone of morality and miscreants. Too often, the selectivity involved, of both misdemeanor and perpetrator, remains unexplored and the embedded meanings unexamined. Whatever of its commercial value, only those labelled as culprits or hypocrites are challenged while the general mass of its consumers may be even further confirmed in their righteousness. Ironically, media discourse, of which these are but two examples, through the use of interviewing protocols in the broadcasting media and the maintenance of a diversity among newspaper columnists and in the letters page, can *appear* to meet the conditions demanded by Habermas for his 'ideal speech situation' – a chance to speak, to initiate conversation, to introduce a new theme, to call a statement into question, and to be free from conditions of distorting influence, etc.

Other possibilities exist for less adversarial public discourse. One such example, which resonates with Young's 'speaking styles', was the technique of 'benign interpretive confrontation' (O'Sullivan, 1982) which was used by the author for many years in adult education. This involved bringing the holders of divergent interpretive frameworks on life into engagement with one another through life history, anecdote, critical incident, etc. as well as exposition, not for the purpose of proving the other wrong or less convincing but with a view to recognising and acknowledging the limitations of one's own frameworks, and questioning how they came to be held and sustained. The objective was not to engineer consensus in understanding the world, but to cultivate a realisation of the complexity, production, situatedness and functioning of interpretive frameworks in our lives. Somewhat apologetically, the author has found himself coming back to education as a corrective, at least in part, for yet another social deficiency. Yet, it is difficult not to recognise the potential, at least in part, of adult education for enhancing the intersubjectivity of the public sphere through the generative role of andragogy, helping people, in Fleming's (1996) characterisation, to become critical and active agents in the reshaping of culture and society. Civic, Social and Political Education, part of the core Junior Cycle curriculum since 1997, has as its objective the preparation of students for active, participatory citizenship (NCCA, 2004). While recognising ongoing issues of staffing, timetabling, support and resourcing (Redmond and Butler, 2003), its emphasis on values education seems appropriate to the age-group involved. Should it be developed into Senior Cycle and the line of argument in this Conclusion suggests that this is compelling, it is valid to propose that 'a significant debate needs to take place in Ireland about what is called "citizenship education"' (Clifford, 2002). In this regard, 'citizenship studies', a curriculum proposal from the CDVEC Curriculum Development Unit, for social and political education in the Leaving Certificate (established) recognises the emerging adult status of students during Senior Cycle in the manner in which its rationale 'detaches the subject from specific political and/or ideological demands of the day and renders it primarily an educational endeavour with its own integrity and its own sovereign space' (Ward, 2002, p. 15).

By bringing the process of 'democratic deliberation', with its specific democratic tools and normative procedures, to the study of citizenship, it aspires to an education that 'meets the affective, pragmatic and cognitive needs of the learner and provides a space within the curriculum for a serious, dynamic and critical engagement with emerging issues' (p. 14). While Habermasian in its focus on democratic deliberation, this seems to me to represent a crucial transitional stage in preparing citizens for the challenges of an expanding public sphere, in its depth and diversity. To simplify the educational project for citizenship, there is a stage of personal development when it is appropriate to teach values, another when it is right that young people be given the norms and procedures for scrutinising these values, and a further more mature andragogical stage when adults are facilitated in meeting the challenges of seeking to accommodate diversity within such principles of deliberation.

The schematisation of the construct of policy paradigm and its application in the study of Irish cultural politics over the past half-century provides a conceptual literacy for deepening the public sphere, and in this regard it addresses itself, in the first instance, to intellectuals. It invites an engagement of political and sociological studies with educational processes and seeks to insert the issues of educational policy into socio-political debate and discourse. As is argued in the Introduction, what little engagement of this nature exists at present is concerned with employing education as a tame manifestation of inadequate public service funding, as a mediator of unequal life chances, or as a provider of skilled workers for the economy. A striking area of neglect has been the role of education in the social and cultural transformation of Irish society since the 1960s. Even if one only considers work-related subjectivities, there is little apart from passing references to well-educated, confident, and outward-looking young people as tropes for detraditionalisation. As for educational studies, there needs to be more of an interrogation than an articulation of discourses. Too often, theorisation in academic studies and policy commentaries reveals itself as an inconvenient necessity, a preamble that ends with an audible sigh of relief as they presume to have established the conceptual and academic credibility of the task in hand. Few revisit the theory in the light of the findings, fewer will have found the need to modify the theory in the first place to accommodate it to local conditions, and scarcely anyone develops theory in line with the particularities of the Irish context.

While recognising the potential in the work of school citizenship programmes and in the contributions of intellectuals for the status of the public sphere, features of the diagnosis of this book, such as the mercantile paradigm and its associated politics of education, reveal constraints on its revitalisation. This is to recognise the interdependence of the forces for change and stasis in education and society – people, social structure and culture. Theoretically integrated and interdisciplinary research is required. Cultural politics is but one dynamic in this, albeit one that is implicated at all levels of society. In this regard, sympathetic with Smith's (2000) more general aspirations, this study has sought to sensitise commentators to the problems and complexities in the production and consumption of meanings, and to redeem this cultural sphere from its 'glossed' status in the study of Irish educational policy by conceptually re-tooling them for this role, while recognising that these linguistic and symbolic systems of representation are themselves both the conditions and effects of social practices and continue to be contested, reproduced and transformed in the manner in which we use them.

Bibliography

Adams, R.S. (1970). 'Perceived Teaching Style', *Comparative Education Review* 14: 50-59.

Advisory Committee on Educational Broadcasting (1979). *Report*. Dublin: RTÉ.

Akenson, D.H. (1975). *A Mirror to Kathleen's Face. Education in Independent Ireland, 1922-1960*. Montreal: McGill-Queen's University Press.

Alexander, J. (ed.) (1985). *Neofunctionalism*. London: Sage.

Allen, F.A. (1959). 'Criminal Justice, Legal Values and the Rehabilitative Ideal', *Journal of Criminal Law, Criminology and Police Science* 50: 226-232.

Allen, G. (2000). *Intertextuality*. London: Routledge.

Allen, K. (2000). *The Celtic Tiger: The Myth of Social Partnership in Ireland*. Manchester: Manchester University Press.

Althusser, L. (1971). 'Ideology and Ideological State Apparatuses', in L. Althusser *Lenin and Philosophy and Other Essays*. London: New Left Books.

Alvarez, B. (1981). 'Educational Research in Ireland: A Bibliography of Empirical Work 1960-1980', *Irish Journal of Education* 15: 41-52.

Alvey, D. (1991). *Irish Education. The Case for Secular Reform*. Dublin and Belfast: Church and State Books and Athol Books.

Alvey, D. (1998). 'Is RSE being Ruled by Catholic Doctrine?' *The Irish Times Education and Living Supplement*, 12 May.

Andersen, N.A. (2003). *Discursive Analytical Strategies*. Bristol: Policy Press.

Andrews, M. (1991). *Lifetimes of Commitment*. Cambridge: Cambridge University Press.

Andrews, P. (1997). 'Irish Education Transformed', *Studies* 86: 149-155.

AONTAS (1980). *National Directory of Adult and Community Education Agencies*. Dublin: AONTAS.

AONTAS Research, Planing and Development Sub-Committee (1986). *Priority Areas in Adult Education*. Dublin: AONTAS.

Apple, M. (1978). 'Ivan Illich and De-Schooling Society: The Politics of Slogan Systems', in M. Young and G. Whitty (eds) *Society, State and Schooling*. Lewes: Falmer.

Apple, M. (1979). *Ideology and Curriculum*. London: Routledge and Kegan Paul.

Apple, M. (1989). 'Critical Introduction: Ideology and the State in Educational Policy', in R. Dale *The State and Education Policy*. Milton Keynes: Open University Press.

Apple, M. (1996). *Cultural Politics and Education*. Buckingham: Open University Press.

Apple, M. (2001). 'Standards, Markets, and Creating School Failure', *Rethinking Schools* 15: 1-2.

Archer, M.S. (1984). *Social Origins of Educational Systems*. London: Sage.

Archer, M.S. (1988). *Culture and Agency*. Cambridge: Cambridge University Press.

Archer, M.S. (1996). *Culture and Agency* (Revised Edition). Cambridge: Cambridge University Press.

Archer, M.S. (1998). 'Social Theory and the Analysis of Society', in T. May and M. Williams (eds) *Knowing the Social World*. Buckingham: Open University Press.

Area Development Management (1999). *Partnerships in Education. Learning the Lessons from Local Development. Conference Papers*. Dublin: ADM.

Arensberg, C.M. and Kimball, S.T. (1940). *Family and Community in Ireland*. Harvard, MA: Harvard University Press.

Ariês, P. (1962). *Centuries of Childhood*. London: Jonathan Cape.

Ashcroft, B., Griffiths, G. and Tiffin, H. (1998). *Key Concepts in Post-Colonial Studies*. London: Routledge.

Ashcroft, B., Griffiths, G. and Tiffin, H. (eds) (1999). *A Post-Colonial Studies Reader*. London: Routledge.

Ashley, C.W. (1944). *The Ashley Book of Knots*. London: Faber and Faber.

Ashley, D. (1997). *History Without a Subject. The Postmodern Condition*. Oxford: Westview Press.

Association of Secondary Teachers, Ireland (c.1994). *Model Policy on Promotion of Gender Equity in Schools*. Dublin: ASTI.

Ausubel, D.P., Novak, J.D. and Hanesian, H. (1978). *Educational Psychology: A Cognitive View*. New York: Holt, Rinehart and Winston.

Avineri, S. and de-Shalit, A. (1992). 'Introduction', in S. Avineri and A. de-Shalit (eds) *Communitarianism and Individualism*. Oxford: Oxford University Press.

Bacchi, C. (1999). *Women, Policy and Politics. The Construction of Policy Problems*. London: Sage.

Bacchi, C. (2000). 'Policy as Discourse: What Does it Mean? Where Does it Get Us?', *Discourse: Studies in the Cultural Politics of Education* 21: 45-57.

Bachrach, P. and Baratz, M. (1963). 'Decisions and Nondecisions', *American Political Science Review* 57: 632-642.

Bacik, I. (2004). *Kicking and Screaming. Dragging Ireland into the 21st Century*. Dublin: O'Brien Press.

Bailey, I. and Coleman, U. (1998). *Access and Participation in Adult Literacy Schemes*. Dublin: NALA.

Baker, J. (1987). *Arguing for Equality*. London: Verso.

Ball, S.J. (1990). *Politics and Policy Making in Education*. London: Routledge.

Ball, S.J. (1994). *Education Reform: A Critical and Post-Structural Approach*. Buckingham: Open University Press.

Bane, L. (1995). 'Thoughts on a White Paper', *The Adult Learner* 1995: 23-27.

Banks, O. (1968). *The Sociology of Education*. London: Batsford.

Bantock, G.H. (1980). *Dilemmas of the Curriculum*. Oxford: Martin Robertson.

Barber, N. (1989). *Comprehensive Schooling in Ireland*. Dublin: ESRI.

Barlow, A.C. (1981). 'Financing Aspects of the White Paper on Educational Development', *Journal of the Statistical and Social Inquiry Society of Ireland* 24 (Part 3): 89-94.

Barrow, R. (1981). *The Philosophy of Schooling*. London: Wheatsheaf.

Barrow, R. and Milburn, G. (1986). *A Critical Dictionary of Educational Concepts*. New York: Harvester Wheatsheaf.

Barry, B. (2001). *Culture and Equality*. Cambridge: Polity Press.

Barry, D. (1989). 'The Involvement and Impact of a Professional Interest Group', in D.G. Mulcahy and D. O'Sullivan (eds) *Irish Educational Policy: Process and Substance*. Dublin: IPA.

Barthes, R. (1970). *S/Z*. London: Jonathan Cape.

Barthes, R. (1973). *Mythologies*. London: Fontana.

Bassett, M., Brady, B., Fleming, T. and Inglis, T. (1989). *For Adults Only. A Case for Adult Education in Ireland*. Dublin: AONTAS.

Baudrillard, J. (1988). *Selected Writings* (Ed. M. Poster). Stanford, CA: Stanford University Press.

Bauman, Z. (1995). 'Is there a Postmodern Sociology?', in S. Seidman (ed.) *The Postmodern Turn*. Cambridge: Cambridge University Press.

Bauman, Z. (1998). *Work, Consumerism and the New Poor*. Buckingham: Open University Press.

Beck, J. (1998). *Morality and Citizenship in Education*. London: Cassell.

Beck, U. (1992). *Risk Society*. London: Sage.

Beck, U. and Beck-Gernsheim, E. (2002). *Individualisation*. London: Sage.

Beck, U., Giddens, A. and Lash, S. (1994). *Reflexive Modernisation*. Cambridge: Polity Press.

Bell, D. (1991). 'Cultural Studies in Ireland and the Postmodernist Debate', *Irish Journal of Sociology* 1: 83-95.

Benford, R.D. (1997). 'An Insider's Critique of the Social Movement Framing Perspective', *Sociological Inquiry* 67: 409-430.

Benhabib, S. (ed.) (1996). *Democracy and Difference*. Princeton, NJ: Princeton University Press.

Bennett, J. and Forgan, R. (eds) (1991). *There's Something About a Convent Girl*. London: Virago Press.

Bennett, N. (1976). *Teaching Styles and Pupil Progress*. London: Open Books.

Bennett, N. and Jordan, J. (1975). 'A Typology of Teaching Styles in Primary Schools', *British Journal of Educational Psychology* 45: 20-28.

Bensman, J. (1988). 'The Aesthetics and Politics of Footnoting', *Politics, Culture and Society* 1: 443-470.

Benveniste, E. (1971). *Problems in General Linguistics*. Miami, FL: University of Miami Press.

Berger, P.L. (1987). *The Capitalist Revolution*. Aldershot: Wildwood House.

Berger, P.L. and Luckmann, T. (1967). *The Social Construction of Reality*. Harmondsworth: Allen Lane.

Berlin, I. (1980). *Concepts and Categories*. Oxford: Oxford University Press.

Bernstein, B. (1961). 'Social Class and Linguistic Development: A Theory of Social Learning', in A.H. Halsey, J. Floud, and C.A. Anderson (eds) *Education, Economy and Society*. New York: Free Press.

Bernstein, B. (1971). 'On the Classification and Framing of Educational Knowledge', in M.F.D. Young (ed.) *Knowledge and Control*. London: Collier-Macmillan.

Bernstein, B. and Davies, B. (1969). 'Some Sociological Comments on Plowden', in R.S. Peters (ed.) *Perspectives on Plowden*. London: Routledge and Kegan Paul.

Best, S. and Kellner, D. (1991). *Postmodern Theory: Critical Interrogations*. London: Macmillan.

Bhabha, H.K. (1994[1985]). 'Signs Taken for Wonders', in *The Location of Culture*. London: Routledge.

Blair, T. (1998). *The Third Way: New Politics for the New Century*. London: Fabian Society.

Blau, P.M. (1964). *Exchange and Power in Social Life*. New York: Wiley.

Blaug, M. (1976). 'The Empirical Status of Human Capital Theory: A Slightly Jaundiced Survey', *Journal of Economic Literature* 14: 827-855.

Blaug, M. (1988). 'Review of *Economics of Education: Research and Studies* (Ed. G. Psacharopoulos)', *Journal of Human Resources* 24: 331-335.

Blaug, M. (ed.) (1968). *Economics of Education 1*. Harmondsworth: Penguin.

Boldt, S. and Devine, B. (1998). 'Educational Disadvantage in Ireland: Literature Review and Summary Report', in S. Boldt, B. Devine, D. McDevitt, and M. Morgan *Educational Disadvantage and Early School-Leaving*. Dublin: Combat Poverty Agency.

Bonel-Elliott, I. (1994). 'Lessons from the Sixties: Reviewing Dr Hillery's Educational Reform', *Irish Educational Studies* 13: 32-45.

Bonel-Elliott, I. (1996). 'The Role of the Duggan Report (1962) in the Reform of the Irish Education System', *Administration* 44: 42-60.

Bonel-Elliott, I. (1997). 'La Représentation du Système éducatif dans des Documents officiels en République d'Irelande (1992-1995)', in *L'Irlande: Imaginaire et Représentations*. Lille: Septentrion.

Bonner, K. (1996). 'Review of *Irish Society: Sociological Perspectives* (Eds. P. Clancy *et al.*)', *Irish Journal of Sociology* 6: 212-220.

Bourdieu, P. (1973). 'Cultural Reproduction and Social Reproduction', in R. Brown (ed.) *Knowledge, Education and Cultural Change*. London: Tavistock.

Bourdieu, P. (1977). *Outline of a Theory of Practice*. Cambridge: Cambridge University Press.

Bourdieu, P. (1988). *Homo Academicus*. Cambridge: Cambridge University Press.

Bourdieu, P. (1991). *Language and Symbolic Power*. Cambridge: Polity Press.

Bourdieu, P. and Passeron, J.C. (1977). *Reproduction. In Education, Culture and Society*. London: Sage.

Bové, P. (1990). 'Discourse', in F. Lentricchia and T. McLaughlin (eds) *Critical Terms for Literary Study*. Chicago: University of Chicago Press.

Bowlby, J. (1953). *Child Care and the Growth of Love*. Harmondsworth: Pelican.

Bowles, S. and Gintis, H. (1976). *Schooling in Capitalist America*. London: Routledge and Kegan Paul.

Breen, R. (1984). *Education and the Labour Market: Work and Unemployment among Recent Cohorts of Irish School Leavers*. Dublin: ESRI.

Breen, R. (1991). *Education, Employment and Training in the Youth Labour Market*. Dublin: ESRI.

Breen, R., Hannan, D.F. and O'Leary, R. (1995). 'Returns to Education: Taking Account of Employers' Perceptions and Use of Educational Credentials', *European Sociological Review* 11: 59-73.

Breen, R., Hannan, D.F., Rottman, D.B. and Whelan, C.T. (1990). *Understanding Contemporary Ireland*. Dublin: Gill and Macmillan.

Brennan, B., Brennan, N., Geraghty, G. and Mullen, K. (1989). *Staff Meeting Reflections. New Syllabi, New Learning?* Dublin: CMRS, Education Commission.

Brookfield, S. (1983). *Adult Learners, Adult Education and the Community*. Milton Keynes: Open University Press.

Brown, A. and Fairley, J. (1993). *Restructuring Education in Ireland. A Report*. Commissioned by the Association of CEOs of VECs. Published by Co. Cork, City of Cork, Co. Kerry and Town of Tralee VECs.

Brown, T. (1985). *Ireland: A Social and Cultural History, 1922-85*. London: Fontana.

Browne, N. (1986). *Against the Tide*. Dublin: Gill and Macmillan.

Browne, V. (2000). 'The Public is Wrong – Teachers must be Accountable', *The Irish Times Education and Living Supplement*, 25 April.

Bruton, R. (1998). 'Measuring Quality', *The Irish Times Education and Living Supplement*, 17 March.

Buckley, D. (1968). 'Comments on "Post-Primary Education: Now and in the Future"', *A Studies Symposium*, 72-80.

Burgess, P. (1996). 'Models of Community Work', in P. Burgess (ed.) *Youth and Community Work*. Cork: UCC Centre for Adult and Continuing Education.

Burkitt, B. and Ashton, F. (1996). 'The Birth of the Stakeholder Society', *Critical Social Policy* 16: 3-16.

Butler, J. (1995). 'Contingent Foundations: Feminism and the Question of "Postmodernism"', in S. Seidman (ed.) *The Postmodern Turn*. Cambridge: Cambridge University Press.

Byrne, A., Byrne, P. and Lyons, A. (1996). 'Inventing and Teaching Women's Studies', *Irish Journal of Feminist Studies* 1: 78-99.

Byrne, K. (1985). 'Review of *Church, State and the Control of Schooling in Ireland 1900-1944* (E.B. Titley)', *Aspects of Education* 34: 77-79.

Byrne, N. (1995). 'Keynote Address on Feminism', in C. Mulvey (ed.) *Women's Power... for a change*. Dublin: AONTAS.

Byrne, P. and Lyons, A. (1999). 'Approaches to Feminist Pedagogy: Teaching Women's Studies', in B. Connolly and A.B. Ryan (eds) *Women and Education in Ireland. Volume 2*. Maynooth: MACE.

Callan, J. (1984). 'The North Mayo/Sligo Project: "Education for Development" 1978-1982', in Department of Education *Preparation of Young People for Work and Facilitation of their Transition from Education to Working Life*. Dublin: Stationery Office.

Callan, J. (1995). 'Equality of Learning in Quality Schooling: A Challenge for Curriculum Implementation', in J. Coolahan (ed.) *Issues and Strategies in the Implementation of Educational Policy*. Maynooth: Education Department, St Patrick's College.

Callan, T., Hannan, D.F., Nolan, B., Whelan, B.J. and Creighton, S. (1988). *Poverty and the Social Welfare System in Ireland*. Dublin: Combat Poverty Agency.

Cannon, P.F.G., McCarthy, C., Milne, K., Ó hEocha, C., O'Meara, J.J. and Marsh, A. (1965/1966). 'Symposium on *Investment in Education*', *Journal of the Statistical and Social Inquiry Society of Ireland* 21 (Part 4): 67-98.

CARE (1972). *Children Deprived*. Dublin: CARE.

Carey, L. (1974). The Objectives of Adult Religious Education in the Roman Catholic Church in Ireland since the Second Vatican Council. Unpublished Ph.D. thesis, University of Manchester.

Carey, L. (1979). 'The History of AONTAS', *AONTAS Review* 1: 10-15.

Carey, L. (1981). 'Aspects of and Reflections on Recurrent Education in Ireland', in M. Jourdan (ed.) *Recurrent Education in Western Europe*. Slough: NFER-Nelson.

Carr, J. (2002). 'Dunboyne Debacle Raises Issues about Religious Education in the New Ireland', *The Irish Times*, 26 August.

Casey, G. (1993a). 'Why I am Opposed to Stay Safe', *Intercom*, June: 10-11.

Casey, G. (1993b). 'Stay Safe Campaign sends Wrong Message', *The Irish Times*, 14 July.

Cassidy, E.G. (1992). 'Irish Educational Policy in a Philosophical Perspective: The Legacy of Liberalism', in D.A. Lane (ed.) *Religion, Education and the Constitution*. Dublin: The Columba Press.

Cathcart, H.R. (1989). 'Adult Education, Values and Irish Society', in D. O'Sullivan (ed.) *Social Commitment and Adult Education*. Cork: Cork University Press.

Central Advisory Council for Education (England) (1967). *Children and their Primary Schools* (Plowden Report). London: HMSO.

Centre for Adult and Continuing Education (1996). *Adult and Continuing Education Report 1992/1995*. UCC: Centre for Adult and Continuing Education.

Chapman, J.D. and Aspin, D.N. (1997). *The School, the Community and Lifelong Learning*. London: Cassell.

Cherryholmes, C.H. (1988). *Power and Criticism*. New York: Teachers College Press.

Chitty, C. (1989). *Towards a New Education System: The Victory of the New Right?* Lewes: Falmer Press.

Chubb, B. (1970). *The Government and Politics of Ireland* (First Edition). Stanford, CA: Stanford University Press.

Chubb, B. (1992). *The Government and Politics of Ireland* (Third Edition). London: Longman.

Chubb, J. and Moe, T. (1988). 'Politics, Markets and the Organisation of Schools', *American Political Science Review* 82: 1065-1087.

Chubb, J. and Moe, T. (1990). *Politics, Markets and America's Schools*. Washington: The Brookings Institution.

Clancy, P. (1982). *Participation in Higher Education. A National Survey*. Dublin: HEA.

Clancy, P. (1983). 'Religious Vocation as a Latent Identity for School Principals', *Economic and Social Review* 15: 1-23.

Clancy, P. (1995a). 'Access Courses as an Aid towards addressing Socio-Economic Disparities in Participation in Higher Education', in *Proceedings of the HEA Seminar Access Courses for Higher Education*. Dublin: HEA.

Clancy, P. (1995b). 'Education in the Republic of Ireland: The Project of Modernity?', in P. Clancy, S. Drudy, K. Lynch and L. O'Dowd (eds) *Irish Society: Sociological Perspectives*. Dublin: IPA in association with the SAI.

Clancy, P. (1996). '*Investment in Education*. The Equality Perspective: Progress and Possibilities', *Administration* 44: 28-41.

Clancy, P. (2001). *College Entry in Focus: A Fourth National Survey of Access to Higher Education*. Dublin: HEA.

Clarke, D. (1977). Focus on Action. A Critical Analysis of the Policies for Adult Education put forward in the Document *Focus for Action* (CMRS, 1974). Unpublished MA thesis, New University of Ulster.

Clarke, D.M. (1985). *Church and State*. Cork: Cork University Press.

Clarke, J. (1990). 'Issues Arising at the Conference', in Combat Poverty Agency (ed.) *Community Work in Ireland*. Dublin: CPA.

Clarke, J. and Newman, J. (1997). *The Managerial State: Power, Politics and Ideology in the Remaking of Social Welfare*. London: Sage.

Clarke, J., Gewirtz, S. and McLaughlin, E. (eds) (2000). *New Managerialism, New Welfare?* London: Sage.

Clegg, S. (1989). *Frameworks of Power*. London: Sage.

Clifford, A. (2002). 'Foreword' to *'Citizenship Studies.' A Curricular Proposal for Social and Political Education in the Leaving Certificate (Established)* (E. Ward). Dublin: CDVEC Curriculum Development Unit.

Clinch, J.P., Convery, F. and Walsh, B. (2002). *After the Celtic Tiger: Challenges Ahead*. Dublin: O'Brien Press.

Coakley, J. and Gallagher, M. (eds) (1999). *Politics in the Republic of Ireland*. London: Routledge, in association with PSAI Press.

Cohen, J.L. (1996). 'Democracy, Difference and the Right of Privacy', in S. Benhabib (ed.) *Democracy and Difference*. Princeton, NJ: Princeton University Press.

Coleman, J.S. (1976). 'Policy Decisions, Social Science Information and Education', *Sociology of Education* 49: 304-312.

Coleman, J.S., Campbell, E.Q., Hobson, C.J., McPartland, J., Mood, A.M., Weinfeld, F.D. and York, R.L. (1966). *Equality of Educational Opportunity*. Washington DC: Office of Education, U.S. Department of Health, Education and Welfare.

Colley, G. (1966a). 'Statement to the Authorities of Secondary and Vocational Schools'. Reprinted in OECD (1969) *Reviews of National Policies for Education. Ireland*. Paris: OECD.

Colley, G. (1966b). 'Our Future in Education', *The Sunday Press*, 9 January.

Collins, M. (1992). 'Racism and Participation – The Case of the Irish Travellers', in DTEDG *DTEDG File. Irish Travellers: New Analysis and New Initiatives*. Dublin: Pavee Point.

Collins, M. (1994). 'The Sub-Culture of Poverty – A Response to McCarthy', in M. McCann, S. Ó Síocháin and J. Ruane (eds) *Irish Travellers: Culture and Ethnicity*. Belfast: QUB Institute of Irish Studies for the Anthropological Association of Ireland.

Collins, N. (ed.) (1999). *Political Issues in Ireland Today* (Second Edition). Manchester: Manchester University Press.

Collins, T. and Ryan, A. (1996). 'Participation in Rural Voluntary Organisations in Ireland: A Case Study', in B. Connolly, T. Fleming, D. McCormack and A. Ryan (eds) *Radical Learning for Liberation*. Maynooth: MACE.

Commins, P. (1995). 'The European Community and the Irish Rural Economy', in P. Clancy, S. Drudy, K. Lynch and L. O'Dowd (eds) *Irish Society: Sociological Perspectives*. Dublin: IPA in association with the SAI.

Commission of Inquiry into the Reformatory and Industrial Schools System (1936). *Report* (Cussen Report). Dublin: Stationery Office.

Commission on Adult Education (1984). *Lifelong Learning* (Kenny Report). Dublin: Stationery Office.

Commission on Higher Education 1960-67 (1967). *Report*. Dublin: Stationery Office.

Commission on Itinerancy (1963). *Report*. Dublin: Stationery Office.

Commission on Mental Handicap (1965). *Report* (Briscoe Report). Dublin: Stationery Office.

Commission on Mental Illness (1966). *Report* (Henchy Report). Dublin: Stationery Office.

Commission on Technical Education (1927). *Report*. Dublin: Stationery Office.

Commission on the Status of Women (1972). *Report*. Dublin: Stationery Office.

Commission on Youth Unemployment (1951). *Report*. Dublin: Stationery Office.

Committee on Adult Education (1970). *National Adult Education Survey* (Interim Murphy Report). Dublin: Stationery Office.

Committee on Adult Education (1973). *Adult Education in Ireland*. (Final Murphy Report). Dublin: Stationery Office.

Committee on Reformatory and Industrial Schools (1970). *Report* (Kennedy Report). Dublin: Stationery Office.

Community Workers' Cooperative (1998). *Local Development in Ireland*. Galway: CWC.

Condit, C.M. (1990). *Decoding Abortion Rhetoric*. Chicago: University of Illinois Press.

Conference of Major Religious Superiors (1986). *Report on Rationalisation*. Dublin: CMRS, Education Commission.

Conference of Major Religious Superiors (1988). *Inequality in Schooling in Ireland. A Discussion Paper*. Dublin: CMRS, Education Commission.

Conference of Major Religious Superiors (1989a). *Inequality in Schooling in Ireland: The Role of Selective Entry and Placement*. Dublin: CMRS, Education Commission.

Conference of Major Religious Superiors (1989b). *Proceedings of the Conference Education for Family and Community Development*. Dublin: CMRS, Education Commission.

Conference of Major Religious Superiors (1991a). *Responses to the NCCA Document 'Senior Cycle: Issues and Structures'*. Dublin: CMRS, Education Commission.

Conference of Major Religious Superiors (1991b). *Response to the Report of the Primary Education Review Body*. Dublin: CMRS, Education Commission.

Conference of Major Religious Superiors (1991c). *Towards an Agenda for The Debate on an Education Act*. Dublin: CMRS, Education Commission.

Conference of Major Religious Superiors (1991d). *The Catholic School in Contemporary Society*. Dublin: CMRS, Education Commission.

Conference of Major Religious Superiors (1992a). *Initial Response to the Introduction to the Green Paper on Education*. Dublin: CMRS, Education Commission.

Conference of Major Religious Superiors (1992b). *Study Guide to The Green Paper on Education: Education for a Changing World*. Dublin: CMRS, Education Commission.

Conference of Major Religious Superiors (1992c). *Education and Poverty. Eliminating Disadvantage in the Primary School Years*. Dublin: CMRS, Education Commission.

Conference of Major Religious Superiors (1993a). *Local Education Committees. A Case for their Establishment and A Tentative Proposal*. Dublin: CMRS, Education Commission.

Conference of Major Religious Superiors (1993b). *Education for a Changing World. Considered Response to The Green Paper on Education*. Dublin: CMRS, Education Commission.

Conference of Religious of Ireland (1996). *The Trusteeship of Catholic Voluntary Secondary Schools*. Dublin: CORI, Education Commission.

Conference of Religious of Ireland (1997a). *Education Bill 1997*. Dublin: CORI, Education Commission.

Conference of Religious of Ireland (1997b). *The Future of Trusteeship*. Dublin: CORI, Education Commission.

Conference of Religious of Ireland (1997c). *Religious Congregations in Irish Education. A Role for the Future?* Dublin: CORI, Education Commission.

Conference of Religious of Ireland (1998a). *The Points System. An Analysis and Review of Some Alternatives*. Dublin: CORI, Education Commission.

Conference of Religious of Ireland (1998b). *Inequality in Education. The Role of Assessment and Certification*. Dublin: CORI, Education Commission.

Conference of Religious of Ireland (1999). *Social Transformation and Lifelong Learning. Towards Policy on Adult and Community Education*. Dublin: CORI, Education Commission.

Conley, V.A. (1992). *Hélène Cixous*. London: Harvester Wheatsheaf.

Conniffe, D. and Kennedy, K.A. (eds) (1984). *Employment and Unemployment Policy for Ireland*. Dublin: ESRI.

Connolly, B. (1996). 'Community Development and Adult Education: Prospects for Change?', in B. Connolly, T. Fleming, D. McCormack and A. Ryan (eds) *Radical Learning for Liberation*. Maynooth: MACE.

Connolly, B. (1997). 'Women in Community Education and Development – Liberation or Domestication?', in A. Byrne and M. Leonard (eds) *Women and Irish Society. A Sociological Reader*. Belfast: Beyond the Pale Publications.

Connolly, B. (1999). 'Group Work and Facilitation: A Feminist Evaluation of their Role in Transformative Adult and Community Education', in B. Connolly and A.B. Ryan (eds) *Women and Education in Ireland. Volume 1*. Maynooth: MACE.

Connolly, B., Fleming, T., McCormack, D. and Ryan, A. (eds) (1996). *Radical Learning for Liberation*. Maynooth: MACE.

Connolly, L. (1997). 'From Revolution to Devolution: Mapping the Contemporary Women's Movement in Ireland', in A. Byrne and M. Leonard (eds) *Women and Irish Society. A Sociological Reader*. Belfast: Beyond the Pale Publications.

Connolly, L. (2003). *The Irish Women's Movement: From Revolution to Devolution*. Dublin: Lilliput Press.

Conway, P.F. (2002). 'Learning in Communities of Practice: Rethinking Teaching and Learning in Disadvantaged Contexts', *Irish Educational Studies* 21: 61-91.

Conway, P.F., Goodell, J. and Carl, J. (2001). 'Educational Reform in the United States: Politics, Purposes and Processes', in R. Griffin (ed.) *Education in Transition: International Perspectives on the Politics and Processes of Change*. London: Symposium Books.

Coolahan, J. (1984a). 'The Fortunes of Education as a Subject of Study and of Research in Ireland', *Irish Educational Studies* 4: 1-34.

Coolahan, J. (1984b). 'Science and Technology as Elements of Education and Socio-Economic Change in Ireland, 1958-83', *Administration* 31: 89-99.

Coolahan, J. (1984c). *The ASTI and Post-Primary Education in Ireland 1909-1984*. Dublin: ASTI.

Coolahan, J. (1989). 'Educational Policy for National Schools, 1960-1985', in D.G. Mulcahy and D. O'Sullivan (eds) *Irish Educational Policy: Process and Substance*. Dublin: IPA.

Coolahan, J. (1990). 'Have We Learned Anything At All? Reflections on Curriculum Development in Ireland, 1972-1992', *Compass* 19: 26-50.

Coolahan, J. (ed.) (1994). *Report on the National Education Convention*. Dublin: National Education Convention Secretariat.

Coolahan, J. (ed.) (1996a). *Increasing Participation. Proceedings of the Irish National Conference for the European Year of Lifelong Learning*. Dublin and Maynooth: TEASTAS and Maynooth College.

Coolahan, J. (1996b). 'The Challenge to Achieving the Learning Society', in J. Coolahan (ed.) *Increasing Participation. Proceedings of the Irish National Conference for the European Year of Lifelong Learning*. Dublin and Maynooth: TEASTAS and Maynooth College.

Coolahan, J. (2000). *Irish Education. History and Structure*. Dublin: IPA.

Cooper, D. (1976). *The Death of the Family*. Harmondsworth: Pelican.

Copleston, F. (1964). *A History of Philosophy. Volume 6 Part II Kant*. New York: Image Books.

Corcoran, M.P. and Peillon, M. (eds) (2002). *Ireland Unbound: A Turn of the Century Chronicle*. Dublin: IPA.

Corkery, D. (1931). *Synge and Anglo-Irish Literature*. Cork: Cork University Press.

Corson, D. (1986). 'Policy in Social Context: A Collapse of Holistic Planning in Education', *Journal of Education Policy* 1: 5-22.

Costello, M. (1999). 'Challenges Posed by the Integration of Local Development and Local Government: Implications for Women's Community Education', in B. Connolly and A.B. Ryan (eds) *Women and Education in Ireland. Volume 2*. Maynooth: MACE.

Coulter, C. and Coleman, S. (eds) (2003). *The End of History? Critical Reflections on the Celtic Tiger*. Manchester: Manchester University Press.

Council of Education (1954). *Report on the Function and Curriculum of the Primary School*. Dublin: Stationery Office.

Council of Education (1962). *Report on the Curriculum of the Secondary School*. Dublin: Stationery Office.

Courtney, S. (1994). 'Adult Education and the Modern Nation State: Reflections on *Social Commitment and Adult Education*', *International Journal of Lifelong Education* 13: 465-476.

Craft, M. (1970). 'Economy, Ideology and Educational Development in Ireland', *Administration* 18: 363-374.

Cregan, Á. and Lodge, A. (2000). 'An Analysis of Policies and Strategies aimed at Tackling Educational Disadvantage in the Primary and Post-Primary Sectors'. Paper presented at the Annual Conference of the Educational Studies Association of Ireland, NUI, Maynooth, 13-15 April.

Cremins, U.M. (1997). Travellers and Intercultural Education. Unpublished M.Ed. dissertation, University College Cork.

Cronin, M. (1957). *Primer of the Principles of Social Science*. Dublin: Gill.

Crook, S., Pakulski, J. and Waters, M. (1993). *Postmodernisation. Change in Advanced Society*. London: Sage.

Crooks, J.A. (1973). 'Humanities in Context', *Compass* 2: 17-18.

Crooks, T. (1999). 'Addressing Social and Economic Disadvantage through Education and Lifelong Learning: The Contribution of Local Development', in Area Development Management *Partnerships in Education. Learning the Lessons from Local Development. Conference Papers*. Dublin: ADM.

Crooks, T. and McKernan, J. (1984). *The Challenge of Change. Curriculum Development in Irish Post-Primary Schools 1970-84*. Dublin: IPA in association with the IACD.

Crotty, R. (1986). *Ireland in Crisis: A Study in Capitalist Colonial Underdevelopment*. Tralee: Brandon Press.

Crowley, E. and Mac Laughlin, J. (eds) (1997). *Under the Belly of the Tiger*. Dublin: Irish Reporter Publications.

Cullen, B. (1989). *Poverty, Community and Development*. Dublin: Combat Poverty Agency.

Cullen, B. (1997). *Integrated Services and Children at Risk*. Dublin: Combat Poverty Agency.

Cullen, B. (1998). 'A Meeting of Mind-Sets: Integrating Approaches to Tackling Education Disadvantage.' *Poverty Today* 40: 2.

Cullen, B. (2000a). *Evaluating Integrated Responses to Educational Disadvantage*. Dublin: Combat Poverty Agency.

Cullen, B. (2000b). *Policy Aspects of Educational Disadvantage: Discussion Papers*. Dublin: Combat Poverty Agency.

Cullen, M. (1987). 'Knowledge and Power: Patriarchal Knowledge on the Feminist Curriculum', in M. Cullen (ed.) *Girls Don't Do Honours*. Dublin: Women's Education Bureau.

Culler, J. (1990). *Saussure*. London: Fontana.

Curtin, C. and Varley, A. (1984). 'Children and Childhood in Rural Ireland: A Consideration of the Ethnographic Literature', in C. Curtin, M. Kelly and L. O'Dowd (eds) *Culture and Ideology in Ireland*. Galway: Galway University Press.

Curtin, C. and Varley, T. (1995). 'Community Action and the State', in P. Clancy, S. Drudy, K. Lynch and L. O'Dowd (eds) *Irish Society. Sociological Perspectives*. Dublin: IPA in association with the SAI.

Dahl, R.A. (1957). 'The Concept of Power', *Behavioural Science* 2: 210-215.

Dahl, R.A. (1961). *Who Governs?* New Haven, CT: Yale University Press.

Daly, M. (1979). *Gyn/Ecology*. London: The Women's Press.

Daly, N. (1978). Provision and Participation in Adult Education in Two Irish Counties. Unpublished MA thesis, New University of Ulster.

Daniels, H. (1996). 'Introduction: Psychology in a Social World', in H. Daniels (ed.) *An Introduction to Vygotsky*. London: Routledge.

Danziger, K. (1971). *Socialisation*. Harmondsworth: Penguin.

Dargan, J. (1992). 'The CMRS Story', *Religious Life Review* 31: 321-332.

Davidson, D. (1984). 'On the Very Idea of a Conceptual Scheme', in *Inquiries into Truth and Interpretation*. Oxford: Clarendon Press.

Davies, B. (1973). 'On the Contribution of Organisational Analysis to the Study of Educational Institutions', in R. Brown (ed.) *Knowledge, Education and Cultural Change*. London: Tavistock.

Davies, S. (1999). 'From Moral Society to Cultural Rights: A Case Study of Political Framing in Education', *Sociology of Education* 72: 1-21.

Davis, K. (1969). *Human Society*. New York: Collier-Macmillan.

de Buitléar, S. (1969). 'Curaclam Nua le hAghaidh na Bunscoile', *Oideas* 3: 4-12.

Deane, C. (2003). *Bridging the Gap. Evaluation Report 2003*. Cork: Education Department, University College, Cork.

Deegan, J.G. (2002). 'Early Childhood Discourse: Problematising Some Conceptual Issues in Statutory Frameworks', *Irish Educational Studies* 21: 77-87.

Deleon, P. (1994). 'Reinventing the Policy Sciences: Three Steps Back to the Future', *Policy Sciences* 27: 77-95.

della Porta, D. and Diani, M. (1999). *Social Movements. An Introduction.* Oxford: Blackwell.

Denzin, N.K. (1971). 'Symbolic Interactionism and Ethnomethodology', in J.D. Douglas (ed.) *Understanding Everyday Life.* London: Routledge and Kegan Paul.

Department of Education (1969). *Ár nDaltaí Uile. All Our Children.* Dublin: Department of Education.

Department of Education (1970). 'Committee Report: Educational Facilities for the Children of Itinerants', *Oideas* 5: 44-53.

Department of Education (1971). *Primary School Curriculum. Teacher's Handbook.* Dublin: Stationery Office.

Department of Education (1984a). *Guidelines for Publishers on Sexism and Sex-Stereotyping in Primary School Textbooks.* Dublin: Department of Education.

Department of Education (1984b). *Preparation of Young People for Work and Facilitation of their Transition from Education to Working Life.* Dublin: Stationery Office.

Department of Education (1985). *Adult Education in Disadvantaged Areas. Discussion Document. Part 1 – Adult Literacy.* Dublin: Department of Education.

Department of Education (1991). 'Parents as Partners in Education', Circular 24/91.

Department of Education (1992). *Education for a Changing World. Green Paper on Education.* Dublin: Stationery Office.

Department of Education (1995). *Charting Our Education Future. White Paper on Education.* Dublin: Stationery Office.

Department of Education (1996). *Gender Matters.* Dublin: Department of Education.

Department of Education and Science (1998). *Adult Education in an Era of Lifelong Learning. Green Paper on Adult Education.* Dublin: Stationery Office.

Department of Education and Science (2000). *Learning for Life. White Paper on Adult Education.* Dublin: Stationery Office.

Department of Education and Science (2004). *Your Education System.* Dublin: Department of Education and Science.

Department of Equality and Law Reform (1997). *Ireland's Combined Second and Third Reports under the UN Convention on the Elimination of All Forms of Discrimination Against Women.* Dublin: Stationery Office.

Department of Health (1975). *Report of the Working Party on Training and Employing the Handicapped* (Robins Report). Dublin: Stationery Office.

Department of Justice (1981). *Annual Report.* Dublin: Stationery Office.

Department of Justice, Equality and Law Reform (2002). *Towards a National Action Plan Against Racism in Ireland.* Dublin: Stationery Office.

Department of the Environment (1995). *Report of the Task Force on the Travelling Community.* Dublin: Stationery Office.

Derrida, J. (1978). *Writing and Difference.* London: Routledge and Kegan Paul.

Derrida, J. (1981). *Positions* (Trs. A. Bass). London: Athlone Press.

Dery, D. (1984). *Problem Definition in Policy Analysis.* Lawrence, KS: University Press of Kansas.

Deshler, D. (1990). 'Conceptual Mapping: Drawing Charts of the Mind', in J. Mezirow (ed.) *Fostering Critical Reflection in Adulthood.* San Francisco, CA: Jossey-Bass.

Development for Full Employment (1978). Dublin: Stationery Office.

Devereux, E.C. (1961). 'Parsons' Sociological Theory', in M. Black (ed.) *The Social Theories of Talcott Parsons*. Englewod Cliffs, NJ: Prentice-Hall.

Devine, D. (2000). 'Constructions of Childhood in School: Power, Policy and Practice in Irish Education', *International Studies in Sociology of Education* 10: 23-41.

Diggins, P.B. (1990). 'Development of Educational Administration in Second Level Schools in Ireland', in G. McNamara, K. Williams, and D. Herron (eds) *Achievement and Aspiration: Curriculum Initiatives in Irish Post-Primary Education in the 1980s*. Dublin: Drumcondra Teachers' Centre.

Dineen, F.P. (1967). *An Introduction to General Linguistics*. New York: Holt, Rinehart and Winston.

Dolphin, E. and Mulvey, C. (1997). *Review of Scheme of Grants to Locally Based Women's Groups*. Dublin: Department of Social, Community and Family Affairs.

Donnison, D. (1991). *Urban Poverty, the Economy and Public Policy. Options for Ireland in the 1990s*. Dublin: Combat Poverty Agency.

Donoghue, D. (1992). *Warrenpoint*. London: Jonathan Cape.

Dorgan, M. and McDonnell, O. (1997). 'Conversing on Class Activism. Claiming Our Space in Feminist Politics', *Irish Journal of Feminist Studies* 2: 67-85.

Dorr, D. (1992). *Option for the Poor. A Hundred Years of Vatican Social Teaching*. Dublin: Gill and Macmillan.

Dorr, F. (1989). 'Values Clarification and Relativism: A Response to Jim McKernan', *Oideas* 34: 105-117.

Douglas, F.G. (1994). *The History of the Irish Pre-School Playgroups Association 1969-1994*. Dublin: Irish Pre-School Playgroups Association.

Douglas, M. (1984). *Purity and Danger*. London: Routledge.

Doyle, E. (1999). *Multiple Intelligences, Curriculum and Assessment Project. Evaluation Report*. Cork: Education Department, University College Cork.

Doyle, P. (1988). *The God Squad*. Dublin: Raven Arts Press.

Dreitzel, H.P. (1973). *Childhood and Socialisation*. New York: Macmillan.

Drudy, S. (1991). 'Developments in the Sociology of Education in Ireland 1966-1991', *Irish Journal of Sociology* 1: 107-127.

Drudy, S. and Lynch, K. (1993). *Schools and Society in Ireland*. Dublin: Gill and Macmillan.

Drudy, S., Gash, H., Lynch, K., Ó Láimhín, P., Moles, R., Lane, C., Ganly, M., Fogarty, C., O'Flynn, G. and Dunne, A. (1991). 'Integrating Equal Opportunities in the Curriculum of Teacher Education 1988-1991: TENET Programme Dissemination Phase', *Irish Educational Studies* 10: 271-288.

Drumm, M. (1997). 'The Place of Theology and Religion in Higher Education', in P. Hogan and K. Williams (eds) *The Future of Religion in Irish Education*. Dublin: Veritas.

Du Vivier, E. (1991). 'How Many Illiterates?' *Studies in Education* 7: 29-40.

Duffy, P. (1967). *The Lay Teacher*. Dublin: Fallons.

Duignan, S. (1996). *One Spin on the Merry-Go-Round*. Dublin: Blackwater Press.

Dunleavy, F. and O'Leary, B. (1987). *Theories of the State*. London: Macmillan.

Dunn, S. and Morgan, V. (1979). 'A Comparative Demographic Study of Student Teachers from the North and South of Ireland', *Comparative Education* 15: 143-157.

Dunne, J. (1991). 'The Catholic School and Civil Society: Exploring the Tensions', in Conference of Major Religious Superiors. *The Catholic School in Contemporary Society*. Dublin: CMRS, Education Commission.

Dunne, J. (1997). 'Symposium. The Future of Religion in Irish Education', in P. Hogan and K. Williams (eds) *The Future of Religion in Irish Education*. Dublin: Veritas.

Durkheim, É. (1952[1897]). *Suicide: A Study in Sociology*. London: Routledge and Kegan Paul.

Durkheim, É. (1976[1912]). *The Elementary Forms of Religious Life*. London: Allen and Unwin.

Durkheim, E. (1982[1895]). *The Rules of Sociological Method*. London: Macmillan.

Eco, U. (1976). *A Theory of Semiotics*. Bloomington, IN: Indiana University Press.

Education (Welfare) Act (2000). Dublin: Stationery Office.

Education Act (1998). Dublin: Stationery Office.

Education Bill (1997). Dublin: Stationery Office.

Education Group. Centre for Contemporary Cultural Studies (1981). *Unpopular Education. Schooling and Social Democracy in England since 1944*. London: Hutchinson, in association with the CCCS, University of Birmingham.

Educational Disadvantage Committee (2003). *Educational Disadvantage Forum. Report of Inaugural Meeting*. Dublin: Department of Education and Science.

Educational Disadvantage Committee (2004). *Submissions Made to the Minister for Education and Science. 2003 Report*. Dublin: Department of Education and Science.

Educational Studies Association of Ireland (1982). *Register of Theses on Educational Topics in Universities in Ireland*. Galway: Galway University Press.

Edwards, R. (2001). 'Editorial: Changing Knowledge? Knowledge Production in the Education of Adults', *Studies in the Education of Adults* 33: 89-94.

Eliot, T.S. (1962[1948]). *Notes Towards the Definition of Culture*. London: Faber.

Ellsworth, E. (1989). 'Why Doesn't this Feel Empowering? Working Through the Repressive Myths of Critical Pedagogy', *Harvard Educational Review* 59: 297-324.

Ellsworth, E. (1997). *Teaching Positions: Difference, Pedagogy, and the Power of Address*. New York: Teachers College Press.

Employment Equality Act (1998). Dublin: Stationery Office.

Employment Equality Agency (1983). *Schooling and Sex Roles. Agency Commentary, Recommendations and Summary Findings of Report*. Dublin: EEA.

Epstein, D., Elwood, J., Hey, V. and Maw, J. (eds) (1998). *Failing Boys?* Buckingham: Open University Press.

Equal Status Act (2000). Dublin: Stationery Office.

Erikson, K. (1966). *Wayward Puritans*. New York: Wiley.

ESF Programme Evaluation Unit (1996). *Evaluation Report. Early School Leavers Provision*. Dublin: ESF Programme Evaluation Unit.

Estes, W.K. (1996). *Classification and Cognition*. Oxford: Oxford University Press.

Etzioni, A. (1964). *Modern Organisations*. New Jersey: Prentice-Hall.

Etzioni, A. (1993). *The Spirit of Community. Rights, Responsibilities and the Communitarian Agenda*. New York: Crown Publishers.

Etzioni, A. (ed.) (1998). *The Essential Communitarian Reader*. Oxford: Rowman and Littlefield.

European Commission (1996). *White Paper on Education and Training. Teaching and Learning – Towards the Learning Society*. Luxembourg: Office for Official Publications of the European Communities.

European Foundation for Management Development (1978). *Management Training in the European Community*. Brussels: Commission of the European Communities.

Executive of the Teaching Brothers' Association (1968). 'Comments on "Post-Primary Education: Now and in the Future"', *A Studies Symposium* 50-59.

Exworthy, M. and Halford, S. (eds) (1999). *Professionals and the New Managerialism in the Public Sector*. Buckingham: Open University Press.

Eysenck, H.J. (1971). *Race, Intelligence and Education*. London: Temple Smith.

Fagan, G.H. (1991). 'Local Struggles: Women in the Home and Critical Feminist Pedagogy in Ireland', *Journal of Education* 173: 65-75.

Fagan, G.H. (1995). *Culture, Politics and Irish School Dropouts: Constructing Political Identities*. Westport, CT: Bergin and Garvey.

Fahey, T. (1992a). 'Catholicism in Industrial Society in Ireland', in J.H. Goldthorpe and C.T. Whelan (eds) *The Development of Industrial Society in Ireland*. Oxford: Clarendon Press.

Fahey, T. (1992b). 'State, Family and Compulsory Schooling in Ireland', *Economic and Social Review* 23: 369-395.

Fairclough, N. (1995). *Critical Discourse Analysis*. London: Longman.

Family Solidarity (1987). *Health Education Courses in Post-Primary Schools*. Dublin: Family Solidarity.

Fanning, R. (1983). *Independent Ireland*. Dublin: Helicon.

Farrell, R. (1982). The Provision of Adult Education in Ireland. Unpublished Diploma in Adult and Community Education dissertation, St Patrick's College, Maynooth.

Farren, S. (1995). *The Politics of Irish Education 1920-65*. Belfast: QUB Institute of Irish Studies.

Faughnan, P. and O'Connor, S. (1980). *Major Issues in Planning Services for Mentally and Physically Handicapped Persons*. Dublin: NESC.

Fay, B. (1987). *Critical Social Science*. Oxford: Blackwell.

Feehan, P. (1979). 'Pearse College Development', *AONTAS Review* 1: 36-38.

Feheney, J.M. (1998a). 'Children of a Lesser God', in J.M. Feheney (ed.) *From Ideal to Action*. Dublin: Veritas.

Feheney, J.M. (ed.) (1998b). *From Ideal to Action*. Dublin: Veritas.

Fennell, N. and Arnold, M. (1987). *Irish Women in Focus*. Dublin: Department of the Taoiseach.

Fennell, D. (1993). *Heresy. The Battle for Ideas in Modern Ireland*. Belfast: Blackstaff Press.

Ferguson, H. (1996). 'Protecting Irish Children in Time', in H. Ferguson and T. McNamara (eds) *Protecting Irish Children. Investigation, Protection and Welfare*. Special Issue of *Administration* 44.

Ferguson, H. and McNamara, T. (eds) (1996). *Protecting Irish Children. Investigation, Protection and Welfare*. Special Issue of *Administration* 44.

Ferguson, H., Gilligan, R. and Torode, R. (eds) (1993). *Surviving Childhood Adversity: Issues for Policy and Practice*. Dublin: Social Studies Press.

Feyerabend, P. (1978). *Science for a Free Society*. London: New Left Books.

Fine Gael Party (1966). *Fine Gael Policy for a Just Society 3. Education*. Dublin: Fine Gael Party.

Fine Gael Party (n.d.) *Winning Through to a Just Society*. Dublin: Fine Gael Party.

Finegold, D. and Soskice, D. (1988). 'The Failure of Training in Britain: Analysis and Prescription', *Oxford Review of Economic Policy* 4: 21-53.

Finegold, D., McFarland, L. and Richardson, W. (eds) (1992). *Something Borrowed, Something Blue? A Study of the Thatcher Government's Appropriation of American Education and Training Policy*. Oxford: Triangle Books.

Finlay, F. (1998). *Snakes and Ladders*. Dublin: New Island Books.

Finlayson, A. (1999a). 'Culture', in F. Ashe, A. Finlayson, M. Lloyd, I. MacKenzie, J. Martin and S. O'Neill (eds) *Contemporary Social and Political Theory*. Buckingham: Open University Press.

Finlayson, A. (1999b). 'Language', in F. Ashe, A. Finlayson, M. Lloyd, I. McKenzie, J. Martin and S. O'Neill (eds) *Contemporary Social and Political Theory*. Buckingham: Open University Press.

FitzGerald, G. (1965). '*Investment in Education*', *Studies* 54: 361-374.

Fitzgerald, R. and Girvin, B. (2000). 'Political Culture, Growth and the Conditions for Success in the Irish Economy', in B. Nolan, P.J. O'Connell and C.T. Whelan (eds) *Bust to Boom? The Irish Experience of Growth and Inequality*. Dublin: IPA.

Fleming, T. (1996). 'The Future of Adult Education: Learning Towards a New Democracy', in B. Connolly, T. Fleming, D. McCormack and A. Ryan (eds) *Radical Learning for Liberation*. Maynooth: MACE.

Flude, M. and Hammer, M. (eds) (1990). *The Education Reform Act 1988: Its Origins and Implications*. Lewes: Falmer Press.

Fodor, J.A. (1976). *The Language of Thought*. Sussex: Harvester Press.

Fontes, P. and Kellaghan, T. (1977). *The New Primary School Curriculum: Its Implementation and Effects*. Dublin: Educational Research Centre.

Fontes, P., Kellaghan, T., Madaus, G.F. and Airasian, P.W. (1983). 'Opinions of the Irish Public on Intelligence', *Irish Journal of Education* 17: 55-67.

Ford, D. (1975). *Children, Courts and Caring*. London: Constable.

Ford, J. (1969). *Social Class and the Comprehensive School*. London: Routledge and Kegan Paul.

Forde, C. (1996). *Making Education Work on Cork's Northside: A Strategy Statement*. Cork: Northside Education Initiative.

Foucault, M. (1973). *The Order of Things*. New York: Vintage Books.

Foucault, M. (1979). *Discipline and Punish*. Harmondsworth: Peregrine.

Foucault, M. (1980). 'Truth and Power', in C. Gordon (ed.) *Power/Knowledge: Selected Interviews and Other Writings 1972-1977*. New York: Pantheon Books.

Foucault, M. (1983). 'Structuralism and Post-Structuralism. Interview with G. Raulet (Trs. J. Harding)', *Telos* 55: 195-210.

Foucault, M. (1985). *The Use of Pleasure. Volume 2 of The History of Sexuality* (Trs. R. Hurley). Harmondsworth: Viking.

Friedman, M. (1989). 'Feminism and Modern Friendship: Dislocating the Community', *Ethics* 99: 275-290.

Frow, J. (1991). 'Intertextuality and Ontology', in M. Worton and J. Still (eds) *Intertextuality. Theories and Practices*. Manchester: Manchester University Press.

Fuller, L. (2004). *Irish Catholicism since 1950. The Undoing of a Culture*. Dublin: Gill and Macmillan.

Future Involvement of Religious in Education (FIRE) (1973). Report of a Working Party set up by the Education Commissions of the Major Religious Superiors and the Hierarchy. Privately Circulated.

Gallagher, M. (1981). 'Societal Change and Party Adaptation in the Republic of Ireland 1960-81', *European Journal of Political Research* 9: 269-285.

Gallagher, M.P. (1997). *Clashing Symbols. An Introduction to Faith and Culture*. London: Darton, Longman and Todd.

Galligan, Y. (1998). *Women and Politics in Contemporary Ireland*. London: Pinter.

Gardner, H. (1983). *Frames of Mind: The Theory of Multiple Intelligences*. New York: Basic Books.

Garfinkel, H. (1967). *Studies in Ethnomethodology*. New York: Prentice-Hall.

Garvin, T. (1981). *The Evolution of Irish Nationalist Politics*. Dublin: Gill and Macmillan.

Garvin, T. (2004). *Preventing the Future*. Gill and Macmillan.

Gaughan, J.A. (1986). *Alfred O'Rahilly 1: Academic*. Dublin: Kingdom Books.

Gaughan, J.A. (1989). *Alfred O'Rahilly II: Public Figure*. Dublin: Kingdom Books.

Geertz, C. (1975). *The Interpretation of Cultures*. London: Hutchinson.

Geraghty, P. (1988). 'Education for the Labour Market. A Critique', *Irish Educational Studies* 7: 118-130.

Gewirtz, S. (2002). *The Managerial School: Post-Welfarism and Social Justice in Education*. London: Routledge.

Gewirtz, S., Ball, S.J. and Bowe, R. (1995). *Markets, Choice and Equity in Education*. Buckingham: Open University Press.

Gibbons, L. (1996). *Transformations in Irish Culture*. Cork: Cork University Press.

Giddens, A. (1984). *The Constitution of Society*. Cambridge: Polity Press.

Giddens, A. (1993). *Sociology*. Cambridge: Polity Press.

Giddens, A. (1996a). *Beyond Left and Right. The Future of Radical Politics*. Cambridge: Polity Press.

Giddens, A. (1996b). *In Defence of Sociology*. Cambridge: Polity Press.

Giddens, A. (1998). 'Risk Society, the Context of British Politics', in J. Franklin (ed.) *The Politics of Risk Society*. Cambridge: Polity Press.

Gilligan, A.L. (ed.) (2002). *Primary Education: Ending Disadvantage. Proceedings and Action Plan of National Forum*. Dublin: St Patrick's College.

Giroux, H. (1983). *Theory and Resistance in Education*. London: Heinemann.

Giroux, H. (1997). *Pedagogy and the Politics of Hope. Theory, Culture and Schooling*. Oxford: Westview Press.

Girvin, B. (1989). *Between Two Worlds: Politics and Economy in Independent Ireland*. Dublin: Gill and Macmillan.

Gleeson, J. (1998). 'Curriculum and Assessment: Some Political and Cultural Considerations', in CORI *Inequality in Education. The Role of Assessment and Certification*. Dublin: CORI.

Gleeson, J. (2000). 'A Social Partnership: The European Union and Irish Vocational Education and Training', in D.R. Herschbach and C.P. Campbell (eds) *Workforce Preparation: An International Perspective*. Ann Arbour, MI: Prakken.

Gleeson, J. (2004). 'Cultural and Political Contexts of Irish Post-Primary Curriculum: Influences, Interests and Issues', in C. Sugrue (ed.) *Ideology and Curriculum: Irish Experiences, International Perspectives*. Dublin: Liffey Press.

Gleeson, J. and Granville, G. (1996). 'The Case for the Leaving Certificate Applied', *Irish Educational Studies* 15: 113-132.

Gleeson, J., Clifford, A., Collison, T., O'Driscoll, S., Rooney, M. and Tuohy, A. (2002). 'School Culture and Curriculum Change: The Case of the Leaving Certificate Applied (LCA)', *Irish Educational Studies* 21: 21-44.

Gmelch, S.B. (1990). 'From Poverty Subculture to Political Lobby: The Traveller Rights Movement in Ireland', in C. Curtin and T.M. Wilson (eds) *Ireland from Below: Social Change and Local Communities*. Galway: Galway University Press.

Goffman, E. (1968). *Asylums*. Harmondsworth: Pelican.

Goffman, E. (1974). *Frame Analysis*. Cambridge, MA: Harvard University Press.

Good, J. (1970). 'The Priest in Education', *Christus Rex* 24: 75-81.

Gorby, S., McCoy, S. and Williams, J. (2003). *2002 Annual School Leavers' Survey*. Dublin: Department of Education and Science and ESRI.

Gordon, J.E. (1968). 'The Disadvantaged Pupil', *Irish Journal of Education* 2: 69-105.

Gore, J.M. (1993). *The Struggle for Pedagogies*. London: Routledge.

Gould, S. (1981). *The Mismeasure of Man*. Harmondsworth: Penguin.

Goulding, F., Martin, K., Frawley, D., Sheehan, M., McCormack, N. and Maguire, P. (1987). 'The Educational Opportunities Scheme', *The Adult Learner* 1: 4-19.

Gouldner, A. (1971). *The Coming Crisis in Western Sociology*. London: Heinemann.

Grace, A.P. (1999). 'Building a Knowledge Base in US Academic Adult Education (1945-70)', *Studies in the Education of Adults* 31: 220-236.

Grace, G. (1989) 'Education Policy Studies: Developments in Britain in the 1970s and 1980s', *New Zealand Journal of Educational Studies* 24: 87-95.

Grace, G.W. (1987). *The Linguistic Construction of Reality*. Beckenham: Croom Helm.

Gramsci, A. (1971). *Selections from the Prison Notebooks* (Trs./Eds Q. Hoare and G.N. Smith). London: Lawrence and Wishart.

Granville, G. (2004). 'Politics and Partnership in Curriculum Planning in Ireland', in C. Sugrue (ed.) *Ideology and Curriculum: Irish Experiences, International Perspectives*. Dublin: Liffey Press.

Greaney, V. and Kellaghan, T. (1984). *Equality of Opportunity in Irish Schools*. Dublin: The Educational Company.

Griswold, W. (1994). *Cultures and Societies in a Changing World*. Thousand Oaks: Pine Forge Press.

Gurin, P. and Marks, H. (1989). 'Cognitive Consequences of Gender Identity', in S. Skevington and D. Baker (eds) *The Social Identity of Women*. London: Sage.

Habermas, J. (1975). *Legitimation Crisis* (Trs. T. McCarthy). Boston: Beacon Press.

Habermas, J. (1979). *Communication and the Evolution of Society* (Trs. T. McCarthy). Cambridge: Polity Press.

Habermas, J. (1996). 'Three Normative Models of Democracy', in S. Benhabib (ed.) *Democracy and Difference*. Princeton, NJ: Princeton University Press.

Hall, P.A. (1993). 'Policy Paradigms, Social Learning, and the State', *Comparative Politics* 25: 275-296.

Hall, S. (1980). 'Popular Democratic vs. Authoritarian Populism', in A. Hunt (ed.) *Marxism and Democracy*. London: Lawrence and Wishart.

Hall, S. (1983). 'The Great Moving Right Show', in S. Hall and M. Jacques (eds) *The Politics of Thatcherism*. London: Lawrence and Wishart.

Hall, S. (1992). 'The Question of Cultural Identity', in S. Hall, D. Held and T. McGrew (eds) *Modernity and Its Futures*. Cambridge: Polity Press in association with the Open University.

Hall, S., Held, D. and McGrew, T. (eds) (1992). *Modernity and Its Futures*. Cambridge: Polity Press in association with the Open University.

Hallak, J. and McCabe, J. (1973). *Planning the Location of Schools: County Sligo, Ireland*. Paris: UNESCO.

Halpin, D. and Troyna, B. (1995). 'The Politics of Educational Policy Borrowing', *Comparative Education* 31: 303-310.

Halsey, A.H. (1972). *Educational Priority. EPA Problems and Policies*. London: HMSO.

Hanafin, J. (1992). Co-Education and Educational Attainment. Unpublished Ph.D. thesis, University of Limerick.

Hanafin, J. (2000). 'Drover and Cloner: The Agency of Intelligence in Structuring Sameness and Educational Exclusion'. Paper presented at the Annual Conference of the Sociological Association of Ireland, Kilkenny, 5-7 May.

Hannan, D.F. (1972). 'Kinship, Neighbourhood and Social Change in Irish Rural Communities', *Economic and Social Review* 3: 163-188.

Hannan, D.F. (1986). *Schooling and the Labour Market*. Shannon: Shannon Curriculum Development Centre.

Hannan, D.F. (1987). 'Goals and Objectives of Educational Interventions', in T. Crooks and D. Stokes (eds) *Disadvantage, Learning and Young People*. Dublin: CDVEC Curriculum Development Unit.

Hannan, D.F. (1993). 'Foreword' to *Restructuring Education in Ireland. A Report* (A. Brown and J. Fairley). Commissioned by the Association of CEOs of VECs. Published by Co. Cork, City of Cork, Co Kerry and Town of Tralee VECs.

Hannan, D.F. (1996). 'School to Work and Adulthood Transitions in Ireland: Problems and Possibilities'. Paper prepared for the NESF.

Hannan, D.F. and Breen, R. (1987). 'Schools and Gender Roles', in M. Cullen (ed.) *Girls Don't Do Honours*. Dublin: Women's Education Bureau.

Hannan, D.F. and Katsiaouni, L.A. (1977). *Traditional Families? From Culturally Prescribed to Negotiated Roles in Farm Families*. Dublin: ESRI.

Hannan, D.F. and Ó Riain, S. (1993). *Pathways to Adulthood in Ireland*. Dublin: ESRI.

Hannan, D.F., Breen, R., Murray, B., Watson, D. and Hardiman, N. (1983). *Schooling and Sex Roles*. Dublin: ESRI.

Hannan, D.F., Hövels, B., Van Den Berg, S. and White, M. (1995). '"Early Leavers" from Education and Training in Ireland, the Netherlands and the United Kingdom', *European Journal of Education* 30: 325-346.

Hannan, D.F., McCabe, B. and McCoy, S. (1998). *Trading Qualifications for Jobs*. Dublin: Oak Tree Press.

Hannan, D.F., Smyth, E., McCullagh, T., O'Leary, R. and McMahon, D. (1996). *Coeducation and Gender Equality*. Dublin: Oak Tree Press.

Hanratty, P. (1973). Evening Students at University. Unpublished M.Ed. thesis, Trinity College Dublin.

Hanratty, P.C. (1982). Distance Education and its Possibilities in Providing Access to Third-Level Education for Students of Mature Years. Unpublished M.Ed. thesis, Trinity College Dublin.

Haran, N. and Tormey, R. (2002). *Celebrating Difference, Promoting Equality: Towards a Framework for Intercultural Education in Irish Classrooms*. Limerick: Mary Immaculate College, CEDR.

Haraway, D. (1994). 'A Manifesto for Cyborgs: Science, Technology, and Socialist Feminism in the 1980s', in S. Seidman (ed.) *The Postmodern Turn*. Cambridge: Cambridge University Press.

Harbison, F. (1967). *Educational Planning and Human Resource Development*. Paris: UNESCO.

Hardiman, N. (1988). *Pay, Politics and Economic Performance in Ireland, 1970-87*. Oxford: Clarendon Press.

Hardiman, N. and Lalor, S. (1984). 'Corporatism in Ireland: An Exchange of Views', *Administration* 32: 76-88.

Harding, S. (1986). *The Science Question in Feminism*. Milton Keynes: Open University Press.

Harrington, M. (1962). *The Other America*. New York: Macmillan.

Harris, J. (1989). 'The Policy-Making Role of the Department of Education' in D.G. Mulcahy and D. O'Sullivan (eds) *Irish Educational Policy. Process and Substance.* Dublin: IPA.

Hartsock, N. (1987). 'The Feminist Standpoint: Developing the Ground for a Specifically Historical Materialism', in S. Harding (ed.) *Feminism and Methodology*. Milton Keynes: Open University Press.

Hastings, C., O'Byrne, D. and Jones, N. (1978). *Learning Problems of Disabled Trainees*. Dublin: AnCo.

Hazelkorn, E. (1986). 'Class, Clientelism and the Political Process in the Irish Republic', in P. Clancy, S. Drudy, K. Lynch and L. O'Dowd (eds) *Ireland: A Sociological Profile*. Dublin: IPA in association with the SAI.

Healy, K. (1998). 'The New Institutionalism and Irish Social Policy', in S. Healy and B. Reynolds (eds) *Social Policy in Ireland*. Dublin: Oak Tree Press.

Healy, S. and Reynolds, B. (1985). *Ireland Today. Reflecting in the Light of the Gospel*. CMRS, Justice Office.

Healy, S. and Reynolds, B. (1993). 'Work, Jobs and Income: Towards a New Paradigm', in B. Reynolds and S. Healy (eds) *New Frontiers for Full Citizenship*. Dublin: CMRS.

Healy, S. and Reynolds, B. (1998). 'Progress, Paradigms and Policy', in S. Healy and B. Reynolds (eds) *Social Policy in Ireland*. Dublin: Oak Tree Press.

Heidegger, M. (1962[1927]). *Being and Time*. Oxford: Blackwell.

Henriques, J., Hollway, W., Unwin, C., Venn, C. and Walkerdine, V. (eds) (1984). *Changing the Subject: Psychology, Social Regulation and Subjectivity*. London: Methuen.

Herrnstein, R.J. and Murray, C. (1994). *The Bell Curve. Intelligence and Class Structure in American Life*. New York: Simon and Schuster.

Hesketh, T. (1990). *The Second Partitioning of Ireland. The Abortion Referendum of 1983*. Dublin: Brandsma Books.

Heywood, A. (1997). *Politics*. London: Macmillan.

Higgins, M.D. (1991). 'Preface' to *Irish Education. The Case for Secular Reform* (D. Alvey). Dublin and Belfast: Church and State Books and Athol Books.

Higher Education Authority (1995). *Report of the Steering Committee on the Future Development of Higher Education*. Dublin: HEA.

Higher Education Authority (2003). *Provision of Undergraduate and Taught Postgraduate Education to Overseas Students in Ireland*. Dublin: HEA.

Hillery, P.J. (1963). 'Post-Primary Education'. Reprinted in OECD (1969). *Reviews of National Policies for Education. Ireland*. Paris: OECD.

Hindess, B. (1996). *Discourses of Power: From Hobbes to Foucault*. Oxford: Blackwell.

Hogan, P. (1982). 'The Central Question in Technological Education', in M. Farry and N. McMillan (eds) *Higher Technological Education in Ireland*. Dublin: Irish Branch, Institute of Physics.

Hogan, P. (1995). *The Custody and Courtship of Experience: Western Education in Philosophical Perspective*. Dublin: The Columba Press.

Hogan, P. and Williams, K. (eds) (1997). *The Future of Religion in Irish Education*. Dublin: Veritas.

Holland, M. (2002). 'It is Time to Stop the School Bullies', *The Irish Times*, 11 July.

Holland, S. (1979). *Rutland Street*. Oxford: Pergamon Press.

Homans, G.C. (1961). *Social Behaviour: Its Elementary Forms*. London: Routledge and Kegan Paul.

Hornsby-Smith, M.P. (1992). 'Social and Religious Transformations in Ireland: A Case of Secularisation', in J.H. Goldthorpe and C.T. Whelan (eds) *The Development of Industrial Society in Ireland*. Oxford: Clarendon Press.

Hughes, C. (2000). 'Resistant Adult Learners: A Contradiction in Feminist Terms', *Studies in the Education of Adults* 32: 51-62.

Humm, M. (1992). *Feminisms*. New York: Harvester.

Humphreys, A.J. (1966). *New Dubliners. Urbanisation and the Irish Family*. London: Routledge and Kegan Paul.

Hunter, F. (1963). *Community Power Structure*. New York: Anchor Books.

Hussey, G. (1990). *At the Cutting Edge*. Dublin: Gill and Macmillan.

Hyland, Á. (1989). 'The Multi-Denominational Experience in the National School System in Ireland', *Irish Educational Studies* 8: 89-114.

Hyland, Á. (1990). 'The Curriculum and Examinations Board: A Retrospective View', in G. McNamara, K. Williams and D. Herron (eds) *Achievement and Aspiration*. Dublin: Drumcondra Teachers' Centre.

Hyland, Á. (1996). 'Multi-Denominational Schools in the Republic of Ireland 1975-1995'. Paper presented at the Conference Education and Religion, Nice, 21-22 June.

Hyland, Á. (ed.) (2000). *Multiple Intelligences, Curriculum and Assessment Project. Final Report*. Cork: Education Department, University College Cork.

Hyland, A. and Milne, K. (1992). *Irish Educational Documents. Volume II*. Dublin: Church of Ireland College of Education, Rathmines.

Hyland, W. (1969). 'Effects of Retardation on National School Pupils', *Oideas* 2: 50-55.

Industrial Policy Review Group (1992). *A Time for Change: Industrial Policy for the 1990s* (Culliton Report). Dublin: Stationery Office.

Inglis, T. (1979). 'Decline in Numbers of Priests and Religious in Ireland', *Doctrine and Life* February: 79-98.

Inglis, T. (1989). 'Adult Education and Government Policy 1979-1989. A Review', *The Adult Learner* 1: 19-25.

Inglis, T. (1997). 'Empowerment and Emancipation', *Adult Education Quarterly* 48: 3-17.

Inglis, T. (1998a). *Moral Monopoly*. Dublin: UCD Press.

Inglis, T. (1998b). *Lessons in Irish Sexuality*. Dublin: UCD Press.

Inglis, T. and Basset, M. (1988). *Live and Learn. Day-Time Adult Education in Coolock, Dublin*. Dublin: AONTAS.

Inglis, T., Bailey, K. and Murray, C. (1993). *Liberating Learning. A Report on Day Time Education Groups*. Dublin: AONTAS.

Inter-Departmental Committee on the Raising of the School-Leaving Age (1935). *Report*. Dublin: Stationery Office.

Investment in Education (1965). Report of the Survey Team appointed by the Minister for Education in October, 1962. Dublin: Stationery Office.

Ionescu, G. and Gellner, E. (eds) (1969). *Populism. Its Meanings and National Characteristics*. London: Weidenfeld and Nicolson.

Irish Business and Employers' Confederation (1999). 'News Release (21 March). Girls Significantly Outperform Boys in Examinations.' Dublin: IBEC.

Irish Foundation for Human Development (1984). 'Report on the North Mayo/Sligo Pilot Project Education for Development', in Department of Education *Preparation of Young People for Work and Facilitation of their Transition from Education to Working Life*. Dublin: Stationery Office.

Irish National Teachers' Organization (1947). *A Plan for Education*. Dublin: INTO.

Irish National Teachers' Organization (1976). *Primary School Curriculum. Curriculum Questionnaire Analysis*. Dublin: INTO.

Irish National Teachers' Organization (1980). *In-Service Education and Training of Teachers*. Dublin: INTO.

Irish National Teachers' Organization (1992). *Travellers in Education*. Dublin: INTO.

Irvine, D. (1974). Participation in Adult Education in the West of Ireland: A Structural and Clientele Analysis. Unpublished Ph.D. thesis, University of Liverpool.

Jacobsen, J.K. (1994). *Chasing Progress in the Republic of Ireland*. Cambridge: Cambridge University Press.

James, A. and Jenks, C. (1996). 'Public Perceptions of Childhood Criminality', *British Journal of Sociology* 47: 315-331.

Jameson, F. (1991). *Postmodernism, or, The Cultural Logic of Late Capitalism*. London: Verso.

Janks, H. (1997). 'Critical Discourse Analysis as a Research Tool', *Discourse: Studies in the Cultural Politics of Education* 18: 329-342.

Jarvis, P. (1995). *Adult and Continuing Education. Theory and Practice*. London: Routledge.

Jenks, C. (1993). *Culture*. London: Routledge.

Jensen, A.R. (1969). 'How Much Can We Boost IQ and Scholastic Achievement?', *Harvard Educational Review* 39: 1-123.

Jóhannesson, I.Á. (1992). 'Capable of Resisting and Entitled to Lead: On the Historical Conditions of the Neo-Marxist Educational Discourse', *Educational Policy* 6: 298-318.

Joint Committee on Lifelong Learning (2001). *Actions for a Learning Society*. Dublin: IBEC, CHIU and CDIT.

Joint Managerial Body (1999). Draft Working Document on Gender Equity. Dublin: Private Circulation.

Joint Oireachtas Committee on Women's Rights (1984). *First Report. Education*. Dublin: Stationery Office.

Jones, H.S. (1968). 'Organisational and Group Factors in Approved School Training', in R.E. Sparks and R.G. Hood (eds) *The Residential Treatment of Disturbed and Delinquent Boys*. Cambridge: Institute of Criminology.

Jones, P.W. (1997). 'On World Bank Education Financing', *Comparative Education* 33: 117-129.

Joppke, C. (2004). 'The Retreat of Multiculturalism in the Liberal State: Theory and Policy', *British Journal of Sociology* 55: 237-257.

Kamin, L.J. (1977). *The Science and Politics of I.Q.* Harmondsworth: Penguin.

Kane, E. (1996). 'The Power of Paradigms: Social Science and Intellectual Contributions to Public Discourse in Ireland', in L. O'Dowd (ed.) *On Intellectuals and Intellectual Life in Ireland*. Belfast and Dublin: QUB Institute of Irish Studies and the Royal Irish Academy.

Karabel, J. and Halsey, A.H. (1977). *Power and Ideology in Education*. New York: Oxford University Press.

Katz, M.B. (1989). *The Undeserving Poor*. New York: Pantheon Books.

Kavanagh, J. (1966). *Manual of Social Ethics*. Dublin: Gill.

Kearney, R. (1986). *Modern Movements in European Philosophy*. Manchester: Manchester University Press.

Kearney, R. (1997). *Postnationalist Ireland. Politics, Culture, Philosophy*. London: Routledge.

Keddie, N. (ed.) (1973). *Tinker, Tailor… The Myth of Cultural Deprivation*. London: Harmondsworth: Penguin.

Kellaghan, T. (1968). 'Review of *The Lay Teacher* (P. Duffy)', *Irish Journal of Education* 2: 63-65.

Kellaghan, T. (1989). 'The Interface of Research, Evaluation and Policy in Irish Education', in D.G. Mulcahy and D. O'Sullivan (eds) *Irish Educational Policy. Process and Substance*. Dublin: IPA.

Kellaghan, T. (2001). 'Towards a Definition of Educational Disadvantage', *Irish Journal of Education* 32: 3-22.

Kellaghan, T. (2002). 'Approaches to Problems of Educational Disadvantage', in A.L. Gilligan (ed.) *Primary Education: Ending Disadvantage. Proceedings and Action Plan of National Forum*. Dublin: St Patrick's College.

Kellaghan, T. and Greaney, B.J. (1993). *The Educational Development of Students Following Participation in a Preschool Programme in a Disadvantaged Area*. Dublin: Educational Research Centre.

Kellaghan, T. and Greaney, V. (1970). 'Factors Related to Choice of Post-Primary School in Ireland', *Irish Journal of Education* 4: 69-83.

Kellaghan, T. and Lewis, M. (1991). *Transition Education in Irish Schools*. Dublin: The Educational Company.

Kellaghan, T. and Ó hUallacháin, S. (1973). 'A Preschool Intervention Project for Disadvantaged Children', *Oideas* 10: 38-47.

Kellaghan, T., Fontes, P.J., O'Toole, C. and Egan, O. (1985). *Gender Inequalities in Primary-School Teaching*. Dublin: The Educational Company.

Kellaghan, T., Madaus, G.F., Airasian, P.W., and Fontes, P.J. (1976). 'The Mathematical Attainments of Post-Primary School Entrants', *Irish Journal of Education* 10: 3-17.

Kellaghan, T., Weir, S., Ó hUallacháin, S. and Morgan, M. (1995). *Educational Disadvantage in Ireland*. Dublin: Combat Poverty Agency.

Kelly, M.B. (1994). *Can You Credit It?* Dublin: Combat Poverty Agency.

Kennedy, J. (1982). *Results of a Questionnaire Study to Ascertain the Present Position of Adult Literacy Provision in Ireland*. Tralee: NALA.

Kennedy, S. (1971). 'The Role of Religious in Child Care,' in *Child Care: Killarney Seminar.* Dublin: Council for Social Welfare.

Kenny, M. (1991). 'Interculturalism and Europe's Nomads', in J. Coolahan (ed.) *Teacher Education in the Nineties: Towards a New Coherence*. Limerick: Mary Immaculate College of Education.

Kenny, M. (1994). 'Final Thoughts: A Case for Celebration?', in M. McCann, S. Ó Síocháin and J. Ruane (eds) *Irish Travellers: Culture and Ethnicity*. Belfast: QUB Institute of Irish Studies for the Anthropological Association of Ireland.

Kenny, M. (1997a). *The Routes of Resistance: Travellers and Second-Level Schooling*. Aldershot: Ashgate.

Kenny, M. (1997b). 'Review of *Travellers and Ireland. Whose Country, Whose History?* (J. Mac Laughlin)', *Irish Journal of Sociology* 7: 138-142.

Kenny, Mary (1997). *Goodbye to Catholic Ireland*. London: Sinclair-Stevenson.

Kenway, J., Bigum, C. and Fitzclarence, L. (1993). 'Marketing Education in the Postmodern Age', *Journal of Education Policy* 8: 105-122.

Keogh, D. (1994). *Twentieth-Century Ireland. Nation and State*. Dublin: Gill and Macmillan.

Keogh, H. and Downes, T. (1998). *VTOSpells Success*. Dublin: Department of Education and Science.

Kiberd, D. (1995). *Inventing Ireland: The Literature of the Modern Nation*. London: Jonathan Cape.

Kiely, E. (2004). Sexing the Curriculum: A Poststructuralist Interrogation of the Politics of Irish Sexuality Education 1960-2002. Unpublished Ph.D. thesis, Department of Applied Social Studies, University College Cork.

Kirby, P. (1997). *Poverty and Plenty. World and Irish Development Reconsidered*. Dublin: Trócaire and Gill and Macmillan.

Kirby, P. (2002). *The Celtic Tiger in Distress: Growth with Inequality in Ireland*. Houndmills: Palgrave.

Kirby, P., Gibbons, L. and Cronin, M. (eds) (2002). *Reinventing Ireland*. London: Pluto Press.

Kleinman, M. (2002). *A European Welfare State? European Union Social Policy in Context*. Houndmills: Palgrave.

Knowles, M.S. (1980). *The Modern Practice of Adult Education: From Pedagogy to Andragogy*. Chicago: Follett.

Komisar, B.P. and McClellan, J. (1961). 'The Logic of Slogans', in B. Smith and R.H. Ennis (eds) *Language and Concepts in Education*. Chicago: Rand McNally.

Kripke, S. (1982). *Wittgenstein on Rules and Private Language*. Oxford: Blackwell.

Kroeber, A.L. and Kluckhohn, C. (1952). *Culture: A Critical Review of Concepts and Definitions.* Cambridge, MA: Harvard University Peabody Museum of American Archaeology and Ethnology.

Kuhn, T. (1962). *The Structure of Scientific Revolutions.* Chicago: Chicago University Press.

Kuhn, T. (1970). *The Structure of Scientific Revolutions* (Second Edition). Chicago: Chicago University Press.

Kumar, K. (1991). *Utopianism.* Buckingham: Open University Press.

Kumar, K. (1995). *From Post-Industrial to Post-Modern Society.* Oxford: Blackwell.

La Rochefoucauld, F. (1940). *The Maxims.* London: Oxford University Press.

Laclau, E. and Mouffe, C. (1985). *Hegemony and Socialist Strategy: Towards a Radical Democracy.* London: Verso.

Lacombe, D. (1996). 'Reforming Foucault: A Critique of the Social Control Thesis', *British Journal of Sociology* 47: 332-352.

Lane, D. (1991). 'Catholic Education and the School: Some Theological Reflections', in Conference of Major Religious Superiors, *The Catholic School in Contemporary Society.* Dublin: CMRS, Education Commission.

Larrain, J. (1979). *The Concept of Ideology.* London: Hutchinson.

Lasch, C. (1980). *The Culture of Narcissism.* London: Abacus.

Layder, D. (1994). *Understanding Social Theory.* London: Sage.

Lee, J. (1989). *Ireland 1912-1985.* Cambridge: Cambridge University Press.

Levin, H.M. (1991). 'The Economics of Educational Choice', *Economics of Education Review* 10: 137-158.

Lévi-Strauss, C. (1969[1949]). *The Elementary Structures of Kinship.* London: Eyre and Spottiswoode.

Levitas, R. (1998). *The Inclusive Society?* London: Macmillan.

Lewis, M. and Kellaghan, T. (1987). 'Vocationalism in Irish Second-Level Education', *Irish Journal of Education* 21: 5-38.

Lewis, M. and Kellaghan, T. (1993). *Exploring the Gender Gap in Primary Schools.* Dublin: Educational Research Centre.

Lindsay, C.N. (1994). 'Quality and Equity in Higher Education', *Studies* 83: 161-169.

Litwak, E. and Meyer, H.J. (1965). 'Administrative Styles and Community Linkages in Public Schools', in A.J. Reiss (ed.) *Schools in a Changing Society.* New York: Free Press.

Lloyd, D. (1999). *Ireland After History.* Cork: Cork University Press.

Lorde, A (1984). *Sister Outsider: Essays and Speeches.* New York: The Crossing Press.

Lovett, T. (1989). 'Adult Education and the Working Class', in D. O'Sullivan (ed.) *Social Commitment and Adult Education.* Cork: Cork University Press.

Lukács, G. (1971[1923]). *History and Class Consciousness.* London: Merlin.

Lukes, S. (1974). *Power: A Radical View.* London: Macmillan.

Lukes, S. (1978). 'Power and Authority', in T. Bottomore and R. Nisbet (eds) *A History of Sociological Analysis.* London: Heinemann.

Lukes, S. (1990). *Individualism.* Oxford: Blackwell.

Lynch, K. (1982). 'A Sociological Analysis of the Functions of Second Level Schooling', *Irish Educational Studies* 2: 32-58.

Lynch, K. (1987). 'Dominant Ideologies in Irish Educational Thought: Consensualism, Essentialism and Meritocratic Individualism', *Economic and Social Review* 18: 101-122.

Lynch, K. (1989). *The Hidden Curriculum: Reproduction in Education: A Reappraisal.* Lewes: Falmer Press.

Lynch, K. (1990). 'Reproduction: The Role of Cultural Factors and Educational Mediators', *British Journal of Sociology of Education* 11: 3-20.

Lynch, K. (1992). 'Intelligence, Ability and Education: Challenging Traditional Views', *Oideas* 38: 134-148.

Lynch, K. (1994). 'An Analysis of the Differences between Educational Policies Based on Principles of Equity, Equality of Opportunity and Egalitarianism', in O. Egan (ed.) *Equality of Opportunity in Third-Level Education in Ireland*. Cork: Higher Education Equality Unit.

Lynch, K. (1995). 'Equality and Resistance in Higher Education', *International Studies in Sociology of Education* 5: 93-111.

Lynch, K. (1996). 'The Limits of Liberalism for the Promotion of Equality in Education', in E. Befring (ed.) *Teacher Education for Equality*. Oslo: Oslo College for the ATEE.

Lynch, K. (1998). 'The Status of Children and Young Persons: Educational and Related Issues', in S. Healy and B. Reynolds (eds) *Social Policy in Ireland*. Dublin: Oak Tree Press.

Lynch, K. (1999a). *Equality in Education*. Dublin: Gill and Macmillan.

Lynch, K. (1999b). 'Equality Studies, the Academy and the Role of Research in Emancipatory Social Change', *Economic and Social Review* 30: 41-69.

Lynch, K. (2000). 'Realising Change: Structural and Ideological Considerations'. Paper presented at the Conference Equality and Social Justice: Challenges for Theory and Practice, University College, Dublin, 15 December.

Lynch, K. and Lodge, A. (2002). *Equality and Power in Schools*. London: RoutledgeFalmer.

Lynch, K. and Morgan, V. (1995). 'Gender and Education: North and South', in P. Clancy, S. Drudy, K. Lynch and L. O'Dowd (eds) *Irish Society: Sociological Perspectives*. Dublin: IPA in association with the SAI.

Lynch, K. and O'Neill, C. (1994). 'The Colonisation of Social Class in Education', *British Journal of Sociology of Education* 15: 307-324.

Lynch, K. and O'Riordan, C. (1998). 'Inequality in Higher Education: A Study of Class Barriers', *British Journal of Sociology of Education* 19: 445-478.

Lyons, F.S.L. (1979). *Ireland Since the Famine*. London: Fontana.

Lyotard, J.-F. (1984). *The Postmodern Condition: A Report on Knowledge*. Manchester: Manchester University Press.

Mac an Ghaill, M., Hanafin, J. and Conway, P. (2004). *Gender Politics and 'Exploring Masculinities' in Irish Education: Teachers, Materials and the Media*. Dublin: NCCA.

Mac Cárthaigh, D. (1980). Adaptation and Socialisation of Male Pupils in Boarding Schools of Munster. Unpublished M.Ed. thesis, Department of Education, UCC.

Mac Gréil, M. (1974). *Educational Opportunity in Dublin*. Dublin: Catholic Communications Institute of Ireland.

Mac Gréil, M. (ed.) (1980). *Report of the Commission of Enquiry into the Irish Penal System* (S. MacBride, Chairman). Dublin: Author.

Mac Laughlin, J. (1995). *Travellers and Ireland. Whose Country, Whose History?* Cork: Cork University Press.

MacIntyre, A. (1981). *After Virtue*. London: Duckworth.

MacKenzie, J. (1999). 'Power', in F. Ashe, A. Finlayson, M. Lloyd, I. MacKenzie, J. Martin and S. O'Neill (eds) *Contemporary Social and Political Theory*. Buckingham: Open University Press.

Mackey, L. (1987). The Role of Positive Discrimination in Education. Unpublished M.Ed. thesis, University College, Cork.

MacSharry, R. and White, P. (2000). *The Making of the Celtic Tiger: The Inside Story of Ireland's Boom Economy*. Cork: Mercier Press.

Maguire, J. (1988). 'The Case for a New Social Order', in M. Hederman (ed.) *The Clash of Ideas*. Dublin: Gill and Macmillan.

Mahon, E. (1995a). 'From Democracy to Femocracy: The Women's Movement in the Republic of Ireland', in P. Clancy, S. Drudy, K. Lynch and L. O'Dowd (eds) *Irish Society: Sociological Perspectives*. Dublin: IPA in association with the SAI.

Mahon, E. (1995b). 'Ireland's Policy Machinery', in D.M. Stetson and A.G. Mazur (eds) *Comparative State Feminism*. London: Sage.

Mahon, E. and Morgan, V. (1999). 'State Feminism in Ireland', in Y. Galligan, E. Ward and R. Wilford (eds) *Contesting Politics. Women in Ireland North and South*. Oxford: Westview Press.

Malcolm, N. (1988). *Wittgenstein: Nothing is Hidden*. Oxford: Blackwell.

Maloney, A. (1980). *Barriers to Higher Education for Apprentices*. Dublin: AnCo.

Manly, D. (n.d.). *The Facilitators*. Dublin: Brandsma Books.

Mannheim, K. (1949). *Ideology and Utopia*. London: Routledge and Kegan Paul.

Marginson, S. (1997). *Markets in Education*. St Leonards, NSW: Allen and Unwin.

Marshall, C. (1997). 'Dismantling and Reconstructing Policy Analysis', in C. Marshall (ed.) *Feminist Critical Policy Analysis 1: A Perspective from Primary and Secondary Schooling*. London: Falmer.

Marshall, J. and Peters, M. (eds) (1999). *Education Policy*. Cheltenham: Edward Elgar.

Masterman, M. (1970). 'The Nature of a Paradigm', in I. Lakatos and A. Musgrave (eds) *Criticism and the Growth of Knowledge*. Cambridge: Cambridge University Press.

Mauss, M. (1990[1952]). *The Gift*. London: Routledge.

May, D. (1971). 'Delinquency Control and the Treatment Model', *British Journal of Criminology* 11: 359-370.

May, D. (1977). 'Rhetoric and Reality', *British Journal of Criminology* 17: 209-227.

Maynard, M. (1998). 'Feminists' Knowledge and the Knowledge of Feminism: Epistemology, Theory, Methodology and Method', in T. May and M. Williams (eds) *Knowing the Social World*. Buckingham: Open University Press.

McAdam, D., McCarthy, J.D. and Zald, M.N. (1996). *Comparative Perspectives on Social Movements*. Cambridge: Cambridge University Press.

McCarthy, C. (1960). 'Purpose and Organisation', *Fundamental and Adult Education* 12: 74-78.

McCarthy, C. (1968). *The Distasteful Challenge*. Dublin: IPA.

McCarthy, P. (1972). Itinerancy and Poverty: A Study in the Sub-Culture of Poverty. Unpublished M.Soc. Sc. thesis, University College Dublin.

McCarthy, P. (1994). 'The Sub-Culture of Poverty Re-Considered', in M. McCann, S. Ó Síocháin and J. Ruane (eds) *Irish Travellers: Culture and Ethnicity*. Belfast: QUB Institute of Irish Studies for the Anthropological Association of Ireland.

McCarthy, T. (1988). *The Critical Theory of Jürgen Habermas*. Cambridge, MA: MIT Press.

McCormack, T. (1989). 'Approaches to Family and Community Education', in Conference of Major Religious Superiors *Proceedings of the Conference Education for Family and Community Development*. Dublin: CMRS, Education Commission.

McCormack, T. and Archer, P. (1998). 'Inequality in Education: The Role of Assessment and Certification', in Conference of Religious of Ireland *Inequality in Education. The Role of Assessment and Certification*. Dublin: CORI, Education Commission.

McCoy, S. and Whelan, B.J. (1996). *The Economic Status of School Leavers 1993-1995*. Dublin: Departments of Enterprise and Employment and Education, and the ESRI.

McCulloch, G. (1998). *Failing the Ordinary Child?* Buckingham: Open University Press.

McDonagh, M. (1994). 'Nomadism in Irish Travellers' Identity', in M. McCann, S. Ó Síocháin and J. Ruane (eds) *Irish Travellers: Culture and Ethnicity*. Belfast: QUB Institute of Irish Studies for the Anthropological Association of Ireland.

McDwyer, J. (1982). 'Adult Education: Some Thoughts and Memories', *AONTAS Review* 3: 71-74.

McElligott, T.J. (1986). *This Teaching Life*. Mullingar: Lilliput Press.

McGahern, J. (1965). *The Dark*. London: Faber.

McGarry, P. (2000). 'Position of Church is Compared to a Monopoly', *The Irish Times*, 7 February.

McGarry, P. (2004). 'The Largest Minority in Ireland?', *The Irish Times*, 10 February.

McGowan, G. (1990). An Examination of the Materials used in the Teaching of Irish Conversation and Reading in Primary Schools for Sexist and Sex-Stereotyping Content. Unpublished M.Ed. thesis, St Patrick's College, Maynooth.

McIntyre, D. (1993). 'The Stay Safe Programme', *Intercom*, June: 6-9.

McKernan, J. (1988). 'In Defence of Education for Living in Post-Primary Curriculum', *Oideas* 32: 65-83.

McLaren, P. (1995). *Critical Pedagogy and Predatory Culture*. London: Routledge.

McLaren, P. (with H.A. Giroux) (1995). 'Radical Pedagogy as Cultural Politics', in P. McLaren *Critical Pedagogy and Predatory Culture*. London: Routledge.

McLaren, P. and Giroux, H. (1997). 'Writing from the Margins: Geographies of Identity, Pedagogy and Power', in P. McLaren *Revolutionary Multiculturalism. Pedagogies of Dissent for a New Millennium*. Oxford: Westview Press.

McLellan, D. (1978). *The Thought of Karl Marx*. London: Macmillan.

McLellan, D. (1995). *Ideology*. Buckingham: Open University Press.

McLoughlin, D. (1994). 'Ethnicity and Irish Travellers: Reflections on Ní Shúinéar', in M. McCann, S. Ó Síocháin and J. Ruane (eds) *Irish Travellers: Culture and Ethnicity*. Belfast: QUB Institute of Irish Studies for the Anthropological Association of Ireland.

McNamara, G., Williams, K. and Herron, D. (eds) (1990). *Achievement and Aspiration: Curricular Initiatives in Irish Post-Primary Education in the 1980s*. Dublin: Drumcondra Teachers' Centre.

McNamara, K. (1987). *Curriculum and Values in Education*. Dublin: Veritas.

Melucci, A. (1996). *Challenging Codes: Collective Action in the Information Age*. Cambridge: Cambridge University Press.

Meredith, D. (1997). 'It's Worth Getting it Right', *The Irish Times Education and Living Supplement*, 18 March.

Mezirow, J. (1996). 'Adult Education and Empowerment for Individuals and Community Development', in B. Connolly, T. Fleming, D. McCormack and A. Ryan (eds) *Radical Learning for Liberation*. Maynooth: MACE.

Midwinter, E. (1972). *Priority Education*. Harmondsworth: Penguin.

Mill, J.S. (1978[1859]). *On Liberty*. Indianapolis: Hackett.

Mills, C.W. (1956). *The Power Elite*. New York: Oxford University Press.

Moody, J. (1979). 'Who is Watching? A Study of the Audience for Adult Programmes', *Irish Broadcasting Review* 4: 44-49.

Morgan, M. (1993). *BITE and LCBEI: Second Year Evaluation Report*. Dublin: Educational Research Centre.

Morgan, M., Hickey, B. and Kellaghan, T. (1997). *International Adult Literacy Survey: Results for Ireland*. Dublin: Department of Education.

Mulcahy, D.G. (1981a). *Curriculum and Policy in Irish Post-Primary Education*. Dublin: IPA.

Mulcahy, D.G. (1981b). '*Investment in Education*: Fifteen Years Later', *Guth agus Tuairim* 1: 16-27.

Mulcahy, D.G. (1989). 'Official Perceptions of Curriculum in Irish Second-Level Education', in D.G. Mulcahy and D. O'Sullivan (eds) *Irish Educational Policy: Process and Substance*. Dublin: IPA.

Munck, R. (2003). 'Review of *Reinventing Ireland* (P. Kirby *et al.*)', *Irish Journal of Sociology* 12: 104-105.

Murgatroyd, S. and Morgan, C. (1992). *Total Quality Management and the School*. Buckingham: Open University Press.

Murphy, A. (1996). 'Comparability and Future-Research in Adult Education: Methodological Challenges in the Euro-Delphi Survey', in B. Connolly, T. Fleming, D. McCormack and A. Ryan (eds) *Radical Learning for Liberation*. Maynooth: MACE.

Murphy, B. (2000). *Support for the Educationally and Socially Disadvantaged*. Cork: Education Department, University College Cork.

Murphy, J.A. (1975). *Ireland in the Twentieth Century*. Dublin: Gill and Macmillan.

Murphy, J.A. (1995). *The College. A History of Queen's/University College Cork*. Cork: Cork University Press.

Murray, C. (1994). *Losing Ground. American Social Policy 1950-1980*. New York: Basic Books.

NALA Research and Development Sub-Committee (1988). *Getting Help with Reading and Writing. Co. Offaly Research Project*. Dublin: NALA.

National Adult Literacy Agency (1981). *Recommendations on the Provision of Adult Literacy and Basic Skills Programmes*. Tralee: NALA.

National Anti-Poverty Strategy. Sharing in Progress (1997). Dublin: Stationery Office.

National Committee on Pilot Schemes to Combat Poverty (1980). *Final Report. Pilot Schemes to Combat Poverty in Ireland 1974-1980*. Dublin: Author.

National Council for Curriculum and Assessment (1990). *Senior Cycle: Issues and Structures. A Consultative Paper*. Dublin: NCCA.

National Council for Curriculum and Assessment (1996). *Relationships and Sexuality Education. Interim Curriculum and Guidelines for Primary/Secondary Schools*. Dublin: Stationery Office.

National Council for Curriculum and Assessment (2004). *Civic, Social and Political Education. NCCA Response to NEXUS Report on Survey of Principals and CSPE Teachers*. Dublin: NCCA.

National Council for Educational Awards (1978). *Discussion Document on an NCEA Award Structure for Recurrent Education*. Dublin: NCEA.

National Council for Educational Awards (1985). *Towards Facilitating Awards for Adult and Continuing Education*. Dublin: NCEA.

National Development Plan 2000-2006 (1999). Dublin: Stationery Office.

National Economic and Social Council (1976). *Educational Expenditure in Ireland*. Dublin: NESC.

National Economic and Social Council (1982). *A Review of Industrial Policy* (Telesis Report). Dublin: NESC.

National Economic and Social Council (1983). *Economic and Social Policy 1983: Aims and Recommendations*. Dublin: NESC.

National Economic and Social Council (1990). *A Strategy for the Nineties*. Dublin: Stationery Office.

National Economic and Social Council (1993). *Education and Training Policies for Economic and Social Development*. Dublin: Stationery Office.

National Economic and Social Council (1999). *Opportunities, Challenges and Capacities for Choice*. Dublin: NESC.

National Economic and Social Forum (1996). *Equality Proofing Issues*. Dublin: NESF.

National Economic and Social Forum (1997). *Early School Leavers and Youth Unemployment*. Dublin: NESF.

National Economic and Social Forum (2002). *Early School Leavers*. Dublin: NESF.

National Industrial Economic Council (1966). *Comments on 'Investment in Education'*. Dublin: NIEC.

National Qualifications Authority of Ireland (2003). *The Role of National Qualification Systems in Promoting Lifelong Learning*. Dublin: National Qualifications Authority of Ireland.

Ní Chárthaigh, D. (1998). *Gender Equity for 2000 and Beyond. Report of Rapporteur*. Dublin: Department of Education and Science.

Ní Aonghusa, C. (1997). *Towards a Critical Awareness of the Marketplace. Consumer Education in Ireland*. Dublin: CDVEC Curriculum Development Unit.

Ní Chuirc, M. (1999). 'The Employment Strategy and the European Social Fund: Future Policy Directions', in Area Development Management, *Partnerships in Education. Learning the Lessons from Local Development*. Dublin: ADM.

Nic Ghiolla Phádraig, M. (1995). 'The Power of the Catholic Church in the Republic of Ireland' in P. Clancy, S. Drudy, K. Lynch and L. O'Dowd (eds) *Irish Society: Sociological Perspectives*. Dublin: IPA in association with the SAI.

Nicholson, L. and Seidman, S. (eds) (1995). *Social Postmodernism. Beyond Identity Politics*. Cambridge: Cambridge University Press.

Nolan, B. and Callan, T. (eds) (1994). *Poverty and Policy in Ireland*. Dublin: Gill and Macmillan.

Nolan, B., O'Connell, P.J. and Whelan, C.T. (eds) (2000). *Bust to Boom? The Irish Experience of Growth and Inequality*. Dublin: IPA.

Ó Buachalla, S. (1977). 'Education as an Issue in the First and Second Dáil', *Administration* 25: 57-75.

Ó Buachalla, S. (1978). 'Non-Traditional Forms of Higher Education in West Ireland', *Pedagogica Europaea* 13: 107-154.

Ó Buachalla, S. (1988). *Education Policy in Twentieth Century Ireland*. Dublin: Wolfhound Press.

Ó Cinnéide, S. (1972). 'The Extent of Poverty in Ireland', *Social Studies* 1: 381-400.

Ó Conaill, N. (1991). 'Girls and Science: Equality in School or Society', *Irish Educational Studies* 10: 82-95.

Ó Donnabháin, D. (1990). 'Republic of Ireland: Minicompanies', in C. Poster and A. Krüger (eds) *Community Education in the Western World*. London: Routledge.

Ó Donnabháin, D. (1998). 'The Work-Related Curriculum', in A. Trant, D. Ó Donnabháin, D. Lawton and T. O'Connor *The Future of the Curriculum*. Dublin: CDVEC Curriculum Development Unit.

Ó Fathaigh, M. and O'Sullivan, D. (2000). 'Five Decades of Adult Education at UCC, 1948-1998: From Roman Catholic Social Reconstruction to Community Partnerships and Empowerment', in A. Cooke and A. McSween (eds) *The Rise and Fall of Adult Education Institutions and Social Movements*. Frankfurt: Peter Lang.

Ó hUallacháin, S. and Kellaghan, T. (1969). 'A Project for Disadvantaged Pre-School Children', *Oideas* 3: 28-32.

Ó Murchú, M.W. (1986). The Role of Irish Universities and University-Level Institutions in Continuing Education. Unpublished Ph.D. thesis, University College Dublin.

Ó Murchú, M.W. (1989). 'Alfred O'Rahilly and the Provision of Adult Education at University College, Cork', in D. O'Sullivan (ed.) *Social Commitment and Adult Education*. Cork: Cork University Press.

O'Brien, C. Cruise (1992). *The Great Melody. A Thematic Biography of Edmund Burke*. London: Sinclair-Stevenson.

O'Brien, J. (1999). 'An Overview of Department of Education and Science Policy in Combating Educational Disadvantage and Promoting Social Inclusion', in Area Development Management *Partnerships in Education. Learning the Lessons from Local Development. Conference Papers*. Dublin: ADM.

O'Carroll, J.P. (1991). 'Bishops, Knights – and Pawns? Traditional Thought and the Irish Abortion Referendum Debate of 1983', *Irish Political Studies* 6: 53-71.

O'Carroll, J.P. (2002). 'Culture Lag and Democratic Deficit: Or, Dat's outside de Terms of D'Agreement', *Community Development Journal* 37: 10-19.

O'Connell, J. (1992). 'Working with Irish Travellers', in DTEDG *DTEDG File. Irish Travellers: New Analysis and New Initiatives*. Dublin: Pavee Point.

O'Connell, J. (1994). 'Ethnicity and Irish Travellers', in M. McCann, S. Ó Síocháin and J. Ruane (eds) *Irish Travellers: Culture and Ethnicity*. Belfast: QUB Institute of Irish Studies for the Anthropological Association of Ireland.

O'Connell, T.J. (1969). *100 Years of Progress: The Story of the Irish National Teachers' Organization 1868-1968*. Dublin: INTO.

O'Connor, J. (1963). 'The Juvenile Offender', *Studies* 52: 69-96.

O'Connor, M.E. (1971). The Juvenile Offender in a Reformatory School: A Sociological Study. Unpublished M.Soc.Sc. thesis, University College Dublin.

O'Connor, P. (1998). *Emerging Voices. Women in Contemporary Irish Society*. Dublin: IPA.

O'Connor, R. and Kelly, P. (1980). *The Dynamics and Vocational Training Implications of Low-Capital Cooperative Enterprises*. Dublin: AnCo.

O'Connor, S. (1968). 'Post-Primary Education: Now and in the Future', *A Studies Symposium* 9-25.

O'Connor, S. (1986). *A Troubled Sky: Reflections on the Irish Educational Scene*. Dublin: Educational Research Centre.

O'Connor, T. (1998). 'The Impact of the European Social Fund on the Development of Initial Vocational Education and Training in Ireland', in A. Trant, D. Ó Donnabháin, D. Lawton and T. O'Connor *The Future of the Curriculum*. Dublin: CDVEC Curriculum Development Unit.

O'Doherty, D.M. (1977). *The Literacy Requirements of Occupations at Semi-Skilled, Skilled and First-Line Supervisory levels in a Sample of Irish Industries*. Dublin: AnCo.

O'Donnell, R. and Thomas, D. (1998). 'Partnership and Policy-Making', in S. Healy and B. Reynolds (eds) *Social Policy in Ireland*. Dublin: Oak Tree Press.

O'Donoghue, M. (1971). *Economic Dimensions in Education*. Dublin: Gill and Macmillan.

O'Donoghue, T.A. (1999). *The Catholic Church and the Secondary School Curriculum in Ireland, 1922-1962*. New York: Peter Lang.

O'Donovan, Ó and Ward, E. (1999). 'Networks of Women's Groups in the Republic of Ireland', in Y. Galligan, E. Ward and R. Wilford (eds) *Contesting Politics. Women in Ireland, North and South*. Oxford: Westview Press.

O'Dowd, L. (1996). 'Intellectuals and Intelligentsia: A Sociological Introduction', in L. O'Dowd (ed.) *On Intellectuals and Intellectual Life in Ireland*. Belfast and Dublin: QUB Institute of Irish Studies and the Royal Irish Academy.

O'Faolain, N. (1996). *Are You Somebody?* Dublin: New Island Books.

O'Flaherty, L. (1992). *Management and Control in Irish Education. The Post-Primary Experience*. Dublin: Drumcondra Teachers' Centre.

O'Grady, S. (1980). '1980 Annual Conference Introductory Address', *AONTAS Review* 2: 53-56.

O'Grady, S. (1982). 'President's Address to the 1982 AONTAS AGM', *AONTAS Review* 3: 58-63.

O'Hagan, E. (2002). *Employee Relations in the Periphery of Europe: The Unfolding Story of the European Social Model*. Houndmills: Palgrave.

O'Hagan, Lord (1870). 'Address at the Opening Meeting of the Twenty-Fourth Session', *Journal of the Statistical and Social Inquiry Society of Ireland* 39: 219-229.

O'Hara, P. (1997). 'Interfering Women – Farm Mothers and the Reproduction of Family Farming', *Economic and Social Review* 28: 135-156.

O'Hearn, D. (1995). 'Global Restructuring in the Irish Political Economy', in P. Clancy, S. Drudy, K. Lynch and L. O'Dowd (eds) *Irish Society. Sociological Perspectives*. Dublin: IPA in association with the SAI.

O'Hearn, D. (1998). *Inside the Celtic Tiger: The Irish Economy and the Asian Model*. London: Pluto Press.

O'Malley, D. (1966). Address to the National Union of Journalists, Dún Laoghaire, 10 September. Quoted in *The Sunday Press*, 11 September.

O'Meara, J.J. (1958). *Reform in Education*. Dublin: Mount Salus Press.

O'Neill, C. (1992). *Telling it Like it is*. Dublin: Combat Poverty Agency.

O'Rahilly, A. (1948a). *Aquinas versus Marx*. Cork: Cork University Press.

O'Rahilly, A. (1948b). *Moral Principles*. Cork: Cork University Press.

O'Rahilly, A. (1948c). *Social Principles*. Cork: Cork University Press.

O'Rahilly, A. (1952). *The Constitutional Position of Education in the Republic of Ireland*. Cork: Cork University Press.

O'Reilly, B. (1984). 'Curriculum and Policy in Irish Post-Primary Education', *Irish Educational Studies* 4: 21-32.

O'Reilly, B. (1989). 'Issues in the Development of Vocational Education', *Administration* 37: 152-170.

O'Reilly, B. (1992). 'Sub-National Structures for Irish Education', *Irish Education Decision Maker* 5: 15-17.

O'Rourke, M. (1991). Address to National Parents' Council Annual Meeting, Rosslare, Easter.

O'Sullivan, D. (1972a). 'Educational Aspects of the Community School: A Review of Related Research', *Studies* 61: 67-84.

O'Sullivan, D. (1972b). 'The Post-Primary School as a Socialising Agent', *Irish Journal of Education* 6: 9-30.

O'Sullivan, D. (1973). 'National School Terminal Leaving and School Delay', *Studies* 62: 63-74.

O'Sullivan, D. (1976). 'Links with Europe for Better Research', *The European Teacher* 11: 34-36.

O'Sullivan, D. (1977). 'The Administrative Processing of Children in Care: Some Sociological Findings', *Administration* 24: 413-434.

O'Sullivan, D. (1978). 'Negotiation in the Maintenance of Social Control: A Study in an Irish Correctional School', *International Journal of Criminology and Penology* 6: 31-42.

O'Sullivan, D. (1979). 'Social Definition in Child Care in the Irish Republic: Models of the Child and Child-Care Intervention', *Economic and Social Review* 10: 209-229.

O'Sullivan, D. (1980a). 'Teacher Socialisation and Teaching Style in an Irish Cultural Context', *European Journal of Education* 15: 387-397.

O'Sullivan, D. (1980b). 'Child Advocacy in the Irish Republic: Social Location, Self-Presentation and Ideology', in N. Kach (ed.) *The Child and Stress in Contemporary Society*. Alberta: University of Alberta, Department of Educational Foundations.

O'Sullivan, D. (1980c). 'Teachers' Views on the Effects of the Home', *Educational Research* 22: 138-142.

O'Sullivan, D. (1980d). 'Socialisation, Social Change and Ideology in Adult Education', *Adult Education* 52: 318-323.

O'Sullivan, D. (1981). *Adult Education and Adult Socialisation. A Study of Student Perceptions of Personal Change associated with the Diploma in Social Study Course.* Cork: Department of Adult Education, UCC.

O'Sullivan, D. (1982). 'Adult Education, Social Change and the Interpretive Model', *AONTAS Review* 3: 57-70.

O'Sullivan, D. (1984a). 'Social Class and Sexual Variations in Teachers' Perceptions of their Pupils', *Oideas* 28: 15-26.

O'Sullivan, D. (1984b). 'Pedagogues under Threat, Paradigms Rule OK', *Sociological Society of Ireland Bulletin* 37: 15-21.

O'Sullivan, D. (1989a). 'The Ideational Base of Irish Educational Policy', in D.G. Mulcahy and D. O'Sullivan (eds) *Irish Educational Policy: Process and Substance.* Dublin: IPA.

O'Sullivan, D. (ed.) (1989b). *Social Commitment and Adult Education.* Cork: Cork University Press.

O'Sullivan, D. (1989c). 'Adult and Continuing Education in the Irish Republic: A Research Synthesis', *International Journal of Lifelong Education* 8: 211-234.

O'Sullivan, D. (1992a). 'Cultural Strangers and Educational Change: The OECD Report *Investment in Education* and Irish Educational Policy', *Journal of Education Policy* 7: 445-469.

O'Sullivan, D. (1992b). 'Shaping Educational Debate: A Case Study and an Interpretation', *Economic and Social Review* 23: 423-438.

O'Sullivan, D. (1993a). 'The Concept of Policy Paradigm: Elaboration and Illumination', *Journal of Educational Thought* 27: 246-272.

O'Sullivan, D. (1993b). *Commitment, Educative Action and Adults.* Aldershot: Avebury.

O'Sullivan, D. (1994a). 'Hands Up All in Favour of Inequality!' *Studies* 83: 191-199.

O'Sullivan, D. (1994b). 'Socially-Committed Learning Programmes: Towards Provider Reflexivity', in P. Jarvis and F. Pöggeler (eds) *Developments in the Education of Adults in Europe.* Frankfurt: Peter Lang.

O'Sullivan, D. (1996a). 'Cultural Exclusion and Educational Change: Education, Church and Religion in the Irish Republic', *Compare* 26: 35-49.

O'Sullivan, D. (1996b). 'Kulturní Cizinci a Rekonstrukce Skolství', *Czech Sociological Review* 32: 159-173.

O'Sullivan, D. (1996c). 'Equal Educational Opportunity: Policy Options and Choices', *TUI Congress Journal 1996*: 53-57.

O'Sullivan, D. (1998). 'Cultural Strangers and Educational Reconstruction in Central Europe in Comparative perspective', in F. Columbus (ed.) *Central and Eastern Europe in Transition.* New York: Nova Science.

O'Sullivan, D. (1999a). 'Educational Disadvantage: Excavating the Theoretical Frameworks', in K. Fahy (ed.) *Strategies to Address Educational Disadvantage.* Galway: Community Workers' Cooperative.

O'Sullivan, D. (1999b). 'Gender Equity as Policy Paradigm in the Irish Educational Policy Process', *Economic and Social Review* 30: 309-336.

O'Sullivan, D. (2000). 'From Theocentric to Market Paradigms in Irish Educational Policy: Equality, Difference, Virtue and Control', in K. Mazurek, M.A. Winzer and C. Majorek (eds) *Education in a Global Society. A Comparative Perspective.* Boston, MA: Allyn and Bacon.

O'Toole, F. (1997). 'Education Bill Offers Little Choice on Church Control', *The Irish Times*, 4 April.

OECD (1961). *Ability and Educational Opportunity*. Paris: OECD.

OECD (1969). *Reviews of National Policies for Education. Ireland*. Paris: OECD.

OECD (1991). *Reviews of National Policies for Education. Ireland*. Paris: OECD.

OECD (1996). *Lifelong Learning For All*. Paris: OECD.

OECD/CERI (1997). *Parents as Partners in Schooling*. Paris: OECD.

Oliver, E. (2001). 'Plan to Streamline Higher Education through Europe could lead to Third-Level Competition', *The Irish Times*, 10 May.

Oliver, E. (2003). 'So It's Goodbye to All That', *The Irish Times*, 18 March.

Oliver, M. (1992). 'Changing the Social Relations of Research Production', *Disability, Handicap and Society* 7: 101-114.

Osborne, R. and Leith, H. (2000). *Evaluation of the Targeted Initiatives on Widening Access for Young People from Socio-Economically Disadvantaged Backgrounds*. Dublin: HEA.

Outram, D. (1995). *The Enlightenment*. Cambridge: Cambridge University Press.

Owens, T. (1989). 'Central Initiatives and Local Realities: Curriculum Change in the County Cork VEC Schools, 1963-1983', in D.G. Mulcahy and D. O'Sullivan (eds) *Irish Educational Policy. Process and Substance*. Dublin: IPA.

Ozga, J. (1987). 'Studying Education through the lives of Policy Makers: An Attempt to close the Micro-Macro Gap', in S. Walker and L. Barton (eds) *Changing Policies. Changing Teachers*. Milton Keynes: Open University Press.

Parry, B. (1987). 'Problems in Current Theories of Colonial Discourse', *Oxford Literary Review* 9: 27-58.

Parsons, T. and Shils, E.A. (1976). *Towards a General Theory of Action*. Cambridge, MA: Harvard University Press.

Passow, A.H. (1970). *Deprivation and Disadvantage. Nature and Manifestations*. Hamburg: UNESCO Institute of Education.

Paz, R. (1990). *Paths to Empowerment. Ten Years of Early Childhood Education in Israel*. The Hague: Bernard Van Leer Foundation.

Peillon, M. (1982). *Contemporary Irish Society: An Introduction*. Dublin: Gill and Macmillan.

Peillon, M. (1995). 'Interest Groups and the State in the Republic of Ireland', in P. Clancy, S. Drudy, K. Lynch and L. O'Dowd (eds) *Irish Society. Sociological Perspectives*. Dublin: IPA in association with the SAI.

Peters, M. and Marshall, J. (1996). *Individualism and Community: Education and Social Policy in the Postmodern Condition*. London: Falmer.

Pinker, S. (2002). *The Blank Slate: The Modern Denial of Human Nature*. London: Allen Lane.

Piore, M.J. and Sabel, C.F. (1984). *The Second Industrial Divide: Possibilities for Prosperity*. New York: Basic Books.

Pitt, J. (1997). 'Reading Resistance Analytically: On Making the Self in Women's Studies', in L.G. Roman and L. Eyre (eds) *Dangerous Territories: Struggles for Difference and Equality in Education*. New York: Routledge.

Platt, A.M. (1969). *The Child Savers*. Chicago: University of Chicago Press.

Pollak, A. (1997a). 'Churches United in Opposing School Management Reforms', *The Irish Times*, 11 March.

Pollak, A. (1997b). 'Parents Urged to Oppose Dilution of Education Bill', *The Irish Times*, 7 April.

Popkewitz, T. (1998). 'The Culture of Redemption and the Administration of Freedom as Research', *Review of Educational Research* 68: 1-34.

Poulantzas, N. (1979). *Class in Contemporary Capitalism*. London: New Left Books.

Powell, F. and Geoghegan, M. (2004). *The Politics of Community Development*. Dublin: A. and A. Farmar.

Primary Education Review Body (1990). *Report*. Dublin: Stationery Office.

Programme for a Partnership Government 1993-1997 (1993). Dublin: Fianna Fáil and Labour Parties.

Programme for Action in Education 1984-1987 (1984). Dublin: Stationery Office.

Programme for Competitiveness and Work (1994). Dublin: Stationery Office.

Programme for Economic Expansion (1958). Dublin: Stationery Office.

Programme for National Development 1978-1981 (1979). Dublin: Stationery Office.

Propp, V. (1958[1928]). *Morphology of the Folktale*. Austin, TX: University of Texas Press.

Proulx, E.A. (1993). *The Shipping News*. London: Fourth Estate.

Prunty, J.J. (1985). 'Signposts for a Critical Educational Policy Analysis', *Australian Journal of Education* 29: 113-140.

Public Policy Institute of Ireland (1993). *Shaping Educational Change. A Response to the Green Paper on Education*. Dublin: PPII.

Putnam, R. (2000). *Bowling Alone: The Collapse and Revival of American Community.* New York: Simon and Schuster.

Putti, J. (1987). 'Papal Strategy for Social Reform', *Social Studies* 9: 61-91.

Qualifications (Education and Training) Act (1999). Dublin: Stationery Office.

Quinn, T. (ed.) (2001). *Desmond Fennell. His Life and Work*. Dublin: Veritas.

Raffe, D. (1997). 'The "Transition from School to Work" and its Heirs', in A. Jobert, C. Marry, L. Tanguy, and H. Rainbird (eds) *Education and Work in Great Britain, Germany and Italy*. London: Routledge.

Raftery, M. and O'Sullivan, E. (1999). *Suffer the Little Children*. Dublin: New Island Books.

Randles, E. (1975). *Post-Primary Education in Ireland 1957-1970*. Dublin: Veritas.

Rath, A. (1999). 'Coming to Know in Community: Voice, Metaphor and Epistemology', in B. Connolly and A.B. Ryan (eds) W*omen and Education in Ireland. Volume 2*. Maynooth: MACE.

Raths, L.E., Harmin, M. and Simon, S.B. (1966). *Values and Teaching. Working with Values in the Classroom*. Columbus, OH: Merrill.

Raven, J. and Whelan, C.T. (1976). 'Irish Adults' Perceptions of Their Civic Institutions and Their Own Role in Relation to Them', in J. Raven, C.T. Whelan, P.A. Pfretzschner and M. Borock *Political Culture in Ireland*. Dublin: IPA.

Rawnsley, A. (2001). *Servants of the People. The Inside Story of New Labour*. London: Penguin.

Redmond, D. and Butler, P. (2003). *Civic, Social and Political Education. Report on Survey of Principals and Teachers*. Dublin: NCCA.

Rein, M. and Schön, D. (1977). 'Problem Setting in Policy Research', in C. Weiss (ed.) *Using Research in Public Policy Making*. Lexington, MA: Lexington Books.

Rich, A. (1979). *On Lies, Secrets and Silences*. London: Virago.

Rigal, J. (1989). 'Some Issues Concerning the Integration of Irish Travellers', *Administration* 37: 87-93.

Robinson, P. (1976). *Education and Poverty*. London: Methuen.

Roman, L.G. and Eyre, L. (1997). 'Introduction' to L.G. Roman and L. Eyre (eds) *Dangerous Territories: Struggles for Difference and Equality in Education*. New York: Routledge.

Rose, N. (1993). 'Government, Authority and Expertise in Advanced Liberalism', *Economy and Society* 22: 283-300.

Rosenau, P.M. (1992). *Post-Modernism and the Social Sciences: Insights, Inroads and Intrusions*. Princeton, NJ: Princeton University Press.

Roszak, T. (1981). *Person/Planet*. London: Granada.

Rouine, B. (1976). An Analysis of the Philosophy of Paulo Freire for the Purpose of Structuring a Community Education Programme. Unpublished M.Ed. thesis, St Patrick's College, Maynooth.

Rousseau, J.-J. (1968[1762]). *The Social Contract*. Oxford: Oxford University Press.

RSE in Catholic Schools. A Resource for Teachers and Boards of Management (1997). Dublin: Veritas.

Rubenson, K. and Field, J. (1987). 'Review of *Philosophical and Other Views on Lifelong Learning* (H.B. Long *et al.*)', *International Journal of University Adult Education* 26: 47-58.

Rudd, J. (1972). *Report: National School Terminal Leavers*. Dublin: Germaine Publications.

Russell, B. (1967). *History of Western Philosophy*. London: Allen and Unwin.

Russo, F.X. (1973). 'Ireland and the Social Studies: Irish Eyes Aren't Smiling – They're Closed', *Compass* 2: 5-16.

Ryan, A. (1970). *The Philosophy of the Social Sciences*. London: Macmillan.

Ryan, A.B. (1997). 'Gender Discourses in School Social Relations', in A. Byrne and M. Leonard (eds) *Women in Irish Society. A Sociological Reader*. Belfast: Beyond the Pale Publications.

Ryan, A.B. (1999). 'Sources for a Politicised Practice of Women's Personal Development Education', in B. Connolly and A.B. Ryan (eds) *Women and Education in Ireland. Volume 2*. Maynooth: MACE.

Ryan, B. (1985). 'The Church and Justice', *Studies* 74: 393-401.

Ryan, L. (1967a). 'Address at University College, Cork "Student Teach-In"', Report in *The Irish Times*, 4 December.

Ryan, L. (1967b). 'Social Dynamite: A Study of Early School Leavers', *Christus Rex* 21: 7-44.

Ryan, S. (1994). *The Home-School-Community Liaison Scheme. Final Evaluation Report*. Dublin: Educational Research Centre.

Rynne, S. (1960). *Father John Hayes*. Dublin: Clonmore and Reynolds.

Sabel, C. (1996). *Ireland: Local Partnerships and Social Innovation*. Paris: OECD.

Said, E.W. (1978). *Orientalism*. London: Random House.

Said, E.W. (1994). *Representations of the Intellectual*. London: Vintage.

Salter, B. and Tapper, T. (1981). *Education, Politics and the State*. London: Grant McIntyre.

Sandel, M. (1984). 'The Procedural Republic and the Unencumbered Self', *Political Theory* 12: 81-96.

Sapir, E. (1933). 'Language', in *Encyclopaedia of the Social Sciences* 9: 155-169. New York: Macmillan.

Sarup, M. (1988). *An Introductory Guide to Post-Structuralism and Postmodernism*. London: Harvester Wheatsheaf.

Saussure, F. de (1983[1916]). *Course in General Linguistics* (Trs. R. Harris). London: Duckworth.

Sayer, A. (1995). *Radical Political Economy: A Critique*. Oxford: Blackwell.

Schama, S. (1995). *Landscape and Memory*. London: Harper Collins.

Schattschneider, E.E. (1960). *The Semi-Sovereign People: A Realist's View of Democracy in America*. New York: Holt, Rinehart and Winston.

Schütz, A. (1972[1932]). *The Phenomenology of the Social World*. London: Heinemann.

Searle, J.R. (1969). *Speech Acts. An Essay in the Philosophy of Language*. New York: Cambridge University Press.

Second Commission on the Status of Women (1993). *Report*. Dublin: Stationery Office.

Second Programme for Economic Expansion (1963). Dublin: Stationery Office.

Seidman, S. (1998). *Contested Knowledge. Social Theory in a Post-Modern Era*. Oxford: Blackwell.

Sertillanges, A.D. (1962[1948]). *The Intellectual Life*. Cork: Mercier Press.

Sexton, J.J., Whelan, B.J. and Williams, J.A. (1988). *Transition from School to Work and Early Labour Market Experience*. Dublin: ESRI.

Sheehan, J. (1979). 'Education and Society in Ireland, 1945-70', in J. Lee (ed.) *Ireland 1945-70*. Dublin: Gill and Macmillan.

Sheehan, J. (1982). 'Education, Education Policy and Poverty', in L. Joyce and A. McCashin (eds) *Poverty and Social Policy*. Dublin: IPA.

Sheehan, J. (1992). *Education, Training and the Culliton Report*. UCD: Centre for Economic Research.

Sheridan, A. (1980). *The Will to Truth*. London: Tavistock.

Shilling, C. (1993). 'The Demise of the Sociology of Education in Britain?', *British Journal of Sociology of Education* 14: 105-112.

Sica, A. (1988). *Weber, Irrationality and Social Order*. Berkeley, CA: University of California Press.

Skilbeck, M. (2001). *The University Challenged. A Review of International Trends and Issues with Particular Reference to Ireland*. Dublin: HEA in association with CHIU.

Slowey, M. (1979). 'Aspects of Women's Participation in Adult Education', *AONTAS Review* 1: 16-24.

Smith, M.J. (2000). *Culture. Reinventing the Social Sciences*. Buckingham: Open University Press.

Smyth, E. and Hannan, D.F. (2000). 'Education and Inequality', in B. Nolan, P.J. O'Connell and C.T. Whelan (eds) *Bust to Boom? The Irish Experience of Growth and Inequality*. Dublin: IPA.

Snow, D.A. and Benford, R.D. (1992). 'Master Frames and Cycles of Protest', in A.D. Morris and C. McClurg Mueller (eds) *Frontiers in Social Movement Theory*. New Haven, CT: Yale University Press.

Snow, D.A., Burke Rochford, E., Warden, S.K. and Benford, R.D. (1986). 'Frame Alignment Processes, Micromobilisation, and Movement Participation', *American Sociological Review* 51: 464-481.

Spivak, G.C. (1988). 'Can the Subaltern Speak?', in G. Nelson and L. Crossberg (eds) *Marxism and the Interpretation of Culture*. London: Macmillan.

St Pierre, E.A. (2000). 'Poststructural Feminism in Education: An Overview', *International Journal of Qualitative Studies in Education* 13: 477-515.

Stanley, L. and Wise, S. (1990). 'Method, Methodology and Epistemology in Feminist Research Process', in L. Stanley (ed.) *Feminist Praxis*. London: Routledge.

Stein, M.R. (1960). *The Eclipse of Community*. New York: Harper and Row.

Stetson, D.M. and Mazur, A.G. (eds) (1995). *Comparative State Feminism*. London: Sage.

Stokes, D. (1999a). 'Working with Early School Leavers: Youthreach's Message to the Mainstream', *Learn* 21: 26-35.

Stokes, D. (1999b). 'Guidance in the 21st Century. The Message from the Margins', *Journal of the Institute of Guidance Counsellors* 1999: 55-65.

Strauss, A.L., Schatzman, L., Bucher, R., Ehrlich, D. and Sabshin, M. (1964). *Psychiatric Ideologies and Institutions*. New York: Free Press.

Strawson, P.F. (1966). *The Bounds of Sense*. London: Methuen.

Sugrue, C. (1997). *Complexities of Teaching: Child-Centred Perspectives*. London: Falmer.

Sugrue, C. (2000). 'Power-Partnerships and the Re-Structuring of Irish Primary Education'. Paper presented at the American Educational Research Association Annual Conference, New Orleans, 24-28 April.

Sugrue, C. (2004). 'Whose Curriculum is it Anyway? Power, Politics and Possibilities in the Construction of the Revised Primary Curriculum', in C. Sugrue (ed.) *Ideology and Curriculum: Irish Experiences, International Perspectives*. Dublin: Liffey Press.

Surber, J.P. (1998). *Culture and Critique*. Boulder, CO: Westview Press.

Swan, D. (1976). 'Is Teaching Reading the Business of the Secondary School?', *Proceedings of the Annual Conference of the Educational Studies Association of Ireland, Galway*, 4-7.

Tajfel, H. (1978). 'Interindividual Behaviour and Intergroup Behaviour', in H. Tajfel (ed.) *Differentiation Between Social Groups: Studies in the Social Psychology of Intergroup Relations*. London: Academic Press.

Tansey, P. (1998). *Ireland at Work. Economic Growth and the Labour Market, 1987-1997*. Dublin: Oak Tree Press.

Taylor, C. (1992). *Multiculturalism and 'The Politics of Recognition'*. Princeton, NJ: Princeton University Press.

Taylor, S. (1997). 'Critical Policy Analysis: Exploring Contexts, Texts and Consequences', *Discourse: Studies in the Cultural Politics of Education* 18: 23-35.

The Federation of Irish Secondary Schools (1962). *Investment in Education in the Republic of Ireland with Some Comparative Statistics*. Dublin: FISS.

The Irish Times (1997). 'Editorial: The Education Bill', 13 March.

The Irish Times (1999). 'Reward for Bringing Business to Schools', 9 December.

The Labour Party (1963). *Challenge and Change in Education*. Dublin: The Labour Party.

The Work of Justice (1977). Pastoral Letter of the Irish Bishops, Dublin.

Theobald, P. and Snauwaert, D.T. (eds) (1995). 'Education and the Liberal-Communitarian Debate.' *Peabody Journal of Education* 70. Special Issue.

Thomas, W.I. (1923). *The Unadjusted Girl*. Boston: Little, Brown and Company.

Thorpe, D. (1997). 'Review Essay: Regulating Late Modern Child Rearing in Ireland', *Economic and Social Review* 28: 63-84.

Titley, E.B. (1979). 'The Historiography of Irish Education', *Journal of Educational Thought* 13: 66-77.

Titley, E.B. (1983a). *Church, State and the Control of Schooling in Ireland 1900-1944*. Montreal: McGill – Queen's University Press.

Titley, E.B. (1983b). 'Rejecting the Modern World: The Educational Ideas of Timothy Corcoran', *Oxford Review of Education* 9: 137-145.

Tobin, F. (1984). *The Best of Decades. Ireland in the Nineteen Sixties*. Dublin: Gill and Macmillan.

Toner, B. (1979). 'Courses for Unemployed People: The CIR Experience', *AONTAS Review* 1: 2-5.

Tormey, R. and Prendeville, T. (2000). *Making Sense of the Cacophony: Understanding the Different Voices on Rural Educational Disadvantage*. Limerick: Mary Immaculate College, CEDR.

Tovey, H. (1999). '"Messers, Visionaries and Organobureaucrats": Dilemmas of Institutionalisation in the Irish Organic Farming Movement', *Irish Journal of Sociology* 9: 31-59.

Tovey, H. and Share, P. (2000). *A Sociology of Ireland*. Dublin: Gill and Macmillan.

Tovey, H., Hannan, D.F. and Abramson, H. (1989). *Why Irish? Irish Identity and the Irish Language*. Dublin: Bord na Gaeilge.

Troyna, B. (1994). 'Critical Social Research and Education Policy', *British Journal of Educational Studies* 42: 70-84.

Tuairim (1961). *Irish Education*. London: Tuairim Pamphlet 9.

Tuohy, D. and Doyle, E. (1994). 'New Directions in Irish Secondary Education', *Studies* 83: 436-446.

Turner, R.H. (1961). 'Modes of Social Ascent through Education: Sponsored and Contest Mobility', in A.H.Halsey, J. Floud and C.A. Anderson (eds) *Education, Economy and Society*. New York: Free Press.

Tussing, A.D. (1976). 'Labour Force Effects of the 1967/68 Changes in Education Policy in the Irish Republic', *Economic and Social Review* 7: 289-304.

Tussing, A.D. (1978). *Irish Educational Expenditures – Past, Present and Future*. Dublin: ESRI.

Tussing, A.D. (1981). 'Accountability, Rationalisation and the White Paper on Educational Development', *Journal of the Statistical and Social Inquiry Society of Ireland* 24 (Part 3): 71-83.

Tussing, A.D. (1983). 'Irish Educational Policy Reconsidered'. Irish Vocational Education Association Annual Congress, Portlaoise, 17 May.

Universities Act (1997). Dublin: Stationery Office.

Van Dijk, T.A. (1985). *Handbook of Discourse Analysis*. London: Academic Press.

Vera Verba (1975). *Have the Snakes Come Back? Education and the Irish Child*. Dublin: Vera Verba.

Vickers, M. (1995). 'Cross-National Exchange and Australian Education Policy', in C.W. Evers and J.D. Chapman (eds) *Educational Administration*. St Leonards, NSW: Allen and Unwin.

Voloshinov, V.N. (2000[1929]). *Marxism and the Philosophy of Language* (Trs. L. Matejka and I.R. Titunik). Cambridge, MA: Harvard University Press.

Vygotsky, L.S. (1978). *Mind in Society*. Cambridge, MA: Harvard University Press.

Waldron, F. (2004). 'Making the Irish: Identity and Citizenship in the Primary Curriculum', in C. Sugrue (ed.) *Ideology and Curriculum: Irish Experiences, International Perspectives*. Dublin: Liffey Press.

Walsh, B. (1981). 'Whither Third-Level Education?', Cork Scientific Council Seminar, Cork, 3 April.

Walsh, B., Breen, R., Hannan, D.F., Rottman, D.B. and Whelan, C.T. (1991). 'Interpreting Modern Ireland: Time for a New View?', *Studies* 80: 400-411.

Walsh, R. (1999). 'The Issue of Rationalisation in Irish Post-Primary Education 1963-96: The Perspectives of the Catholic Church and the State', *Oideas* 46: 7-25.

Walsh, W.R. (1997). The Christian Brothers and the Management of Change in Irish Post-Primary Education 1966-1990. Unpublished Ph.D. thesis, Department of Education, UCC.

Walshe, J. (1999). *A New Partnership in Education*. Dublin: IPA.

Ward, E. (2002). *'Citizenship Studies.' A Curricular Proposal for Social and Political Education in the Leaving Certificate (Established)*. Dublin: CDVEC Curriculum Development Unit.

Waters, J. (1997). *An Intelligent Person's Guide to Modern Ireland*. London: Duckworth.

Waters, J. (2004). *The Politburo Has Decided That You Are Unwell*. Dublin: The Liffey Press.

Waters, M. (1994). *Modern Sociological Theory*. London: Sage.

Watson, I. (1996). 'The Irish Language and Television: National Identity, Preservation, Restoration and Minority Rights', *British Journal of Sociology* 47: 255-274.

Weber, M. (1964[1930]). *The Theory of Social and Economic Organisation*. New York: Free Press.

Weber, M. (1972[1922]). 'Class, Status, Party', in B.R. Cosin (ed.) *Education: Structure and Society*. Harmondsworth: Penguin.

Weber, M. (1978[1922]). *Economy and Society*. Berkeley, CA: University of California Press.

Weiss, P.A. (1998). *Conversations with Feminism. Political Theory and Practice*. Oxford: Rowman and Littlefield.

Wells, H.G. (1967[1905]). *A Modern Utopia*. Lincoln, NB: University of Nebraska Press.

Wertsch, J.V. (1991). *Voices of the Mind*. Cambridge, MA: Harvard University Press.

Wheeler, S. (1969). *On Record: Files and Dossiers in American Life*. New York: Russell Sage Foundation.

Whelan, B.J. and Walsh, B.M. (1977). *Redundancy and Re-Employment in Ireland*. Dublin: ESRI.

Whelan, C.T. (1994). 'Poverty, Social Class, Education and Intergenerational Mobility', in B. Nolan and T. Callan (eds) *Poverty and Policy in Ireland*. Dublin: Gill and Macmillan.

Whitaker, T.K. (1958). *Economic Development*. Dublin: Stationery Office.

White Paper on Educational Development (1980). Dublin: Stationery Office.

White, T. (2001). *Investing in People. Higher Education in Ireland from 1960 to 2000*. Dublin: IPA.

Whitty, G. (1985). *Sociology and School Knowledge*. London: Methuen.

Whorf, B.L. (1954[1927-41]). *Language, Thought and Reality* (Ed. J.B. Carroll). Cambridge, MA: MIT Press.

Whyte, J. (1980). *Church and State in Modern Ireland*. Dublin: Gill and Macmillan.

Wickham, A. (1980). 'National Educational Systems and the International Context: The Case of Ireland', *Comparative Education Review* 6: 323-337.

Williams, K. (1997). 'Religion in Irish Education. Recent Trends in Government Policy', in P. Hogan and K. Williams (eds) *The Future of Religion in Irish Education*. Dublin: Veritas.

Williams, K. (1999). 'Faith and the Nation: Education and Religious Identity in the Republic of Ireland', *British Journal of Educational Studies* 47: 317-331.

Williams, K. and McNamara, G. (1985). *The Vocational Preparation Course*. Dublin: ASTI.

Williams, R. (1983). *Keywords: A Vocabulary of Culture and Society*. London: Fontana.

Willis, P. (1977). *Learning to Labour*. London: Saxon House.

Willmott, R. (2002). *Education Policy and Realist Social Theory: Primary Teachers, Child-Centred Philosophy and the New Managerialism*. London: Routledge.

Wilson, R. (1985). 'Community Education and Community Action', Proceedings of the 1985 AONTAS Conference *Community Education*, 3-5 May.

Winch, P. (1958). *The Idea of a Social Science*. London: Routledge and Kegan Paul.

Wittgenstein, L. (1961[1921]). *Tractatus Logico-Philosophicus* (Trs. D.F. Pears and B.F. McGuinness). London: Routledge and Kegan Paul.

Wittgenstein, L. (1967[1953]). *Philosophical Investigations*. Oxford: Blackwell.

Women's Representative Committee (1976). *Progress Report on the Implementation of the Recommendations in the Report of the Commission on the Status of Women*. Dublin: Stationery Office.

Women's Representative Committee (1978). *Second Progress Report on the Implementation of the Recommendations in the Report of the Commission on the Status of Women*. Dublin: Stationery Office.

Wood, E. and Attfield, J. (1996). *Play, Learning and the Early Childhood Curriculum*. London: Paul Chapman.

Woodward, K. (1997). 'Concepts of Identity and Difference', in K. Woodward (ed.) *Identity and Difference*. London: Sage.

Worton, M. and Still, J. (eds) (1991). *Intertextuality. Theories and Practices*. Manchester: Manchester University Press.

Wrong, D. (1961). 'The Over-Socialised Conception of Man in Modern Sociology', *American Sociological Review* 26: 183-193.

Yearley, S. (1995). 'The Social Shaping of the Environmental Movement in Ireland', in P. Clancy, S. Drudy, K. Lynch and L. O'Dowd (eds) *Irish Society. Sociological Perspectives*. Dublin: IPA in association with the SAI.

Young, I.M. (1990). *Justice and the Politics of Difference*. Princeton, NJ: Princeton University Press.

Young, I.M. (1996). 'Communication and the Other: Beyond Deliberative Democracy', in S. Benhabib (ed.) *Democracy and Difference*. Princeton, NJ: Princeton University Press.

Young, M.F.D. (1977). 'Taking Sides against the Probable', in C. Jenks (ed.) *Rationality, Education and the Social Organisation of Knowledge*. London: Routledge and Kegan Paul.

Young, M.F.D. (ed.) (1971). *Knowledge and Control*. London: Collier-Macmillan.

Youth Employment Agency (1982). *A Policy Framework for the Eighties*. Dublin: YEA.

Youth Employment Agency (1983). *First Report and Accounts to December 31st, 1982*. Dublin: YEA.

Zappone, K. (2002). *Achieving Equality in Children's Education. National Forum Primary Education: Ending Disadvantage*. Dublin: St Patrick's College.

Zigler, E. and Muenchow, S. (1992). *Head Start. The Inside Story of America's Most Successful Educational Experiment*. New York: Basic Books.

Index